The Thirty Years' Wars

V

The Thirty Years' Wars

Dispatches and Diversions

of a Radical Journalist

1965-1994

◆

Andrew Kopkind

Edited by JoAnn Wypijewski

VERSO

LONDON • NEW YORK

First published by Verso 1995
© Estate of Andrew Kopkind 1995
All rights reserved

Verso
UK: 6 Meard Street, London W1V 3HR
USA: 180 Varick Street, New York, New York 10014

Verso is the imprint of New Left Books

ISBN: 1-85984 902 4

British Library Cataloguing in Publication Data
A catalogue record for this book is available from the British Library

Library of Congress Cataloging-in-Publication Data
A catalog record for this book is available from the Library of Congress

Printed and bound in the United States of America

This book is dedicated with deep love and respect to John Scagliotti.

It was made possible only through the invaluable work of a superb editor, JoAnn Wypijewski, and the timely support of many who jumped in when the going got rough for me; they include Katrina vanden Heuvel, Maria Margaronis and Tom Gogola.
For this project, both in conception and execution, the importance of my dear friend Alexander Cockburn was incalculable.

This book represents maybe 10 percent of André's life...

EDITOR'S NOTE

"Life is not an unbroken narrative," Andy Kopkind said to me one day early in our discussions about this book. I had finished reading through tall stacks of his writing, and was intent that the final collection reproduce the incandescent journey I had just made through lived history. But perhaps because of the breadth of that journey, plotted out through more than a thousand articles, I felt oddly suspended in time and overly sensitive to gaps. Where was Sirhan Sirhan? I wondered, or Watergate? or the reunification of Germany?

Andy had rich tales about each of the moments I'd noted, but as for a written record, he'd been doing something else (travelling to Hanoi, making political commentaries and documentaries for WBCN radio in Boston, fighting off cancer for the first time). Remembering the conversation now, I think how finally ridiculous were my worries that *something might be left out*. This book represents maybe 10 percent of Andy's life work (not counting the radio scripts). It is his walk, quickening sometimes to a trot, through the history of the late twentieth century. In life-as-it-happens, unlike calculated reconstructions of the past, something is always missed out. Indeed, it is not an unbroken narrative. But how fresh are the scenes as they unfold!

Andy began his career as a political journalist in 1965, at Gil Harrison's *New Republic*. He concluded it at *The Nation*, where he wrote until he died, in October of 1994. In between, his work appeared in the *New Statesman*, where he was US correspondent in the late sixties; in *Mayday*, later *Hard Times*, the newsletter he founded with James Ridgeway and Robert Sherrill towards the close of that same decade; and in varied publications, from *The New York Review of Books* to *Ramparts* to *The Boston Phoenix* and *The Village Voice* to *Il Manifesto*. Here some pieces are titled differently from the original. Some have been cut to avoid repetition and to dispense with detail that, while highly relevant at the moment of writing, is obscure in its specificity today. Some have been shortened for space. All have been copy-edited for style. But there has been no attempt to trim the sails of exuberant idealism or to readjust analysis in light of later events. Andy was a sense-maker, never a revisionist. Nor have conformities of style been imposed where style itself is a political expression. Thus, with time, "Negro" transmutes into "black" transmutes into "African-American" and back again to "black." Thus, too, "'the movement'" as a concept in inverted commas evolves into "the Movement" and thence "the movement" as its fortunes rise and fade.

The book is arranged chronologically, with a Prologue—drawn from interviews conducted in early 1994 by Tom Gogola and Jean Stein—that captures Andy's character, evokes the world before his political coming-of-age and opens a window onto the history that it anticipates. Occasionally in the last two parts of the book the rules of temporal sequence are suspended for the sake of the narrative's thematic arc. Also, some of the later pieces from *The Nation* are assigned their publication date rather than their much later issue date in cases where the proximity of analysis to events under discussion is meaningful.

Throughout his years at *The Nation*, Andy had a special affection for the magazine's interns, and I am most grateful to Theo Emery, Jennifer Ferrara, Kyra Holland and Lawrence Levi for their assistance to Andy and to me. I want to thank Richard Lingeman and Katrina vanden Heuvel for their generosity when work on the book limited my participation at the magazine. Also Peter Meyer, Jeffrey Blankfort, Tom Gogola, Christine Haggerty, Bob Lescher, Yuri Shutovsky and Kio Stark, who were helpful and kind in times of need.

This book was produced under fierce pressures, eased greatly by the spirit and talent of Deborah Thomas, who did the design and production, Sandy McCroskey, who did the typing, Beth Stroud and Emily Gordon, who proofread, and Marty Jezer and Shoshona Rihn, who did the index. Lists such as this have a flatness that drains the most deserving of credits. For John Scagliotti, Andy's tender comrade, these lines must contain the whole of my gratitude.

In the aftermath of Andy's death, the raw material of this book, through all of its refinements, has been for me like a glorious conversation. It is with some sadness, amid the joy in Andy's legacy, that I now let it go.

— J.W.

CONTENTS

INTRODUCTION

Unfolding in the pages that follow is the history of an era, the evolution of a sensibility at once personal, generational and national. It is written by the greatest radical journalist of his time, in many episodes and in many venues. Andrew Kopkind was 29 when he wrote the first pages on the road from Selma, and 59 when he was done. It is the history of America, and the history of an American. It belongs on the shelf next to *The Education of Henry Adams*.

The history of the sixties, which is told in the first part of this book, has mostly fallen into enemy hands, dismembered by the sourness and rage of those who missed the boat, got the wind up, got it wrong. As Andrew described them looking back from the vantage point of the 1980s:

> Many members of that generation found themselves facing choices in their own lives that required them to deny or redefine their earlier experiences. Whatever else the sixties did, the decade seemed to promise its children an honest, humane, useful and communitarian life. Those promises were always exaggerated, and when they could not be fulfilled, the ageing children labelled them "lies," and the whole decade a "failure." . . . those who feared they had "sold out" resented those whose continued activity according to the old patterns of thought presented a constant reproach.

So students in American Studies these days have had the wrong maps and untrustworthy interpreters. Now they will have *The Thirty Years' Wars*, the recovered memory of the left, an eyewitness account from a radical who never lapsed into profitable apologies, an idealist who never discarded realism or judgement. He had passion, but also a sense of history.

Andrew "saw" history, whether in Selma, the trial of Capt. Howard Levy, the battles in Newark, the evolution of the Weathermen, Woodstock, Hanoi in '68, Prague in the same year, the rise of gay liberation and also the New Right in the seventies, the birth of postcommunism, in Moscow and Tashkent. Many people "see" history, but often without knowing what to make of it or without even being sure that some decisive heave in the Zeitgeist has transpired. Andrew was always alert to the new shapes history was taking.

What, then, are these wars of thirty years?

They are hot, starting with Vietnam and ending with the Persian Gulf. They are cold, in Cuba, Russia, Czechoslovakia and here in America, in the entire texture of the politics and the culture that Andrew described with so unerring a sense.

They are race wars, whether Watts in 1965, Detroit in 1967 or Los Angeles in 1992. They are class wars, described with the unsentimental compassion—I am thinking of his portrait of the Wallace voters—that Joan Didion isolates rightly as one of Andrew's great qualities. They are sex wars, over the emergent gay movement and feminism; and culture wars, from the Free Speech Movement through Woodstock to disco and beyond.

In these discrete histories there are core themes:

§ Race and racism's persistence, from the struggles of King to SNCC to the black power movement and the Panthers; from bussing in Boston to Bernhard Goetz in New York.

§ Power, the modes whereby it is exerted, overtly in imperial wars or covertly through the imposition of the closet and of cultural conformity; and whereby it is contested, by blacks, students, gays, alienated Middle Americans and revolutionaries overseas.

§ Liberalism, its blunting edge, its failures, its bad faith.

§ Authenticity, the struggle to achieve it.

No one had a more sensitive ear than Andrew to the mutant declensions of liberalism, as expressed in JFK, RFK, MLK, Eugene McCarthy, Jimmy Carter, Bill Clinton, Paul Tsongas, the cold war liberals born of the forties, *revenant* in the early eighties.

And no one explored more feelingly the issues of authenticity, whether at *Time*; in the struggles within the anti-war movement; in the persons and personae of John Lennon, Janis Joplin, David Bowie; in the author's own political and psychosexual itinerary.

Such themes in this history weave through each other down the years, and from time to time coalesce, nowhere more strikingly than in the pages on Allard Lowenstein. Here in one swoop Andrew takes us from the refusal, in part engineered by Lowenstein, at the 1964 Democratic convention, to seat the Mississippi Freedom Democrats, to its consequence in the emergence of black power, the fragmentation of the multiracial civil rights movement, the Jesse Jackson campaigns of 1984 and '88, perhaps the rise of Louis Farrakhan; then on to Lowenstein's possible belated stumble towards sexual authenticity before his murder took away that chance.

"You are the music/while the music lasts" is a line Andrew liked to quote from Eliot's *Four Quartets*, and the music in which Andrew expressed this history and these themes took the form of a perfect style. Try the first paragraphs in the chapters of these histories. Unfailingly they capture you and carry you forward. It was the way I first came to know Andrew, in dispatches read in England at the *New Statesman*, where I was an editor and he the

US correspondent in the late sixties, not long before we met and forged a friendship that lasted till he died. There in the print shop in High Wycombe, to which Andrew telexed his weekly pieces, the teletyped paragraphs had the urgency of time on the march:

> Those who did not live before the revolution will never know how sweet life is, Talleyrand said, and perhaps for such knowledge there is a desperate sweetness as the disaster spreads in this summer of the American crack-up. *Sergeant Pepper* blares from ten million phonographs, they're feeding the bears in Yellowstone Park, and the odor of barbecue wafting over the suburbs is suddenly mixed with the fragrance of pot. Hear it, see it, smell it while there is still time. For although there will be no revolution in the ordinary sense, the quality of life in the society—the values, the expectations, the perceptions—is radically changing. Things are not likely to be so sweet again.

Later, as the seventies began to unfurl, there was a more meditative but no less compelling tempo:

> The topography of American political culture in this strangely suspended season is strewn with the skeletons of abandoned movements, lowered visions, dying dreams. . . . Ideologies based on mechanistic analyses of power and history may not be wrong, but they are seen to be external to the lives of many whom they once moved, and irrelevant, too, to long-untended needs for peace of body, soul or mind.

Andrew never wrote a graceless line, but that style, with its supple syntax, smooth rhythms, playful allusions and puns, was always mustered in the service of a considered thought. As participant as well as observer, Andrew knew how to weigh excitement and reason both. Even in 1969, announcing a revolutionary moment, he qualified its arrival immediately with the news that the numbers were few, the performance uncertain, and the prospects dim to non-existent.

And in writing of changes in consciousness and culture, as he did in 1968, he never let paradox stray far from his typewriter:

> This is not a revolutionary situation; if it were, Tom Hayden wouldn't be on television, Country Joe and the Fish would be underground and Eldridge Cleaver would be shot.
>
> Sometimes it seems that if Tom Hayden, Country Joe and Eldridge Cleaver did not exist, America would have to invent them. And so—in a way—America *did* invent them: to satisfy revolutionary longings. They are aphrodisiacs in the air-conditioning system, hallucinogens in the water supply. To the extent that the forces

they represent can be contained, society will be safe. But if the forces reach a critical mass, the mild hype becomes hell broken loose. Repressive tolerance is an exquisitely subtle game.

He was urgent but never shrill. The harshest lines of Andrew's I can find here were written on the occasion of LBJ's death:

I can't imagine why people from so many political positions now find Johnson's craziness, his crassness, his malevolent *machismo* so charming. I'll always remember LBJ as a demented half-drunk mockery of manliness, a dirty young, middle-aged and old man who called in secretaries to give him head and generals to give him body counts with equal relish, while mind-bent America lied to itself about him.

The first duty of a journalist, a historian is to get things right, and Andrew did. 1966: "What will end the war? At heart it will be an acquaintance with death." 1968: "One of these days—when the 'German problem' is solved—the Czechs will find a new way out of the Soviet sphere and others will follow." 1977: "The victories of the right this year have been permitted, to some extent, by the failure of a liberal opposition—the consequence of the left's own cynicism, disillusionment and isolation." 1986: "Even the most pervasive totalitarianism has gaps, and history has a way of evading even the most ingenious plans for its cancellation." 1988: "If the Jackson campaign allows itself to be folded into the Democratic Party like egg whites into a soufflé, it will have betrayed all those who put their faith in and pinned their hopes on empowerment." February 3, 1992: "The more America declines, the better will Clinton's chances be to become president. . . . But in terms of making any meaningful change in the way America works—from the delivery of health care to the redistribution of power—Clinton offers nothing of interest. . . . This is a status quo election. America is still a one-party state."

Then there's the matter of Andrew himself. Hear his voice in the Prologue—so chatty, ironic, evocative. To his friends and acquaintances, Andrew was vivid at all times. He could be fearful. What radical, what gay person, what sane person in late twentieth-century America would not be? But he was an idealist, and captured beautifully the idealism of the generations seeking to make their own history:

To be a revolutionary is to love your life enough to change it, to choose struggle instead of exile, to risk everything with only the glimmering hope of a world to win.

Twenty-six years later, on Independence Day, just over three months before cancer claimed him on October 23, 1994, Andrew looked back on the Stonewall riot and wrote:

Somewhere in the existential depths of that brawl of screaming transvestites were all the freedom rides, the anti-war marches, the sit-ins, the smoke-ins, the be-ins, the consciousness-raising, the bra-burning, the levitation of the Pentagon, the endless meetings and broken hearts. Not only that, but the years of gay men and lesbians locking themselves inside windowless, unnamed bars; writing dangerous, anonymous novels and articles; lying about their identity to their families, their bosses, the military; suffering silently when they were found out; hiding and seeking and winking at each other, or drinking and dying by themselves. And sometimes, not often, braving it out and surviving. It's absolutely astonishing to think that on one early summer's night in New York that world ended, and a new one began.

As Andrew liked to emphasize, our end is *always* in our beginning. For him, that anniversary piece on Stonewall ended the narrative that began in Selma. For those who would carry that narrative forward, *The Thirty Years' Wars* now takes its enduring place on their bookshelves, their bedside tables, in their knapsacks on the road ahead.

—Alexander Cockburn
Petrolia, California

PROLOGUE

I'd assumed ever since the beginning of junior high school that I was going to go to medical school and that I would be a psychiatrist, primarily because when I was a kid I embarked on a two-year course of deep, intense, five-day-a-week non-directive, on-the-couch psychoanalysis. This was in 1946, and the analyst didn't say a word from the beginning of the time I went there, when I was 11, to until he said, "Well, you're through now," when I was 13. I invited him to my bar mitzvah, and that was sort of that. Very nice man. Dr. Milton J.E. Senn.

He was head of pediatric psychiatry and director of the child study center at Yale, which was a pioneer child development institute. At places like Yale and in big cities, what was then called the Freudian movement was like the left. The thinking was that the socialist left in itself was not going to make it, and—this is a long story, but basically the idea was that a kind of revolution was being fought on a psychodynamic battlefield. And by and large, the analysts, the Freudians, were left-wingers and Jewish intellectuals and people who would have been radicals if the radical movement at that time was viable. They were attacked by the conventional right as commie shrinks, and made fun of—men with beards, you know. So for a long time I just assumed that being analyzed was part of my political journey, that being part of the Freudian analytical movement was a political act.

Anyway, I started writing in junior high school. When I got to high school I wanted to be editor of the *Hillhouse Sentinel*, but the woman who was the faculty adviser—the hated English teacher, Dr. Sheridan, Dr. Marion C. Sheridan, this big right-wing Irish fascist—hated me for political reasons, and she installed the brown-nosing Judy Finman. Goody good two shoes, Judy Finman.

When I went to college I was in pre-med, but I started writing for the *Cornell Daily Sun*. At Cornell the campus was pretty apolitical, but I thought of myself as some sort of socialist. I had no idea why. I think it had to do with Bob Goldburg, my commie pinko rabbi. My father was a Republican, and I don't know how I got the idea that I was a socialist. But I did and I got a subscription to the *New Statesman* when I was very young and read it all through high school and college. I always wanted to write like a British political journalist. I thought that was the coolest. I remember one day having a talk with my friend Frank Clark, who was president of the Student Council—I was crazy about Frank Clark. He was kind of a mousy, quiet, soft-spoken guy, incredibly sweet, who was in air force ROTC to pay for college. (He was killed on a training flight right after he graduated.) So Frank Clark and I were talking—I remember this so well—walking down one of the campus quads having this college kids' rap, and we both came out to each other as socialists. It was sort of weird.

Culturally this was the beginning of the beat period, and there was a very active beat community around Cornell. There was Pynchon, Richard Farina, C.M. Kaplan, a wonderful science fiction writer called Darryl Turgeon. I thought it was kind of crazy, but exciting. Then I also remember the first spring weekend that "Rock Around the Clock" came out. It was a whole new thing, just morning, noon and night. For a closeted gay man, rock-and-roll meant dancing was suddenly not this heterosexual ritual that involved intimate touches. You just jumped up and down. I think also the speed and the blackness of it all—deep down somewhere, even when white people were doing it—was exciting. It was the beginning of an outlaw culture.

I was pretty conventional, though. Susan Brownmiller did a piece about Cornell in the fifties for *Esquire*—this was in the 1960s, and she liked me— she wrote that Kopkind in the fifties was a nightmare. She was in my class and was kicked out for being a lesbian—no, she *claims* it was for being a lesbian (which I don't think she is anymore); I remember her being kicked out for stealing her sorority sister's engagement ring. She once told me she did it as a political act. Anyway, when she said I was a nightmare, I think what she meant was that I was conventional. And I *was* having a very good time within the boundaries of conventionality, but the political editorials I wrote for the *Sun* were very left. When McCarthy was censured, I wrote one called something like "The Ism Outlives the Man."

Part-way through my time at Cornell there was this trip, sort of a boon-doggle, being organized to Iran. Twenty students—all men—were invited as guests of the Shah. The minister of education, I think, had been at Cornell, and there was this whole idea of modernizing the Shah. He had just been reinstalled by the CIA, after Mossadegh was overthrown. So we went, and we spent a month in Iran, and we had all these adventures with the Shah. I had my picture taken with him.

After that, my friend Peter Hern and I went to Cairo, arrived there on the 26th of July, 1956, which was the day that Nasser nationalized the Suez Canal. Great days in the history of Middle East nationalism. And there were American consuls and vice consuls in blue-striped suits out at the airport telling Americans to get on the next plane, anywhere. I said, Bullshit, I want to see the pyramids and I want to see the Sphinx, and I've come here . . . We stayed there and had a great time.

Then we went to Yugoslavia and from there to Moscow. It was the first year that Americans were allowed—by our government—to go there. We got there in August, a few months after Khrushchev had given his famous speech at the Twentieth Party Congress; and although this had not been made public, everyone was talking about it—all the crimes of Stalin. Stalin was still pickled out in Red Square, along with Lenin, but everyone said, "He's not going to last." So I saw Uncle Joe.

Now, while I was away there was this whole *megillah* going on back home, with professors calling my parents, saying, "He's doing very well in everything else, but he's flunking organic chemistry." My parents were very upset, but when I got back I realized, God, this is wonderful; I don't have to go to medical school. It was so liberating. I started taking political science, and it turned out that I majored in philosophy. My super-adviser was this very wonderful man named Norman Malcolm, who was the American anchor for Wittgenstein; he figures all over the Wittgenstein movement. I thought it was pretty interesting, but I never really got it. It was very useful, though, for journalism—as a methodology, in terms of analyzing things linguistically, in terms of what the language really means and what's going on in a text. I remember Norman Malcolm had this whole riff on Reason and Cause. He said, "You're sitting"—all these Wittgensteinians talk this way, about Wittgenstein's dog and the fly and the fly bottle, all these paradigmatic stories, which I never completely understood, either. Anyway, he says, "You're sitting in a room and the doorbell rings, and you jump up and you go to the door and you open the door. Now, I could say to you, What caused you to go to the door? Or I could say, What was the reason you went to the door?" These mean two different things. If you sort of hate your mother, what caused you to hate your mother, and then what's the reason for you hating your mother? That stuff proved useful in terms of analyzing and deconstructing, and I realized that American journalists, like Americans in general, just don't like to apply any kind of analytic tools to anything that they're doing. It has something to do with anti-intellectualism, which is pervasive, even among intellectuals. It's one of the reasons that Americans for the most part are such poor Marxists, because Marxism, after all, is nothing more than an analytical construct to understand history. But people are so afraid of using those constructs that they refuse to ask what causes things, what are the reasons. They just write words, but what does it all mean? It means I'm king of the cats.

I went to Europe after college, at the end of the Eisenhower period, in 1959. There was no reason to stay in the United States. I had this sense that there was no historical energy here, and it was terribly repressive and boring—not just sexually but in general. So much of America seemed like Norman Rockwell, and then there was the McCarthy legacy. Nowadays when kids go to Eastern Europe, it's an economic thing. There's nothing for them to do here, at least nothing equal to what they always imagined for themselves. Back then it was different, and there were these whole communities of American students in Paris and London. I felt like an expat, and although I knew I couldn't stay abroad forever, I also didn't feel like coming home. I went to the London School of Economics and never came home for two and a half years.

When I did, finally, in October of 1961, I took the last westward sailing of the *Liberté*, the great French ocean liner. It was sort of the end of that whole era of trans-Atlantic liners. It was part of the end of a lot of things, part of the end of the postwar world. And, strangely enough, there in second class, which is cabin class, meaning you didn't have to dress up in tuxedos for dinner, were Alexander Calder and his wife, and Mark Rothko by himself, being very depressed. They were not travelling together, but they of course knew one another. Calder was wonderful. It was during this period when he was making these miniature mobiles for art jewelry, and his wife, his *then* wife, would model them. Every night she'd come down for dinner with these Caldermobiles dangling from her ears. Calder was this marvelous Ed Wynn/Santa Claus figure—all twinkly and curly white hair. He always had on a plaid shirt, and she had on Connecticut tweeds. After dinner, he would lead us—there were maybe eight students at the table and Mark Rothko—up into the first-class lounges and just brush aside the stewards who were trying to keep us down, and buy us drinks. And, oh, it was just so much fun.

I got to the dock in New York not knowing what the hell I was going to do with my life, and I was met by Bud Trillin. He had been to Europe a couple of times, and we had travelled to Spain—it was still the Hemingway era. I think I went twice to Pamplona, ran with the bulls through the streets, with the wineskins and everything.

Bud was working for *Time* then, and after I'd been back a while he said, "Do you want me to talk to some *Time* people?" I had been pretty much a lefty, especially living in England, and I thought, well, doesn't sound like my principles, but I needed a job. So I was interviewed by Dick Clurman, the chief of correspondents, who sort of hired me on the spot and said, "Can you be in Los Angeles?" I got my little red Alpha Romeo that I'd bought for $1,800, and I drove to LA.

I had a great time there, for a while. At one point I lived in Laurel Canyon, just above Sunset Strip, in a great, crazy house. That was the part of LA that I really loved; it was still part of the Raymond Chandler seedy Hollywood from the thirties. Sort of campy without knowing it—low camp. Also it was such a sexy town. I hated the narcissism, but I loved it too because it was exciting. The vulgarity. The one thing in England that I had missed about America was the vulgarity, the kind of down-and-out vulgarity. LA was so much like that, and San Francisco was so pretentiously trying not to be, so calculatedly not-vulgar and sophisticated, and it was a complete farce.

So I loved LA, but I was also heading for a fall there. I got involved with all this sexual cruising which ended up very badly a couple of years later. It was the summer of '64 when I got busted for running afoul of the sexual perversity laws, and I had known that something was going to happen; it was just in the air. Afterwards there was really no way out for me except to play that through, because the alternative was to come out, which was unthinkable, or to go straight. At *Time*, they said I had to change trains or be terminated. So I found this shrink who said he could set me straight, so to speak, and *Time* would pay the bills. (The whole thing was kind of a milder version of what Marty Duberman describes so well in *Cures*.)

It so happened that I had to commute by air shuttle three times a week to these psychiatric sessions, and my therapeutic homework was to sit next to any female passenger I found remotely attractive (or else approach a stewardess) and try for a pick-up. In the sessions I rehearsed these opening lines—"Do you fly the 8 o'clock shuttle often?"—and the psychiatrist assumed the role of pick-upee. It worked just fine in the office; not so well in midair.

But I digress. Very soon after I got out to LA, I put aside all my simple political reservations about *Time*. The line I had, which I used all the time, was, "You don't know the half of it . . ." I hated these liberals who would berate me for working at *Time* because it was for Eisenhower instead of Adlai Stevenson. This was so stupid because what's wrong with *Time* isn't that they have Republican politics; it's all institutional. People who worked there understood that and hated it for that reason.

Henry Luce had this dream of corporate journalism, which had two inspirations—capitalism and Calvinism—and two central features: the corporate *process*, by which writers, reporters and editors are reduced to assembly-line production components; and the corporate *adventure*, by which Time Inc. amassed power on a national and ultimately international scale. What was most important was the isolated individual; only the process mattered. And, you know, the basic Calvinist contradiction—the necessity of work as against its unimportance—drove most *Time* staffers to distraction, or bars, or other jobs. Everyone would always say three years is the limit; take what you can get, but don't forget to leave.

I started working there when I was 26, and I left when I was 29. And it was just about one of the best jobs that you could get in American journalism in 1961. They gave me what I thought was a lot of money for those days—I think it was about $18,000. In 1961 dollars, that's like earning $70,000 today as a beginning wage. Plus, you could bank your salary. That was the line they told you the minute you got there: "Bank your salary." And the other great line was, "Put it down as a lunch." I'd fly to Aspen for a week, put it down as a lunch and never pay for anything. There was always some excuse and always some story, and the thing was, they would encourage you to do this. A couple of times I was brought into the bureau chief's office and told that my expense account was too low. Dick Clurman came into our whole bureau one time and told us, "You've got air travel cards; use them." And we were to ride first class. There was nothing terribly evil about it; it was just corrupt. It was all old boys' net; it was all Ivy League. But even more than that, when abroad, you were like this celebrity. You were taken seriously at 25-years-old by movers and shakers and corporate leaders, and it wasn't because of you at all; it was because you represented *Time* magazine. It was the golden age of the newsmagazine.

I was the low person in a seven-person bureau. I had the room that had no windows. I subsequently got a great room with a great picture—this huge pin-up of Rita Hayworth in a black negligée—across one entire wall. It was like a billboard. I always loved Rita Hayworth. There was something about her . . . And she danced like an angel. Poor thing—talk about Alzheimer's. Her daughter took care of her. Jasmine. I adored Rita Hayworth. "Put the blame on Mame, boys . . ."

Now, everyday at the bureau there'd be ten or twenty queries to do a little bit of reporting on some subject. I think maybe the second assignment I got was to do an item for this little feature called "Time Clock," which was basically a bunch of one-paragraph stories about business. Mine was about department store sales: find out if Broadway stores had a very good year. So I called the public relations office for Carter Hawley Hale: "This is Andy Kopkind calling from *Time* magazine, and we're doing an item on the Broadway stores' business last year. Can you tell me what your gross was?" Well, she said, "I'll get back to you." Fifteen minutes later there arrives in front of our office a limousine bearing Ed Carter, the president of the company. He was on the California board of regents, and I guess he wanted to be governor. But more than anything else, he wanted his picture on the cover of *Time*. And the girl at the front desk, Lois, I'll always remember her—she was from Chandler Hollywood, or maybe the fifties, with big boobs and an angora sweater and lipstick, and she knew all the gossip about everything—she buzzes me: "Ed Carter's coming back to see you." I said, "Who's Ed Carter?" And she said, "You'd better find out quick, honey. But he's a bigshot, so be very careful." So here comes probably one of the biggest corporate honchos in Southern California to see Andy Kopkind. He's in Mike Davis's book *City of Quartz*. He was a big player in the globalization of Los Angeles in the sixties, in making it a world-class metropolis and sort of putting together museums and educational facilities. And he says, you know, "What can I do for you?" And I think, What is going on here? And I see out my door the bureau chief and all these people are looking in: What is Ed Carter doing holed up with Andy Kopkind? I couldn't believe it. You know, "Anything else you need, just call my people." This was for a one-sentence kind of story. When he left, the bureau chief came in and told me, "That guy will do anything to get in *Time* magazine." And, you know, about seven or eight years later, Ed Carter did get his picture on the cover of *Time* magazine.

So that was how it was. I could do anything I wanted, really, but finally I felt I had to leave—partly because of my little brush with LA law but also because working at *Time* just got awful. Nothing that you did ever counted for anything. That was the absolutely horrible thing about it. If you were a correspondent, you'd write these funny, long or brilliant (or not) files; then you'd give them to Ed, the telex operator, and his little machine, and soon you realized that you were writing for Ed, working for Ed, because Ed would send them in, and basically you would never hear from anyone again. In New York the writers, with their bottles of gin and their Maalox in the desk and their sleazy paws on the little research girls from Bryn Mawr, hated the correspondents. The writers were stuck on the twenty-third floor of this ridiculous building, and they'd never see the world or do anything or talk to any of the people that they were writing about. All they had were the clips, and the correspondents' file was just another clip. They hated the idea that someone was having fun out in the real world, and they pretended that it wasn't real unless it was in *The New York Times*. And still to this day, you know, journalists don't believe it unless it's in *The New York Times*. I think some of them at *Time* are still slugging down the martinis and still pawing the Bryn Mawr kids as they come by. It's Sleaze City, and that was the real reason why you couldn't stay. It was too alienating.

I was across the bay from Berkeley in '64, when the Free Speech Movement was revving up. I was working for *Time* in San Francisco, but I didn't want to get involved in this. I didn't want to go even for my own interest, because I didn't want to have to feel bad. If I wrote about it, I knew that people would say, "What are you interested in that shit for? Bunch of creeps." The whole culture of *Time* was so anti-student and anti-black, anti-beatnik and whatever. There were all these names one would be called, and so the response was not to get involved. And that's what produced the culture of the *Time* correspondent being alienated, the detachment and the cynicism.

It was interesting because a couple of months later, after I'd left the magazine, Berkeley was like the biggest thing in my life. I was working for *The New Republic* and doing a different kind of journalism, and I got involved in all the movements that I had avoided. I think that was the key to the sixties: if you were in an institution that protected you from expressing yourself, you couldn't make a commitment of any kind. And the defense against that was the fifties values of intellectualism and cynicism, the tendency to analyze everything away. Even if you were sympathetic, you'd say, "Oh, it's not going to amount to anything," or "these people are stupid," or "they're immature," or "they're acting out against their parents," or dat-te-da-da-da. There were a million ways for our generation to delegitimize any kind of commitment.

But when I worked for *The New Republic*—it's hard to imagine now—this world of possibilities opened up. I could actually have some authenticity and integrity doing the work that I liked. Those were the two things—authenticity and integrity—that *Time* robbed you of. One of the first things that happened, about six weeks after I got to Washington, was the Selma march. This is early 1965. I had never been to the South to report before, but I went off to Alabama and hung out at Brown's Chapel Church and got to know all these people and all the SNCC workers, black and white. This world had opened up. They were saying exactly what I'd been thinking all these years, but had never actually heard. I didn't know that anybody was acting out these ideas, and it was great.

It wasn't just about civil rights, not just about laws, but about power, and power to the people, power to the community. And they were analyzing the white power structure. At the same time I started reading all this New Left stuff, *The Power Elite* and all, about this sociology of power, and it made a tremendous amount of sense. And then it was like Paul Simon's line, "When I think back on all the crap I learned in high school . . ."

Anyway, I just thought these people were real heroes. The SNCC workers and the black workers from the counties; we would just go and hang out in the sharecroppers' houses and in the little chapels, and this was so beautiful. I thought I was part of this tremendously exciting historic, romantic movement. And . . . I was. So I came back, and I wrote the first piece sort of discovering SNCC for a national left-liberal audience. After that, I was talking to Arthur Waskow, and Arthur said it was a great piece and I said, "Is anyone doing this kind of thing up North?"

"Funny you should ask; there's a group called Students for a Democratic Society."

"S—, D—, is that as in Dog? Really?"

He said they were running this project called ERAP.

You have to know that a lot of these words were not in use at the time. I remember trying to explain what "project" meant. To most people at that time, "project" meant your school project or something, but all of a sudden "project" began to mean this kind of organization. That was a new use for an old word that I remember having to explain to people.

Waskow said you should go to Cleveland and talk to my friends Carol McEldowney and Paul Potter, and go to Chicago and talk to Todd Gitlin and Rennie Davis, and go to Newark and talk to Tom Hayden and others. And I don't think I'd heard of any of those names at all. So off I went. This was the spring of 1965, and I became really emotionally involved with this whole experience. In Cleveland, Carol McEldowney, who was this sort of Swedish ivy plant that we're still trying to clone, took me around the inner-city, through these scenes of urban desolation, over the Cuyahoga River, which was on fire. It was the first time I'd seen a river burning—from the oil pollution and the chemicals. It looked like some sort of Tolkienian harbor, post-nuclear.

At the same time I had a good friend from college, Dan Silverberg, who had married and lived in Cleveland and was in investments or something.

He was a happy-go-lucky guy. I called him and he said, "Come out to my country club for dinner." We couldn't make an arrangement until late in the week, and by that time I was going through what R.D. Laing calls an ontological break. I was becoming radicalized, but I couldn't put a name on it. I was trying to be calm: I was a reporter; I had on my reporter's clothes; I was doing my little thing, interviewing everybody, but I knew this was different.

When the appointed night came, I was staying at a grubby motel right near the SDS project house. I remember it was the week that Dylan's *Bringing It All Back Home* had come out, and "Mr. Tambourine Man" was playing endlessly on the little Webcor hi-fi in the house. I dressed up in my tie and jacket and rented a car and went way out away from the inner-city. Dan Silverberg had grown up in Shaker Heights, but even Shaker Heights was too close now. *They* were moving in. So I drove to Pepper Pike Boulevard or Parkway, way out. At the club it was all plush banquettes and Mediterranean fixtures, young executives and their lovely wives. I remember sitting there absolutely blanking out. Other people apparently were there, I have no recollection. My mind was back in the house, and that reality was so strong, and this reality so different and unpleasant to me. They were talking about their houses, their careers and their kids, and I started dissociating; there I was watching this person who used to be Andy Kopkind sitting with his old friend Dan Silverberg. And between the filet and the cheesecake with strawberries I suddenly got up and said, "Oh, I have a meeting I have to go cover."

I got up and got in my rent-a-car and went back to the west side of inner-city Cleveland and realized that I could never do that other thing again without it being a performance of some kind. Later on I integrated all these things into some sort of social matrix. But the matrix at that point was elusive. And my behavior and my self-presentation started changing from that day: who I could be comfortable with and what I was comfortable doing. I was still the journalist, but I was part of the movement too. The genie was out of the bottle.

PART ONE

Chapter I

◆

DREADFUL OPTIMISM

A Walk in Alabama

Selma

There are easier ways to get to Montgomery. The massed power of the army, the national guard, state troopers and the Justice Department does not lessen the sun's glare or the force of thunderstorms. The pavement along the fifty miles of US 80 from Selma is just as hard on the feet, and the muddy campsites just as cold and disagreeable for all the complex battle plans of the marchers and their protectors. By Tuesday, when even the television cameramen began to lose interest, the march had been transformed from a carnival for 3,000 into a crusade for 300. That night, a Presbyterian clergyman—one of the few whites left in the column—leaned against the clay-caked tailgate of a farm truck and picked at a cold pork chop. "This," he smiled, "is our finest hour."

Whatever the original point of the march—and it has been lost in the events of the last few weeks—the most immediate significance is for the marchers themselves. The young Dallas County Negroes who walk singing freedom songs confirm their commitment to the movement as their fathers and older brothers never did. The thousands of whites who have come to Selma from the North will never, of course, be the same.

When the Selma campaign started two months ago, Brown's Chapel AME Church was a black citadel; now it is the most thoroughly integrated place in the South. At the Saturday night meeting before the march, there were more white faces than black, and Andy Young, one of the best of Martin Luther King's organizers, told the outside agitators that they were being taught as much as they were teaching. "You can't live with us down here without understanding poverty. We could have put you up in fancy motels [they couldn't] but we wanted you to see how we live. We wanted you to live in Negroes' homes and see the poverty of our lives. Because before we get out of this movement, we'll have another one going up North." For the first time in the lives of most of the whites, a Negro ghetto was their home, and when they walked through it at night they were among friends. If they ventured into the white center of town or the residential areas, they were in enemy territory.

"This is not a spectacle; it's a pilgrimage," Andy Young said, but as the marchers flooded over the Pettus Bridge Sunday morning, the scene owed more to Cecil B. De Mille than to Saint James of Compostela. It was a kind of instant history, like "You Are There" on the radio, and everyone tried hard to feel it: two Negro Nobel Peace Prize winners walking hand in hand down an Alabama highway, the majesty of the federal government protecting a ragged band of revolutionaries, the radical change the civil rights movement was effecting in the country.

But it was not until Monday noon, when the four-lane highway narrowed to two and the column was cut to 300 under a federal court rule, that the march took on more than ceremonial meaning. Just before lunch, the marchers crossed into Lowndes County, the heart of darkness in the Black Belt. Last week, the first Negro since Reconstruction was "processed" as a voter (he has not yet officially registered). Negroes outnumber whites more than three-to-one, but they live in unrelieved squalor, and pervasive fear. A few miles into the county, the column passed a ramshackle frame building, which looked like a burned-out barn but turned out to be the certainly separate but grotesquely unequal Rolan elementary school for Negroes. A small group of students gathered at the side of the road. And Dr. King, Reverend Ralph Abernathy and Young talked with them. "Do you want freedom?" Young asked a Negro boy on a bicycle. "Yes, sir," he answered. "Well," said Young, "in a few years Uncle Sam's going to send you over to Vietnam or Korea to fight for the white man's freedom, but you've got to start fighting for your own freedom right now." The boys were terrified, and excited. Later that night, one came to the campsite and asked what he could do. He talked with a leader of the students from Selma in a small trailer, found out how to start a protest movement and then slipped home across a cornfield.

Tuesday it poured, but the songs were louder, and the evening camp was, if anything, more full of high spirits. A few Northern whites wondered whether it was all a meaningless gesture; the long fight for the right to march was after all the real victory. At the moment the right was conceded, the march became unnecessary. And on Wednesday, when thousands more joined the 300 where the four-lane highway resumed, and the City of St. Jude Hospital was turned into a kind of civil rights Copacabana, it was again a stagey pageant. But next week, the young Lowndes County boy will ride out on his bicycle to talk to his friends about the movement, and the Negroes of Dallas County—despite the real danger of retaliation—will move into surrounding Black Belt counties, and there is no merchant on Broad Street in Selma who does not know that there will be other walks on other days.

April 3, 1965, THE NEW REPUBLIC

New Radicals in Dixie

A labama Governor George Wallace has unexpected allies in his efforts to discredit the civil rights movement. They are not racists or segregationists or even Southerners, but white Northern moderates who have decided that the movement is being infiltrated by communists and is heading towards left-wing extremism. From Wallace, the accusations have little impact. There are scores of billboards on Southern highways this week showing Martin Luther King at a "Communist training school" and few take them seriously. But from Northerners, the charges suddenly are real, and they hurt.

"The Red issue is the one thing that could break up the movement," a white director of the Mississippi Summer Project said last month. Since then, a Pittsburgh rabbi has made headlines in every Southern paper by denouncing civil rights extremists; columnists Rowland Evans and Robert Novak are howling that the Student Nonviolent Coordinating Committee (SNCC) is "substantially infiltrated" by communists; and the *New York Post*'s James Wechsler, a perennial poet of liberalism, is convinced that militants are "staging an uprising against the major civil rights blocs . . . encouraged by a fragment of Communists (Chinese rather than Russian in orientation)."

Why it has taken them all so long to discover that the movement is extreme in both its concept and execution is not clear. Civil rights leaders, and particularly those in the South, have been proclaiming their radical intentions for five years or more. Before the marchers left Selma for Montgomery, King's most cautious and conservative adviser, the Reverend Andrew Young, told them: "Actually, we're at war. We're trying to revolutionize the political structure of America." Perhaps it is only as the movement is increasingly successful in the South—as it has been during the last half year—that its meaning becomes obvious.

When the first sit-ins began in Greensboro, North Carolina, and then in Nashville, Tennessee, in the spring of 1960, they were denounced by older leaders of the movement (which was hardly a movement at all in those days) as tactically too dangerous. Dr. King himself withdrew support from the Freedom Rides of 1961, and it was not until a month or so ago that Roy Wilkins of the National Association for the Advancement of Colored People got around to agreeing that demonstrations were a valid tactic in the civil rights war. Recent critics do not misread the signs: the history of the movement had been a record of its evolution from Tomism through tokenism and gradualism to militancy and radicalism. However, the critics do misunderstand what is happening and for two reasons: generation and geography.

Studies of the battles in left-wing politics of the thirties and forties, or factionalism within the International Ladies Garment Workers Union do not shed much light on the current conflicts within the civil rights movement.

SNCC, which is rightly considered the most radical civil rights group, bears little resemblance to the popular front organizations of a generation ago. SNCC is part of the "new radicalism," or the "student left," and is closer to Mario Savio than to Marx. It is anarchic rather than monolithic, social more than economic, downward-pointing rather than pyramidal in organization. It is supremely undisciplined. There is no plan, no program. SNCC's major effort in the South this summer will be "Let the People Speak" conferences held in several states and then, perhaps, regionwide. "We want the people to tell us what we can do. We'll do anything they tell us," said John Lewis, SNCC chairman.

SNCC's leaders avoid rather than command the publicity spotlight. Bob Moses, the brilliant young Negro who directed the Mississippi Summer Project, is so anti-leader that he has changed his name and has slipped out of the state. SNCC despises the "cult of personality" that has surrounded King and the leader-worship within his Southern Christian Leadership Conference (SCLC). The SNCC kids mock his Baptist rhetoric; they dislike the way SCLC "tells people what to do." Moses's idea is to keep SNCC workers in a Southern town only until they can help the local Negroes organize their own protest movement, and then leave. Now SNCC field workers are clearing out of Mississippi, having spawned dozens of indigenous action groups and a statewide anti-establishment political party.

There are no doubt those in SNCC who have read Marx, and some socialist theory may inform their political ideas, as it does for almost everybody these days. The organization also has instrumentalist links to the National Lawyers Guild and the Southern Conference Education Fund, whose activities probably figure prominently in the annals of the House Un-American Activities Committee. But this is a far cry from interpreting SNCC's vague longing for social and economic equality and its rather pervasive anti-establishment behavior as evidence of a communist plot. Since Russia is now so firmly part of the establishment, Maoism or Castroism probably are closer to the romantic yearnings of the SNCC kids who bother to think about it, but there is no evidence that Mao or Castro are taking advantage of their young fans. There is no Manchurian candidate in Mississippi.

There is, however, the beloved Fannie Lou Hamer and her fellow zealots of the Mississippi Freedom Democratic Party. The MFDP (one learns, slowly, to put up with the proliferation of initials) got 80,000 votes in the mock Freedom Election of 1963, and 60,000 in the mock congressional election last year, surely more than any other radical political party could pick up in any election in the US. The MFDP originally had the participation of most of Mississippi's older and most respected Negro leaders. But in the past two years, the bigger names and older leaders have fallen away, and the new leadership has little respect for the tradition of political compromise. The crucial moment was the 1964 Democratic National Convention in Atlantic City, where most of the other civil rights leaders and Democratic Party operatives tried to convince the MFDP to give up the claim to be the lawful Mississippi delegation in exchange for two national at-large seats, and a promise by the convention to exclude discriminatory delegations in future years. SNCC alone was against the compromise, and the MFDP delegates refused. Their point was that they had no interest in or hope of assimilating into the Democratic establishment. They wanted to demolish it. It was rotten to the core, not just eroded here and there. They believed in their rights to political power, and they wanted them in 1964, not at some unnamed future date. Despite a masterful plea for compromise by Bayard Rustin (who ironically is head man on Wallace's personal list of unreconstructed civil rights communists), the MFDP decided that rights delayed were rights denied.

To understand the Southern Negro's radicalism from Washington or New York is impossible. The current crop of critics are not only too old-fashioned to make sense out of the movement, they are also too far away. In their March 28 broadside at SNCC, Evans and Novak quoted an "aggressive young Snic worker" at a civil rights strategy meeting: "You people just don't know what it's like down South." The worker's impertinence was compounded, they said, because he spoke not just to any old Northerner, but to "respected liberals who were crusading for civil rights before he was born."

What the "respected liberals" do not know is that in the South a Negro rarely sees a friendly white face. Worse, he never meets a white Southerner who will treat him as an equal. The Mississippi Freedom Democratic Party was an inevitable development because Negroes are not allowed to assimilate into the white world. It is a mercy that the revolt of the outcasts is not more violent. It is a civil rights truism that wherever the movement goes, the community is polarized. Moderates evaporate, because their role has been built on the foundation of white paternalism and black Tomism which the Negroes must destroy to achieve equality. The segregationists are in a sense right: race relations are more strained after the civil rights agitators finish with a town. There is more tension and more conflict, but there is at least equality. The whites face the Negroes across a sea of hostility, but they face them as equals. It's a necessary beginning.

The "respected liberals" of the North see King in Stockholm or San Francisco, but they do not see a SNCC worker in Amite County, Mississippi. Evans and Novak think that "SNCC and its leaders aren't really interested in the right to vote or any attainable goal." They are dead wrong. Only SNCC, in fact, working through its Mississippi alter ego, the Council of Federated Organizations, has bothered about voter registration; county by county, with the threat of white violence always in the air, SNCC has organized the Negroes in Mississippi and has helped them form a political movement as King has never done, and as the NAACP has never even considered. In terms of local action, SNCC (with help from the Congress of Racial Equality, which is only spottily in the South) is the only successful organization.

King's SCLC is no less militant than SNCC. It is, however, less radical in its approach to the problems of society. SCLC is a strategic command; SNCC is an ideological army. King's incomparable success is largely due to his ability to convince the Northern whites that they can fight for Negro rights as a moral issue and not be concerned with the political and economic consequences. SNCC makes no such distinction, and the harshness of its demands jangles Northern ears. King is concerned with arousing the "national conscience"; SNCC wants to organize the rural Negroes in the South. As the only charismatic leader the movement has produced, King can provide the voice and create the mood that gets legislation through Congress, but he has not yet done the basic work that can change the Southern climate of attitudes.

There may come a day when radicalism in the movement passes white liberals by, and there are some who are working to keep it far hence. But there is danger in the growing gap between Negro expectations and achievements. Legislation will not in itself do much to change the lives of Southern Negroes. As frustrations grow, so will the demands for radical action. Many civil rights leaders think that the problem in the North has only begun to be understood. If the ghettoes explode, the white liberal critics will look back at SNCC radicalism as the mildest of manners.

It embarrasses some liberals to have extremists working for the same causes they support. But there is no good way to make the movement moderate and "respectable." The Confederate flag still flies atop the Capitol in Montgomery, and there are no Negroes in the white waiting room in the bus station in Jackson, four years after the Freedom Ride. The successes of the past few years have been won by increasing militancy and more determined radical action, and there is much further to go. The civil rights effort is a movement, not a disciplined political party or a dues-collecting union or a closed corporation. It needs more militants and more radicals, not fewer.

April 10, 1965, THE NEW REPUBLIC

✦

Of, By and For the Poor

For the students of the sixties, Birmingham and Albany and the Mississippi Summer was the new American Revolution. At the core of the Berkeley Free Speech Movement last fall was the same battle cry that had been heard in the counties of Mississippi: "Let the people decide."

It is the same slogan that the SDS organizers wear on buttons as they work with the Negroes of Clinton Hill, a slum in the South Ward of Newark, New Jersey. It is the same phrase that SDS organizers in Cleveland's Near West Side, a poor white slum, use in protesting the politician-run poverty program.

Students for a Democratic Society has a prehistory as the unfortunately named SLID—the Student League for Industrial Democracy. Without the students, the parent league is a kind of camp for itinerant old-leftist intellectuals—or those who think old. In the summer of 1962, the new SDS students met near Port Huron, Michigan, and approved a statement of ideas and principles. The "Port Huron Statement" is the seminal document of the new left—or "the movement." Its analysis of society was blunt: "America rests in national stalemate . . . its democratic system apathetic and manipulated rather than 'of, by and for the people.'" The framers had no detailed prescription for a change, but a determination to "search for truly democratic alternatives to the present, and a commitment to social experimentation with them. We seek the establishment of a democracy of individual participation governed by two central aims: that the individual share in those social decisions determining the quality and the direction of his life; that society be organized to encourage independence in men and provide the media for their common participation."

SDS chapters opened on several campuses—there were twenty-three with 900 members at the beginning of the academic year; there are now about seventy-five, with 2,000 members—but except for crisis breaks for civil rights activities in the South, the students had no program for putting the Port Huron concepts into practice. In fact, the distrust of authority and dislike of manipulation were so strong and so pervasive that the idea of any program at all was suspect. Programs imply leaders, strategy, preconceived notions of what is good for people. But somehow the students got that particular philosophical fly out of the bottle, and in early 1964 began setting up SDS projects in a number of Northern cities. A special department called ERAP (Economic Research and Action Project) administered the community organizing work, initially with a $3,000 grant from the United Auto Workers. Students are now organizing in eleven Northern cities.

They moved into the communities in groups of six or a dozen. In Cleveland, they rented an apartment in a tacky old frame house in one of the poorest white neighborhoods. They had an idea that they would help the local "community people" to change the condition and quality of their lives, but they were not at all sure how they would do it. ERAP was committed to building an "interracial movement of the poor"; it was thought reasonable to begin reshaping the community among the classes who had the least stake in its preservation, and the most immediate need for improvement. The Near West Side of Cleveland looked at first like fertile ground. Poor whites from Southern Appalachia lived in squalid "hillbilly heavens," in small, roach-infested apartments that rented for $25 a week. There was a WPA-vintage housing project nearby, with an unobstructed view of a clangorous barge-loading canal, and easy access to the city's most notorious rat-breeding grounds.

For three weeks, the SDS kids (they are called that, or "students," by their friends in the community, and while the terms are, strictly speaking, inaccurate, they do not object) canvassed the neighborhood on a voter-registration drive. They were able to get into hundreds of living rooms, and they talked easily about the concerns people had. In late July, they put together their findings. There were three major problems the people of the Near West Side had more or less in common: the inadequacy and mindless application of public welfare (particularly Aid to Dependent Children), unemployment among men and conditions in the public housing project.

Organization of the community was to begin around these issues. First off, the staff helped women on welfare to revitalize an organization called CUFAW (Citizens United for Adequate Welfare), which had been active two years previously when Ohio's Governor Rhodes cut welfare payments drastically as an "economy move." The cut had never been restored, but CUFAW was dormant.

"We just talked with the women. We said we'd help them do whatever they wanted," said one of the SDS staff. CUFAW's first target—less ambitious than the restoration of full welfare payments—was the institution of a free school lunch program in Cleveland public schools. With the SDS kids always in the background, the women held rallies and meetings, protested to official boards, and complained so loud in public—and with such force—that the city caved in.

In the housing project the SDS kids talked with residents, and a tenants' meeting was held. Lack of recreation facilities became the issue. The housing project officials were terrified, but the recreation director—whose enthusiasms had not previously included an interest in recreation—was convinced to make immediate reforms. The tenants' meeting became the Tenants' Council, but the whole movement in the project touched a sensitive nerve in Cleveland officialdom. SDS activities were investigated by the city's "Red Squad," a kind of miniature FBI. Some older women residents of the housing project were convinced that the students were communists, and the first of a continuing series of Red-baitings began. The pressure finally became so strong that SDS withdrew its support from the Tenants' Council, the president of the Council resigned, and organizing was abandoned.

The unemployment issue proved difficult to "organize around." As it turned out, unemployed men in the neighborhood had little in common. In the process, though, some of the SDS students spent days in "spot labor" employment offices, and began to learn what it was like to be in the lowest ranks of American life. They also saw how uninterested organized labor was in reforming the employment patterns of the area. "Spot labor"—short-term or part-time jobs for minimum wage or less—was non-unionized, but the spot laborers could work in union shops, often for long periods of time under gentlemen's agreements between the employers and the unions.

Organizing in a poor white community was much tougher than the SDS kids had feared, but they did make their existence felt in Cleveland. They fought the official anti-poverty program (like most in the country, controlled by politicians for its political benefits), and helped residents draw up alternatives. They also made friends in the Negro near-slum area of Glenville, and planned to start an organizing project there this summer.

As the year progressed, the SDS staff—which now included one young mother on welfare—were attracted more and more to the idea of a "community union" rather than specific issue-groups as a basis for organizing. Their model was the SDS project in Newark, which had gathered scores of local Negroes into the Newark Community Union Project (NCUP), called by everyone "en-cup."

NCUP began at the same time as the Cleveland project, but the SDS kids found more immediate response in the Negro ghetto than their friends had among Cleveland's poor whites. The Negroes of Clinton Hill had a wide range of grievances: housing, education, police harassment, welfare—and simply the feeling of being "left out." The organizers easily found local residents to work with them, and there are now about as many Negroes as "students" on the staff.

The students roamed the streets of the "lower hill" neighborhood in Newark; they took "housing surveys" and met the residents. Those who were most eager to "do something" were encouraged to have informal meetings of their neighbors, and soon a system of organized streets—called blocks—developed. Hunterdon Street held weekly meetings, so did Hillside and Peshine; and every Tuesday there would be a general meeting for all the blocks.

So far, it is difficult to measure the extent of NCUP's effect on Clinton Hill. In the way of immediate improvements, there have been a number of building repairs made by landlords, and at least detectable housing inspection and code enforcement by the city. Sanitation and garbage pick-up (NCUP demands) have been improved, and an urban renewal scheme that would have turned much of the area into an industrial zone—with drastic results for the poorest residents—has been quietly shelved. These are small victories, but they have done something more for the Negroes of Clinton Hill: they expect something will happen.

Organizing the poor is not so much a political act as a psychological process. There is no street haranguing, no cadre discipline. Spontaneity is all-important. "The most significant thing," says Tom Hayden, who drafted the Port Huron Statement and is now a NCUP organizer in Newark, "is the development of a group of people with no previous political connections who are able to speak and act without being embarrassed or dependent on the higher-ups."

It is a long jump from a statement of theories to a block meeting, but they are jumping in Newark. Last week, after she and her son were arrested by Fifth Precinct policemen in Clinton Hill, Mrs. Georgia Lewis sat in the office of an aide to Mayor Hugh J. Addonizio and told him she didn't want to take any more harassment, that she was tired of arbitrary arrests and threats and brutal treatment (Mrs. Lewis's daughter was arrested in front of the

NCUP staff's apartment a few months ago, also for no apparent reason). With her in the office were a dozen NCUP members—both students and community people. Mrs. Lewis, a shy, frail Negro, was suddenly not afraid to speak back to the "higher-ups." The mayor's aide was annoyed, but he could not help being impressed.

To visit with the SDS projects for a week is a wrenching experience. Someone said the official war on poverty might be far more effective if Sargent Shriver spent a few days—perhaps incognito, like Peter the Great among the shipwrights in Amsterdam—with the poor whites on the Near West Side, or the Negroes in Newark. Long before Adam Clayton Powell thought of it, the SDS kids knew that social change cannot come from the top down and decided they had to become as nearly as possible part of the community they are helping.

Hardly anyone on the "outside" can imagine the completeness of their transformation. They are not down there for a visit in the slums. They are part of the slums, a kind of lay-brotherhood, or worker-priests, except that they have no dogma to sell. They get no salary; they live on a subsistence allowance that the project as a whole uses for rent and food. Most of the time they are broke. In the dining room of the Cleveland "project house" last week was a sign: "Panic point. Bank balance $4.09." Newark project workers have to call "friends in the suburbs" every so often for $5 or $10, so the necessities of life can continue. The kids are the very antithesis of paid organizers the unions or political parties have to hire. Most of them have committed their lives to "the movement"; no matter if in a few years they change their minds. It is important that they now have the expectation of remaining.

Most of them went to college. Their experience runs from drop-out to Ph.D. The two major collegiate springs are Swarthmore and the University of Michigan. Most of them come from middle-class and professional-class families; many of their parents do not approve. They are subject to the same psychological motivations as everyone else of their age in America. They believe it is their conscience, not their psychology, that counts in their society. They hear about SDS at college, and the projects cannot absorb all the organizers who apply to work. The urge to *act* is the strongest force of the new left.

The students will never, of course, assimilate themselves entirely into poor communities. There is a psychological distance between the newcomers and the older residents, and even though it is shorter than one would imagine, it bothers some of the kids. A few of the NCUP students have gone to another New Jersey city, have taken low-paying jobs, much as the indigenous poor would have, and they lead an "ordinary" life without any kind of plan for organizing. It is more than the Fabian idea of "getting to know the poor," and much less than the old communist idea of infiltrating the proletariat. One girl has gone to work in a garment shop; when her friends and co-workers learn that she is a college graduate and ask why she is working for $1.25

an hour as an unskilled laborer, she replies, truthfully, "because I was tired of the rat race."

But most of the SDS kids do not go so far. They balance their desire to build a working movement with their anti-strategy and anti-leadership beliefs. They hate the system of manipulation and authoritarianism more than they dislike the injustices it produces.

It is hard for liberals traumatized by both Stalinism and McCarthyism to understand the new left's attitudes about communism. First, SDS called itself a "non-Communist organization." The students dropped the designation a few months ago, because no one could see its relevance. (The Daughters of the American Revolution, for instance, does not call itself a non-communist group.) They do not seek allies in the middle-class liberal world, because their analysis of society tells them that the liberals have as much stake in the status quo as the conservatives, and are equally biased against change. The Red-baiting in Newark has come from liberal Democratic politicians—and from some of the older civil rights organizations.

Relations with the League for Industrial Democracy are far from friendly. League leaders—especially Bayard Rustin—want a coalition of liberal movements (unions, civil rights groups, the churches) to improve the condition of the poor. The students see the coalition idea as merely an extension of New Deal welfare politics. They want to do more than lift a few poor people into the middle class. "The New Deal brought socialism to the middle class and free enterprise to the poor," a Protestant minister who works with SDS in Cleveland said.

The organizers are anything but apolitical. But they believe they must shake up the politicians before any changes can be made, that they must start the poor moving—as the civil rights movement got the Negroes in the South moving—before the "power structure" will acknowledge their existence. SNCC workers in Mississippi march with Negroes to courthouses every day in a futile attempt to register to vote, not because they think that the rolls will suddenly open but because the Negroes learn that they are systematically excluded from democratic participation. SDS organizers march with the poor in Newark for the same reason. If Mayor Addonizio thinks this is a subversive development, he is right.

At the April 17 March on Washington to End the War in Vietnam, which SDS sponsored, the organization's president, Paul Potter, asked the demonstrators as they massed at the base of the Washington Monument, "What kind of system is it that disenfranchises people in the South, leaves millions . . . impoverished and excluded from the mainstream and promise of American society, that creates faceless and terrible bureaucracies . . . that consistently puts material values before human values—and still persists in calling itself free and in finding itself fit to police the world? What place is there for ordinary men in that system and how are they to control it, make it bend itself to their wills rather than bending them to its? We must name that system. We must name it, describe it, analyze it, understand it and change it."

Someone in the crowd yelled "capitalism," and he was shouted down by others. The system Potter means to name—and change—is much more complicated than that. It is an intricate set of interlocking relationships that is called "power." It doesn't really matter who is holding it—a Negro leader or a white, a liberal or a conservative.

The old left says that community organization was tried in the thirties, among the unemployed; it did not grow into a movement then, and will not in this generation. They suspect that the students would not know what to do with power if they should suddenly achieve it, and they think that indeed the students would rather remain in opposition than start planning. More than that, they do not know how in the world a community union or a group of protesting welfare mothers can win over the entrenched power of city or state administrations and their vast economic allies.

What is to be done with power is the crucial question in SDS, as it is with SNCC. Last week in Newark a slate of NCUP community members (including some SDS staff organizers) was elected to run one of the area boards of the city's official war on poverty. Newark's machine politicians were aghast, but NCUP's joy at political victory (the slate won a vote of area residents by two-thirds majority) was not unalloyed. Running even part of an anti-poverty program (the area board will determine the needs of its neighborhood and then help administer the funds granted) might lead to the creation of the kind of bureaucratic, leader-heavy organization that the students abhor. In Cleveland the SDS staff shies away from attaching itself too closely even to the opposition anti-poverty plan, which calls for the participation of the poor. The tension within the "freedom movement," between those who want more freedom and those who want more movement, will surely increase as the doors to power open.

June 19, 1965, THE NEW REPUBLIC

✦

Not So Great Society

Six months is not a very long time in which to build a Good Society, much less a Great one. But President Johnson is no Fabius; his political science does not admit the tactic of delay, and by his own rules (which we are bound to follow) the US should be passing from Good to Great just about now. Last week the President signed the Medicare bill, prepared to approve the housing law and the Voting Rights Act, and saw labor and immigration measures move towards passage. Congress is obviously willing to enact the whole of the Administration's program, and a lot it did not have the nerve to ask for.

Already it is possible to see what life will be like in that best of all possible worlds. The Aid-to-Education Act gives federal funds to local state and religious schools, more or less for the first time on a universal basis (previously, there had been exceptional cases of aid in various disguises). The aid program has tortuous formulas for grants that avoid constitutional (and sentimental) restrictions on mixing church and state, and it contains not particularly stringent rules for racial integration. Incredibly, it represents the first serious attempt of the federal government to improve the quality of general education, and is about twenty years late.

The Medicare program will provide people over 65 with "free" hospital care for two months a year, providing they pay the first $40 themselves. It is about one-tenth of the national health program introduced by President Truman nearly twenty years ago and killed by the doctors' lobby.

The housing bill has very little to do with building new housing, but it does provide "rent subsidies" for poor families who would like to live in middle-income flats but can't quite afford it. Like much of the current welfare legislation, it is a sort of short-cut to status. One can imagine a poor Negro family in Harlem receiving a telegram from the White House: "Greetings! You have been selected at random to enter the Middle Class. Please report on 1 October to Apartment 17-B, 710 Riverside Drive, with a 21-inch television set, the *Saturday Review of Literature* and a set of Danish-modern silverware."

The Voting Rights Act will let Negroes in the South register to vote and perhaps even vote, providing they can (1) withstand the economic threats and the physical harassment of their plantation bosses and the local white "power structure"; (2) shake off the political apathy produced by 350 years of educational and social deprivation; and (3) be convinced that voting can change their lives. Congress has so far ignored a small but intensive campaign by civil rights workers to unseat five Mississippi representatives chosen—in violation of a specific provision of the federal Constitution—in an election from which all Negroes were systematically excluded.

Federal aid for Appalachia—a dismally depressed region stretching from Tennessee up the Appalachian Mountain ridge into New York State—consists mainly in building highways to attract tourists and in the process give some out-of-work coal miners construction jobs.

The appropriation for the War on Poverty is twice last year's sum—almost $2 billion. It is a complete mystery what the "war" has done, is doing or can do. A great many people in Washington talk about nothing else; the Poor Corps is this year's *in* job, as the Peace Corps was last year's. But neither the Poor Corpsman nor anybody else has an idea of what winning the war would mean.

There is some small hope that President Johnson is not finished building his Great Society, and that next year's legislative program will attempt to change the structure of the social complex instead of merely adding rooms. But the President has yet to look at the problems he so often deplores—

poverty, racial discrimination, social fragmentation—in any programmatic way. He is still tied to the New Deal concept of welfarism: poor people are responsible for their poverty; Negroes are responsible for their oppression; and the middle class is responsible for its alienation. Give them all a little money, and the minimum freedom in which to exercise it, and they will be all right. Except that is not how it worked out in 1935, and it is doubtful, from the look of things in the Great Society so far, whether it will now.

August 6, 1965, NEW STATESMAN

♦

Bureaucracy's Long Arm

In the flat cotton counties of Mississippi, the federal government has come close to subsidizing a movement of poor Negroes to change the pattern of their short, nasty and brutish lives. The unlikely vanguard of the poor is the Child Development Group of Mississippi (CDGM), which runs eighty-four preschool centers and attendant adult action programs in seventy-five communities throughout the state, under a $1,460,748 Project Head Start grant from the Office of Economic Opportunity.

It hardly sounds like the makings of a revolution, but for many Mississippi Negroes, CDGM *is* the civil rights movement this summer. The spirit and momentum of last summer's brilliant social drama has thinned. "The movement" is in disarray, and while no one imagines the US government could ever replace the angry organizers of the Negro poor, it is obvious that some kind of test is under way. How far can—and will—the government go?

Not so strangely, people at two different geographical poles may arrive at different interpretations of the results of CDGM's eight-week program. From Washington, the romantic idyll of Negro sharecroppers running little schools in the cotton fields is marred only by the disorderliness of the CDGM central staff, which for some reason cannot data-process and quadruplicate their activities in the Harvard Business School manner. From Mississippi, the overwhelming problem of running an independent school system with totally inexperienced people in a continually hostile society is complicated by the OEO's lack of empathy and its sensitivity to political pressure. Early this month, Washington and Mississippi collided. How they got to that point illustrates the central problem of the War on Poverty: how to ensure (as the legislation demands) the "maximum feasible participation" of the poor.

CDGM is an outgrowth and an elaboration on the "freedom schools" which workers for the Mississippi Summer Project set up last year. Political action had to involve education. The schools were in the middle of what CDGM's first director, Tom Levin, calls the "natural community," the urban neighborhoods and rural groupings where Negroes lived and knew each other.

Levin, a 41-year-old lay psychoanalyst with a long involvement in civil liberties and civil rights activities, worked with the Medical Committee for Human Rights and the freedom schools last summer in McComb, Mississippi. Late in the winter, he got together a group of civil rights organizers in his New York office to discuss the possibility of starting "freedom preschools" in Mississippi. The day before the meeting, an OEO officer heard about the plan, immediately related it to the embryonic Project Head Start program, and rushed to New York to convince Levin to join up.

Neither Levin nor his colleagues, principally Protestant ministers from the National Council of Churches' Delta Ministry (the churches' civil rights program in Mississippi), were overwhelmed by the offer of government funds. For the same reason that Mississippi politicians dislike the federal government—"control"—Levin thought the preschool project should be a volunteer, independent effort.

But the possibilities of Poverty Program help were enormous. With healthy ambivalence, Levin and the Delta ministers agreed to become part of Head Start. It fit the OEO's plan perfectly: Washington was searching for a way to attack poverty in Mississippi from outside the "white power structure." To avoid a possible veto by Governor Paul Johnson, CDGM was to be set up under a grant to an educational institution (which by law is veto-proof). Tougaloo College was frightened and refused; finally Levin convinced Mary Holmes Junior College, an obscure institution in West Point, Mississippi, to sponsor the program. The *quid pro quo* was a $12,000 "administrative fee" requested by the college.

The theory of Head Start is to give poverty's children a leg up on their richer schoolmates when they enter kindergarten or the first grade in September. There is no very strong evidence that eight weeks of preschool activities, even in the best of circumstances, will make much of a lasting difference. But even if the educational benefits of Head Start are not enormous, it offers obvious opportunities for community action and development, particularly in the poorest areas of the South. Included in the program were a medical examination and treatment plan, meals for the children and nutrition education for the parents, a counseling project for the most distressed children, a book printing project, and a drama and film-making project. There were hundreds of ways to train parents and volunteers in patterns of living that had always been closed to them.

The central staff Levin assembled was largely composed of young civil rights workers. At a SNCC convention in the spring, Levin proposed that the organization actively support CDGM. Nothing could have been further from the SNCC mystique of anti-government, anti-bureaucracy, anti-control and—some might say—anti-program. But some SNCC workers came along, and Levin put them to work canvassing the rural counties, finding local Negroes who were interested in setting up centers, and forming local parents' committees to do all the planning and management. No one else but civil rights workers had the dedication and the experience to organize the local centers.

White harassment began early. Sharecroppers who registered their children for a Head Start center were threatened by the plantation bosses. One tenant was evicted; many withdrew their children. There was physical violence, too. Someone shot into the CDGM headquarters at Mt. Beulah, and at the center in Rolling Fork. Levin's car was forced off the road by two white men in a radio-controlled pickup truck in a Delta county. A cross was burned at the Anguilla center. To deflect some of the attacks, the OEO gave money to white county school boards to set up their own Head Start projects in competition with the CDGM centers. The rationale was that CDGM could not handle the demand. In reality, the two rivals often fought for the same children, and in the poorest areas, where Negroes were most vulnerable to economic pressure, the white Head Start often as not won.

All Head Start centers are technically open to both Negroes and whites, but there is little race mixing in Mississippi this summer. Except for a few white CDGM staff members' children, the eighty-four centers are all Negro. In almost all, however, there are white workers from the North (there is one white Mississippian—a secretary—on the central staff). The county Head Starts, meanwhile, are controlled by whites but have neither white students nor teachers. They deny the possibility of community action, rather than encourage it. There are no functional parents' committees. All power is in the hands of the white politicians, and the Negro principals and teachers who have been hired (to the general exclusion of the poor) are in the unenviable role of "Uncle Toms." The emphasis in these centers is on discipline and regimentation. On the other hand, the best CDGM centers make a conscious effort to let the children express themselves as freely as possible; they will not have much of a chance to do it again in Mississippi.

The only local Negroes in the poor Delta counties who would start a CDGM school, naturally, were "movement" people. Sidney Alexander, a wise and charming carpenter in Rolling Fork, was a leader of the town's Freedom Democratic Party precinct; he became the organizer of the Head Start parents' committee. The experience was repeated throughout the state. Reverend J.F. McRee, the powerful leader of the civil rights movement in Canton, started the Canton CDGM project, the biggest (with 560 children) in the system. They all had the experience and the confidence of leadership. They could withstand the consuming hostility of the whites, who refused to cooperate almost everywhere except Gulfport and the "moderate" Gulf Coast cities. Facilities were hard to find; school boards refused to lease the public schools, and in most cases would not contract out the school buses. Buildings in the white neighborhoods, or buildings owned by whites, were unavailable. In the backwoods, CDGM found small Negro churches and unused shacks. The community volunteered to repair and paint them, build equipment and put in the necessary sanitary facilities.

Incredibly, all eighty-four centers were operating on opening day, July 12, but the troubles had just begun. A central staff of about forty non-administrators, most of them under 30, was running a school system with about 5,600 children spread out over a vast area, in the face of antagonism from the people who controlled the state.

The CDGM headquarters was located on an old Negro college campus called Mt. Beulah, now leased by the Delta Ministry, and used like a 1930s labor union camp in the Catskills. From it, the staff began to fan out to the countryside. Ten yards from the campus gate they met their first obstacle: police lay in wait for CDGM cars and gave them tickets for every possible traffic violation, real or fancied. In the first week or so, CDGM employees collected $1,100 in fines. In the counties, the local committees were having more serious problems. They were to be reimbursed for supplies and food and the usual expenses, but they had no operating capital and local white merchants would not extend credit, even with the government behind them. In one community, the Negroes could not get credit for buying a stove, and the OEO would not authorize payment until the purchase was made (the stalemate was broken by an elaborate leasing agreement). The OEO demanded receipts and all kinds of official documents for every purchase, which would have been easy enough in Chicago but difficult in Sharkey County, where the Negro store owner's idea of a receipt was a scrap of paper bag or, at best, a slice of tape from the old adding machine. Neither, of course, went down well with Washington.

For some reason, the lack of bureaucratic efficiency did not seem to bother the program, which was going miraculously well. Some of the schools were having their difficulties, in a few instances because of conflicts between forceful Negro matriarchs and the parents' committee members. The CDGM staff was attentive to their needs, but Levin demanded that the community committees work out their own problems. Two of the centers were temporarily suspended for a few days because they were not coping with personal problems and the program was falling apart; their disappointment and embarrassment—and the support offered by central staff coordinators—moved the parents' committees to resolve the conflicts.

Visitors were shuttling back between Washington and Mississippi, and they all were excited by the centers. The staff was justly proud. It is hard not to be moved by the experience of people sensing freedom for the first time.

August mornings in the Delta are hot when they dawn, but the children stand patiently at the roadside for the cars or rickety buses to pick them up. Many of them have no shoes; some wear rags for clothes. In one county, a bus driver spends two-and-a-half hours fetching children, and the same amount of time taking them home. In Sharkey County, one of the poorest in the country, parents pick up children for the Hopedale CDGM center in their own cars and trucks. They rumble down the narrow highway and then bump along narrower dirt roads, and at a corner they turn into a rutted path that leads to the school, a one-room shack with no electricity, and fresh water carried in in big cans from heaven-knows-where. In the field in back is a huge pecan tree, with a low table underneath and forty small children playing with blocks and finger paint and picture books. Louis Robinson, the head of the local committee, is fixing a stair to the center. Four or five mothers are playing with the children. A white "resource person" (there are no "teachers") is setting out breakfast—eggs, bacon, grits, bread, milk.

"Some of the parents was threatened by the boss man," Louis Robinson explained. "But the kids come anyway. It's our school, so it's their school. Well, I think they like it pretty good."

Hopedale is a small victory, and so is Rolling Fork and the centers at McComb and Holly Springs and Itta Bena and Second Pilgrim's Rest (which was set fire to, but saved from destruction). Together, they are a huge triumph and no imaginary threat to the architecture of white control. Mississippi racists cannot tolerate the example of Negroes running their own affairs. Small wonder, then, that the political attacks began even before the centers opened, and increased in number and intensity as they were seen to be successful.

The *Jackson Daily News,* a paragon of the white Mississippian's point of view, warned in May:

> Here is one of the most subtle mediums for instilling the acceptance
> of racial integrity and the ultimate mongrelization ever perpetrated
> in this country. The most frightening parallel of these so-called
> Head Start programs . . . are some similar programs which have
> been a part of some anti-American countries for years.

US Representative John Bell Williams, the Goldwater Democrat who was stripped of his seniority by the House leadership in January, "represents" the Mt. Beulah area and wants dearly to get CDGM out of his district. He managed to convince Senator Stennis (a *bona fide* Mississippi politician but not a fanatic) to use his position on the Senate appropriations committee to lead the attack. Stennis put the chief committee investigator, Paul J. Cotter, on CDGM's trail. An investigating team went to Mt. Beulah, pored over CDGM's books, and snooped around in desk drawers and filing cabinets. Cotter went to Levin's home in New York (where his wife and children are staying) and asked Mrs. Levin personal questions about her husband's personality and his activities.

The OEO, whose $1.9 billion appropriation is before Stennis's committee, was understandably anxious. The news went quickly to Sargent Shriver and to the White House. OEO auditors and evaluators began to descend on Mt. Beulah. Dr. Julius Richmond, the director of Head Start, came down with an inspection team. The staff was nervous and harried, and with good reason. On August 1, the OEO called a special meeting of the CDGM board of directors at Mary Holmes Junior College. Levin heard about it during the day; he and his assistant, Jim Monsonis, a former SNCC worker, chartered a plane and flew to West Point.

Three OEO representatives presented Levin and the board with an ultimatum in the form of fourteen "recommendations" to clean up CDGM. The first thirteen were not unreasonable. Levin recognized the administrative deficiencies, and was eager to eliminate them. The OEO wanted more complete receipts, strict accounting of petty cash, logs kept on travel and phone calls, and more financial responsibility for the board of directors. Their fourteenth request was the shocker: CDGM was to move immediately from Mt. Beulah to West Point, and an OEO official would be installed from Washington to act as a "liaison" between the president of Mary Holmes College and Levin.

With three weeks to go in the summer Head Start project, Levin argued, a move would destroy the program. He was not thrilled about the set-up at Mt. Beulah: the quarters were inadequate, there were too many non-CDGM activities interfering with the central staff's work, and some minor friction had developed with the Delta Ministry. But to move to West Point would be killing: it was more than 200 miles from most of the centers, telephone and transportation facilities were extremely difficult, supplies could not be found in the area and would take weeks to arrive from Jackson (which is a half hour by car from Mt. Beulah), community people would not be able to come to the headquarters, and living arrangements were poor.

The more-or-less official OEO explanation (the entire matter was never made public) was that the move would somehow improve CDGM's administration. Levin thought it would do precisely the opposite. He insisted that the real reason was pressure from Stennis. That was true enough: OEO hoped that it could give Stennis a symbol of retreat and maintain the substance of the program. But more than that, the OEO wanted more control of Levin, which is to say more control of the program. It was almost impossible to do that at Mt. Beulah; at Mary Holmes, the dancer might be separated from his dance.

The next day, Levin returned to Mt. Beulah, called a meeting of the staff, and presented the "recommendation" to move. There was a violent, emotional reaction. A secret vote was taken; only three staff members wanted to accept the move and stay with the program; two were undecided; five said they would resign and leave CDGM; and twenty-five voted to resign from OEO employment and try to continue CDGM without federal funds. Staff members who were used to fighting power structures (and were, in fact, rather fond of it) painted a distressing picture of what a forced move would cause: Negro pickets in front of Head Start centers and action by civil rights workers to undermine OEO projects. Someone suggested getting all 1,200 CDGM local employees to return their weekly OEO paychecks to their congressmen, or to President Johnson, with publicity fanfares.

Washington was horrified. Two negotiators flew to Mississippi and met again with the staff. Through a long night session, the staff battered the Poverty men: how could CDGM maintain its credibility as champions of poor Mississippi Negroes if it gave in to "Mister Charlie," in this case Senator Stennis, at the first attack? By the middle of the week, the OEO caved in. Or did it? It was agreed that CDGM could stay at Mt. Beulah for the rest of the summer. Levin would be eased out of all administrative functions; he would be assigned to develop proposals for the vastly expanded program that CDGM hopes to sell to the Poverty Program in the fall, all things and Senator Stennis willing. Levin's assistant would take over administration, and the board of directors would try to assert itself, most vocally through Reverend Art Thomas, of the Delta Ministry; Miss Marian Wright, a young lawyer from the NAACP Legal Defense and Educational Fund; and A.D. Beittel, the retired (white) head of Tougaloo College. The federal bureaucracy allowed the insurgents to win one skirmish, but there was little doubt who would win the long war.

The trauma of the sudden OEO barrage, and the resulting engagement of the board of directors' role, has damaged staff morale. When the board called a meeting to, among other things, set up a four-man executive committee and did not invite Levin's replacement, he quit. Not only had the board gone over his head, but he felt its action to concentrate power in the hands of just four people, none of them community representatives, had diminished the role of the poor in the administrative control of the program. The fall program, if it is ever funded, will suffer too. Eight weeks of Head Start is, as its name implies, only a first step. To be meaningful, the program has to continue.

Despite the OEO's concessions to the Head Start staff at Mt. Beulah, things will not be the same again. The SNCC workers who thought they could run a US government program like a Freedom House (which is to say, not run it at all) know that the strings attached to all that money are constricting, and have no end. OEO's anxiety about Mt. Beulah and Levin and CDGM may have been simply a response to ill-kept finances and political pressure. Underneath, there is a deeper concern about the radicalism of a program like CDGM.

The independent civil rights workers in Mississippi see that the Negroes in the small communities lose some of their motivation for protest when they get small government jobs at the Head Start centers. The inevitable gulf opens between those who want to tear down the whole "system" and those who want to slip into it. If CDGM can keep its course, it may prove that if it cannot be the whole civil rights movement, it can at least be a strong ally. The sharecroppers who are tasting power and money this summer for the first time are developing into political men faster than anyone expected. The civil rights workers who could find no program to push after the protest marches have seen what real changes can occur in people's lives. They are growing up, too.

August 21, 1965, THE NEWREPUBLIC

The First Falling Domino

The best that can be said about the domino theory is that it works in reverse. The deeper America's involvement in Vietnam becomes, the less effective is its deterrence value. It is one thing to lose a war with 17,000 "advisers" and quite another to lose it with 125,000 battle troops; to win it (whatever that means) with a land army of half a million would be worst of all. That kind of victory is the death of policy, not the foundation of it.

The President's melodramatic high-noon announcement of increases in America's Vietnam force and the doubling of the draft was something of an anticlimax. Most people expected more, and many wanted it. The Republican leader of the House of Representatives, Gerald Ford, would like a declaration of war and bombing of North Vietnamese cities. It is a fair guess that the Republicans will attack the Administration's policy from the right, rather than the left, in the 1966 congressional elections. To forestall some of the criticism, Mr. Johnson will have to think in terms of escalation. How Americans got to be war-lovers is difficult to say. One would have thought there was very little enthusiasm for long casualty lists and a traumatized economy. Still, hardly anyone questions the President's latest escalation.

Opposition now has polarized into two schools: the desperate and the ineffectual. Not that the desperadoes have very much effect; but they do make a splash. Last weekend, several hundred marched on the Capitol to "declare peace." A few thousand students have threatened to tear up their draft cards (and a Democratic congressman threatens to make that act a high crime). A group of Mississippi Negroes, returning from the funeral of one of their townsmen killed in Vietnam, declared that they would not serve in the armed forces. The story was reported nationally and served only to discredit the civil rights movement.

The ineffectual opposition is much more respectable, but they do not make any noise at all. A dozen liberal congressmen hold meetings to "discuss" Vietnam and announce that they think some solution ought to be sought. They hope for the Titoization of Vietnam, but are unwilling to base their suggested policies on the more realistic possibilities. There is still no broad movement for peace in Vietnam.

Without any external or internal brakes on policy, Mr. Johnson does not have to entertain seriously the alternative of withdrawal, or even serious negotiations. Despite his denials, there have been several occasions for him to de-escalate, and they have been ignored. As soon as Mr. Khanh, the last South Vietnamese premier but three—or is it four?—cleared his throat in a way that sounded like "negotiate," he was allowed to be democratically deposed by a coup which could not have succeeded without at least tacit American support. The US embassy in Saigon gives no sympathy to the noncommunist elements who would like to try for a negotiated settlement.

The only hope for a way out of this dismal trap, at least the only hope visible in Washington, is a change in the American domestic political situation. Sooner or later, the human cost will get too high, and the defense budget will become unmanageable. Already, the Republicans are calling for drastic cuts in welfare legislation to pay for the war ("Uncle Sam has to take off his Santa Claus suit and put on his khakis," a Republican senator said). There will have to be the same kind of dissatisfaction with the way things are going in Vietnam as there was with the war in Korea. It all puts Americans who oppose the Administration in a very curious position. "I don't like it much," one left-wing Democrat in Washington said, "but I keep on cheering for the Vietcong and the Republicans. Both ways, the end will come sooner."

August 13, 1965, NEW STATESMAN

✦

Call Me Ma'am

A fter the Beatles and Scotch whisky, the Royal Family is Britain's most entertaining export to the US. Three weeks with Princess Margaret and Lord Snowdon is perhaps a bit longer than hosts like visitors to stay, but their presence has been a welcome relief amid the afflictions of a grey November—the war, the blackout and the passing of Dorothy Kilgallen. And after all, this is a big country and there was a lot to see. They departed, tastefully, on the eve of Thanksgiving, which commemorates the Pilgrims' deliverance from the tyranny of the British Crown as well as the abundance of the American wilderness. The fruits of that earlier migration were laid before the Princess and the Earl. They had sumptuous meals and lavish receptions wherever they went, but if they fulfilled their desire to "meet all kinds of Americans" they must have done it on the sly. In the course of their official tour, they came across only those picked and prepared (everyone was told to say "ma'am") for the royal encounter. In San Francisco they met descendants of late-nineteenth-century robber barons, in Los Angeles they met movie stars and Barry Goldwater, in Arizona they met bankers and a prominent member of the John Birch Society, in Washington they met "the gay young fun" set, and in New York they met the successors to The Four Hundred.

Everyone else had to be content to catch a glimpse of the Royal Limousine (Rolls Royces in California, white Cadillacs in Arizona) as it sped by with police sirens wailing, or read about the banquets, parties and balls on the society pages of the newspapers. Someone had written, "Margaret is much more than a princess, she is a personality," in one of the innumerable pre-visit puffs which were designed to ready the American public for the visit. But at the end very little about the Princess's "personality" was known. She had the sneezes and a bad case of laryngitis in Los Angeles (San Franciscans hinted darkly that it came from the smog), and that at least established that she was subject to familiar human ailments. But otherwise the Princess remained two-dimensional at best, and every-other-inch a Queen. Perhaps that is the most one can expect of tourists; people are always reduced to stereotypes when they go abroad.

Aside from the unlikely possibility that the couple wanted to see America just for the fun of it, there has been no convincing explanation for the tour. There was no political motivation, of course, and as for "goodwill," Americans probably think too well of the British upper classes already. It was said at the beginning that Britain was going to show off its new fashion-consciousness, and there was a great deal made of the royal wardrobe (white wool coat with bronzed seal lapels, yellow feather toque and sky-blue organza gown with diamanté embroidery for Her; patent leather jodphur boots with high loops, fitted blue jacket and cuffless pegged pants for Him). The couple even began to act like Barbie and Ken.

After a while, the clothes business went slack. Reporters still felt obliged to tell what the Princess was wearing, but notice slid from the first to the fifteenth paragraph. It was hard for the Royal *couture* to compete with Jax slacks in Southern California or the latest imports in New York. Then the papers started talking about the fuss everyone made over the visit. "Agog" became the favorite word some time during the end of the first week. "Hollywood Agog," "Tucson Agog," "Desert Agog." When no one was agog anymore, the real effect, if not the purpose, of the tour began to become apparent: Princess Margaret and the Earl of Snowdon were exchange status symbols, like exchange Nigerian students at the University of Oklahoma, sent to infuse vitality into a bored aristocracy that had begun to doubt its own importance.

It was all very clear when they came to Washington. Nothing else but the Royal Visit was talked about in drawing rooms of status, but it was not talked about at all anywhere else. A careful check of twelve taxi drivers turned up not a one who knew that a regular princess was in town. The millions of civil servants in the area had no idea of the visit, probably because they were not given the afternoon off, the custom when big shots come to the capital for a parade in an open car. News of the visit vanished from front pages and lodged in the fashion pages under recipes for pumpkin pie and cranberry sauce.

It has always been true that difference between the upper classes in England and America is this: in England everyone takes the aristocracy seriously, and in America no one takes it seriously but the aristocrats themselves. Thus, except among her own acquaintances, Mrs. Nicholas deBelleville Katzenbach (wife of the Attorney General) is not a famous social lioness. But among the few who know (according to *The New York Times*) "Lydia Katzenbach is considered to be the most 'with-it' wife in the Cabinet." Mrs. Katzenbach gave a small party for seventy friends and the royal couple, which had at least 200 other, slightly less with-it people agog because they were not invited. Mrs. Katzenbach was no paper lioness; she asked all her guests to bring baby pictures for a souvenir album for the Princess and the Earl; she herself knitted a woolly pullover for Lord Snowdon, and she attached black ties to it so that he might be prepared for any level of formality in swing at the palace; she had Jim Symington, the son of the Missouri senator, play "John Henry" ("was a steel-drivin' man, Lord, Lord") on the guitar. When the party broke up in the wee hours, one of the seventy guests was asked whether it was indeed fun. "The fun," he said dismally, "was intense."

November 26, 1965, NEW STATESMAN

✦

Radicals on the March: But Where to, and by What Route?

Thirty thousand people marched in Washington to seek peace in Vietnam. They blazoned peace on banners, proclaimed it from platforms and demanded it in pamphlets. Whereupon, the Administration began to lay plans for the next escalation of the Vietnam conflict into a major war in Asia. No logical connection need be drawn between the two events; it remains that the protests of the last seven months—bearded or beardless—have been largely irrelevant to what official decisions are made.

There may have been some who came to Washington during the Thanksgiving weekend with hopes of influencing Vietnam policy. Few had them when they left. The older, respectable protesters who came out to demonstrate in the SANE march saw plainly enough that 30,000 voices, or votes, is not much of a bite out of President Johnson's consensus on the war. The students, who have been at the anti-war game since last spring, were reacting for the most part out of chronic anger. They had lost most illusions of their power a long time ago.

But there was more to the weekend than the Saturday march, and there were other consequences than despair. In the development of the radical politics of the last few years—the movement of civil rights workers, war protesters, students and organizers of the poor—the weekend was an informal first Party Congress of the "New Left." When it was clear that all the elements of the political left, both old and new, would be in town, events began to proliferate. There was a convention of more than a hundred national and local end-the-war organizations grouped under the loose National Coordinating Committee.

This broad encampment of the left was diffused in Negro churches, expensive hotels, under trees on the Mall and in scattered apartments all over Washington. And over all there was a mood of uncommon pessimism. The activities of the radicals have not been able to keep up with the evolution of their rhetoric. The civil rights effort, both South and North, has been stymied for months; there is no obvious strategy for integration of the Negro and white communities after the legal barriers are removed. The students find they have no workable program for effecting the changes, on campus or off, that their analysis tells them are necessary to broaden democratic participation; authority seems everywhere to be consolidating itself. The organizers in the ghettoes cannot move from the small victories to major alterations in political power; how can the leap be made from street and block organizations and the incorporation of a few poor people on anti-poverty boards to changing the political life of a city? Above all, the war protesters can do nothing to end the war.

It is almost impossible to exaggerate their concern with that war. The young people of "the movement" make no polite protest; they rage against the war because they see it as the embodiment of all they are fighting in American society. It is a product of "the system" from which they are alienated. It is a system that will not hear the voice of the poor in a world that is mostly poor, and that will not allow even the rich the right to affirm in their own lives their own values, rather than the values of the institutions they serve. Now their alienation is complete.

This frustration is particularly apparent in the tension between the radicals and the liberals, such as those who planned the SANE march. People and events do not come in neat boxes and well-defined categories. But the New Left does exist in some recognizable ways. It is not easy; "it's like digging Bartok or Bird when you've been listening to Bach all your life," an older observer said. Bach is "the system": "good liberals" in Congress, fair-housing laws, slowly desegregating schools, slum clearance, more college buildings and higher salaries for teachers, negotiated settlements for wars and much more. The new tunes are more jangling: power blocs of the poor, all-Negro third parties, "freedom schools," a student voice in college policy, sexual "liberation," rich mixtures of rich and poor in housing and schools, support of popular revolutions throughout the world and, again, much more. Some objectives of the different outlooks converge, and others do not. Styles of action and modes of behavior are totally disparate.

Thinking such thoughts or at least assuming them, the young people began arriving in Washington on the eve of Thanksgiving. The next day, when most others were eating their turkeys in Norman Rockwell tableaux, the war protesters were meeting in a church called the Lincoln Memorial Temple, in the capital's vast Negro ghetto. The National Coordinating Committee convention was, in effect, a convenient way to examine the extent of their helplessness.

In many ways, all of them unpleasant, the convention was a recreation of the sectarianism of the left of the thirties. Middle-aged radicals at the sessions—there were only a few among the hundreds barely past teen age—must have been possessed of a terrible *déjà vu*. By their leaflets they were

known. There were the Trotskyists—all twenty-eight flavors. There were
the Stalinists, and to bring matters up to date, the Maoists, the Russian
revisionists, the Castroites and the various shadings in between. A tall,
solemn girl in a dark blue dress took the rostrum at one point in the proceedings and announced herself as the representative of the American
Committee for the Fourth International. The students looked puzzled; the
old radicals remembered.

But the thirties-style ideologues did not represent a majority of the students in town, most of whom eschewed the older styles for the new fashions
in leftism; they would claim to believe in "participatory democracy," or something of that sort, if anyone was square enough to ask. Up to now, their view
of political reality did not include a clear picture of what the traditional leftists looked like. Trotskyists were like vampires—creatures with foreign
accents seen late at night in old movies from their parents' era. Suddenly,
they came face-to-face with the "Trots" in the same room, and lo and behold!
they were young people like themselves, concerned with the same issues (the
war). But now, in a series of baffling "plenary sessions" of the convention,
the Trots were trying to "take over" the organization, form their own national organization and control the Vietnam protest! And they were doing it not
in order to deliver the protest movement into the hands of some hideous
international conspiracy but merely to do things their own way, and to use it
to increase their own power.

Perhaps in that distant day when the New Left sounds like Bach, and
graduate students write about radicalism in the sixties as they do now
about the nineteenth century, the intricacies of the National Coordinating
Committee convention will be catalogued. At this point, it is enough to say
that it was a tangle of conflicting ideas on the uses of a very small amount
of power. If the convention had been the whole New Left, it could have
smothered the SDS-type students. But in the unstructured, pluralistic style
of the new politics, the SDS people coped with the situation by avoiding it.
They stopped going to the convention sessions. A few who were more interested in studying the zoology of sectarian politics stayed behind to raise
objections where necessary, and the Trotskyist factions and some independent allies went off to fail in forming a new national organization on the
"peace issue."

For the radical democrats of SDS it was all an educating experience. And
if there is any future to "the movement"—from the student radicals to
those beleaguered souls in government agencies working for participation
of poor people in federal programs—the confrontation of the New Left with
the inheritors of the old ideologists is an important milestone. The students of the new style learned that the forms organizations take mean
something to what they can do, and what attacks they can withstand.
Some of the SDS members think that they can muddle through a social
revolution with a movement structured as tightly as a bull session at a

Freedom House in Mississippi (and if they can't, it's no use revolting). But if they are to be taken seriously, they will have to be more than "students for a *small* society," as one cynic suggested.

The experience of the National Coordinating Committee convention had shown some of the SDS and SNCC activists that the old revolutionists were as boring as most of the speakers at the SANE march. The students want to work, not just talk. But a willingness to work does not tell them how, or where, or even why. They must define their methods. The "hang-up" is strategy. SNCC has been slowed in the South because the students are not able to devise the next grand strategy. What is to follow the sit-ins, the Mississippi Summer Project, voter registration and the Freedom Democrats' convention and congressional challenges? The movement in the rest of the country has the same hang-up. The problem of how far the radicals can go in accepting liberal forms of action (two-party politics, government welfare programs, the Peace Corps and the like) and remain truly radical, and not just reformist, continues to be the central issue of the new politics.

The tension revealed itself all through the weekend. In yet another meeting, SNCC and SDS students, having recently disposed of Trotskyism by turning their backs on it, turned to, or perhaps *on,* liberalism. They met with the older activists who shared some of their analysis and methods, and with political workers from reform movements and coalitions around the country. The results, predictably, were inconclusive. The radicals would like to convince the liberals to give up reform politics and join "the movement."

The movement already represents enough power to interest some conventional politicians. Politicians in Mississippi who want to break the stranglehold of the old establishment will have to deal seriously with the Freedom Democratic Party, which for all its contradictions and weaknesses is a successful instrument of the new politics. Robert Kennedy is said to be interested in seeing what political alliances are possible with "movement" organizations in New York City; it would certainly suit his strategy of an "opening to the left" to do so. The campaign of Carl Stokes, a Negro candidate for mayor of Cleveland this fall, was in many ways a "movement" election contest, and Stokes came close to defeating the Democratic machine.

It was in the big march itself that the lines between the radicals and the liberals were most sharply drawn. The organization of the day was in the hands of the liberals. SANE wanted to produce a good public relations march: no beards, no Vietcong banners, not very much noise and, above all, no politics that could not have been accepted in the Johnson consensus, vintage 1964. Such a reasonable approach, presumably, would convince the President that a great many of the people on whom he depends for love and money would support a rapid, and perhaps face-losing, end to the war. It is still in dispute whether the SANE organizers at first agreed to use the Washington police to enforce their clean-up campaign for the march—against unauthorized signs and unwelcome slogans. Although in the end beards and "bad politics" were plentiful, SANE had made a lot of marchers feel they were unwanted.

The liberals' analysis of the Administration's policy and the possibilities for change was frontally assaulted by the radicals. For them, the pressure necessary to force—or allow—the Administration to settle for a "no-win" war could not be measured by tens of thousands of polite, slightly agitated people carrying unobjectionable signs for a few hours around Washington. It would take a mass movement of tens of millions, such as clearly was not abuilding; or the threat of widely disruptive disorders based on anti-war sentiment, such as was not likely; or the slow accretion of unhappiness and disgust at the mounting casualties and the cost of war, which had little to do with marches or protests but would be a function of the escalation of the conflict.

The marches could be helpful in developing a permanent protest movement—not to end the war in Vietnam but to end (as Richard Rothstein of SDS said) "the seventh war from now." But that movement would not be advanced by fussy attention to respectability. The experience of protest can turn the slightly interested into the deeply committed; there were many people at the Washington Monument last month who first tasted political activism in the civil rights March on Washington in 1963. A lot more had the experience of Selma, or merely the signing of a petition or participation in a teach-in behind them. If the protest is manipulated and protesters are kept strictly in line, that process of radicalization is not so likely.

That, at least, is how the student radicals saw things, and although they marched along with the safer and SANEr grown-ups, their hearts were not in it. One result was the blandest of all possible demonstrations. In a hundred football stadiums on the same afternoon there was infinitely more excitement. There was a theory bruited about in the crowd that the speakers were deliberately chosen for their soporific effect, or at least that they were instructed to sing their politics in the rhythms of a lullaby. Whatever the reason, people were demonstrably asleep until the penultimate speech of the long afternoon. Then Carl Oglesby, the president of SDS, gave the march, and for that matter the whole weekend, its definition and a new dimension. He was the only "movement" speaker, and while he may not have transformed the New Left, he at least gave it new life.

Oglesby accused the liberals of underpinning the elements of the very system that the New Left attacked: the military and industrial "corporatism" that keeps too many unemployed and foreign intervention frequent; the anti-communist ideology that inhibits the formation of peaceful policies; the welfarism that keeps the poor alive but powerless and, in the end, still poor. The war in Vietnam, Oglesby pointed out to liberals in the audience, came after three decades of liberal government: "Maybe we have here two quite different liberalisms—one authentically humanist, the other not so human after all."

"We do not say these men [Johnson, his advisers, the liberals in the biggest corporations] are evil. We say rather that men can be divided from their compassion by the institutional system that inherits us all. Generation in and out, we are put to use. People become instruments. Generals do not hear the screams of the bombed, and sugar executives do not see the misery of the cane-cutters; for to do so is to be that much less the general, that much less the executive," Oglesby told the marchers.

And the war in Vietnam: like it or not, it was a real revolution—a dirty, brutal, contradictory, uncompromising, authentic revolution. And there is no political percentage, or moral justification, in America's opposing it. "Revolutions don't take place in velvet boxes," he said. "It is only the poets who make them lovely." Oglesby offered that "ideological" basis for protesting the war: not support or apologies for the Vietcong but an affirmation of their right to revolution. It was non-communist, not anti-communist, as the New Left students have been trying to explain all along. His speech gave the students the intellectual transfusion they needed. The long and diffuse meetings of the weekend showed them a way—building small movements around the country and acquiring power (in slums, ghettoes, on campuses, in the black South, among the middle-class who feel powerless and unspoken for)—to end "the seventh war from now."

"Those allies of ours in the government," Oglesby asked, "are they really our allies? If they are, then they don't need advice, they need constituencies; they don't need study groups, they need a movement. And if they are not, then all the more reason for building that movement with a most relentless conviction."

When Oglesby left the rostrum the crowd rose from the grass and clapped and shouted. It was the electric moment of the afternoon, and Sanford Gottlieb, organizer of the SANE march, knew it. He had been walking a tightrope between the old liberals and the new radicals all week. Perhaps it was what the speaker had said, and perhaps it was the way he said it; Gottlieb retrieved Oglesby from the wings of the platform, brought him back to the microphone, and raised up his arm in a victory salute.

December 11, 1965, THE NEW REPUBLIC

✦

Dreadful Optimism

There is a mood of dreadful optimism in Washington this week. The diplomatic to-ing and fro-ing of the last ten days confirms the first break in the year-long war fever, but if it is only temporary the patient may die. And as time goes on, there is not much to indicate permanence. "We have thrown everything into the peace basket but surrender," Vice President Humphrey said on his return on Monday from an Asian trip. More accurately, he and the other diplomatic couriers have asked Hanoi and the Vietcong to throw themselves into the peace basket *and* surrender, and they have so far refused.

The Administration's "fourteen points" look tempting, but they do not include the minimum condition for ending the war. The National Liberation Front in the South and its allies in the North are fighting for nothing less than control of the government of South Vietnam. It need not be immediate, and it may be well-disguised; the art of coalition is not unknown in Indochina. The Front would probably negotiate while American troops are occupying their bases, while the war continues, and even through some "representatives" to save the US government the embarrassment of dealing with a government-in-exile. But the Vietcong are not defeated, and it is foolish to suppose that they will settle for less than their primary objective in South Vietnam.

"Free elections," whatever they are, do not seem to be enough. The Vietcong will not play Republican-and-Democrat with us. They have not been fighting for two generations to end up with a gentleman's agreement out of John Locke or the Federalist Papers.

It is still unfair to accuse President Johnson of insincerity in his desire for peace. He is not a moral ogre, and more than that, he knows that the war can do him little good with his 200 million constituents, at least in the long run. But he is unlikely to get the peace he seeks on the terms he now judges acceptable. He must either give up the US position in South Vietnam to the enemy, or expand the war to a new and terrible tempo. Not even a stalemate seems possible now. "We're hoping for a *deus ex machina*," an Administration official confessed recently. Other than that, there is no vision of the end.

No one says anymore that the US is "defending freedom," no one says that the bombing of the North for eleven months (it will probably resume) is in "retaliation" for attacks on US barracks and bases by the Vietcong. "It is not because of what the Vietcong are doing that we have gone to war, but what they are," Charloton Ogburn Jr., an author and former State Department officer, said on Sunday in *The Washington Post*. It becomes irrelevant to argue the US strategic requirements in Vietnam; the only consideration is the ideological necessity of "defeating communism," and war is as good a means as any for the job. *Time* quotes Churchill to that effect this week in its "man-of-the-year" story on Gen. William Westmoreland: "Nothing is worse than war? Dishonor is worse than war. Slavery is worse than war."

The Administration has its critics, but they are likely to be undercut by the current "peace thrust." There was talk of a major congressional debate over Vietnam (it is a measure of our distance from parliamentary democracy that one has not taken place in all the years of US involvement in the war), but the Administration can now answer, quite plausibly, "we tried." Many senators and representatives are known to be unhappy with the war, but they are buffaloed by the Johnson consensus. It is still more or less un-American to criticize while American soldiers are dying in the jungle. And would the President be distraught beyond consolation if twenty or thirty hawkish Republicans replaced the cautious but unsympathetic Democratic doves in the November elections? Someone joked that this would even advance Mr. Johnson's ambition to be the nominee of both parties in 1968; whereupon everyone laughed. *Joked?*

If all this "jet-propelled diplomacy" turns out to be nothing more than a prelude to the new "hard decisions" about the war—hundreds of thousands of additional troops and more bombing targets—it will leave a residue of bitter disappointment in a well of hopelessness. The war is already having predictable (but generally unpredicted) effects on the home front: inflationary pressures, cutbacks in welfare projects, worry about the Negro "revolution." Perhaps a tax increase. It may become necessary to further restrain credit, prices and wages. Reductions—or the curtailment of normal expansion—in anti-poverty programs are under consideration. More and more families are feeling the effects of the draft. More coffins reach Travis Air Force Base in California every day. Last year 1,350 Americans were killed in Vietnam; 5,300 more were wounded (11,000 South Vietnamese troops were killed, but it's still hard to evoke sympathy for them here). Great Society agencies have already built up sizable followings; as their programs are depleted of funds, the dependents will be less tolerant of the war. It is difficult to estimate the impact of all these elements. One can only piece it together from newspaper cuttings and Washington office gossip. Yesterday a plan for a national park in the California Redwood country was reported in danger because of lack of money for land purchase. Who is angry about that, and to what extent? Tomorrow the Negro poor in Washington may learn that their promised anti-poverty aid will be shelved. What will they think about the war?

And over all, the utter immorality of this beastly business in Vietnam will take a toll. If there was ever a just war, this is not it. It is no good saying that a benevolent America is helping the freedom fighters of South Vietnam. We are killing, burning and impoverishing them all. We have created a race of refugees. The picture magazines, as justification, show American GIs performing little acts of kindness among the carnage: "candy in the morning, napalm in the afternoon." But this war doesn't wash. When it gets bad enough, and if there is still time, we will end it. The rationalization will be the taxes or the politics or the Redwoods or the frustration—the deprivation of the goods and goodies of American prosperity. At heart it will be the acquaintance with death. The candy first. Then the napalm.

January 7, 1966, NEW STATESMAN

Chapter II

✦

WAITING FOR D-DAY

The Outlook for Bosch

Santo Domingo

There are times when Juan Bosch would rather be almost anything else than president of the Dominican Republic. "I want not to win this election," he said morosely in the course of a long conversation one rainy afternoon in May. But Bosch is not likely to get his wish. The elections that many people thought impossible now appear inevitable: they are set for June 1; Bosch is the odds-on favorite.

There is nothing unnatural about Bosch's occasional fits of gloom. If he wins, his troubles begin. Today, he sees his country from the prison that is his own house, which he has left just twice during the campaign—both times for personal emergencies and at night. He spends his days under a palm-thatched pergola in a tiny walled-in patio, receiving callers and taping speeches for the daily radio broadcasts. Campaigners, officials, friends are admitted through a circle of guards, across a sandbagged front yard, through a maze of locked doors leading to sitting rooms, offices and nondescript antechambers. In one of them there is a bookshelf: *Land Reform in Taiwan* and Erich Fromm's *The Heart of Man* stand next to thinly bound volumes in Spanish. In an alcove next to the pergola, two Dominican women scrub clothes in a soapy tub.

The visitors swirl around Bosch, following as he moves swiftly around the enclosure; he greets them with a warm, open-armed *abrazo*, talks for a few minutes, then sends them off with the same gesture. Just outside the circle, a navy "frogman"—one of the small elite corps fiercely loyal to the pro-Bosch "constitutionalist" rebels in last year's revolution—stands guard in his black uniform, black canvas shoes and black kepi, with a submachine gun slung over his shoulder.

"If I left this house and went to the city—or any city in the country—thousands of people would surround me," Bosch said, relaxing as best he could in a straight-back kitchen chair. "I want most of all to avoid a disturbance." His opponents put off the guards and the seclusion to personal fear (which is why, they say, he remained in Puerto Rico for five months during and after last April's revolution), or to an exaggerated sense of indispensability, or to campaign demagoguery designed to dramatize Bosch's persecution by terrorists in the military forces. But Bosch, and most Dominicans, believe the dangers are real. Although there are no more snipers in Santo Domingo and the terrorism has largely subsided in the past few months (after scores, perhaps hundreds, were murdered), there is no end to anxiety. "The extreme right might try anything to stop the elections at the last minute," a former government official told me. An attempt on Bosch's life, even if unsuccessful, would provoke mass demonstrations.

It is a small miracle that the election program has proceeded so far without interruption. A year after US military intervention (at one time there were 23,000 troops), politics in the Dominican Republic are hardly "normal," even if the edge of violence has been dulled. The country is still in that condition that McGeorge Bundy called "an interrupted civil war," or, more accurately, an interrupted revolution. There is a pervasive expectation of another act to come. Order, such as it is, is maintained by an uneasy and certainly temporary equilibrium of forces. The most obvious component is "La FIP," the 7,447-man Inter-American Peace Force of the Organization of American States. For most purposes, it is a US army of occupation (some Brazilians, Hondurans, Paraguayans and Nicaraguans are included, but there is no doubt about who is in control). La FIP, popularly interchangeable with *los Yanquis*, no longer patrols the main streets with tanks and armed jeeps, or searches citizens "from the head to the foot," as a Dominican engineer complained bitterly, "with no tact at all." It has been ordered away from the highly political University of Santo Domingo, and FIP soldiers were pulled back from checkpoints late last month—both after the kind of "unfortunate accidents" (natives killed or hurt) that an occupying force cannot easily avoid.

But the army is by no means invisible. Troops inhabit two of the major tourist hotels and part of the third. Convoys rumble through town and helicopters whirr overhead. The best residences have been taken over for such support activities as the "USFORDOMREP Library," the US Army Service Club and various staff headquarters. There are about 900 people in the official US mission—one of the biggest in the world. There are CIA and FBI agents, and special forces soldiers in civilian clothes wander throughout the countryside. There has been the usual sprouting of hamburger stands, black-market cigarettes (sales of the local product dipped 40 percent after the US invasion), Coca-Cola. Waiters in the restaurants, as a matter of course, bring "fren' frie'" to anyone who looks vaguely *Norteamericano*.

Exactly what the helicopters and the convoys whirr and rumble for is not at once apparent. By and large, the FIP is here as a symbol of control, as a guarantor of the semblance of order and as an umbrella for the provisional government of Hector García-Godoy. Installed by the US in early September after the Act of Reconciliation ended the civil war in its rawest form, García-Godoy is provisional in almost every way. He survives (there have been rightist coups attempted) at the sufferance of the FIP. He has his share of problems with all factions and has only narrowly squeezed through: the US had to remove General Wessin y Wessin bodily from the country and plant him as a military attaché in Miami. When two of Wessin's anti-revolutionist colleagues refused to leave, García-Godoy told the US embassy he wanted a "Dominican solution," and kicked the military chiefs upstairs to positions in the government. He talked his way out of a widely successful general strike by the revolutionists in February, and finally won peace at the university by granting recognition (and funds) to an "insurgent" pro-revolution administration. Like almost every other Dominican politician, he has called for the removal of the FIP; no doubt he would like the troops to go before his term of office expires in a few weeks, as his parting shot at history.

The FIP and the provisional government are the caretakers; they are the constants in the equilibrium. The other forces—the military, the politicians, the militants in the streets—jockey for advantage underneath the imposed "tranquillity."

The Dominican military, like its counterparts in many Latin American countries, has been traditionally the instrument through which the small industrialist and landed upper classes can maintain their position. Civil government is largely irrelevant to the military's power. The dictator Trujillo appeased his generals and colonels with generous favors, but in the end even he became their victim. He trusted only the air force under his son, Ramfis, and he gave it ground weapons of its own to keep the army in check. Since Trujillo's assassination in 1961, no government has been able to cut into the military's independence. General Wessin (of Trujillo's beefed-up air force) led the coup against Bosch's short "constitutional" government in 1963; Bosch's greatest failure in his seven months in office was his unwillingness—perhaps his inability in the face of US pressure to the contrary—to change the structure and command of the armed forces.

The young colonels and the lower officers who overthrew the junta of Donald Reid Cabral to start the revolution a year ago represented a new and still ill-defined force in the country. Many of them had not been cut in on the beneficence distributed to the commanders. "The lower officers are poor, hungry and barefoot," Hector Aristy, the civilian leader of the revolutionary government, explained recently. That is perhaps hyperbole, but in general the lower military officers were an aggrieved class. How "revolutionary" they are is problematic, but their disaffection with the classic role of the armed forces—the support of the *oligarquía*—has been taken into account: most of the rebel military leaders of last year have been sent abroad. Except for Wessin and navy chief Francisco J. Rivera Caminero, most of the anti-revolutionist military leaders remain in the Dominican Republic, and for a year the armed forces (now 30,000 strong, counting the paramilitary national police) have been under commanders of the very oldest guard.

It is an article of faith in the pro-Bosch ranks that all the power of that old guard is as nothing compared with the fervor of the people aroused: it is taken for granted that the rebels would have easily defeated the generals if the US had not given Wessin assurances of its support, and if the intervention (on the fifth day of the revolution) had not taken place. There is good internal evidence for such faith. General Wessin himself acknowledged that his junta forces had been virtually defeated in the first few days of the revolt. In any case, the ex-rebels, would-be rebels and potential rebels in Santo Domingo now claim that the old military men are "finished," and that only the FIP gives them the appearance of power.

The people who made the revolution—those in the streets and the huge numbers of urban slum-dwellers, *campesinos* and idealistic youth—have a new sense of dignity this year and a feeling that they "can do" something about their country. It is difficult to avoid comparisons with the atmosphere in a Southern city after a civil rights demonstration, or for that matter with Watts after last summer's revolt (Bosch told me, in passing, "You had the Dominican revolution in Los Angeles"). But for the moment the interrupted revolution is expressed in the political maneuvering.

There are a dozen or more political parties, movements and groupings, representing every political interest, style and opinion, but in fact the parties make little difference to what is actually going on. At bottom, there are only three approaches to Dominican problems: return to the paternalistic control of a Trujillo and the juntas; remake Dominican society under a kind of "revolutionary" regime; or try to mediate between the incredibly poor and troubled populace and the small but immensely hostile upper classes by means of a government of the "democratic left."

Juan Bosch, with his *Partido Revolucionario Dominicano*, is dedicated to trying the third way. He must therefore suffer attack from both sides. The old guard is quite convinced that he is a communist; the far left says it will vote for him but disagrees with his objectives. He dislikes those in both camps with equal passion. Still, he must grant enough concessions—the economic and political reforms he promises—to keep his large following among the "masses" (as he calls them), and to keep the right-wingers and the military that supports them from kicking him out of office.

Americans in Santo Domingo tend to see the Dominican Republic in terms of their own experience—as a slow-moving, slowly improving society. But the Dominicans are in no mood to play the game in which one side can lose and (more or less) good-naturedly hope to come back another day. There is no underlying consensus of interests here. Winner takes all. Bosch seems to understand very well what is happening.

"The right wing feels that nothing can stop its power after the US intervention," he told me. "And the intervention has also caused a tremendous increase in communism in the new generation. You can see it in activity in the unions, in the schools and on the streets. These are two irreconcilable forces, and they could cause an explosion at any time."

To deal with them, Bosch has been trying to put together a coalition of center forces broad enough to assure the stability of the government he hopes to form. He turned down an offer of support by the radical 14th of June Movement—called "1J4"—on the reasonable grounds that it might give him 25,000 votes but would lose him perhaps 125,000. He has been outspokenly anti-communist, has reacted sharply against attempts to form a "united front" (there are two communist parties, one pro-Chinese and the other vaguely pro-Russian). He refused to endorse one general strike, and supported the other, in February, only when it appeared to be a success. His speeches on economic affairs more and more emphasize the need to build the "infrastructure"—roads, dams, schools—before changing the relative standing of the poor and the upper classes by more drastic means. "Bosch is certainly moving to the right," an economist remarked to me. "If he wins, the PRD will be the party of the center and the right."

In the election campaign, Bosch has smooth sailing in the seas of the left. He is the hero of the revolution, and there is no one on the constitutionalist side who will actively oppose him. His two opponents for the presidency both represent the right, and of them Joaquín Balaguer is far and away the stronger. He is a soft-spoken slip of a man, who derives at least some of his strength from the Trujillo era. He was the last puppet president under the old tyrant, but he emerged with much of his "prestige" (a very, very big word here) intact. He left the nastier duties of the dictatorship to others. He is considered to be the "brains" of the government in those days. Balaguer is wooing the *campesinos*, who for generations saw Trujillo as a father or at least a rich-uncle figure (there are still pictures of Trujillo on the walls of many a shack in the *campo*). "Who will lower the price of rice for you?" the posters ask. "Balaguer!" Among the anti-Trujillistas, Balaguer's popularity is not helped by the travelling companions he chooses for his campaign caravan—a collection of Trujillo's thugs whom he leads, like George Raft trailing an entourage of movie gangsters. His supporters say that Balaguer, like Bosch, needs whatever protection he can get.

Balaguer's party is called *Reformista*, but it is generally thought that reforms are what he will not provide. "Balaguer will win—or else the communists will take over," a well-to-do manufacturer told me. "If Bosch wins, my friends say we had better learn to row!" The manufacturer lives in a pleasant house with a swimming pool in a small rural village several miles from the capital. He has two cars and a pack of maids, some land, and a towering television antenna atop a bamboo pole in his back yard.

To win, Balaguer would need the unanimous support of the manufacturer's friends, as well as a very large proportion of the *campesinos*—the unpredictable key to the elections. The first families of the republic, the *oligarquía*, are now behind a third presidential candidate, Rafael Bonnelly. There are rumors that Bonnelly will withdraw at the last minute and hand his votes (probably not more than 25,000) to Balaguer. But three weeks before the election, it does not seem likely that any combination can defeat Bosch.

Everybody has been told how important the elections are, and they are beginning to believe it. The buses and the *publicos*—usually rattling old cars that serve as jitneys—carry signs announcing, "To vote is to open the road leading to progress." There are billboards and newspaper ads: "The vote means full sovereignty." The radio is full of spot announcements, speeches, endless exhortations. People talk of politics in the *publicos*, in their homes, on the streets. I listened for hours to an emotional political discussion among fifty or more youths on a street corner in the Los Pepines barrio in Santiago de los Caballeros, the second city of the republic. It is a highly charged country.

From the very first, the new president will be confronted with demands that will be hard to meet. Bosch, particularly, will have his hands full: he must decide whether to chop up the military and install his own commanders. He will then have to tell the *Yanquis* to go home, presuming he wants them to, which is not entirely clear. The FIP could guarantee Bosch's election, and keep him in power during the crucial first few weeks and months of a government. But anti-FIP sentiment is so strong that it will be difficult to keep from making public exhortations against it. Bosch sees the dilemma: "We cannot have democracy against the Americans, and we cannot have it *with* them."

The anti-FIP agitation will come largely from the young people in the left-wing parties, and perhaps most of all from 1J4. To a great extent, the *catorcistas*—the "fourteeners"—are the most significant political force in the country, not because of their numbers (in the thousands) but because their movement expresses the hopes of so many of the children of the April revolution. It is difficult to define what 1J4 is, exactly: it does not follow an identifiable ideological line, as the communist parties do. It has no national leaders, not very much of a party structure and little discipline. It is a collection of romantic revolutionaries—inheritors of a small band of guerrillas who started a futile campaign against Trujillo (on the 14th of June, 1959), and then politicked until the next opportunity to take to the hills—after Bosch's overthrow in 1963. In a few months all but a few of the fighters were massacred. One of the survivors, Fidelio Despradel, explained something of the movement: "We are not a liberal party; we are not reformers. Middle-class parties are always more influential in elections. We go to the elections because people believe in them and they want them. We have time; we are not desperate for power. We are not alone. There is not only one Vietnam, not only one Santo Domingo. We do not keep quiet. We tell the people here what we want. We fought for the constitution last year, but we could not control the revolution; it was in the hands of the PRD. What we could do was important; what we *wanted* was not important." What 1J4 wants has not been coherently stated—perhaps it is a kind of Castroism-in-one-country. But it has captured the aspirations of young revolutionaries, and its force will be felt.

How successfully would Bosch juggle the military, the upper classes, the *catorcistas,* the Americans? "We are sure that in the first year or two we will lose popularity," José Francisco Peña Gómez, a brilliant young Bosch advisor, suggested. "Those who will be disappointed will go to the 14th of June or the Social Christians. We will have to promote austerity, reduce expenditures of the government in all sectors, increase production, build the infrastructure, reform agriculture. We will begin to redistribute government-owned land first. Then we hope the government will begin to produce results, and our popularity will increase."

There is a general feeling that the only way to encourage such a process is for the US to leave the Dominican Republic alone, giving aid and comfort when the Dominicans ask for it and in the ways they want it. US aid has gone for all the wrong things here—budget supplements, credits for the purchase of expensive US products, military training. The legacy of the US intervention four decades ago was the Trujillo regime; the legacy of the intervention last year has been equally destructive.

"Now we are less than a colony," Bosch said as our interview was ending. "An underdeveloped people is very hard for you to understand. We have the problems of 200 years ago in the middle of the problems of the modern world. You do not try to apply the same rules to Mississippi as you do to Connecticut, but in foreign policy you do not understand it. The US should be able to help us out without ruling us; I know it is a very difficult task. I shall die without understanding why the United States did what it did last year. It was natural to defend its interest, but it was not right for the United States to give orders to this government from the embassy. Well, the damage has been done, and the cost will be high. Our history has been distorted by the invasion. You are strong enough to pay the cost, but we are not. To be a president in this situation is a very sad task."

May 21, 1966, THE NEW REPUBLIC

Afternote: Balaguer gained the presidency in 1966, and for Dominicans, history since has had a terrible consistency. On May 16, 1994, Bosch, Balaguer and Peña Gómez contended for the presidency—Balaguer engineering a bare "victory" over Peña Gómez, while the military vowed "to guarantee public peace" lest anyone protest too strongly this seventh term of the 87-year-old blind arch-conservative.

✦

Watts—Waiting for D-Day

Los Angeles

Towards the end of these warm, dusty spring afternoons, small knots of men begin to form at street corners, in front of liquor stores and pool halls, and on the stoops of shabby houses all over south central Los Angeles—a vast, undefined area that is "Watts" to everyone who doesn't live there. School is out; jobs are over. It has been another day of frustration and failure and, overall, boredom. Students and the marginally employed mix with the drop-outs, the permanently idle and the hustlers. The whites—merchants and social workers, mostly—scurry home to the western and northern suburbs. What is left is the police and "us."

Ten months after the riot or the revolt (depending on where or who you are), Watts is still in a state of siege. The police keep order by their numbers, the extent of their weaponry and the sophistication of their tactics. They cruise the avenues all night long, breaking up gatherings, arresting as many as possible, searching everyone who looks suspicious. And almost everyone looks suspicious. Few men in Watts do not know how to spread-eagle against a wall or a police car; they have learned from experience.

From time to time the siege is broken. In March, two people were killed in an extended battle that some people call Watts II. Now the incidents hardly rate front-page treatment. Deep in the *Los Angeles Times* are stories such as the one last week that began: "Angry crowds hurled rocks and bottles at police in two Negro areas of the city early Saturday. . . ." The tension is below the surface, but there is an almost universal belief another "explosion" is inevitable.

It is this belief, as much as anything, that could produce Watts III. Both sides are girding for war. The police have developed new anti-riot tactics: at the call of "Code 77" (the Watts precinct number) they move out in troop carriers bristling with shotguns. The young Negroes of the ghetto have their battle plans, too: gangs are organized to converge on one preselected target, then scatter in souped-up cars and regroup at the next unannounced site for another attack. Naturally, neither side wants to be the first to charge. But in the context of a mounting arms race (there are rumors that Molotov cocktails are being prepared and cached, and most Negro men have guns) an "accident" could trigger a fresh revolt.

It almost happened last month. On May 7, police officer Jerold M. Bova shot and killed a Watts Negro, Leonard Deadwyler, after a forty-block auto chase up Avalon Boulevard. Deadwyler's pregnant wife said she was having labor pains and her husband was speeding her to the hospital (the car had a white handkerchief, as a signal of distress, tied to the radio antenna). Bova said he was justified in stopping the car (his cruiser forced it to a halt) and approaching the passengers with a loaded .38 revolver. Bova reached in through the window of the passenger's side, across Mrs.

Deadwyler, and stuck the gun in the Negro's side. The next instant Deadwyler was shot. Bova claimed the car "lurched" and the gun discharged accidentally. Mrs. Deadwyler said Bova was negligent. The Negroes of Watts called it murder.

There were rallies and rioting after the killing, and an ad hoc Committee to End Legalized Murder by the Cops was set up. Two *Newsweek* reporters covering a riot at a liquor store were beaten. Then the police moved in and busted four young Negroes who seemed to be among the ringleaders. One of them, Tommy Jacquette, was picked up for "suspicion of robbery," but by the time the police were through, that charge was dropped and he was booked for "inciting to riot" and three attendant charges. The arrests did not do much to reduce tensions; predictably, they had the opposite effect. White social workers and sympathetic white journalists were warned by their Negro friends to keep clear of Watts.

The coroner's inquest into the Deadwyler case lasted eight days. Last week the nine-man jury (in good Hollywood style it included one Negro, one Oriental, one woman) found the homicide "accidental," and the district attorney dropped the case. But the Negroes in Watts were not in a charitable mood. Tuesday night, they went on a window-smashing rampage.

A lot of chickens (in a phrase much appreciated in Watts) are coming home to roost. No matter how such incidents may be explained in white society, every time a white man kills a Negro (or is even mildly disrespectful, for that matter) the difficulty of building an integrated community comes that much closer to impossibility. As it is, black alienation from white Los Angeles is almost total.

What is "happening in Watts"—the question everyone here asks—is a strong surge of the black nationalist tide. It is a logical response to the conditions of the ghetto: the powerlessness of the Negro, and the unwillingness of the whites to move towards "integration" on anything more than a token basis. The McCone commission report—issued last December to explain the nature of the August revolt and suggest some kinds of solutions—was discouragingly inadequate on both counts. It placed much of the responsibility on the Negro, who couldn't cope with "the conditions of city life" (Bayard Rustin pointed out that the city couldn't cope with the conditions of Negro life). There were some things that the city could do to help out: build a hospital, run a bus line through Watts to employment centers, put cafeterias and libraries in the all-Negro schools. But at bottom, the conflict was some sort of communications breakdown; nothing wrong that a human relations commission and some bricks and mortar couldn't cure.

It would be hard to find a Negro in Los Angeles who has the slightest faith that the report's recommendations, even if they were all effected, could make a significant difference in ghetto life. "There's been a complete failure of white leadership," a white businessman active in civic affairs told me. "No one understands that the Negroes just can't stand being second-class citizens anymore. Patching up living conditions or finding a few people jobs won't help."

The nationalist "reaction" focusses on that state of second-classness. There had been a base of nationalist feeling before, but the August revolts charged the entire Negro population with that sense of "black power" that combines dignity, pride, hatred of whites and Negro brotherhood.

In Watts, there is no single form for its expression. There are organizations like SLANT (Self-Leadership for All Nationalities Today), Us (a somewhat cultish but powerful following of Malcolm X), the Black Muslims, the Afro-American Citizens' Council, the Self-Determination Committee, the Afro-American Culture Association and more. It is hard to estimate their numbers (SLANT, which is Tommy Jacquette's group, has about 500 young members), but the important point is not members but sentiment. They catch the deepest aspirations in the ghetto, and they can command the "troops" when the crisis comes.

Nationalist feeling goes beyond these particular clubs. It permeates even the "moderate" institutions—the self-help organizations, the community development agencies, the Teen Posts. Many of them are moving to all-black staffs; whites are relegated to minor positions, as helpers or "resource people."

"What's happening in Watts is what's happening in the rest of America," a nationalist leader told me. "The ghetto is no promised land. There are no jobs to be integrated into. There's no way to move to the so-called integrated areas. The accepted liberal means don't work. The white power structure has no intention of giving up anything without demands, and power yields only to power. I want to see black people organized for power—now. There are enough black people in Los Angeles right now to have a great amount of power *as blacks*. Every other ethnic group in America did it—the Jews, the Italians, the Irish, all of them. The black people have to do it even more, because they were slaves and they started with absolutely no power at all. The feeling is there, though the organizational unity isn't there yet. But the only healthy sign is the feeling of black unity, the feeling that people will have to look to themselves for the solution to their problems."

There is no single ideological line for "black nationalism." Jacquette, for instance, calls himself "more liberal" than others because he sees nationalism as a more or less temporary stage: black men (they all disdain the "slave" word "Negro") have to build up their own community before integration is anything more than continued subservience. Jacquette does not isolate himself from whites, but he recommends that they work in their own worlds, trying to force changes that could allow Negroes acceptance as equals.

But the line moves quickly to extreme positions. As it does, behavior as well as philosophy becomes more removed from white standards. Leaders of Us wear green felt "bubas" (a sort of poncho, of no particular national origin) to set themselves apart (their followers sometimes wear Malcolm X sweatshirts). "Black" is the common referent for all that is good or true. There are black holidays (Malcolm's Birthday, the Sacrifice of Malcolm, Uhuru Day), black language (Swahili), black schools (teaching "soul," nationalist doctrine), black history and, in a sense, black logic.

"You can't mix with the power structure that you're going to deal with," Us's chief, Ron Karenga, explains. Karenga, a 24-year-old graduate student (African linguistics) at UCLA, speaks with a biting, slyly contemptuous air of an old mandarin. "We can't share power that we don't have. We could someday share city or state power, but not community power." At a youth rally after the Deadwyler killing, Karenga said, "We are free men. We have our own language. We are making our own customs and we name ourselves. Only slaves and dogs are named by their masters" (Karenga's name used to be Everett). The Deadwyler case, Karenga thinks, "could be the catalyst that sets off a community-wide revolt."

White Los Angeles is convinced that the Negroes want another violent revolt, and black Watts is sure the whites will provoke it. Observers who have wandered around the 77th Precinct say the mood of the police swings from deep hatred to deep fear of the Negroes. The Negroes feel much the same way, in reverse.

On both sides there are increasing pressures to keep the lid on. For the whites, another blow-up could upset an already delicate political situation— there are state, congressional and county elections this year, and Watts is a major issue in all of them. Governor Brown is sensitive to the charge that his office did not quickly call up the national guard last August. (Brown was initially out of the country.) He is said to be a little quicker on the trigger these days. In the wake of the Deadwyler killing, national guardsmen were alerted and advance men were moved into the area in the middle of the night. Brown sends aides into Watts to "talk things over" with Negro militants, and while nothing tangible comes of the conversations, the Negroes are pulled into a talking situation.

On the ghetto Negroes' side, there are new organizational pressures for "cooling it" that did not exist before last August. Watts was the paradigm non-community. It had a wide variety of leaders and practically no followers. In the past year, the traditional leadership has been discarded—first went the clergymen, then the politicians and the older civil rights chiefs who used to talk mainly to the whites. There are rudiments of new kinds of organization, but it is barely visible (especially to the white eye). "Before August there were gangs," Tommy Jacquette explained; "now they're organizations." There are also the new self-help agencies, like Operation Bootstrap ("Learn Baby, Learn") which does job training, literacy and personal behavior education in a strongly nationalist atmosphere. The local poverty program has funded the Westminster Neighborhood Association and the Neighborhood Adult Participation Project, which sponsors training and education projects, block and tenant organizations, and various social services. Local residents are hired (including some of the most active young militants) and they quickly develop an interest in community stability. The activist groups perhaps would not mind a good fight—if they could lead it. But none of them feels that they are yet in a secure leadership position. For the time being, they all would rather keep things just below boiling point.

There is nothing very important being done to change people's lives in Watts, and until there is, outbursts of fresh violence should be expected. The official War on Poverty has some $33 million to spend, but two-thirds of it goes to shore up the public schools. Sargent Shriver has been shopping for a new LA poverty czar, but at least two of those asked have said privately that Shriver would not assure them of his political support for whatever "controversial" activities they might try.

Times are bad in the power broker business; many of the middlemen seem to be losing their accounts. In Watts, the whites—and even the middle-class Negroes—cannot do much to win the confidence of the ghetto. There is suspicion all around. One Watts nationalist leader told me, when I called for an interview, "I don't think you'd give us a fair shake because like most liberals you're probably a Jew and very sensitive to anti-Semitism, and you just don't want to understand black nationalism." The impression is strong that, in every way, it is already too late in Watts.

Although whites will be increasingly irrelevant in the ghetto, it does not mean the death of "leadership." Ignored for years, natural leaders are now quickly rising to the top. On the first day of the Deadwyler inquest hundreds of furious Watts residents jammed into the courtroom and threatened, if only by their presence, to break up the proceedings. Appeals from stern and respectable whites failed. Finally, a black man in a Malcolm X shirt climbed into the judge's chair and directed the scores of Negro clergymen to get out. They did. Then he said the rest of the black folk without special business in the court could go, too. The people filed peacefully into the corridor, and the man in the Malcolm X shirt climbed down.

June 11, 1966, THE NEW REPUBLIC

✦

Mini-Star for Governor

In the fantasy world of California's pop politics, people vote for comic-book characters, not public officials. Small wonder, then, that the Republicans have chosen Captain Marvel as their candidate for governor. In real life (as the comics say) he is, of course, movie mini-star Ronald Reagan; he won easily over San Francisco's boring ex-mayor, George Christopher, whose campaign style was that of an ageing, broken-down Joe Palooka.

In a funny way, Reagan is the perfect candidate for hyper-America. He is tanned, healthy and springy; he looks fifteen years younger than his 55. His philosophical line is an entirely incomprehensible jumble of every myth and cliché in American life. On television, at political meetings and on handshaking tours of suburban shopping centers, he affects a manner somewhere between a TV doctor's and a Methodist minister's.

What is unfunny is that Reagan's two-to-one victory sets him up to beat Governor "Pat" Brown in the November election, and could propel him into a commanding position among Republican contenders for the presidency in 1968 or 1972. Reagan may not be (as Brown claims) the inheritor of the Goldwater estate, but he derives a considerable income from its holdings. The far right is stronger in California than in any other populous state in the US. Reagan's election to the governorship would give some credence to the (probably valid) notion that the right continues as a strong force in American politics, despite the disasters of 1964.

That is not to say that Reagan's successes so far count as an undoubted victory for ultra-conservatism. No right-winger has ever done as well in California: he obviously appealed to what politicians nowadays call the "great white whale"—the mass of white middle-class voters who consider themselves both "moderate" and "independent." He did it by an adroit use of public relations based on his onstage charm. The PR men (Spencer-Roberts, who also ran the Rockefeller campaign) followed him around with huge cue cards with single words or phrases printed on them (Reagan is shortsighted) for easy reference: BIG GOVERNMENT, CRIME, TAXES. Reagan struck moderate poses as the campaign progressed. He talked of the Creative Society as an alternative to the Great Society, and the idea was that business should be "partners" with government for the common good.

On the other hand, he easily identified the emotional issues and hit hard at them: beatniks and perverts were fouling the University of California, the "poor" (whatever color they were) were wasting good tax money on welfare, and the rabble was ready to riot in the streets. He seemed to suggest that a good strong hand could whip everybody into place. At a speech to navy officers' wives in Los Angeles, he warned that "you can't be a little bit socialist, a little bit free," and that America was being transformed from "a republic to the mobocracy of majority rule"—the fault, probably, of school textbooks chosen by leftists, in which "entire chapters are devoted to public welfare and not a single line to Patrick Henry." When he was through, a woman slid up to the head table and whispered in Reagan's ear: "I'm getting tired of poor people."

June 17, 1966, NEW STATESMAN

✦

Average American Boy

The best that may come from America's current string of mass murders is a gun-control law that would have prevented none of them. The man who killed eight nurses in Chicago evidently preferred ropes of bedsheets and long knives to firearms. The Texas sniper could have assembled most of his arsenal quite legally under the provisions of the bill now before Congress. Under those regulations, President Kennedy's assassin would have had to use a domestic rifle (the Italian Carcano would be banned primarily to protect native manufacturers), but that hardly would have stopped him. Murder will out.

There have not been many convincing analyses or explanations of Charles Whitman's rampage thirty floors above the University of Texas in Austin. The small brain tumor discovered in the autopsy appears not to have been the cause of his psychosis. Blame has shifted between his authoritarian father and over-protective mother, and the university psychiatrist who heard Whitman say he wanted to "go up on the tower with a deer rifle and start shooting people." Perhaps the killer had read a recent (but little-known) novel by Ford Clarke, called *The Open Square,* in which a man snipes at passers-by from the clock-tower on a Midwestern college campus. Or he may have been somehow struck by the line from Poe: "While from a proud tower in the town death looks gigantically down." Governor Connally wants Whitman's brain studied by physicians, but they probably cannot tell us much.

Whatever his specific motivations, Whitman in his last ninety-six minutes played out a metaphor of the pathology of contemporary society. He is the American dream turned nightmare. Albee could not have created a more perfect archetype: Eagle Scout at 12 (the youngest in the country, they say), piano lessons, altar boy, marine corps, B-student at a state university, handsome, blond, an aqualung diver and karate fighter. "The average American boy," *The Washington Post* called him, with only semi-conscious irony.

But beneath the banality was the unintegrated man. Pressures built on all sides: his father, a "moderately successful plumbing contractor" (said *Time*), demanded performance. His mother, who left her husband in Florida and moved to Austin to be near her son, demanded love. Whitman could provide neither. Security was elusive: guns, the marines, karate, an early marriage—proofs to all but himself of his manliness, his worthiness.

For a while regimentation and the impersonality of large institutions (the armed forces, the 25,000-student university) kept him functioning. Then the most vulnerable institution—his family—cracked apart. And so, in ways that no one now can explain, did Charles Whitman. In long, rambling typewritten confessions, he expressed his total alienation by condemning his father. Then he destroyed everything he thought was pulling at him: his mother, his wife, his world. He climbed the tower (the symbol of suicide to students in moments of despondency), armed with knives, hatchets, two pistols, two rifles and a revolver. In a satchel he carried provisions: water, petrol, food, lavatory paper, a transistor radio and spray deodorant. Like pharaohs who took their worldly goods in solar boats to the afterlife, Whitman took the symbols of his own world for comfort in his materialistic heaven.

Perhaps that is not the way it was at all. It may be only the movie script, but it is doubtful whether the film will ever be made. Most Americans would rather believe the tumor theory, or the uncontrolled sales of guns, or some undetected congenital disease. It was easier to understand the others: Richard Speck, accused of murdering the nurses, was a marginal character, a "bad boy" who drank and whored and served time in jail. Oswald was a communist. Howard Unruh, who killed nineteen people in New Jersey in 1949, was war-scarred. The Clutter killers were "born to lose."

But the picture of Charles Whitman smiling out at America from newspaper front pages and television screens is almost too much for people to bear. Who is that nice young man with the blond crew cut? A lot happened last week. Did he score two touchdowns in the college all-stars football game with the Green Bay Packers? Did he marry the President's daughter on Saturday? Did he win the car safety teenage Road-E-O? Did he kill sixteen human beings and himself? How can we tell the good guys from the bad?

Someone called it "middle-class Watts." Another, more irreverently but perhaps accurately, said that "Charles Whitman died for our sins." In any case, the feeling remains that Whitman's life, and his death, was very much like our own, with all the violence, alienation and anxiety pushed just above the surface instead of kept just below. We are all hung up, the literary critics say, on love and death. There are "acceptable" ways of working out such problems: in the jungles of Vietnam, for instance, or in the boardrooms. But when they are inconvenient, the campus in Austin will do. That is not a very pleasant thought, but Americans have learned now to live with death and Texas.

August 12, 1966, NEW STATESMAN

✦

The Lair of the Black Panther

Montgomery

They say in Alabama that Black Belt soil is so rich a peg-legged man's got to run through it quick or he'll take root. For 200 years it has produced bountiful crops of cotton, corn and poor Negroes. The profits go to a hereditary white gentry—a class of feudal flies in amber, fixed in a permanent state of moral decay and financial advantage. A kind of tranquillity is maintained by an elaborate system of controls: "white power" is the bullying sheriff, the segregated courthouse, the inferior Negro schools, the white bankers and businessmen, the Uncle Tom teachers and preachers. Demands for change are answered by foreclosures, evictions, loss of jobs and violence. From time to time it is thought necessary to kill an "uppity nigger" or a white carpetbagger, *pour encourager les autres.* The gentry rarely dirties its hands; such tasks are performed by poorer whites who roam plantation roads in armed pickups or stake out positions from command posts in rural stores and gas stations. In their own way, they too are as much the victims as the executioners.

Of all the Black Belt counties, Lowndes is the very heart of darkness. There are four times as many Negroes as whites (12,000 to 3,000), but the blacks live in poverty, subservience and fear. The median family income for Negroes is $935; for whites it is $4,400. Until last year not a single Negro was registered to vote. In 1964 about 118 percent of the 1,900 eligible whites were registered: there are a lot of dead souls in Lowndes County.

The median educational level for Negroes is 5.1 years of schooling; 80 percent of the people, black and white, are functionally illiterate. Elementary schools for Negroes are shacks in the fields. The larger Negro "training schools" are poorly staffed and equipped, and fall rapidly into dilapidation. In one, the "library" is a cinderblock closet in a drafty auditorium; the washrooms have the appearance and redolence of a Mexican railway station.

Jonathan Daniels was murdered in Lowndes last summer; Tom Coleman, a hanger-on at the courthouse, was acquitted in the case. Mrs. Viola Liuzzo was shot in Lowndes last year, not far from the place on Route 80 where evicted farm families now live in a "tent city." About seventy Negro families have been forced off their plantations. They had committed the extreme discourtesy of registering to vote—and besides, most had for various reasons ceased to bring a good return to the landowner. Court cases to restore their homes have not proved successful. "For something so elementally inhumane, it's damn hard to prove illegal," a civil rights lawyer explained.

Most of the Negroes in Lowndes are sharecroppers or tenants, but some also have salaried jobs. Half of the women workers are maids in Montgomery, at $4 a day and a "little bit" for carfare: It is a forty- to sixty-mile daily round trip. Farm hands get $3 to $6 a day in the planting season. Some Negroes own little plots of land; a few have small farms. But 90 percent of the land is owned by eighty-nine white families. There is one major industrial plant—the brand-new, wondrously automated Dan River Mills textile factory, which employs no local Negroes above the menial level.

It is hardly surprising that the breezes of change that had been blowing through Alabama for more than a decade were late in reaching Lowndes. Its isolation was complete. Until demonstrations began early last year in Selma, in neighboring Dallas County, the civil rights movement seemed to belong to another century, in another country. Then, on the second day of the march to Montgomery, it was suddenly in Lowndes County.

A few weeks earlier, a small band of Lowndes Negroes had gone to Selma to talk with organizers in Martin Luther King's Southern Christian Leadership Conference and field staff from the Student Nonviolent Coordinating Committee. They came home with the vaguest encouragement to "do something." Others in the country were entertaining similar notions, and without realizing it, they were a "movement." Jesse Favors, one of the originals, recalled: "We just decided to hold a meeting. One night we went from place to place looking for a hall, but everyone said, 'I ain't gettin' in that mess.' Well, I had to trick a boy out of a key, but we found a place, and we had our meeting."

Soon they were down at the courthouse. "The white people had a kind of bad attitude, you know," Sidney Logan Jr. said recently in an interview with a SNCC newspaper, *The Movement.* "We went down and I said, 'It's come time for the colored people to get reddished.' The registrar said, 'Many of 'em?' And I says, 'A lot of them.' He said, 'Y'all done get along all right with us. Y'all want anything, we'll let you have it. We don't want all those outside agitators in here.' I said, 'Well, it's time for all of us to get reddished now.'"

Thirty-seven Negroes were turned away that day, but two weeks later two were able to register. That week they formed the Lowndes County Christian Movement for Human Rights.

What has happened since then is a small triumph of democracy in Alabama and a large crisis for the civil rights movement in the US. Lowndes is the lair of the Black Panther, "a vicious animal, as you know," the remarkable local leader John Hulett likes to say. "He never bothers anything, but when you start pushing him, he moves backwards, backwards and backwards into his corner, and then he comes out to destroy everything that's before him." Under the symbol of the panther, the Lowndes County Freedom Organization (a political parallel to the Christian Movement) has gathered thousands of poor Negroes into one of the most broadly democratic political parties in the country. Their immediate aim is to "take over the courthouse" this year with the election of seven county officials, the next time by completing the slate. After that they can provide some services for the poor and begin to think about more ambitious economic development—with taxation (Dan River Mills pays no county taxes, and most white estates are more than favorably assessed), land purchase, cooperatives or any other means at their disposal.

It all amounts to "black power" in its most logical sense, and it is here that SNCC's Stokely Carmichael first began using the idea. Politicians, editorial writers and white (and light brown) intellectuals may argue about it in the North, but it remains an abstraction. In Lowndes, it is a simple case of Negroes having things their own way. Negroes were shipped to Alabama as slaves, and in the Black Belt they have always been in bondage. The Emancipation Proclamation changed little; they had been robbed of any sense of themselves, and they have never retrieved it. They are not "qualified" to lead or do the white man's work; they are not worthy of paved roads or good schools or running water or brick houses or the vote or a fair trial or the simple title of "mister." When they talk to the white man, they must scratch their heads and surround all words with echoes of "yes, suh, yes suh." Their natural condition is fear—of their own inadequacy as much as the white man's hostility.

The outsider can only dimly perceive how Lowndes Negroes live, in their paintless wood shacks, up the dark-red dirt roads and across the flat fields. "I was born and raised here," John Hulett said, "but until I started going around to talk to people with the movement, I never would have believed it myself." Families are huddled in small dusty rooms crowded with beds, a wood-burning stove and, usually, a television set, for which they will pay an itinerant salesman for years to come. The better houses have glass windows; the poorer ones have wooden shutters that close in the darkness when it is cold or rainy outside. If there is anything on the walls inside, it is a coating of old *Saturday Evening Post* pages.

The Black Panther organizers set for themselves the overwhelming task of changing both the psychology and the living conditions of the black people in Lowndes. Carmichael came in just after the Selma march. With the local Negroes, he fanned out from the first communities "on the move" into the reaches of the county. He would talk all day with people in their houses and in the fields, then try to get them to hold a community gathering or come to the weekly "mass meeting," which travelled every Sunday from church to church. It was hardly like ringing doorbells in New Canaan. The scared tenants knew that political activity of any kind would mean trouble.

Late last month I travelled with John Hulett as he went from house to house in the fields of Lowndes. The areas we visited were the least "organized" of the twenty-one communities in the county. It was oppressively hot, and the corn was burnt from lack of rain. Some of the men were away working in the fields. Others sat on their porches or on the beds inside looking at television. Women were fanning themselves quietly; even the children were subdued in this torpid season.

The people were "shaky," Hulett said. They were wary of "that mess" and of the white Northerner. But Hulett approached briskly and confidently. "Baby," he told a child, "tell your mother to step to the door." He introduced himself and asked the woman whether she had heard of the Freedom Organization—"with the emblem of the black panther"—and whether she would register to vote when the federal registrars came to town. She was unresponsive. "We got to do something," he went on. "You know it, we need good schools and running water for our houses. We been pushed around too long." The woman nodded perfunctorily; "uh huh," she answered, in the way the people do in Baptist church services, but now with less faith. "You don't need to be afraid," Hulett said. "If we all stand together, there ain't nobody can turn us 'round." Hulett talked a while longer, then asked if she and her family would come to a community meeting at the church two nights later. The woman was noncommittal.

"They'll come, I think," he said as we left. "You got to go back to these people and talk to them about their problems. They know what can be done." Two nights later, at a ramshackle church in a stand of pine trees, the meeting had just begun when the woman and her husband—dressed in their Sunday finery—walked in.

It took the Lowndes movement eight months to form its political party. By last May, they were ready to enter politics all the way. Carmichael and the two or three other SNCC secretaries working in the county had always conceived of an independent third-party structure. SNCC ideology aside, there was little point in trying to "integrate" the white supremacist Democrats in Lowndes (and there was no Republican Party at all). More than that, there would be no enthusiasm among Negroes for joining the political party that had kept them down for so long. "It's like asking the Jews to reform the Nazi Party," Carmichael said. "It didn't make sense to join the Democratic Party, when they were the people who had done the killing and had beat our heads," Frank Miles Jr., another local leader, said. John Hulett said, "To me, the Democratic primaries and the Democratic Party are something like a gambler who carries a marked card around in his pocket and every now and then he has to let somebody win to keep the game going."

In any case, the Lowndes Democrats had no intention of integrating in even a token way. They upped the qualifying fee for political candidates from $50 to $500 just before filing time for county offices. The Freedom Organization set about its own primary. It was called for May 3 on the courthouse grounds in Hayneville (Alabama law stipulates that nominating conventions be held at or near a public polling place). By the merest coincidence, it was also the day of the Democratic primary. There were no easy ways out for the Negroes; if they wanted their own party, they would have to forget about the Democrats. The county sheriff refused to let the Freedom Organization use the courthouse. To make sure his order was executed he deputized 550 white men. Hulett (the chairman of the Freedom Organization) said that the blacks would come armed too. At the last minute, Attorney General Richmond Flowers and the US Justice Department worked out a compromise, and the Black Panther leaders agreed to hold the convention at a Negro church near the courthouse. But the show of courage was not lost on the whites. As the Negroes began to feel "like somebodies," the whites knew that things would never be the same.

They haven't. Nine hundred people came to the convention and nominated a slate of candidates: Sidney Logan for sheriff, Frank Miles for tax collector, and others for coroner, tax assessor and school board members. There were no teachers, ministers or funeral directors among them; the candidates were farmers, construction workers and housewives.

Carmichael left Lowndes after his election in May as SNCC president. There are a few other staff workers still in the county, but much of the hard work is being done by the candidates and the Black Panther leaders.

None of them has any previous political experience, but they are boning up on the duties of their offices and they all have learned political organizing the hard way.

The logistics of politicking under such limitations are formidable. There are no voting lists, no telephones, no address directories. There are no door-bells to ring, and even if there were, the population is not lined up in neat houses; it is thinly dispersed over a vast area (the county seat, Hayneville, is not large enough to be incorporated; the largest town, Fort Deposit, has 1,300 inhabitants). Transportation is difficult and often the Black Panther organizers cannot find money for gas. Potential voters would not know a vot-ing machine from an IBM 1401, and most cannot read or write; the symbol of the panther is not only psychologically reassuring, it is necessary for voting.

Local leaders are trying hard to educate the people to issues; they do not want them to vote for a black man simply because of his blackness. SNCC has printed up pamphlets and political "comic books" to get the message to the farms. The latest one is called, "A Vote for the Lowndes County Freedom Organization Is a Vote for US." In comic-strip style, it begins: "Once upon a time . . . in a country called America . . . in a state called Alabama . . . in a coun-ty called Lowndes . . . lived a man named Mr. Blackman. . . . One day while walking by the courthouse, Mr. Blackman thought: 'Us colored people . . . been using our mouths to do two things: Eating . . . and saying yes suh . . . it's time we said NO. . . . Yes, it's time we get in this mess. . . .'"

What it will all mean November 8 is still problematic. Already, there are more Negroes than whites registered (by about three to two). But intimidation by whites, sometimes blatant and often subtle, could cut into the majority. With a few exceptions, the ministers of this God-fearing (more accurately, God-loving) populace have not been "with the move-ment." Some are working against it, as are the hundred-odd Negro teach-ers who have been plugged securely into the white power structure. Many Negroes are still not convinced that black people are entitled to hold office. "We've been educated for fear too long," a young local organizer, John Jackson, told a mass meeting.

The movement in Lowndes needs to do a lot more than elect officials. Already it has become involved in the Poverty Program: the Christian Movement has a $240,000 grant for literacy and vocational training, but it is in a morass of political trouble. Governor George Wallace attacked the Office of Economic Opportunity for supporting "black power," and said that one of the movement's leaders, Robert Strickland, was a "convicted murderer." Actually, Strickland, at the age of 17, in 1940, had shot one of four white boys who had hit him and were chasing him into a house; he was sentenced to life imprisonment for "premeditated murder," but paroled after five years and finally given a full pardon. And the OEO grant was not given to the Black Panther Party but to the Christian Movement, which is the only viable organization in the Negro community. But Wallace's main concern was that control of money and people was being taken out of his hands. Outside Democratic politics, his influence is cut.

Competing organizations of two classes of Negroes will make it difficult to replicate Lowndes's success. In other counties, even in the Black Belt, there are small "voters leagues" and civic associations, made up of professional-class Negroes and committed to the "national" wing of the Democratic Party. In the primaries last May, they all did poorly; they could not develop mass support (even with the help of Dr. King), nor could they convince the whites to integrate. More important, only eleven of Alabama's sixty-seven counties have Negro majorities. Most of the Negroes live in the bigger cities, which still contain more whites. In those places, it would be extremely unlikely that Negroes could be elected to major political offices. SNCC workers say that they will still work to form independent parties in predominantly white counties, in order to have bargaining power for the Negro bloc. But if the major decisions continue to be made in Democratic primaries, it is hard to see how to apply the leverage.

Although the development of third parties is a tricky business at best, and future results are uncertain, counter-examples do not offer much more hope. The well-reported "Tuskegee plan"—where a majority of Negroes voluntarily gave whites political control in order to win their confidence—seems to be foundering. The Negro organization, run by educators at the Tuskegee Institute and middle-class blacks, refused finally to endorse a Negro candidate for sheriff. He won without their support, and he knows that his constituency is the poor Negroes in the city and Macon County who see that "integration" has not meant much to them over the years. In fact, they have been kept down by both the educated Negroes and the whites. The politics of accommodation is breaking down. The hope for racial reconciliation assumed that whites would give up power gracefully if they were not harassed. That is neither good sociology nor good history.

August 13, 1966, THE NEW REPUBLIC

✦

Far-Out Kids Strike a Blow

A hearing of the House Un-American Activities Committee may not be the greatest show on earth, but it usually has a full complement of freaks, clowns, daredevils, wild animals and peanut-vendors. The current series was as diverting a circus as Washington will see this year. Ringmaster was Big Joe Pool of Texas, ballooned out like one of those life-size dolls that can't be toppled. The twelve young witnesses, skimmed from the thinnest margins of the war protest movement, fouled the hearing room with all the contempt and charm of monkeys in a cage. Lawyers shouted and pouted before an indifferent panel of congressmen; the audience, recruited in large part from the beat scene at Dupont Circle, responded at frequent intervals with clinically accurate demonstrations of autistic behavior.

Pool had it in mind, in a manner of speaking, to discredit the Vietnam protest by exposing its most embarrassing followers. Most of the witnesses were members of the Progressive Labor Party, a small Maoist fragment specializing in ghetto insurgency; a few, like the indomitable Jerry Rubin, had had their flings at stopping the Super Chief troop train in its tracks, or giving blood to the Vietcong, but were not particularly attracted to communist ideology. But HUAC jabbed unerringly at the movement's most vulnerable spot.

Or so the committee members thought. From the beginning it was clear that HUAC would be more jabbed into than jabbing. Unlike the docile, middle-aged ex-radicals strung out before the investigating committees of the fifties, the new breed courted contempt right up to the members' dais; these witnesses had no jobs to lose, reputations to ruin or families to shame. "Well, Joe-Joe," a tieless young man from Stanford University began when called before the honorable Mr. Pool. (Would Owen Lattimore ever have dared *think* such disrespect?) Another, when asked to swear the oath of truthfulness, snapped his heels and stiff-armed a Nazi salute to the startled chairman. No one invoked the Fifth Amendment provisions against self-incrimination, although one formulated an adequate (if extra-constitutional) paraphrase: "I will not answer that question on the grounds that it nauseates me and I might vomit all over the table."

Meanwhile, the (somewhat) less disrespectful battery of American Civil Liberties Union lawyers were challenging the committee's right to exist. They claimed that HUAC's very nature threatened the essential freedoms of witnesses. For the most part, it was a legal exercise, a warm-up for the weeks of litigation that would surely follow. But a (possibly unnerved) federal judge surprised them all and granted an injunction against the committee and its hearings. Congress responded with self-righteous rage. Speaker McCormack predicted the end of the entire framework of separation of powers, checks and balances, the independent legislature and the rest of Chapter Three in every high school civics textbook.

Pool said that he had no intention of obeying the injunction. In any event he didn't have to; at 10 the next morning, minutes before the hearings began, an appeals court dissolved the order and the case was continued to a later date for arguing. After an hour's worth of lawyers' objections, Pool called his first witness, a young ex-leftist and new-rightist named Philip Luce, whose duty it was to play the title role in "Son of Whitaker Chambers." He was, unfortunately, miscast. No tortured, guilt-ridden, mystical *Time* senior editor was he; in fact, he turned out to be a rather boring, low-key tattler of tales that the investigators already knew, and that the "hostile" witnesses corroborated with pride.

HUAC had a chance to hear only one hostile witness declare "I certainly am a communist" before Pool blew the whole show. He grew angry as ACLU lawyer Arthur Kinoy argued—"vigorously" or "boisterously," depending on one's politics—an objection to the proceedings. Pool ordered the federal marshals to remove Kinoy from the room, which they did, by a persuasive combination of hammerlocks, strangleholds and the bum's rush. Before anyone knew what had happened, Kinoy—who possesses one of the finest legal minds of his generation—was being booked for disorderly conduct at the nearest police headquarters.

Now the hearings had fallen apart completely. Wave after wave of spectators were dragged from the chamber—for applauding, shouting or merely *appearing* to be involved in such demonstrations. Witnesses, lawyers, cameramen, marshals, policemen, reporters and curious congressmen milled around the dais. Finally, Pool recovered enough cool to call a recess. When the committee returned, the eight lawyers for the witnesses declared their inability, under the circumstances, to represent their clients, and in close order, double-file, they marched out of the hall.

Pool hastily called a few more "friendlies": a Yale student who had "infiltrated" a Progressive Labor office and lived to write about it in William Buckley's right-wing *National Review*; and the assistant district attorney of Oakland, California, who presented a rather more impressive picture of the war protesters' efficiency, support and *esprit* than the youths themselves might have been moved to give.

The other "hostiles" (except for the one with the Nazi salute) never got to testify; Pool surrendered and closed the "investigative phase" of the hearings. The other committee members were visibly relieved. At that point, a quick curtain might save the actors, if not the show. Only Jerry Rubin was disappointed. He had waited patiently for three days, dressed in a Revolutionary War soldier's costume to make the point that he was upholding the spirit of 1776. "I want to testify," he demanded as Pool gavelled the hearings to an end. The marshals closed in and hustled Rubin off to jail—the last prisoner taken, after the battle was over.

There had been a great deal of speculation about the implications of the hearings, and some disquieting predictions that a new wave of McCarthyism was rolling in. Doubtful. HUAC no longer has a constituency in either the congressional establishment or the executive department. It lost much of its support in 1960, when witnesses and spectators pitched their first battle against hearings in a wild scene in San Francisco. There have been more debacles since then, and the one last week probably served to prove to the leadership that HUAC is more trouble than it's worth. If need be, there are subtler, and perhaps more effective, ways of stifling dissent in the country.

Huffy editorialists have been condemning both the committee and the "hostiles" for their bad manners, but from any distance the strategy of total disruption seems both logical and successful. HUAC invented its game and set the rules: any counterattack is bound to break them. To play along is to give credence to HUAC's authenticity. Certainly the policy of cooperation within the rules could not cut into the committee's power in the fifties. And it was useless to wait for the courts to do the job (the last attempt failed in the Supreme Court) or for liberals in Congress to get up enough nerve to work for abolition. Each year only a handful of congressmen vote against the appropriation of funds to the committee. It fell to a dozen far-out kids to bring HUAC near to its deserved end, and, if they did not make their points against the war (as they had hoped), they at least struck a very smart blow for civil liberties.

August 26, 1966, NEW STATESMAN

✦

The Birth of Black Power

Jackson

"Black power" may have been the rallying cry of the Meredith march, but "white power" is still the Mississippi way. Its expression was in the shotgun blast that felled James Meredith, in the sullen faces that greeted marchers in the Delta towns, in the cherry bombs and axe handles of Philadelphia, the tear gas in Canton, and the wall of troops guarding the capitol at Jackson. The black panther is not yet at the throats of Mississippi's whites; after the marchers and the loudspeakers and the television crews have gone, the whites are still in control.

If the long, brutally hot trek through darkest Mississippi did not noticeably soften the white power structure, it did at least give many Negroes an appreciation of the changes that are possible in their lives. The main column and its outrunners passed through dozens of towns that had never been touched by "the movement," or had not felt its national influence. The appearance of an NBC camera in Yazoo City is not necessarily a sign that the revolution is at hand, but it does mean that things will never be quite the same again.

Meredith began the march as a rite of exorcism, a way to work out those fears that had made him something less than a man. He has said over the years, since his adventures at the University of Mississippi, that his chief objective was to become "unadjectived": not a Negro man, but a man. Mississippi had denied him that privilege, as it had reduced all Negroes to psychological serfdom.

The march never lost the character of a crusade. The cries of "black power" in its last week were a natural expression of its original intent. SNCC workers from Alabama imported irridescent orange bumper stickers carrying the black panther symbol and the proclamation, "We're the Greatest." There were printed posters with the same snarling panther and the warning: "Move on Over—or We'll Move on Over You!" They were usually read by Northerners on the march as sinister statements of policy. But for almost everybody en route, "black power" (some SNCC kids prefer "black conscious-ness") was simply the denial of fear and the assertion of manhood.

The old cries of "Freedom" and "We Shall Overcome" are still good for public relations, but they no longer represent the mood of the marchers. Dr. Alvin Poussaint, a Negro psychiatrist who heads the Medical Committee for Human Rights activities in the South, seemed to make the most sense to the marchers at the rally in Jackson: "For many years we've been singing 'We Shall Overcome,' and this song is almost obsolete and too passive. A new day is here, brothers, and we should begin to think, act and feel that 'We Shall Overthrow'. . . the vicious system of segregation, discrimination and white supremacy."

It is difficult for whites (and many Negroes) to understand a "march against fear," much less a march for identity. When Meredith was shot and national civil rights leaders rushed to Hernando, all the conflicting ideas about the movement began to appear. Dr. King, the first on the scene, want-ed to make the march another in his series of national civil rights spectacu-lars. The country needed one. White sympathies were flagging; the 1966 civil rights bill was in trouble in Congress. More than that, King has fallen upon bad times. His Southern Christian Leadership Conference had not had a vic-tory since Selma, a year and a half ago, and King's own significance was increasingly problematic.

He has been, more or less, shut out by the White House, perhaps because of his criticism of the war in Vietnam, or more likely because he does not, after all, have much to offer in the way of politics. At the recent White House conference "To Fulfill These Rights," King was all but ignored. The Administration's smiles were reserved for the most "responsible" leaders, those who have given up any ideas of militancy.

The "responsible" leaders, probably with White House approval, had little to do with the march. In the first hours after the Meredith shooting, when Dr. King and his friends issued a "manifesto" containing some mild criti-cisms of President Johnson, the NAACP's Roy Wilkins drew away in horror, denouncing the march and the marchers. Whitney Young, of the Urban League, was on-again, off-again. He finally appeared in the last twenty-four hours of the march, but when introduced at the rally on the eve of entry into Jackson, he was roundly booed. No one even thought to ask whether Ralph Bunche was coming.

King found himself in the role of the most conservative leader on the march. Ignored by Washington, he was treated barely more cordially by the SNCC bloc. SNCC could have hardly refused to take part; the movement in Mississippi started when Bob Moses came to Amite County in 1961. Most of the civil rights work in the counties began with SNCC or its allies.

Local Mississippi Negro leaders saw the march as a way to organize move-ments in the towns and counties, and as a stimulus for voter registration. Their major worry was that nothing would happen after the column of marchers came and went. Nothing much happened, they argued, in other cities where King has staged national demonstrations: Selma, Birmingham, Albany, St. Augustine. SNCC, the Freedom Democratic Party and the Delta Ministry (of the National Council of Churches) had to fight with King to get the march off Highway 51 and into the Delta. He reluctantly agreed.

White Mississippi finally began to realize that the march was something more than the publicity stunt their newspapers were calling it. Governor Paul Johnson withdrew most of the state troopers he had assigned to "protect" the marchers. Hostility increased in the towns, but there were only minor incidents until Philadelphia. There, under the watchful eyes of a sheriff and his deputy—under indictment for the murder of three civil rights workers in 1964—the local populace attacked King and a group of marchers who had come for a memorial service (it was two years since the murders). Sheriff Lawrence Rainey and Deputy Cecil Price have hardly been chastened by two years of demonstrations and national legislation. During the last days of the march, Rainey sealed off the Negro quarter of town at sundown and kept it under a kind of siege. From time to time he made armed forays into the area—in his big white Oldsmobile 98 fitted out with four antennas, five spotlights, and carrying (on the day I saw it) a machine gun, a rifle, two leather slapjacks, a set of brass knuckles, a wooden truncheon and a boxful of packages of Red Man chewing tobacco (Rainey himself carries a .38 and an ammunition belt).

It is not easy for Negroes to give non-violent answers to brutality in such an atmosphere, and after two years of civil rights work, many are no longer sure what the point is. Two days after the attack in Philadelphia, a white man fired into the Freedom House in the middle of the night. One of the young workers inside fired back. Later, he told me:

"Ralph Abernathy (King's lieutenant) says, 'If you fight back you're a coward.' That's crazy. It's just a question of being a man. What's my non-violent response to a guy shooting at me in the dark and running away through the streets? Do I go limp somewhere inside the house? What the hell am I supposed to do? The assumption of non-violent protest is that the other guy has a conscience you can appeal to. That's just not true in Mississippi.

"People get hung up when Martin tells them to be non-violent down here. Nobody wants to hear that non-violent stuff anymore. The real issue isn't violence *versus* non-violence; it's self-defense *versus* accepting anything white people want to do to you—including death."

Much the same attitude was heard in Canton after the state police gassed marchers as they prepared to pitch tents for the night on the grounds of a Negro school. The troopers' attack was obviously ordered in Jackson. The police approached in tight formation, cleared away the doctors and nurses, saturated the area with gas and then waded in with clubs, rifle butts and jackboots. Scores were hospitalized, most from the beatings.

Whether or not Governor Johnson ordered the gassing himself, he benefited from it. He had been under pressure from the militant racists to "deal" with the march. Withdrawal of the state police patrols was obviously not enough; he had to escalate to tear gas. When the march came to Jackson, he put hundreds of national guardsmen around two sides of the capitol square, and stationed state police and special Game and Fish Commission guards on the other sides. The marchers were kept within 200 feet of the building, and nobody missed the aptness of an unintegrated guard (federally subsidized) around the capitol.

Governor Johnson was admirably supported by the White House. President Johnson turned down requests for federal protection of the marchers, even after the Philadelphia attack. After Canton, the Administration took the position that the Negroes brought the trouble on themselves by refusing three private campsites offered to them. A delegation of church leaders called on Attorney General Katzenbach the next day and argued that the federal government should not concern itself with the choice of tent grounds. "What do you think about trespassing?" Katzenbach shot back.

It is probably a characteristic of the new mood of the Southern civil rights movement that the young marchers did not care one way or the other about federal help; if anything, they tended to disdain it. After Canton, many of the Negroes found arms. At the second Canton rally (held on the school grounds under a battery of rooftop machine guns manned by state troopers) the hero was Ernest Thomas, the leader of the Deacons for Defense, who argued very convincingly that the Negroes could not rely on others to defend them.

No matter how much whites would have liked it, the march would not come un-black. "This black power thing is very serious," one Northern church official complained. "The folks back home are scared. They aren't using their air travel cards and coming down like they used to." Many of the young militants would just as soon have it that way. They doubt the value and the depth of the "national sympathy" that is presumed to be the vehicle for giving Negroes what they demand. "I wouldn't care if we never get another civil rights bill if they'd just enforce the ones we've got," a SNCC staffer said. The experience of the county organizers has been that whites are *too* competent; the local poor Negroes fall into the old patterns of reliance on "the man." When he leaves, the organization falls apart.

Whether "black power" or "black consciousness" solves such problems remains to be seen. What is more certain is that Negroes in the South (as well as the North) are perhaps irreversibly heading in that direction. The Meredith march was probably the last "freedom march" and the first "black power march." It may also have been the last that included "white liberals" in any sizable numbers. "From now on," a white journalist who has been in the South for a long time said, "color the movement black." "You know," a former SNCC officer replied, "what gets people isn't the *power*; they understand that. It's the *black*."

October 1966, RAMPARTS

Chapter III

✦

ALL SYSTEMS FAIL!

In Wartime

"I will not war against women and children. I have ordered my air force to restrict itself to attacks on military objectives." For weeks now, the atmosphere in Washington has been heavy with such promises of humility and restraint. That particular promise happened to be made by Adolf Hitler, on the occasion of his declaration of war against Poland in September 1939, but it serves to illustrate the universal desire of statesmen to make their most monstrous missions seem like acts of mercy. In the case of President Johnson, the quality of mercy is not strained; it drops on Ho Chi Minh and General Ky, on pacified Vietnamese villages and the Thai Nguyen steel works, on Senators Robert Kennedy and Edward Brooke, Premier Kosygin and U Thant, Governor Romney and Buddha. If mercy burns like napalm or stings like rebuke, that's not his fault. The President—as Senator Kennedy said early in his annual speech on the war—has a "grave and painful responsibility," and is entitled to our "sympathy, understanding and support."

It is not easy to give him that due; nor is it always clear what he expects. He pulls benign and malign faces like an actor rapidly alternating the classic masks of Comedy and Tragedy. In Tennessee he bristled with threats of wider war. At Guam, he talked about Vietnam under pacification as a green and pleasant New Jerusalem. In mid-Pacific, he released the record of his correspondence with Ho to indicate the extent of Washington's willingness—and Hanoi's reluctance—to negotiate a settlement. Soon afterwards, Johnson achieved Senator Brooke's conversion to hawkdom. In a moving display of blue-eyed soul, Brooke burst into real tears and announced that he dug the war. Finally, Johnson instructed Secretary Rusk to "accept" U Thant's truce proposals, pending preliminary talks before bombing of the North stopped, and provided assurances of reciprocity were given. With an acceptance like that there was no need of a rejection.

Such is the state of the President's credibility that both critics and sup-
porters of US policy assume his behavior to be disingenuous. After Rusk's
embrace of the Thant peace plan, *The New York Times* concluded that the
groundwork was now laid for "further military pressure against Hanoi."
The important question was what form the escalation would take. *The
Wall Street Journal* guessed that there would be bombing of North
Vietnamese airfields, or some sort of assault on Haiphong. Former
Strategic Air Command *kapo* Curtis LeMay delighted an Air Force
Association convention by advocating the use of tactical nuclear weapons,
but the idea found little favor in the White House. There was speculation
about a rapid build-up of troop strength (now about 435,000 in Vietnam,
and untold multitudes in the Pacific area as a whole), or an attack on rail
lines closer to China, or bigger and better raids of the type now employed
against North Vietnam. In any case, the general idea was *more*.

The Administration's objective in Vietnam is now "victory"—interpreted
in a variety of possible ways, perhaps, but all within the common-sense
meaning of the word. There is no more talk of finding a means to "save
face" so that the troops can leave.

The history of proposals for a negotiated settlement of the war is little
more than the account of a tiresome game that long ago lost interest for
the spectators. The pattern has been for a new act of escalation to follow
every diplomatic move. In December 1965, the Fanfani-La Pira message
(that Hanoi might not insist on recognition of its Four Points for negotiation) was followed by the first bombing of the Haiphong area. On June 20,
1966, U Thant put forward his Three Points, which called for a cessation of
bombing in the North after a scaling-down by both sides; on June 29, the
US bombed oil storage depots in Hanoi and Haiphong. Last December, the
Polish peace initiative was frustrated by the bombings of Hanoi proper.

Senator Kennedy, among others, pointed out that the US could have fastened onto any number of acts of *apparent* de-escalation by North Vietnam
as a "signal" to end the bombing and begin talks towards negotiations. But
President Johnson wasn't buying it.

The only "clear signal" either side will recognize is a white flag. Since none
are unfurled, the war will continue, and the President feels he is bound to
pursue it. But despite some rather ambiguous and altogether minor "victories," the war is not going at all well for the US command. The generals predict the imminent collapse of the enemy, but they are unable to produce that
god from the military machine. "I wish I could report to you that the conflict
is almost over," the President said in his State of the Union message. "This I
cannot do. . . . I cannot promise you that it will come this year—or the next."
In the recent Senate hearings on a supplemental military appropriation,
Defense Secretary McNamara admitted that the balance of military control
of South Vietnam had not changed appreciably in a year: the Ky government
controlled about half the population, the Vietcong about a quarter, and a

quarter was disputed. (Even that was wildly over-optimistic; US intelligence uses very flexible criteria for "control.") Desertions from the communists are said to be high, but reporters say that the deserters are from the "soft shell," not the hard core of the main force. And desertions from South Vietnamese government forces are much greater.

The recent US "beachhead" in the Mekong Delta was high farce; the NLF knew the Americans were coming, slipped out of sight and returned when the invaders left. The huge area-wide sweeps have been more productive of casualties but not of victory. Operation Junction City, the largest US attack of the war, used 30,000 troops, cost $25 million to launch and caused more losses to the US than to the enemy. Paradoxically, the Vietcong have been launching smaller attacks, but they are inflicting more casualties on US forces than ever before in widespread guerrilla raids. In the last week of March, 274 Americans were killed, a record, the papers said, for the war. (Preserving the theoretical ten-to-one kill ratio, 2,774 communists obligingly dropped. It was the kind of statistical coincidence that suggests army intelligence officers in Saigon are getting lazy about their work.)

The pacification program has been sold to the American public as a kind of modified Vietnam Summer Project. It seems to have a great deal of success in *The New York Times Sunday Magazine*, but less in the field, where 20,000 armed community organizers putter around villages trying to convince the inhabitants to support the Saigon government. Lately they have been doing voter education work ("Y'all come to the votin'"), but in their spare time they turn over "suspected Vietcong" (i.e., young men in the villages who get in the way) as prisoners to the government troops. Most of the pacifiers are afraid to spend the night in the villages; exceptions are so rare that the head of the program, Gen. Nguyen Duc Thang, personally commends the courage of sleep-in cadres as American reporters rush to write stories about them.

At best, the US effort in Vietnam (and indeed in the whole Southeast Asian "theater") is a mixed bag of costly advances and even more costly frustrations. It doesn't make sense to talk about victories and defeats in the terms that were invented for the wars of European nation-states of the nineteenth century. The NLF and the North Vietnamese do not decide to make war or peace on the basis of industrial production statistics or even casualty lists. They are in the process of making their nation, and while that process can be brutal and painful and often contradictory, it cannot be turned off except by total annihilation.

April 1967, RAMPARTS

✦

Waiting for Lefty

In America, the cult of personality is the faith of the outcast, the politics of salvation. To be revered beyond reason, the cult hero need not be particularly talented (Barry Goldwater, for example) or especially commanding (Adlai Stevenson). But he must express, however ambiguously, the unrealized hopes of the disaffected of his age for a new order of life. The only mandatory article of faith is the belief that the qualities of his personality can somehow become the values of their society. The unhappy few who were madly for Adlai saw in their hero all the elements of compassion, intelligence and wit that a generation of official liberalism had failed to secure. Twenty-six million Americans knew in their hearts that Goldwater would infuse his own virtues of individualism, morality and simplicity into the social fabric. Disconfirmation of the prophetic vision by electoral defeat served only to strengthen the faith and spur the efforts of the believers. Stevensonism's wildest expression was in the galleries of the 1960 Democratic convention. The biggest batch of bumper stickers for Barry was affixed after the rout of November 1964.

Now Stevenson is gone and Goldwater forgotten, and the hero who has succeeded them is Senator Robert Francis Kennedy. By luck and pluck he has become the last, best hope of the sixties and the first of the seventies. The luck is his family, his fortune and the assassin (or assassins) of Dallas. The pluck involves the development of a style and a rhetoric compounding some of the more attractive aspects of Bob Dylan and Fidel Castro: tousled hair, plaintive croon, underdoggedness, undefined revolutionism. His special charm is for those temporarily or permanently out of power; they sense that he is, either directly or metaphorically, their ticket to the top. They are more than willing to overlook his shortcomings; they invent virtues and powers for him quite beyond the possibilities of natural endowment. His past is rationalized into a prologue for greatness, and his future is divined as its realization.

It is neither dishonorable nor impolitic to ask upon what meat our caesars feed, but as Ralph de Toledano* will see, it is useless. Cult heroes cannot be destroyed by looking at their records or exposing their mistakes. Everybody knows that Robert Kennedy was soft on McCarthy and vicious to Hoffa, that he plays rough in touch football and tough in election campaigns, that his father is a scoundrel and his social life a three-ring circus. But those who believe in him don't much care; they apologize for his faults and anticipate his perfection. They see his ruthlessness as pragmatism, his sentimentality as humanism, his single-mindedness as dedication.

Mr. de Toledano took the precaution of avoiding all contact with his sub-

*Author of *R.F.K.: The Man Who Would Be President*, 1967

ject. He talked with no one in Kennedy's entourage, and if he saw the senator it was from the Senate gallery or on TV. He was wise, because proximity to Kennedy easily confuses the objective researcher. To think the worst of Kennedy, as the author was determined to do, it is better to stick to old newspaper clippings and secondary sources in remaindered books. There are dangers in such a method: errors will be repeated, and distortions will be magnified. The author has escaped neither pitfall. But by keeping his distance, de Toledano is at least saved the trouble of sorting out his prejudices from contradictory firsthand impressions.

Anyone who has spent even a few minutes with Kennedy knows how he can get under the skin—by a word or the omission of it, by a glance or the diversion of it. Those who must deal critically with Kennedy *should* stay as far from him as possible or, alternatively, tie themselves like Odysseus to a mast of opposing politics and sympathies if they must listen to his songs. For he gives an impression utterly at odds with the one taken from the clippings. He is charming and tender, not brutal and rough; he is spontaneous, not scheming; witty, not humorless; self-critical, not cocky. More than the other ninety-nine senators and as much as any public official, he abjures the easy political response, the hypocritical canned answer to serious questions. He is the only non-Rotarian in the club, the one who tells it like it is: as they all say, he is "one of us."

What all that has to do with Kennedy's promise as a political leader is quite another matter, and a very important one to consider, but de Toledano manages to miss it. He is too busy trying to document the hero's vices. What happens, finally, is that he secures them as virtues.

In the end, de Toledano's deprecation is useless in the same way that the liberal appreciations fail to make sense of the Kennedy phenomenon. They both assume that Kennedy's personality is the substance of his politics, that a putative Kennedy Administration will institutionalize all the characteristics that one finds so appealing and the other so appalling. De Toledano translates Kennedy's personal traits into a ruthless, repressive socialist society run by labor leaders, Negroes and other dubious characters, each one trying to push the other into a swimming pool. Some older, schmaltzier liberals share his description of Kennedy but fear that the new society would *not* be socialistic. Anti-Johnson Democrats consider Kennedy's fondness for peaceful change and economic development and foresee a state free from imperialism. Moderate civil rights leaders watch him wander through Brooklyn and Mississippi and fantasize an end to racism and exploitation. The near-New Left and the half-hippies hope that somehow Kennedy can create a world of love and pot and participation.

History and social analysis suggest that the outcome would be like none of the above. Whatever his hang-ups and his moods, Kennedy's politics are determined by the same perceptions that have produced Lyndon Johnson and George Romney, and in the long run his Administration would have

much the same effect as theirs. There is no way of knowing whether
Kennedy will continue to be a cult hero, much less whether he will become
a candidate for the presidency. There are too many variables, which are
best left to the newspaper columnists to pick over in the next five years.
But, at this point, there is an assumption of popularity and eventual candidacy on the part of the political commentators, Kennedy and his staff, and
a large population of demoralized and frustrated voters waiting for the
coming of the once and future Kennedy.

As the future Kennedy moves to a position of political power and responsibility, the latitude he allows himself decreases. He may or may not predicate his actions on a cold assessment of political reward, but that is not the
point. He has to deliver, he has to show his effect, and he has to keep winning. Because he cannot think of doing that outside political convention, he
must become increasingly conventional.

At first, Kennedy appeared to be on the outer margins of the "system,"
poised for a swing beyond, into a position of attack. He exhibited a certain
identification with the insurgents of this world: the grape-pickers in
California, the Negro political movement in Mississippi, the rebels in
Santo Domingo, the blacks in South Africa—even the Vietcong, whom he
thought entitled to the blood of his countrymen. It was not entirely clear
how far that identification went: Kennedy always had an inexplicit appreciation for the poignant, the powerful and the talented. But his support
remained primarily moral. He was no insurgent himself.

Whatever swing has come has been inward, towards traditional methods of
dealing with social problems. Kennedy supported the grape-pickers' merger
into the AFL-CIO, which may have been helpful to their strike but which
surely limited their capacity to attack political and economic institutions
beyond immediate objectives. He made television commercials for
Representative Jeffery Cohelan to use in his Democratic primary fight
against the peace-and-civil-rights campaign of Robert Scheer in California.
He helped raise funds for the Young Democrats in Mississippi, an elitist,
"moderate" grouping allied with the national Democratic Administration and
opposed to the politics of the Freedom Democrats. He chided critics of the
CIA's activities by reminding them of the complexities of international affairs.

Kennedy's interest in foreign policy waxes and wanes with the phases of
some private moon which he alone observes. Perhaps his cult, and not his
own behavior, is responsible for the incredible fuss when he goes abroad—
to Latin America and Africa last year, to Europe recently. But in spite of
the returns in newspaper column inches, they seem to be more trouble
than they are worth. Back home, he delivers occasional speeches on Latin
America that describe in fine detail the malignancy of the established
order, the misery of the poor and the failure of US policy. But he makes no
assault on the root causes of that failure—the manipulation of US corpo-

rate interests and the habit of military support. He saves his complaints for the examples of obvious breakdown. One can look in vain in his speeches for a convincing critique of the sources of imperialism, although it is clear that he would like to clean it up a bit. The same is true for his treatment of South Africa. Kennedy's visit there last year gave heart to both internal and external opponents of apartheid, and he seemed to understand the depressing realities of resistance. But there his understanding stopped: never a mention of his friend the mining kingpin Charles Engelhard, or of the Chase Manhattan Bank, nor a recommendation that the US withdraw support from the South African regime.

Most perplexing, because most tantalizing, has been his position on the war in Vietnam. In February 1966 he proposed acceptance of the National Liberation Front's role in any Vietnamese settlement, then backed away when questioned sharply and remained silent (or contrite?) for a year. His second annual Vietnam address, presented to an expectant Senate this year on March 2, criticized the President for a reluctance to negotiate with Hanoi and included a moving account of the horrors of war. It was a fine attempt to legitimize the moral issues, which hard-nosed politicians would like to ignore. Kennedy's staff claims the second speech went further against official policy than did the first, but to many listeners it seemed somewhat less of a break. In any case, it came at least two weeks too late to have any specific effect on negotiations for de-escalation. Kennedy knows now that he waited too long; he confided recently that the Administration fooled him into thinking that real progress towards peace talks was being made and that a critical speech might ruin its chances of success.

What is maddening is that Kennedy *always* appears to know better. Staughton Lynd and Tom Hayden emerged from a lengthy interview (which Kennedy requested) believing that he understood the basic error of the Administration's policy: that the refusal to entertain the possibility of a unified, communist-controlled Vietnam only prolonged the war. "We're in the same ballpark," Kennedy told the two visitors as they left his East River apartment. But that was not the way it came out on the floor of the Senate. Some weeks later, after General Westmoreland's bullying visit to the mainland, Kennedy indicated to friends that he thought the war would soon get much worse, that there would be new escalation and that the dangers were enormous. He thereupon made only a few mildly critical comments about Administration policy in the course of an exchange among "doves" after the wide-ranging assault by Senator George McGovern. Even then Kennedy could not see himself risking his place inside the system to lead the attack—the only attack that might mobilize effective opposition to the war in the foreseeable present.

It should hardly be surprising that Kennedy acts like a normal politician. There is nothing in his background, his performance or his prospects that suggests that he would behave otherwise. He may be impulsive and keen on the issues, but he sees them with the eyes of a traditional political operator. It is not necessary to suppose that he feeds every alternative into some Lou Harris poll or a computer to see which one will get him the most number of votes in some future election. He goes out of his way to talk with poor sharecroppers in the Mississippi Delta, or attacks LA's racist mayor, Sam Yorty, or supports legislative reapportionment because he is genuinely concerned. But it is all perfectly safe. His impulses never take him beyond the limits of accepted behavior. He would not join a peace march in Central Park or withdraw his account from a bank supporting the South African economy or make a TV spot for a peacenik candidate against a good Democrat. Nor will he fail to support the Johnson-Humphrey ticket for re-election in 1968. He can conceive of doing no less.

All that may be obvious to the politically sophisticated, but the Kennedy cult is based on the hope, if not the tenet, that the man can operate without as well as within the boundaries of the system, that he can lead a revolution of attrition against the dominant institutions of society. The myth will die hard. It is based on the shaky assumptions of pluralism: that the structure of American life if open enough and democratic enough to allow for whatever reforms are necessary, if only a formula for gathering political power can be found.

Arthur Schlesinger Jr., a peripatetic theoretician in Kennedy's Lyceum, appears to have arrived at such a formula. In an article in the April *Progressive*, he restates his argument that Americans have most of the things they need for the good life. What they want now is quality control. The new "qualitative" issues replace the old "quantitative" ones. Instead of "a job, a suit of clothing, three meals a day, a roof over one's head, and a measure of security for old age," people now are concerned with "civil rights, civil liberties, education, urban planning, the state of the arts and the beauty of the environment . . . and, in addition, foreign policy." These issues, he concludes, "are no longer social and economic so much as they are cultural and moral. It is no longer the common man against the economic royalist or the worker against the boss so much as it is the rational against the indignant, the tolerant against the bigoted, the planner against the spoiler, the humanist against the materialist, the educated against the uneducated, the young against the old."

To deal with them, Schlesinger would weld a new coalition of urban innovators, the unorganized (or Reuther-organized) poor, the newly diplomated middle class, the remaining progressive ethnic groups, the churches—"and the most vital group of all, the youth." Discarded are the regressive elements of the old New Deal coalition—the satisfied labor unions, the grasping lower-middle class and the backlashing minorities. To lead the new forces must be a leader "sufficiently free, cool, and brave, to relate to the young and recover their allegiance for American society." Schlesinger need be no more specific.

Despite the echoes of Dylan and Marcuse, Fannie Lou Hamer and Erik Erikson in Kennedy's speeches, Schlesinger's formulation indicates the basis and the limits of the new Kennedy politics. It can all be seen in Kennedy's project in the Bedford-Stuyvesant section of Brooklyn. In January 1966, Kennedy presented a series of speeches on urban problems that included several policy suggestions for community development but no specific plans for action. A few weeks later he began to hear complaints from Negroes in Bedford-Stuyvesant about the lack of follow-up. Kennedy's New York staffmen went to work, and by the end of the year they had developed a "total program" for employment, education, community organization, social services and economic growth such as Kennedy outlined in the second of his addresses.

A committee of influential businessmen—Thomas Watson of IBM, William Paley of CBS, financiers Douglas Dillon and André Meyer—was established as a development corporation. A local organization of the poor was set up to "govern" the project. City and state officials were asked to help, and proposals for federal aid (including financing from a Labor Department program that Kennedy pushed through Congress last year) were drawn. Before long, however, the poor people's organization developed a malfunction. It was being controlled by the traditional manipulators in the community. The Kennedy men in New York had not known how to reach the underclass, but when they saw that the council was making no impact in the area, they abandoned it and established a new *poorer* people's organization as a rival. The Citizens' Crusade Against Poverty, a liberal coalition of community action organizations set up by Walter Reuther, was called in to get the poor moving. The Astor fortune was requisitioned to build "superblocks" in the slums.

It is far too early to tell whether Kennedy's plan for Bedford-Stuyvesant will develop the new forms of community government and achieve the physical and social rehabilitation its backers envisage. The basic scheme suggests that something less than radical reconstruction will result. The Kennedy assumption is the Schlesinger thesis: that the highly motivated poor can work with the corporate elite and the planners with the politicians to produce a "qualitatively" Greater Society. It does not, however, seem likely. The cultural and moral issues are still inextricably bound up with the social and economic ones. Air pollution may be an aspect of the quality of life, but all the technological adjustment in the world will not reduce the smog one particle if economic pressure cannot be applied against the polluting industries. Urban planning is still a political problem. Banks and factories for the slums might be nice, but something more profound—"more social and economic" in the sense that Schlesinger's formula rejects—has to be done to bring the poor out of the culture of poverty. Kennedy's men in Brooklyn will find that the poor and the middle class do not share a universe of interests. In trying to improve education, for example, they will see that new buildings and bright teachers and modern curricula make little difference in learning among the poor. As the parents of East Harlem's IS 201 have been trying to say for a year now, changes in educational quality will not come until the community gains new measures of power—money and status and social effect. That process comes through political struggle; it will not be freely given by businessmen or social workers, much less by senators or mayors or directors of human resources. For the act of *taking* power is the condition of *being* powerful.

At best, the Bedford-Stuyvesant plan seems to be an attempt to apply the principles of American development aid overseas to an "underdeveloped" community at home. The idea of local counterinsurgency obviously appeals to Kennedy. Riot control is the first responsibility of the modern Prince. But there is no assurance that the local effort will have any more success than the foreign one has had. Overseas, AID programs have largely failed because of an inability to arrange a redistribution of power in the "target" countries. US money and technical assistance is monopolized by the elites, who use it to tighten their grip on the underclasses. The same has been true of the anti-poverty programs in this country; city machines and welfare bureaucracies have been the major beneficiaries of the money and the effort expended so far.

Still, it is difficult to criticize the Kennedy project in Brooklyn, as it is to bad-mouth his efforts and exercises in other fields. There is precious little in the country that is any better. Only a handful of senators criticize the war, few even *talk* about Latin America, and in any event Kennedy is so much brighter and more appealing personally than any of them. But it may be a serious mistake to consider what Kennedy is doing—in Bedford-Stuyvesant as elsewhere—a healthy "first step" towards significant change. For Kennedy would impose his own kind of elitist reform before any independent forms of social reconstruction could begin.

In foreign policy Kennedy would tend to strengthen, not weaken, the structure of imperialism: by encouraging American overseas corporations to behave liberally, to allow foreign governments to exert superficial control over corporate operations and to keep cool when political currents seem to threaten their interests. At the same time, Kennedy would encourage the development of a large counterinsurgency capability (as begun by his brother) to put down the really serious threats.

At home, Kennedy would be drawn to analogous illusions of reform. Larger governmental units might be decentralized to bring policy-making "closer to the people," while the old power relationships are maintained. It would always be necessary to control independent political constituencies, whether they are Freedom Democrats in the South, or liberation parties in the ghettoes, or unaffiliated labor insurgencies on the farms. The job of a political leader is to force such groups into coalitions that he already manipulates: the national Democratic Party, the city machines, the big labor unions.

A Kennedy Administration would try to implement the Schlesinger formula on a grand scale. There is a strong suggestion in that thesis that there is a "crisis" in the order akin to the failure of American institutions in the years before the New Deal, which Schlesinger has chronicled so well. The New Deal saved the order then by appearing to reform it. If things are really falling apart now, if the war and the Negro revolt and the alienation of the suburban middle class and the loss of "allegiance" of the young is as serious as Schlesinger supposes, Kennedy may indeed be the only leader able to maintain the order, however readjusted it may have to be internally. Certainly the Bedford-Stuyvesant coalition—corporation heads, liberal intellectuals, welfare politicians, progressive unionists, militant Negroes and eager young volunteers—offers the best hope to keep the center holding. But it is absurd to suppose that the social finagling will produce essential change. The Schlesinger doctrine invests the "free, cool, and brave" leader with powers he cannot logically have. The kind of top-down reforms he is capable of will result only in the superficial readjustments that can buy off the cutting edge of resistance. To do more requires the kind of dislocation and reconstruction of underlying relationships that can come only from a new politics, based on movement and conflict, not coalition and consensus. It is not Kennedy's fault that he can do no other; it is his situation.

For those who cannot believe in the essential efficacy of "cultural and moral" (or technical and legislative) solutions to basic social and economic problems, the next few years will present a series of painful choices. The Kennedy camp will gather much of the brightest, most energetic, most effective talent in the country. Some may join up in full agreement with the prospects as they now appear; others may try, as Robert Scheer recommended in a recent *Ramparts* profile of Kennedy, to "up the ante," to make Kennedy's reforms a little more broad than they might otherwise be. Only a few will remain outside. Only a handful will continue to build independent constituencies—of intellectuals, of the poor, of the Negro underclass. It is far from clear what the outsiders will accomplish. But in the end Kennedy will not remake the society, either by his personality or by his programs, and we will have need again of a saving remnant.

June 1, 1967, New York Review of Books

✦

Doctor's Plot

Captain Levy

At 11 o'clock in the morning of a drizzly day in June, Capt. Howard Brett
Levy, MD, was seized and manacled, hurried from a courtroom and
carried off in a staff car to the stockade at Fort Jackson, South Carolina. He
stayed the night in a small bare cell behind a crude wood-and-wire door, and
the next day was inexplicably moved to an empty ward at the post hospital,
where he had served for nearly two years. There he is confined, under constant watch by an MP, as he begins a sentence of three years at hard labor
for crimes of conscience and belief. In a sense, Levy concurred with the findings of the court martial. He did what they said he did, and he is not sorry.
He killed no guard, threw no bomb, raped no white woman, stole no secrets,
packed no pumpkin. Nobody framed him; he is the wanted man. What is in
contention is not the fact of his actions, but their meaning. Levy refuses to be
complicit in a war he abhors; the army calls that disobedient. He accepts
responsibility for the consequences of his acts; that is unbecoming conduct
and it promotes disloyalty. Levy did not seek to change the army, but to
ignore it, and he wanted not martyrdom but expression. The army, in the
way it often does, gave him just what he did not want.

Levy's progress from Brooklyn, where he was born thirty years ago, to
the Fort Jackson stockade is lined with milestones familiar to his generation. He was the only child of conventionally nice Jewish parents. Towards
the end of high school, he became vaguely aware of politics: "If I had been
old enough I would have voted for Eisenhower." At NYU he studied hard
("I had to, I wasn't brilliant"), assembled a respectable record and became
the president of a fraternity that he helped found. "It was designed to do
everything that fraternities don't do," he said. In that case, it was a useful
way of avoiding the conformism of the era without actually opting out.

"The most radical thing I did in the fifties," Levy said in the course of a
long conversation one afternoon in the middle of the court martial, "was to
go to folk music concerts or read the Elektra Records catalogue." He went
to Downstate Medical Center in 1958; in 1962 he interned at Maimonides
Hospital in Brooklyn. "I was interested in the money part of medicine," he
said. "But then a real change happened. I took part of my residency at
Bellevue, and I was working with people who were destitute and down-
trodden and completely cynical about the system. I began to identify with
their problems in a real way."

There were others in America who were turning off "the system" in those
years, but the effect of the new "generational" mood was indirect at best.
"There was absolutely nobody to talk to. I tried to talk all the time.
Everyone I knew disagreed. You know, if you hang around with old socialists all the time, you begin to think that everyone's a socialist; it just ain't

true. If you hang around with liberals, you think that everyone's a liberal; that just ain't true. But the people I hung around with were racists, and most people are racists. Period."

Levy read Paul Goodman and C. Wright Mills and went to lectures by Negro radicals. He listened to WBAI, the audience-supported radio station, and when its license was in jeopardy, he wrote a letter to the FCC. The license was renewed, and Levy was encouraged to write to President Johnson and the New York senators—"all those irrelevant people"—on weightier matters. But now the letters did not do much good. The first "really activist thing" he did was join a welfare workers' picket line in 1965 in New York. "I was uncomfortable as hell," he remembered. "It was freezing and raining and a terrible day. But most of it was just the fear of having my friends see me."

At about that time, Levy's marriage began to disintegrate. He had married right after medical school, before his ideas of himself and his world began to change. "I said screw all the materialism; I don't want to be poor, but I'm not interested in the money part." Like many of his contemporaries whom he had never met and who were also changing, Levy began to believe that he might spend a part of his life in jail. There was nothing romantic about it. "Individual martyrdom is irrelevant in this society," he thought, "but sometimes you get yourself into situations. At Bellevue I saw people lined up in the morning defecating without even screens between them. That's just degrading. The *aim* is degradation. I feel more strongly about that than about Vietnam."

In medical school, Levy had signed up with the army's Berry Plan, which allows doctors to finish their training before accepting the inevitable draft call. There is no "selective" service for doctors; it is an across-the-board sweep, with no deferments for family status, few for physical impairments, and eligibility until the age of 36. Levy was to report to the army in July 1965. Because of the crush of new commissions at the end of the academic year, there was no room for him in the orientation course given most army doctors at Fort Sam Houston, Texas. He was expected at Fort Jackson, and for weeks beforehand he was anxious and depressed. He drank a lot and came home sick. His marriage was about over, and it was hard for him to separate the two traumas of change.

"It wasn't the regimentation of the army that bothered me," Levy said, "although I didn't like it. It was Vietnam; it bothered me a lot then, and it bothers me a lot more now." He was two days late for duty at Fort Jackson (car trouble). He checked into the BOQ the first night, discovered there was no hot water in the shower, and moved to an off-post apartment the next day. The second rebellion came soon afterwards, when he found a $12 bill for officers' club dues on his desk. He never paid it—or the bills that followed. He was not terribly popular with his superiors.

Fort Jackson is a basic-training center with a large transient population and not much connection with the neighboring city of Columbia. "Fort Jackson is barren of intellect, barren of life; the people aren't really alive in any sense of the term," Levy said. He felt isolated. One Saturday morning in a Columbia coffee shop he noticed an item in the paper about a Negro voter registration drive in a town called Newberry, South Carolina. Levy had no idea where it was. But he quickly paid his check and started out to find the action. Somehow, he made his way to the county courthouse, where a demonstration was in progress. He found the local organizer, a young white army veteran named Bill Treanor, and volunteered his services.

"It was very simple then, very romantic. The next afternoon we registered an old man in his 90s," Levy recalled. "He was all bent over, a sharecropper all his life, and he was so proud with his yellow registration slip. It made us feel so good. I don't think I'd feel the same way today."

Levy went to Newberry every weekend that summer, and in the fall joined in civil rights work in Columbia. Later he staged a fundraising rhythm-and-blues show ("it was monumentally unsuccessful financially but extremely successful artistically"), and last year began to publish an eight-page newspaper for the movement called *Contrast*. But civil rights organizing is not a usual pastime for a white army officer in South Carolina, and Levy soon piqued the interest of the Counter-Intelligence Corps. Investigators got to him shortly after the summer project was over and questioned him closely about his politics, his reading matter and his organizational affiliations. They were worried about the sponsorship of the Negro radicals' lectures (Trotskyist), and were not calmed by Levy's assurances that he only went to listen. They asked him to take a lie-detector test, and he refused. Finally, they asked whether he would follow an order of a superior officer under any circumstances, and Levy said, of course he would not.

All along, there had been minor run-ins with authority. Levy never could manage to wear his uniform correctly, or keep his shoes shined, or remember to have his hair cut. His manner is abrupt and defensive at times, but he can easily be warm and eager with those for whom he feels some companionship. More than anything, he is Brooklynesque, with none of the assimilated "shoe-ness" of the med-student style. That suits Levy and his friends, but it is not always successful with the types at Fort Jackson. One day he had an argument with an MP officer: something about a parking ticket. "I was short with him," Levy admitted. In his report, the MP gave more details:

> When told to come to attention and salute, subject smirked, came to attention on one leg and half-heartedly put his hand near his head with his fingers in a crumpled position, then threw his hand in the direction of the wall. His left hand remained in his pocket. Throughout the conversation, CAPT. LEVY was insubordinate by facial expression, bodily movement and vocal inflection. Subject needed a haircut and his branch and US insignia were in reverse manner.

Colonel Fancy

On post, Levy spent his time running a small dermatology clinic for soldiers (VD), dependents (acne) and retired personnel (psoriasis). He was well thought of professionally. Col. Chester H. Davis, the hospital's executive officer, had no complaints about the way Levy treated him for a dry spot on the buttocks ("Don't wash so much"). Then Fort Jackson initiated a training program for special forces medical aidmen—the part-combat, part-medic complement of the Green Berets—and Levy was assigned to give each of them five days of instruction in dermatology.

He trained them for three or four months—"with some reservations"—and found them the most interesting people on the base. There was a striking similarity between the backgrounds of the Green Berets and white civil rights workers: the alienation from middle-class families, the feeling of being trapped by the society, the urge to have some effect of one's own.

"I talked to them about the war and about themselves," Levy said, "but after a while I realized that it wasn't doing any good. For a time, I pulled the kind of crap that some of the other doctors did—they just let the aidmen hang around and never really trained them. Then, last June, I just kicked them out.

"It wasn't intellectualized in the beginning, but I had two reasons. First, I don't think you can possibly train guys for five days in dermatology to a point where they'll do more good than harm. And second, I don't think medicine should be used for political purposes. You can't separate it from the war. It's part and parcel of the same thing."

Levy's earlier commander heard that the aidmen had been refused training, but he let the matter slide after an inconclusive interview with the captain. But Col. Henry Franklin Fancy, who took command of the hospital in mid-summer of 1966, was not quite so complaisant. He had noticed the "flag" on Levy's personnel file, denoting a security risk; "communistic," Colonel Fancy thought to himself (as he testified later). Then Fancy began hearing reports that Levy was telling aidmen and patients that the war in Vietnam was wrong, that he would not serve in Vietnam if ordered and that if he were a Negro soldier he would come home to fight for civil rights. As for Green Berets: they were "liars and thieves and killers of peasants and murderers of women and children." Worst of all, Levy had been talking like that to *enlisted* men, in violation of the responsibilities of rank.

Colonel Fancy was wondering just what to do when an intelligence agent told him the little secrets of Levy's "G-2" dossier. The full richness of its 180 pages has not yet been revealed even to Levy's civilian lawyers, but it contained such spicy information as this interview with a sergeant:

> Levy expressed very leftist ideas and viewpoints. He spoke favorably about those persons who burned their draft cards, feeling that this was their right, and they should not be prosecuted for this. Source

does not consider subject a loyal American because of his statements condemning US policies. . . . Levy was quite pro-Negro, to the side of the Negroes when discussing civil rights matters and appeared to think more of the Negroid race than that of the White race.

Colonel Fancy told his executive officer, Colonel Davis, that Levy was a "pinko." Then, after consultation with army lawyers, Fancy issued a formal order to Levy to train the special forces aidmen. Levy did not comply. Colonel Fancy was ready to take non-judicial disciplinary action when, after another close look at the G-2 dossier, he and Heaven knows who else decided to escalate the proceedings. Fancy charged Levy with willful disobedience of an order (a capital offense in wartime), and with promoting disloyalty and disaffection among the troops. A general court martial was convened.

Levy is convinced that the ante was raised because of his politics, or Colonel Fancy's reading of them. There is nothing to suggest that the commandant was in any way flexible on the subject of pinkness. In a preliminary hearing, Colonel Fancy testified that the communist line, as he understands it, includes "the requirement for world domination . . . and the lack of what we consider God and their requirement not to believe in God. The requirement to agitate and propagandize in such a way that non-communist people's minds are maintained in a state of chronic anxiety in the hope that this will not impair their will to resist the communist domination." The civil rights movement, he said, might well create such anxiety, and the anti-war protest was communist-based. That seemed to take care of Captain Levy. Colonel Fancy felt it necessary to warn a class of aidmen, in a graduation speech, to disregard the blandishments of left-wingers who might have infiltrated his hospital. Still, there was a touch of sentiment in the old bureaucrat. One day after the preliminary hearing had been concluded and the court martial was to begin, Howard Levy received a birthday card in the mail: "Look to this day for it is life," the message read. "For yesterday is already a dream and tomorrow is only a vision. But today makes every yesterday a dream of happiness and every tomorrow a vision of hope. Hope your birthday is happy and the year ahead is full of all that means the most to you." It was signed, "Bud and Cooksie Fancy."

Captain Shusterman

Exactly why the army permitted the Levy trial to blow up out of all rational proportions is still unclear. But the proceedings seemed to take on a life of their own. The actors were swept along by a play they never wrote. Last fall Levy told his girlfriend, an art student at the University of South Carolina named Trina Sahli, that he believed no final action would be taken before he left the army in July 1967. Levy's lawyers gave the authorities any number of escapes—including an application for conscientious-objector status, which was promptly refused. But the charges kept increasing. In February a third count was added, for "conduct unbecoming an officer and a gentleman," on the basis of the conversations with enlisted men. A few days later two more came. They stemmed from a letter Levy wrote to Sgt. Geoffrey Hancock in Vietnam, at the suggestion of Bill Treanor, the civil rights worker in Newberry. Treanor had been stationed in Hawaii with Hancock. The two regularly corresponded, and Hancock (a white man married to a Negro woman) had expressed some concern about the Vietnam protest movement at home. Treanor thought Levy could tell Hancock how it was. Levy wrote:

> I am one of those people back in the states who actively opposes our efforts there and would refuse to serve there if I were so assigned. . . .
> I do not believe that you can realistically judge the Vietnam war as an isolated incident. It must be viewed in the context of the recent history of our foreign policy—at least from the start of the cold war.
> . . . Geoffrey, who are you fighting for? Do you know? . . . Your real battle is back here in the US, but why must I fight it for you? The same people who suppress Negroes and poor whites here are doing it all over again all over the world and you're helping them. Why? You . . . know about the terror the whites have inflicted upon Negroes in our country. Aren't you guilty of the same thing with regard to the Vietnamese? A dead woman is a dead woman in Alabama and in Vietnam. To destroy a child's life in Vietnam equals a destroyed life in Harlem.

The letter went on for eight pages, with a great deal of explanation and obvious passion. It ended with an invitation for reply (the two had never met), but Hancock did not answer. He kept the letter for fourteen months in a pile of trash, and when he saw a television news broadcast about the Levy affair on Okinawa, he turned it over to his superiors.

At some point, the army began to worry about the effects of the trial. Its tactics began to seem a little more cool. Col. Earl V. Brown, the service's chief law officer, was sent down from Washington to be the "judge." The Fort Jackson commanding general appointed a court martial composed of ten men of rank higher than Levy's, all career line officers, four of them combat veterans of Vietnam, and all but one Southerners. The line-up was out of a Frank Capra war movie: one quiet Negro, one inscrutable Nisei (both quite junior) and a major whose eye had been lost in a ("friendly") mine explosion in Vietnam. There were no Jews, or doctors, or captains, or enlisted men, or women, or non-career officers. For the prosecution, the army found a young Jewish lawyer in a camp in Georgia and brought him to Fort Jackson. Someone in the Pentagon had been reading Zola.

Capt. Richard M. Shusterman presents only one of the countless ironies of the Levy affair. Amiable, ambitious, square, deferential, liberal and crew-cut, Shusterman is everything that Levy is not. He believes in military necessity and good order, the proper balance between the rights of men and the demands of institutions, the mutability of moral standards. He asserts that the world is too complex to be understood, and he makes a positive value of that incomprehension. It gets him off the hook. If he had any doubts at the beginning, he had convinced himself of the moral rightness of his side by the time the court martial began. He even seemed to have allayed some of the difficulties he may once have had in supporting US policy in Vietnam.

Shusterman is Levy before Bellevue. He is the part of the generation of the late fifties—by far the larger piece—that is continuous with its past, unmindful of its future. He votes for liberal Democrats and moderate Republicans, his favorite magazine is *The New Republic,* and he wishes that New Left students would shave their beards and dress neatly. It would help them sell their ideas in the marketplace. Phi Beta Kappa at Lafayette, a full scholarship to Penn Law, and a job, perhaps, with a tony firm in Philadelphia that now and then takes a few well-turned-out Jews. He doesn't mind the officers' club at all, but would defend to the death anyone's right not to like it. Except, of course, when he is the chief prosecutor.

Major Llewellyn

The trial began on May 10, in a small low-ceilinged hut on a sandy knoll at Fort Jackson. The court assembled each morning at 0900 hours, as everyone was fond of saying, in the way tourists on their first trip abroad enjoy the simplest Berlitz phrase. Newsmen and spectators drove to the court through fields of recruits doing calisthenics, romping over the "confidence course" (formerly, the obstacle course) or charging aimlessly with fixed bayonets. Women remarked sadly on the youthfulness of the soldiers marching down the roads.

Shusterman had an easy job. He had to prove that all the facts of the case were as everyone agreed they were, that Colonel Fancy's order was lawful, and that Levy had said and written the words ascribed to him. Colonel Brown, the law officer, ruled that the truth of the statements was immaterial, as was evidence of their effect. As a matter of fact, Howard Levy was not much of a subversive. No one became disaffected or disloyal. Shusterman did, however, have to prove Levy's intent to commit his crimes, but the court was permitted to draw its conclusions on that matter from the circumstances of the case and from the pattern of Levy's political behavior. Colonel Fancy was first on the stand, reciting softly and with no feeling the tribulations of life in the hospital with a trouble-making pinko. During much of his long testimony, he stared at the thin red carpet beneath him. The men on the court seemed sympathetic; no officer likes to be disobeyed. Levy's civilian counsel, Charles Morgan Jr., tried to establish from the succession of aidmen who followed that they were essentially combat soldiers, not medics. Some carried Red Cross insignia on their ID cards, and some did not. The point was never established.

The first indication that Levy was not alone in his concern about complicity and responsibility at Fort Jackson came in the testimony of another Brooklyn Jewish doctor named Ivan Mauer. Levy had once told him: "You're no better than the rest. You're in sympathy with me, but you want to walk the tightrope." At last, Captain Mauer got off the tightrope. He was not teaching aidmen at present, he said, and he would not participate in the program if he were assigned. There seemed to be a small "doctors' revolt" brewing. A Negro ophthalmologist (who, in the thousandth irony of the case, was treating the wounded one-eyed major on the court) testified for Levy that he had serious doubts about training aidmen. He compromised with his scruples by merely letting the students look over his shoulder as he worked, with no formal instruction. He told the law officer he was afraid to say even that much, for fear of prosecution.

Morgan had begun the defense's case with a battery of character witnesses—Levy's father, Negro civil rights workers—and was admittedly creating "an aura of Nuremberg" when the law officer interrupted. If Morgan wanted seriously to invoke the Nuremberg defense—that soldiers have a duty not to obey orders to commit war crimes—then he had to prove that the US was following "a general policy or a pattern or practice" of war crimes in Vietnam. Morgan was stunned. "Give me an extra day," he asked Colonel Brown, half-seriously.

Morgan actually had five days, but the task was hopeless from the start. For tactical and political reasons (for example, dissension within the American Civil Liberties Union, for which Morgan is southern regional director), he decided to limit his testimony to criminal actions by the small special forces contingent in Vietnam. That eliminated evidence of saturation bombing, napalming and genocide. A platoon of ACLU lawyers and staff assistants flew into Columbia from New York, accompanied by scores of new reporters. There were rumors of famous witnesses on the way—Sartre, Bertrand Russell, leaders of the NLF. At the end, there were only three: Robin Moore, the author of *The Green Berets*; Donald Duncan, the *Ramparts* editor who had served in the special forces himself and had told all in a magazine article; and Peter Bourne, a British-born US army psychiatrist just back from a study tour in a special forces camp in Vietnam.

Moore was never actually a Green Beret. He was a Sheraton Hotels PR man who went through special forces training to write his book (three and a half million copies sold) and has not yet gone back to the PR business. He was embarrassingly chummy on the stand ("no sweat," he told the judge, and he called the Montagnards "Yards"—which indeed was kinder than a prosecution witness who called the Vietcong "Luke the Gook"). But, like Duncan after him, he did provide some grisly tales of the tactics of special forces when they are done winning the hearts and minds of the natives. No one seemed particularly moved. Moore, Shusterman and Colonel Brown kept chatting about the cheapness of life in the Orient, the superstitions of the Vietnamese and the exigencies of war.

Peter Bourne provided the most convincing testimony about the way in which the special forces turn over prisoners to the South Vietnamese to torture them as they please. The US maintains no prisoner-of-war camps, and "military necessity" demands the transfer to the South Vietnamese. Under the rules of war, military units that take prisoners are responsible for their well-being, but none of the testimony satisfied the law officer. He ruled the next day that a case for war crimes as a policy had not been made, and he did not allow the testimony of "isolated incidents" to go before the full court.

Nuremberg Day was followed by Ethics Day. The defense went back to its original line, that Colonel Fancy's order to Levy need not have been obeyed if it was contrary to the principles of medical ethics—that is, the rules against teaching medicine to those who will not practice it ethically. Three physicians (Victor Sidel of Harvard, Louis Lasagna of Johns Hopkins and Benjamin Spock of everywhere) and a non-physician faculty member at Harvard, Jean Mayer, testified lucidly about the role of ethics in a physician's life. Shusterman tried to get them to admit that whatever good the special forces aidmen might do in Vietnam justifies their military role, or at least is distinct from it. But they would not buy his cheerful pluralism. The aidmen's role is inextricable from the war policy. The aidmen and the pacification teams and the winners of peasants' hearts and minds do not make war any better; they merely make it (possibly) more complete, more effective, more legitimate.

Shusterman produced a physician from Duke Medical School to refute the defense's experts. Doctors may train "paramedical personnel," the witness said, but they need take no responsibility for what the paramedics do with their training. But the most frightening witness of all was Maj. Craig Llewellyn, a 30-year-old special forces physician who ran the program in Vietnam for a year and a half and now directs training at the John F. Kennedy Special Warfare Center at Fort Bragg, North Carolina. Llewellyn arrived in paratroop boots and an open shirt, his head shaved almost bald and his manner something like a karate instructor's. With cold passion, he argued that the special forces are the best thing that ever happened to Vietnam, or any other counterinsurgency situation, for that matter. The aidmen bring modern medicine to areas that know only "Chinese doctors"— "neither Chinese nor doctors." Llewellyn's case was as strong as any Calvinist missionary could ever have made, and with precisely the same logic. He proclaimed the new doctrine of participatory imperialism—let the people decide to accept American intervention. The court was impressed, and Shusterman rested the prosecution's rebuttal.

Charles Morgan

No one could reasonably believe that the court martial would not convict Levy. Aside from the disadvantages of military procedure and the rather disorganized if often brilliant defense, there was simply too much at stake for the army. Levy was a symbol of anarchy and willfulness.

But at the motel in Columbia where the defense lawyers, Levy and his family, and most of the press hung out, there was a disturbing kind of euphoria. The out-of-towners were isolated and distracted by the strangeness of the small Southern capital and the otherworldliness of the army base. More than that, they had developed a sympathy—for many, a commitment—to Levy for which there were no appropriate forms of expression. In civil rights marches and peace demonstrations the committed can shout and stomp and wave banners. If they like, they can make faces or fists at hostile segregationists or pro-war hecklers. But there was no visible enemy to be angry at in Columbia. The substitute was a bizarre, compulsive hilarity. There were gags and songs and cocktails late into the night. Levy joined in as thoroughly as anyone; his parents looked somewhat baffled but they did not leave the scene. No one really could leave. The motel was like some moored ship carrying a cargo of doomed but laughing passengers.

The party began to wear thin in the last few days. Sgt. Charles Sanders, a quiet Southern army lawyer serving as Levy's military counsel, was wrenched out of shape. He had started the case as a routine assignment. By the time it was over, he had to question his values, his background, his deepest sense of himself. Levy's act seemed to touch Sanders directly, at the same personal level on which it was made.

Morgan had been working hard on the case for six months, and he was utterly involved and completely worn, but he managed to pull the pieces of the case together for a moving and masterly summation. Where it touched the law was not entirely apparent. But it was so painfully personal and so profoundly felt that even the court may have been moved to mercy.

"Events occur in the life of the world that are irrational, and the reason that they occur is that good men don't stop them," Morgan said. He is a great whale of a man, rumpled and sweaty at the slightest exertion, and he ranged around the small courtroom, talking without a script. "This case shouldn't be here. Dr. Levy shouldn't even be in the army. Someplace down the line, there was a place for this to stop, but it didn't. Now it's your responsibility to stop this thing as it monumentally cascades on to some crazy, wild conclusion."

Morgan knew how things get out of hand. He had been a lawyer in Birmingham, Alabama, in 1963, when he spoke—tentatively at first— against white racism. He was forced to leave the state. "Men are constantly being fitted into structures, and sometimes they conform and sometimes they don't. Sometimes men become martyrs by inadvertence, and around them swirl great movements. I don't want a martyr. I want acquittal, and we're entitled to it and the army will not fall if Levy goes free.

"More lives have been taken for heresy and witchcraft than for all the crimes in human history. More people have been tried for crimes that do not exist than for whose which exist. Men are constantly put on trial for their minds and words. Your whole lives are involved in the context of freedom; true patriotism involves a man's right to dream and believe and think and speak and act. This trial has to do with free men and responsibility. I truly do not want a martyr. I want a free man."

The court did not oblige. Levy was found guilty on the three major charges, and of a slightly less serious offense on the two counts arising from the letter to Hancock. Shusterman seemed to be having some last-minute doubts about his severity; he asked for a dismissal of those two charges, and Colonel Brown agreed. The next morning Levy was sentenced. As the court rose, Col. Chester Davis—the hospital executive officer now cured of the dry spot on his buttocks—took Levy by the arm and pushed him into a chair. Flushed and trembling, Davis pulled a pair of silver handcuffs from his pocket, fumbled awkwardly and clasped them around Levy's wrists. The lawyers shouted, Trina Sahli cried and Levy started moving through the door. He had a most peculiar smile on his face, which was captured in all the news photos—something between sorrow and contempt, but for whom it was not possible to tell.

June 29, 1967, NEW YORK REVIEW OF BOOKS

✦

Battle of Newark

A t high noon Tuesday, in Plainfield, New Jersey, the bells of a church began to chime "Onward, Christian Soldiers." Down the street, an armored vehicle crunched over layers of broken glass and stopped in the driveway of a cluster of small neat cottages. The army militiamen on board clicked open the safety catches of their weapons, then jumped to the ground. "Get your ass on the double," a sergeant shouted. The troops charged into the houses. State and local policemen, armed and helmeted like the soldiers, took up positions in the streets and gardens, behind car doors and trees. The militiamen battered down doors and scrambled through rooms full of black people, looking for "snipers." But they found none, and in half an hour the whole crew moved on to play the war game elsewhere.

It is a brutal war and an absurd game that has afflicted northern New Jersey this summer. In downtown Plainfield, about thirty-five miles from New York, whites went busily about their affairs in the shops and banks, only a few hundred yards from the war zone. Along its perimeters, past the chiming bells, a teeny-bopper couple in an open red MG glided from checkpoint to checkpoint, surveying the scene. They could smell the danger but felt safe from it, like runners far ahead of the bulls in the streets of Pamplona. Inside the "riot area," in occupied Plainfield, Negroes stood in small crowds. Whites who ventured past them in cars were taunted with angry obscenities. The few stores—it is primarily a residential section—were stripped and burned. Cars and motorcycles lay smashed and overturned in the streets, and glass covered everything, sparkling on the streets and sidewalks like precious stones. By Tuesday one young Negro girl had been killed. The policeman who shot her was stamped and beaten to death by the people in the streets. Plainfield seems only a skirmish in the shadow of Newark. There, for five days and nights, the city's 250,000 Negroes (the majority of the population) were in total "insurrection," as Governor Richard Hughes admitted. It began as a protest against the beating by police of a Negro taxi-driver who had been arrested for tailgating an unmarked plainclothesman's car. That first night there was looting of liquor stores, and a group of Negro youths threw a firebomb at the wall of a police precinct station. But the city officials, who have been fearing a riot for three years, played it cool. They did not gas the crowd or fire upon it. By dawn the ghastly ghetto which is Newark's Central Ward was quiet, and the mayor announced that it was all a "minor incident" with no racial implications.

The next night was different. Thousands of Negroes poured into the streets, looting and burning white-owned stores. The primary targets were those known for overcharging ghetto-dwellers. White government officials found the scene unimaginably mad, but there was more rationality than they would admit. For the most part the Negroes concentrated their attacks on shops carrying highly prized merchandise—liquor, clothing, drugs, cars parts. Even more rationally, they left alone those few businesses in the area owned by Negroes. Not one that had posted the shibboleth "Soul Brother" on the windows and doors was touched.

When the big night of looting was over, the insurrection had little to feed on. Half the shops in the Newark ghetto had been attacked. But Governor Hughes—a "liberal" Democrat with respectable credentials in the run of civil rights legislation—either did not believe it was finished or did not want to. He activated the national guard and moved into Newark himself to take control of the city. The local administration, which had been playing a role in the middle between white anxiety and black anger, retired helplessly before the military power of the state.

From then on there was a war of revenge in Newark, with the army and police on the offensive. Up to that point three people (all Negroes) had been killed. But the troops came in with guns blazing. Governor Hughes toured the ghetto and decided, in (perhaps) unconscious parody of a white colonial governor in Africa, that "the line between the jungle and the law might as well be drawn here as any place in America." The troops were told: "Use your shotguns and revolvers—that's what you have them for." They followed orders meticulously. In the course of looking for "snipers," the police and guardsmen killed twenty-three Negroes. Not one sniper was arrested, not one killed. Many of the dead were women and kids.

There were probably a few professional snipers in the battle but they were certainly insignificant. Others fired back in self-defense or in counterattack if their homes and families were attacked by the troops. But the police rampaged through the ghetto, spraying public housing blocks with bullets up the walls for six floors. Houses and apartments were ransacked and bystanders beaten. Some of the Negroes fought back, but not many—not nearly enough, people thought later. In any case, if there were snipers, they were impossibly poor shots: only one policeman and one fireman were killed, the latter probably by a police bullet. When it was all over, a Negro who had been fighting and trying to organize the community told me sadly: "What can you say to a kid who asks why they got twenty-three of us and we got only two of them?"

Early this week it began to occur to Hughes and his staff (which includes a former director of the Ford Foundation) that the occupation of the black city of Newark was producing something close to a guerrilla war. Some of the militants who met with him suggested that its logical consequence would be mutual massacre or concentration camps, or an entire state in "insurrection." He hardly knew how to respond, but after a day of flip-flopping on strategy, he suddenly pulled out the army on Monday afternoon. Crowds on the sidewalks cheered as the troops marched off, as if it were Liberation Day.

The battle of Newark was more than just a cry of frustration. If its politics were primitive and ambiguous, it was still a mass uprising in which tens of thousands—perhaps half the black people of the city—participated in some way. Governor Hughes was appalled at the holiday air he felt in the ghetto, but to anyone who understands what it means to be black in the white American century, that was a liberating spirit.

July 21, 1967, NEW STATESMAN

✦

All Systems Fail!

Those who did not live before the revolution will never know how sweet life is, Talleyrand said, and perhaps for such knowledge there is a desperate sweetness as the disaster spreads in this summer of the American crack-up. *Sergeant Pepper* blares from ten million phonographs, they're feeding the bears in Yellowstone Park, and the odor of barbecue wafting over the suburbs is suddenly mixed with the fragrance of pot. Hear it, see it, smell it while there is still time. For although there will be no revolution in the ordinary sense, the quality of life in the society—the values, the expectations, the perceptions—is radically changing. Things are not likely to be so sweet again.

For people who have difficulty seeing it clearly, the gods have created a ghastly metaphor in the disaster of the *USS Forrestal*. That mighty engine of war, that marvel of technology, that brilliantly organized institution exploded and burned not from enemy attack but from its own mundane malfunction. As an airplane prepared to take off for North Vietnam on a bombing mission, fire from its jet afterburner ignited a missile on a nearby plane. Then its fuel tank exploded and a chain reaction of explosions was set in motion.

We have been accustomed to think about America as the same kind of invulnerable fortress of power and technique. It is a tightly run ship, resilient and flexible when necessary, but always under control. If bugs develop, they can be worked out; if attack threatens, it can be resisted. But now the bombs are bursting and the flames are shooting. The well-laid plans cannot be followed, the fail-safes fail. The technological marvels have only limited value, if that: perhaps they do more harm than good. Above all, the institution is vulnerable to its own internal snafus. One blast can destroy the whole system.

It is always hard to describe the moment of failure from the inside, and harder still to see what led up to it. The crack-up is terribly complex. For twenty years the arrangements of the American system worked well enough to maintain control. Classes were roughly balanced, status was generously apportioned and demands for mobility were generally satisfied. The ideology of liberal corporatism, which is another way of saying "the American way of life," was neatly developed by established intellectuals like Stevenson and Schlesinger, and diffused by any number of agents—from the CIA to *The New York Times,* the great universities and the mega-corporations. Resistance was unsubtly crushed by the anti-communist purges of the late forties and McCarthyism in the early fifties. After that the methods were subtler. It was clear sailing, or so it seemed.

The first problems, however, were noticed almost as soon as the process of consolidation began. Cracks were discovered in the picture window of middle-class life: it somehow was not the utopia everyone had predicted. In the early days the trouble was called phoniness (by J.D. Salinger) or other-directed-ness (by David Riesman) or status-seeking or apathy. Now the terms are powerlessness and alienation, but the idea is the same: ordinary people are helpless to find expression or achieve participation in the huge governmental and corporate bureaucracies that control their lives. The system was still working well enough to make protest against that condition seem unreasonable. Students in the fifties may not have been entirely happy about what was in store for them, but they were mostly compliant and "silent." They slipped easily into the army and into IBM because there were no obvious alternatives. It was best to be cool.

The next problem was not so easy to ignore. For 300 years black people had been slaves, or as good as slaves, in the US. They neither demanded liberation nor were granted it. All of a sudden they were in the streets—boycotting the bus lines in Montgomery, Alabama, in 1956, and sitting-in and freedom-riding through the South a few years later. They were pushed both by the force of worldwide anti-colonialism (the US Negro movement coincided exactly with the African experience) and the vast discrepancy between the promise of American life and its reality for the huge underclass of the poor. Whites were victimized too, but Negroes had a heightened consciousness of their position in a racist country.

The example of a whole class of people aroused and marching to protest their powerlessness energized a new generation of white students—and later their elders—to do the same. In his brief years, John Kennedy tried to use that new spirit by employing its compelling rhetoric. Lyndon Johnson may have toyed with the idea of emulating his predecessor, but he never got very far. For one thing, he did not have the foggiest idea of what it was all about, and for another, he had to act in a number of ways to deny the legitimacy of the best rhetorical figures. He proclaimed the doctrine of community action and the "participation of the poor" but conveniently forgot it all when his larger political interests were threatened. At length the sense of impotence throughout the whole society grew so strong, and the sense of imminent disaster became so overpowering, that the revolt of the "slaves" began: in the streets of the black ghetto, in the suburbs, in the churches, in the universities.

It has come to a head, although hardly a conclusion, this summer with the insurrections in a dozen cities and towns. But what is most startling is the complete failure of the collective leadership—the politicians, the bureaucrats, the corporate managers, the liberal elites—to save the system. What appeared two years ago to be the most successful state power structure in history turns out to be a paper tiger. There is neither resiliency nor determination and no genius at all. The old intellectuals have been discredited by the recent disclosures of CIA involvement in just about everything, by the irrelevance of their anti-communist doctrine and by the failure of their strategies for reform to coincide with the realities of power. The politicians have been discredited simply because their solutions have failed to meet the society's most distressing problems: imperialism, war, racism, poverty, powerlessness.

There's certainly nothing new about such failure. Systems fail, crises arise and changes—often violent—are made. How violent America's change will be is uncertain, but it is perhaps foreshadowed by the summer's events. In Los Angeles, during the demonstrations against LBJ, whites fought back against police for the first time since the labor wars of the last era. The black uprisings are among the bloodiest civil conflicts in the nation's history. Already cities have been occupied "preventively" by troops, and civil liberties have been suspended before riots begin. It is not unlikely that in the next months or years vast urban areas will be under long-term military rule.

There is really no way of knowing where it will lead. No one could have seen the end of the chain reaction on the *Forrestal* when the first missile exploded. What is clear, however, is that there is a tremendous amount of energy left in America, even if there is little at the top. This is not Rome in the time of the barbarians, or even Britain at the end of empire. If there is greatness here it consists of that intense vitality and sense of purpose. In lots of ways, America is swinging.

August 4, 1967, NEW STATESMAN

✦

Soul Power

The Movement is dead; the Revolution is unborn. The streets are bloody and ablaze, but it is difficult to see why and impossible to know for what end. Government on every level is ineffectual, helpless to act either in the short term or the long. The force of army and police seems not to suppress violence but to incite it. Mediators have no space to work; they command neither resources nor respect, and their rhetoric is discredited in all councils, by all classes. The old words are meaningless, the old explanations irrelevant, the old remedies useless. It is the worst of times.

It is the best of times. The wretched of this American earth are together as they have never been before, in motion if not in movement. No march, no sit-in, no boycott ever touched so many. The social cloth that binds and suffocates them is tearing at its seamiest places. The subtle methods of co-optation work no better to keep it intact than the brutal methods of repression; if it is any comfort, liberalism proves hardly more effective than fascism. Above all, there is a sense that the continuity of an age has been cut, that we have arrived at an infrequent fulcrum of history, and that what comes now will be vastly different from what went before.

It is not a time for reflection but for evocation. The responsibility of the intellectual is the same as that of the street organizer, the draft resister, the Digger; to talk *to* people, not *about* them. The important literature now is the underground press, the speeches of Malcolm, the works of Fanon, the songs of the Rolling Stones and Aretha Franklin. The rest all sounds like the Moynihan Report and *Time*-Essay, explaining everything, understanding nothing, changing no one.

Martin Luther King once had the ability to talk to people, the power to change them by evoking images of revolution. But the duty of a revolutionary is to make revolutions (say those who have done it), and King made none. By his own admission, things are worse in the US today—for white people and for black—than when he began the bus boycott in Montgomery eleven years ago. Last summer in Chicago he was booed at a mass meeting, and later, as he lay in bed unsleeping, he understood why.

For twelve years I, and others like me, had held out radiant promises of progress. I had preached to them about my dream. I had lec-
tured to them about the not too distant day when they would have
freedom, "all, here and now." I had urged them to have faith in
America and in white society. Their hopes had soared. They were
now booing because they felt we were unable to deliver on our
promises. They were booing because we had urged them to have
faith in people who had too often proved to be unfaithful. They were
now hostile because they were watching the dream they had so
readily accepted turn into a nightmare.

The fault is no more King's than it is ours, though no less, either. He has
been outstripped by his times, overtaken by the events that he may have
obliquely helped to produce but could not predict. He is not likely to regain
command. Both his philosophy and his techniques of leadership were products of a different world, of relationships that no longer obtain and expectations that are no longer valid. King assumed that the political economy of
America was able to allow the integration of the mass of poor Negroes into
mainstream society with only minor pushing and shoving. White liberals
would be the thin edge of the wedge, the Democratic Party the effective
agency of change, a marching army of blacks the sting to conscience. The
trick lay in finding the best tactics, presenting the most feasible programs
and putting on the most idealistic faces.

It worked well for a while. Southern feudalism began to disintegrate (it
was already unsupportable), voters were registered, lunch counters integrated and civil rights acts passed. But there were stonier walls behind the first
defenses of segregation. A society infused with racism would not easily discard the arrangements by which it confers status. Unlike anachronistic feudalism in the deep South, the national system of industrial and technological
capitalism was practically invulnerable. Marches and freedom songs were
unavailing. The "power structures" of the Mississippi Delta may have trem-
bled when they heard "Ain't Gonna Let Nobody Turn Me 'Round," but the
one in Cook County was unmoved. It had better weapons: an anti-poverty
program, an Uncle Tom congressman, available jobs and huge stores of tolerance. When that failed, as it did, there were armies of police and soldiers
prepared for final solutions.

King may have first realized his predicament as he sat, silently, in the
caucus of the Mississippi Freedom Democrats in Atlantic City three years
ago this month. The National Democratic Party in which he had placed his
faith for change denied their petition for representation; it had no intention
of altering the balance of power between blacks and whites in Mississippi.
Worst of all, the liberal vanguard of that party, Hubert Humphrey and
Walter Reuther, were wielding the heaviest hatchets, to protect their own
skins and secure their own interests.

If that lesson was unclear, King could have seen a half-year later how the party of peace embarked on the most barbaric imperialistic war of this century. At best, he might have understood that the institutional demands that induced the war—the politics and economics of anti-communism—were parallel to the ones that kept the underclass in its place—the politics and economics of racism. At least he began to realize that social destruction in Vietnam was somehow incompatible with social advancement at home.

When the going was good, King still had his white liberals and his black marchers. But then the going was bad and getting worse. The white liberals had apparently misunderstood, or had been misinformed. They were willing supporters when the goals of the movement were integration and the *embourgeoisement* of poor Negroes. When the goal was liberation, the slogan "power" instead of "freedom," and the consequences were convulsions in the society they wanted desperately to preserve, the liberals dropped back, with their marching feet and then their checks. At the same time, and for the same reasons, King's black base had begun to thin. With no agents for change responsive to his demands, there would be no goods to deliver. It was not that King had chosen the wrong tactics or picked the wrong allies. He had simply, and disastrously, arrived at the wrong conclusions about the world. No coalitions available and no programs imaginable could "succeed" even in his own terms. Insofar as his objectives were revolutionary, they could not come out of status quo institutions; insofar as they were not, his followers were not interested.

King's response was to fly out in all directions in search of a new constituency. He arrived in Chicago last summer with fanfares in the national press and commensurate ballyhoo in the streets. The thrust of his attack was the formation of community organizations to End the Slums. His strategy had three phases: tenants' councils would harass landlords, mass (integrated) marches would arouse the country, and the Democratic Administration in Washington would push an open-housing bill through Congress.

Within a few months he had failed in all three endeavors. The local councils were haphazardly organized by staff workers with no understanding of the problems of building a solid base of local people. The marches were premature—the community was not ready to support them to the end—and King had to surrender to Mayor Daley and his friends for a worthless list of promises that would never be fulfilled. The national Democratic Party was unable to pass a housing bill, although it was theoretically in charge of the most "liberal" Congress in thirty years.

King retired in defeat to write his book*, surfacing only a few months ago to condemn the war in which his movement had been drowned. As always, his speeches were fluent and moving, but as always, they never quite got to the heart of the problem. For like his formulation of the race

Where Do We Go From Here: Chaos or Community?, 1967

conflict, his conception of the war is devoid of historical perspective and a sense of the processes of society. He seems to believe that progress is inevitable because compelled by an abstract moral force. Reality is seen as a series of episodes: "Every revolutionary movement has its peaks of united activity and its valleys of debate and internal confusion." Life is just one damn thing after another.

It is not easy to reconcile King's morality and his history—or the lack of it. Conventional commentators these days like to speak of King's "nobility" and the purity of his humanism, and then they sigh that the world is not ready for him. But it is more accurate to say that King is not ready for the world. His morality derives from where *he* is, not from where his followers are. The black people of America are at the losing ends of shotguns, outweighed by thumb-heavy scales, on the outermost margins of power. King's invocation of love and integration and non-violence may embody what he likes to call the Judeo-Christian tradition, but in the US in this generation those are basically the demands of the boss, the preacher, the publisher and the politician. Turn-the-other-cheek was always a personal standard, not a general rule; people can commit suicide but peoples cannot. Morality, like politics, starts at the barrel of a gun.

In spite of King's famous sincerity and the super-honesty that he exudes, there is something disingenuous about his public voice, and about his book. He is not really telling it like it is, but as he thinks his audience wants it to be. His readers will be white, and his book sounds as if it were intended to be read aloud in suburban synagogues and ADA chapter meetings. He recounts the heroic deeds of American Negroes, such as the Guianan immigrant Jan Matzeliger, who invented a shoe-lasting machine that developed into "the multimillion-dollar United Shoe Machinery Company," and Norman Rillieux, "whose invention of an evaporating pan revolutionized the process of sugar refining." Then he tells personal tales of discrimination against his family. The tone is that of a middle-class Negro having the same old conversation about race with his white liberal friend.

At the end, King suggests a few "programs" for action, and they amount mostly to legislative demands that either will not be passed, or, if they are, will result in none of the "structural changes in society" to which he occasionally refers. He likes the idea of a guaranteed annual income, more Negro elected officials, better schools, more jobs and protection of rights. Those are unexceptionable goals, but King has no real notion of how they are to be attained, or to what they may lead. Although he speaks of structural changes, he assumes structural preservation.

What is hardest now to comprehend—remembering the *Time* covers and the Nobel award—is King's irrelevancy. Almost seven years ago, in *Harper's,* James Baldwin wrote that King has "succeeded, in a way no Negro before him has managed to do, to carry the battle into the individual heart and make its resolution the province of the individual will. . . . He has incurred, therefore, the grave responsibility of continuing to lead in the path he has encouraged so many people to follow. How he will do this I do not know, but I do not see how he can possibly avoid a break, at last, with the habits and attitudes, stratagems and fears of the past."

Baldwin's skepticism was wise. The break has not come, and the heart is no longer the battleground. Yet King still counsels:

> Our most fruitful course is to stand firm, move forward non-violently, accept disappointments and cling to hope. Our determined refusal not to be stopped will eventually open the door to fulfillment. By recognizing the necessity of suffering in a righteous cause, we may achieve our humanity's full stature. To guard ourselves from bitterness, we need the vision to see in this generation's ordeals the opportunity to transfigure both ourselves and American society.

This summer, King is shuttling between Chicago and Cleveland. He has all but abandoned the End the Slums campaign in Chicago, and instead is pushing Operation Breadbasket, a program of economic pressure against large food-marketing corporations in an effort to get more jobs for Negroes. A similar tactic had some limited success in Philadelphia many years ago, but its gains have not been significant anywhere else. From a Chicago base, King hopes to get ministers across the country who are affiliated with his Southern Christian Leadership Conference to start local Breadbaskets— against National Dairy Products, Kellogg and California Packing Company goods. The theory is that the ministers will negotiate for jobs with company representatives; if no progress is made, congregations will be mobilized to picket and, if necessary, boycott proscribed products. At the same time, King's staff in Chicago has a federal grant to do vocational education so that some untrained Negroes off the streets may be able to fill the new jobs if they appear.

There is no reason to believe that the national Breadbasket will make more headway than the local ones. The organization is crude, and, more than that, many of the assumptions are questionable. The few jobs that may open will not noticeably change the character of ghettoes; at best, a few more black people will pop out into the middle class, like overheated molecules in a brimming beaker of water. Many of the jobs would go to Negroes who are either skilled already (and may leave slightly less desirable employment) or at the very top of the underclass. Local groups backing up the demands for jobs will be thoroughly controlled by SCLC staff workers, in consultation with the odd black businessman in town. There is little implication for permanent organization or real movement. Breadbasket amounts to an escalation of rhetoric but a diminution of power over a broad base. More than anything King has attempted so far, it assumes the permanence, and even the desirability, of present economic relationships. The only change would be the imposition of a few black faces behind desks and counters.

In Cleveland, King's staff is working on a larger scale, but his campaign there is new, and it is likely to suffer from the same deficiencies found in the Chicago experience: top-heavy organization, premature action, orientation towards small goals (instead of movements). If there is violence there, King's position will be all the more precarious. He has maneuvered for several years now between white anxieties and black anger. On one side, he tells whites that he alone can control the ghettoes, if they support his work and give him goods to deliver; on the other, he tells the black people presumably under his influence that rioting will get them nowhere and that he alone can give them what they want. It is a complicated game requiring consummate political skill, and although King abides by the rules, he has not been winning many points. Whites have ceased to believe him, or really to care; blacks hardly listen.

It is not that the ghetto listens to anyone else. No black "leaders" with national reputations speak in understandable accents. The only authentic black hero of this revolutionary generation was Malcolm. Stokely Carmichael comes closer to that standard than most, but he is somehow unscarred, not deeply cynical enough to evoke the radical funkiness of black America. Carmichael, like the rest of the sharp SNCC organizers of his early sixties era, is still hung up on white culture. What happens when a child of Camus grows up? There is something stagey about his public performances; each is too much a *tour de force*—"Stokely Carmichael, the tee vee starmichael," his SNCC friends called him in Mississippi in 1964. Until now, at least, he has had too good a time. His successor, Rap Brown, lacks Carmichael's smile and brittle brilliance, but he seems more at ease with the slowly moving black poor. He may well sound too dangerous to be tolerated. "We going to burn this town to the ground," he says. Apocalypse is the normal mood of ghetto talk, but on the outside it sounds like criminal anarchy. Brown must choose between understanding from his audience or tolerance from the enemy.

SNCC decided last winter to move into Northern urban centers and begin the kind of organizing there that it had once done in Southern Black Belt counties. The stated political objectives of the Southern campaign—politicians elected, schools desegregated, economic improvement—have not been fulfilled, but SNCC had been able to devise radical new models for the organization of communities. The projects in Mississippi and Alabama had suddenly given people a sense of themselves and their power.

It worked so well for the wrong reasons as well as the right ones. SNCC's black and white intellectuals charmed the rural "folks" as much as they organized them. When the SNCC kids left, the local communities often slid back—if not into the lives that they had led, then to a less sophisticated kind of political organization than SNCC had envisioned. A kind of black Tammanyism began to arise in the counties where SNCC and the Freedom Democrats had worked hardest. SNCC became largely irrelevant, and its staff members more or less uninterested in hanging around to see the after-effects.

The Northern campaign never really happened. A few workers in a small number of cities are still at it, but their total effort is small, and its effect diffuse. Since the spring, SNCC has been most actively involved in energizing Negro campuses, for, after all, Carmichael and most of the other SNCC breed relate best to people like themselves. SNCC started at Southern black colleges, and its return is both logical and useful.

Of the other "national" organizations, only CORE is attempting to reach the bottom layers of blackness. Still, there are few cities where CORE is more than a journalistic reference point.

We have been accustomed—trained, even—to think of social change as the work of visible political organizations. That perception is produced by reliance on the "media," which respond mindlessly to the sheer size and solidity of the institutions that are to be changed. The Lowndes County (Alabama) Freedom Party, the Black Panther, was considered unimportant because it could not effectively take power in the state. It could not quickly and decisively shatter the existing social arrangement over a wide area. Parties—traditional or revolutionary—are assumed to be the only agencies of social movement, and their size is of crucial importance. The significance of a political party, a demonstration, a publication or an organization is thought to be directly related to its weight in raw numbers.

But somehow that perception lies. In the past few years, dislocations have taken place that utterly destroy the numbers theory. Political parties did not cause tanks to rumble through the heart of the nation's biggest cities in July; they did not bring out soldiers by the thousands, or destroy billions of dollars' worth of property. Something much more subtle is happening, much more difficult to locate in time or place. The "civil rights" organizations of last year's headlines are observers like the rest of us, no matter how loud their preachings or insistent their press releases. Black politicians, from Tom to militant, have all they can do just to stay on camera. Representative John Conyers in Detroit—heralded as the model of the new breed—is as irrelevant to his war zone as Representative William Dawson is to Chicago's. History moves at breakneck speed. Adam Powell had better stay in Bimini.

So all that has come until now is prologue—not the first steps in a long flight of equal gradations, but preliminaries of a different order from the main event. The maneuverings of the last half-decade have been predicated on King's assumption that the American system can somehow absorb the demands of its underclass and its alienated. Now this summer we all know that it cannot. Those who speak in seats of power seem not to have the slightest idea what those demands are, much less know how to meet them. Jerome Cavanaugh of Detroit is the most "progressive" mayor in the country; his battleground is bloodier than Sam Yorty's LA was. The United Auto Workers tried in Detroit to integrate Negroes into the economic community;

no other big union will be nearly so helpful. Anti-poverty programs, swimming pools, free trips to the ballpark, aid to education: if that was riot control, it failed.

Martin Luther King and the "leaders" who appealed for non-violence, CORE, the black politicians, the old SNCC, *are all* beside the point. Where the point is is in the streets of Detroit and Plainfield, New Jersey, and Cambridge, Maryland. There has been no response by government because there can be no adequate answers, save suppression and investigation, to people who by their actions indict the very legitimacy of the government. "The name of the game," a movement operative in San Francisco said recently, "is chaos."

But not quite. What observers called indiscriminate "rampage" was the deliberate and selective destruction by thousands of people of white-owned stores. The kind of unanimity of purpose (any one or two looters could have invaded a black merchant's store, but they did not) suggests that the rebellions have an authenticity beyond chaotic mob action.

Both Governor Hughes of New Jersey and Mayor Cavanaugh watched in horror as the looters hauled out television sets and furniture. But in a strange way, those reactions may be exactly what the looters meant to inspire. Ghetto life has always been a mean caricature of middle-class values: the pink Cadillac bought on credit, the TVs in every crowded flat, the boozing on Saturday nights just as they do in the country clubs. The riots, too, mocked the materialism of the suburbs and the legal violence committed in the name of government. The man tells black people to amass goods and to kill enemies of the state; the people comply in the way they know how. Seen from afar, the riots were scenes in a vast, spontaneous morality play, staged by guerrilla actors in the only real theater.

There was some sense in the riots, and from them a primitive new kind of politics has come out of the ghettoes this summer. There are tough black street leaders who have emerged as local heroes, and although they are not interviewed on *Huntley-Brinkley* nor appeal to suburban fundraisers, they are legitimate and powerful. The first wave came out of Watts—Tommy Jacquette, Brother Crook and a dozen others. They were street rumblers before the summer of 1965; now they are the new political organizers of the LA ghetto. More like them are spinning out of Newark and Detroit. They are half guerrilla, half ward heeler. They work between organization and revolution, groping for a way in which a bitter and mobilized minority can change a system they know will never accept them as they are. They disdain the numbers game, they avoid the "visibility" hang-up. They are told it is hopeless, but they are beyond hoping. The strategy is to keep people moving and working, to make noise and trouble, and always to disrupt. Slowly, others in the ghetto learn how to do the same. There is no talk yet of revolutionary institutions; there cannot be, for there is no revolutionary context, and now there can be only approximations. At best, there may be new ghetto organizations: community schools, block councils, tenant unions, police patrols, labor groups. The point is to extend democracy radically, and that task will involve whites as well as blacks.

The insurrections of July have done what everyone in America for thirty years has thought impossible: mass action has convulsed the society and brought smooth government to a halt. Poor blacks have stolen the center stage from the liberal elites, which is to say that the old order has been shattered. It is at once obvious that the period of greatest danger is just beginning. The political establishment will swing wide to the right and "buffers"—the Committees of Concerned Citizens, the defenders of dissent, the liberal politicians who give cover to the left—may be obliterated. Those who are working in the streets need to have a new coalition behind them to absorb the inevitable calls for repression.

The civil war and the foreign one have contrived this summer to murder liberalism in its official robes. There are few mourners. The urgent business now is for imaginations freed from the old myths to see what kind of society might be reconstructed that would have no need for imperialism and no cause for revolt. At least we know now that even if all Martin Luther King's programs were enacted, and all Jerome Cavanaugh's reforms were adopted, and the Great Society as it is described materialized before our very eyes, there would still be the guerrillas.

August 24, 1967, New York Review of Books

✦

The Defense of Hue

It is a sad symptom of a war which is more than sad that Americans cannot appreciate the heroism of the defense of Hue by the Vietnamese guerrillas. At another time, given a different history, we would see the three weeks in the citadel (at this writing) as a storybook inspiration—a new Stalingrad, the Blitz, the Alamo. As it is, all the pictures and all the perceptions come from over the shoulders of the marines. In the papers and on television, the defenders are gooks, their defense is a suicide mission and the only heroes are the imperial invaders with their God-given firepower. The conscience of the republic was best expressed by the *Washington Star*, which declared the Vietcong guilty of the greatest material crime of the war by bringing on the destruction of Hue with their defense of it.

The indicators on the chauvinism scale are all up. At the end of the Tet offensive, the Gallup poll found that 62 percent of the American people considered themselves "hawks"—up ten points from December. In the same period, confidence in President Johnson's handling of the war dropped seven points, presumably because he was not hawkish (that is, successful) enough.

As a consequence, the President is scrambling to make his determination clear. A few hours after the NLF's "second wave" barrage against US bases and South Vietnam's cities, the President decided to express his solidarity with the troops. Naturally, he picked the paras and the marines for his visit; their reputation for brutality enhances his image of toughness. There followed a visit to General Eisenhower, who might or might not have understood what was happening, but in any case was good for a few mumbled words of encouragement for the war, in between mashie shots on the Palm Springs links. Mr. Johnson uses the ageing, somewhat distracted ex-President as his private Republican oracle: the earth shakes lightly, the vapors thin, and whatever groans are heard can be interpreted to bestow historical legitimacy on the petitioner. (Palm Springs even *looks* like Delphi: lush valley, black precipitous cliffs, hard blue sky.) Safely removed from reality in Mr. Eisenhower's desert retreat, the President took the opportunity to declare the guerrilla offensive a positive blessing, not even disguised. Walt Whitman Rostow, who keeps track of such things, advised Mr. Johnson that the widespread attacks had given the Saigon government and its army a new sense of togetherness. Only the irreverent I.F. Stone pointed out that after a few more victories like that, the US would be lucky to end up with a coalition government in Hawaii.

February 23, 1968, NEW STATESMAN

✦

The Liberal's Progress

History is full of last chances, lost opportunities and unperceived possibilities. The history of political liberalism in America for the past twenty years is composed of very little else. Now, in the winter of 1968, when the country is practically *in extremis*, the keepers of that liberal heritage have found themselves confronted by the severest—and the final—test of their legitimacy. There is no way within the system to save the system except by the presentation of a practical, possible political alternative to the present impossible choices.

For a year or more, liberal activists have been fussing about with one project or another, searching for a pool of political energy and a way to exploit it. Finally, after all the trying, the very core of the liberal tradition has brought forth its candidate for the last, best hope of America.

He is, of course, Eugene J. McCarthy, and now it appears that he is no hope after all. McCarthy is a sympathetic, intelligent man, sincerely rational and profoundly cynical. If politics were nothing more than a show of sensibility, McCarthy would be counted a success; there is a touch of the (minor) poet that conceals the corruption and compromise of his role. But of the uses of power he knows little, and cares less. His campaign for the Democratic presidential nomination has had its occasional moments of exuberance, but mostly it has been flat, tasteless and strangely out of context with the crisis of its time.

"I don't know whether it will be political suicide," McCarthy joked at his press conference on the day when, at the end of November, he announced his candidacy. "It will probably be more like an execution." All along, the message of his campaign has been its hopelessness, and McCarthy seems to derive a certain reassurance from his lack of effect. "It's nonsense to set my mind on the presidency," he said some weeks later in his Senate office, as he sunk into a dark, fragrant leather chair. "The challenge on the issue—that's the important thing." In the windmill-tilting racket, the tilt is all; no one wants—or expects—the blades to stop. "I'm testing the system," McCarthy concluded softly, and then nodded his head to acknowledge that he had no doubt that the system would be found wanting.

What lays beyond the rhetoric of challenge in McCarthy's mind is still obscure. In the campaign legend, the germ of the idea was planted by his daughter, Mary, who from the margins of Radcliffe radicalism chided her father for not making good on his liberal ideals. Father had indeed been cautious. In private he worried about the war, but in public he said little, and in Congress he lined up with the Democratic leadership more often than not. He had voted for the Tonkin Resolution, extension of the draft and the various war appropriations. Suddenly he grew uneasy. "If you've been around for thirty years passing moral judgements on politics and society, you've got to take a stand," he said one morning a few weeks ago. "You can't go waving your wooden sword forever."

Once motivated, McCarthy began sniffing out the dank places of liberal politics for possible sources of support. He had seen the ads for dissident and concerned Democrats in the usual liberal publications, and he assumed that most of them, whoever they were, would welcome a "peace" candidacy, as long as the candidate was over 30 and shaved regularly. Most of the political preparation had been done by the Vietnamese in winning the war. And the liberal space had been stretched by the radical war protest movements, which had been at work all during the time McCarthy had been agonizing over the national honor and keeping his mouth shut in the Capitol.

McCarthy declared his intentions in a press conference in the Senate Caucus Room (where John Kennedy had done the same thing eight years earlier), then flew to Chicago where the Concerned Democrats were conveniently assembled for endorsement of his candidacy. The affair had been arranged by Allard Lowenstein, who at age 40 was in the process of casting off his role as the oldest student leader in America in exchange for a more adult profession. Lowenstein saw his political future in the Kennedy camp, but his entreaties to Bobby to run for the presidency in 1968 had been unavailing. In September, Lowenstein made a determined effort to talk Kennedy into the campaign, and when it failed, he reconciled himself to supporting a lesser figure. By the time of the Chicago conference, McCarthy was the only possibility, but Lowenstein was not completely happy. McCarthy, he thought, was pitched in too low a key for a "peace movement" campaign. More than that, the senator's position on Vietnam— stop the bombing, withdraw to enclaves and try to negotiate—was considerably behind that of his most militant supporters. Lowenstein found the 500 Chicago delegates restless, bored and a little disappointed even in anticipation of McCarthy's appearance; whereupon he proceeded to deliver an enormously exciting speech to the convention, to the accompaniment of a brass band's rendition of "Hello, Dolly." McCarthy waited in the wings, "kicking paper cups," someone said. Lowenstein soared higher and higher. "He didn't just warm up the crowd," a McCarthy campaigner said later, "he overheated it."

It was more than a letdown when McCarthy finally gained control of the rostrum. His own speech was dry and dull, and the audience response was in the same vein. It was there that the image of McCarthy as a cool fish was born, and it haunts the campaign to this day. Lowenstein's tentative relationship with the campaign also appears to date from the Chicago speech, although McCarthy is at a loss to explain why.

Like many bright men, McCarthy likes to surround himself with aides who are distinctly duller. There are a few outsiders with whom he talks on political subjects and the great issues of the day—Joseph Rauh Jr. of Americans for Democratic Action, Gilbert Harrison of *The New Republic*, Robert McAfee Brown, the Stanford theologian, and some of the more clever journalists around the country—but with few exceptions, his office and campaign staffs are inexperienced or worse. By early February, Lowenstein's role in the campaign was unclear, even to the McCarthy staff. There were stories that he was out, then in, then half-out or half-in. In the back of his mind, Lowenstein was still hoping, if not working, for a Bobby miracle. On January 31—the day after Kennedy made another in his series of disavowals of candidacy—Lowenstein flew to Washington to tell Bobby how sorry he was.

Al Lowenstein is not alone in his sorrow. Much of what is left of the liberal community in America was waiting for the Camelot plot to fulfill itself. As Kennedy later told Lowenstein, however, he simply could not put the thing together—not yet, at any rate. He felt that Johnson could manipulate opinion and demand Democratic loyalty with sufficient strength to stop any attempt at an organized dump.

In their own separate ways, the Kennedy forces and the McCarthy minions were acting in response to the same constellation of political circumstances: the break-up of the Democratic coalition, the disenfranchisement of the remaining liberals and the fluidity of the general political scene. Intuitively, the McCarthy men began to emulate the vintage 1948 model for the reorganization of the liberal bloc. In the original version, intellectuals and trade unionists formed the Americans for Democratic Action and secured control of major labor groups, local political parties and private parapolitical organizations. To legitimize their claims as well as to rid themselves of their fiercest rivals, the liberals cleansed existing organizations of all radical elements, and when that was not possible, they formed parallel groups that excluded the unwashed left. ADA countered the Progressive Party and supported Truman over Henry Wallace; the Liberal Party in New York was aimed against Vito Marcantonio's American Labor Party. In Minnesota, Hubert Humphrey and Orville Freeman, with a little help from their friends (like Eugene McCarthy), drove the Reds out of the Democrat-Farmer-Labor Party. Walter Reuther did the same in the CIO.

One of McCarthy's younger campaign workers—who must have been in grammar school when all of that took place—said last month that it was his hope that McCarthy would build an "enclave" within the Democratic Party as a home for liberals and a launching pad for social change. That was the line in the old days. The liberals were safe and secure as long as they could translate the demands of their constituencies into benefits from a Democratic Administration.

In fact, the liberal leaders were simply entrepreneurs of the system. They held title to a base of union members, intellectuals, Negroes, ethnic minorities, young professionals and ex-radicals in wide assortment. If all went well, they could gather up bloc votes, money, campaign work and general support to offer the party politicians. In exchange, they were given labor legislation, peace and civil liberties, civil rights, welfare and a bagful of reforms to deliver to the folks at the grass roots. The power brokerage game has a vocabulary of humanitarian virtue and popular idealism, but it is played as rough as machine politics or wheeler-dealer business. Explicit bargains involving the lives and hopes of millions of people are struck in Capitol Hill offices and Washington lunch clubs. Implicit deals are arranged more subtly, in the regions of men's minds: labor leaders, for instance, understand that they must cut the edge of militancy in their unions if they are to be welcome in Administration councils. The status of the brokers depends on how smoothly they can keep the system flowing.

During the Eisenhower years, the middlemen—Joe Rauh, Reuther, Schlesinger, Humphrey and the rest—clung to their positions on the promise that the Democrats would be back in power before long and the goods would roll once more. For recreation, they formulated ideologies to rationalize their own interests and confirm the historical mission of the system they served. The theories were elaborate: "end of ideology," anti-communism, neo-Keynesianism. With Kennedy's election, the liberals achieved their finest, if briefest, hour. Many of the top men came straight into the Administration; the others could buzz in and out as they pleased.

But the liberal perceptions of even the most steadfast are warped by the experience of power. The most obvious—and most pathetic—example was

Adlai Stevenson; as Kennedy's ambassador to the United Nations his elo-
quence proved equally appropriate to lies as it once was to truth. There was
a lot of selling out, as there always is, and the great movements for change
never seemed to be launched from the enclaves. But by the time of the assassination—and for a year afterwards—the entrepreneurial system was working as well as it ever could.

The war and its domestic consequences changed all of that. The intellectuals dropped out first, then the Negroes, the ethnic minorities and the young
professionals. The AFL-CIO's George Meany discovered that he needed no
middlemen to represent his interests to the power structure. He was *in* it.
Fresh disasters befell the Administration (the black uprisings, tight money,
the backlash). All, in their own ways, reinforced the total effect of disintegration. After a while there was no role for the middlemen; they had no base to
trade and no goods to deliver. And the legitimacy that they had won with
anti-communism was destroyed by the exposure of their complicity with the
CIA establishment.

It may not have been in McCarthy's mind, but it must have been in his
guts to recreate the 1948 scene. This time the peace movement would be the
base of support, the anti-war intellectuals would supply the rhetoric, and the
Negroes and student activists would provide the necessary energy. Like the
communists before, the most radical elements would be purged. It was a nice
idea, but divorced from real politics. The peace movement is not some
dependable union; it is not organized or structured, nor does it have much
potential in those directions. Few whites, least of all the McCarthy liberals,
can talk with the ghetto Negroes. On the same hand, the liberals can *only*
talk to the white radicals, but there is no guarantee that they will listen.
Most of all, McCarthy could not hope to deliver the necessary pay-off—an
end to the war—from the Democratic Administration.

Despite the contraindicative arguments and evidence, McCarthy cannot
help identifying himself and his campaign with the "respectable" peace constituency. It is a comfortable, middle-class, white and well-educated family.
They believe that they are the only effective political agents in the land; they
have not yet learned the truth of their own powerlessness. Like his people,
McCarthy is a gentle elitist, with that mixture of good intention, self-delu-
sion and arrogance common to the breed. His own history is the perfect scenario for the Liberal's Progress.

McCarthy's first job was in the "intelligence community" as a War
Department spook during World War II. He taught sociology at a Catholic
college in St. Paul, then began dabbling in Democrat-Farmer-Labor politics,
on the Humphrey side. He helped Humphrey purge radicals from the DFL
and was rewarded with a congressional nomination in 1948. In those days
McCarthy seemed more aggressive than he is now. He played the *old*
McCarthyist game on both sides of the street, speaking out against the
witch hunts and then, in a sense, legitimizing them. He bitterly attacked

Joe McCarthy (the two once debated on the air) for threatening the civil liberties of non-communists, and he offered a successful amendment to a security bill in Congress that gave the right of appeal to civil servants who had been fired for suspected subversion. But in 1954 he supported the Humphrey bill outlawing the Communist Party. And he later said: "It seems clear enough that the Communist Party gives lip service to freedom only to exploit and abuse it."

In the mid-fifties it was perfectly acceptable for a liberal politician to take an imperialist line on foreign policy. The following statements have an authentic Dullesian ring:

> The US must undertake to preserve Western civilization and the peoples who value it . . . [and] guard and protect our lifelines to vital materials and necessary supplies of oil, tin, manganese, uranium, etc. . . . preserve our national honor . . . and raise the economic and cultural level of peoples of other civilizations and thus promote the cause of justice and world peace.

> . . . It is to the interest of the United States to protect non-communist countries against communist combination, even to the point of using American troops under certain conditions.

It was not John Foster Dulles but McCarthy who said that (the first statement in 1951, the second in 1954). The point is not that McCarthy should be hung on his words of fifteen years ago. He is aware of his inconsistencies, and in his campaign speeches is careful to say that the nature of international communism has changed, and that the US response should now change with it. In a real way, however, liberals of the cold war period laid the foundation for today's anti-communist imperialism. They never challenged the whole framework of ideology which, as it turned out, was of their own construction. In theory, they said, it was perfectly all right to wage the world counterrevolution, if the consequences were not too disagreeable. Naturally, those in power, whose interests are really at stake in foreign policy, will accept the premise and feel free to disregard the qualification. The conception of America's role in world politics that McCarthy formulated in 1951 led almost inevitably to John Kennedy's policy of counterinsurgency in 1961, and from there to the Cuban missile crisis and, at the end, to the genocidal war in Vietnam. Unresponsive now to demands of the power centers, McCarthy can easily see the necessity for the liquidation of a particular imperialist adventure. But it is not hard to imagine what line he would take if he were in the seat now occupied by his soul brother Hubert Humphrey.

In Congress, McCarthy voted for most of the standard liberal programs, worked his way up into the ranks of the ways and means committee, and quickly discovered the political and social benefits that its membership conferred. When he moved to the Senate in 1959, he slid easily into the finance

committee and settled down to a casual life in that most boring of all parliamentary bodies. The finance committee was where it was at, and it was the
custom of members to trade favors for political support, senatorial status
and—in the case of the more venal types—campaign funds and personal
"contributions." McCarthy never stooped to venality (he is, unfortunately,
the poorest of the current presidential candidates), but he was not above
playing the bill-swapping game or using his influence within the committee
for little political gambits. It was all harmless enough. He voted for oil depletion allowances in 1964 and has generally been considered a friend of the oil
and gas industries, with only a few regrets—mostly on the Senate floor,
where they are for public consumption, and not in committee, where they
count. He justifies his oil votes to his liberal audience by arguing that depletion allowances have been "built into the structure of the industry, its price
structure and capitalization." To his critics, he gently thumbs his nose: "The
oil depletion allowance is not really a great liberal issue."

There were other favors for large corporations and their managers that
did not fit into McCarthy's definition of "great liberal issues." In sum, it is
pretty much small-time stuff, but then McCarthy has never been in the big
time. His Senate record is not exactly barren, but he has yet to sponsor a
major piece of legislation. His biggest moment in the Senate in years came
during the last session, when he introduced a resolution creating a congressional watchdog system over the CIA. But then, out of boredom or peevish-
ness, he let the matter drop in mid-course.

It is startling to compare McCarthy's pervasive cynicism in congressional
politics with the exalted idealism of his campaign. He acts under the
assumption that individual acts of political courage make little sense in
Washington, but proclaims that they mean everything on the stump. At the
beginning, McCarthy had hoped that his candidacy could frighten the
President into changing his war policy. Perhaps a different campaign might
have done just that—one that mobilized large numbers of people for a direct
attack on the legitimacy of the Johnson Administration, with the explicit
threat of making a mass defection from the Democratic Party in November.
But McCarthy refrains from such tactics and remains a good party man.

Even if he could not help defeat Johnson or bring an immediate change in
foreign policy, some benefit might come out of the campaign if McCarthy
could educate an active group of voters for future political work. To do that,
he would have to give them information and help draw the connections and
relationships between forces that the Democratic center tries to obscure. But
McCarthy never even begins to talk about the underlying causes of the war,
the fundamental imbalances that produce poverty and support racism, or
the real dimensions of the crisis of America's empire. He feels more at home
lecturing about the superficial inequities and injustices. Perhaps he underes-
timates his audiences; they know the war is wrong and that black people are
oppressed. What they want to know is *why*, and what can be done.

At St. Anselm's College in Manchester, New Hampshire, McCarthy gave his typical answer: "Change will really not come in response to what I have to say. It will come in part, I hope, from that. I suppose it will really not come in response to what you may say or do here in New Hampshire and how you may vote. But I think that, in part, that change can be influenced by what does take place here in New Hampshire in March. And I ask . . . that you be aware at least of that share of the burden of citizenship which you carry in the United States, that what you say in some way will be heard, and that what you do—even though it may seem to be unimportant and minimal—will also be noted."

It is not surprising that a lot of people walked out puzzled. They were not worried about his "style," which the daily press keeps attacking. Like any sensitive adult, McCarthy disdains the extroverted, arm-grabbing approach to politics. "People don't want to be shouted at," he said on opening day of his drive for the New Hampshire primary vote. "This is a confrontation of issues, not a presentation of a personality." On the trail he chats amiably with newsmen and passers-by, and although he seems to find it a little tiresome, he presses on. He spends as little time as he has to in campaign appearances—his is the first campaign in recorded history that runs ahead of schedule—and seems embarrassed and awkward with ordinary citizens.

But the problem at heart is not McCarthy's inability to thrust a personality on the public. Candidates have overwhelmed voters and still lost elections, and shy men have made revolutions. It is what McCarthy's campaign means that makes the difference. He says he is providing an "alternative" to the frustrations of the protesters, and he is applauded for that effort by both the establishment press and the frightened liberals. At the end, however, he may be causing more frustration than he relieves. A campaign without a political focus is hopeless from the start.

McCarthy's failure, both personally and politically, is a perfect metaphor for the failure of liberalism in the American sixties. Liberalism is where people are not. In another age, McCarthy's gentle appeals to reason and his touching loyalty to the Democratic Party might have found wide acceptance. Their audience now is distinctly limited.

The importance of the McCarthy campaign lies in its unimportance; its pathos is its unreality. McCarthy sets his political objectives as a "test of the system," and a "challenge to the war." These goals are worthy only if the campaign has a reasonable chance of success. But even McCarthy knows that it does not, and the inevitable consequences rob the effort of its essential morality. McCarthy himself may find contentment in the belief that he has committed "suicide"—the final act of personal morality. But political morality cannot exist outside political reality; it's not how you play the game but whether you win or lose. To believe you will win and then lose is excusable; to know all the time that you will lose is not.

The real victims in all this are the frustrated and alienated people, as McCarthy speaks of them, who trudge through the snow to get a glimpse of the candidate, or stuff envelopes in wretched campaign headquarters on the off chance that it will do some good. They must believe in the campaign for they have nothing else. They hate the war and they are terrified by the failure of the institutions they once relied on. They will not vote for Johnson, they cannot vote for Bobby Kennedy, they are made physically ill by the sight of Nixon or the thought of Reagan, and they cannot bring themselves to storm the steps of the Pentagon. Their last, best hope is indeed in McCarthy, and now he cannot tell them what his campaign means.

It is small consolation that even he sees his predicament. "It's worse than I thought," he said at the end of a long talk in his office a few months into the campaign. "It might have been better to let things run wild—to have a peasants' revolt. Maybe it would have been better to stand back and let people light fires on the hill."

March 1968, RAMPARTS

✦

The Trial of Captain Levy: II

On a bright day in early November, I returned to Fort Jackson, South Carolina, for a visit with Capt. Howard Levy, who was then still detained in the prison ward of the hospital in which he had served as an army doctor for almost two years. That day, he was led in handcuffs from the small post courtroom and put in the stockade; he was transferred to the detention ward the next day when the army realized that Levy in irons did more damage to its image than Levy in comfort would do to its security. Since then a series of somewhat frenetic legal maneuvers to free him on bail—or failing that, to keep him at Fort Jackson—had ended in failure, and Levy and his lawyers supposed that he would soon be removed to the US Disciplinary Barracks at Fort Leavenworth, Kansas, for the remaining thirty months of his sentence. So it was probably a last visit for the duration of his term; at Leavenworth, Levy would be allowed to see only his lawyers and a short list of relatives and intimate friends.

In May, I had arrived at the Columbia airport on a midnight flight with a cadre of lawyers, legal PR men and reporters. We swarmed into town in a fleet of rent-a-cars and camped out with the rest of the Levy entourage at a huge motel built in the Waikiki-Antebellum style. For two weeks the trial unfolded as a kind of morality pageant with a Brechtian *mise-en-scène*: circus clowning, flowing booze, running gags, shackings-up and puttings-down. We moved through the town and the base like actors in street theater, using the surroundings as props, alienating the audience and playing only to ourselves. Through it all, the moral—the commitment of a man, the confusion of a generation, the agony of the times—bounced and bumped against the surface action, until at the end it emerged almost too clearly by comparison.

In November there was no theater in the streets of Columbia, no way of shutting out the depressing surroundings. Objectively, the town was in all ways unchanged, give or take a new A&W Root Beer stand or a McDonald's Golden Arches. But for us (I was with another journalist and an American Civil Liberties Union lawyer), it was all different. Columbia was no longer a prop but a completed universe; it shut *us* out, isolated us, made our visit a marginal event. It was like walking through an Alabama county the day after a civil rights march passed by, or visiting a college campus in the summer after one's own graduation.

That sense of isolation, or something close to it, was with Howard Levy at Fort Jackson in the years before the pageant arrived, and it reclaimed him—despite his efforts—when everyone left. Levy could have visitors without limit, and a few came or phoned (he had an incoming line) almost every day. But it was of course a life apart that he was forced to live, and the personal relations he built from his cell were necessarily partial. To the local radicals and political activists, he was the guru; for the scattered GIs at the post who dared make or continue friendships with him, Levy was a moral (emotional?) inspiration. He would hardly admit the existence of his former colleagues. Dr. Ivan Mauer, who admired but could not emulate Levy's defiance, came often to the prison ward. At first Levy filled each visit with brutal assaults on Mauer's caution and failure to share his protest. Then anger cooled to contempt, and Levy simply ignored the other doctor. Mauer would come and read a newspaper and slip out without a word of conversation; his wife brought gifts of food, which failed to appeal to Levy's appetite.

Col. Henry Fancy, the commander of the hospital, who brought the original charges against Levy, wandered in during the first few weeks of his confinement. "You should get something light to read to take your mind off your troubles," he advised Levy. During the Arab-Israeli war Colonel Fancy sought Levy's political interpretation; the colonel always made good use of his officers' talents. Col. Chester Davis, the hospital executive officer, who manacled Levy that day in the courtroom and hustled him to the stockade, came later to make his courtesy call, but Levy would not see him. No doubt the post officers were put off by Levy's uncompromising attitude; but then they never could comprehend his refusal of complicity in the system that he loathed and they accepted. For that matter, neither could many of his friends. One sympathetic journalist reported Levy's behavior each day of the trial as a case study in manic-depressive syndrome. Even Levy's father, somewhat less clinically, whispered once in an aside, "Why couldn't he have held out just a few more months?"

I had heard the stories of Levy's first months in prison, and I approached the hospital that morning with some apprehension, and a feeling—as we walked the long wooden corridors towards the ward—almost of regret that I had come. Some of that ambivalence, which the three of us felt, was a version of the familiar personal dread and self-consciousness that people have when they visit a dying relative or a hopeless cripple. But now there was a threat of a different quality, an impending judgement, even if it were never articulated, of existential failure: Mauerism. The corridors were impossibly long, or so they seemed to be, and branches led off in all directions without sign or explanation. We kept losing our way in the maze and had to ask for help several times. The last person we found—a serious and respectful GI— set us pointing right, and as we began walking, he added, not really as an afterthought, "Good luck."

The day with Levy was not nearly so awkward as I had feared. He was the only prisoner in the ward, which was filled with unused, stacked-up hospital beds, and guarded—not very convincingly—by two MP's. (One evening, Levy told us, he had found the outside guard asleep, and saw that he could easily unlatch the screen door to the ward and leave the grounds. "I toyed with the idea of going into Columbia for the night, and then reappearing the next morning, just to embarrass them," he laughed. "But I went back to bed instead.") Levy had not yet been stripped of his rank, and the guards were dutifully deferential to a member of the officer class. They all watched television together. Levy's own "cell" was a narrow screened-off room; there were political posters on the wall and an array of books and magazines in a large shelf: "Skin," Styron, the *Monthly Review.*

The weather was fine and warm, and we sat all afternoon in a screened porch. For a long time, we talked about the war, the strategy of protest, the condition of the peace movement. Two shy black girls came to visit, and then, at the end of the day, four white students from the University of South Carolina. The students had been to the Pentagon on October 21—some had been arrested—and they were planning further political action at home. Levy suggested that they begin with moderate programs to attract middle-class support, but he told them sternly that if they were going to pass out leaflets or hold peace vigils in the adult community they would have to modify their hippie appearance. They seemed unconvinced by the tactical advice, but obviously awed by Levy himself. "I know I'm hard on them," Levy said later. "They're good kids. But I don't have much time, and I've got to use the position I've got with them."

From the prison ward, Levy was conducting an impressive organizing effort in Columbia. He had used the authenticity of his condition to set up antiwar groups at the university and in the community—a large delegation had gone to the Pentagon—and he was "working" on a slum organizing project in a section of town called Black Bottom. There was already an embryonic resistance movement on the post which drew both inspiration and leadership from Levy. He hoped, most of all, to reactivate a civil rights newspaper called *Contrast,* which he had put out himself in 1966.

As we were going, Levy began to talk about his expectations of Leavenworth. He had thought about non-cooperation, but he was not sure what that meant for him, or how he would react to actual conditions. But he knew he could not play the army's game. "The whole point, of course, is castration—to rob soldiers and prisoners of their manhood and their identity, their pride," he said. "Sex deprivation in prison is the most blatant tactic for that, and if they can take away your manhood, they can do anything with you they want."

I left the hospital quite unsure of what I felt about Levy and the meaning of his trials—the one in May and the others since and to come—and about myself, as a journalist who wrote about it, a friend (although distant) and a minor political actor. Levy of course was a star; supporting players must always be blinded by the glare.

We flew North by way of Atlanta. On the short leg of the trip from Columbia, we sat with a Navy pilot who had been stationed on the carrier *Kearsarge* in Asian waters, and was on his way back to Vietnam after a brief time at home. He kept kneading his flat-top hat as if it were a soft cap, and it was wet in his hands. From time to time he would jump up from his seat and roam the aisle of the plane. Soon he began talking with the other writer in our group, who was sitting next to him. He had no idea of who she was, or who we were, or where we had been that day. He talked about the war, and there must have been a slight suggestion in the conversation that we were politically interested. "I suppose you and your friends are against the war," he said to the other writer. "We are," she answered. "How would you feel if you were out there risking your life, and your buddies were getting killed, and the people back home didn't support you?" he asked. "That's why we're against the war," she said. They talked a little while longer, and he said that he had been to William and Mary, he was a Catholic, his father was a Foreign Service officer, and he was in the States to visit his wife. And then he said what was obvious from the very beginning, although none of us wanted to hear it. "You know," he said, "I'm terribly afraid." He got off before us, but we caught sight of him again briefly in the Atlanta terminal, boarding another plane, and we waved goodbye with a slight gesture that I do not think he saw.

A light plane came for Levy, one day just before Christmas, and took him to Leavenworth. On the day of his departure, several of his friends or supporters at Fort Jackson—no one knows how many, but some say hundreds—planned to "see him off." But the post commanders confined them all to their barracks or work stations, and Levy's send-off party consisted only of officials. There was a good deal of banter all around, and Levy was characteristically sarcastic and funny. The last and best line was the provost marshal's, who admitted that he disagreed with everything Levy said, but would defend to the death his right to say it.

Unfortunately, the provost marshal's premise is not shared by the boards and courts of justice that have reviewed the case so far. Levy's lawyers argue that he has a constitutional right to speak against the war, inside the army as well as out, and that his refusal to train aidmen for Vietnam service was protected by rights of conscience and medical ethics. The appeal process is complex and, at least on the lower levels, almost hopeless. Neither army boards nor federal civilian courts are likely to overturn decisions of military justice in time of war. An injunction to stop the court-martial before it began was denied in successive civilian courts. The appeal for bail was refused through the military and civilian process, and the Supreme Court has denied a hearing on the issue. On the substance of the charges themselves, appeals for dismissal or reduction of the sentence have been turned down by a variety of officials, and they are now under consideration by the Military Board of Review. After that, the case can go to the Court of Military Appeals, and then to the civilian courts, on the lowest level. Most, if not all, of Levy's sentence will probably have been served by the time the final appeal is heard. Possibly Levy can get six months off his term as "good time," but that is a discretionary matter and it is difficult to predict the manner in which discretion in the army will be exercised.

Levy shares quarters at Leavenworth with a half-dozen other officers—a forger, a black marketer but no other frankly political criminals. Watching television coverage of the Tet offensive, Levy seemed rather pleased by the success of the guerrillas, and two of his cellmates threatened his life. Levy remains unconcerned, although he is a bit apprehensive at the prospect of his next cellmate—a Green Beret officer convicted of murdering a Vietnamese civilian. Levy never had many kind words for the Green Berets (although the accuracy of one of his indictable statements—that special forces men were "murderers"—is now proved). He has applied for work as a physician at the prison, but action has not yet been taken on his request. Other prisoners with special qualifications are usually allowed to use them. As an alternative, Levy volunteered to teach American history at the prison school. That seemed acceptable, the director of custody said, if Levy would teach "facts, not his opinions." "Fine," Levy agreed.

A visitor who saw Levy shortly after his arrival reported that he had found the first week severely dislocating: the "depersonalization" which he had expected was still shocking when it began. Levy's hair was cut, he had his regular clothes exchanged for a prison uniform, and the privileges of reading, seeing outsiders and writing letters were drastically cut. Prisoners at Leavenworth are allowed five correspondents, who are also the only five permitted visitors. Four of those on Levy's list live on the East Coast, and are effectively out of visiting range. Letters to him seem to be passed or returned on an arbitrary basis; letters from close friends have been sent back, but a large quantity of hate mail gets through. He was told at first that he could receive a certain number of publications, but when he specified his choices, the officials said some were not on the "approved" list. *Ramparts* and *The New Republic* were banned; *The New York Times* and *New York Review* were allowed.

One prison psychiatrist, a young doctor serving his two years in the army, offered Levy work in his mental health department and, incidentally, a chance to read his own subscription copy of *Ramparts*. Levy was unmoved by the offer. The psychiatrist, he thought, put on liberal airs while functioning as a crucial part of the system of authority. Psychiatrists sit on disciplinary and review boards, and in the name of therapy act as part of the judicial and controlling process. For the psychiatrist as well as the commandant, the chief virtue of a prisoner is his capacity for "adjustment." Both their jobs are to induce docility. When Levy objected to that use of medicine, another psychiatrist promptly diagnosed him as pathologically hostile, passive-aggressive and paranoid. "He thinks I'm paranoid," Levy wrote in a letter, "because I call him the enemy." The inimical quality is Mauerism, and Levy has the radical perception—or ill-luck—to see it in all its incarnations.

Levy's only major confrontation with the prison authorities occurred during the initial depersonalization period, when an MP guard entered his room at midnight and turned on the light. Levy wanted it off, and said that prison rules gave him the right to the luxury of darkness. The guard remained steadfast; Levy called him a "neofascist." Levy was reprimanded, but when the guard repeated the light-torture, Levy repeated his accusation. This time, the commandant found him guilty of disobedience and sentenced him to two weeks in solitary confinement on bread and water. Then the sentence was suspended.

There is a certain amount of freedom within the prison, and Levy spends his days talking with enlisted men. The Fort Hood Three are at Leavenworth, and in all, Levy says, there are about forty "political prisoners," although the army classifies most of them as AWOLs or puts them in other non-political categories. In a way, Levy now sees his role as an organizer, and he has told his few visitors that he thinks "inside" political organizing in the army can be effective.

"Outside," the effect of Levy and his trial on particular political developments is difficult to assess. At Fort Jackson a nucleus of Levy's friends began open anti-war activity in January, and in a month's time they were strong enough to move from town onto the base for a protest "meditation" service at the chapel. About thirty soldiers appeared, but before it began, Col. Chester Davis called in one of the leaders and ordered him to cancel the meeting, or "you will end up in prison like Dr. Levy." The soldier reluctantly obeyed (for his troubles, he has been denied a minor promotion), but two others who came refused to leave the chapel grounds and fell to their knees in "prayer." MPs dragged them off, and Colonel Fancy brought charges. Charles Morgan, Levy's flamboyant ACLU lawyer, took their case, and the sky at Fort Jackson grew dark with chickens coming home to roost.

Signs went up on bulletin boards: "Morgan's Back." Finally, Colonel Fancy dropped the charges. Attempts at more "pray-ins" have been made, but the authorities have managed to break them up. They have also been able to frighten away some original supporters, but the protest effort seems to be growing. "Levy is spiritually responsible for it all," a political activist in Columbia reported recently. "He single-handedly turned on the half-dozen people who started it all down there. It's the best example of direct personal organizing I've ever seen."

Away from the post, the activities that Levy generated or encouraged continue in a less dramatic way. A nucleus of activists was created during and after the trial, and separately if not together they will go on working. Around the country the pray-in "movement" spawned at Fort Jackson is spreading to other military camps: there was a similar demonstration in Fort Ord, California. There are also a few more cases of individual resistance like Levy's. Air force Capt. Dale Noyd has just been sentenced to a year in prison at Clovis Air Force Base, New Mexico, for refusing to train airmen for Vietnam. A private at Fort Dix, New Jersey, applied for conscientious objector status and when it was denied refused to wear his uniform. He has been sentenced to a year at Leavenworth. A lieutenant at Shaw Air Force Base, South Carolina, refused to assist in training for the war and has also been convicted and sentenced. Perhaps a dozen other cases of overt resistance have been tried in the past eight months.

I thought at the time of the trial, and see more clearly now, that Levy was as much a metaphor for a generation as a political leader. He "turns people on" not by the force of his arguments (which have grown more sophisticated with his prison reading and reflection) but by the power of his example. Everyone who was at the trial was touched in some way: many came to see that their perceptions of their lives were profoundly changed. Of course, that happened in the context of the war and a society in crisis, but Levy supplied the live model. An army doctor who testified in the trial found himself increasingly bound up with Levy and has become a working political activist. A lawyer who helped with the defense realized in the months after the trial that his own association with liberal causes and action never extended to the roots of his existence, and he is undergoing a painful, and probably irresolvable, reevaluation of his life. Capt. Richard Shusterman, the cool young prosecutor who did more than his duty in arguing against Levy (he added two charges to the case) has recently ended his army service; together with his assistant at the trial, he is reported to be "pretty much against the war." Shusterman has joined a Philadelphia law firm. His former assistant is now an anti-poverty lawyer in Florida. Neither has yet had public second thoughts about Levy. Col. Earl V. Brown, the law officer ("judge") at the trial, suffered a mild change of heart. He has left the army to become assistant dean of the Columbia University law school; in February, he signed an advertisement published in the *Times* calling for an end to the war. "We believe that the terrible violence the war is inflicting on the people of Vietnam is destroying the society we seek to protect. . . . We believe that the US cannot by *acceptable* means succeed in its attempt to secure and maintain control of the Saigon government," the ad said. In May, Colonel Brown had denied the existence of any "pattern or practice" in the US conduct of the war which was *un*acceptable to generally held moral standards.

Levy's example extends to medical students (who are being organized in one of the most energetic radical movements in the country) and doctors (several, led by Dr. Spock, visited him in Fort Jackson in November) and others across the spectrum of political action. But most of all, it has an impact on those who are most like him in age and class and social role—the "generation of the fifties" that exists in confused transition between the security of liberal careerism and the support of the radical movements. Burt Austen, a biomedical engineering researcher at Downstate Medical Center in Brooklyn (where Levy was trained), lived on that margin, and what has happened to him in the last half-year seems to represent the experience of others.

"Last summer an ACLU man spoke at Downstate about the Levy case, and I became quite interested," Austen told me not long ago. "I talked with him for two hours or so after the meeting, and before long I was volunteering for work on the Committee for Howard Levy, MD. We had a demonstration in Times Square on Hiroshima Day, and in November we went to Fort Jackson. I more or less organized it. It was really the first time I had done anything like that—for years my wife and I looked at TV and she said we shouldn't pay our taxes, but I just scoffed at her. What happens can be very strange. When we went down to visit Howard, he told us not to waste our time on him, but to do more. Do more. He even told Spock he wasn't doing enough. I think it made me want to do more, sort of reflect on what I had done up to that point.

"Most people take the attitude, 'it can't happen to me.' When I met Howard I realized I knew so many people like that in Brooklyn where I grew up. I realized that it didn't take much to be there: I mean circumstances could have placed any one of us in that stockade. The more each person does, the more he can't stop, the more he has to see it through to the end. I ran a press conference for the doctors at Fort Jackson; I never thought I could do it, but then when I did it, I said, well, I can do it again. I felt in thirty-six years I had not really matured, and then in six months I came of age. I can't really look at things the way I used to. Sometimes a person comes in via the back door and before he knows it he finds himself organizing without really knowing what happened to him. You see, the more you do the more you have to do."

All Fools' Eve

Policies fail; governments fall; heroes return. The progression is a constant in the histories of modern democratic states, and somewhere within the incoherence of these weeks' events that very simple outline might be found. The problem now is in selecting the proper dots to connect with lines of interpretation. The starting place must be the success of the guerrillas in Vietnam and the collapse of the American military initiative. From there, the line extends to the monetary crisis, the failure of confidence in the President and Mr. Johnson's bizarre performance on All Fools' Eve, announcing a pause in the bombing and his own imminent retirement. The last fixed point was the emergence of Robert Kennedy as the agent of national renewal.

But the pattern is incomplete and the rules do not clearly advise the next move. For eight months the country has been in eruptive turmoil; for three weeks it has been in acute crisis. At last there was an expectation that things were falling into place. The dead hand was lifted, the war was coming to an end. People could begin to breathe again, which is to say that there was space for life, for an enlivening spirit. It wasn't simply the President's speech, or the New Hampshire primary, or the Kennedy candidacy. Singly, those events were politically incomplete or morally ambiguous. Taken together with everything else—with Poland and Prague and Hue, with Wall Street and Wisconsin and the Old Senate Caucus Room—they infused energy into a system that was practically miserable but unable to move.

I was in New York on Sunday, and I heard President Johnson's speech in a small apartment in a brownstone in Greenwich Village. At the end, when he promised he would not run again, a cheer went up from inside all the other flats in all the blocks in the neighborhood. Isolated, insulated New Yorkers, living for years in the very depths of *anomie*, had the extraordinary sense of communal happiness. The sound echoed against the big brick buildings. We all ran into the streets below, and although everyone had heard the news, people told each other again, for the sheer release of expressing it. A hippie came up and said softly, "Johnson said uncle, exclamation point," and then skipped down Christopher Street. The telephone lines were jammed. It struck me that Americans had taken no political event so personally since November 1963, and that the need for a public expression of feeling was the same then as now, although the feeling itself was so different. The expectation of relief was as high as it has been for twenty years. It was lifted still further on Wednesday when news came of Hanoi's willingness to talk—if only about the bombing—and the White House's first "interested" reactions to the Hanoi broadcast. The hope lives. I am not at all sure what America will do if it dies.

April 5, 1968, NEW STATESMAN

Chapter IV

✦

A CORD SNAPS

A Cord Snaps

There is a cord that is strung from the winter of 1948 until now, and along it hang the politics, the events and the personalities of one long, cold season of history. The length of span is far less than an epoch and still greater than a generation, and one day the period may seem to be not much more than a journalistic conception: the "cold war decades." But now people have been seized with the sense (it is as vague as that) that the strands have come together and the cord is somehow complete. It is only when such periods end that we can begin to describe them (and much later to define them), for only in their endings do their beginnings make sense. For Czechoslovakia, the sending-down of Novotny and the ascension of Dubcek seems to complete a course that began with the throwing-out of Masaryk twenty years before, even if what will follow remains unclear. For the US, there is stark symmetry between the election of Truman and the abdication of Johnson; the formation of the cold war coalition in the Democratic Party in 1948 gains an essential clarity of relief against its dissolution in 1968.

The events of these weeks hardly constitute a revolution, but they do seem to follow Lenin's description of a revolutionary time, in which things fall rapidly out of place and historical space is compressed. The motive force, of course, has been the war in Vietnam, and the prime movers are the guerrillas of the South and the armies of the North. Their Tet offensive, despite its limited military accomplishments (and objectives) had the power to wrench the vision of Americans—and others to the extent that America touches them—from one perspective of the world to another. The realities of the war were not much changed: troop ratios, supply lines, areas of control and the distribution of firepower are not significantly different today from what they were in late November, when the Johnson Administration's great optimism

campaign began. What has changed radically is the way the war is perceived, and it is from that new expectation that a new politics has developed.

The expectation that the expedition in Vietnam was doomed destroyed
worldwide confidence in the ability of America to solve its monetary problems and led directly to the gold crisis (really a dollar crisis). That set the
teeth of the American corporate and financial establishment on edge; both
the money managers and the industrial directors yearned for retreat.
Reinforcing their misery, profit declined in some of the biggest, most highly
technological defense industries. The war turned out to be a bear. Crucial
confirmation was supplied by *The Wall Street Journal*, which in an editorial
on February 23 advised its readers to "prepare for defeat," and be more or
less grateful for it. Not only the professional anti-war protesters had seen
what was coming. Business magazines and investment newsletters had been
as full of protest, in their own ways, as any liberal journal. But those who
had learned their lessons early (David Rockefeller, for instance, began to
fear imperial overextension last year) could conceive of no way to translate
their fears into political action. American corporatists, with all their immense
resources, have never figured out how to play their roles as political actors.
Now the politicians have struck out on their own. They have gained legitimacy for an anti-war position indirectly from the Vietcong, by way of the
ranks of desperate voters and nervous business leaders. While the
Administration could still pretend that there was a hope of military victory
in Vietnam, the old cold war vetoes obliged politicians to maintain a respectful anti-communism and a determination to contain the world revolution.
With that hope gone in Vietnam, the restrictions were removed.

Eugene McCarthy saw the opportunity earliest of all. His own intense dislike of the war led him into the presidential campaign, but his feeling of isolation from the center of political power probably made him underestimate
the possibilities for a broad "peace" candidacy, and for several months he
refused to believe that he was doing much more than creating a "dialogue."
Robert Kennedy was no less unhappy about the war, but much more hung
up on power. For him, dialogue was insignificant; the presidency was not.
But he feared that Johnson could finagle the war—escalation here, a bombing pause there—and outmaneuver his own campaign strategy. The results
of the Thanksgiving week optimism speeches gave confirming evidence: the
President's popularity rose to its highest point in a year, and support of the
war gained commensurately.

The NLF (or General Giap, or whoever) had to sacrifice thousands of
lives and use large reserves of its power simply to destroy the President's
fantasies. But it worked, and the political situation was suddenly more
fluid than it had ever been. Johnson was in a box. The Senate foreign relations committee, in its hearings with Secretary of State Rusk, made serious congressional politics out of the war for the first time. A panel of some
of the most important men in the Senate spent two days on national net-

work television staking out a hard opposition to the war; at the very least, they voted a blanket "no confidence" in any future escalation the President might attempt. The hearings, like the New Hampshire primary in the same week, were held under the cloud of "rumors" that General Westmoreland had requested 206,000 more troops. There is no telling how many votes all that cost Johnson in the primary, but the ratio of rumored troops to real votes was probably no more favorable to him than that of soldiers to guerrillas in Vietnam. Even at ten to one, and even with a technical "victory," Johnson lost.

The political difficulty of escalation was only half of the President's predicament. The other part was the difficulty of de-escalation because of the weakened structure of the Saigon government in Vietnam. As the Kennedy strategists figured it, the US command could stop the bombing or begin negotiations only at the enormous risk of destroying the remnants of General Thieu's authority, and pushing many of the provincial administrators (and perhaps whole South Vietnamese battalions) into the NLF's arms. Already Thieu was proposing a new *bac tien* ("march to the North"), as former President Nguyen Khanh had done in July 1964, when his government was in similar straits. Then, the US had supported him with the manufacture of the Tonkin "incident" and the resulting air strikes on North Vietnam. This time, domestic policy made support all but impossible.

Kennedy concluded easily if prematurely that Johnson was trapped. From all reports, Kennedy's vision on the morning after the New Hampshire primary was not terribly clear. It sounded as if he were half-way up the wall before the final returns were in, and his aides had all they could do to restrain him from declaring his candidacy before noon. He suddenly understood what many of them (Arthur Schlesinger, Adam Walinsky, Burke Marshall) had been saying for months: silence this spring would do him more political damage than defeat this summer. If Kennedy misjudged the President's ability to de-escalate, he guessed that any major change in the war strategy would go to his own advantage. As it turned out, of course, Kennedy was right; Johnson could not seriously sue for peace in Vietnam without admitting the vanity of his four-year strategy. In his April Fool's Eve speech, Johnson implicitly confessed that he had condemned 150,000 Americans to death or injury, and had completed the obliteration or subjugation of much of Southeast Asia, for reasons that were now unimportant or irrelevant. He had no choice but to leave the presidency. At least his epitaph might now be kinder than his press.

Even after New Hampshire, McCarthy had little hope of convincing those who enjoy power, rather than dialogue, that he could be in a position to deliver goods to them next year. His role was something like the demonstrators'—even the dirty ones, whom he dislikes: he opened a space for more conventional (and therefore more real) politics to operate. Kennedy shares the peaceniks and the "kids" with McCarthy, but he does not stop there. He is out to build a new coalition, with nasty elements as well as nice ones, and he has an ability to attempt it that McCarthy, so far, does not. Kennedy rushes off to Watts. McCarthy had to suffer the embarrassment of Kennedy's success in the streets before he would venture into a Milwaukee ghetto. Kennedy immediately began calling in the political loans he had made over the years to the active new edge of labor. Even before his campaign announcement he flew to California to join a rally for Cesar Chavez's grape-strikers. McCarthy has no political methodology for gathering major labor support. Kennedy is not above brazening his way into working-class neighborhoods and playing the old JFK line for the ethnic vote, no matter how racist or reactionary it may be. McCarthy may be tempted by the same prospect, but he has no taste for it, and he leaves much of the work to his lieutenants.

Anyone can make a list of the stylistic differences between Kennedy and McCarthy, and everyone will before the campaign is over. But it is a stylistic difference, not one of basic politics, that distinguishes the two candidates. McCarthy's main bloc of popular support so far (or at least the leading edge) comes from the old Stevensonian party and its spiritual heirs. The older types never liked the Kennedys in the first place (although they were sucked in eventually like everyone else). They remember that McCarthy's noblest effort was his nomination of Stevenson at the 1960 Democratic convention. McCarthy's "second choice" that year, he told an interviewer at the time, was Lyndon Johnson. The "Clean for Gene" crew is a widely mixed bag of earnest young people, not unlike the Kennedy youth brigade, and both are led by cadres of decidedly unalienated young operators. Like Sam Brown, the Harvard Divinity School student who has been a principal in the McCarthy drive in New England, they are the kind of kids who have been making their way in the youth "establishment" by adopting the rhetoric of the radical movements while maintaining the politics and style of the liberal system. Brown, for instance, was a National Student Association advisory board officer who helped save the organization after its CIA connection was disclosed. No doubt Kennedy will have counterparts to Brown in plenty. There is more than one way of making it in the youth bag this year.

All of this helps to determine the political locus of the campaign. Under it, both Kennedy and McCarthy had been working for the same broad objectives: to "save" the Democratic Party, and by extension the country, by reforming the most undemocratic aspects of the one and liquidating the worst failures of the other. In the dead of winter the US was deep in a kind of despair that had not been felt since the pre-Roosevelt depression. Whether the institutions of the republic were in the state of degeneracy they appeared to be is arguable; what was obvious to everyone was that there were no enlivening political alternatives and, in a sense, no politics. For a society that so completely identifies its nature with its political structure, that is a killing weakness.

The Vietcong made politics possible again; McCarthy made it thinkable; Kennedy made it seem workable. The importance of the campaign is not that it will solve America's problems, or that either Kennedy or McCarthy will even win—in August or November. But even if they ultimately lose, the political system will have been seen to work. It has produced alternatives, which is its function. The fact that even those alternatives present secondary, not elemental, choices, is by and large ignored. Neither Kennedy nor McCarthy will even think of breaking up the concentration of corporate power which is at the heart of America's un-democracy and produces the effects of imperialism and racism that the candidates decry. Neither will move to disengage the power of America from its necessarily domineering role in the world; indeed, both have said that only by ending the war in Vietnam can the country get on with the business of consolidating its power elsewhere. Neither, finally, can encourage the development of institutions of black unity which, for the moment at least, seem to be the only way for black people to fight the nightmare oppression of racism. What it will take to do all that is a politics independent of a Kennedy or McCarthy or Nixon administration; radicals have their work cut out for them.

The two candidates together (more successfully than either one could have done alone) have let loose a surge of energy in the society which is essential if anything good is to happen. It is the direction of that energy that confirms the end of the last "twenty years' crisis." It is focussed against the cold war. It opposes the centralization of bureaucratic power which has characterized the organization of government since the New Deal. It implicitly establishes many of the values of "liberation" which the youth movements have produced. And it denies the pre-eminence of anti-communism as the dominant ideology.

What politics may follow are completely unpredictable, for the rush of events is by no means over. Whatever the NLF and the North Vietnamese do now will have powerful effects on US politics. So far, there is no reason to doubt the brilliance of their strategy; the Khe Sanh siege and the Tet offensive broke the resolve of America to pursue the war, as they always predicted (and Johnson always feared) they would. Reports from Vietnam indicate that US officers in the provinces—through the rank of colonel—think the war has been much of a bad bargain, and would just as soon be out of it. Defense informants have told McCarthy of preparation for use of tactical nuclear weapons, and *The New York Times* heard all about General Westmoreland's absurdly optimistic appraisal of the war in January.

Humphrey could now enter the campaign on his own, or the President could endorse (or seem to endorse) one or another candidate; perhaps the favor McCarthy did for Johnson in 1960 could now be returned, as a means to "stop Kennedy." Humphrey would be a logical focus for the affections of the Johnson diehards, who cannot bear the thought of a more contemporary candidate: labor, the state machines, the conservative corporatists and the unreconstructed New Dealers. They might try to promote Humphrey on a peace-and-continuity platform. And if the projected pre-negotiation "talks" between the US and North Vietnam are more immediately productive than now seems likely, the President himself could emerge as a draft candidate at the Democratic convention in August. We will all need a strong stomach.

But already the first effects of the thaw can be seen. The New Left, which had hoped for a grand breakthrough into aboveground politics this summer, finds suddenly that its potential base (which it never organized) has evaporated into the Kennedy phenomenon. Draft resistance work will go on, but now many youths hope they can win a little time with draft appeals boards before the war ends and their resistance becomes moot. The "hippie thing," which blossomed in a time of political stasis, is showing signs of rapid decay. The "old liberalism," which died with the end of the Johnson consensus, is being replaced by a newer form, which is no closer to radicalism but has an originality and contemporaneity no one could foresee. Throughout, there is a sense of breathing space in the society at last, a hope that the next months will not bring the boot heel down on everyone who is trying to resist.

Best of all, the war is coming to an end. Not that there won't be much more fighting, and not excluding the possibility that an act of rage or duplicity could elevate that conflict again into a still larger calamity. But it is hard to see how any now or future president can again maintain a winning face. The huge problem of liquidation remains—for Kennedy as well as Nixon, or for President Johnson. But the old cord has snapped, and the new one begins with at least the expectation of peace.

April 25, 1968, NEW YORK REVIEW OF BOOKS

✦

The American Nightmare

What happened last weekend was an American convulsion. With all nerves naked and the system pulsing with new energy, the murder of Martin Luther King provoked a violent national twitch, a soul-writhing, practically involuntary reaction. We have grown accustomed to the face of urban violence in the last half-decade: Harlem in 1964, then Watts, next Chicago, and then Newark, Detroit and a hundred cities last year. But this was somehow different. The earlier riots began with local incidents, and over the course of weeks or months produced a national pattern; this April's uprisings in eighty cities were responses to a single national stimulus. That very immediacy gave an authentic aspect to the long black rebellion, and for those who had not yet understood, Friday was a night loaded with omens.

It is no longer possible to see the sacking of cities as merely the work of "criminal elements," although whites wish desperately that it were so. President Johnson calls it, simply, "lawlessness," but he must have an idea of its nature because in the next breath he calls for "needed reforms." If he could spend a day in the ghetto, he would see that law or the absence of it has little relevance for the mass of Negro poor. To much of black America, the law is what white men use to rationalize their oppression of blacks. If there was ever a social contract joined freely by the two races in this country, it has been abrogated.

In his brief decade of work, Dr. King tried vainly to make whites enforce such a contract. He had to assume that the races could, with a minimum of conflict, find ways of living together peacefully and on the basis of equality. Dr. King's methods were noble—saintly, even—but his assumptions seem to have been wrong. A society so suffused with racism does not reform itself by moral example, and the "white power structure" (a phrase he used) does not fall before a sit-in, a march or a freedom ride.

Dr. King's immense importance, however, derived from both his success and failure. To Negroes, he was a spiritual savior; to whites, he was a political leader. The attention he brought to the Negro freedom movement and the legislative gains he won for civil rights secure his place in American legend. That he failed finally to change the system that brutalizes his race is a profound relief to the white majority. As a reward they have now elevated his minor successes into major triumphs and have given his failures a significance that they do not really deserve.

His death has become the occasion for an extraordinary "pacification program" conducted on TV and in the press. Any previous controversiality that might have been attached to Dr. King has been removed almost by national consensus, and last week's bigots are today proclaiming his nobility. But no one has had a change of heart; Dr. King represented the white man's last hope for racial stability and minimal change, and his death brings as much fear as sorrow to whites.

It carries a threat to blacks, too, but for a different reason. White men have murdered blacks for hundreds of years in America, and indeed the pace has quickened in the recent past. The three most revered figures in the black movement—Medgar Evers, Malcolm X and Dr. King—have been assassinated within five years; two appear to have been killed outright by whites, and the third was slain in an internecine quarrel against the backdrop of racist pressures. But there have been dozens of other leaders killed in the course of their struggle, and every week in every ghetto of the country blacks die, in jails or on the street, simply for their blackness. Then there are the "little murders"—the countless indignities and humiliations and deprivations that round out the lives of black people. In a sense, white America has committed a kind of genocide. The death of Dr. King, the white man's hope as well as the black's, could mean that the murders will get bigger.

The latest wave of "riots" (a loaded noun, like all the others that describe these events) spring not so much from the ghetto's anger at the assassination as from the sudden confirmation of the hopelessness of non-violent protest. The guerrilla looters and firebombers did not rise to avenge the death of Dr. King but to attack the system that makes them, as well as him, all victims.

The long hot summer came a little early this year, and it scorched cities that have been spared in the past, as well as some of the familiar targets. Those who said that Washington would never blow, despite the obvious tensions and the dreadful conditions for the huge black population (65 percent), see now that no ghetto is immune. Long avenues in the center of the Negro districts are completely gutted—with the exception of a "soul brother" barbershop or Negro-owned store here and there. The 5,000 who were arrested were unusually well educated and well employed, many in government jobs. The curfew takes up half the day. Some 11,600 army troops patrol the streets, and thousands more are encamped on the outskirts of town. There is an army machine-gun nest on the steps of the Capitol. Ruins are still smoldering, and there is sporadic tear-gassing. The Cherry Blossom Festival has been cancelled.

Around the country, dozens of people have been killed (mostly blacks, said to be "fleeing" from looted stores). Ten detachments have been moved into three major cities so far, national guard units patrol many more, and state and local police are trying to deal with the rest. There is more to come. News programs are interrupted for "special bulletins" as the next city explodes: Sunday it was Pittsburgh; Monday night, Cincinnati. No doubt "order" will be restored—whether based on the thin promise of future reforms or on terror. In Oakland, the police cornered the entire leadership of the Black Panther Party in a slum house and opened fire. Bobby Hutton, one of the young leaders, was killed when he emerged with his hands high in the air. All the others were wounded and jailed.

Who killed Martin Luther King? There is no easy answer, and if the man who pulled the trigger is caught, the question will still remain. For the culprit is not one psychotic individual but a complex of men and institutions, all very sane in their own terms. That which killed King killed Bobby Hutton and Malcolm X; it runs the slum housing supermarkets and the "easy credit" shops in the ghettoes; it sends black soldiers to Vietnam and Guatemala. And white ones too. In effect, it forces black leaders to kill themselves: King's non-violent protest raised hopes that had to be frustrated, and the result was predictable violence. It is a brutal, blind and violent society hung up on the myth of its humanity, dedicated to equality and founded on racism, proclaiming democracy and practicing exploitation. It corrupted King and country, and in a tragic sense has driven them both to an ambiguous suicide.

April 12, 1968, NEW STATESMAN

From Hanoi With Love

"Try not to idealize that place," the United States Information Service man said in Vientiane, knowing that his advice would probably be unheeded. From time to time he sees Americans on their way to Hanoi, and he feels somehow obliged to make a last attempt to shore up their patriotism. In a California ranch house hard by the Mekong, the brutal necessity of America's imperial mission in Asia is put forth, to the accompaniment of a good Continental dinner (served by the Vietnamese refugee houseboy), baroque music and Baez on the hi-fi, and the soft smiles of complaisant Laotian royalty. But the next day the International Control Commission plane comes in and sweeps his guests away over the paddy fields and jungle mountains, and so the effect is destroyed. After all, there is no good defense against the realities of "that place."

North Vietnam shatters an American's vision and displaces comfortable categories of thought: not because "that place" is immediately convincing and charming but precisely because it is not. Expectant visitors find neither pitiable victims nor hard heroes, not the warm romance of the Sierra Maestra nor the violent precision of East-is-Red Square. Americans have to fight their way to understanding through their own misapprehensions, the accumulated refuse of two generations of revolution, reaction and cold war rhetoric. "I hope you can find out if Ho Chi Minh is a Stalinist," a friend in Washington said before I departed. Now, the issue seems as irrelevant as Lyndon Johnson's Confucianism.

The struggle to understand finds its greatest obstacles in the barriers that the Vietnamese themselves take pains to erect. Like Hassidim who mask their simple souls with alternating masks of mysticism and vulgarity, the Vietnamese hide behind ritual courtesies and opaque language. No doubt the wall is constructed of Confucianist culture, colonial patterns, communist ideology and Vietnamese tradition; but in what measure it is impossible to say. What is important is a life beneath of extraordinary dignity, discipline, pride and sensitivity, and if any Westerner in Hanoi can catch even a glimpse of it—from a corner of the mind's eye—he will be lucky. If he is an American, he may at last know why the "enemy" has won.

Taking the Tour

There have been almost fifty Americans in North Vietnam in the last two and a half years—not counting the ones who bail out on bombing runs—and almost all of them get what is known in the lobby of the Thong Nhat ("Reunification") Hotel in Hanoi as "the tour" or "the treatment." It is a route of formal interviews and semi-state visits, arranged for maximum comfort with embarrassing solicitude. A trip around the corner proceeds in a motorized procession; a stroll through a museum begins with a reception by the director and staff. One cannot pop in on a class at school; the principal and teachers (and usually an official from the education ministry in Hanoi) arrange themselves in greeting at the entrance, and instruction is suspended while the children perform musical selections, folk dances or poetry recitations. At an evacuated secondary school north of Hanoi, I asked if I might sit in on an actual class session. The officials seemed puzzled but finally obliged. The result was hardly worth the imposition. Teachers were nervous and the pupils distracted; they would have preferred the ritual to the real thing. Guests must remain guests.

So the first difficulty is the hardest to overcome: a feeling that "the tour" is meant to inhibit understanding rather than enhance it. Americans equate spontaneous "discovery" with honest reporting; anything programmed or packaged is supposed to be rigged. But the Vietnamese place small value on casual spontaneity, which is considered to be a strange form of escape from social obligations. Why do Americans always want to go off by themselves? If they are pressed, the Vietnamese guides let visitors wander about Hanoi on their own (I took several long walks, all alone, every day I was in the capital), but the pressure must be insistent, and the Vietnamese worry that their guidance has been taken as a method of ideological control. On both sides, habit and personal style cannot always be separated from questions of good faith.

I had been in Hanoi less than a day when I realized that the whole fortnight's visit would be a fight against that feeling of entrapment. I had been taken to the Museum of History, and the tour began formally with tea, bananas, cigarettes ("Dien Bien" brand), slightly soggy biscuits and long speeches of welcome and introduction by the assistant director, who for some reason thought it necessary to detail the contents of the museum before we saw the displays. I listened as patiently as I could during the "tea ceremony" and then went on to follow a solemn guide through centuries of Vietnamese history.

It began in Mesolithic times, with models of ape-men in their natural surroundings. I may be prejudiced, but all ape-men look alike to me; I can't tell one from the other. But these were the pre-ancestors of the Viet race, indigenous to the soil of the Indochinese peninsula, "contrary to the old theories of some Western scholars," the guide said. Then I noticed for the first time the faint gestures and intonations of an easy, natural pride—more, a confidence in the Vietnamese identity—which has only perverse and distorted analogues in the Western mentality. "Nationalism" in America, at least, is a base emotion, and its expression is despised by intellectuals; pride, of course, is a sin. But the Vietnamese can celebrate themselves and their past without guilt or embarrassment. Probably this facility is a subjective, cultural attribute—or is it that they have less to be guilty about?

Next to the ape man maquette was a case of stone arrowheads, which seemed to be as neutral as historical objects can be. "They were used to fight against foreign aggressors," the guide said, and walked away without further explanation. "Didn't they *hunt*?" I asked one of my companions. (I travelled with two other Americans: Susan Sontag, the novelist, and Professor Robert Greenblatt, a mathematician who works full time in the US anti-war movement.) We both shrugged and continued through the exhibition hall.

If there are any other themes in Vietnamese history, from ape-man through the Tet offensive, they failed to materialize in the museums or anywhere else in the next two weeks. Like music on the single-stranded bao, the traditional and popular instrument, Vietnamese history is played on only one string: the permanent resistance of the indigenous race to alien attacks.

When the war is over and reconstruction is done, the Vietnamese may want to fill in the obvious holes in their historical displays, and their historical consciousness. The pervasive cultural influences of the Chinese invasions is hardly mentioned, and the history of the French period is abstracted as a continuous campaign of resistance to colonialism. But for now, history is not a luxury but a weapon, more important than any Russian missile. Every schoolboy has seen models or diagrams of the famous victories of his race, from the battle of the Bach Dang River against the Mongol navy in 1288 to the battle of Dien Bien Phu in 1954 and Junction City in 1966. They speak one lesson: repel the invader. The posters and slogans that are written everywhere in the city and countryside flow directly from that motif. It is a transitive injunction: not enough to struggle in the abstract, but to win. The object now is the *giac My xam luoc*—the "pirate American aggressors"—and the phrase is part of every poster. Translated it becomes uncomfortable jargon in our sense (which is not to say that it is untrue), but the words have a very specific meaning to the Vietnamese. The *giac xam luoc* were the Mongols, too.

Americans—the *My*—may be pirates in the sky, but they are welcome guests down below. The Vietnamese seem to prefer them to any others. The choice is good politics—even US correspondents who are "neutral" on the war make good propaganda simply by reporting what they see in North Vietnam—but the favor goes beyond that. Vietnamese are fascinated by America and Americans, by novels as well as presidential politics, by Walt Whitman along with Walt Whitman Rostow. Part of the attraction must derive from a love/hate feeling for the enemy, but there are other levels of sensitivity as well. Ordinary people in the hamlets stared at us with a piercing curiosity, as if they might ultimately divine what mysterious mechanism compels Americans to destroy their land. Officials and intellectuals get more news of the US (they are very well informed about government politics and the protest movement, vague about day-to-day life and psychology), and their interest is at once more practical and more emotional. They want to understand the American mind for political reasons and at the same time are drawn to those American sensibilities that are strangely similar to their own: power, pragmatism, obstinacy and even a certain frontier honesty.

Of course, we were always greeted and introduced as *cac ban*—"dear friends"—which conferred a special role; no American can go to North Vietnam without serving some political function. Whatever our importance in politics at home (minor indeed in my case) we were taken to be representative of "the movement" against US policy. I tried to conceal my embarrassment when officials offered compliments for our help in ending the war, but perhaps not many of them took us all that seriously.

Far beyond its effect on US policy, the peace movement has a symbolic value for the Vietnamese. Every peasant knows that Norman Morrison cremated himself as a protest to the war, and the leading poet and composers have written works in his honor; few Americans now would recognize his name. But Vietnam has little more on its side than pride in the justice of its cause, and the fact of American support has an enormous effect on morale.

The "socialist countries" give Hanoi military aid and help of other kinds, but it is sparse, to say the least, and the politics behind seems qualified. One night in the Thong Nhat lobby, a fat, baldish man approached me and introduced himself, in a music hall Russian accent, as "second secretary, Soviet embassy." He said he was the "American policy expert," although he had never been to the US, and he would enjoy talking with me. By way of introduction, he laid out his political position: "Are two wings in embassy. I am spokesman for wing which believe should not object American power in Southeast Asia. America is great power, Soviet Union is great power. Great powers have many problems, many responsibilities." We could get no statistics, of course, on the exact amount of the Soviet (or Chinese) subsidy to Vietnam, but there is evidence that the government has refused weapons that would require Russian technicians to operate them, or that would have to be installed at permanent, vulnerable sites. The basic military strategy is mobility, and the fundamental political consideration is self-reliance.

A Walk With War

Vietnam has been "at war" for twenty-eight years, on and off, and is by now very much at home with all its consequences. An American visitor is more appalled by the deprivation, and more romantic about the danger, than any Vietnamese. The skies above Hanoi are now peaceful, except for an intrusion of the occasional US robot reconnaissance plane, which is customarily shot down. When the alert sounds, people on the streets move in the direction of the nearest shelter—they are seldom more than a few yards away—and perhaps make mental contingency plans for a dash inside should bombs actually fall. Mothers toss their children into the streetside cement "wells," and then squat patiently on the rim. The day's rhythm is hardly broken.

Robot planes are easier to down, but if less skill is required, less ambiguous pleasure can be taken at the sport. The US chooses not to count the drones on its airplane casualty list, but it is all the same to the Vietnamese, and when the day's tally is announced on Hanoi radio, the figures on chalk-boards all over the country are changed with prideful ceremony. When I arrived, the total was 2,886 "US pirates," and a fortnight later it was up to 2,921. There is no reason to doubt the accuracy of the count, give or take ten or a dozen. Bird-bagging is the national sport, and rewards go to provinces, districts, militia units and individuals who hit on target. In Ninh Binh province, near the coast, we met a girl—"Miss Dream" or "Miss Apricot," depending on the translation of her given name—who had three planes to her credit. She was well placed for the hunt, in a militia group directly under the point where navy bombers enter Vietnamese airspace from the sea. She was 20 years old and very shy.

The alerts are the only active reminders of war in the northern provinces; the other aspects are passive: military vehicles in the streets, mobile work-shops at the roadside, pith helmets decorated with bits of plastic "camou-flage," the shelters, the slogans, the SAM missiles peeking out from canvas covers on mobile launchers on the highways, the bombed-out bridges and railway carriages, the news broadcast twice each day over loudspeakers in the city squares. Hanoi is "drab," as Westerners like to say when they can see no neon, but whether that describes a quality of life or simply its surface is hard to tell. Everyone is poor; that is an immediate impression. At night the lights are dim—not for curfew but to save electricity—and bicycles move quietly down dark brown streets. Crowds at theaters and cinemas, and in the long beer queues in Hanoi, are shabbily dressed, and there is hardly a hint of "bourgeois" style. I have no scale for measuring the state of " happiness" or depression, but it did not occur to me (as it did in Vientiane, or years ago in Eastern Europe) to apply the adjective "grim."

Outside Hanoi, life is harder and the people are, if anything, poorer, but it seems to matter less. Most of the provincial cities are destroyed or evacuat-ed, and expectations of comfort or style are low in the villages. There is usu-ally enough fruit on the trees, and in the paddy fields prawns and crayfish swim beneath the rice plants. Ducks and chickens seem to be plentiful enough, and eggs are not rationed.

Less than a mile outside Hanoi, the bombing destruction begins (there are ruins closer to the center, too, but the damage is not pervasive). At first it appears that only one or two settlements have been bombed, but the damage extends further and after a while it is clear that there will be no break in the dismal scene. South from Hanoi, I drove sixty miles through the Red River delta, and in two days along the national routes and the vil-lage paths, in towns and hamlets, there was not a single frame building of more than one storey still standing, not a church or a hospital or a school or an administrative center, not a shop or a block of flats. Every bridge, across large rivers or streams or irrigation ditches, was destroyed, and huge rain-filled craters were clustered around the banks. Any houses by the bridges had been obliterated in the fire. Phu Ly, with some 60,000 inhabitants, had suffered more than fifty raids; it was levelled lower than a Roman ruin. A few roofless walls remained. Snakes crawled through the rubble, and a few birds perched on the edge of bomb craters. There was no other sign of life.

Ninh Binh, the chief city of the province, was the same, and so was Phat Diem, the country's center of reed-product manufacture. From the highways, we could see the outline of ruins of other towns across the paddy fields; perhaps the bombers spared a village here or there, but I could not be sure. For most of the targets, there could be no pretense of "military necessity." Hospitals far from cities were destroyed, and the ravaged hulks of enormous "romanesque" cathedrals stood in isolated absurdity in the fields.

"We were a psycho-social target," the chief official of Kim Son district said as we walked through the ruins of the city of Phat Diem. "The American strategy was to destroy Catholic churches and Catholic cities in order to turn those people against the government. But it was not very clever. The French were smarter; they spared the churches and bribed the priests."

The destruction of Phat Diem began in April 1966, and continued until March 11 of this year. The district committee's office building had been ruined, and its functions were removed to makeshift quarters in an adjoining hamlet. The People's Council "chamber" was a pit, sunk into the floor of a room, with earthen steps leading down about three feet to the mud floor. The legs of short stools, placed around a table for our reception, dug into the soft ground. "We can meet during alerts," the official said.

The March 11 raid, he said, destroyed a Catholic settlement on the far end of the city; the Seminary in Praise of the Cross, a church and several houses were hit, and five nuns were killed. We were walking through the bombed seminary when one of the surviving nuns appeared in a doorway, barefoot, toothless, with a ragged habit and shawl. An ornate gold crucifix hung from a chain around her neck. One of the guides asked her to tell him what had happened.

Her name was Agnes Hoang Thi Ngo, she began, and she served as the assistant mother superior at the seminary. She was 66 years old. "We had twenty-five students and nine teaching sisters. The bombs came just before noon, when we were at prayer. They killed the mother superior and four sisters; many others were injured. Why do they want to bomb us? We live by ourselves, we take no part in the society. We just pray and do no one any harm." She was crying very hard and could not finish the story. Just then, a young man carrying a baby in his arms arrived at the chapel and whispered a few words to the interpreter, who explained that he was secretary of the parish. The man went on with a description of the day's events:

"Many people were killed; I don't know how many. When the bombing came that day, I was home with the four children; they are 4, 7, 10 and 12. I took them into the shelter with me, but my wife was in the fields collecting reeds. She ran home, but the bombs caught her as she was approaching the

Great Church. They blew out her eyes and cut off her hands. Then she died. She was 29 years old. We were married twelve years."

We spent that night in Ninh Binh province in a "guest house" maintained by the provincial council in a hamlet several miles from the wreckage of the chief city. The little house seemed to be a converted stable. It was wedged into the base of a huge outcropping of limestone covered with thick foliage, a "mountain" of a kind common in that region, scattered like gigantic boulders at random in the rice fields. The hostel had neither electricity nor plumbing, but it was relatively safe from air attack; back of the building was a deep cool cave, the roof dripping with bats, where guests would be safe.

A provincial administrator came to have dinner, a much too elegant meal of pork, beef, chicken, white dove and various vegetables and soups. He had been in the First Resistance War with two of our guides, and they told old stories and recounted adventures to one another, with translations for us at first, but mostly in Vietnamese. I slipped out, primarily to escape the mosquitoes, and walked down the path to the highway. Military trucks were rumbling past in both directions with their lights out. From far away I heard low thunder, and in the hamlet beyond the hostel the amplified squawking of a film (North Korean, someone said later) echoed off the overhanging rocks. Suddenly I realized that I was being followed; I looked around and a militiaman smiled at me from across the road. I moved on; so did he. I backed up; he did too. He tailed me to the guest house, and I asked one of the interpreters what the militiaman's mission was. "He has been with us all during our visit to the province," the interpreter said. "We are guests of the provincial council. He looks after our safety."

There were other questions I wanted to ask about the controls over our movement, and about the things we had seen: rural religion, the Catholic minority, the Workers Party, agricultural cooperatives, social hierarchies. Information was available, but most of it had too much of an "official" tone; it was probably accurate, but outside an analytical context. Analysis, like rice, is rationed in North Vietnam, and the "detached" Western observer has to rely on sketchy impressions and speculative assumptions. It was my *impression* that the "ancestor cult" is widespread and tolerated among the peasants, that the remaining Catholics are not persecuted (hundreds of thousands fled to the South in 1954, at the urging of the French, the priests and the CIA), that the party is firmly in control but not entirely monolithic, that the cooperatives are successful (98 percent of peasants belong) and that the society still retains elitist patterns. But I am sure of none of it.

A cynical visitor can ascribe the difficulties of analysis to "Stalinist" suppression or, less evilly, to the pressures of a war society. Perhaps there is some of both, but a great deal more. Our questions often made no "sense" to the Vietnamese because they assumed a context of issues in our own society, not theirs. Once, in a village of the Meo minority in Hoa Binh province, I tried for an hour to understand the nuances of inter-tribal and majority-minority social relationships. In the back of my mind I had fixed notions of racism derived from the American experience, and I was determined to fit Vietnamese problems to them. What would a Muong mother say, for instance, if her daughter—secretly in love with a Meo boy—bounced into the house one afternoon and asked, "Guess who's coming to dinner?"

Finally, I posed that very problem, and instead of defensive evasion, there was laughter. Inter-marriage had been less frequent when the mountain tribes were isolated in their villages, but as communications improved, there was more integration. Obvious problems—"the most serious in the country"—still existed in such relationships: different levels of education, acculturation and expectation. But they were not put in a racist setting, nor one of social status, in the American way. The loudest laugh of all came from our chief guide, who said that he had always wanted to marry a Meo woman and had in fact been engaged to one before the war against the French interrupted the courtship.

On the opposite side, the Vietnamese were equally baffled; there were issues in their lives that could not be "translated" into a Western context, and I could only guess at what they might be.

Hardest of all were questions about politics. Hanoi seems to be the last place to find out what the Vietnamese will do in the Paris negotiations, how they are dealing with the Russians and the Chinese, what the military situation is in the South and how relations stand between North Vietnam and the National Liberation Front.

For North Vietnam, the Tet offensive of the NLF was a consummate victory of the Resistance, but then there are no "defeats" against which it can be compared. The official position is that the war is a steadily mounting series of victories for the NLF, with undefined "support" from the Northern "region." That is probably much closer to the truth than the American line, which persists with the invasion-from-the-North theory, but it lacks serious analysis, and it was impossible to find out very much more.

It was mercifully early in our visit when the first slip about "North Vietnamese troops" in the South was made. The Vietnamese official with whom we were talking seemed to gel there on the spot: "You mean the 'infiltrators'?" We cleared our throats, or made whatever apologetic noises seemed appropriate, and asked more politely whether there were *any* North Vietnamese troops in the South. "There are the regroupees, but no others," the official said (under the Geneva Accords, Viet Minh soldiers from the South were allowed to regroup in the North, and Hanoi admits that "some" have returned to fight with the NLF). We explained that most Americans, of whatever political sympathies, assume that North Vietnam has sent soldiers over the 17th parallel. The official seemed more hurt than angry that we doubted him. We heard no contradictory word in the next weeks. Adherence to the Geneva Accords is a paramount policy; so is Ho Chi Minh's decree that "in a people's war the people must be told the truth." By the time we left, none of us was prepared to take Averell Harriman's word over Pham Van Dong's, but the doubts remained.

Military issues are subjects for debate outside, but not inside North Vietnam. There is no question that people trust the directors of the Resistance, and one another. But a great deal of energy—and some controversy—surrounds the extraordinary "decentralization" of Vietnamese life; it has become the major issue of the society. Decentralization is not an abstract concept, as it is now in the streets of Paris or the universities of America. The totality of Vietnamese life has been broken into elemental components by the war, and the process has meant survival. Masses of people have been moved into the countryside, central provincial schools are scattered among several villages, factories are found in grottoes, hospitals hide in caves. The museums of Hanoi are closed much of the time to avoid concentration of the population (and department stores are shut during the daylight hours for the same reason), but travelling exhibitions are sent by bicycle and lorry to the reaches of the country. "Warehouses" are mountain meadows strewn with wooden crates. Vehicle repair is done in "mobile workshops" set up in the streets and squares of Hanoi and along the provincial roads.

Decentralization has spiritual roots in Vietnamese life: "the village could overrule the king," people repeated. But the war made it the central principle of social organization. Partly because of the difficulties in communication, but also because of ideology, authority is atomized along with function. For example, our guides (who were representatives of the quasi-governmental Committee for the Defense of Peace) had to ask the permission of local authorities before we visited a factory or hospital, a province or a village. Provincial officials met us at the borders of their jurisdictions, as much to assert their authority as for welcome; in fact, the two notions were combined. Many Vietnamese expect institutional decentralization to continue after the war, and it may be that North Vietnam will—almost by accident—develop the crucial tool for social harmony.

Near Hoa Binh City, American planes had destroyed the seven buildings of a hospital complex completed in 1960. Now there are dozens of "hospitals" distributed among the villages as part of the decentralization scheme. Mai Chau district—one of nine in Hoa Binh province—has three of the hospital units, and twenty-two infirmaries, for its 23,000 inhabitants. At the Chieng Chau village hospital, the chief doctor, a fully trained MD, told us that malaria had been entirely eliminated in the district (it was endemic ten years ago), and there are no more cases of cholera, smallpox, trachoma or polio. Under French rule the district had no hospital at all. "Every five or ten years a doctor came to inoculate against cholera, but only for those between 16 and 30 years old."

Chieng Chau hospital is a cluster of bamboo huts between the paddy fields and the mountains. Each hut is marked for its function by a sign over the door: Delivery Room, Pharmacy, Operating Room. The rooms are clean, the floors raised off the ground on stilts in the manner of Thai minority architecture, and the equipment is neatly arranged. One room is set aside for "Oriental medicine," with instructions for acupuncture therapy hanging on the wall, and a cupboard full of herb preparations. The village practitioner has been "integrated" into the Western medicine system.

The last room, apart from the others, was set into a cave in the hill. Its floor had been planed smooth, except for a few immovable boulders which still protruded. In the center was a long metal table, and across the roof was strung a silk parachute, dropped by a US plane during a bombing raid on a nearby hamlet. "This is our second operating room," the doctor said, pointing to the sign "Buong Mo" over the mouth of the cave. "We use it during alerts. The parachute keeps dirt from falling from the roof, and it reflects the lamplight. Look, you can see writing on it, in English."

I left the cave and headed back across the rice fields, hopping over the trenches (several kilometers long in each village) which the people use instead of walkways in the bombing season. "Do you believe all this?" one of my companions asked. "Try not to idealize this place," I said.

As it turned out, idealization was not really the issue. North Vietnam cannot be an "ideal" for an American, although it can be, and was, an object of admiration and some bafflement. It is possible, after all, to turn back the American empire in its full fury and develop a society that is more self-reliant, more equitable and, if anything, more humane than when the struggle began. For Americans, it is almost impossible to understand that, but it is absolutely necessary, for North Vietnam's victory takes a direct object: us.

May 31, 1968, NEW STATESMAN

✦

No Hope From Miami Beach

Miami

Committed by intuition and interest to the sinfulness of mankind, Republicans have always shown a fine sensitivity to the futility of political action. Liberal columnists remark on the Republican "death wish," but the instinct is really pre-Freudian: they are prisoners of a deadly grace that does not allow the efficacy of good works. The party found its perfect hero in Barry Goldwater because he expressed the inevitability of human defeat; now its choice of Miami Beach for the 1968 convention completes the metaphor.

Nothing tangible or spiritual in this desolate sandpit resort holds hope for repairing a wounded nation. The 1,333 delegates, the journalists without number, the Pepsi-Cola girls, the flag-wavers, sign-carriers and security guards must have the sense that they have been cast east of Eden. From the air, the skyline is stupefying, but from below the great hotels are seen to be made of plaster of Paris, the statues of Winged Victory and the Medici Venuses are of papier-mâché, the sun-tanned holiday-trippers are geriatric specimens. Inside the enormous public rooms, the wallpaper is peeling and the carpets are soiled and threadbare.

Like the place, the party is terribly vulnerable. Ordinarily, the median age in Miami Beach is said to be 56, and the presence of the delegates must raise that considerably. They are old and tired and they look bored. Demonstrations for candidates are smaller and less enthusiastic than at any previous convention anyone can remember. Television cameras shoot from low angles to make the crowds appear bigger, and newsmen inflate their estimates of the excitement in order to justify the importance of their own assignments. But hardly anyone claims that there is much to report. "This is the lull before the lull," a convention veteran said dispiritedly last weekend.

The Republican Party may well rule the country for the next four years, and the delegates suppose that the man they nominate for president a few days from now may have more luck than most Republican candidates in the past thirty-six years. But somehow these possibilities fail to enliven the proceedings or dispel a certain subtropical ennui. Geography and mentality combine to remove the Republicans from poverty, race conflict and war; the hum of air conditioning—in cars and hotels and the convention hall— drowns out all outside noises.

To be fair, the major candidates have done their best to revive the imagery of convention hoopla. They have pretty girls in neat uniforms passing out buttons and bumper stickers. Governor Rockefeller hired a steamboat to puff along Indian River on the landward side of the beach strip. Airplanes trailing banners fly along the seaward coast promoting one or another candidate. *The Nixon Nominator*, *Rockefeller Roll-Call* and other convention newspapers are slipped under the doors of hotel rooms, but it is hard to believe that any adult would take seriously the tone of their "news": "New York, NY—the powerful people-appeal of Richard M. Nixon's presidential campaign is turning up massive support among independents and organized labor and their families."

But half-way through the convention (as this is written) there is unusual agreement among press and politicians that it is an expensive non-event. Not many conventions in other years have been relevant to the country's problems; what is unusual now is the agreement that this one cannot connect with the outside crisis. In the past three years Americans have been politicized to a degree that the professional politicians cannot imagine. The mythology of convention politics simply is no longer credible, and while most people cannot easily see the change in themselves, they all know that the steamboats and slogans are unimportant to what really matters in their lives.

It will take a long time for the institutions of politics to reflect those changing ideas. The parties have built bases of their own elites, and the choice of a nominee must follow their narrow interests. A convention vote merely legitimizes the process. Rockefeller has called for an "open convention," which means one in which his popularity exceeds Nixon's. But it is only a matter of popularity—either man would be an acceptable candidate, and provide acceptable administrations with no basic policy difference between them.

With full knowledge of the implausibility of anything unexpected happening at the conventions, people are still drawn to attend. Rumors abound ("Billy Graham for vice president?") because they offer relief from dull certainty. As often happens at circuses of other kinds, the freak shows on the side become more interesting than the main event. Here they are fascinating but depressing. The funniest and most pathetic oddity is Harold Stassen, a boy-wonder governor of Minnesota twenty-five years ago, who has run for the presidential nomination four times, and this week will be nominated by his nephew, a member of some delegation or other, predictably to the accompaniment of patronizing laughter.

Others are sadder, because more real: the "concerned Afro-American Republicans," who are barely recognized by the delegations (98 percent white); the handful of returned Peace Corps volunteers and students who hand out leaflets protesting against the war; the "poor people's campaign" stragglers parading down the hotel strip with their mule-train; workers for a "new party" coalition trying to pick up disaffected Republicans to join New Left radicals and McCarthy liberals in an improbable realignment. The Republicans welcome their presence because it makes the convention seem important, but they cannot take any of it seriously. Issues are considered only once—in the party platform, which is discarded by common consent on the day after it is adopted. Candidates are then free to say and do what they please.

Political science professors used to say that such "pragmatism" is what democratic politics is all about, that America's political strength lies in its relegation of "ideology" to an evening's consideration once every four years. If that is true, America should be strong and healthy. Perhaps it is, but if you listen carefully—even here in Miami Beach—you can almost hear the rats in the walls.

August 9, 1968, NEW STATESMAN

✦

Prague Under Red Guns

Prague, August 28

Yesterday, in Wenceslaus Square, a tall student stood at the base of the statue of Czechoslovakia's patron saint/king/national hero and watched the disorganized groups of people wandering, talking, reading posters. A group of *huligani* (the local combination hippie-activists) was trying to stir up a teenage following. Wenceslaus's statue was plastered with posters; the uppermost one read, "Kids, be affectionate in front of the Russian soldiers and drive them crazy." On the pavement in front of the monument was a chalk-marked square where the first martyr of the resistance—a 14-year-old boy—had been killed by the Russians.

The parallel with the 1939 German invasion is obvious, but the startling dissimilarity is the spirit of the Czechs in the face of the Russian occupation. The trauma of the invasion has produced a kind of national unity and determination that in its most hopeful aspect could be the beginning of a strong resistance. Clearly, this surprised the Russians—but as anyone here will admit, it surprised Czechs more. Until now, balls have not exactly been the national emblem of Czechoslovakia.

Whatever their source of inspiration may have been, the Czechs met their Russian occupants (as they call them) with ingenuity, bravery and a curious sense of humor. News broadcasts on the clandestine radio stations are interspersed with jokes and funny stories about the occupation, and in the underground newspapers there are collections of cartoons and magazine parodies. The popular sports daily, produced in the traditional form, has become a resistance sheet with mock scores of mock games and captions in sports jargon under photos of occupation scenes.

At nine o'clock every morning the entire country observes a brief "general strike" which consists primarily of the production of a great deal of noise. In Prague people line the streets and blow whistles, cars stop and drivers lean on their horns, church bells ring and fire sirens blare. While the Russian soldiers sit impassively in their tanks, the people laugh and clap their hands. It is a peculiar struggle. A young Czech artist said to me, "We are fighting half a million troops with fifteen minutes of noise."

There are other tricks in the Czech bag. All road and street signs were painted over within a few hours of the invasion, and the armies were appropriately confused. Outside Prague an entire tank column went round and round in an area of twenty square miles for six hours until the commanders were able to find their way into the city. In the square in front of Prague Castle, armored trucks and tanks spent an hour trying to get proper directions to the army barracks half a block away. When Russian secret police began to round up "liberal" activists, the underground radio sent out an appeal to citizens to tear the numbers off their doors; within twenty minutes, every house in Prague was de-numbered.

The clandestine news services were the major organizers of the first week's resistance. Television programs suddenly appeared on channels that were normally empty. The programs originated from secret studios, and the location and transmission channel changed every fifteen minutes.

Mobile radio units moved from quarter to quarter to avoid detection. On the first day of occupation, radio announcers told the Czechs how to stop trains carrying Russian equipment. Instructions were broadcast to destroy all maps, to transfer provisions from food shops to shoe stores (to evade Russian requisitions) and to ignore the occupiers. At least as far as anyone can see, the orders were universally obeyed. One morning there was a rumor that a man who was seen giving bread and sausages to Russian soldiers on the Charles III Bridge had been surrounded by angry citizens and hurled into the Moldau River; it may be an apocryphal story, but it is a parable that everyone believes. Russian troops have to drink from the river because the Czechs deny them water, and the invading armies' food supplies are dwindling.

The Russians have not responded to Czech practical/political joking with the same good humor in which it is extended. In the Great Power bully contest, the Russians are making an ambitious effort for the prize. In the first few days, the soldiers killed a hundred or more Praguers, almost entirely at random. Machine gunners shot up the facade of the National Museum for the fun of seeing the plaster fly. At night the soldiers shoot tracers and live bullets into the air for fifteen minutes at a time, just to see the pretty patterns; every once in a while the bullets hit a hospital or a school.

One evening on a small street near Prague Castle, Russian soldiers came upon an elderly couple who were sitting on a garden bench; the soldiers stuck guns into their necks, marched them down the road to an empty newspaper kiosk and made them remove the posters and signs from the facade. Then they fired over the couple's heads and forced them to jump up and down on the rubbish. The occupants of one Russian tank commanded passers-by—at cannon point—to offer flowers to them while a camera crew photographed the touching scene for the papers back home.

Bullying mixed easily with brutality in the first few days of the attack. Yesterday a woman running from one streetcar to another was blown apart by a Russian cannon fired at a range of forty feet. She lay on the ground until a Czech car happened along; the driver picked her up and drove off. Kids with long hair are often shot at and occasionally killed.

Now, however, a minor Russian "peace offensive" is beginning, perhaps an attempt to win the hearts and minds of the people. The tanks have retired to side streets, and some of the roadblocks in the middle of Prague are completely abandoned or maintained with only perfunctory searchings. Today the tank crews had little to do, and at midday the soldiers were dozing in the open cockpits or smoking and talking in the streets beside their vehicles.

Perhaps there is a culture of occupation that makes all occupiers look alike. The soldiers could have been Americans; they looked bored, slightly stupid, somewhat arrogant and frightened at the same time, and strangely abstracted from the time and place of occupation.

Several times a day, helicopters swoop over Prague and drop leaflets putting forth the Russians' reasons for "answering the Czech government's invitation" to occupy the country. But the commanders are apparently imprecise in explaining these reasons to their troops. Last night, one Russian soldier in Wenceslaus Square said he had come to help put down the "Mensheviks who wear long hair and believe in God." Another thought the Czech border had been opened to West German troops and that the country was now full of German and American soldiers. When they first arrived, many of the Russians were surprised to learn they were in Czechoslovakia at all; they had been told they were being sent to West Germany to stop the invasion.

However, most of the soldiers have no answers at all when the Czechs ask why they have come, and a few seem genuinely unhappy in their roles. Yesterday a very young soldier began to cry and knock his gun against his knee in despair; he said he had just shot into a crowd. There are stories of Russian soldiers killing themselves after a skirmish. Such stories may be part of the rumor mill, but it is true that the Russian command has changed the guard composition every night to counteract "demoralization" after contacts with citizens. Perhaps there will soon be a Russian book called *Why Are We in Czechoslovakia?*

Not only the Russian troops find that question difficult to answer. The Czechs are baffled by the invasion. "We did nothing to you," people tell the soldiers. And indeed they hadn't; it never seemed likely that Czechoslovakia was planning to leave the Soviet defense system, as the Nagy government was attempting to do in Hungary in 1956. Czech economic and social reforms appeared to be no more (if no less) threatening to Russia than the Rumanian or Yugoslavian experiments. At some point in the distant future, the Kremlin may give up its secrets, and the reasons for the invasion of Czechoslovakia will emerge in the dirty wash; until then there is only conjecture, and the more informed conjecturers in Prague suggest an analysis that is mostly based on the old myths of ideology.

Of course myths emerge from real settings. The context of economic reformism is crucial to the Czech problem. At the beginning of the reform movement, the socialist economy in Czechoslovakia was in a state of dismal stagnation. "We had ten years of dissolution and dissatisfaction and depression," a Praguer told me yesterday.

The bureaucrats of that dreary era seemed determined to make matters worse at every opportunity: incompetent hacks were kept in the most sensitive managerial positions, and if the occasion ever arose, even more incompetent replacements were made; inefficient industries were protected from any pressures for improvement. Minor reforms proved insufficient to repair the major faults of the system.

Czech workers were probably no worse off than their counterparts in other Eastern European countries, but their expectations were higher and their economic progress slower than elsewhere in the bloc. The obvious foci for their discontent were the local Communist Party machines and labor unions; in time, pressure at the grass-roots level had built to the point where local leaders were forced to support reform—and in so doing, to discredit the central party apparatus. There were strikes and petitions and implied threats of more to come, and all at once it appeared that the whole party structure was on the verge of decomposing.

Whether or not socialism can be reformed from within is a point that theoreticians will argue for decades. But the Czech reformers decided to have a good try at it. The mastermind was Ota Sik, an economist who has been around the party for more than twenty years, although at the moment of the reform wave he was outside the official leadership. It was thus easy for the Novotny government to accept Sik as a kind of "consultant" without elevating his recommendations to the level of party dogma. Sik proposed steps to increase competition, make industry more efficient and prepare for eventual free-market socialism—but not too quickly, for fear of inflation. There were three principal points: first, the encouragement of local private small industry, such as service operations with two or three employees; second, state-controlled imports to compete with inefficiently produced Czech goods; third, encouragement of individual initiative to set up state-run industries and to let competent factories take over incompetent ones.

In classic style, Antonin Novotny finally contracted the occupational disease of minimal reform: he was caught in a crossfire. His orthodox colleagues would not let him carry out Sik's proposals, while his liberal constituency demanded even more than his moderate program promised.

And then the roof fell in. The small amount of reform that had been instituted served to produce more economic problems in the short run than it promised to solve in the future, and the workers—having tasted change—were beginning to want more. At the same time, the spirit of reform had stimulated the frustrated intellectuals to protest restrictions on their freedom of criticism. The intellectuals' revolt came to a head in the Writers' Congress last June. Novotny threw three popular liberal intellectuals out of the party and banned their red-hot magazine, *Literarni Noviny*.

As dissatisfaction among workers and intellectuals mounted, the Novotnyites nervously began to sidle over to the reformers—both to save their own skins and to "save the system" in which they had invested their careers. Finally, in January 1968, Novotny was overthrown and Alexander Dubcek was installed as first secretary.

For a time, it seemed as if the reformers' best friends were in Moscow, which had adopted the New Frontier/*Alianza* approach of encouraging reform now to head off revolution later. At one moment in the middle of the last big battle, Novotny attempted to arrest Dubcek, who fled to the Soviet embassy for protection. In Russia, party theoretician Mikhail Suslov (*The New York Times*'s favorite "party theoretician") argued for the Czech reformers; later in Bratislava he told the Warsaw Pact summit conference, "We must support reform in Czechoslovakia because sooner or later we will all have the same thing."

Somewhere between Suslov's support speech and the coming of tanks to Wenceslaus Square, there was a blinding short circuit in Soviet decision-making. The overloading element was fear. It was hardly a question of the liberalization itself. A liberal Czechoslovakia presented only small problems to Russia; an *independent* Czechoslovakia would pose an enormous threat.

The precipitating cause of panic seems to have been the reception the Czech people gave to the state visits of Yugoslavia's Tito and Rumania's Ceausescu after the Bratislava conference. Both were welcomed with unpremeditated enthusiasm. A Czech said it was the biggest outpouring of people and sentiment since the Second World War. To the Russians, the demonstrations were all the more impressive and frightening because they were so clearly spontaneous. It began to seem to some Muscovites in Eastern Europe that a new socialist bloc was being formed on the southern tier of the Soviet frontier defenses. If support for the Czechs continued to grow in Hungary (Premier Kadar is said to consider himself a potential "Hungarian Dubcek"), the Russians would be confronted with a neutral, if not exactly hostile, alliance of four countries on its western flank.

In this instance, the panic button was pressed by first secretary of the German Socialist Unity Party, Walter Ulbricht, who returned from his visit with Dubcek carrying reports of impending catastrophe. No doubt Ulbricht saw that East Germany would be in a most vulnerable position if the southern tier should slide away from Russian control. He predicted that Czechoslovakia would make its first approaches to the Common Market before the end of the year and that De Gaulle would heartily approve. He told the Russians about intelligence reports that American businessmen were flooding into Prague and that the CIA was hard at work. One of his most impressive pieces of evidence was the fact that former State Department consultant Zbigniew Brzezinski and former State Department policy planner William Griffith had visited Prague in the last spring; Brzezinski's mission was to make an anti-communist speech while Griffith snooped around town.

No one knows all the gory details of Ulbricht's message to Moscow, but it apparently got Brezhnev and Kosygin home from the Crimea in a hurry. Those in the Soviet leadership who worry about such things immediately began to think about the Fourteenth Congress of the Czechoslovakian Communist Party, which was preparing to eliminate every vestige of pro-Moscow sentiment from the new Central Committee; not one "conservative" had been nominated. And within Czechoslovakia the anti-Russian press campaign, which Dubcek had promised to control, was in fact intensifying. Putting all those pieces together, the Russians saw an impending calamity, and the troops began to move.

In Prague, the Czech party presidium was to meet on August 20 to discuss the September party congress. Moscow's plan was to have its partisans in the meeting force a vote against Dubcek; he would be accused of allowing undirected demonstrations, of promoting an anti-Russian campaign, of allowing the party to be overly criticized and of building up his personal popularity at the expense of the party. The presidium would form a new anti-Dubcek majority and invite Russian and Warsaw Pact troops into the country. To dramatize the issue, Brezhnev sent Dubcek an ultimatum around which a new friends-of-the-Kremlin majority could rally.

Of course it was all a terrible bungle. Russian intelligence had utterly misread the sympathies of the Czech party (as well as the Czech population). The presidium rallied in favor of Dubcek instead of against him, and as the tanks were rolling, Brezhnev announced his "acceptance" of an invitation that had not and never would be given.

"Not only a crime," Talleyrand said of Napoleon's order to execute a certain French nobleman, "but a mistake." In one blow, Russia has done irreparable damage not only to Czechoslovakia but to its own plan for a viable single communist community in Europe.

If there was even a vague sentiment for neutrality in Czechoslovakia before the invasion, it is now a nearly unanimous demand. One of these days—when the "German problem" is solved—the Czechs will find a new way out of the Soviet sphere and others will follow. Beyond that, Russia has discredited leftist parties and the left in general for years to come. And within the Warsaw Pact countries, and perhaps even in Russia, Czechoslovakia has already become an embryonic "Vietnam."

The invasion is a big help for the deteriorating United States policy in Europe, a strategy that has always been centered on the US-German alliance. The main stimulus for unity among the "Western Allies" has always been pressure from the East. As such pressure diminished, the United States tried to find pretexts to whip up "demand" for atomic weapons from Germany. Now the Russians have provided one—and, incidentally, dealt a crippling blow to Gaullist foreign policy, whose stated goal is to create one Europe from the Atlantic to the Urals.

It seems unlikely that internal pressure from the Czechs and Slovaks will soon be able to change the seemingly tightening Russian control. For one thing, the main reformist intellectuals are in hiding or already in exile. There has been some activity among workers, but thus far no resistance. Dubcek co-opted the people after he himself had been co-opted by the Russians—but his days in office seem numbered. Shortly after returning from Moscow, Dubcek went on the air to thank everyone for their resolutions of support and their resistance, but would they now please go home and stay quiet.

One man, a highly reliable source, told me that he has seen Dubcek and that Dubcek is in very bad physical condition, having been beaten by Russian soldiers on the first night of the invasion. The same man was told by a friend in the government that the Soviet secret police has a list of 20,000 "reformers," intellectuals and anti-Moscow types in general, and it remains to be seen what will be done with them.

Scientists in particular are rushing to leave the country in the next few days, before mass round-ups begin. Four people have stopped me in restaurants or on the street to ask me for letters from abroad requesting them to travel outside the country on whatever urgent business I can invent. All are scientists, engineers or technocrat types.

An unimpeachably accurate government source says, "The Red Army will be here forever." He thinks they will be stationed on the Western frontier inside Czechoslovakia, if not closer to populated areas, but that wherever it is all power will flow from it. This government man says further, "The puppet master will pull whatever strings he chooses."

There is still a lack of any substantial organization among the populace. One main reason for this is the impossibility, during the twenty years of the Stalin regime, of developing independent institutions outside the party—or even within it. That is one of the tragic consequences of Stalinism. Though this may have begun to change during the brief period of the Dubcek reforms, the people are still unprepared for the formation of a base of organized resistance. For twenty years, despite rhetoric to the contrary, apathy and depoliticization were encouraged.

"What do you think we should do now?" a student asked me. I said I didn't know. He answered his own question: "Perhaps we should think about organizing ourselves."

"Do you know what that means?" I asked.

He thought for a moment. "I guess we'll find out," he said.

September 1968, RAMPARTS

✦

Blue Collars and White Racism

Cleveland

Wallace country—in Northern industrial expanses—is a land of the forgotten. Not the excluded or the oppressed or the dispossessed: this Wallace public has simply slipped out of mind. While the blacks are baited, the poor programmed, the students beaten, the elites honored and the New Class celebrated, the white working men are ignored. They inspire neither fear nor admiration. In Cleveland, the Wallace neighborhoods lie tentatively between the scrubbed suburbs and the unwashed ghettoes—not quite bad enough for slum-clearance or quite good enough for segregation. Around them the atmosphere is thick and heavy—with smoke and dust, boredom and frustration.

For thirty years or more, the demands of blue-collar workers—as a class—have been expressed through two institutions: the unions and the Democratic Party. By one means or the other, working people could establish a social identity, however incomplete. Now, both have ceased to serve that purpose in any substantive way. It would be hard to find a labor official who does not admit, with everybody else, that the unions have "lost touch" with the rank-and-file. As a mediating force, the Democratic Party has fallen even further into disuse. Local party clubs that once served as vehicles for up-mobility for the myriad ethnic groups are no longer in running order. In the past few years, the politics of ethnicity has blended into a color-conscious pattern: race wars have melted Poles, Italians, Irishmen and Bohemians into a pot of whites. Now the Democratic Party is seen as an active opponent of "ordinary people": it drafts their sons into pointless wars, plows up their communities for freeways, lets rioters roam their streets, and appropriates their wages in taxes for someone else's benefit. The union is considered only slightly less offensive: it sacrifices local issues to national bargaining, plays along behind the scenes with the company, and pushes the unskilled and unqualified into well-paying jobs.

Whether those complaints are real or not, they are deeply felt. The "real" gains that white working men have won through unions and party politics do not produce eternal gratitude, nor do they alter the objective frustrations of blue-collar life. Now, from the well of those frustrations, bubbles of racism and anti-communism are exploding on the surface, and it is hardly surprising: America gives that gas to everyone. But for many blue-collar workers, the Wallace campaign is the first new means of expression they have found in years.

As a national candidate with a country-wide constituency, George Wallace can mean many things to many publics—even if he has only one speech. To Bradley Jefferson, a 53-year-old auto worker at the Fisher Body plant in Cleveland's industrial suburb of Euclid, Wallace is neither a messiah nor a maniac, but he is at least better than "the others." Wallace *talks* to people like Bradley Jefferson, and Jefferson returns the compliment of such unusual attention by wearing a Wallace button to work.

"I was a brainwashed Democrat," Jefferson began in a long conversation we had last week. "I thought there wasn't anything else than a Democrat— they were for the little man, the working man. I voted for Frank Lausche every time except this year, but the unions said Gilligan was 100 percent on my side, so I just switched. I never voted for a Republican, not even Eisenhower: I just can't see a Republican president. I voted for Johnson in '64 because he was against Goldwater, but I thought he was purely a politician, 100 percent for personal gain. Now, Nixon—he's a loser; that Checkers speech didn't lay so good. Humphrey—everything good; check, check, check, but he's too easy on race, that's a minus. (Boy, am I making myself out a racist?) Wallace—I only like him 40 percent; it's not what he can actually do in his own power if he became president, but the fact that he won, or got a lot of votes, would get people together. So I'm for Wallace. But you know, sometimes I'm not sure why I vote for someone. Does that make sense?"

Bradley Jefferson's presidential choice seems to be shared by at least a third of the plant's 1,800 employees, according to a poll taken by the company newspaper before the conventions. He is a gentle, quiet man with nine children, a house that he (almost) owns, one son in the marines. Several other of his children have married and left home. A long time ago, Jefferson and his wife planned to open a drygoods store, but he spent his savings in California during the war, and nothing ever came of the idea. In 1963, he did manage to buy a "little sandwich shop" in the neighborhood, but he lost it— and half his investment—two years later. Now in his spare time he tinkers with old television sets and watches football on the new one. He was born in Cleveland, not far from his present house, and the immediate neighborhood is still white. A mile and a half up the avenue, the black section begins. For one reason or another, he is thinking about moving out of the city.

For many years, Jefferson worked "on the line," installing floorboards in cars as they moved past him, one every eighty seconds. It was, as all the assembly-line workers say, "a killing pace." Now, his age and seniority entitle him to an easier job off the line—putting "four or five bolts, some nuts and screws, a piece of rubber and a piece of chrome" in quarter-glass assemblies for the rear windows of Cadillacs and Oldsmobiles. The union contract requires that Jefferson finish twenty-one assemblies in an hour, or 189 in a day; but he can do more if he works faster, and sometimes he finishes quickly and sneaks off to look at the paper or the *Reader's Digest*. He is not allowed to leave the plant during the workday.

This is the high-production season, and Jefferson works six days a week. Like everyone else, he counts on overtime pay as a necessary component of salary; the forty-hour week (or whatever is the current slogan) is an economic fiction. A while back, he was union financial secretary at a different plant local, but although he counts himself a "militant," he does not take part in union affairs to any significant degree.

It is hardly worth saying that life in an auto plant is thoroughly dehumanizing; fluorescent lighting and a union contract have not materially changed the social effect of the industrial system since the days of the dark satanic mills. What is harder for American non-workers to understand—against the myths of cushy conditions and executive wages—is that the union contributes to the dehumanizing process. Labor officials in Cleveland believe that the United Auto Workers has the largest component of Wallace supporters, and while there are many possible explanations, the UAW's extraordinarily manipulative structure has to be counted a critical factor. "It almost seems as if the UAW is *designed* to shut out the rank-and-file," one worried union official told me. "We tell the members nothing and ask them only to come to our meetings to endorse our decisions." It is not surprising that the members refuse even that minimum demand. At one large Cleveland local with 4,500 members, only 1 percent of the membership participates in union business, according to the estimate of the local's leaders. At another, less than 10 percent use the grievance procedure, and almost three-quarters failed to vote in the last union general election. For three months running, membership meetings at a huge General Motors local have had to be cancelled for want of a fifty-man quorum. In the UAW system, day-to-day work problems are handled right on the plant floor by two dozen stewards and supervisors who can make shift-assignments and fit workers to company rules in the manner of management experts. The workers see "their" stewards as unresponsive bureaucrats, doing the company's dirty work.

As a social force, the labor movement (in all but a few odd sectors) stopped all forward motion long ago, and now concentrates on the huge effort of running in place. Its "progressive" politics are expressed in a flood of rhetoric—and pamphlets—from the International headquarters, but at the local level the few remaining liberals (and fewer radicals) have all they can do to keep abreast of the tide of racism and reaction. Sometimes, they drown. At a Chevrolet local in Cleveland the leadership was so racist that the union president put up a Confederate flag on the wall of his office to proclaim his sympathies; the International headquarters sent men down from Detroit to tear it off. At another GM factory many members of the local's executive board are openly for Wallace, despite the International's disapproving propaganda. The recently retired president of the Cleveland area UAW—the largest union in the state—led a thinly disguised racist attack against Carl Stokes, a Negro, in his first, unsuccessful primary campaign. Conveniently, Stokes's white opponent in the primary was the organization's man. "Labor leaders have been winking at racism for years," a Democratic politician said recently. "Now it's jumping up to bite them."

Attempts by some labor activists to form political blocs outside the Democratic Party—or to oppose orthodox Democratic positions—are quickly crushed. "The leadership actually fears new organizing," one union official reported. "They're afraid the members will vote 'wrong' in the next election." When a small caucus of "radicals" in a Cleveland UAW local started agitating against the war a year or so ago, a representative from the International flew into town to put down the anti-Administration revolt. He told a meeting of workers called by the caucus, "half of you guys will be out of jobs when this war ends." Big labor's swordwork on independent political action is terrible and swift: when a non-party organization, set up to campaign against a right-to-work referendum in Ohio, tried to continue its highly successful operations in electoral campaigns, state and national labor leaders cut off all funds and support. Along with it died the most promising new political force in Ohio in a generation.

For all the obvious reasons, the national labor establishment is spending its fortunes to defeat the Wallace campaign. Workers are deluged with literature chronicling Wallace's anti-labor record in Alabama, and along with appeals to the pocketbook, they get appeals to reason. But in a way, the whole effort may be counterproductive. For one thing, people do not like being told they are "racists" when in their hearts they have at least a sneaking suspicion that other motives are at work. More important, official labor's stern anti-Wallace position often becomes identified with its abrasive authoritarianism in other matters. "Labor has tried to deliver its votes to racists in the past in the same tone of voice it uses against racism now," a union man said in Cleveland. "Leaders sign national contracts that the rank-and-file know are screwing them, or the union heads support integration drives that the rank-and-file think are at their expense. They get it from both sides, and they take it out against the union. Now the union tells them to vote for Humphrey, and they're likely to vote for Wallace just for spite."

There is an underlying paradox of "anti-union unionism" that can explain much of the Wallace syndrome in the industrial North. To Ben Nash, an assembly-line worker at Fisher-Euclid (rubber molding on car windows), the paradox is easily resolved.

"I'm a union man," he told me quickly. "I wouldn't be anything else. I don't believe it's possible to have anything without a union. But that doesn't mean I've got to listen to what the leaders say about politics. They don't know how it is with us. Our son is in the army; he's going to Fort Benning, and then it's either Vietnam or Germany for him. I don't want him getting hurt in Vietnam; that war is just like our way of running things—like our South against our North, the black against the white, the West against the East. We've got a lot of boys killed just to force two types of government in a country that wants only one government. Now I would have voted for Bobby Kennedy, because his morals were higher, and he had a lot better thinker on him than H.H. Humphrey. Our kind of government today is all promises and no action. I thought a lot of Wallace, going back to the time he stood up against the federal government. Now I'm not against color, but I'm against riots. I'm getting older; am I going to live with the thought of the riot coming through? I want my home to be as close to heaven as it can be. I'm building my home and I hope the Lord is going to let me live to enjoy it."

In his fifteen years in Cleveland, Ben Nash has lived in a dozen apartments and houses, with and without his wife and various numbers of their eleven children. Before that, he crawled around in "thirty-two inches of coal" in the West Virginia mines; beginning wages were 36 cents a ton (about ten tons a day on the average)—"and you furnish your own powder." His first apartment in Cleveland cost $30 a week—the standard exploitative rate for "hillbilly" families in those days—but he was forced to move by a rather aggressive army of bedbugs that began to attack his children. Now he can make $200 a week, counting overtime, in the busy season, and he is remodelling a ramshackle frame house he bought for $7,400 five years ago. The other day, a "dark" family moved in down the street, but the Nashes have yet to determine whether it is "colored" or "Puerto Rican." In any case, the threat of violence—in some undefined way—hangs over the Nash household.

"During the Glenville riots [in July], I just lay in bed wondering what I would do if it came through," Libby Nash said nervously. "We don't have no gun or anything." Ben Nash thinks everyone should have a gun, but for some reason won't keep one himself in his house. "We thought that Stokes would have kept them quieter," he said, "but he hasn't. I'm with the police 100 percent, because they take an oath to protect me, and in a hundred ways they protect me every day. It's not just the riots, it's everything."

Anyone with or without a year of freshman sociology can dismiss Ben Nash and Bradley Jefferson as racists, and there would be some truth in the description. But racism is only part of it, and only one symptom in the whole syndrome. "I don't think that factory people are real racists, at least any more than anyone else around here," a college drop-out who worked in an auto plant near Cleveland told me. "People were really frightened when they heard about the riots. But in the factory, black people were treated fine— better than in middle-class colleges." The older workers agree: there are no racial fights in the plants.

What has happened in working-class Cleveland, as in almost every other sector of institutionalized life in the US, is that the liberal "center" has crumbled, and in the vortex produced by that cataclysm the social rubble is spinning. Wallace is available to pick out some of the pieces. In his campaign, he gives them a framework of issues and a rough structure of ideology that for the most part is arbitrary. If another political campaign got there first, different forms could as easily be constructed. In many ways, it is uninstructive to study the Wallace campaign: Wallace himself carries around all the rhetorical and political baggage from his several bum trips, and it is too tempting to put all his supporters into the same trunks.

The Wallace people are not so easily categorized. The basic unit of Southern support cuts across class and caste, from Black Belt redneck to

"New South" suburbanite. Outside the South, the true-believer Birchers and diehard Goldwaterites are at least as important as the blue-collar "forgotten men." The various constituencies are frequently at war with one another. In Ohio, there have been two distinct Wallace campaigns: "the racists and the bombers," as the liberal Democrats call them, a bit too glibly. The industrial workers' campaign fixes on the riots, but it has a pseudo-Populist air about it too. Wallace's direct attacks on the banks, the foundations and the "pointy-headed intellectuals" are almost as appealing as his indirect attacks on Negroes. The middle-class campaign has a stronger obsession with "communism." As many of the working men who organize for Wallace are crypto-Democrats, the middle-class organizers are Republican drop-outs. They were lifted to new heights of enthusiasm when Wallace chose Gen. Curtis LeMay as his vice-presidential candidate, but that same choice may cause some workers to defect. "Wallace's appeal on the war," a factory worker said, "has gotten to many of the younger guys at the plant. They don't want to go, but they're afraid to surrender. Basically, they're as scared as the students; they don't want to die." They could be more terrified than elated at LeMay's fanatical anti-communism.

The two ends of the Wallace campaign spectrum seem to merge in the skilled tradesmen and the aspiring small businessmen, those who are either just outside or inside the promised land of status and achievement. In the auto plants, Wallace support is highest among the young apprentices, many of whom tried—and failed—to jump up into middle-class careers and now feel trapped in factory life. Just across the center, the *lumpen-salariat* and struggling "professionals" recently out of the inner-city flee into the Wallace camp with the hot breath of their former classmates still on their necks. In substance, Wallace can do nothing for any of them. He has neither programs nor plans to fit either of his Northern publics. Many politicians in Ohio—like Mayor Stokes—believe (hope?) that the Wallace candidacy will lose its appeal for voters at the last moment, when the full horror and futility of the campaign occurs to them in the privacy of the voting booth. That may be true, but if the campaign is really only one expression of a "new politics" of frustration, it will soon reappear in another monstrous form. For Wallace and his constituents know that the campaign itself has already given them both a certain power they never had before. People take them seriously now, and there's no going back from there.

October 11-18, 1968, MAYDAY

✦

Sabotage: 'This Is Number One and the Fun Has Just Begun'

People are used to thinking of wars of nerves, or wars against poverty, or wars of all-against-all. But the new "underground" war in America is not just a metaphor for political action or social unrest. This campaign has dynamite, firebombs and *plastique*. It is fought on hilltops in California, in the hollows of Appalachia, on scores of college campuses, in black ghettoes and downtown shopping districts. The targets are not people but property—perhaps the only valid object of attack in a super-industrial, technological society: police cars, draft boards, military facilities, power stations and mining equipment. Although no lives have been taken, property damage runs into the millions.

Very slowly, the possibility creeps into public consciousness that all the explosions fit some political pattern. Exactly what the outlines are is difficult to discern. The few newspaper accounts of the various "incidents" do not distinguish between the Cuban exiles' bomb project and the others. Rather, everything is lumped into a category of "violence," which seems to have arrived for no reason at all, like an aberrant tornado on a summer's day.

But at bottom, the campaign of sabotage grows logically from very real conditions. The failure of traditional mediators of change, on the one hand, and the increasing militancy of the forces of change—on the same hand—provide a framework in which violent action is at least thinkable. The experience of "real" warfare in Vietnam and widespread violence in urban ghettoes lends a certain practicality to any plans that might be hatching. There is no need for national coordination, and there is no evidence at all that any exists. Related action springs naturally and spontaneously from similar causes.

The first attack—four Molotov cocktails thrown at a Berkeley ROTC building in February—was followed by the burning of a similar center at Stanford. At about the same time, electric power cables strung over the Berkeley hills were cut. Then, three giant electric towers in Oakland were blown to the ground, leaving about 30,000 houses without power and stopping work at the Lawrence Radiation Laboratory at Berkeley. A few days after the tower was destroyed, a University of Colorado drop-out student turned himself in to police to publicize his "crime." "I had to do something to stop their machines—so maybe they would listen, so that this war would be stopped," he said.

Other bombers have not been so open; few have been caught, and police and FBI seem to be going about their investigations in a curiously low-key way. Most of the attacks on police facilities—in Oakland and in the Detroit area—have been unsolved. Last week police rounded up several suspects in the anti-Castro campaign, but not many of the war protesters or the other "revolutionary" saboteurs have been apprehended.

ROTC buildings and draft boards remain favorite targets. The Stanford ROTC building attacked last winter was hit again a few months later, and destroyed. On September 18, a Naval ROTC hall at the University of Washington, in Seattle, was blasted, with damage estimated at $85,000. Hundreds of students watched the building burn, and a cheering-section chanted, "This is number one, and the fun has just begun. Let it burn, let it burn, let it burn." Five days previously, a Naval ROTC building at Berkeley was dynamited and an ROTC hall at the University of Delaware was hit by a Molotov cocktail. Last spring, an ROTC building at Nashville Agricultural and Industrial College burned to the ground while the school's students (all black) kept firemen from fighting the fire effectively. In Eugene—hard by the University of Oregon—a series of explosions destroyed the Naval and Marine Corps Training Center in late September. Damage was put at $106,000.

Draft boards have been attacked in North Hollywood, California; Xenia, Ohio (near Antioch College); and Berkeley. In early September a building near Detroit housing two suburban draft boards was bombed. Last March an office used by employment recruiters for defense contractors at San Fernando Valley State College (Los Angeles) was firebombed. In Ann Arbor, the unmarked office of the local CIA agent was bombed—and permanently closed. Policemen's private automobiles in station-house parking lots in Detroit have been blown up or damaged.

Sabotage of strip-mining operations in Appalachia does not fall into exactly the same category as the university-military attacks, but there are some obvious political connections. The new radical movements have been active in Appalachia since the early sixties. The poverty of the "poor whites" and unemployed miners in the region was one of the first major issues for the New Left—even before the Negro civil rights movement took center stage. President Kennedy capitalized on sympathy for Appalachia's poor in his 1960 campaign, and the Southern mountains became a fashionable hard-core poverty area for welfare bureaucrats and economic development experts. VISTA volunteers and assorted anti-poverty organizers venture to the area, but the economic decay continues and the political stranglehold of company-owned local officials is hard to break.

Strip-mining is the most distressing external expression of the ills of Appalachia. Coal companies have succeeded in winning legislative rights to destroy surface land to get at mineral deposits, and in the process have laid waste thousands of square miles of farms and wooded hillsides. The landscape is now barren and unreclaimable. Small farmers and rural residents have no power to push conservationist demands against the influence of the companies and their political allies.

But in the past few months the people of Appalachia have asserted a new kind of power for themselves. On August 24, four men invaded a mine office in Middlesboro, Kentucky; they bound up the night watchman, carted him away and set off the company's own explosives. A million dollars' worth of equipment went up with the dynamite charge. Throughout the summer, the "Appalachian guerrillas" roamed Kentucky, blowing up strip-mining equipment where they could find it. State authorities would like to blame out-of-state organizers, but so far most of the activity seems to have been carried on by inside-agitators: townspeople, union men, people who have been run out of the hollows by strip-mine landslides. It would be hard to say they don't have enough to be agitated about.

Appalachian sabotage has a parallel with "civic-action" projects in many black communities across the country—not the well-publicized and televised riots, but the nightly bombings and burnings which police and municipal officials would rather not talk about. In Washington there were several nights of looting and street demonstrations last month after a white policeman shot and killed a black man whose crime had been to cross a street against a red light. (The policeman has been indicted for homicide.) Tear gas filled the streets and the mass media were on hand. But when the crisis subsided, public interest disappeared—and still, firebombs explode on the same streets and the white-owned stores that remain are being picked off one by one.

November 1-8, 1968, MAYDAY

✦

Are We in the Middle of a Revolution?

R evolution is a serious business. It is not the Dodge Rebellion, the miniskirt revolt or the McCarthy movement, however beneficial or entertaining those campaigns may have been. People talk now about the coming of the revolution as they would discuss the arrival of the latest hurricane; it is thought to be imminent, or upon us, or just blowing by. But real revolution is a wind of longer passing.

It is at once the most tragic and redeeming social experience. It is what societies do instead of committing suicide, when the alternatives are exhausted and all the connections that bind men's lives in familiar patterns are cut. Death and transfiguration is the ultimate human drama; revolution combines those two acts in a single transcendent scene.

Whatever else may be going on in America, it is not very much of a revolution. Despite some unruliness, a few perilous moments and a great deal of intramural bickering, the strongest fortresses of "the system" remain in the hands of the same elites that have held power for years. The only change is that the capability of those hands can now be questioned. But Ralph Nader and his irate consumers have hardly dented General Motors. The New Left and the Yippies will find the Cook County Democratic machine still running. All the power of poor people's organizations, community-control projects and black economic-development schemes have failed to impede the extravagant growth of corporate capitalism at home and abroad in this generation. *RAT* does not threaten the hegemony of *The New York Times*; Luckies outsell grass; Andrew Cordier still outranks Mark Rudd in anybody's hierarchy of power.

By usual definition, revolution means the displacement of the rulers by the ruled, a redress of the imbalance of power in a social system. The classic model—a seizure of the state in violent struggle—is of course unthinkable in America now. Potential revolutionary classes—black people, students, blue-collar workers, hippies—are either ill-placed or ill-disposed for such battle.

If there is a revolutionary program in anyone's head, it involves action along all kinds of fronts to soften the system—by blowing kids' minds, frightening the comfortable classes, organizing the oppressed, questioning the legitimacy of everything. But that would be only a preliminary stage; plans and programs would have to grow out of the experience. The Declaration of Independence detailed tyranny but presented no formula for constitutional democracy. Marx carved up capitalism but laid out only the foggiest conception of a communist state.

Conventional politics should be the last place to look for revolutionary change, and with only one possible exception—the distressing example of the Wallace campaign—no exercise of electoral politics has carried revolutionary values along with it. But the Wallace movement is strongest where America is least vulnerable—in the decaying rural South or the shrinking near-slums of the blue-collar North—and it can amount only to a permanent (if permanently dangerous) minority.

Across the center spread, the left margin of politics is even thinner. The McCarthy campaign was conceived (if not plotted) as an *anti*-revolutionary reform movement, to "channel protest" into the two-party system, to strengthen the Democratic liberals, and to replace evil and incompetent managers with humane and wise ones—at the head of the same machine.

Understandably, the McCarthyites focus their attack on segregation and unequal opportunity, and on the war in Vietnam. But the war they sought to end is only the deformed child of too-healthy parents: the Joint Chiefs and the defense intellectuals, Lockheed Aircraft and IBM, the Rand Corporation and the AFL-CIO, the nice and the nasty, the actively conniving and the merely complicit. Sterilization of the parents might have been revolutionary; abortion of the child could not be.

The art of holding onto power is the American system's special grace. The trick is to make reform seem so tantalizingly close as to dull the edge of militancy and force the purest revolutionaries into the peripheries of political action. Dissent has a political function as well as a constitutional position; it legitimizes and supports the status quo. Only the dumbest establishments practice open suppression of dissidence; what Marcuse calls "repressive tolerance" is far more effective. In practice, it is the art of letting dissident minorities say whatever they please within a system loaded in favor of the most powerful elites. The dissidents let off steam; the controllers keep power. A shirt-sleeve walk through a riot area works better than a police charge—and for the same ultimate objective.

America is cleverest when it protects its oppositions and neutralizes them: by buying them (War on Poverty), channeling them (Clean for Gene) or marketing them (turn on with cars). The last method is the most fun—and the most profitable. To a society that is suffering from too much internalized repression already, the sale of vicarious liberation can bring a bonanza in cash returns. Radicals, hippies and "black-power extremists" have only to sit by the phone or collect their mail these days while the invitations pour in. Newspaper syndicates are searching for lefties to run alongside their regular columnists on the editorial pages of a hundred provincial papers. The mass-circulation magazines can't seem to get enough of SDS. Hearst is publishing a head magazine for the straights. The performing rebel is urged to tell it like it is and do his own thing—*pour épater les bourgeois*. Media fortunes will be made or broken on a company's ability to swing with the liberation movements. It is all proof enough that this is not a revolutionary situation; if it were, Tom Hayden wouldn't be on television, Country Joe and the Fish would be underground and Eldridge Cleaver would be shot.

Sometimes it seems that if Tom Hayden, Country Joe and Eldridge Cleaver did not exist, America would have had to invent them. And so—in a way— America *did* invent them: to satisfy revolutionary longings. They are aphrodisiacs in the air-conditioning system, hallucinogens in the water supply. To the extent that the forces they represent can be contained, society is safe. But if the forces reach a critical mass, the mild hype becomes hell broken loose. Repressive tolerance is an exquisitely subtle game.

The forms that radicalism has taken are familiar enough to everyone. There are the student revolutionaries, the hippies, the drug-heads, the middle-class marchers, the black nationalists and other less virulent types fading out into the gray center. Among them there are scores of ideological bits and pieces, some amounting to no more than a phrase and others constituting a regular *Weltanschauung*. Chunks are borrowed from one or another foreign model or historical example, and strains spring as well from native American soil. But what unites them all is more interesting: a common thread of values and needs that people in this technologized, over-productive, post-industrial land seem so desperately to lack. Participation, recognition, loving, honesty, caring; the list is so "corny" that the values must be expressed in cooler clichés: "Do your thing," "Like it is," "Listen, whitey," "Share in the decisions," "Make love, not war."

The thread is woven in no particular pattern throughout all the areas of disaffection. Single events or a series of them occasionally make it very clear. The four kids who sat in at a lunch counter in Greensboro, North Carolina, in 1960 were enacting the *idea* of individual effectiveness in a pure and simple form. For the decade of the 1950s, at least, no one had dreamed that one person could effect change by beating on the anonymous and impassive system. It was not so much that people had wanted to be "silent" in that generation; they had no notion that speaking out would make the slightest difference.

The roots of radicalism in both its major streams and all its forms lie in that existential ground that the Greensboro kids plowed. The politics came later, and is of secondary importance for understanding (although of primary importance for the strategy of change). What it meant to be "under 30" (in 1964) was to identify yourself with that surge of resistance against the old values. Whatever supported or legitimized them became a fair target: university administrations and their IBM-card rules, political machines and their hypocritical reforms, college professors and their self-justifying intellectualism, parents and their suburban aspirations, unions and their unfulfilled promises. When the kids and the blacks excoriated America in four-letter words, they were talking of more than the war or segregation. They meant that America had lied to them—and in a way that was the original sin.

Now what the war has done to the society—quite apart from the cost in lives—is only beginning to be understood. It introduced politics to a generation that had been taught that politics—in the ideological sense—was dead in America. The war's duration and pointlessness have "radicalized" some numbers, if not hordes, of previously bored and apathetic liberals. That process is easy to describe in terms of personal perception: (1) The war is an unfortunate necessity. (2) The war is an unnecessary aberration of US foreign policy. (3) The war is one of many mistakes. (4) The war is one mistake in a generally unprotested pattern of mistakes. (5) The war is a product of the same political structure and the same economic relationships that "institutionalize" racism, brutalize the poor and alienate the middle classes, and creates that oppressive reality of powerlessness which is at the bottom of it all. (6) Pig! (7) Brother . . .

Not everybody goes all that distance. The radicalizing process depends on many variables of background and station in life, and it is rather more experiential than rational. The McCarthy delegates in Chicago, for instance, were poised in midprocess when the Democratic National Convention opened. The police charges put many of them in a personal confrontation with authority which in one explosive moment stripped a layer of myths from their conception of America. Some have described it almost in psychoanalytic terms. "I had this sudden insight," or "I didn't know I felt that way."

Millions of others were carried along to lesser degrees by the television coverage, and the pictures reinforced other images that had been registering for many months. Grant Park meant more after three years of burned

Vietnamese villages; Mayor Daley's cops somehow hark back to Bull Connor's. The shock of recognition is a potent force.

Marches, vigils, teach-ins, draft-refusal rituals and the myriad protests of these protesting years have involved a sizable fraction of the population, personally or once removed. No one is quite the same after he has marched in a demonstration, however tame, and it is at least half as good to hear about the adventure from a close relative or friend. Legitimacy mounts, and one experience can be transplanted to another "issue" via the familiar routes. The 200 parishioners who walked out on Cardinal O'Boyle's anti–birth control sermon in a Washington cathedral were to some unknown degree spiritual heirs of the peace marchers and the freedom riders.

Separately or together, the radical streams seem to have no real revolutionary potential. From the beginning it was hard to conceive of a strategy for radical reconstruction of America. Some looked to Marx or Castro or American Populism, but none of those was seen then, or now, to be singularly applicable. The "center" of the system was too securely in control, at once too flexible and too commanding to allow the development of mass action.

But the history of the last three years is the chronicle of the center's disintegration, of the failure of the methods of political liberalism to cope with systemic disorders. The mediating institutions that have been dominant from the New Deal through the Great Society delayed the day of confrontation but could not remove the causes. In their last incarnations the mediators were anti-poverty programs, peace offensives, methods for humane riot control, urban-renewal projects, counterinsurgency schemes, foreign-aid grants, anti-segregation laws, the McCarthy campaign, "dove" candidacies, the "politics of joy": in short, most of the things that editorialists from *The New Republic* to the *Times* endorse. All of them sought to reduce the real conflicts of our lives, and all of them were inadequate. The rising sense of hopelessness and helplessness this summer—the widespread fear that there were no more "alternatives"—followed from the realization that the mediating forces were out of commission.

There is a real failure of the left in America as well, but it follows the collapse of the middle. Radicals can provide no believable alternatives for many of the people spinning out of the center as the vortex widens and deepens. The white radicals have no program to appeal to the working class or to newly radicalized middle-class adults. Black militants do not appeal organizationally to the mass of black people.

That may be too bad, but the left should not bear all the blame. America does that to its radicals. It fragments and isolates them, illegitimizes them and scorns them. However rebellious children may be, they have their parents' genes; American radicals are Americans. They cannot easily cross class lines to organize groups above or below their own station. They are caught in the same status traps as everyone else, even if they react self-consciously.

Yet for all the disarray, there is something happening here, as Dylan says, but we don't know what it is, at least not exactly. People are right when they sense something new in their lives, even if they cannot touch it or see it. Sexual freedom, the kids, the riots, assassinations: they all seem to be related, but the bonds are obscure.

The connections are all underground, in a root mass of rapidly growing and changing new relationships, of men to men and institutions among themselves. For four decades the material basis of American life has been in the process of real transformation, from classic industrial development to the "new system" of post-industrialism, or post-capitalism, or technologism, or whatever it's called. The politics, ideologies, mores and life patterns of the old system obviously cannot work well with the new. Marx described the same kind of shift 120 years ago:

> Does it require deep intuition to comprehend that man's ideas, views and conceptions, in one word, man's consciousness, changes with every change in the conditions of his material existence, in his social relations and in his social life?

Work has new meaning, personal space is compressed, leisure looms large, consumption has a different function. Notions change accordingly. Good taste becomes prudery, adjustment is conformism, surplus is waste, success is self-indulgence, status is paralysis, pragmatism is hypocrisy, welfare is slavery. Those who hold steadfastly to the old values are true conservatives; those who only sense the new are worried liberals; those who see the whole pattern very clearly are radicals, and they don't know what to do about it.

Perhaps for that reason, cultural change has been far more successful than the political kind; the radical movement has moved from Lenin to Lennon in one generation. It is easily spread by a thousand rock stations and the big record companies, and it is carried by the winds that blow the burning grass. Not for nothing has *The Wall Street Journal*, for one, questioned the wisdom of anti-marijuana laws. Apart from any inherent injustice, enforcement is turning an entire class of pre-elite kids against established authority. If the House Un-American Activities Committee had any sense, it would leave Dave Dellinger alone and investigate Big Brother and the Holding Company.

"The Great Bourgeois Cultural Revolution" can change people's lives in a way, but it is too easily manipulated by the same old economic forces, and the pot and the music end up reinforcing their positions of control. Any revolutionary content is soon drained, and all that remains is a new style.

Only political change can build the new (or rediscovered) cultural values into the life of the society. Whether any of the preconditions for a political revolution now exist on top of the basal changes is most difficult to say, but for the first time in years, people have begun to talk seriously about such change taking place. Half a year ago the issue of revolution was not considered quite legitimate for conversation, even on the left. Only this summer did white radicals begin to refer to themselves as "revolutionaries" with less than total irony. They are looking for "allies," in the spiritual more than the material sense, in Western and Eastern European movements, as well as in Cuba or Vietnam. Anyone hacking away at the American empire from abroad is an ally of those chipping away from within.

The problem is where to start chipping. The revolutionaries, of all degrees, are as baffled as anyone else. If the need for change is obvious, the strategy remains obscure. Whether they can hold out for very long in the face of little or no success is still more problematic. They need patience now (later, after the revolution, they will need irony, as the hero said in *La Guerre Est Finie*). But their genius so far has been the ability to redefine "success." It consists no longer simply in electing a militant city councilman or passing a local anti-discrimination law, in paralyzing the Selective Service System or occupying a college hall. The objective really is closer to the Beatles': to "free minds" by forcing people to re-examine their beliefs about their world.

That has been a more successful campaign than anyone would have thought possible. Street fighting is only one tactic. There are a thousand projects yet untried, and radicals of all types are finding support for their efforts in their own haunts. Education and electoral politics were clear initial targets; the press and the mass media may be next. No one need plot the attacks. One wave can break on several shores. The kids in Chicago, for instance, touched many reporters at the core of their consciences. One result has been the publication of a new Chicago monthly paper by journalists who objected to their papers' convention coverage. In Washington some young reporters are talking about refusing to cover events or write stories when to do so would violate their own political commitments. People are finding allies everywhere.

At an impromptu street rally in Paris last May, I heard a student speaker from atop a car remind his fellows: "The unique and essential enemy is America." To him, it meant the America that is on everybody's back, spreading herbicide in Indochina and sociology at the Sorbonne and spies in Africa. To his American revolutionary ally, the enemy is the system that victimizes its own people. Both revolutionaries share an affection for (and derive imagination from) American spontaneity and energy. They love the music and the movies, the style and the sweep of American adventure. The Frenchman might easily reject it all in a critical moment; the American cannot throw it all away—not the kids with the cops, the underground press with the TV networks, the hard rock with the Muzak, Harlem with Scarsdale, the High Sierras with the automobile graveyards. To be a revolutionary is to love your life enough to change it, to choose struggle instead of exile, to risk everything with only the glimmering hope of a world to win.

November 10, 1968, THE NEW YORK TIMES MAGAZINE

Chapter V

✦

BAD MOON RISING

Blacks v. Jews

A few years back, when the civil rights movement seemed ready to make its final assault on racial injustice in America, Norman Podhoretz wrote in *Commentary*, the Jewish journal, about "My Negro Problem—and Ours." Generalizing from his own admitted prejudice, he argued that hatred of blacks (or blackness, really) was so deeply set in culture and society that whites could never grant Negroes equality and acceptance. It was a sensationalized and silly essay, for all its sophisticated self-condemnation, and not much more than an apology for racism when all was said. But its point might be remembered now by Jews who have belatedly discovered "black anti-Semitism" and in a fair frenzy of fear and anger can find no reason in their own lives for the blacks' rage.

Bigot for bigot, all sections of the white population in the US are pretty much in the same league. At the same time, it may also be true that of all the white "minorities" the Jews have more than their share of civil rights activists, just as they produce more political liberals and radicals. But casual liberalism does not exclude casual racism; a suburban Jewish housewife may give $25 a year to the NAACP, but her actual relationship to her black maid is no different from the gentile's in the next suburb. For the maid, of course, the Jewish mistress induces the sharper conflict; gratitude is much harder to deliver than hostility. Nice colonial masters usually get it in the neck sooner than nasty ones.

Frantz Fanon—a good antidote to Podhoretz—detailed the phenomenon of the colonial dependency relationship, in which the colonized always despises the colonizer *for his kindness* as the master always patronizes the slave. There is a good deal of that in the interaction of blacks and Jewish liberals, and in that case it has little to do with any subjective hypocrisy in the Jews' behavior. For even the most sincerely committed white radicals must be seen by blacks—from one angle at least—as "objectively" hypocritical. The whites can never make the last leap into black souls—the final act of good faith.

Jews took the lead among whites in the early civil rights campaigns. Tom Kahn, a young Jewish social-democratic intellectual, instructed Stokely Carmichael and the first wave of Northern black militants in prerevolutionary political theory when they all were at Howard University in the early sixties. Jewish students flocked to the South for the great rural organizing drives, and some were murdered by white segregationists. But the blacks finally expelled white activists from their organizations for qualities that are epitomized by but not confined to American Jewish culture: elitism, social manipulation, intellectual superiority. The super-competence of the Jewish organizers and intellectuals made the young blacks realize quite clearly that they had to master the techniques of their own revolution.

Such subtle and even tragic confrontations are not the whole story of the black-Jewish antagonism. There is the obvious problem of Jewish "visibility" in the ghetto. Jews are the small shopkeepers, the landlords, the teachers and the social workers for much of the urban black population. Rage against "whitey" takes the form of attacks on the Jews. Anti-Semitism is a convenient way to needle the closest white man, who often turns out to be a Jew. Earl Raab, a Jewish community leader in San Francisco, writes in a current issue of *Commentary* that the kind of anti-Semitism now found in the black ghetto has little of the political content of historical European models, but simply draws on the pervasive gentile cultural prejudice to get one particular brand of whitey at his most vulnerable point.

The "problem" of black anti-Semitism—if it is one—came into public consciousness during the recent New York school strikes. The teachers' union is predominantly Jewish; it struck in protest against a decentralization plan that is supposed to give blacks increased authority over the next generation of ghetto schools. The stated complaint of the union was that teachers' professional qualifications would be compromised if black community groups gained the power to hire and fire local school staffs, at least partly on the basis of race. But the union quickly adopted a different unofficial line with strong racist overtones. White radicals who "broke" the strike picket lines to support the black position were harassed and in some cases physically attacked by white teachers, who called them "nigger-lovers."

New York has the largest Jewish population of any city in the world (including Tel Aviv), and anti-black feeling runs high. It is fanned by events in the Middle East; blacks tend to sympathize with the Muslims of the Third World, but white New York is solidly pro-Israel. The mass-circulation newspapers never deviate from support of Israel, but one small radio station that appeals to the hip/radical underground chanced to let a black schoolteacher read an anti-Semitic poem (dedicated to the head of the teachers' union), and hell broke loose. The station—one of the few in the country that is supported by listener-donations and has no commercial advertising—may lose its license. Then the old gray Metropolitan Museum of Art published a catalogue for its show of Harlem photographs, and the introduction—written by a Harlem schoolgirl—contained a criticism of Jewish shopkeepers. "Fun City" has suddenly become a winter festival of Jewish paranoia.

What few Jews understand is that in the half-century since most of them came to America as an oppressed minority, their situation has so changed that to today's underclass they are inextricably part of the oppressing class. Enough Jews act like gentiles of comparable status to make the differences of motives and mentality irrelevant to the distant black poor. Jews fight "bussing" of children for school integration with the same tenacity as Irish-Americans or Italian-Americans. Long before black anti-Semitism was an issue, worshippers at one fairly enlightened synagogue in Connecticut raised an unholy stink when their leftist rabbi invited a black militant to speak. If the Jews' hearts are in the right place, the Negroes can't see the anatomical difference.

Racism in American life is not a sometime thing. It is integrated into every institution in the society, and well-intentioned Jewish liberals are as complicit in its operation as Southern segregationists. "Black anti-Semitism" is hardly an evil comparable in its social effect to the pattern of oppression of blacks in the US. Jews will be taunted and may suffer some personal pain, but they now enjoy virtually every "opportunity" for social and economic status, while blacks are light-years away from equality.

What in many ways is just as frightening as black anti-Semitism itself is the "issue" that surrounds it. Liberal intellectuals (the *Commentary* types) have begun to use the "issue" to bait black and white radicals. Confrontation politics, Earl Raab says, has produced a pre-fascist atmosphere that gives rise to black anti-Semitism now and God-knows-what later. The argument parallels (and often specifically recalls) the notion that the communists in Germany brought Hitler to power. Of course it could happen here, but if it does the black and white radicals will not have produced fascism like a rabbit from a hat.

February 7, 1969, NEW STATESMAN

✦

The Year of the Heroic Convict

The Oakland 7, the Fort Hood 43, the Catonsville 9, the Milwaukee 14, the Presidio 27, the SF State 486, the Moses Hall 3: they sound like athletic clubs, but they are teams in a different American league, formed to play the new national game of resistance. It's not much fun. The players have been grouped by the police and the courts to stand trial, at one level or another, for crimes of resistance, disruption and insurgency. Defense is tedious, expensive and demoralizing; worst of all, it is usually conducted in vain. The jails are filling; in this game, the rules are stacked against all the players.

The Year of the Heroic Guerrilla gave way logically to the Year of the Heroic Convict. Last season's street-fighters are today's defendants. For instance, the Oakland 7 are charged with conspiracy (a felony) to commit the minor acts of disruption (misdemeanors) that occurred during Stop the Draft Week in October of 1967. If any of the seven were actually involved in the demonstrations, they hardly thought of themselves as secret plotters. Articles were written detailing and discussing every aspect of protest theory and strategy. But Stop the Draft Week was too clearly successful: white radicals took to the streets for the first time in formations less containable than marching columns. Demonstration leaders no longer "cooperated" with police captains to keep protest within manageable bureaucratic limits. In response, the police set upon the demonstrators with chemicals and clubs, and the Oakland judicial establishment followed later with indictments.

Others were caught in different acts, but all were finding new ways to challenge policies and institutions that had long ago adjusted to the conventional tactics of petitions, vigils and polite marches. The Fort Hood 43 (that team's membership varies with the legal maneuvers) are black soldiers who refused to go to Chicago last summer to search-and-destroy white and black demonstrators at the Democratic convention. The Presidio 27 are charged with "mutiny" for objecting to the murder of their fellow prisoner in the army stockade in San Francisco. The Catonsville (Maryland) and Milwaukee groups are accused of destroying Selective Service records in their symbolic protest against the war system. The Moses Hall 3 are charged with conspiracy in leading the protests against the ban on Eldridge Cleaver's lectureship at Berkeley (the Alameda County prosecution gave the case a nice ironic twist by indicting representatives of different political factions, who do not speak to one another, let alone agree on strategy). The San Francisco State College 486, together with the 173 arrested earlier, were busted for attending a political meeting on the campus in the face of a prohibition on their freedom to assemble.

The game does not end with league play. Singly and in twos and threes, local and state prosecutors and military authorities have been picking up political activists and cultural antagonists on the handiest charges. Two dozen draft resisters are indicted each week in San Francisco. There were over 50,000 pot arrests in the State of California last year. Jails are beginning to look like college dormitories (the reverse phenomenon had been noted long ago) as they fill up with white youths with droopy mustaches and blacks with bushy Afros. In San Francisco's city jail, for example, guards have abandoned their insistence on clean shaves and short haircuts: "hair" is now reluctantly accepted as a useful safety valve for the energies of resistance. On a recent weekend I visited a prisoner there, the crowd of convicts and their visitors seemed to have been abstracted, in essence and actuality, from the very heart of the Bay Area hip-black-radical community. Prison visiting rooms—along with rock-and-roll ballrooms and airport boarding lounges—have become the grounds of assembly of the new generation.

Few radical actors or militant black leaders are working these days without the threat of legal prosecution over their heads, or actual charges on their shoulders. How it all affects their work is the crucial question of the Movement this year. Unschooled and indisposed for real conspiracy, the new radicals are vulnerable targets for the authorities they seem to threaten. The Movement's openness has been its genius: it has been a creative characteristic until now, and it may soon become a fatal one.

February 3-10, 1969, MAYDAY

✦

Football, American Rules

Sixty million Americans plugged themselves into their television sets one afternoon this past January to see Joe Namath play football in a Miami stadium. A few days later a crowd only a fraction of that size watched Dick Nixon's inaugural swear-in on the Capitol steps. Namath's popularity is accurately represented by that ratio: he is the unquestioned "superstar" of his generation.

Last week in a tearful press conference held in Bachelors III, the bar he owns in midtown Manhattan, Joe Namath quit professional football. "We blew it," he said later; what he meant was that he blew away an estimated $5 million in contracts with his team, the New York Jets, and commercial advertisers. Namath was, as the sportswriters say, at the peak of his career. His winning performance in that Miami Super Bowl championship game was the kind of athletic *tour de force* that wins players all the season's awards. Joe Namath won them. He was leaving football, he said, "on principle": to keep his ownership of the bar. For the overlords of organized football had found that Bachelors III was a haunt of big-time gamblers, and to protect the purity of their sport, decreed that Namath get out of the business. And nobody tells Joe Namath what to do.

In a sense, Namath merely chose one business over another. Not only does he have the bar; he owns a company that leases the franchises of Broadway Joe restaurants to local operators around the country. (Namath's share is worth about $1.4 million.) He has a thriving industry going on the basis of his "personality": a Hollywood movie, TV spots, books, advertising and personal appearances. But, as much fun as all that is, it hardly measures up to the profits of professional American-rules football.

Contracts with the major networks for television rights to the games will be worth about $37 million this year, and closer to $45 million in 1970—when, for the first time, thirteen games will be played during weekday-night "prime time" instead of the traditional Sunday afternoons. Actual attendance at the games accounts for another annual $40 million, plus or minus. The various team franchises are worth $10 million to $20 million, depending on their popularity on the open market.

Automobile manufacturers, commercial airlines and men's cosmetics firms pay large fortunes for the privilege of "sponsoring" the television broadcasts of the games. And uncounted (because illegal) millions are wagered on the games each week. All told, football is an enormous economic force, and an important cultural one, too. In the last five years or so, attendance and viewing has increased beyond predictable proportions. The Sunday-afternoon session with the tube has become every American male's home church service. Those who are bored by it all dare not admit it; football has become the last great act of personal *machismo* possible in a neuter, electronic society. The profits flow accordingly.

Joseph William Namath—once "Joe Willie," later "Broadway Joe"—is both master and victim of the football phenomenon. Now 26, he grew up in the coal-mining town of Beaver Falls, Pennsylvania; his father still pumps petrol at a corner station. After high school, he turned down a $5,000 offer to play professional baseball, then began to choose one among fifty-three universities that offered him football scholarships. He took Alabama—the "Crimson Tide"—where "Bear" Bryant was thought to be the best college football coach in the country.

Namath was a collegiate football star, and the Crimson Tide won all the appropriate championships. After graduation he signed up with the New York Jets—a member of a decidedly second-rate league—for $400,000. Now, four years later, he has created so much interest in the Jets, its league and football in general that the leagues have decided to realign themselves into new divisions of equal competence. Vast increments of income will come to the team owners and players from that move too. There was one flaw in Namath's success. Early on in the agonizingly brutal sport of pro football, his slender knees were so battered that he can now hardly climb stairs of get in and out of automobiles. He has had three knee operations, and wears bandages or braces at all times.

Still, he was having a great deal of fun. He grew his hair long, affected mod fashions and at one point appeared in public with a drooping Fu Manchu mustache, which he then agreed to remove for $10,000 in a televised commercial for an electric shaver. Football commissioner Pete Rozelle—the industry's "czar," who has been given extensive police powers—took a dim view of Namath's affectations, but he made no move until his investigators spotted the gamblers at Bachelors III. Rozelle's investigating service—directed by a former FBI agent—costs the teams $100,000 a year, which they consider money well spent to keep up the sport's clean-cut image.

But Namath always knew how selective the commissioner's code really was. Everybody gambles on football, he said at his press conference; the former owner of the Jets bet on the Super Bowl game, he told the reporters. Furthermore, the present owner is also the president of a horse-racing track in New Jersey.

Namath's resignation is this week's morality playlet. The plot makes perfect sense: a poor small-town kid wins fame and fortune with his own personal resources. Then he tells the patronizing, hypocritical millionaires who make their profits from his skill (and the silent bystanders who get their kicks from his courage) to stuff it. He sets out to torment them by making it in their own game—on his own terms. If the moral lesson is to be seen, both Namath and professional football would have to destroy themselves: the one for his hubris, the others for their crimes. Of course, neither is likely to happen. But this is America, and there's a new morality; and what will surely happen is that Namath will rescind his resignation, and go on to make more money than any petrol jockey's son ever dreamed possible, weak knees or not.

June 13, 1969, NEW STATESMAN

✦

The Real SDS Stands Up

Chicago

There have been many acts of rebellion in the American sixties, and countless scenes of insurgency, but for white radicals, the Students for a Democratic Society has always been the only show in town. Like all political shows, it is both shadowy and substantial, plagued by missed cues and tardy prompts. But SDS still speaks the lines of the young white left in this country. The material of movement is stored in its wings, and the running plays out front reflect that unique collection.

What happened in SDS's convulsive convention last week was not a death rattle but a life struggle. At stake was the survival of the radical sensibility of what used to be called the New Left—until its immediacy overcame its newness.

From the beginning, SDS has been attacked at close quarters for its self-confident, often smug independence from older and wiser heads. The League for Industrial Democracy, a moribund social-democratic (now Humphrey-Democratic) pamphleteering society, expelled SDS as its youth branch for refusing to follow an anti-communist line. Over the years, Trotskyists, communists and the range of left sects have spent much of their energies bad-mouthing the growing SDS organization. But the greatest challenge of all has come from the Progressive Labor Party, which decided four years ago to take over SDS as a youthful base for power.

To an untrained eye, PL people look much like their SDS counterparts. Although there are fewer beards, shorter hair and straighter clothes seen in PL caucuses than in SDS ones, the differences in appearance are not enormous. Distinctions begin to grow on the level of attitude and style: against SDS types, PL cadres seem mechanistic and dour, with a tone more suited to the street-corner than the street.

But the real clash comes in terms of basic views of how the world works (or doesn't). SDS people seem intuitively to recognize the variety of insurgency in the US, and while they may prefer some kinds to others, they feel a bond with the insurgents and attempt to fit their politics to a wide range of needs. Beneath all the definitions of line and strategy, SDS has always had the ability to look at radicals in their movements and say: "Us." The black rebellion, women's liberation, culture freakdom, workers' struggles, students' strikes, GI demonstrations: obviously, some must be more strategic than others, but all have a reality that PL seems determined to overlook.

PL derives its ideology not from its experience up against the American empire but (it often seems) from a detailed study of late-nineteenth-century Europe combined with an analysis of the wall posters in East-is-Red Square. No doubt post-industrial capitalism in the US has something in common with German and Russian society in the time of the kaisers and czars. Doubtless, too, the American Movement can learn a great deal from the development of the Chinese revolution, the most cataclysmic political event in the history of the modern world. But there is more to fighting the empire than the application of a labor metaphysic and a position on the Sino-Soviet split. PL peoples a Tolkien middle-earth of Marxist-Leninist hobbits and orcs, and speaks in a runic tongue intelligible only to such creatures. It is all completely consistent and utterly logical within its own confines. But that land, at last, is fantasy. The real world begins where PL ends.

PL has inherited many of the worst traits of the old left and only a few of its virtues, but it is not its ideology and derivative politics that give the most trouble: there's enough wrong-thinking all around in every part of the Movement. What is so destructive is the way in which the doctrine is applied. For some time now, PL has been organizing young people into its Worker-Student Alliance caucuses inside SDS chapters. Trained by and responsive to PL, the WSA members divert much of the organization's energy from outside action to internal hassling. Because of its emphasis on working-class revolution—and its own rigid definition of what that class is and how it functions—PL discourages support of the Black Panthers, of organizations of black workers, of black and brown community control campaigns, of anti-racist protests on campus, of Cuba and the NLF, of "people's parks," of women's liberation organizations—in short, all the activities that the Movement finds most important and attractive.

SDS has been fighting hundreds of local skirmishes with PL since the "take-over" process began, and in a few areas—Boston and the Berkeley campus, for two—the Movement tradition has lately been very much on the defensive. PL overwhelms newly politicized students with its sophisticated Marxism-Leninism on the one hand, and its simple promises of workable "work-in" programs on the other. It proclaims the inevitability of revolution in America given conditions now at hand. Like Calvin's state of grace, PL's state of socialism requires patience for salvation, not sacrifice for action (although both Calvinists and PL people feel a curious urge to work in spite of its irrelevance). In that, PL denies the central existential agony at the core of the Movement of this generation.

With its simple strategy of instant revolution by the working class and its logical and disciplined structure, PL appeals to young people who are tired of the tentative experimentalism and un-discipline of SDS organizing. More than that, the distracted and contradictory leadership of SDS's national office plays into the hands of PL's rationalized leader-base relationship: in a stormy season, a disciplined party is a comforting port for repair.

To see the divisions at last week's convention—and the eventual split between SDS and PL into rival organizations—as merely factional fights is to ignore their historical context and underlying meaning: the Movement fighting off a destructive force. To succeed, SDS had to reaffirm the traditions of native American radicalism of which it is the guardian, without losing the sense of worldwide revolution that had driven people into the streets in the first place. In mechanical terms, it had to throw off the PL incubus and accept the challenge to define its own self-conscious revolutionary ideology. Whether SDS can survive that struggle and remain a viable political organization is hard to predict now with any certainty. But what is more certain—and entirely exhilarating to the Movement "side"—is that SDS has at least taken the challenge seriously.

From the beginning, there was a *High Noon* quality to the convention week, a promise of a shoot-it-out on the Coliseum floor—if not with guns, then at least with low-caliber word-bullets and ideological grenades. Inside the ratty, batty old auditorium, it was not long before the first test of strength between PL and SDS developed. The issue was procedural, but it contained an attractive substantive twist: delegates had to vote speaking permission for Chris Milton, a young American who went to school in China and joined a platoon of the Red Guards in a "long march" through the countryside. PL was against the idea: Milton apparently espoused a "bad line" on American politics, although few of the non-PL delegates were able to tell just what was the trouble.

The most vociferous bloc in favor of Milton was the "Action Faction" of the Ohio-Michigan SDS region. At one heated point in the debate on Milton, the entire bloc—fifty people or more—jumped on their chairs, whipped out their Little Red Books, and began a joyful parody/performance of a Red Guard rally: "Ho, Ho, Ho, Chi Minh: NLF is Gonna Win!" and "Mao Tse-tung, Mao Tse-tung: Dare to Struggle, Dare to Win!" Those in the hall who could not yet identify the factions were puzzled and perhaps appalled, but the obvious hilarity on the chanters' faces placed them clearly outside the dead-serious PL style. It was the best kind of guerrilla theater, in which the action means something both for itself and for a lesson, and the spirit is both enlivening and instructive.

The Ohio-Michigan group was only one of a dozen or more major factions, tendencies and caucuses on the SDS regulars' side. To tell the players, or at least tell the plays, scorecards of a kind were provided in the appearance from time to time of proposals, resolutions, papers and uncategorizable ideological documents representing the various caucuses. The San Francisco Bay Area Revolutionary Union (called the RU) distributed its "Red Papers"; an SDS national office *groupuscule* (known as Klonsky-Coleman) passed out its "Revolutionary Youth Movement—II" proposal; and there were papers from anarchists, left-social-democrats, Harvard Marxist intellectuals, campus coalitions and local action projects.

But the most significant ideological force within SDS was a group of eleven New York and Midwestern activists and intellectuals who had drawn up an analytical and programmatic thesis called, simply, "You Don't Need a Weatherman to Know Which Way the Wind Blows" (the title is from Dylan—a characteristic weapon for that group to use against PL). "Weatherman" was a 16,000-word paper which made the first and crucial attempt of defining an ideology and a program for SDS as a movement of the most aggressive part of white radical youth. As a basic platform, it was the first major overhaul SDS has had since the "Port Huron Statement" and "America and the New Era," long ago (five years seems like a century) in the organization's post-liberal infancy and puberty.

The paper was both too short and too long, too rambling as an action guide and too sketchy for a coherent work of political philosophy. It was assertive in places where reasoned explanation was needed, and obtuse in other places where definition and delineation were required. A viscous rhetoric suffused the whole. But despite all those disabilities, Weatherman produced a valuable and honest set of notes for a native American revolutionary youth movement, in a setting of worldwide liberation struggles.

In simple summary (Weatherman itself is a barely reducible summary), the paper presented this argument: Opposition to US imperialism is the major international struggle today, and the "primary contradiction" of capitalism. Those who are leading the fight are the guerrillas of the Third World (principally, now, the Vietnamese and the Latin American *guevaristas*) and those of the "internal" black colony within the US. The empire will lose its grip as its resources are over-extended in dealing with the combined foreign and domestic rebellion. The US military and economic system cannot successfully maintain itself against intensive, expanded and protracted insurgency.

That central idea implies several consequences: first, the black liberation movement in the US is the most important element of the whole process. As part of the Third World opposition, it could eventually bring down the imperial system; the role of white radicals is primarily (although importantly) supportive and extensive.

Second, the way in which the various foreign and domestic colonies arrive at the revolutionary stage is through their own fights for "self-determination." Of course, the nature of that process is vastly different in Vietnam and black America, but in both cases the colonized community must become conscious of its own identity: that is, blacks will organize themselves separately from whites, and form whatever alliances they need on their own terms.

Third, the youth movement did not spring full-blown from abstract idealism, but is a specific response to the black movement and the worldwide "war" against the American empire: it must now reach out of its middle-class origins to a base in the white working-class and the permanent drop-out culture—without giving up what it has already done to organize students at all the "best" schools. For as the lower classes come increasingly up against the system (often symbolized by police or military authorities), they can move to fight it more surely than the "privileged" students higher up on the class ladder. Strategically, work should concentrate on building city-wide movements, based on intensive youth organizing across a whole range of issues.

Fourth, the several community "movements" should begin to think of themselves as cadres and collectives in the first stages of formation of a revolutionary political party.

In concept, Weatherman's chief distraction seemed to be in its specific reference to PL ideology. It was written in Aesopian style: each section meant something in itself, and another thing in reaction to PL. The treatment of the idea of black people in the US as a "caste" and a "colony" contained an implicit reference to PL's notion that blacks have no functional quality outside their "class" condition as super-exploited workers. The emphasis on the Third World was specifically aimed at PL's arrogant, carping criticism of the Vietnamese and Cuban revolutions.

Weatherman's ideological point-making did not grow out of an intellectual construct (as PL ideology does), but from the real concerns of SDS organizers—in their local fights with PL as well as their organizing work. PL has frustrated SDS's attempts to develop and energize the anti-war movement around the identification its members feel with the NLF. In the same way, the document tried to justify the natural inclination of SDS people to ally with the Black Panthers (and counterpart Chicano groups, such as the Young Lords in Chicago)—against the opposition of PL, which finds both the Panthers and the Lords guilty of "chauvinistic nationalism." There was some attempt—not very complete—to integrate women's liberation into the theoretical whole; for it is a movement that SDS people now find immensely important. The idea of city-wide, neighborhood-based youth organizing comes out of the Action Faction's work in the cities and campuses of Ohio, and similar operations in the New York and New Jersey area.

If it was difficult to understand Weatherman without knowing its referents in SDS's experience, it was just as hard to understand the many levels on which the convention seemed to be operating. Every procedural debate contained ideological implications and one-upmanship games that only a handful of the delegates could fathom. The "panel discussions" of the first three days degenerated into polemic-slinging contests between PL and SDS, at a rock-bottom level of debate. The one on women's liberation was a gross horror show; another on racism was little more than a screaming match.

But what went on off the platform—the things that are never reported in the straight press and rarely even in Movement papers—was the exact antithesis of the events onstage. Many of the caucuses and informal workshops on the SDS side and within WSA as well—where they were not dominated by PL cadres—worked in the close, undogmatic style that is the best tradition SDS keeps. And although very little about ideas and ideology could be learned from listening to the speakers at the podium, people did glean a great deal of understanding by bouncing ideas off one another.

The low point in the official proceedings was reached early Thursday night, when a clutch of Black Panthers arrived to speak. PL's sullen reception turned to noisy hostility when the first of the Panther speakers began baiting the delegates about women's liberation, and proceeded to promote "pussy power" as a revolutionary tactic. White delegates from the two sides all but shouted him down; a second Panther tried to retrieve the situation but drew even sharper catcalls from the audience. Finally, the third Panther combined part of an apology with an attack on white radicals' intellectual game-playing, and seemed to salvage some part of the disastrous performance. Typically, SDS people treated the affair as a healthy opening of criticism between allied movements; PL kept crying "male chauvinism"—in part, surely, as an opportune defense against the same charge SDS makes against PL ideology.

The Panthers' alliance with SDS, formalized by the white organization last winter in Austin, is a fragile affair at best. But it is the best attempt since the break-up of the "integrated" Southern student movement four years ago to align black and white radicals for joint action: this time on the basis of separate organizations with socialist ideas. Both the Panthers and SDS are anxious to preserve the relationship; the Panthers agreed to come to the convention to advance it, despite the predictable hostility from antiwhite militant forces in the black community. PL, naturally, saw the Panthers' appearance as a bald power play by Mike Klonsky, the spearhead of SDS's alliance with both the Panthers and the Young Lords. And PL's perception was reinforced Friday night, when—in an atmosphere of growing rivalry between the two sides—the Panthers reappeared for the specific purpose of attacking the PL contempt for black self-determination.

PL people screamed at SDS for its "racist" use of the Panthers as a weapon of debate; SDS shouted back that that very argument revealed PL's "racist" notion that blacks cannot arrive at their own independent politics. PL's Jeff Gordon and a wedge of supporters seized the platform. The noise level in the hall rose to new peaks of intensity, along with the tension. Mark Rudd moved to recess for the evening, and when that motion failed, the SDS walk-out began. As the delegates left, PL's cheerleaders began their last chant: "No split, no split, no split!"

Somewhat less than half the people in the meeting hall filed into the dark, dusty sports arena next door, and arranged themselves in rows of bleachers. SDS security guards were posted at the passageway connecting the adjoining rooms. No one then had the slightest idea of how the walk-out would resolve itself, but some kind of order in the "caucus" was assembled, and speakers paced the boarded floor as they shouted to the bleachers what sense they made of the move. Jim Mellen, a solemn, analytical "Weatherman," conceded that the SDS side had not acquitted itself impressively in the tactics of the split; for a while, some of the national leaders seemed to entertain fantasies of doing the whole business over again, only this time more cleanly and clearly.

It was true that neither side had acted with much nobility during the final stages of the confrontation. But if fault could be assigned in broader context, it seemed to lie with PL. Gresham's Law applies in paraphrase: bad politics drives good politics out. PL had made contributions to the Movement in its association with SDS (nobody loses all the time) but its overall effect had been deformative; it forced SDS into two years or more of reactive maneuvers, inevitably hypocritical and unproductive. So the discussion dragged on in both halls until midnight.

When the SDS side met again in the arena late Saturday morning, spirits were sailing. All night, meetings of regional groups and political blocs had given people the idea that the split was not only inevitable but somehow liberating. "We feel like we did inside one of the Columbia buildings," a girl told the crowd.

It was left to Bernardine Dohrn, one of SDS's three national secretaries, to sum up the meaning of the break and suggest a course of action. In what was obviously the outstanding political speech of the whole week, she explained the split with PL in the stream of Movement history, and claimed legitimacy for SDS as the keeper of a tradition that now was finding increasingly radical expression. The youth movement in America, she said, was spawned by black student sit-ins in the South and energized by the guerrillas of Vietnam and Cuba. It was not now going to deny its sources for the sake of PL's metaphysic. It was a thorough, tight—and devastating—job. "We are not a caucus," she said at the end. "We are SDS." And suddenly it all became true to the crowds in the bleachers, and they knew that there was no going back.

By evening, the strategy of "exclusion" was developed, and when the order was done and approved, the bleachers emptied and the SDS delegates filed silently back into the hall for the reading-out of Progressive Labor. Bernardine Dohrn presented the bill of particulars, which now seemed more like a bill of divorcement. The SDS delegates stood in aisles on the perimeters of the auditorium. The PL cadres sat scowling; the WSA kids sat uncomprehending. At the end of the order, PL people responded with a planned mass nervous giggle. Then, flanked by a dozen SDS delegates (chicks up front) who stood Panther-style on the podium, Bernardine Dohrn started to speak in explanation of the exclusion. But after initial attempts to quiet hecklers, the PL leaders began to cheerlead the hecklers themselves, and the speech sputtered to its conclusion: "Long live the victory of the people's war!" From Dylan to Lin Piao in forty-eight hours.

For the last day of the convention, PL met in the Coliseum to ponder the most perplexing strategic question in its history: What to do about its coveted "mass base," which had suddenly cut out? In a church across town, around the corner from its national office, SDS met in a much more upbeat mood. A tentative list of unity "principles" was drawn up for circulation and discussion at the local chapter level; national demonstrations against the war were set for Chicago in late September, to coincide with the beginning of the Chicago 8 conspiracy trial. Delegates took on the continuing problem of leader-base relations between the SDS national office and the local chapters. Finally, a slate of three national secretaries and an eight-man national interim committee was elected. All three secretaries—Mark Rudd, Jeff Jones and Bill Ayers—had been "Weathermen."

The significance of their election lies in that document. Although it never came up for convention action of any kind, it was an expression (chief among many) of the crucial theme of the week: the attempt to begin work on a New Left revolutionary socialist ideology and program. SDS's main problems have grown up in the failure to do that job. It has never really defined what it is—and how it differs from, say, Progressive Labor. And for that neglect, SDS alumni have strayed, because SDS could not identify itself as the critical center of the Movement.

The reasons SDS has failed so far in those respects are for the most part good ones. The original tensions within the Movement between personal liberation and political mobilization still play themselves out at every level. SDS contains both traits. What has to happen finally for SDS to survive is an integration of those traditions, probably in response to outside challenge and as a result of internal synthesis. Only then will the New Left become an American liberation movement.

June 30–July 5, 1969, HARD TIMES

✦

We Aim at the Stars (But Hit Quang Tri)

A t certain moments in history, the rules of irony transcend even the laws of Nature, the writ of God and the operation of the Dialectic. The landing of the module Eagle in the Sea of Tranquillity (or was it Bethpage, Long Island?) seems to be just such an epochal cusp. As America's society breaks apart, America's technology comes perfectly together. The proportion is exactly inverse: to the degree that social values collapse, in the same degree do computer values take hold.

There is no cause to deny the impressive engineering feat performed by the space planners or denigrate the competence and courage of the astronauts. A walk on the moon is every bit as difficult as a swim across the English Channel; a moon landing is certainly as complicated as the construction of the Golden Gate Bridge—if considerably less useful to real people afterwards. But neither history nor *The New York Times* records that a twenty-three-mile Australian crawl or the swing of a long suspension cable is equivalent to the emergence of earth-animals from the primordial ooze.

The idea that Neil Armstrong's "one small step for man" represents an evolutionary quantum leap seems to derive from the movie *2001*, and it's no wonder: Arthur C. Clarke devised both the theme of the film and the theory of space visits. But Clarke was dealing in metaphors. The *Times* really believes the whole shuck:

"It [the moon trip] is a *willed* step in the evolutionary process, one made deliberately and in the full consciousness of its import. . . . There are comparable precedents in nature, though for one as full of meaning for the future one might have to go back to the first fishy creature that emerged from the Devonian sea to make a feeble try at life on dry land."

That was on Sunday. The next day, still drowning in its own Devonian imagery, the *Times* wrote: "In the long evolution of the human race up from the primeval ooze, no more significant step has ever been taken than yesterday's when man the worldling truly became but 'little lower than the angels' and first set foot upon another planet." If there is any doubt where the ideology underlying such extravagance comes from, Bernard Weinraub made it clear in his interview with Dr. Kurt H. Debus, 'the little-known director of the Kennedy Space Center who was a rocket expert under the Nazis in World War II."

"We have come out of the ocean in our past history and have taken over the land," Debus said. "We have left the land and taken over the air and have moved mankind really together." (Readers can supply their own dialect imitations.)

Aside from its small error (the moon is not a planet) and its large absurdity, the *Times*/Debus thesis is monstrously inhumane. And not only editorial writers have been taken in; a kind of technological Hitlerism has taken hold of everyone in Apollo's shadow, from Walter Cronkite to Ralph Abernathy. In essence, it is a "willed" disregard for the agony of that obsolete creature, human being, in favor of the adulation of a new Uebermensch: Spaceman. With uncommon hubris and uncontrolled *chutzpah*, the space planners have defined "evolution" as a rocket ride, and have themselves decided it is imperial America's "national purpose." Today, Bethpage, Long Island. Tomorrow, the worlds.

It's appropriate to see the whole lunar hype in terms of the media—the *Times* and CBS—because the moon landing is really more an event in media history than in chordate evolution. As a television entertainment, it left a lot to be desired (personally, I liked the assassinations much better—much more televisual, with blood, death, fire, insurrection and horses). But the moon "epic" was the ultimate *media* event. At that great moment in universal history, 500 million people were watching a relayed television picture of a television camera televising one robot-astronaut photographing another.

If Walter Cronkite were honest, he'd have to admit that the moon landing was less important, and certainly less exciting, than Denny McLain's last winning inning, or the moment when a torero faces the bull alone, or the rush across Grant Park to the Conrad Hilton, or the cure of one case of lymphocarcinoma, or the birth of a baby. It had to be *made* to touch people by the amplifications of the media. Mankind was programmed last weekend, just as surely as Eagle was, or Luna 15.

Why the wizards of ooze want us all to be programmed should not be hard to imagine. For one thing, it allows them to spend scores of billions in a way that swells the profits of the biggest military/space corporations without changing the system of distribution of those profits one whit. The old liberal criticism of the space program on the basis of its diversion of public expenditures from public works and welfare is good-natured but irrelevant. The $24 billion (probably a lot more, counting disguised costs) spent on Apollo would never have been put to better use, any more than the money "saved" by ending the war in Vietnam would be spent on worthier causes. Welfare doesn't increase profits; hardware manufacture does.

For another thing, and all too obviously, the nauseating togetherness of the space trip seems to dull the edge of discontent, at least in the short run. Ralph Abernathy got thirty seats in the VIP section at Cape Kennedy for his SCLC poor-campaigners, along with Governor Kirk of Florida, Jack Benny, Spiro Agnew, the L.B. Johnsons and other assorted worldlings. Abernathy returned the compliment. "For a moment," he said, "I forgot about poverty." In the longer run, media-glut kills the capacity for discontent. If post-humans can be programmed to plant an American flag in a simulated flapping mode in a flapless environment, they can be made to do anything—or nothing.

Is it all over for man?—man of the Lascaux caves and the Pyramids, of the Agora and the Forum, of Horyuji and Angkor Wat and the Benin temples, of the Globe Theater and the Fillmore and the Roxy? Does it end in a funless farm twenty feet beneath the lunar phenocryst? Mission Control is trying to kill fantasy by mediating reality. Grumman Aviation wants to destroy illusions by simulating certainties. Kurt H. Debus wants the whole world to look like airports, and all the people in it like the computer freaks who swarm around Cape Kennedy and Downey, California, and Route 128, and Bethpage, Long Island. Dick and Pat don't even have the imagination to be as funny and awful as Ferdinand and Isabella. ("Hello, Chris and Amerigo. This has got to be the most historic phone call ever made from Seville . . .") It's been downhill for him since Checkers.

Walter Cronkite certainly wants everyone to enter the programmed age. At the moment of touchdown, all he could think of was a put-down: "I wonder what all those kids who pooh-poohed this program are saying now?" he said, rising slightly from his ooze. And maybe it is all over, for if the kids had any spirit left in them they would have broken every television set in sight, smashed every transmitter, and burst into CBS Grumman space simulation headquarters in Bethpage, Long Island, screaming as loud and as long as they could: "POOH POOH."

July 28–August 4, 1969, HARD TIMES

✦

Coming of Age in Aquarius

I looked at my watch, I looked at my wrist,
I punched myself in the face with my fist;
I took my potatoes down to be mashed—
And made it on over to that million-dollar bash.
                                        —Dylan

The Woodstock Music and Art Fair wasn't held in Woodstock; the music was secondarily important; the art was for the most part unproduced; and it was much of a fair as the French Revolution or the San Francisco earthquake. What went down on Max Yasgur's farm in the lower Catskills last weekend defied casual categories and conventional perceptions. Some monstrous and marvelous metaphor had come alive, revealing itself only in terms of its contradictions: paradise and concentration camp, sharing and profiteering, sky and mud, love and death. The urges of the ten years' generation roamed the woods and pastures, and who could tell whether it was some rough beast or a speckled bird slouching toward its Day-Glo manger to be born?

The road from the Hudson River west to White Lake runs through hills like green knishes, soft inside with good earth, and crusty with rock and wood on top. What works of man remain are rural expressions of an Other

East Village, where the Mothers were little old ladies with *sheitls*, not hip radicals with guns. There's Esther Manor and Siegel's Motor Court and Elfenbaum's Grocery: no crash communes or head shops. Along that route, a long march of freaks in microbuses, shit-cars and bikes—or on thumb and foot—passed like movie extras in front of a process screen. On the roadside, holiday-makers from the Bronx looked up from their pinochle games and afghan-knitting and knew that the season of the witch had come.

"Beatniks out to make it rich": Woodstock was, first of all, an environment created by a couple of hip entrepreneurs to consolidate the culture revolution and extract the money of its troops. Michael Lang, a 25-year-old former heavy dealer from Bensonhurst, dreamed it up; he then organized the large inheritance of John Roberts, 26, for a financial base, and brought in several more operatives and financiers. Lang does not distinguish between hip culture and hip capital; he vowed to make a million before he was 25, beat his deadline by two years and didn't stop. With his Village/Durango clothes, a white Porsche and a gleaming BSA, he looks, acts and *is* hip; his interest in capital accumulation is an extension of every hippie's desire to rip off a bunch of stuff from the A&P. It's a gas.

The place-name "Woodstock" was meant only to evoke cultural-revolutionary images of Dylan, whose home base is in that Hudson River village. Woodstock is where The Band hangs out and the culture heroes congregate; it's where Mick Jagger (they say) once ate an acid-infused Baby Ruth right inside the crotch of a famous groupie. A legend like that is good for ticket sales, but the festival was always meant to be held in Wallkill, New York, forty miles away.

By early summer Woodstock looked to be the super rock festival of all time, and promoters of a dozen other summertime festivals were feverishly hyping up their own projects to catch the overflow of publicity and enthusiasm: rock music (al fresco or recorded) is still one of the easiest ways to make money off of the new culture, along with boutique clothes and jewelry, posters, drugs and trip equipment, *Esquire*, Zig-Zag papers and Sara Lee cakes. But the Woodstock hype worried the burghers of Wallkill, and the law implemented their fears by kicking the bash out of town. Other communities were either less uptight or more greedy; six hard offers for sites came to the promoters the day Wallkill gave them the boot. With less than a month to get ready, Woodstock Ventures, Inc., chose the 600-acre Yasgur farm (with some other parcels thrown in) at White Lake.

Locals there were divided on the idea, and Yasgur was attacked by some neighbors for renting (for a reported $50,000) to Woodstock. But in the end, the profit motive drove the deal home. One townsman wrote to the Monticello newspaper: "It's none of their business how Max uses his land. If they are so worried about Max making a few dollars from his land they should try to take advantage of this chance to make a few dollars themselves. They can rent camping space or even sell water or lemonade."

Against fears of hippie horrors, businessmen set promises of rich rewards: "Some of these people are shortsighted and don't understand what these children are doing," he said. "The results will bring an economic boost to the County, without it costing the taxpayer a cent."

The vanguard of freaks started coming a week or more before opening day, and by Wednesday they were moving steadily down Route 17B, like a busy day on the Ho Chi Minh Trail. The early-comers were mostly hard-core, permanent drop-outs: their hair or their manner or their rap indicated that they had long ago dug into their communes or radical politics or simply into oppositional life styles. In the cool and clear night they played music and danced, and sat around fires toasting joints and smoking hashish on a pinpoint. No busts, pigs or hassle; everything cool, together, outasight.

By the end of the next day, Thursday, the ambience had changed from splendor in the grass to explosive urban sprawl. Light and low fences erected to channel the crowds without actually seeming to oppress them were toppled or ignored; cars and trucks bounced over the meadows; tents sprung up between stone outcroppings and cow plop. Construction went on through the night, and already the Johnny-on-the-Spot latrines were smelly and out of toilet paper, the food supply was spotty, and long lines were forming at the water tank. And on Friday morning, when the population explosion was upon us all, a sense of siege took hold: difficult as it was to get in, it would be almost impossible to leave for days.

From the beginning, the managers of the festival were faced with the practical problem of control. Berkeley and Chicago and Zap, North Dakota, were the functional models for youth mobs rampaging at the slightest provocation—or no provocation at all. The promoters interviewed 800 off-duty New York City policemen for a security guard (Sample question: "What would you do if a kid walked up to you and blew marijuana smoke in your face?" Incorrect answer: "Bust him." Correct answer: "Inhale deeply and smile."), chose 300 or so, and fitted them with mod uniforms. But at the last minute they were withdrawn under pressure from the police department, and the managers had to hire camp counselors, phys ed teachers and stray straights from the surrounding area.

The guards had no license to use force or arrest people; they merely were to be "present," in their red Day-Glo shirts emblazoned with the peace symbol, and could direct traffic and help out in emergencies if need be. The real work of keeping order, if not law, was to be done by members of the Hog Farm commune, who had been brought from New Mexico, along with people from other hippie retreats, in a chartered airplane (at $16,000) and psychedelic buses from Kennedy Airport.

Beneath the practical problem of maintaining order was the principal contradiction of the festival: how to stimulate the energies of the new culture and profit thereby, and at the same time control them. In a way, the Woodstock venture was a test of the ability of avant-garde capitalism at once to profit from and control the insurgencies that its system spawns. "Black capitalism," the media industry, educational technology and Third World economic development are other models, but more diffuse. Here it was in one field during one weekend: the microcosmic system would "fail" if Woodstock Ventures lost its shirt, or if the control mechanisms broke down.

The promoters must have sensed the responsibility they carried. They tried every aspect of co-optation theory. SDS, Newsreel and underground newspapers were handed thousands of dollars to participate in the festival, and they were given a choice spot for a "Movement City." The idea was that they would give hip legitimacy to the weekend and channel their activities "within the system." (They bought the idea.) Real cops were specifically barred from the camp grounds, and the word went out that there would be no busts for ordinary tripping, although big dealers were discouraged. There would be free food, water, camping facilities—and, in the end, free music, when attempts at crowd-channeling failed. But the Hog Farmers were the critical element. Hip beyond any doubt, they spread the love/groove ethic throughout the farm, breaking up incipient actions against "the system" with cool, low-key hippie talk about making love not war, the mystical integrity of earth and the importance of doing your *own* thing, preferably alone. They were the only good organizers in camp. They ran the free food organization (oats, rice and bulgur), helped acid-freaks through bad trips without Thorazine and (with Abbie Hoffman) ran the medical system when that became necessary.

The several dozen Movement organizers at the festival had nothing to do. After Friday night's rain there was a theory that revolt was brewing on a mass scale, but the SDS people found themselves unable to organize around the issue of inclement weather. People were objectively trapped, and in that partial aspect the Yasgur farm *was* a concentration camp—or a hippie reservation—but almost everyone was stoned and happy. Then the rain stopped, the music blared, food and water arrived, and everyone shared what he had. Dope became plentiful and entirely legitimate; in a soft, cool forest, where craftsmen had set up their portable head shops, dealers sat on tree stumps selling their wares: "acid, mesc, psilocybin, hash . . ." No one among the half-million could not have turned on if he wanted to; joints were passed from blanket to blanket, lumps of hashish materialized like manna, and there was Blue Cheer, Sunshine acid and pink mescaline to spare.

Seen from any edge or angle, the army strung out against the hillside sloping up from the stage created scenes almost unimaginable in common-place terms. No day's demonstration or political action had brought these troops together; no congress or cultural event before produced such urgent need for in-gathering and self-inspection. The ambiguities and contradictions of the imposed environment were worrisome, but to miss the exhilaration of a generation's arrival at its own campsite was to define the world in only one dimension.

Although the outside press saw only masses, inside the differentiation was more impressive. Maybe half the crowd was weekend-hip, out from Long Island for a quick dip in the compelling sea of freaks. The other half had longer been immersed. It was composed of tribes dedicated to whatever gods now seem effective and whatever myths produce the energy needed to survive: Meher Baba, Mother Earth, street-fighting man, Janis Joplin, Atlantis, Jimi Hendrix, Che.

The hillside was their home. Early one Saturday morning, after the long night of rain—from Ravi Shankar through Joan Baez—they still had not abandoned the turf. Twenty or forty thousand people (exactitude lost its meaning; it was that sight, not the knowledge of the numbers, that was so staggering) sat stonily silent on the muddy ground, staring at a stage where no one played.

No one in this country in this century had ever seen a "society" so free of repression. Everyone swam nude in the lake, balling was easier than getting breakfast, and the "pigs" just smiled and passed out the oats. For people who had never glimpsed the intense communitarian closeness of a militant struggle—People's Park or Paris in the month of May or Cuba—Woodstock must always be their model of how good we will all feel after the revolution.

So it was an illusion and it wasn't. For all but the hard core, the ball and the balling is over; the hassles begin again at Monticello. The repression-free weekend was provided by promoters as a way to increase their take, and it will not be repeated unless future profits are guaranteed (it's almost certain now that Woodstock Ventures lost its wad). The media nonsense about death and ODs has already enraged the guardians of the old culture. The system didn't change; it just accommodated the freaks for the weekend.

What is not illusionary is the reality of a new culture of opposition. It grows out of the disintegration of the old forms, the vinyl and aerosol institutions that carry all the inane and destructive values of privatism, competition, commercialism, profitability and elitism. The new culture has yet to produce its own institutions on a mass scale; it controls none of the resources to do so. For the moment, it must be content—or discontent—to feed the swinging sectors of the old system with new ideas, with rock and dope and love and openness. Then it all comes back, from Columbia Records or Hollywood or Bloomingdale's in perverted and degraded forms. But something will survive, because there's no drug on earth to dispel the nausea. It's not a "youth thing" now but a generational event; chronological age is only the current phase. Mass politics, it's clear, can't yet be organized around the nausea; political radicals have to see the cultural revolution as a sea in which they can swim, like black militants in "black culture." But the urges are roaming, and when the dope freaks and nude swimmers and loveniks and ecological cultists and music groovers find out that they have to fight for love, all fucking hell will break loose.

August 25–September 1, 1969, HARD TIMES

Going Down in Chicago

I prefer the philanthropy of Captain John Brown to that philan-
thropy which neither shoots me nor liberates me. . . . I do not wish to
kill nor to be killed, but I can foresee circumstances in which both
these things would be by me unavoidable. We preserve the so-called
peace of our community by deeds of petty violence every day. Look at
the policeman's billy and handcuffs! Look at the jail! . . . We are hop-
ing only to live safely on the outskirts of this provisional army. So we
defend ourselves and our hen-roosts, and maintain slavery. I know
that the mass of my countrymen think that the only righteous use
that can be made of Sharpe's rifles and revolvers is to fight duels
with them when we are insulted by other nations, or to hunt
Indians, or shoot fugitive slaves with them, or the like. I think that
for once the Sharpe's rifles and revolvers were employed in a right-
eous cause. The tools were in the hands of one who could use them. . . .
The same indignation that is said to have cleared the temple once
will clear it again. The question is not about the weapon, but the
spirit in which you use it.

—Henry David Thoreau, 1859

There were twelve people in our two-man cell at the Chicago police head-quarters last Saturday after the SDS Weatherman march through the Loop. Our charges ran from disorderly conduct (my own) through possession of explosives to attempted murder. The styles and situations of the dozen were as widely disparate as the charges: a black student (explosives) in bou-tique bell-bottoms stretched out cooly on one of the two wooden benches, sur-veying the rest of us with amusement as well as attachment. A long-haired New York Weatherman, who said he had written and produced a musical version of the Columbia University insurrection, skillfully sang both the instrumental and vocal parts of Cream's "I Feel Free." A very young, very rich kid (mob action) spouted heroic slogans intermittently during a compul-sive, anxious monologue about himself. An uncommonly tender gang type from a Michigan Weatherman collective washed a cell-mate's wounds with wet toilet paper and went to sleep on the crowded cement floor. Brian Flanagan, a bright and sensitive upper-middle "moderate" who found his way inside a Columbia building last year and had now come to be charged with attempted murder (of Chicago's toughest judicial figure), rested in another corner, dealing quietly with his own fear and a large still-bleeding gash in his head.

The events of the afternoon were common to us all, whether we had been busted in the La Salle Street melée or a mile away (as I and two friends were). Solidarity and spirit grew easily from the experience of fear and force; it was expressed through the long first night in jail with songs and chants and good talking. But beyond the fellow-feeling and gallows humor, much more drastic changes were running down within us, and they could not be expressed at all, at least not then and there. The protean rebellion that was born ten years ago in the South; that found forms to fit the Mississippi Delta, the Cleveland slums, the Berkeley campus, the hundred colleges and parks and army posts; that appeared bloody last summer in Grant Park and stoned this summer at Woodstock: it ran that day in the Loop. Almost everyone else now thinks that the spirit of the sixties has found its end, but at night in the cell-block, we believed that it had found a new beginning.

Weatherman demands the willing suspension of disbelief. As an ideology of communism and a strategy of revolution, it shatters the reliable categories of thought and modes of action that white radicals have developed in the last ten years. It challenges the validity of an intellectual left, which functions as a comfortable culture of opposition; instead, it asks that radicals become revolutionaries, completely collectivize their lives and struggle to death if necessary. Nothing could be more threatening to the investments of thought and action that Movement people have made. Weatherman asks them to leap— in life-expectations as well as political ideas—over a distance fully as wide as that which they crossed from liberalism (or whatever) into the Movement.

Since the civil rights movement moved North in 1964, white radicals have been working within a politics that was defined in SDS's ERAP community organizing projects in Newark, Cleveland, Uptown Chicago and a half-dozen other urban centers. Although the organizers used some revolutionary rhetoric, they were never able to find a strategy for mobilizing masses of people to restructure "the institutions that control their lives." Marches, sit-ins, tenant strikes and election campaigns inconvenienced but did not seriously threaten the welfare departments, housing agencies and city administrations against which they were directed. At length, the project workers— mostly white college kids—realized that those institutions could not be overhauled without wholesale shifts in power inside the "system" itself.

Since ERAP began to dissolve in 1966 and 1967, radical organizers have used basically the same strategy in other areas: campus strikes, draft resistance, army base movements. The common principle was the organization of people in one locale (or in various branches of the same essential locale) to change the immediate institution that most oppressed them. It was hoped that such action might lead, in an always undefined way, to a chain reaction of structural changes throughout the whole system. But, of course, nothing like that ever happened.

Taken together, that effort can hardly be counted a political failure, even if it did not accomplish its rhetorical objectives. What did happen was the creation of a race of radical organizers who are extraordinarily competent to do the work that their strategy defines. But there are obvious limits to the strategy, and after years of operational failures, a feeling of frustration and even desperation has set in. Many of the early organizers went off to the peripheries of politics: journalism, the academy, legal aid, teaching or even "liberal" government welfare jobs. Others went completely into personal "lifestyle" retreats in one or another wooded grove.

As the repository of the political forms in the Movement, SDS has been struggling to break out of the frustration of repeated failure—or at least dispiriting un-success. The factionalism that has now become rampant is a direct result of that situation; politics without promise rapidly loses its coherence. Weatherman is the newest and most adventurous expression of that frustration. It is, in theory and practice, a revolutionary "army," and it flaunts that notion: "Come to Chicago. Join the Red Army," its leaflets called out.

The life-arrangements that have been built to deal with both the personal and political consequences of Weatherman are collectives—numbering now about a dozen in Ohio, Michigan, Illinois, New York, Maryland, Washington State and Colorado. The intensity with which they work is almost indescribable; they are crucibles of theory and practice, action and self-criticism, loving and working. They are widely experimental: some now are considering rules against men and women living as "couples"—a form of privatism that inhibits total collectivization. Often, members of collectives are revving at such high speed and intensity that they sleep only every other night; the rest of the time they are working—reading, criticizing, writing, travelling, pushing out the problems of the collective and talking to other people.

The Weatherman perspective treats collectives as "pre-party" organizations, building eventually to a fighting communist party. A structure of leadership is developing with the Weather Bureau at the top, regional staffs under that, and the collectives providing local cadre. The principle of authority is a form of "democratic centralism," with as much self-criticism thrown in as anyone can bear—probably *more* than anyone can bear.

But despite that formal plan, Weatherman is still primarily an organizing strategy, not a fighting force. Heavy actions are undertaken more for their "exemplary" effect on potential Weatherpeople than for their "material" aid to the Vietcong. Weatherman wants to get at high school and community-college drop-outs—not middle-class university kids—and it believes that the way to do it is to convince them that they can fight the authorities who daily oppress them: cops, principals, bosses.

There's no denying antagonism to Weatherman within the radical left—not to mention the sheer horror with which liberals and conservatives view it. In some places—Detroit, for instance—unweatherized radicals have tried to form coalitions specifically aimed at destroying Weatherman. Some of the best New Left radicals believe that Weatherman is destroying (or has destroyed) the Movement. Movement spokesmen, such as the *Guardian* and Liberation News Service, are almost viciously anti-Weatherman; the underground press, for the most part, thinks Weatherman is positively insane. Such hostility is more than mere factionalism. It represents total rejection of Weatherman's revolutionary form.

Weatherman itself doesn't help matters. Perhaps because of the intensity of their own lives, its members cannot accept the relative lethargy of other radicals. More than that, Weathermen have built such elaborate political and emotional defenses against their fears of death and imprisonment that any challenge to the meaning of their work directly threatens their identities. It is obvious that Weatherman is quasi-religious and "fanatic" in a way; the members see those who stand apart as the early Christians must have seen the pagans. It is difficult to die for a cause that your peers reject.

The Movement's antagonism is particularly wounding because Weatherman has so far failed to attract the large numbers of people it hoped would follow "up-front" fighting. All summer and in the early fall, Weatherman tried to organize its drop-out constituency by running through schoolrooms yelling, "Jail break!", fighting with hostile kids and carrying NLF flags down beaches literally looking for trouble. When trouble came, the Weathermen fought, and in many instances "won," but the actions did not mobilize the hordes of kids the organizers had expected. There were famous Weatherman horror shows: in Pittsburgh, where members ran through a school and were arrested with no organizing effect; and in Detroit, where a group of Weatherwomen (now called the Motor City 9) entered an examination room in a community college, locked the doors, subdued the teacher and then took two hostile male students out of action with karate blows.

It's hard, too, for many outsiders to grasp the dramatic—often comic—quality of Weatherman's political style. That element has carried through into all aspects of weathering, so that at times it is difficult to tell whether the entire phenomenon may not be a gigantic psychodrama. Most Weathermen, in their own self-criticism sessions, are aware of the dangers of the emotional "trip" that revolutionism entails. At a meeting one night during the Chicago weekend, speaker after speaker warned against the "death trip" or the "*machismo* trip" or the "violence trip."

Because Weatherman is still so young, it would be fatuous to condemn it as worthless or elevate it to heroic proportions. Its contradictions are apparent, even to most Weathermen, who are defensive outside their collectives but truly self-exploring within. What seems most troublesome right now is Weatherman's simple-mindedness about the varieties of political experience in America; as revolutionaries usually discover, violent struggle and less intense organizing are not mutually exclusive. Other radical groups are still producing organizers who can serve a variety of functions; to put all radical eggs in a weatherbasket would be unutterably foolish.

Nor is there much evidence that violence can mobilize thousands of kids, even in Weatherman's chosen drop-out pool. Real revolutionaries have a contempt for violence, not an adoration of it; it is used only as a last resort, as a response to specific oppression. As yet, most people do not comprehend the relationship of the police in America to the B-52s in Vietnam. A revolutionary party finds its moral authority in leading an oppressed people in retaliation against their intolerable oppressors: that's how the Vietcong did it in Vietnam and how People's Democracy is doing it in Northern Ireland. To most people outside, Weatherman is a vanguard floating free of a mass base.

But there's more to it than that. What appeal Weatherman has comes in part from its integration of the two basic streams of the movements of the sixties—political mobilization and personal liberation. Since the break-up of the ERAP projects, few radical organizations have been able to contain and combine both streams. Those in the "liberation" stream have gone off on private trips; those in the political stream have been reduced to old left sloganeering and dreary demonstrations. Weatherman does break through, with its liberating collective sensibility and its active mobilization. However disastrous or brilliant its strategy may turn out to be, its spirit, purposefulness and integrity ought to command respect.

I had come to Chicago last week to see the range of actions planned in and around the trial of the conspiracy—the eight men charged with conspiring to incite a riot at last year's Democratic convention. The trial itself is a depressing affair, as political trials almost have to be—played as they are on hostile turf with no real chance of gaining the offensive. Slogans such as "Stop the Trial" seem too inflated even to shout, and except for a spirited action on opening day staged by the Panthers outside the Federal Building (Bobby Seale is one of the "conspirators"), radicals have stayed away in droves. Meanwhile, the defendants are picking up support from *Life* and *Time* and liberal civil-libertarians—all of which may be helpful to them but does not seem to move the radical movements this year.

The Weatherman march was political psychodrama of the best and worst kind. It began dully at the site of the statue of the Chicago policeman, a singular symbol of power, in Haymarket Square, which had been blown up earlier in the week. It was hard not to fear that Weatherman's history might be as tragic as the Knights of Labor or the Wobblies; that it would never even have the trigger effect of John Brown's raid; that before it developed, death or long prison sentences would cut off the experiment at its inception.

The crowd was small and the weather was cold and wet. Just after noon, a posse of plainclothes detectives fell upon the small crowd of marchers and arrested Mark Rudd and several other Weatherman leaders. No one was at all sure that the march would ever happen. Then from around a corner came the sound of shouts and cheers, and a brigade of about a hundred Weathermen burst into the street, fists raised, chanting and laughing: "Ho, Ho, Ho Chi Minh . . ." Then there was a send-off speech, and people joined arms and stepped quickly down the street into the deserted Loop. After a mile of marching, the column suddenly lurched, and there was fighting and rock-throwing and wailing sirens and the paddy-wagons were soon filled to overflowing. For an hour afterwards, police picked up Weathertypes on the streets and brought them in on various minor and serious charges.

Now some say that the police attacked first, and others say that the Weathermen took the offensive, but it is true that the Weathermen did not shrink from the fight, and we all thought in the cell-block that night that simply not to fear fighting is a kind of winning.

October 20-27, 1969, HARD TIMES

✦

To the Comfort Station

There was something for everyone last weekend in Washington. North Vietnam and the NLF got their big, peaceful march. The white radical movement got its street-fighting. The liberals got the speakers' platform. The Nixon-Mitchell Administration got its rocks off gassing the kids. The plate-glassed banks, brokerage houses and stores down Connecticut Avenue got their comeuppance. And the New Mobilization Committee to End the War in Vietnam, after endless negotiations, rebuffs and delays, finally got its portable toilets.

The Mobe's arrival at the comfort stations on the grounds of the Washington Monument did not signal the start of the New American Revolution. To no one's surprise, the masses of workers and peasants who marched there from the tennis courts in front of the Capitol were in a mood to do little more than raise a limp "V" sign or dance idly to plastic tunes from *Hair*. Scorpio was still in the house of Aquarius.

"Give peace a chance" was a lyric specifically appropriated by Mobe leaders in response to threats of repression by the government and predictions of trouble in the press. What has come to be known as "Mobe politics" was infused in the weekend's events by a number of subtle (and not-so-subtle) means. First, the New Mobe reversed its 1968 policy of *apertura a la sinistra* and moved precipitously to its own right. It blended easily with the post-McCarthy shades of the Moratorium and foreshadowed the colors of the pre-McGovern campaigns of the seventies. By week's end, it had successfully internalized the consciousness of the Justice Department. Mobe marshals—under the direction of peace bureaucrats—were used by federal authorities in Washington much as African natives were used by British colonial police in, say, the Gold Coast: to carry the white man's burden. The "peace pigs" were freaky and friendly, but whom were they working for? Were they us or them? Late Saturday, when 10,–15,000 people split from the monument grounds to march on the Justice Department, they were met first by Mobe marshals, not city cops—although the Mobe had explicitly disavowed participation in that march. The Mobe's chief lawyer gabbed with police officials over his walkie-talkie, and at one point he was overheard describing the demonstrators as the "hard-core helmeted few."

There were other ways, too, by which the Mobe froze the politics of the day into a moderate mold. Eugene McCarthy was chosen as the kick-off speaker in front of the Capitol, and George McGovern was a principal speaker at the rally (he had asked that numbers of the Moratorium kids sit near the platform so that he would not be pelted with stones). Except for one or two speakers, no one talked to the political consciousness of the crowd; rather, they spoke to defuse protest and drain it of militant energies. No one up there is likely to be charged with incitement—of any kind. Those few representatives of the radical movements that originated anti-war demonstrations in this decade and had given the Movement its motive force through the years were drowned in the thick Mobe soup.

The use of groovy marshals to protect Washington, not the marchers; the eagerness of the Mobe to "negotiate" what should have been considered its right to parade; the glib acceptance of the Justice Department's deformed category of "violence" as the major issue of the weekend; the careful construction of the line of march to avoid even a glimpse of the White House; the insistence on a narrow and selfish message—stop the killing of US soldiers—rather than a broader one: it all went to ensure that the left would act on its own to express the real rage of this winter in America.

Few of the 300,–400,000 young marchers in town for the actions have ever been exposed to a basic, definitive national "political struggle." There may have been examples in the past: the battle for control of the labor movement's future in the thirties, for instance, when socialists and communists fought with a "coalition" of New Dealers, middle-roaders and the right. (The brief contest in the late forties around the Henry Wallace campaign never amounted to much more than a capitulation by a left at once too tired, settled and terrified to put up a fight.) Since then all the contests have taken place within the center ring of establishment politics: Republicans against Democrats, reformers against traditionalists, New Politics against Old Politics. But the past is really no guide; the conditions that have given rise to the movements of the sixties have no parallels in other eras of this century.

Now a major political struggle is shaping up, and it's an extraordinary event in American history. While the mechanics of the fight are byzantine to a fault, the lines of force are relatively clean: liberals who see political change coming from a reformed or realigned Democratic Party are battling with radicals who see the need for a deep, systemic reconstitution of American society. The object of struggle now is definition of the "peace movement" and the terms on which it will develop.

At present, the thousands who stood in the cold in Washington last weekend (and the millions, perhaps, at home or at provincial demonstrations) make up a more or less unselfconscious assemblage—less than a movement, really, although more than a mass. Its level of political understanding of the society from which it has tentatively turned is low indeed. The right-wing of the movement would just as soon leave that the way it is. To restrict the peace movement's politics to a condition of existential anguish and practical discomfort (napalm on the one hand, inflation on the other) allows large numbers of people to be drawn in quickly—and it keeps their temperature down. If the white, privileged marchers on Pennsylvania Avenue really grasped the connections between the war, the imperial system, racism, economic exploitation, cultural manipulation, consumerism and police power (the way most blacks and working-class people instinctively do), they wouldn't have turned so sheepishly away from the White House.

The left wants to define the peace-mass in anti-imperialist and anti-racist terms. "Give peace a chance" is nice but nowhere; why not "Give revolution a chance"? The left emphasizes growth in understanding of society and action against the state, rather than the mindless collection of bodies. Both sides use symbolic action, but the symbols stand for totally different perspectives on political change. The liberals assemble crowds to petition a basically legitimate government for a redress of grievances; the radicals fight in the street, tear up draft records, shut down militarized schools or blow up corporations' headquarters to demand destruction of illegitimate authority. United on the issue of the war, the two sides are actually poles apart on the meaning and quality of politics in America.

There are roots of the present struggle in the late forties (at least), but the immediate origins lie in the McCarthy campaign. In the fall of 1967, the liberal-left coalition finally and permanently split, on the basic principle of support for the black liberation movement. Until that time, the coalition had been led by those in the process of becoming radicals—the civil rights workers, the SDS anti-war demonstrators, the community organizers. But a new set of social and political conditions was turning young people's heads around, and the papered-over splits began to widen. At the convulsive National Conference for New Politics convention in Chicago that September, the blacks and the white left refused to realign the coalition with liberal leadership. Martin Peretz, a Harvard teacher who helped bankroll that convention, stalked out of the Palmer House ballroom and announced to the TV cameras, "the Movement is dead."

And so it was, on its old terms. But implicit in the political system was the need for a "liberal" front to mediate divisive political conflict; thus, it was not long before Peretz, Allard Lowenstein and several other drop-outs from the old movements began putting together a New Politics coalition focussed on capturing the reformist wing of the Democratic Party. The form for their efforts became the McCarthy campaign (and to a lesser extent, the Bobby Kennedy campaign). But the effort did not end with Kennedy's assassination and McCarthy's collapse. It began again last spring with the formation (on Marty's Peretz's bread among other sources) of the Moratorium committee, directed by old McCarthy and Kennedy hands, and organized by Clean-for-Gene kids, according to their privileged perspective on politics. The October 15 Moratorium was their show (although it was open enough on the local level to allow others to do their various things).

After that, the Moratorium people were at a loss as to how to move. In one sense, they were trapped by their own weapons: they had been attacking "violence" on the left for so long that they did not know how to operate in a situation that might be "violent." But they also were not sure of where they stood politically in relation to the movement they were seeking to lead.

For a year or more now, the "moderates" in and around the peace movement have been "violence-baiting" the left. But their attacks are more autobiographical than descriptive. The "new liberals" of the late sixties gain respectability by agreeing with the categorical definition of violence used by press, politicians and government. Without analyzing the source of violence in the society and its near-monopoly within the power of the state, they accept the notion that it is the radicals who cause violence against a "neutral" social system. By rights, the issue of "violence" last weekend ought to have been the genocidal bombings of Vietnam, the exploitation of the people of Latin America, the brutalization of the black community in the US and all the institutionalized forms of violence perpetrated against ordinary people every day. Against that, a pop bottle thrown at the Justice Department is as a bird-dropping against an atom bomb.

Still, the Moratorium people were stuck with their definitions and their categories, and it wasn't easy for them to know what to do when they saw the peace movement, for all its docility, moving on to Washington against their own wishes.

Not to be cut out, a delegation of McCarthy-Kennedy men fell upon Washington to heighten the struggle for control of the terms on which the November actions would be projected. John Kenneth Galbraith, Adam Walinsky, Peter Edelman, Richard Goodwin and Jeremy Larner helped Moratorium leaders Sam Brown and David Hawk write a response to President Nixon's November 3 speech on Vietnam. Walinsky tried to get the Reverend Richard Fernandez, a member of the Mobe steering committee, to kick the Communist Party's delegate, Arnold Johnson, off the Mobe board. Then, having failed, he began working on Senators Goodell and McGovern to stay off the Mobe rally platform. Do we want American students to follow David Dellinger or Sam Brown? he asked his fellows at one meeting.

When it was obvious that the march would be a numerical success despite their own predictions of violence, the Moratorium people abruptly changed tactics and began taking over Mobe logistics. Moratorium leaders frankly stated that their own people were going to act as marshals. Senators and congressmen were convinced to join the action because, as one of Senator McGovern's assistants said, "If you don't join in, you leave the demonstration to people outside the system." The more the Mobe grew bland and unoffensive, the more the politicians joined in.

All the time, the government was playing an elaborate game of chicken with the march organizers. The trouble was that the Administration wanted contradictory things: violence and peacefulness. Violence would (in Nixon's terms) discredit the entire peace movement and remove pressure on Vietnam policy; it would also allow the White House to crack down on radicals and make a show of force for lawnorder against disruption. At the same time, Nixon hardly wanted a huge riot in Washington on his hands—or on his record. The image of armed struggle going on in his own front yard was quite properly terrifying.

The tactic the Administration used to deal with both objectives was negotiation—of every aspect of the march, from route to toilet. Issuance of a permit was purposely delayed until the last minute, so that the Mobe could make no firm plans until a few days before the action was scheduled to begin. At the same time, various government agencies worked to keep people away from Washington. The Justice Department kept the schools from opening up to the public. The FBI checked with bus companies across the country, ostensibly to determine the size of the crowd coming to Washington; predictably, many companies backed out of their commitments to travellers after the FBI came around. It was clear that at least part of the Administration was looking for trouble. Deputy Attorney General Richard Kleindienst (who talks about locking up "ideological criminals") recently told a staffer for a Republican House member, "We can't wait to beat up those motherfucking kids. If you thought Chicago was bad, wait till you see DC."

As it happened, Chicago was worse. The Washington police were about as "restrained" as police can be these days—not because they were groovy or sympathetic but because they were disciplined according to the political strategy of the weekend. Already, Mayor Daley had given pigs a bad name; Washington police did not want to stimulate the kind of national resistance to police power that last year's "police riot" in Chicago had done. So when the police wanted to clear the crowds Friday night near the Saigon embassy and Saturday at the Justice Department, they used a great deal of CS gas and a minimum of public clubbing.

What the police, the Justice Department and the Mobe marshals failed to do was break the left, as they all, in their own ways, had hoped to do. Their use of fear, force and co-optation produced its own contradictions in militant actions Friday and Saturday.

As the weekend had approached, there was a feeling in Washington that perplexing questions about political alignment, the future of the Movement and the course of US policy in Vietnam might be answered. But when the revels were ended the questions remained. The "new liberalism," swinging desperately from Woodstock to redwoods to MIRV, is torn as surely as the "revolutionary contingent," and it is feeling Nixon's repressive wrath as much as the radicals. It's hard to believe another mass march can soon be mounted, and "local actions" cannot be successfully channelled into a liberal frame. And the war drags on. Interest seems to be focussing now on GI organizing; revolt is rife at army bases all over the country, of a tougher kind than people have seen on college campuses. If the "peace" coalition attacks the army system, the Movement, rather than the right-of-the-left, could once more assume the leadership role.

The left may have a real chance now, but its tactics and its organization are so fragmented that it still provides small threat. Friday's and Saturday's street actions were truly anarchic—spontaneous in the worst sense. The "organizers" organized nothing but the time and site of launch. A disciplined force as large as those seen at either action (the size and heaviness were curiously understated in the otherwise sensationalist press) could have played havoc with Washington. There was no want of revolutionary fantasies as people surveyed the targets and possibilities, but there was a total lack of tactical leadership. And that, obviously, cannot develop until new left political institutions mature.

No one was interested in speeches Friday night when a crowd of about 4,000 young people gathered in Dupont Circle—locus of Washington's small street culture—to begin a march "in solidarity with the Provisional Revolutionary Government of South Vietnam." An anomalous thunderstorm that had drenched the city was just ending, and the night was wet-cold in the most awful Washington way. Someone started to speak from the white marble fountain in the circle's park center, and then people were streaming into Massachusetts Avenue, up "embassy row" four blocks to the Saigon embassy at Sheridan Circle. Just before the far circle, a line of helmeted, gas-masked police in full riot gear stood firm, guarding the Saigon embassy in the US just as they have to guard the US embassy in Saigon. In back of the police, searchlights went on and blinded the oncoming crowd. For a few minutes there was the familiar face-off: cops and kids, with a narrow DMZ in between. Then one bottle flew from the crowd towards the police line, and the gas grenades started popping. The marchers freaked for a moment, then marched back down the street and regrouped. A second assault was mounted, but this time the grenades came more quickly, and it was the atrocious CS gas, which cuts like a million knives in back of your throat and makes you move out fast. But people were more orderly in their retreat this time, and then small groups broke out of the main march and began "trashing" the windows of the banks and stores in the posh neighborhood nearby.

Friday night's action clearly sparked the militance Saturday at the Justice Department. People seemed up for it: "affinity groups" of sixes and dozens were getting together through the night and day.

For many thousands, the formal rally was a bummer: just a cold day with a little music and not much dope. People began drifting off soon after they arrived at the Washington Monument, and by 4:30 it was time to move on out. The "organizers" of this march—called to protest the "conspiracy" trial in Chicago and other political trials—handed out flags and banners, and four twelve-foot puppets of Nixon, Agnew, Mitchell and Judge Julius Hoffman were raised to guide the march.

The tone and tempo were drastically different from that of the Mobe's Pennsylvania Avenue march earlier in the day. The red banners and the NLF flags were streaming and the chants were quick and loud: "Free Bobby Seale!" "Off the Pig!" "Stop the Trial!" "Power to the People!" The line swung around the Justice building, then came up against the Mobe marshals "protecting" the Constitution Avenue entrances. In seconds, the marshals were knocked aside, and people filled the streets for blocks in front of the building. Someone ran an NLF flag up the flagpole, and everyone cheered. Then a pretty pink smoke bomb went off in the bushes in front of the building. And then the gas attack began. This time, few people panicked, and when the first barrage had settled they came back, in close. Then there was another wave of gas, and another, and the whole building and the streets in the heart of the Federal Triangle were thick with smoke. When it was clearly overwhelming, the crowds began moving back towards the monument. And then a strange thing happened. In the middle of all that gas, with the rockets going off in front of us as well as behind, people joined arms and began chanting: "Free Bobby Seale! Free Bobby Seale!" People were together in a way they hadn't been all weekend, for some maybe never before, and in the thick of the gas we were laughing and cheering and not yet done.

November 24–December 1, 1969, HARD TIMES

✦

Bad Moon Rising

I hear hurricanes a-blowin'
I know the end is comin' soon
I fear rivers overflowin'
I hear the voice of rage and ruin

Hope you have got your things together
Hope you are quite prepared to die
Looks like we're in for nasty weather
One eye is taken for an eye
                    —*Creedence Clearwater Revival*

That monstrous monsoon coming over the horizon is The Repression. No doubt about it: it's been predicted, pre-analyzed, prevented and now it's here. The first rains drop on just about everybody who is still outside: *The New York Times* and the Black Panthers, the Moratorium and the Weathermen, hippie communards and suburban bureaucrats. Although the quality and quantity of repressive action—and rhetoric—differs from case to case, it is all clearly of a piece.

Just what that piece is becomes difficult to see. The activities of an increasingly repressive ruling class are as various as an increasingly probing insurgent class. But it's obvious that Panthers or Mobemen or hippies don't cause the repression—any more than the Vietcong cause American intervention or the civil rights movement causes racism. Repression happens when those who command the levers of the political system can no longer get them to work, when the accepted methods of governance are ineffective, when the crisis brought on by the failure of leadership overtakes the leaders.

Within the US, no single party of opposition has suffered repression as consistently and as harshly as the Panthers. Twenty-one Panthers have been killed by police so far this year; twenty have been exiled from the United States; ninety-eight are currently in jail and at least twenty-seven others are under indictment for various charges. Bobby Seale's trials are so numerous that they have almost ceased to be news (the transcript of his "contempt" in the Chicago "conspiracy" process, published in the current *New York Review of Books,* is at once beautiful and frightening). Last week, Seale was beaten in jail in San Francisco and put in solitary confinement for possessing "contraband papers"—which turned out to be Black Panther Party documents given him by his attorney, Charles Garry.

Next to the Panthers' troubles, the problems of SDS's Weatherman contingent seem small. But the stuff coming down on their heads is the heaviest the white radical movements have felt so far. Almost every Weather collective has been busted, in nine cities. In Boston, twenty-six Weathermen were arrested after two bullet holes were found in the window of a police station. (The evidence was so thin that charges have already been dropped for twenty-three in the group, but the hassling damage has been done.) In Chicago, 284 people were arrested during the early October SDS demonstrations; most were arrested on charges of looking peculliar—an indictable offense in many jurisdictions. Last week twenty-nine Weathermen were indicted on felony counts growing out of those demonstrations, and conspiracy indictments are expected any week now. Close to a million dollars in bail is on Weathermen, and the ideological campaign against the group is so intimidating that most Movement lawyers won't take Weatherman cases. The FBI is investigating the activities of Weatherman—along with other radical action groups, and peaceful liberals too—during the November Moratorium days in Washington, and there are suggestions of imminent indictments (for conspiracy, extortion or what-have-you) in the capital.

As the GI protest movement deepens and extends, it too feels the hot breath of police power at closer range. Pvt. Richard Chase refused last January to participate in "riot-control" training at Fort Hood, Texas. At that time, his commanding officer granted him "unofficial conscientious objector status." In June, Chase began to participate in the Fort Hood movement against the war in Vietnam. He helped organize a petition campaign for GI political rights, and started working with the Oleo Strut, a GI coffee house in Killeen. On September 11, Chase was given a direct order to undergo riot-control training. He refused, and was placed in the stockade for "pre-trial confinement." He is now awaiting a general court martial. Last week he was placed in solitary for the second time in a month (for swinging from the rafters in the latrine). During his first spell in the hole, he was beaten four times.

In October a group of thirty-five GIs held a meeting on base at Fort Lewis to discuss ways to build a servicemen's union. MPs tried but failed to break up the meeting by removing from the room five people they took to be the leaders. Since then, several of the GIs who participated have been severely harassed. One of the group, Bruce McClean, a conscientious objector who had a discharge pending, was taken under armed guard soon afterwards to the overseas replacement station and almost shanghaied to Vietnam. Just before boarding the plane to leave the United States, he received permission to go to the latrine; guards blocked the doorway, but he escaped through the window, and is now AWOL. Another GI who took part in the meeting has disappeared from the base since that time, and his friends have been unable to locate him. One participant went to speak at an SDS meeting at Tacoma Community College recently; when he returned he was put in the stockade for four days for "speaking disloyally." Two other GIs are now in the stockade for refusing to serve on the "reactionary force" (a reserve riot-control unit) during the October Moratorium; the two assigned to this force were known beforehand to be among the most politically dissident GIs on base.

The government is cracking down on its own civilian employees, too. HEW issued a directive on November 1, which has now been extended to all government agencies, drastically limiting the freedom of civilians to hold meetings on government property. State officials are also increasingly active in the repression. In Camden, New Jersey, a black-owned factory which manufactures dashikis was recently ransacked by police who wrecked $20,000 worth of equipment and arrested several people. The factory was doing well financially, beginning to get out-of-state contracts and plowing the money back into black movement work. The police claimed they had heard stories of a weapons cache hidden in it.

All over the country, longhaired freaks are arrested on spurious charges. A few months ago, police set up a roadblock in Chatham, New Jersey, in order to stop and check "suspicious" cars. In Atlanta, police came down heavily on the hippie community during the summer and fall, busting street people for such crimes as "clogging the sidewalk," and enforcing petty laws—like that against jaywalking—in areas with a high hippie population, as well as making numerous drug arrests.

The Justice Department approves of, and in many cases helps plot, the local attacks; and officials at the department are busy planning their own strategy for quashing rebellion. Justice orchestrates the collection of intelligence and decides what to do with it. John Mitchell, the bond attorney who was Nixon's law partner, managed his campaign and is now his Attorney

General and closest adviser, has Kevin Phillips, the mastermind of the Republicans' "Southern strategy" for wooing racist whites, working in his office. Mitchell concerns himself with "dissent" across the country. During the past few weeks, he has authorized hundreds of new wiretaps every day. The real business of running the Justice Department is left to his deputy, Richard Kleindienst, who was a campaign manager for Goldwater in 1964 and, according to Goldwater, the man who "suggested to me that I make law and order my principal issue." Kleindienst transferred his loyalty to Nixon after his candidate was defeated. "I'd do anything for Nixon," he told a congressional aide recently, explaining that he feels Nixon has been appropriately tough with dissenters. (Kleindienst was attracted to Nixon in the early fifties, when they both supported Joe McCarthy.) Justice is not the only federal agency concerned with policing rebellion. HEW already has two offices to gather intelligence about students and is now planning a propaganda campaign to show the public what students are really thinking about.

At the same time that the repression is rolling, there are ameliorating influences at work, too. Although pressure from the great international corporate managers to end the war decreases as it becomes obvious that "end" means "lose," there is still some thrust in the direction of liquidation. The liberal institutions—media, churches, the professions, education—are still pressing for some kind of disengagement, and although Nixon seems committed now to stay on in Vietnam, he must throw the anti-war sector of his own class a few promises when its anger rises.

The most favored form of co-optation of the insurgency is in the terms of the new culture, rather than in the old political and economic ways. The Administration is acting with astounding speed (for a bureaucracy) to give heads their head—that is, to lessen the penalties for light dope. And it may go further than that: in Washington, city council "president" Gilbert Hahn, a Nixon appointee who was head of the District Republican Committee, announced last week that the council will soon hold hearings on the legalization of marijuana. He fears that the evils of the Prohibition era will be repeated. In any case, the theory is that a turned-on generation can't be a revolutionary one. Perhaps people are beginning to realize that 1984 is an election year.

December 8-15, 1969, with Frances Lang, HARD TIMES

✦

To Off a Panther

The Black Panther Party has found more sympathy in its moment of extermination than it ever did in its whole tragic life. But such brutal irony fills the history of black people in white America: a black man must be a victim before he is a hero.

The decapitation—at least—of the Panthers appears now to be complete. The killing of Fred Hampton in Chicago, the siege of the Panthers' headquarters in Los Angeles, and the arrest of David Hilliard and Bobby Rush just about finished the ability of Panther leaders to move freely—or at all. The party's work continues in some aspects; the newspaper *The Black Panther* appears weekly and provides the main source of revenue. In several cities a breakfasts-for-children program operates and there are a few free medical clinics run by Panther chapters. Political education classes are held for Panther members, and some high school organizing is going on. But it's obvious that the forward motion of the Panthers has been seriously slowed.

Whether the Black Panther Party—in its present form—can thrive again is problematic, but in the aftermath of the events of December, it has been consigned by whites, and many blacks, to a certain grave. Upon Fred Hampton's tomb, liberals of both races sing funeral songs with words full of pity but little praise. Like palefaces who wrote heroic ballads about the redskins they slew, the "civil rights establishment" has bestowed upon the Panthers a folkloric role, the while denying its own part in the slaughter. There are already nine separate investigations of the Panthers' troubles. The great corporate foundations are fairly falling over themselves trying to get into the act: Ford has granted the Arthur Goldberg/Roy Wilkins Commission of Inquiry a cool quarter-million to confirm the obvious fact that the Panthers are being destroyed.

The twenty-eight commission members,* individually and with their organizations, have spent the last three years condemning the Panthers' "violence," and thus helping to create the climate in which revolutionary blacks could be easily repressed. Even a cursory glance through the newspaper clippings shows how the anti-militants have used their standing in the white political system to illegitimize militancy.

Roy Wilkins, for example, has condemned black power, ghetto insurgencies, black studies programs, reparations to the black community, separate black labor organizing and just about everything that is up-front in the black

---

* Arthur Goldberg, Roy Wilkins, Clifford Alexander, Julian Bond, Sam Brown, W. Haywood Burns, Kenneth Clark, Ramsey Clark, John Conyers, William T. ("Bumps") Coleman, John Douglas, Melvin Dymally, Marian Wright Edelman, Jean Fairfax, Jack Greenberg, Richard Hatcher, Philip Hoffman, Jesse Jackson, Arthur J. Lelyveld, Morris Abram, John de J. Pemberton, Louis Pollack, Joseph Porter, Charles Palmer, A. Philip Randolph, Cynthia Wedel, George Wylie, Whitney Young.

liberation movement. He has indulged in sly Red-baiting: "If you ask me whether Mr. Carmichael is his own man, I am sorry I don't know Mr. Carmichael and his connections well enough to guess." Wilkins, Whitney Young and the others have continually belittled the significance of militancy: "Carmichael's following amounts to about fifty Negroes and about 5,000 white reporters," Young wrote in a right-wing magazine in the month that Panther Bobby Hutton (and Martin Luther King) were murdered. Dr. Kenneth B. Clark, the academic establishment's favorite "militant" Negro, used to say things like "black power is a shoddy moral product disguised in the gaudy package of racial militance," and he warned Negroes not to be "cowed into silence by unrealistic Negro racists." When black students occupied a building at Cornell last year, Clark—a member of the New York State Board of Regents, which has partial jurisdiction over Cornell—said, "The spectacle of American college students concluding their armed occupation of a campus student union building by a victorious exit with sixteen rifles and three shotguns at the ready restimulates the feelings of revulsion and sadness one felt when viewing the Birmingham police use of cattle prods on human beings." By excluding the militants from the "masses" of the black movement, the liberals gave the necessary assurance to government and police that repression would not seriously be opposed. And so, except in words, it has not.

It was only three years ago that the Black Panther Party slid into public consciousness. The mood of those days was most evocatively recalled by Eldridge Cleaver, who wrote that he "fell in love" with the Panthers at the first sight of them—at a meeting of black militants in San Francisco:

> I spun around in my seat and saw the most beautiful sight I had ever seen: four black men wearing black berets, powder blue shirts, black leather jackets, black trousers, shiny black shoes—and each with a gun; in front was Huey P. Newton with a riot pump shotgun in his right hand, barrel pointed down to the floor. Beside him was Bobby Seale, the handle of a .45 caliber automatic showing from its holster on his right hip, just below the hem of his jacket. A few steps behind Seale was Bobby Hutton, the barrel of his shotgun at his feet. . . .

The party had been formed a few months before by Newton and Seale, who had begun organizing "black power" action in Oakland's Merritt College. The name Newton chose reflected his affinity with Stokely Carmichael's Black Panther organization in Lowndes County, Alabama.

Like the Lowndes project, the Black Panther Party has its historical roots in the transitional period between the break-up of the integrated civil rights movement in the rural South and the development of a black liberation movement in the urban ghettoes. Newton and Seale drew more on the revolutionary thrust in the black streets than on the reformist ideals of the white universities. "What we are doing," a California Panther once remarked in those early days, "is putting Malcolm and Mao together."

The Panthers dug the Little Red Book (and made money from selling it), but they never went completely *chinois*. The material of their politics conveyed the authentic weight of the black experience in America. Newton's program, which is still the party's basic platform (it is printed each week in the newspaper), put traditional demands of Negroes in the US in a revolutionary context:

> 1. We want freedom. We want power to determine the destiny of our Black Community.
> 2. We want full employment for our people.
> 3. We want an end to the robbery by the white man [later changed to "Capitalist"] of our Black Community.
> 4. We want decent housing, fit for shelter of human beings.
> 5. We want education for our people that exposes the true nature of this decadent American society. We want education that teaches us our true history and our role in the present-day society.
> 6. We want all black men to be exempt from military service.
> 7. We want an immediate end to Police Brutality and Murder of black people.
> 8. We want freedom for all black men held in federal, state, county and city prisons and jails.
> 9. We want all black people when brought to trial to be tried in a court by a jury of their peer group or people from their black communities, as defined by the Constitution of the United States.
> 10. We want land, bread, housing, education, clothing, justice and peace. And as our major political objective, a United Nations-supervised plebiscite to be held throughout the black colony in which only black colonial subjects will be allowed to participate, for the purpose of determining the will of black people as to their national destiny.

The statement of demands ended with a quotation from the American Declaration of Independence. Explicit in the points was the conception of a "black colony" within imperial America, similar to—but functionally distinct from—the colonies of the empire in the Third World. That notion had been hanging around for a number of years, but what was different was the Panthers' implicit Marxist analysis of the imperial system. The racism that permeated everything was not a self-contained and self-supporting phenomenon but a consequence of imperialism. Because of their colonial history, black people had to struggle against the system as blacks, but liberation could not come until the entire imperial machine was destroyed.

From that ideology flowed a number of crucial implications. First, the enemy wasn't simply "whitey," but specifically the white ruling class, and the final struggle was not between races but between classes. Second, black people should organize for that struggle as blacks, and not—as "orthodox" Marxist-Leninists insisted—as members of an integrated working class. Third, liberation did not depend on the establishment of a separate territorial black state but on the defeat of US imperialism. Fourth, white revolutionaries had a valid role in the whole process—as allies of black revolutionaries, at work "behind the lines" of the Mother Country. Finally, the Panthers' demands could not be co-opted by corporate or federal hand-outs and cash-ins; only a revolution could satisfy them.

It took some time for whites—even white radicals—to dig the Panthers. At first, the Panthers were objects of amusement. Posters of Huey in his cobra chair, flanked by spear and gun and African artifacts, had an appeal that was more pop than political. But then Eldridge Cleaver began writing and speaking, and his words weren't funny at all.

Inevitably, the Panthers became a media event. *Ramparts* built circulation on Cleaver's writing; television and the mass-circulation press inflated the Panther image and marketed it along with nudity, drugs and rock music. Cleaver became the paradigm native revolutionary hero, an American Che. Pressures grew on the Panthers to move out of their base in Oakland; soon, black hustlers as well as black political activists were calling themselves Panthers whether they were actually in the party or not. Any dude who wanted a little money or excitement could pass himself off as a real live Black Panther and hijack a plane to Havana or raise funds from willing white leftists.

It is doubtful if there have ever been more than several hundred *bona fide* Black Panther Party cadre in the country, or more than several thousand who identified themselves in any specific way with the party organization. But the Panther myth was so outsized that it must have seemed as if there were 100,000 of them. Local and federal police agents began to infiltrate Panther organizations—as thoroughly as they had done in Communist Party cells a generation earlier.

The real Panther leadership was hard put to deal with the overblown national image. At the same time that key figures were feeling the first predictable blows of repression, pressures to expand were mounting. Even the development of the solid Oakland "foco" was stunted as the party began to think of itself as a powerful national organization. At that point, the contradictions were formed that led at last to the Panthers' extreme distress. The emergence of a nationwide Panther presence aroused the authorities before the Panthers were really ready for defense, and before they had organized a wide enough circle of support for political protection.

Panthers would shout "Off the pig," and while it may have been a promise or a metaphor to ghetto people, uptight whites took it literally. As a matter of fact, the Panthers never formulated—or practiced—an aggressive strategy against the cops. For all the reported "gun battles" between Panthers and police, there are no cases of armed forays by Panthers, or even sniping. From the start the ruling metaphor was: "It is not in the panther's nature to attack anyone first, but when he is attacked and backed into a corner, he will respond viciously."

The Panthers' primary strategy was to organize people in the ghettoes around their demands—and even to begin implementing the easier ones, such as black education and food, medical and clothing services. Because those demands carried a revolutionary force—they could not be granted by the system as presently constituted—the Panthers expected repression, and armed themselves for it. Huey Newton said: "Without protection from the army, the police and the military, the institutions could not go on in their racism and exploitation. Whenever you attack the system, the first thing that the administrators do is to send out their strongmen. If it's a rent strike, because of the indecent housing we have, they will send out the police to throw the furniture out the window. They don't come themselves. They send their protectors. So to deal with the corrupt exploiter, you are going to have to deal with his protector, which is the police, who take orders from him. This is a must."

The attacks began early enough. Cleaver was warned that his prison parole (from a pre-Panther conviction) would be revoked if he continued to engage in political activity. The police began following the Panthers around Oakland, and the Panthers began counter-patrolling the police. To a certain extent, the Panther patrols were effective in keeping cops off the backs of ghetto people. But the police counterattacked by harassing and arresting the Panthers, and in one "routine check" of a Panther car, Newton was arrested. In a flash there was gunfire; Huey and one policeman were wounded and a second policeman was killed. Huey, of course, was charged with the murder. For several days afterwards, Panther members in the San Francisco Bay Area were rounded up and arrested on irrelevant charges.

Six months later, Cleaver and several other Panthers in three cars were stopped by police in Oakland; they were out getting provisions for a big barbecue picnic to be held in a park the next day. Again, there was an "argument," and shooting—at the Panthers. Cleaver wrote about it in his cell at Vacaville: "Common sense told me that I'd best have my hands up by the time I cleared the front of my car. But before I cleared, the cop on the passenger side of his car started shouting and firing his gun, and then the other cop started shooting. . . . The explosions from their guns sounded right in my face and so, startled, I dove for cover in front of my car. . . . It took only a split second to see that they had us in a cross fire, so I shouted to the brothers, 'Scatter!' . . . As we started across the street, one of the Panthers, Warren Wells, got hit and let out an agonized yelp of pain. . . . A cop with a shotgun was running after me, shooting. I didn't have a gun but I wished that I had! (Oh, how I wish that I had!)"

Cleaver and Little Bobby Hutton made it into the basement of a nearby house. The cops shot into it: "We lay down flat against the floor while the bullets ripped through the walls. . . . The pigs started lobbing in tear gas. . . . I took the opportunity to fortify the walls with whatever we could lay our hands on: furniture, tin cans, cardboard boxes. . . . We decided to stay in there and choke to death if necessary rather than walk out into a hail of bullets. . . . One of the shots found my leg and my foot with an impact so painful and heavy that I was sure I no longer had two legs. . . ."

Then the police shot firebombs into the basement, and Cleaver decided to surrender. "I called out to the pigs and told them that we were coming out. . . . There were pigs in the windows above us in the house next door, with guns pointed at us. They told us not to move, to raise our hands. This we did. . . . The pigs pointed to a squad car parked in the middle of the street and told us to run to it. . . . Then they snatched Little Bobby away from me and shoved him forward. . . . After he had traveled about 10 yards the cops cut loose on him with their guns."

The crackdown in the Bay Area was met by mass demonstrations and solid support by blacks and white radicals. Huey Newton's trial was the political event of the year, and "Free Huey" was the leading slogan; and Huey's amazingly light sentence—two to fifteen years—attests to the Panthers' success. But outside of Oakland the repression was more successful, and the arrests and murders mounted with only weak protests in their wake. At length, the total effect of the nationwide anti-Panther campaign weakened the Oakland base, too, and the whole organization entered a nightmare period of siege.

As their troubles deepened, the Panthers began to redirect their activities and emphasize different aspects of their strategy. There was less talk of armed struggle and more work to "serve the people." The breakfasts-for-children program was successful in many cities. But the liberal approval of the project did not allay fears that there was a bit of politics being served with the corn flakes. The crackdown continued.

At the same time, the Panthers were intensifying their fraternal relations with white radicals. "Coalitions" were formed with the Peace and Freedom Party (Cleaver ran for president of the US), with the Oakland Seven (white youths charged, and acquitted, of conspiracy in anti-draft demonstrations) and, most important, with SDS.

What followed was the organization of a white base to support the Black Panthers, and although it was an attractive idea to many whites, it had the effect of eroding the Panthers' black following. Many black militants had always opposed the Panthers' openness with white radicals. Cleaver was widely criticized for writing for whites, speaking to white college audiences and generally "relating to white reality." Non-Marxist black militants and black "cultural nationalists," whom the Panthers consistently bad-mouthed, treated Newton and Seale as "traitors to their race."

Last summer, the Panthers called a national conference in Oakland to build a "United Front Against Fascism." By all accounts it was a dispiriting affair. Most of the participants were white leftists, and it ended in factional argument. The program that was supposed to emerge—a petition campaign for community control of police—has never come off the ground. The Panthers were understandably bitter—both at the lack of black support for UFAF and the disputes among the whites. In the next months the Panthers began violent rhetorical attacks against the white radicals who did not single-mindedly follow them: in particular, the Weatherman element of SDS.

The difficulties that the Panthers have endured have as much to do with the fragmentation of the left as they do with the un-togethernesss of the black movements. The groups with whom the Panthers coalesced are for the most part weak and struggling. The celebrated "Rainbow Coalition" in Chicago—the Black Panthers, the Young Lords (Latinos) and the Young Patriots ("hillbilly" greasers)—sounded glorious but has yet to make much sense as a coalition, although both the Lords and the Panthers have a certain strength on their own turfs. The alliance with SDS has not been noticeably effective in recent months.

The Panthers may in theory be the "vanguard" of the new American revolution, but in practice they have yet to win legitimacy—especially in the black community. There, a hundred parties contend; in almost every city there are black organizations across a range of politics of almost indescribable complexity. In terms of national consciousness, the Panthers' supremacy is being challenged by two groups in particular: the Republic of New Africa and the League of Revolutionary Black Workers.

RNA demands a separate black nation, made up of five Southern states; how it will pry them loose from the Union is not yet clear. RNA is doing low-level organizing of high school kids in a few cities (Detroit, Brooklyn, New Orleans), generally on the basis of anti-white black nationalism. The League seems to be moving much faster. Organized at first in Detroit as an insurgent campaign within the United Auto Workers, it has now expanded into a city-wide black movement. It publishes a weekly paper, *Inner City Voice*, and has just about taken control of the West Central Organization, an old Saul Alinsky project. The League is training high school cadre in "freedom schools," readying candidates for UAW leadership, and struggling for union power inside various factories. For the time being, the League seeks to avoid the pitfalls of national expansion; it chooses to concentrate its effort in Detroit, but its example is widely watched.

The Black Panther Party is still in the forefront of black liberation, even if it is not universally acknowledged as the vanguard. It played a heroic role at a moment of historical necessity; its tragedy is that the ranks were thin and disorganized.

Fred Hampton was murdered because he was a black man, and because he was a revolutionary. He was born black; he chose revolution. So the persecution of the Black Panther Party is part of two grim American traditions:

the casual extermination of black people and the repression of real radicalism. But the determination of the assault against black revolution only
underlines its seriousness. Huey Newton saw it: "As long as there are black
people there will be Black Panthers."

January 12-19, 1970, HARD TIMES

✦

The Trial

Chicago

It was said of the 1945 World Series that both the Detroit Tigers and the
Chicago Cubs were so war-weakened that neither team could win.
Something like that judgement has been applied in these closing weeks of
the trial of the Chicago 7 (or 8, 9, or 10, according to whichever of the available calculi is preferred). The certain fate of the defendants and their
lawyers—regardless of verdict—and the expense of energy and leadership
suffered by the radical movements is balanced against the months of insult
to the judicial system: "A loss for all," mourns *Time* this week. But neither
politics nor baseball is a zero-sum game. The Tigers, after all, won the '45
series. And although the scoring is obscure in the current contest, it seems
clear that the orderly administration of justice—as she is practiced now in
America—has lost the most. For that is what the trial was all about.

The Nixon Administration, not the defendants, chose to make the trial a
political event. As former Attorney General Ramsey Clark had predicted, the
Justice Department's invocation of the conspiracy law against anti-war
movements signalled the imposition of general political repression such as
the US had not seen since Nixon's earlier involvement with McCarthyism.

The Chicago all-stars—the original eight defendants—were picked for
their symbolic value and their leadership roles: Bobby Seale, the Panther;
Tom Hayden and Rennie Davis, the SDS veterans; Abbie Hoffman and Jerry
Rubin, the anarcho-Yippies; Dave Dellinger, the Mobilization coalitionist;
John Froines, the activist professor; and Lee Weiner, the street organizer
and second-level cadre. It was important to have as much of the Movement's
spectrum represented as possible (next time there will be women, too) for the
effect to be truly chilling. In political trials, final depositions are of secondary
importance: the act of prosecution is primarily intimidating and decapitat-
ing. Ramsey Clark and the Justice Department "liberals" who brought the
indictments against Dr. Spock for conspiracy to aid and abet draft resisters
in 1967 may have sincerely (if secretly) hoped for ultimate acquittal, but the
damage they did in bringing the case could never be undone by verdict or
higher court reversal.

To mean anything at all, the defense must also be political. To accept the
convention and conceit of common criminality consigns the defendants to
defeat in the real terms of the trial. The government may contend that Dr.

Spock or Dave Dellinger are no different from car thieves or wife-beaters, but everything about its conduct of the cases confirms the pretense of that contention. The several "conspirators" are seen by the government as "ideological criminals," in Deputy Attorney General Kleindienst's ominous phrase, and their political positions prove them guilty as charged.

Short of seizing judicial power, there is no foolproof way for radicals to conduct a political defense against political prosecution. The courtroom is the government's turf and it commands the range of options. It has informers and agents willing to testify to anything. It controls the selection of a jury and it can keep tabs on the feelings of jurors as the trial progresses. The judge is not an impartial arbiter but a member of the government team only thinly disguised (whether he knows it or not). The Justice Department has immense resources; the defense is impoverished in every way inside the court. Most important of all, the government can define the issues at hand; the defense has either to accept them and hope for a lucky break or attack the definitions at their roots.

The Chicago defendants tried hard to politicize their trial: that is, to expose the meaning of their prosecution and present it to the jury and the country. And in a sense they succeeded almost in spite of themselves. There was never a clear strategy for the eight. The government assured confusion at the defense table by bundling widely disagreeing fellows in one bed. Dellinger's militant pacifism, Abbie Hoffman's theatrical anarchism, Hayden's visionary pan-radicalism and Bobby Seale's black Leninism defied neat packaging.

Certainly the eight, or most of them, expected some amount of "confrontation" to go on at the trial. If there were to be real politics presented, they would have to reflect the sensibilities of the radical generation that arrived in Chicago in August 1968 for the Democratic convention. The demonstrations of that month could make no sense now—to the jury or the people outside—without a re-creation of their models as well as a recitation of their ideologies. How could Abbie explain the Yippies' call for "public fornication" (in their 1968 manifesto) in that sterile glass courthouse before a judge so uptight that he had to spell out b-a-l-l-s and b-i-t-c-h when reading the record of contempt? How could the jury understand the deep-rooted rage of radicals in the streets when the defendants and their lawyers had to sit listening to informers' lies and a judge's obtuseness? It may have been unwise for Dellinger to say "bullshit" or William Kunstler to embrace Ralph Abernathy, but it was necessary and it was true.

After all, it was Judge Julius Hoffman, not the defendants, who set the terms of the courtroom confrontations, just as Mayor Richard Daley had set the terms of the actions in the streets. The judge could have cooled it in court as Daley could have cooled it in the streets; both men chose violence. Hoffman was an extension of Daley by other means, as the laws of the rulers are extensions of their politics.

Judge Hoffman's conduct of the trial contained elements of both *Grand Guignol* and *petit mal*. Variously characterized as Mr. Magoo and Adolf Eichmann, he was rather a character wholly unto himself: shrewd, cruel, stubborn, arbitrary, bizarre—and not without a certain wit and an amount of perverse compassion. He understood his part in the drama he made: a foil too perfect for the desperate hijinx below his bench.

There's no doubt that Judge Hoffman enjoyed it all immensely—his power over the defendants and their lawyers, his dramatic notices (even the bad ones), even his place in the history of the revolution. He postured, grimaced, nodded, dozed, cackled and wisecracked with maximum effect. The outbursts he created by outrageous rulings were merely scenes in which he could get back to center stage. And all along he knew that he alone would deliver the curtain line—and *exeunt omnes*, in tears.

A large part of the defense consisted of responses to the judge's antics. He baited the culture heroes whom the defendants called as witnesses and even feigned a mild bemusement to Ginsberg's "Om." He prohibited a delay of less than two months in the trial's commencement, so that Bobby Seale's lawyer, Charles Garry, could not join the defense. When Seale demanded his right of self-defense, the judge bound and gagged him to encourage the spectacle. The other defendants and the other lawyers behaved just as they had to—and just as Judge Hoffman knew they would.

The defendants' basic problem was making the events of 1968 understandable a year and a half later. It was not enough for them to insist that they had done nothing wrong; obviously, they had done *something*, but its definition could not be isolated from the political context of that dreadful year: the war, Johnson's retirement, political assassinations, the riots of April, Daley's "shoot to kill" order, the hippie "cultural revolution," the military defense of Chicago, the convention itself. If the jury understood all that, it just might be sympathetic; if people outside understood, the meaning of a whole generation might come a little clearer.

The judge, of course, tried to block contextual testimony at every turn. Ramsey Clark was not allowed on the stand because, the judge ruled, nothing he would say could possibly be relevant to the case. Ralph Abernathy was barred because he arrived a few minutes late in court. Those who made it to the witness box were silenced at the merest mention of testimony that might explain the defendants' actions. And all the time the government built its case against them by exploiting the atmospherics of radical protest. What acts of contempt that occurred in the courtroom—certainly the most serious ones—flowed from that essential imbalance. In a contemptible court, only the contemptuous are just.

During the trial, however, the meaning of the disruptions was not always so clear as it seems now in retrospect. Early on, differences developed among the defendants. The first major point of departure was the removal of Bobby Seale from the other seven; then there was talk of a general refusal to continue, as a protest against the inherent racism of Judge Hoffman's decision to call a mistrial for the one black man among the eight. Seale asked the others to go ahead with the trial, but even so, they felt impotent and trapped. Later, when Dellinger's bail was revoked for saying "bullshit," several of the defendants wanted to disrupt the trial so ferociously that the judge would have to revoke their bail too.

But the remaining six stayed out of jail until the end. One model for their behavior seemed to be Jerry Rubin's famous appearance at the House Un-American Activities Committee hearings in 1966, when he dressed in Revolutionary War costume and the proceedings dissolved in farce. The contrary model was Tom Hayden's appearance before the same committee in 1968, when he seemed to play along with the rules but in effect succeeded in turning the hearing on its head—so that he controlled the show. There was, however, no way to integrate Hayden's subtlety with Rubin's directness, and the total effect did not synthesize the two styles but merely mixed them.

Because the government sought to discredit and decapitate the Movement by indicting its leaders, it was the defendants' responsibility to connect themselves to a popular base and legitimate the Movement's objectives. At least that was the theory. In practice it was a difficult duty to discharge, not only because of the essential disparities among the defendants but because of the utter fragmentation of the Movement as the sixties ended. Abbie and Jerry had a considerable following in freak nation (and a lot of media visibility) but Yippie! was admittedly a put-on party, and neither Simon and Schuster nor Random House seemed to be the agents of revolution. Tom Hayden and Rennie Davis had some attachments with active radical organizations, but they had also accumulated a decade's natural resentment here and there, and they were floating on the edges of current organizational politics. Dave Dellinger is universally respected in the Movement as an avuncular Ho, but it would be hard to find three other people who share his particular brand of politics. Alone among the defendants, Bobby Seale was connected to a real base—the Black Panther Party—but its heavier problems elsewhere (and his, too) made it unlikely that much organizing would go on around his conspiracy indictment.

The Panthers staged the best demonstration in Chicago during the trial— on opening day in September—and there were dozens of good rallies around the country when the defendants flew out to speak after the daily court adjournments or on weekends. Abbie and Jerry, in particular, hoped that the Justice Department demonstrations during the Washington Mobilization march last November would lead to a national movement around the conspiracy, but although the action was exhilarating, the movement did not materialize. In too large a part, support action was organized through the old boys' net of early SDS people, Mobe functionaries and personal friends of the defendants. If there were a large national radical organization, it might have made the conspiracy its winter project: action would be undertaken by chapters on campuses, in communities or wherever. But nothing like that organization exists.

As the trial drew to a close, spirits seemed to pick up. The press, which had been treating the case perfunctorily for months, suddenly regained interest. In the long middle of the case, reporters were satisfied simply to fill the requirements of their editors for a daily story. They fixed on a set of conventional categories into which each session's events were placed: the "antics" of the defendants, the weirdness of the judge, the freak-outs of the spectators and the frustration of the defense lawyers. Bobby Seale's moments made the front page, and the silenced songs of Phil Ochs, Country Joe and Judy Collins were good for a few laughs, but most of the time the stories were buried. It was hard for the real importance of the trial to be broadcast.

Towards the end of January the jury realized that the end of the trial was upon them. Full-time spectators and participants say that an entirely different feeling was projected from the jury box (seeing those fourteen stone-cold faces, it is a bit strange to imagine any feeling at all). By then, everyone knew that both defendants and lawyers would be packed away for contempt whatever the actual verdict in the case; the judge had practically said as much himself. Still, no one could have been prepared for the final week.

MONDAY: Judge Hoffman accepts eighty-six of eighty-eight instructions suggested by the government for his charge to the jury, and thirty-four of seventy-nine offered by the defense. Chuckles. The judge turns angrily to the defendants' table: "The conduct is continuing right down to the last observation." He then turns down a defense motion to show films of the 1968 demonstrations—already entered and used in evidence—in its summation. (The films would probably show the unprovoked, brutal police attacks on demonstrators.)

TUESDAY: Assistant US Attorney Richard Schultz, the dogged and somewhat prissy prosecutor on the government's legal team, begins his summation. The August 1968 demonstrations, he says, were to signal "the start of the revolution" and establish "a National Liberation Front—the political arm of the Vietcong—in the United States." The government's police and informers and intelligence agents were "impartial observers"; the defense's big-name witnesses (Jesse Jackson, Dick Gregory, Julian Bond, Judy Collins, Allen Ginsberg, Terry Southern, Norman Mailer, Arlo Guthrie, Phil Ochs, Richard Goodwin, etc.) were "duped." The defendants were like "Lenin and Mao Tse-tung."

WEDNESDAY: Leonard Weinglass begins summarizing the defense case. The government's witnesses could not be trusted as "honest men," he says, because they were paid informers and agents. (Objection. Sustained.) "Violent statements are not violent," he says; the trial is "an act of vengeance" by Chicago authorities.

THURSDAY: Weinglass finishes his portion of the summation; he says that in the sixties people such as Martin Luther King took their protests into the streets. "There is no proof" that King would have had anything to do with the 1968 demonstrations in Chicago, the government says in objection. Weinglass argues that the events of August can't be understandable outside of the larger context. (Objection. Sustained.) Weinglass tries to quote from Clarence Darrow's defense of communists in a famous Chicago case fifty years earlier, but the government and prosecution won't let him explain. He does manage to get in a line from the Passion (according to St. Matthew).

Kunstler begins his summation—the defense's last word. It doesn't work: he's too rhetorical, somehow inauthentic (as Weinglass had been movingly honest). He gets bogged down in a detailed recitation of the events of an alleged "bomb plot" by one of the defendants in an underground garage; people feel he may have raised new doubts about his own client rather than quell them.

FRIDAY: Kunstler recoups. He slips out of the garage incident, then moves on to his final flourishes: "The hangman's rope never solved a single problem, except that of one man. You can crucify Jesus, poison a Socrates, hang a John Brown or a Nathan Hale, jail a Eugene Debs or a Bobby Seale, kill a Che Guevara, assassinate a John F. Kennedy or a Martin Luther King. But the problems remain."

"Look what happened to all of them," one of the defendants remarks mournfully.

US Attorney Foran winds it up. The defendants lured innocents to Chicago with promises of sex in the streets. The defendants are "evil men"; Jerry Rubin worked best at night "like most predators." He appeals to the jury's philistinism and tells the members (ten men and two women) not to be swayed by intellectual arguments but to rely on the evidence of their senses—that is, how the defendants looked and acted in the courtroom. The defendants, he says, "corrupted" innocent children: "We can't let people do that to our kids. The lights of Camelot that kids believe in needn't go out." He finishes with a quote from Jefferson: "Obedience to the law is the major part of patriotism."

SATURDAY: Judge Hoffman gives his two hours' worth of instructions to the jury. He begins by quoting the long indictments in full (he has done it before in the trial), so that the jury can see just how guilty the defendants are. The jury leaves at noon, and the rest of the people in the courtroom are about to file out when the judge says he has a few other "matters" to take up. Then he begins reading the contempt citations. Dellinger gets thirty-two counts. Before sentencing, he asks Dellinger if he has anything to say: "There are two issues the country refuses to take seriously and refuses to solve—the war in Vietnam and racism," Dellinger answers.

"I don't want to talk politics with you," the judge says angrily, cutting him off. Dellinger continues:

"You want us to be like good Jews going quietly to the concentration camps while the court suppresses the truth. It's a travesty on justice. The record condemns you, not us."

Dellinger's two teenage daughters applaud and shout approval. Court marshals fall upon them; a woman cop tackles the elder daughter and drags her out. Kunstler stands before the bench, sobbing, his arms outstretched: "My God! What are you doing to us? My life is nothing. Put me in jail now, I beg of you." Dellinger is led away. "Right on, beautiful people," he says softly, smiling. As the door shuts, Rennie Davis approaches the bench: "You have just jailed one of the most beautiful and courageous men in the country."

"You're next," the judge snaps to Davis. He gets twenty-three citations, then is allowed to make a statement. "You represent all that is old, ugly, repressive and bigoted in this country," he tells the judge, who cuts him off and sentences him to two years, one month and nineteen days in jail.

Then Hayden. This time, the defendant works his way brilliantly through an hour of "argument" and explanation, and the judge seems confused, apologetic and self-justifying. Hayden tells how two Justice Department gooks tried to convince Ramsey Clark not to testify, and one of them followed Clark to Chicago and right into the courtroom. Hayden's argument is so skillful that the judge is impressed: "A fellow as smart as you can do awfully well under this system." Abbie shoots back: "He doesn't want a place in the business, Julie."

Finally, Hayden is asked if he has anything to say in mitigation of punishment. He stands motionless by the defense table, his arms at his sides. His eyes are red and wet and his mouth is trembling. "I would like to have a child . . ." He can't finish the sentence. The judge is crueler than he has ever been. He cracks: "That's where the federal judicial system can't help you." (No laughter.) Hayden answers fiercely: "And the federal judicial system can't help you prevent the birth of a new world." Hayden picks up his papers and his coat and walks towards the lockup, the marshals following.

Abbie is next. He ends defiantly, then walks to the spectators' section, gently kisses his wife and smiles: "Water the plant."

SUNDAY: Weiner and Froines get theirs. Then Kunstler's citations are read. When told he can reply, the lawyer approaches the bench and leans on the lectern. He reads from a prepared statement:

"Yesterday, for the first time in my career, I completely lost my composure in court. I felt such a deep sense of utter futility that I could not keep from crying, something I had not done publicly since childhood. I am sorry if I disturbed the decorum of the courtroom, but I am not ashamed of my tears.

"Neither am I ashamed of my conduct in this court for which I am about to be punished. I have tried with all of my heart faithfully to represent my clients in the face of what I considered and still consider repressive and unjust conduct towards them. If I have to pay with my liberty for such representation, then that is the price of my beliefs and sensibilities.

"I can only hope that my fate does not deter other lawyers throughout the country who, in the difficult days that lie ahead, will be asked to defend clients against a steadily increasing governmental encroachment upon their most fundamental liberties."

Kunstler gets four years and thirteen days. Judge Hoffman finishes off his contempt extravaganza with Weinglass, whose name he misstates for the umpteenth time during the trial. Weinglass never raised his voice or uttered a discourteous word during the trial, and he does not begin to do so at the end; his crimes consist mainly in attempting to get important testimony before the jury against the prosecution's wishes and the judge's unheeding rulings. Weinglass gets a year, eight months and five days. All told, the eight defendants (including Seale, who is at present serving his four-year contempt sentence) got nineteen years, one month and three days for contempt, before any verdict was rendered.

The jury took four days to reach a verdict, and when it was in, there was more a sense of anticlimax than surprise or dismay. A "compromise" was what the defendants had always thought would be most debilitating; it would split the coherence of the conspiracy, confuse the public and make hard-line organizing that much more difficult. The government and the judge would look a bit better than if there had been a straight conviction—or a total acquittal. But "compromise" is what the defendants got. As it is, the defendants face long prison terms on the contempt charges and—except for Weiner and Froines—sentences on that part of the indictment on which they were convicted.

But the trial wasn't just about winning acquittal, which was always thought unlikely for the six chief political actors among the defendants. Its purpose was to expose the unlawfulness of the new law, the disorderliness of the old order. If the trial had taken place in one or another of those countries that Americans dismiss as "totalitarian," it would be universally recognized as an outrage. It's a little more difficult for people to make the same judgements about Chicago.

But there's no substantial difference between other repressive regimes and ours. American tones may be softer and the colors more muted, but underneath the effects are the same. Repression is real, and if the politics necessary to fight it are not always so clear, at least they are available. There's energy now to wage a heavy campaign against repression around the issue of the trial, and the events of the last week—from congressional speeches to marches in the streets—suggest that more will happen in the days after. For the issue isn't the freedom of the ten; at last, it is the freedom of us all, and those who think that they are neither in conspiracy nor in contempt will have to fight to prove their innocence, or their right.

February 23–March 2, 1970, Hard Times

PART TWO

Chapter VI

✦

REFUGEES

A Sense of Crisis

*But you see, we all believe in what Bakunin and Nachaev said: that
a revolutionary is a doomed man. . . . So you come to terms with the
idea that you may be killed. And when you have to live with the
prospect of being wiped out in a flash, you either stop doing what
you're doing and remove yourself from that situation, or else you
have to accept it and kind of repress it, and get it off your mind.
Otherwise, you'll be non-functional. You can't walk around afraid
and watching and looking over your shoulder. Anyway, I think
many people these days have learned to live with that understanding. I learned to live with it somehow.*

—Eldridge Cleaver

Ralph Featherstone lived in Neshoba County, Mississippi, for two years,
off and on. He had first come there one day in the summer of 1964 to
meet three fellow civil rights workers in a church in the county seat of
Philadelphia. The three had left Featherstone in Meridian in the morning;
he was to catch up with them in Neshoba later in the afternoon.
Featherstone waited all afternoon in the church in Philadelphia. Mickey
Schwerner, James Chaney and Andy Goodman never did come.

Black folks in Philadelphia gave Featherstone a place to sleep and food to
eat, and he'd pay them a few dollars every now and then with money he'd
get from Northern white contributions to SNCC. Then the money stopped,
and Featherstone began working on economic development projects that
might make the Southern movement, and the black community, self-sustain-
ing. I spent some time with Ralph in Neshoba, and the one day I remember
most vividly was framed by two visits: by the FBI in the morning and by the
notorious Sheriffs Rainey and Price in the late afternoon. Neither visit was

pleasant; the FBI was polite and menacing and the sheriffs were rude and menacing, but Ralph dealt coolly and good-naturedly with both. At the end of the day he drank a lot of milk and took medicine for his stomach. He kept a shotgun next to the medicine.

The economic development project didn't work, and Featherstone came back to Washington, where he had grown up and had gone to college, to try a similar scheme. That one came to little, too, and he went back to Mississippi for a spell. As the movements of the sixties progressed, he went to Japan to talk to young people there, and he travelled to Cuba to see what that was like, and to Africa. SNCC pretty much stopped functioning as an organization, but Featherstone and some of the best of the SNCC people kept working. In the months before he was blown to bits by a bomb in Bel Air, Maryland, Featherstone and several others were running a bookstore, a publishing house and a school in Washington. Ralph lived a few blocks from me, and we'd bump into each other every few weeks, chat briefly and make vague plans to get together for a meal or a longer talk. As we both knew, the plans would not be followed. Somewhat mindlessly, I would slip Ralph into a category called "the black thing," a locked box decorated with exotic Benin artifacts and a tag: "Do Not Open Until . . . " I shudder now at the thought of the tag on the bag he had for me.

The road from Meridian ended in many more ways than one last week. Ralph's progression in the last six years was, like the road itself, an attenuated metaphor. Strung out along the way were the mileposts of a generation, the markings of a movement, passed as soon as they were come upon, quickly out of sight. It's hard to say how one or another man or woman is bound to travel, and it can't be known where anyone is going to stop. Ralph missed a meeting in Neshoba; but then he kept his appointment in Bel Air.

A desperate irony of history, a dialectical pun, put Featherstone's death next to the explosions in the Wilkerson house in Greenwich Village and the bombings a few nights later of three corporations' offices in Manhattan. In evidentiary terms the events of that week seem totally disconnected. Featherstone and his companion, Che Payne, were most probably murdered by persons who believed that Rap Brown was in their car. Featherstone had gone to Bel Air to make security arrangements on the eve of Brown's scheduled appearance at his trial for arson and inciting a riot in connection with the 1967 conflagrations in the nearby town of Cambridge. Brown had good reason to fear for his safety in that red neck of the woods. No one who knew the kinds of politics Featherstone was practicing, or the mission he was on in Bel Air, or the quality of his judgement believes that he was transporting a bomb—in the front seat of a car, leaving Bel Air, at midnight, in hostile territory, with police everywhere.

The police and newspaper accounts of the goings-on in the Wilkerson house on West Eleventh Street seem—in outline, at least—consistent within them-

selves and probable in the (dim) light of developments after the recent
break-up of a formal Weatherman organization. The tensions within
Weatherman, both organizationally and politically, were always as explosive
as any bomb; Weatherman collectives changed their course almost fortnight-
ly: puritanical one week, totally uninhibited the next; druggy and orgiastic,
then ascetic and celibate; concerned with a mass line and liberal movements,
then deep into guerrilla training. And all the time they were dealing—not
very successfully—with open repression from the Man and open hostility
from most other radicals. It was clear at the Weatherman convention in
Flint last December that the organization was not going to grow in size and
legitimacy, and as early Weathersymps and cadre from the collectives
dropped out of contact, the core hardened. In a few months, the distance
between the guerrilla center and the discarded cadre and lost sympathizers
could be measured in light-years; people who had once worked closely with
the women who were reportedly in the Eleventh Street house knew nothing
of their recent activities, and could not begin to find out.

The corporate bombings in Manhattan on the night of March 11 appear to
be the work of people with politics quite different from the post-Weathermen
of Eleventh Street. Even a cursory analysis of the messages the bombers left
indicates that they were of the same anarchist strain as those who hit similar targets last November. The notes spoke in terms of "death culture" and
life forces, but contained few of the internationalist, anti-police, anti-racism
and pro-Vietcong references that mark the Weather ethic.

Although the week's three events are disconnected in all particulars, they
are at the same time tied at some radical bottom. Guerrilla attacks by the
revolutionary left and counterattacks by the extreme right seem almost natural in America this winter. When students demonstrate they do not merely
sit-in but burn-up: they firebomb a bank in Santa Barbara, snipe at policemen in Buffalo. Few peaceful marches end peacefully; both marchers and
police are ready to fight.

The newspapers have begun calling the current crop of radicals "revolutionaries," but they have removed the quotation marks and have dropped
such skeptical qualifiers as "self-styled" or "so-called." For the first time in
half a century, at least—and perhaps since 1776—there is a generalized revolutionary movement in the US. It is not directed at organizing labor or winning civil rights for minorities or gaining power for students in the administration of universities. Wholly unorganized and utterly undirected, the revolutionary movement exists not because a handful of young blacks or dissident middle-class whites will it but because the conditions of American life
create it; not because the left is so strong but because the center is so weak.

It's worth saying that what the revolutionary movement is *not*. First of all,
it's not big. All the people who are into demolitions this year could gather in
a townhouse or two in the Village—and probably have. There have been
scores of bombings in the past six months—in New York, Seattle, the San

Francisco Bay Area, Colorado and scattered college towns. In Madison, Wisconsin, someone predicted *Zabriskie Point* and bombed an ROTC building from an airplane (the bombs did not go off). But a hundred or two hundred people could have done all that, and there are no vast divisions preparing for the next assaults.

Second, it's not yet a revolution. A bomb in Standard Oil's headquarters in Manhattan does as much material damage to Standard Oil as a tick does to a tiger. Universities have not ground to a halt, draft boards have not been shut down, the war in Indochina hardly has ended. The resources of the corporations and the government that make public decisions and social policy are complete.

But then, the revolutionary movement is not isolated in its few activists, nor confined to its few acts of violence. There was a general sense of depression in the liberal left when the Eleventh Street house blew up, and there was a genuine sense of exhilaration when the bombings followed. For that reason, the guerrilla acts cannot be dismissed as "isolated terror" by a "lunatic fringe"; they draw a positive response from a surprisingly large number of ordinary people—even those who venture out of their conventional lives for nothing more exciting than a Moratorium rally, and who will tell you before you ask that they "deplore" violence. The contradictions of the society as a whole exist within each of them as well.

Finally, the revolutionary movement is not professional, nor is it politically mature, nor tactically consistent. Nor is there much chance that it will get itself together in the coming months. If it was a "tragic accident" that killed three young people in the Eleventh Street house, it was in one sense no accident: those who seek to build a revolution from scratch must inevitably make such mistakes. (For a description of how amateurish revolutionaries can be, read Che's diaries.) The politics of guerrilla acts are not always self-explanatory, even to committed radicals. One New York radical activist said recently that the corporate bombings could have contextual meaning only if the messages demanded US withdrawal from Vietnam and Laos, say, or freedom for Black Panthers in jail. A note that threatened continued attacks until the war ended, for example, would make sense to many more people than the seemingly "nihilist" statements made last week.

The escalation of radical protest into revolutionary action will produce two major social effects: a sense of crisis in the society as a whole, and a need for more repression by the authorities. The two effects are inextricably related. The sense of crisis is not the work of the bombers or bank burners or demonstrators or Panthers alone. It develops easily when the phones don't work, the beaches are oil-slicked, the blacks are bussed to white schools, the priests are marrying, the redwoods are toppling, the teenagers are shooting up, the women are liberating themselves, the stock market is falling and the Vietcong are winning.

Neither does repression happen in a single tone of voice. Even in the most critical of times (*especially* in the most critical of times) the state acts, as Lenin put it, like hangman and priest. In the same months that Fred Hampton is killed or desegregation is postponed in Mississippi, millions of dollars go to black urban bureaucrats; black students are streaming into previously white colleges and white jobs; and the government makes plans to give preferential hiring to blacks in construction jobs. Of course, the "Philadelphia plan" for hiring black construction workers is also a way to limit the power of labor unions. But in the near and middle distances, all those measures—the repressive and the co-optive—are reasonably successful in blunting the chopping edge of the black liberation movement.

Likewise, in the same week that Vice President Spiro Agnew is denouncing "kooks" and "social misfits," and Chicago 7 prosecutor Foran is talking of a "freaking fag revolution," the Nixon Administration and a coalition of politicians from (and including) Goldwater to Kennedy are proposing lowering the voting age to 18, and plans are going ahead for an all-volunteer army. Again, those measures will not accomplish much in the way of changing social values in America, but neither are they exactly Nuremberg Laws to be used against a radical force or a distasteful element of society.

In the wake of the bombings and deaths last week, the FBI fanned out to question anyone known to have a connection with the Eleventh Street people. Agents were unusually uptight; one set of FBI visitors called a New York man who declined to speak to them a "motherfucker." There were police agents with walkie-talkies standing around major airports all week long. The newspapers—especially in New York—bannered scare headlines and speculated endlessly, and foolishly, on the connections between the events. Authorities "leaked" word to Richard Starnes, a Scripps-Howard reporter in Washington who often acts as an unofficial flack for the FBI, that both Featherstone and the three Eleventh Street people so far identified had visited Cuba—and that attorney Leonard Boudin, whose daughter's papers were found in the house, represented the Cuban government in legal matters in the US. Senator Eastland has now called for an investigation of the Venceremos Brigade of Americans who have gone to Cuba to harvest sugar cane. No one believes that the natives in America can be restless all by themselves.

The level of fear (that is, paranoia with good reason) has risen to exorbitant heights, but that too affects the general sense of crisis in the society. Seen in relief (if there can be any), that crisis is the most serious organizing effect of the bombings. If the radical movements are to win middle-class people—or those, black and white, who aspire to middle-class comfort and security—they must devise ways of forcing real existential choices upon them. At one time, marches and rallies or sit-ins or building occupations provided a setting for those choices. But privileged Americans do not easily make the revolutionary choice. Only if their privilege is worthless are they free to act. Now, the sense of crisis is the specific contradiction of privilege:

that is, all the things Americans want to get and spend are without meaning if the world no longer holds together. At such times, people choose to fight—one way or the other.

March 23-30, 1970, HARD TIMES

◆

Bringing It All Back Home

New Haven

The first time I was in the streets in New Haven was twenty-six years ago, when I marched alongside my father in the civil defense contingent of a Fourth of July parade, during the Second World War. My father was a divisional leader of the Air Raid Wardens, and he kept a small stockpile of gas masks in the attic of our house, for use in the event of enemy attack. The masks were objects of wonder and pride to me, and I carried one in its canvas case, tied around my waist, in the parade. Much to my disappointment, the war ended without an enemy attack. The German Spy who carried on extensive clandestine operations in the wooded lot across from our house disappeared without a trace in May 1945. He was replaced only briefly by a Japanese Spy assigned similar duties. After the war my friends and I played out our fantasies with the surplus gas masks, the large galvanized metal hand-pumped fire extinguishers and the rest of the disaster-control paraphernalia made obsolete by peace. Then the wooded lot was levelled and "developed" with one-family brick or wood houses. Our fantasies took other turns.

My next demonstration in New Haven came nine years later, on a mild May afternoon at the end of my senior year in high school. An argument had erupted between the Good Humor ice cream man and the Jack and Jill ice cream man over trading rights for a choice corner in the middle of the Yale campus. Student partisans of each side argued boisterously among themselves for a while, then joined in a united front against the university and the downtown business establishment. I came upon the scene after my school let out that afternoon, at the point that the squabbling around the ice cream issue was turning into a general insurrection. The riot lasted well into the evening. The mayor, a lugubrious undertaker named William C. Celentano, arrived at one corner of the Green on board a fire engine and read the Riot Act to the unruly crowd through a bullhorn. I had never heard the Riot Act read before that afternoon, nor have I since. Undeterred, the rioting students assaulted the Hotel Taft, ran through its rooms and streamed toilet paper from its windows onto the streets below. At length, we were pushed back into the Old Campus, doused with water from fire hoses and locked in the quad. No one took it very seriously. My father was the New Haven DA at the time, and I believe he was in charge of prosecuting those few students who were arrested. I doubt that any of them served a day in jail.

There have been other riots in New Haven since then; panty raids gave way to ghetto uprisings, but I have kept my distance. I went away to college, and except for brief family visits over the years, I have not wanted to return. The city underwent drastic changes in its physique and its politics, but my nostalgic curiosity in the new New Haven was hardly equal to my sense of alienation from the whole scene. My father, a Republican, was removed from the prosecutor's office by a Democratic administration which seized state power in the fifties and has maintained its hold to this day. Richard Lee, the reformist Democratic mayor, bulldozed much of the city to the ground, and after a decade of delays, built rows of glassy office blocks, lyrical parking garages and chic townhouses atop the rubble. Inhabitants of the "slums" torn down were left to shift for themselves. The mindless "community action" programs that Lee laid on the blacks provided new careers for the upwardly mobile, and very little else. Nothing he did in his years of rule could prevent the full-blown black revolt that convulsed the city in 1967.

Yale's rulers embarked on a similarly wasteful building and expansion program, in so close a relationship to Lee's as to invite indictment for incest. Lee was a Yale PR man before he assumed the mayoralty, but that was only the most up-front connection between town and gown, whose political and economic interests are inextricably tied. According to the excellent pamphlet "Go to School, Learn to Rule," published this month by two radical research and political groups, Yale holds almost $100 million worth of tax-free property in New Haven—one-third of all untaxed real estate in the city. It controls the principal health and psychiatric services for the community; commands the important cultural institutions; constitutes the social elite; instigates or vetoes public works that touch its extended interests. Moreover, it hardly pays lip-service to the rhetoric of "community involvement" which other great universities now feel compelled to produce. All in all, Yale is the dominating force in a wide New Haven community of almost half a million people, which the university treats as a kind of support population for its 8,000 students.

When I was growing up in New Haven, Yale provided the models and set the standards for acceptable values and behavior. Sons and daughters of the white middle class were showered with Shetland sweaters, bathed in button-downs, inundated with natural-shoulders from the tweedy boutiques of York Street. We went to all the Yale sports events, the Yale concerts, the Yale museums, the Yale libraries, the Yale movies. New Haven's only three high schools (in those days) were clustered in one compound in a corner of the campus. (They all fell under Yale's expansion program, and were replaced by high-art university dorms.) As high school students, we competed with Yale underclassmen for dates with the more desirable local girls. The Yalies always won.

The attributes of a Yale man—snobbish, super-cool, careerist—were transmitted through all Yale's contacts to the community around, and if those values were always resented on some level, they were respected on another. Subcultures of New Haven society—particularly New Haven youth—might react to Yale with hostility or affection, but it was to the over-whelming fact of Yale's presence that they were reacting.

In the fifties there was a lively institution practiced by the gentlemen of Yale called the "pig party." In this instance, the animal metaphor had noth-ing to do with an oppressor in the police force or the ruling class, but referred rather to an ugly and promiscuous girl—usually of local origin and with few educational credentials. On certain occasions in the school year, Yalemen in a fraternity or secret society would invite a bevy of such women to a party in whatever Gothic chapel they called home. The men alone knew the "key" to the affair; the women were delighted to attend such a tony func-tion, and did not recognize what they had in common with one another. Invariably, the evenings ended in drunken orgy, and the Yalies dined out for weeks afterwards on stories of the party.

Of course, that was Yale at its very worst, but it symbolized what I thought was the universal corruption and hypocrisy of the Yale spirit. It never sur-prised me, in the mid-sixties, that there was no big radical movement on the Yale campus. Long after Berkeley blew and Columbia collapsed, Yale's cathe-dral towers stood unstained on New Haven's Green. Conventional wisdom attributed the absence of movement to president Kingman Brewster's liberal reign, but New Haveners knew that there was a lot less to Brewster than met the eye. More than anything else, Yale was quiet because Yalies didn't care.

Now that has all changed, and again it is not because of Brewster but in spite of him. The anger of a generation finally reached the ivied tombs, blew away the pig parties, discredited J. Press and, last weekend, for May Day, filled the Green with shouting, fist-waving freaks. No need to exaggerate: God, Country and Yale still stand. But the student strike and the weekend rally in support of Black Panthers now in Connecticut jails on murder charges are the biggest things to hit Yale since Dink Stover, and in their own way constitute as important an event in the radicalization of elite edu-cation in America as the uprisings at Berkeley or Columbia.

The route to the Green is marked with signposts familiar enough in this age. In 1966 the "peace" campaign of Yale professor Robert Cook for Congress developed into an independent Movement organization, AIM. Cook did poorly in the election, but he and his organizers kept AIM alive as a cen-ter for political activity, in closer or looser coalition (as those things will be) with a militant black group called the Hill Parents Association. Those few New Left students at Yale who wanted to do political work in New Haven naturally gravitated to AIM and HPA.

AIM went through all the changes common to Movement organizations in the late sixties, but unlike many, it managed to stay alive and active. AIM people published a newsletter, started a coffee house, took jobs at communi-ty colleges, formed communes and collectives, focussed on Yale and New Haven issues with a radical approach.

Because Yale had been polarized by radical actions, there was a predictably large McCarthy/Moratorium constituency: predictable, too, was its vocal anti-radicalism. But by 1969, connections were being made between people and movements at various points, and it all came together one night last spring in the Ingalls Skating Rink, a soaring Saarinen structure on the edge of the Yale campus. The issue that night was ROTC at Yale, and there was a multiparty struggle to decide its future and, by extension, the political temper of the student body. SDS members, Moratorium types, "moderates," faculty and administrators battled it out at the podium, while Yale's rulers sat in the bleachers in back, looking more like a Greek junta than a Greek chorus. The result was a "compromise" of some sort, the dimensions of which are lost in my memory. I was in New Haven that night because my father had died a few weeks before, and I wandered into the rally to see what was happening. It was not a very revolutionary affair; I had seen more struggle over the issue of ice cream. But in a back row I saw four young blacks—a woman and three men—who alone in the vast hall appeared not to be Yale students. I watched them for a moment and heard them shout "Right on!" at an appropriate juncture in the debate. After an hour or so, they rose and left. "The Panthers," a friend said to me with a nod. "The woman's Ericka Huggins."

I can remember having only one black friend at high school in New Haven. He had light skin, spoke posh and went on to Williams or Amherst after graduation. I had one gentile friend, too. Everyone else I knew was a middle-class Jew. *Gentlemen's Agreement* was the defining movie of my childhood. Ericka Huggins grew up in New Haven, also, but I would have known her, or her brothers and sisters, only if we were in the same room at the same school. Hillhouse High School was "integrated" in that way.

I don't know exactly how Ericka got from high school in New Haven to a jail in New Haven (people say her mother is a "very nice lady" active in the Urban League), but now she is one of the nine Black Panthers charged with murdering Alex Rackley a year ago this month. The police say the Panthers believed Rackley was an informer and murdered him—on Bobby Seale's orders—after a lengthy interrogation and a torture session. The interrogation was supposedly recorded for use as instructional material for other Panther chapters.

The Panthers say Rackley was a party member in good standing and that he was murdered by undercover agents in order to set Bobby up for a murder rap. They say Seale was brought to New Haven by a Yale administration official to speak at the university; that official has vanished. George Sams, the "Panther" who supplied police with details of the alleged murder, is thought to be an agent, or crazy, or both. Warren Kimbro, another member of the New Haven Panther chapter, has confessed to participation in the crime, in exchange for which his murder charge was reduced by one degree. Kimbro pleaded guilty after his brother, a Florida policeman, was flown to the New Haven jail by the DA and closeted for a long talk with Warren.

Such "evidence" will be pored over when the trial begins, probably at the end of the summer. But although the popular press insists that the question of who killed Alex Rackley is the only thing that counts, that is at bottom not the issue at all. "The facts," Tom Hayden said at the rally on the Green last Saturday, "are irrelevant." Murder, after all, is a category defined by the interests of those with weapons. No one was punished for executing Benedict Arnold, no one stands accused of the murder of Che Guevara, no trial will be held for the national guardsmen who shot the four Kent State students. In all those cases, like so many others, the murders were acts of war, outside the concern of a judicial system. Seen one way (at least) the killing of Alex Rackley was an act of war, whether committed by Panthers or pigs, and if Bobby Seale pulled the very trigger (an act not even the police accuse him of; he never saw Rackley) and were convicted of murder, he would be neither a criminal nor a political prisoner: he is a prisoner of war.

The people who came to New Haven for the May Day events were drawn by the perception of a war game, not a civil liberties issue. The Panthers had organized the rally—primarily through the genius of Douglas Miranda, the 19-year-old Panther who directs the support campaign in New Haven—and the whites who helped were struggling to submit to Panther discipline. It was not always easy. Internally, Panther politics is every bit as disputatious as other Movement examples, and for weeks before the rally it was never clear what the Panthers wanted whites to do in New Haven. In the May 2 issue of *The Black Panther,* the official party newspaper, New York Panther leader Afeni Shakur excoriated the "so called revolutionaries of Babylon" for "jiving, pimping . . . but not waging revolution." Shakur continued: "You have not delivered one political consequence to the planned execution of a humanitarian. And to further your laziness, your cowardice, you allowed David Hilliard and Emory Douglas to be kidnapped. There isn't enough fire power being heard or felt in Babylon. Demonstrations have got to be on an even-steven basis. You start demonstrating with .357s on your hips."

It hardly matters that Shakur was wrong (white kids in New Haven were so active that they forced Judge Mulvey to release Hilliard and Douglas, who had been sentenced to six months for contempt). Her anger at the white movement springs from all the disappointments Panthers have had with whites, all the broken promises, all the failures of support when it would have been crucial. Last summer, the Panthers tried to make an alliance with SDS and other white radicals at the United Front Against Fascism conference in Oakland. It came to nothing. Until New Haven, whites had not committed themselves to the Panthers' struggle.

Nixon was giving his Cambodia invasion speech on the radio as I turned off the Connecticut Turnpike into New Haven last weekend. The President was denouncing "anarchy" as I pulled up in front of a house where one of the radical collectives was billeted. The building was elegantly reconstructed from a dilapidated townhouse in what was long ago the richest section of town. From under a street light across the way, three or four fat middle-aged men watched me and a few friends approach the house. After a round of suspicious self-identifications, a young man opened the door. He had short blond hair and wore wire-rim granny glasses and work clothes. He carried a shotgun in his hand, and as we entered he pointed it rather awkwardly at his own chin. Three young white women sat doing paper work at a desk in the front room. A shotgun rested in a window bay. The windows were covered by bed sheets. The women raised their fists in greeting and said, "Power to the people." The interior of the house was glass and brick and white wall and indirect lighting. I had a flash of Godard, and then felt mildly disgusted with myself for succumbing so quickly to allusion.

We drove around the city in the night. Most of the stores and public buildings were boarded with plywood. Police cars prowled the streets. Everyone we met told us how tense they were, and how uptight the city was. Later that night, Kingman Brewster held a little meeting with some of the Chicago "conspirators" who were in town for the weekend. Cyrus Vance, a leading member of the Yale Corporation, sat quietly through the meeting; he had had ample experience with civil insurrection in Cyprus, Detroit and Vietnam. The Reverend William Sloane Coffin sauntered into the meeting and invited himself to stay. ("Brewster is Sihanouk," Hayden said in his rally speech Saturday; not much of a ruler but committed to a "progressive" role so long as those above and below keep him in power. Sooner or later, he will be deposed by those who feel he is selling out or by those who feel he is cashing in. But for now, Hayden said, he will protect us and he should be supported.)

I suppose that other demonstrations and college uprisings last week could be described in just as dramatic terms as the Yale action and have as much importance. New Haven had seemed critical at first because it had been building for weeks as a media as well as a Movement event. By chance, it was the first college demonstration after the invasion of Cambodia. In fact, the renewed bombardment of North Vietnam was taking place as the events in New Haven were going on, and the announcement came while 10,000 people were still sitting on the Green. The Panthers and the white organizers quickly decided not to broadcast it to the crowds, and instead sent everyone home abruptly to avoid the "violence" that might be expected if word of the bombing went out. What followed in the next week—the convulsive collegiate twitch against the war, the murders at Kent State, the calls for national actions—seemed almost to erase memories of New Haven. But that weekend was no minor meeting. If the elements on the Green were already old, still the mix was new. The crowd was freaky, dopey and rocky, but it was beyond Woodstock; or perhaps it was Woodstock Nation, Marxist-Leninist, the revolutionary part of the whole.

It was not so much the events of the New Haven weekend as the context that gave it meaning. The Panthers finally settled on a strict rule of non-violence (urged by attorney Charles Garry), not because it would lead to a better deal for the defendants but rather as a way to ensure bigger and heavier actions in New Haven when the trial begins. The combination of Panther discipline, press hysteria and the presence of army and national guard troops enforced the rule. The days were bright and warm, and there was just enough dope and good feeling to keep spirits high. The speeches, for the most part, did not ruin the fine days; the best of the lot were made by Miranda and Hayden. They defined the terms of radical coalition, set goals for the developing revolutionary movement and generally encouraged Long Marching. There were suggestions for further actions this summer—and hopes were raised for enormous rallies in New Haven and at the UN in the fall. Abbie Hoffman got the biggest response with his usual Woodstock rap, and if it was devoid of much logic, it still made sense as a connection-on-the-spot.

Yale loved every minute of it. Those students, teachers and administrators who were not into the revolutionary aspects of the action maintained a proper Lord and Lady Bountiful attitude and dispensed services with almost obsessive zeal. Everywhere you looked there was someone with a sandwich, an apple, information, a toilet or a bottle of eyewash. Signs were printed with symbols for various services: a little house for housing, a cup and saucer for refreshment, a plate and fork for food, a toilet, a red cross and so on. It was like an autobahn somewhere.

New Haven weathered it all with only mild hysteria. Much to my disappointment—once again—the city did not suffer enemy attack. A peaceful demonstration marred an otherwise promising holocaust. The tweedy haberdashers boarded their windows against Alaric and the Visigoths, but the most Gothic thing about the weekend were the flying buttresses on Dwight Chapel. There was sporadic tear-gassing on the Green at night, but no one got very alarmed. The mayor did not read the Riot Act. I looked in my attic for a gas mask, but found only an old saxophone and a pile of 78 RPM records.

May 11-18, 1970, HARD TIMES

Afternote: Charges against Seale, Huggins and one other Panther in the Rackley case were eventually dropped; Sams and Kimbro were convicted.

✦

Andy Weil and the Search Beyond Reason

Frontiers may come and go, but the regions within one's mind remain grounds for exploration forever. No dark jungle, no cold star, has drawn more intrepid travellers than the *terra incognita* of consciousness. Notwithstanding President Nixon's boasts, the "greatest days since creation" have involved trips quite different from those propelled by rocket fuel.

Things being what they are, the shores of the known universe are crowded these days with pioneers departing for God-knows-where in search of the inner light, the god within, the still, small voice that makes some sense when Reason fails. By no coincidence, the émigrés include many scientists who staked their careers on the triumph of Reason—and now have most to lose from its failure. One example is John Lilly, who, after trying for many years to dispute the great issues with dolphins, has now entered into a dialogue with his own head; his book about it is called *Center of the Cyclone*. In a somewhat related phenomenon, many psychiatrists who believe they have not got through to their patients or themselves are turning to trans-rationalist or "mystical" disciplines, such as the Arica course, for a new start.

The latest "invert" scientist (from external/objective to internal/subjective concerns) to hit the bookstores is Andrew Weil, whose tantalizingly and determinedly incomplete survey of trans-rationalist doctrine is called *The Natural Mind*. Weil is a romantic explorer, a stoned guru, a doctor-in-spite-of-himself. His own odyssey from Cambridge (Harvard College and Med) to Shantih-town has taken him through Psychedelia to the Amazon, where he is investigating tribal ways of getting and staying high within a "stable" community. No doubt he has a long way to go. But his trip is in some ways archetypal of his generation (he turned 30 this year, when the sun was in Gemini). I'll get to that generation-shift later (and my own brief journeys with Weil). First, at the risk of giving myself away as un-holy, un-stoned and lowly-of-consciousness, I'll attempt an old-fashioned rational exposition of Weil's new-fangled "intuitions" about consciousness and drugs:

1. The urge to alter one's consciousness and enter states of non-ordinary reality (daydreaming, tripping, psychotic episodes, trances, general anaesthesia, meditative states, etc.) is a basic drive, like sexual desire or hunger. Children who whirl to get dizzy, dervishes who whirl to get holy, hippies who turn on with grass, and suburbanites who drop martinis are all in their own ways fulfilling that urge.

2. Drugs—all intoxicants from glue to alcohol to heroin—are a tool, and only a tool, to enter such non-ordinary states of consciousness. But the "trip" is not in the drug; it is in the mind. The drug is an "active placebo" whose pharmacological effect merely triggers the alteration of consciousness. Unpleasant pharmacological effects of some drugs (nausea, impotence, liver failure) should not be confused with the trip.

3. Ego-attached, "straight" thinking, Reason-bound Western society is so threatened by alterations of consciousness that it has created a drug problem: "what we are now doing in the name of stopping the drug problem *is* the drug problem."

4. Come to think of it, "straight," rationalist, cause-and-effect, non-intuitive, inductive, "materialist" epistemology is the source of most social ills and the obstacle to alleviating personal ills. That is, social oppression and individual illness can be avoided not by aggression (war, antibiotics) but by alteration of "straight" categories to "stoned" ones.

5. The consciousness revolution is beginning. Sooner or later, we will be able to accept transrational categories and use them in everyday life: intuition, ambivalence, unity, infinity. Eventually, we will all be able to control our hitherto "autonomic" or involuntary nervous system, effect healing without toxic medicines or surgery, and get high without drugs.

There will be pie in the sky by and by—not after death (cf. Christianity) or after the proletarian revolution (cf. Marxism) but rather after the collective elevation of consciousness. Not-thinking about it will make it so. In his expectation of peace-through-mind, Weil is very much in the wake of the great Eastern religious philosophies. But he is Western enough to relate Nirvana to a social context, however tentative that may be at this early stage of his own "stoned" thinking.

It is only one irony of Weil's work-in-progress that he builds his argument with fine Cartesian logic. Weil's ideology is based on the necessary and inevitable acceptance of "stoned" thinking and its triumph over the bad consequences of straightness. Along the way, there are echoes of Freud, Jung, Laing, Lao Tzu, Prince Gautama, Baba Ram Dass, Carlos Castaneda, H. Rider Haggard and assorted witch doctors, organic gardeners and yogis. If you sense a certain contradiction between the construction of ideology and the destruction of rationalism, no matter: ambivalence is the nature of all things.

I'm not sure why Andy Weil wrote his book in the first place, since books (this kind of book, surely) are products of a "straight" way of thinking. Perhaps one can still half-believe in the notion that stoned people can argue rationally with straight people, or that social repression of stonedness will decrease as more people become convinced, through argument, of its virtues and necessity. Or perhaps one can't believe in that notion at all. How hard does rationalism die?

Such questions probably don't bother Weil much. He has spent the last year in Central and South America, and from such reports as filter back, he has gone beyond where his book ended. I suspect he also sees his naïvetés, superficialities, biases more clearly. Since I met him three years ago, I've always had the sense that Weil was "on to something" and that "it" was too evanescent to catch at any given point in time. His book—like his conversation—unnaturally stops the process of development of his consciousness and warps what picture happens to be there in a "straight" time-frame.

Weil enjoyed a flamboyant career at Harvard, playing practical jokes, writing clever articles and generally larking it up with the funniest people. He also had a remarkable drug life (e.g., mescaline in 1960) before anyone had heard of psychedelics. Drugs did not turn his brain to oatmeal or produce "amotivation," whatever the hysterical claims of the Harvard Health Services might be. At Harvard Medical School, Weil and psychiatrist Norman Zinberg did strategically important research on the effects of marijuana on humans (conclusion: all things considered, it's better to smoke grass than not). He then interned in a psychiatric hospital in San Francisco, accepted a commission in the Public Health Service to escape the draft and was assigned to the National Institute of Mental Health in Washington. At length, the dissonance between stoned institutions and bureaucratic institutions became too loud, and Weil quit the NIMH. (He continued to avoid the military by stating that if drafted as a doctor he could no longer in good conscience practice Western medicine; the army recoiled in fear.)

I met Weil when he was sliding out of NIMH and I was sliding out of "straight" journalism in Washington. We shared many of the same ambivalences, fears, excitement about that process. I was "into" radical politics and he was "into" mystical politics, but those trips seemed somehow analogous. We got stoned together a lot. In the course of a year, Weil became a vegetarian, began rather intensive meditative disciplines, and gave up Western science and medicine. I jumped in and out of Weathersymp actions and began a de-urbanization process that eventually took me to a rural commune in Vermont. I took acid for the first time and read Zen parables and Lao Tzu. We had a totally informal but nonetheless recognizable "group" that was moving around the same poles together. We talked about "stone consciousness," among other things, and took various trips. The "group" or set broke up for the usual hundred reasons, and we would all have different ways of seeing that dissolution. My own feeling is that we all failed to take one another's emotional life into account in our zeal to see the lord.

What I mean to suggest with this autobiographical fragment is that the flight from the confines of an oppressive rationalism may be a generalized phenomenon in young, white middle-class (male?) America, and that it finds particular expressions in many ways: tripping, revolutionary ecstasy, sexual liberation, commune-ism, religious disciplines. Andy Weil's denial of allopathic medicine and inductive science and my own rejection of objective reporting and political science were indicative of that flight. Was my political progress only that—a flight from hyper-rationalism? I think not. The process is shot through with ambiguities. But surely that is part of it. Weil and another of our friends once printed up slogan-stickers with the simple motto: "You Never Know," and started pasting them on refrigerator doors all around town. We never knew. One of my recurrent "flashbacks" recollects an LSD trip on Memorial Day almost two and a half years ago. Under an exquisite waterfall near Harper's Ferry, West Virginia, I asked a Movement friend who was tripping with me: "Do you think the revolution will be like acid?" "It *is* acid," she said, and laughed. I knew she didn't mean it in the simple hippy-trippy way.

Andy Weil is in some sense premature in projecting an ideology beyond rationalism; his identification of Straight Reason as the primary contradiction is no more valid, if no less, than the naming of a dozen other factors by ideologues with primary contradictions to flog. But every pot smoker knows "something" that non-heads don't know, and trippers know it more, and no doubt those who can achieve one-pointedness by drugless concentration know it best of all. The substance of that knowledge-beyond-knowledge is probably not statable, or perhaps Andy Weil said all there need be said about it on his refrigerator stickers years ago.

October 3, 1972, THE BOSTON PHOENIX

✦

Lady Sings Dem Kozmic Blues

There are no second acts in American lives.
—F. Scott Fitzgerald

Somewhere between Port Arthur, Texas, where she was born, and the Landmark Hotel in Hollywood, where she died on October 4, 1970, Janis Joplin relinquished the terms of ordinary existence and became a "metaphor" for her generation and its times. Drop-out, doper, hooker, rock star, sex freak, super-hip—Janis did not merely make the scene; she *was* the scene. There was almost nothing about the youth subculture of the late sixties that Janis did not embody in her raucous white blues style and her reckless white lifestyle. But it was her style of death that now seems to be the *beau geste* of her twenty-seven years. Nearly finished recording an album (*Pearl*) that was to determine the future of her popularity, and torn between lesbian longings and an impending heterosexual marriage, Janis picked up the heroin needle which she had earlier abandoned and shot herself into the ultimate down. Now, even her death is not her own; it merely extends the metaphor.

Like Marilyn Monroe, with whom she shares some striking mythic qualities, Janis remains a topic of conversation and an object of curiosity long after the ubiquitous Los Angeles County medical examiner has closed his files on another OD. Both women crumbled under the strain of the same central contradiction: public adoration against inner inadequacy. What was worse was that the adoration fed on the image of inadequacy, and the inadequacy increased as the adoration grew stronger. There was no good way out of that double bind beyond the drug black-out typical of the years in which both women died.

None of the current retrospective biographies of Janis deals effectively with the nexus of personal, social and historical catastrophes that led logically, if not inevitably, to her destruction. Myra Friedman's careful chronicle, *Buried Alive,* applies a shallow psych textbook description of Janis's affection/rejection complex and mixes it with some smug sneers at the rock culture to produce an annoying analysis free of any ties to the history of the sixties and its complicated consciousness. Peggy Caserta's raunchy *Going Down With Janis* tells us more about the inside of Janis's thighs than the inside of her head, which give the book a certain organic accuracy that Friedman's detached accounts lack but renders it otherwise irrelevant.

What's missing is a sense of Janis struggling both to dominate and escape a progression of existential roles that are common to many women brought into high relief by the pressures of performance, stardom and the youth culture. In Janis's case, the most critical role was that of sexual actress. Aware of her lesbian feelings since adolescence at least (and probably earlier; Friedman's uptight accounts can't be trusted), she was forced into heterosexual patterns by both the straightness of Texas and the newer, and in some ways more aggressive, straightness of the sixties generation. Her compromise with the closet was a sad proclamation of bisexual do-your-own-thingism, which may have satisfied publicity requirements (Friedman was her PR agent) but did not deal directly with her need for a love connection. As so many other homosexuals have discovered, drug and alcohol connections are easier to make.

"Why is it," a friend of Janis's asked Myra Friedman, "when Janis was talking to a chick, she had a low, relaxed kind of voice and when talking to a cat her voice got all high and uptight?" Why indeed? Janis had long and complex relationships with several women, and unlike her thousands of sexual encounters with men, many of her "affairs" with women did not directly involve sex. It's obvious, for example, from Friedman's straight-faced writing of it, that Janis felt the kind of intimacy with her PR lady that she never had with any man. Once, Janis suggested that she and Myra stop going together to a restaurant they frequented lest people begin to gossip. Near the end, when Janis contemplated marriage to a young Berkeley hanger-on named Seth Morgan, she offered to share him with Friedman: "You can fuck him if you want to," Janis said to Myra over the long-distance phone from California to New York. Friedman takes the better part of a page to record her astonishment at Janis's "extremely bizarre" behavior and to proclaim her own "inflexible" heterosexuality. Several other times Friedman rails against the "militant lesbian movement" and various named and unnamed radicals for distorting reality to claim Janis as one of their own.

Those stories and many others that both Friedman and Caserta recount speak pretty plainly for themselves to anyone with the slightest understanding of the defensive consciousness of gay people in a "straight" career and social context. Homosexuals in the closet are far more worried than heterosexuals about going out in public with friends of their own sex. Gays often fantasize—and sometimes act out—sexual relations with reluctant straight sweethearts via a third party in bed, according to the syllogism of repressed sexuality: if A screws C, and B screws C, then A and B *almost* . . .

All of this is bizarre or astonishing only to those who will not admit their own role in producing such very predictable behavior. Superstar or super-hip, Janis suffered the same impossible pains as a million other lesbians who don't simply want everybody to do their own thing but want those they love to do one particular thing—and have that love validated by the world they inhabit. What was behind Janis's suffering? I'd look to the fearful indifference of her friends as well as the "infantilism" of her psyche that Friedman diagnoses.

Beyond the tortured tensions of Janis's sexual role were the demands of performance and stardom in an incomplete and historically immature culture that had no real standards for excellence. In their absence, performers and publicists alike elevated those ineffable and largely impressionistic qualities of style, soul, spontaneity, charisma, energy and heavy vibes to the level of brilliance of technique. But what journalists ordain as qualities of spirit change with every concert or album, and good vibes one day may be a drag the next. Rock stars are always riding for a fall, and they know it; they haven't the slightest idea what gave them stardom, but whatever it was can and just as surely will take stardom away. Agents, PR people (such as Friedman and her boss, the ursine Albert Grossman), record industry A&R men, other rock performers and fickle fans fit roles in that system of impossible dreams that are bound to bring everyone down in the end.

Naturally, the stars stand to go down the farthest—and still more if they are women. Jerry Garcia does not fall into deep despair if he fails—or thinks he fails—as a sex god. Janis did, because the role of sex goddess went along with her kozmic blues and she could not have one without the other. Of course, her own needs constitute an important aspect of that equation. But so do the needs of a culture that is forever looking for sex stars, creating them and moralizing over their destruction.

The cult continues after Janis's death, like rituals to a sacrificed virgin, because of those same quaint sexual demands of the late-twentieth-century American culture. Janis and Marilyn are as important in their heavenly incarnations as they were in mundane form: objects of mass male masturbatory worship, one way or another. It's easy to see in Marilyn's case, but Janis, too, was a hippie sex-ideal—for all her funky weirdness, bad skin and autistic presentation.

There aren't a lot of books about a Jimi Hendrix or a Jim Morrison cult; nor is Mick Jagger—a sex god in his own right—in the same spot as Janis was. Men, even those pretending sexual ambiguity, are rarely trapped in the same way that women are in performance situations. And when men do find themselves victimized, they have options as individuals that are simply not open to women. Myra Friedman is rather pleased to say that Janis eschewed the nonsense of the "collective" ethic of the new culture, as if individualism were such a virtue that even in the abstract it transcends the obvious cases where it is counterproductive. Janis couldn't make it out of the sex-star-smack world alone. Friedman hoped she would get a man (Albert Grossman, if you can believe it) to pull her out. What she needed was other women— not, perhaps, a romantic careerist like Peggy Caserta, but others who could at least understand the Janis behind the *Newsweek* cover, behind the crazy-lady myth, behind the feather boas and velvet dresses, even behind the persona of Pearl.

Janis's life and death seem doomed to be taken as a moral tale, and the typical lessons drawn concern the wildness of the hippie scene, the disintegration of American families, the evil of heroin and similar comfortable cautions. Myra Friedman blames the unselfconscious artist, Janis, who "did not quite comprehend the whole circle of her partnership with the public, stopping at a frightening perception that did not include a recognition of her half of the bargain. 'Maybe my audiences,' she declared, 'can enjoy my music more if they think I'm destroying myself.'"

It always makes me angry to hear people talk about life-struggles as a "bargain," the way parents conceive of "deals" in which children get Pontiac GTOs if they are accepted into law school. Janis and the fans had no partnership; the rock business is no bargain; the blues ain't no deal. Janis needed to be what the blues made her feel, what the hip culture promised her, what the audiences thought she was. People out there in concert-land and stereo-land were fighting to feel those same things through her. Janis didn't merely lose. She was overwhelmed.

The lesson in the Janis legend has little to do with Janis's lack of bargain-sense, her emotional infantilism or the flaws in the flower scene. It's mainly about the meeting of one woman with the dreadful demands of the American monster of sex, money and love; and how, as Hemingway didn't quite say, one woman alone ain't got a bloody chance.

November 1973, RAMPARTS

✦

Which Way the Wind Blew

"The Seventies" may be a mere journalistic joke, a category whose only coherence is the accident of decimal enumeration. But that day at the dawn of the decade when three Weathermen blew themselves to death while making bombs in the basement of a townhouse in Greenwich Village marked a generational watershed for me and my cohort of "The Sixties." One of the three was a close and cherished friend who had drawn me into the New Left several years earlier; the other two I counted as political comrades, whom I saw frequently at meetings and demonstrations. The explosives they were concocting so carelessly were intended for use against draft centers, police headquarters, corporate offices, banks and other imperial command posts in the Weather war against the American military machine. Their cause may have been correct, but their recipe was wrong, and on that winter's day the Weather Underground detonated itself prematurely in a political vacuum, all sound and fury, signifying nothing, except death. The explosion seemed to be the end of politics, the senescence of the youth culture, the negation of idealism, the death of hope. For a short span of years that looked as long as a century our world was in turmoil and then . . . nothing happened.

Around midnight on the day of the townhouse explosion I was visited in my apartment in Washington by a young man who had been tangentially involved with surface-level Weatherman activities. He wore a long gray coat with its collar pulled up to meet the rim of an oversized cloth cap, giving him the appearance of Victor McLaglen in *The Informer*. He stood in the doorway and asked for money to help those "friends" who had escaped the blast. I asked no questions, but scoured the flat for spare change and hidden bills and came up with $50 for the cause. I then flushed a half-ounce of marijuana down the toilet.

In the sixties I had been to more marches than I could count, trashed everything in my line of sight, travelled to Hanoi and other enemy redoubts, spent white nights in jail and long days in political congress. After that winter I went to one last demo—the "Free Bobby and Ericka" weekend in New Haven, Connecticut, on May Day 1970. There were speakers from every walk of the Movement, including the first appearance of a gay liberation representative. He received scant applause. Late that afternoon leaders of the demonstration asked if they might use my family's house, on a quiet suburban street, for a meeting to plan campus protests against the Cambodian invasion for the following week. The Panther leaders were invited, along with such luminaries as Tom Hayden, Jean Genet and William Kunstler. I accepted, of course, and sped home to remove the "Visit Israel" posters my parents had tacked to the knotty-pine walls in our basement rumpus room, where the meeting was to take place. "They don't like Israel?" my mother asked as I rolled up the colorful photographs. "Not at the moment," I told her.

In those early days of the decade, I did not exactly decide to sit out the seventies, but I wasn't marching anymore. I found myself a new set of friends who swallowed rather large quantities of LSD on a regular regimen and listened to Baba Ram Dass raps on tapes. I bought a motorcycle and a black leather jacket to go with it. One night I threw all my suits, ties and button-down-collar shirts into an enormous packing box and dragged it to a street corner where the hippie quarter and the black ghetto intersected in Northwest Washington. Then I went to dinner with a friend at a nearby Cuban *gusano* restaurant much favored by anti-imperialist radicals despite the prominence of an enormous portrait of Fulgencio Batista in the entrance way. When I returned to the packing box after dinner, every piece of clothing was gone.

The next morning I set out on my Honda 450CB for Vermont, where I camped out in a waterless, heatless, phoneless, powerless and floorless shell of an eighteenth-century farmhouse nestled in a spectacular niche of hills and meadows. I planned to return to Washington and my career as a political journalist at summer's end, but by September a small commune had accreted around me and we were busy putting in water, a telephone, electricity and floors. I bought a $90 chain saw and cut up fifteen cords of wood, most of it green or rotted. Somehow we got it to burn in the stoves that winter, and while the snow piled up past the window line, we sat in the half-heat and talked about the topics of the day: our lives, our loves, our bodies, our selves. Everyone fell in and out of love with everyone else. The dogs ran a deer through crusty snow one day, and cornered it in an icy brook. Its neck was broken in the fray, and we decided to shoot it for mercy's sake. The deer turned out to be a pregnant doe, and when the game warden came to supervise the disposal of the animal, he cut out the fetus, which he left to lay upon the snow, a perfectly formed aborted fawn, like a stuffed miniature toy.

The women in the commune all came out as feminists that winter and I came out as gay. At Christmastime I made a quick trip to Washington to close up what was left of my business in the capital. I went to a New Year's Eve party and met the man in the long gray coat who had raised money for the townhouse fugitives the year before. He had just come up from "underground," having discovered (with some disappointment, I thought) that no charges were pending against him. We both took a hallucinogenic drug of some kind and began a love affair that lasted for three days and three nights, during which time we saw the movie *Trash* and drank about two gallons of Tropicana orange juice from concentrate. I can remember no other material from that affair. We never talked about the explosion or the friends who had escaped. . . .

January 5, 1980, THE REAL PAPER

✦

Refugees From the New Left

> *To communicate with Mars, converse with spirits*
> *To report the behaviour of the sea monster,*
> *Describe the horoscope, haruspicate or scry,*
> *Observe disease in signatures, evoke*
> *Biography from the wrinkles of the palm*
> *And tragedy from fingers; release omens*
> *By sortilege, or tea leaves, riddle the inevitable*
> *With playing cards, fiddle with pentagrams*
> *Or barbituric acids, or dissect*
> *The recurrent image into pre-conscious terrors—*
> *To explore the womb, or tomb, or dreams; all these are usual*
> *Pastimes and drugs, and features of the press:*
> *And always will be, some of them especially*
> *When there is distress of nations and perplexity*
> *Whether on the shores of Asia, or in the Edgware Road . . .*
> — *T.S. Eliot*
> *"The Dry Salvages"*

> *Everybody in our house is here, but we're marching under*
> *the banner of Crunchy Granola and Vitamin E.*
> —*Fragment of a conversation overheard at an*
> *anti-Inaugural demonstration, Chicago, 1973*

The topography of American political culture in this strangely suspended season is strewn with the skeletons of abandoned movements, lowered visions, dying dreams. No truces but tacit cease-fires have stilled the war on poverty, the war of the classes, the war of the worlds. In the white and middle-class field of action, at least, explicitly political energy and imagination are in short supply. Ideologies based on mechanistic analyses of power and history may not be wrong, but they are seen to be external to the lives of many whom they once moved, and irrelevant, too, to long-untended needs for peace of body, soul or mind.

Anyone who looks around can see the force behind the spiritual, religious and existential cults that have developed in the spaces where political organizations are usually found. Gurus, swamis, roshis, dervishes, gods and therapists are building impressive movements and extensive institutions, while the traditional left sects contract in size and influence. Rennie Davis, once the New Leftist *par excellence,* has become a devoted organizer for the aggressive religion of the Satguru Maharaj Ji, the teenage Avatar (that is, God). Davis draws enormous crowds of both the curious and the faithful at a time when it's hard to summon a *minyan* for a political demonstration.

Although stars of Davis's magnitude have not, as yet, appeared in other cosmic constellations, it is apparent at once from a browse through any bookstore, a stroll through a college campus or a glance through an underground newspaper that mystic chic has replaced radical fashions on the trend charts this year.

It is easy for an unreconstructed radical to dismiss the New Mysticism as bourgeois escapism, mass-psychological deviation or an inevitable (and insignificant) historical retreat before the next revolutionary offensive. Perhaps it is all of that, the varying interpretations implying only the various perceptions and ideologies. But it is more, too: there is a spirit that connects the political movements of the last decade with the spiritual movements of this one, and a style as well. Although a community of yogis and a collective of radicals may see their lives and their work as vastly different in content and purpose, in the current American context they appear driven by many of the same incessant impulses, haunted by the familiar fears, baffled by the old perplexities. Class, race and sex; bureaucracy and authority; love and distance; alienation and integration; rationalism and spontaneity: the energies that create and destroy social movements act on the cosmic ones as well. It's more than coincidence (and even more than economics) that lures foreign mystics and masters to America in these last/first days of an imperial era. The spreading decay nurtures a full garden of revolutionary and mystical blooms, which grow together from the same rich and rotting soil. And it is neither wise nor useful to call them flowers of evil or of good.

The *Zeitgeist* of the political generation of SNCC, SDS and Weatherman—the "student" radical movements—always had its existential and spiritual side beneath the hard edge of political action. I'm thinking of Bob Moses disappearing from SNCC when he felt his ego attaching itself to the organization and its policies; of SDS turning on with dope and rock in the *Sergeant Pepper* summer of 1967; of the Liberation News Service spinning off a magical mystery commune in the Massachusetts woods from its Manhattan Marxist center; of women and homosexuals leaving "anti-imperialist" politics for what was condemned then as "the politics of personal liberation." Seen from the radical perspective, there was an anti-political contradiction to every political style, a non-rationalist counterpoint to every reasoned position.

But from another vantage point—the apolitical, spiritual perspective of good vibrations—transcendent consciousness, not social upheaval, was the basis of the times that were changing. Politics was simply (or perhaps not so simply) an old-fashioned obstacle in the way of universal enlightenment. It surprised me to hear young communards in Vermont—in conversations with older radicals who were discussing oppressive racism, sexism, corporatism or whatever—name "politics" as the source of their oppression. Acid, yoga, flower power and bucolic communalism were base substances of the generational revolt. For people in that frame of mind, Marxism, Marcuse and Mao got in the way of the development of a passionate, non-rational, transcendental sensibility.

Historically, those two perspectives existed in more or less the same space: that is, in the institutional, psychological and existential lives of young white people in America. Acid freaks in the East Village and Weatherpeople in Chicago were in most ways different—and yet they were in the same "space" in the culture. A balance was struck so that the political and the personal, the external and the internal, the organizational and the existential forces, did not seriously encroach upon each other, either in the population or in any one individual. A political organizer, for example, could go off for a month tripping by the sea and it would be cool; or a student strike leader might join a lamasery in the mountains and the balance would not tip.

But the historical redefinition of the sixties generation and the student movement now has drastically altered the relationships within the culture, distorted the elements of that "space." *Institutionally*, there are few ongoing political organizations on the left, and those that remain keep limiting their appeal by hardening their lines and stiffening their demands. The Communist Party, the Trotskyist sects, the Revolutionary Union, the Labor Committees and Progressive Labor gave up long ago on white middle-class youth. The temporary anti-war coalitions have no significant lives beyond this or that demonstration. As a matter of fact, it is impossible for most people to express their ideas politically in an organization that takes them seriously.

Psychologically, the political perspective has become alienating and unsettling as support drains and the circumstances of the "real world" seem to change only for the worse. Many people who once found the universe of political action and ideology meaningful and enlivening now seem to find it empty and boring—and on top of that, they feel guilty for being bored.

Finally, in *existential* terms, it is particularly difficult nowadays to lead an integrated, authentic, sense-making life in a political way; that is, to live out in everyday terms those social values that are inherent in the political perspective. The projects, collectives, newspapers, offices of the political movements, are mostly gone or transformed, and there are few ways to find support—of any kind—for the good political life in the workaday world.

In the sixties, young people who were "radicalized" could (if they looked) find activities, homes, communities and work in which to express those radical values that had changed their lives. Now, mysticism, spiritualism and therapeutics provide the ready shelters for the politically lost or strayed—and also pick up naturally those who have no other home.

The spectrum of trips is extremely broad. These things change rapidly, but as of this week I have friends in a Zen community on the coast of Maine, an Arica house on the beach at Santa Monica, a Gestalt-Sufi retreat in Berkeley, an ashram in New Hampshire, a messianic religious organization's headquarters in Colorado and several related non-geographical regions of the mind. All of these New Mystics were New Leftists, feminists, radicals and activists of one kind or another a few years ago. I've spent time with two of them in recent weeks.

Rennie Davis became a devotee of the Satguru Maharaj Ji at the end of a course of events that included dreams and mystical experiences, the Indochina cease-fire and a visit with the NLF's Madame Binh in Paris. In the first of the dreams (as he related it to me), Davis was at the speaker's rostrum in an enormous auditorium. He felt some anxiety because he was not sure what he was supposed to say. Suddenly "every Vietnamese I ever knew" and a lot more came into the hall. They were " blissed out," brimming with joy and confidence and a sense of victory. Davis awoke similarly joyful, some of his anxieties allayed about his deeply felt responsibility for carrying on the anti-war political struggle.

A few days later he awoke from a deep sleep at 4:30 in the morning (his tale continued) sensing the presence of a close woman-friend on his bed. He reached out to touch her but she was not there, at least on the level of "ordinary" reality. Just at that moment the phone rang. It was that woman. She asked him to come to her apartment, not far away. Davis dressed and went to her; when he arrived, she was in a yogic prayer position, her palms together in the "namaste" gesture, her head lowered and her eyes closed. Silence. Then, she spoke as in a trance: "All your sins are forgiven. You go for all of us."

The next day Davis was off to Paris to see Madame Binh, but at the airport he met an old friend—from the May Day organization which directed the demonstrations in Washington in 1971—who had become a devotee of the Guru Maharaj Ji. In the course of a trans-Atlantic conversation with the friend and his companions, Davis was given an airline ticket to India. He did stop in Paris, saw Madame Binh, found her—of course—"blissed out" and flew off to India. After several ambiguous encounters with the Guru Maharaj Ji and His entourage, Davis found himself holed up with the young God himself in some Himalayan retreat, where one day he received "the Knowledge" in a blinding transcendent experience that seems to be the sum and substance of the Satguru's theology. The other several days were spent discussing the bureaucratic and organizational development of the Divine Light Mission and the now-in-formation Divine United Organization. Davis will probably direct the DUO; he has just been appointed vice president in charge of the Divine Light Mission.

"I was impressed by the fact that an organization like this could exist worldwide," Davis said in an interview not long ago, "and that I would have so little consciousness of it. The strength of the organization is just absolutely remarkable. It's not just a spiritual strength, either. The Guru Maharaj Ji has 5,000 mahatmas [disciples with direct experience of "the Knowledge"]. Most of them are based in India, but increasingly they're learning English and other languages, and are travelling to other nations. He's in every continent now except for the socialist countries, and He announced that next year He's going to Russia and the year after that He's going to China and by 1975 everyone on the planet will know that He's here.

"In the United States there are now 150 centers oriented around the Guru Maharaj Ji. They're all hooked up with Telex machines and WATS lines. Next year Guru Maharaj Ji is going to build, probably in California, a city that will use all the advanced methods of technology to ensure that the air is pollution-free; cars will be run on electricity instead of gasoline. It will be an architectural wonder, and it will be—according to Him—a concrete demonstration of what it means to have Heaven on Earth. When you see the organization that He's assembled in two and a half years and you see the forces that are coming together for this city, for a huge festival in the Houston Astrodome next fall, which is going to launch the Divine United Organization—you realize that there is an incredibly serious force here at work that really means to have people roll up their sleeves and get down to work with the problems of this material world. I think the combination of a politics and a spirit joined together in one form led by God Itself is a very far-out vision."

The social organization of the Divine Light Mission, the religion and the ashrams (the centers where people work, live and pray) has a lot in common with the administration of New Left offices, activities and project houses. There's a warmth and good feeling that has not been around the "straight male left" for many years, although some feminist and gay projects have experienced similar relationships. In the Guru Maharaj Ji's ashrams there is a "house mother" who cooks, washes up, irons clothes and serves the food. The heavies are, of course, all men. According to Davis, consciousness of sex roles is still, regrettably, low among the Guru Maharaj Ji's devotees because of their own political backgrounds, the Indian influence and such factors. But in any case it doesn't matter. "Are you oppressed as a woman in the ashram?" Davis asked the "house mother" of a Manhattan ashram as she was serving up our health-food lunch. "Oh no," she laughed gently. "We all serve the Guru Maharaj Ji."

The playful 15-year-old Satguru (Perfect Master, or Avatar) prophesies global apocalypse, although how good or bad it turns out depends on the extension of His teaching and the universal acceptance of "the Knowledge." Politics as Rennie Davis knew it has no function; Davis's own decade-long involvement in the Movement was simply "preparation" for his organizational role as "Rajdut," or Messenger of God, or Divine Organizer (the Hindi word was the brand name on the Divine Motorcycle that the Guru Maharaj Ji let Davis ride in India; Davis took it as a symbol of his new position *vis-à-vis* the Satguru).

A few days after I saw Rennie Davis in the ashram in New York City, I visited Sally Kempton in the Arica headquarters on the ocean-front in Los Angeles. Kempton is a rather well-established writer who helped organize the Radical Feminists in New York and generally identified with radical, left and women's movements in the sixties. A nexus of personal and professional circumstances, some friendships with people enjoying enlightenment trips, and a traumatic death in her family prepared her for the Arica course, a systematic body of physical, psychological and meditative disciplines developed by a Bolivian intellectual named Oscar Ichazo.

For what it's worth, in the world of professions and performance Kempton is considered a remarkably intelligent and sensitive writer; perhaps, as an old SDS mover told me recently, "the smartest one of us all." She was not herself a leader of the male left, but her articles (in *The Village Voice* and *Esquire*) and organizing activities in radical feminism were important to the development of the women's movement. I know her well; she spent a lot of time at the farm commune in Vermont where I once lived, and I was always aware of the ongoing struggle in her consciousness between contending values of intellectual performance and emotional integrity—in simpler (and perhaps too simplistic) terms, work against love. It was a kind of struggle I found replicated in myself, in many other radical men and in a few women. I'm not surprised to see such women in a place like Oscar Ichazo's Arica.

"Oscar," who is in his 40s, learned various mystical disciplines and Eastern martial techniques at an early age, and developed a more or less coherent body of eclectic mysticism and psychotherapy which he taught to a small number of students/patients/followers in the city of Arica, in Chile, where he settled. Claudio Naranjo, the Berkeley post-beat, proto-hip, trans-Esalen therapist, heard of Oscar's work with psychiatric patients and in time sent several dozen Big Sur types and arty freaks to Chile to take the long course that Oscar had worked up. They returned to America little less than a year later, and at Oscar's urging and direction set up an Arica Institute in New York City. Ads in *The New York Times* and elsewhere announced the $3,000 three-month course to be given in a big hotel on Central Park South. But the expected hordes of corporate executives and ruling-class representatives did not sign up to save themselves and America, and the scale of the operation was quickly reduced in price, length of training and expectations for universal salvation. It did, however, attract a number of show-biz and literary types, who underwent serious psycho-cosmic traumas and emerged somewhat more "awake" than they had been previously. Oscar's technique is *sui generis*, but generally employs elements of Gestalt, Sufi, yoga, Zen, T'ai Chi and other disciplines to achieve high consciousness, self-awareness and joyful social relations.

The atmosphere in the Arica beach house was comradely and communal, as it had been in the Guru Maharaj Ji ashram. But the Aricans were different in their hip sophistication and their trippy irony. Arica, of course, is not a religion and Oscar is not God, or a god, but a very high, awake and wise teacher with an apocalyptic vision of the world and a slightly less than obsessive proselytizing instinct. Sally Kempton claims that women's caucuses within the various semi-autonomous Arica schools around the country have promoted sexual egalitarianism in the once male-dominated outfit, and that relations between members of an Arica community are "worked" more successfully by Oscar's techniques than with the methods of political and emotional struggle we all used in our late communes and collectives.

Both the Divine Light Mission and Arica involve communities of the faithful. After receiving "the Knowledge" or "waking up," students or devotees of both systems tend to find work and pursue lives within the organizational structure. Aricans are busily finding students for the various courses ($600 for the popular forty-day "Open Path" session); Divine Missionaries are organizing the Houston rally, building the Divine City of Peace near Santa Barbara, running the slick magazine *And It Is Divine*, and operating the Divine Sales business that helps support the entire organization. (Both movements rely on the financial kindness of rich and super-rich devotees.)

There is not much agreement, trust or friendship between followers of one discipline or religion and another. Rennie Davis says that all other cults, as well as political organizations, have "the blind leading the blind," because the Guru Maharaj Ji is God in human form. Aricans think that the strict belief system of the Guru Maharaj Ji is anti-enlightening. Then again, some organized students of yoga and Zen call Arica "spiritual fascism" under Oscar's authoritarian dictatorship. "We're not 'Arica robots,'" Kempton insisted, "even though we all have the same haircut."

It's too early to draw hard psycho-historical conclusions about the movement of personnel from politics to mysticism; and the art of psychohistory is underdeveloped at best. A brief glimpse at Rennie Davis or Sally Kempton provides only the roughest sketch for a psychological interpretation of the phenomenon.

Of course, there are other examples. Greg Calvert, a former SDS national secretary in the "participatory democracy" days, has been seriously into Sufism and Gestalt therapy. Jerry Rubin has been experimenting, as he says, "with anything that has claims in that direction," and is especially fond of bioenergetics, est and Gestalt therapy. I encountered Rubin recently and found him fairly glowing with mellow vibes. And the list goes on.

I'm not entirely sure what shades of a sensibility or patterns of consciousness all the cults share, but there are some obvious springs that feed them all:

1. The "failure" of revolution, according to the hyperboles employed by the political movements of the late sixties, freaked out the people who had set their life-clocks according to the apocalyptic timetable. What happens "when prophecy fails"? In a study (under that title) of an end-of-the-world cult of the fifties, the sociologists Festinger, Riecken and Schachter saw that the moment of disconfirmation—the day that the world does *not* end—creates extreme dissonance in the minds of those whose belief systems are based on the fulfillment of the prophecy. In other words, it becomes positively painful to experience reality rubbing against belief.

The un-success of rapid, radical political change in America; the re-election of Nixon; the "winding down" of the war in Indochina without the unconditional surrender of the Pentagon—all that created an amount of dissonance (not to mention despair) among those who had invested the most in the expectation of a quick victory. Everyone has a way of blunting that dissonance, and one of them is the acceptance of a new belief system that either *confirms* the success of the left in new terms, or *invents* drastically new terms. So, you can say that the American radical anti-war movement and the Provisional Revolutionary Government of South Vietnam have won the war in Indochina; or you can say that radical politics is irrelevant and God is where it's at. Or, as in the example of Rennie Davis, you can say both.

2. The pressure many men feel, from external and internal sources, to "open up" emotionally, lower their intellectual defense and relate to other men and women in a spontaneous, sensual, non-competitive way is widely experienced and largely unheeded. In groups, men have been unable to get it together themselves, while women have usually had the opposite experience. But the pressures are real and cannot be entirely disregarded. The political organizations and projects surviving into the seventies have all been traumatized by the crisis of sex roles, and the outcome of the resulting struggles is usually dissolution of the group—or male-dominated reaction.

Some young, white middle-class men understand that they should find a way from their conscious behavior into their unconscious mind, to integrate action and feeling, detach their egos from matters and materials, break the barriers between intellect and emotion. By no means is that easy. "Consciousness-raising" groups, on the joint model of Red Guard and radical feminist struggle sessions, are threatening, limited and long. Traditional psychotherapy is expensive, somewhat discredited or tainted in the political and youth culture, and perhaps a bit too German and Jewish to be exotic anymore. But mysticism provides several escapes. It offers the alternative of an altered cosmic consciousness to a changed unconscious—a new reality of self rather than a new relationship with self.

Some wise and with-it gurus, philosophers and therapists are trying to put the two ways together, to blend the Freudian and the Buddha nature. But most of the organized cults I've encountered remain strongly male-dominated. At least, the terms of the religion of therapy are set by men—precisely to deal, by evasion or attack, with those male problems of the mind/emotion, conscious/unconscious split. It seems many of the women who are heavily involved in that kind of work also see their personal crisis in that "male-defined" way of blockage between the conscious and the unconscious. It's not surprising that mysticism in America is a white and middle-class trip; when one thinks about it, it is not surprising that it's essentially a male trip, too.

3. In an analogous way, mysticism is a kind of back door or side window to the non-rational side of humans. Western rationalism is undergoing another wave in the series of assaults that mark the intellectual history of this cen-

tury. There is, after all, that tradition of Western intellectuals seeking philosophic counterweights to Reason and Science, materialism and logic. What's so paradoxical is that many of the new mystical cults outdo Western philosophies in their excessive categorization of psychic and cosmic states. Arica, for example, presents trainees with endless lists of ego states, levels of consciousness, physiognomic points for attention and so on. Ultimately, an Arican assured me, the categories can be internalized by the trainee.

4. The quest for peace-of-mind encouraged the development of psychiatric schools and psychological sects throughout the twentieth century, and there has been an increasing spill-over into peace-of-brain techniques and peace-of-soul ideologies. Moral re-armament, positive thinking and Dianetics/Scientology have their hip analogues in est, Silva Mind Control, biofeedbackery and the various occult systems. A Gestalt theoretician writes, "Freud's famous statement, 'Much has been accomplished if we can change neurotic misery into common unhappiness,' is no longer sufficient. . . . Now we use words such as enhancement, intimacy, actualization, creativity, ecstasy, and transcendence to describe what we wish for ourselves and others. [These] theories . . . offer as the alternative to misery, not unhappiness, but joy."

For middle-class Americans, the world offers the promise and the expectation of joy as it does the abundance of material goods, a job when needed and interesting ways to fill up a day. The fact that most people somehow don't get the joy that's coming to them is a source of unending perplexity—and the impetus for the development of techniques, organizations and corporations to make good on the promises. The politics of joy having failed, perhaps the mystique of joy should be explored.

5. The half-true, half-mythic sense of "participation" and communitarianism that the New Left was supposed to achieve is still a relevant dream in much of the old new culture. It has been said that Rennie Davis found the Satguru in his never-ending search for the participatory democratic spirit that was supposed to infuse SDS's ERAP organizing projects, which he developed and directed. In fact, much of the nostalgia is both mistaken and misplaced: Davis and a few other early New Left men manipulated some fuzzy notions of participatory democracy and communalism for rather standard organizational and personally political ends. Still, the myth survives, and it is probably true that some people look for its realization in one or another mystery house or magical project.

6. At last, there is the gnawing notion some have that somewhere out there humanity is on the verge of an evolutionary leap forward, a quantum jump beyond what we now understand as "humanness" into some as yet un-understood mode of higher being. Both the Divine Light people and Aricans talk about *biological* changes that are occurring to raise and change the quality of being human. Rennie Davis says that *homo sapiens* is itself the "missing link" between what is now and what will be—soon. The message is that we do not have to wait out some Darwinian infinity for this next evolu-

tionary stage. Aricans say that they have achieved a "one body" state among members of an Arica living and working unit.

Central to all these theories is that single, essential mystical experience, the famous insight into the "oneness" of the universe, the Acid test, the yogic perfection: the "knowledge" that all the energy and all matter in the universe are somehow infinite and undifferentiated except in our minds.

"Men's curiosity searches past and future/And clings to that dimension," Eliot says near the end of the "Dry Salvages":

> But to apprehend
> The point of intersection of the timeless
> With time, is an occupation for the saint—
> No occupation either, but something given
> And taken, in a lifetime's death in love,
> Ardour and selflessness and self-surrender.
> For most of us, there is only the unattended
> Moment, the moment in and out of time,
> The distraction fit, lost in a shaft of sunlight,
> The wild thyme unseen, or the winter lightning
> Or the waterfall, or music heard so deeply
> That it is not heard at all, but you are the music
> While the music lasts. These are only hints and guesses,
> Hints followed by guesses; and the rest
> Is prayer, observance, discipline, thought and action.

July 1973, RAMPARTS

Chapter VII

✦

SPECTACLE

See Dick Run: Politics-into-Spectacle

The confusion of spectacle with politics is now so complete that there is no way to distinguish between them. The only remaining standard of judgement is the comparison of *live* and *simulated* phenomena, and even that distinction is breaking down. It's fair to say, however, that the Nixon-simulation seen last week on TV from Miami was generally better than the Nixon-live model seen occasionally in the past (except for the simulated right-arm motion, which was just a bit too jerky). The same high marks go to the convention-simulation, but the cops-and-kids simulation definitely needed more work. It was better live four years ago. Looking ahead, it is estimated that by 1980 an entire Administration can be simulated for at least three out of four years, and Bell Labs are now working on total audience-simulation by the end of the 1980s.

It appears a real breakthrough was made this week in that last technological feat. The people at the Republican convention and the various outside-shows looked and acted as though they were made of Styrofoam, with Fresca running coolly through their veins. Or perhaps it's just that in 1972 everyone wants to look like mentholated cigarette smokers in the TV commercials. (If my set was equipped for smellovision, menthol would have been the dominant odor all week, disrupted only on Wednesday evening by the heady synthesis of tear-gas, cannabis resin and Patchouli oil.)

The network commentators and the newspaper columnists talked about Nixon's script for the convention, but I didn't get the sense, at least from in front of the screen, that such unimaginative minds as inhabit the White House and the Republican National Committee could have invented all of it. Some higher hand—higher than Eric and Harry and Walter and John in their isolation booths; higher even than Teddy White, if that's possible or permissible—wrote the Total Script, the one that included

Sammy Davis Jr.'s coy hug of Nixon; or the band's playing "Lovely to Look at, Delightful to Hold" when Pat walked on stage; or the hustling of the paraplegic Vietnam vets out of the hall when Nixon appeared; or John Chancellor's memorable line about the street demonstrators: "For the life of me, I can't understand what these people are trying to prove."

During a break between an automobile sales commercial and an automobile wreck commercial some TV "reporter" related the historical note that prior to Eighteen Twenty Something, presidential candidates were chosen by a caucus of congresspeople and senators. As America moved to "democratize" (which sounded like "Vietnamize" to me), "King Caucus" was abolished in favor of the Open Convention. A lot of good *that* did. The consequence of the new openness was not a succession of Andrew Jacksons but a presidential line of simulated insurance agents and quiz show emcees.

"It's great to see all you young people out there," Nixon shouted at the Young Voters assembled in Marine Stadium Tuesday night; it seemed as if his next line would be: "Our next contestant is a black Jewish singer from Hollywood, California." (Here the programmers slipped up a bit: Nixon's volley of smiles and the Young Voters' bursts of applause were out of sync.)

It's hard to believe that anyone who isn't paid to watch these stone drags on TV is staying very close to the set. (The Democratic bash last month wasn't less of a simulation; it was just a bad simulation.) If I were a network executive, I'd call the whole political show this fall *ENNUI 72* and sandwich it in, pre-recorded, between *Love of Life* and an arthritis ad. After all, it's all dots anyway.

August 29, 1972, THE BOSTON PHOENIX

✦

Munich: Terror on the $3 Million Stage

To hear Howard Cosell tell it, "politics" invaded the Olympics with the Palestinian commandoes. That certainly was politics with a vengeance, but it was a new Olympic event only in its ferocity. In its many other aspects, politics is the oldest Olympic game.

Governments have always seen Olympic medals as political objects; they spend vast sums of money to gear their athletes up for victories over competitors from hostile countries: Americans over Russians, East Germans over West Germans, Latin Americans over North Americans, Israelis over Arabs. Race is pitted against race, and that didn't end with Jesse Owens. This year, US boxing heavyweight Duane Bobick was touted in every interview as a "great white hope." (He lost to a Cuban.)

As a global political event, the Olympics is a natural focus for political activity, and it doesn't seem strange at all that the Palestinian guerrillas picked it for their latest adventure. The Olympics' media magnitude alone—

the real "new politics" in McLuhanist terms—made it a natural: more so than a space spectacular, or an Archducal tour through the Balkans. Any event that enters the public consciousness, not to mention the public's living room, on such a mass scale must be recognized as an exercise of *power*, and up for grabs, no matter how high the price. The "terror" issue has to be normalized—that is, put into a sense-making context—before it can be comprehended. A great deal of the hysteria that surrounded the events in Munich seemed to derive not from the nature of the action, which was ghastly enough, but because it was considered to be outside of a "political" context. Put back into politics, it is somewhat defreaked, if no less horrifying.

Terror, like treason, never prospers; if it prosper, none dare call it terror—but something like "protective reaction," or "retaliation," or "selective targeting," or "relocation." No TV broadcaster ever called Richard Nixon a terrorist for all the dead peasants and destroyed villages he's ordered. No sports announcer called Moshe Dayan or Golda Meier a terrorist for the Israeli policy of brutality against a million Palestinian Arab residents and refugees, and Israel's captured Arab populations. Terror is almost by definition an attribute of the outcast, the oppressed, the political desperado.

Even the nature and quality of "terrorism" changes according to the status of the actors. The Palestinian guerrillas set out on a kidnapping mission: it ended disastrously, of course, for reasons that were not entirely in the kidnappers' power to control. Still, kidnapping (or hijacking) is not the same kind of "terror" as bombing a cafe (see *The Battle of Algiers*), dropping atomic bombs on Japanese cities or mowing down passengers in an airport. For real terror, Operation Phoenix, a CIA escapade in Vietnam which, according to US congressional reports, killed upwards of 9,000 civilians prone to anti-Saigon sentiments, takes some kind of bronze medal at least. No memorial services are being televised round-the-world via satellite for the dead Vietnamese, or for the Arab refugees who die of disease and starvation in their "temporary" camps, or for the black Americans terrorized by white police every night, etc., etc. We know all this, and more, and yet we get carried away by Munich.

There is the well-known good reason for the emotional response: the dreadful irony of the Jewish return to death in Munich (only ten miles from Dachau). There are some reasons, too, that come from darker springs: the unpopularity of Arab nationalism, the adopted "Westernism" of Israel, the recent success of Israel and diasporic Jews in war and games, from Sinai to Spitz. "A little competitive edge can make a world of difference," the Brut toiletries commercials were saying all week.

Terrorism, even when it's not meant to be very terrible, is not *supposed* to be popular. Like industrial strikes—a form of terrorism, after all, and as prone to violent ends as the Munich kidnappings—acts of political terrorism are committed to irritate, infuriate, threaten and overall destabilize civilian populations. In the way that electroconvulsive shock therapy jumbles and shakes a brain, terrorist acts shake up social and political relationships in non-specific ways. There's no predicting the result when the shock is over. Things may be better or worse, but they are not likely to be the same. So by their nature, terrorist acts are outside chances, last resorts, blind throws.

That's exactly where the Palestinians are at: outmaneuvered by Israel and Arab governments, discarded by China and Russia, ignored by the American and European left. They represent a depressed and hopeless population that has practically no revolutionary resources: no rich allies, no vulnerable enemies, no supportive political culture, no enlivening revolutionary history.

Fawaz Turki, an exiled Palestinian now living and teaching in Paris, wrote in his journal, "The Disinherited":

> As a Palestinian, the prospect of an end to my isolation from the mainstream of other men's ordered activities and purposes exercises an intensely strange fascination on my mind. I am lured by the agony of wanting, *now*, in my own lifetime, to know what it feels like, how the experience would sense in my brain, to be, for the first time since I was a child, the citizen of a country, a native of a land that is my own, all my own, with hills and mountains, and children in brick houses, where I could sit with my people, no longer menaced, no longer destitute.

That is a vision as true for Palestinian Arabs as it was for Zionist Jews.

Before anything good happens to the Palestinians, one or more elements in the equation of defeat must change, and the guerrillas believe, or hope, that kidnapping or hijackings will do that. One Arab in a refugee camp told a *Washington Post* reporter last week: "Maybe the world will start asking now, Where is this Palestine those commandoes come from?"

There's no way of telling whether they're right or wrong. If the Palestinian liberation struggle succeeds in some yet unknown way in changing the dismal condition of the refugees and captive "aliens" in Israeli-occupied areas, the vanguard guerrillas may be justified, if not absolved, by history. After all, some of our favorite nationalist movements were conceived in terrorism—among them Zionism. Israel owes something to the Stern Gang and the militant Irgun commandoes who blew up British buildings and people—as well as Jewish collaborators—in the days before Israel was finally let go by London.

It's hard to find the line sometimes between comprehension and apology for political action, and indeed there may be no line at all but only points of perception and definition. One person's comprehension of a ghetto rebellion, for instance, may be called an apology by another.

But sooner or later one must come to terms with politics, and to make those definitions and perceptions for one's self. That's not easy (perhaps not possible or even wise) to do in the atmosphere of emotion that the Munich events have generated. But at some point politics doesn't work when TV analysis overwhelms hard judgements. If revolt is any kind of a solution to oppression, it is not going to be clean enough and pretty enough for prime time.

"The revolution 'logically' does not demand terrorism," Trotsky wrote, "but just as 'logically' it does not demand an armed insurrection. . . . [It] does require of the revolutionary class that it should attain its end by all methods at its disposal—if necessary, by an armed rising; if required, by terrorism. . . . The question of the form or of its degree, of course, is not one of 'principle.' It is a question of expediency. . . . Terror can be very efficient against a reactionary class which does not want to leave the scene of operations. *Intimidation* is a powerful weapon of policy. . . . War, like revolution, is founded upon intimidation. The . . . terror of a revolutionary class can be condemned 'morally' only by a man who, as a principle, rejects (in words) every form of violence whatsoever—consequently every war and every rising. For this one has to be merely and simply a hypocritical Quaker."

September 12, 1972, THE BOSTON PHOENIX

✦

Are Two Sexes Too Many?

A s the front wave of the new culture, rock music brought us the first intimations of the changes that were eventually to transform our lives. Political protest, drop-out alienation and drugs were heralded by music that in one way or another—rhythm, lyric and mood—expressed an underground consciousness on its way up. I don't think *Sergeant Pepper* created the drug culture or Dylan caused the times to a-change. But they made mass what was only minor. After all, revolutions—even cultural ones—are self-adjusting and need no tin pan allies to legitimize them.

Distinctions between honesty and gimmickry, authenticity and exploitation on any of these culture fronts are hard to make. In the end, a gimmick for one person can be an act of perfect truth for another. And historical time (even a matter of months) can turn the sweetest song sour. For a long time it never occurred to me that the Rolling Stones were exploiting violence for its commercial value. Was all that driving energy once honest and positive? The advertisements for the movie *Gimme Shelter* said, "Altamont changed a lot of heads"; or was it that a lot of heads changed Altamont?

These contradictions keep coming back to me like a song as I've watched David Bowie, Alice Cooper, Elton John and several other big-time rock musicians ride a new wave of sexual "liberation" to the top of the charts. In one way or another, each of them toys with ambiguity in sexual roles, as the men play with manners and mannerisms that are not strictly "male."

Some are more ambiguous than others. Alice Cooper performs in drag but makes it known that the boys in the band are closet straights. Elton John now wears campy, glittery clothes and features a cockettish drag number in his travelling show; he and Bernie Taupin have also written a new love song ("Daniel") to a man, who may or may not be his biological "brother." The Kinks had a hit single last year about a transvestite named "Lola." The J. Geils Band's new album, *Full House*, displays on its cover five large playing cards: three jacks, a king and a queen. The queen seems to be either blind in one eye or winking—a very strange hand, indeed.

Of course, there have been such undercurrents in rock music since the beginning, from Elvis through Little Richard to James Brown and Mick Jagger. It would not be accurate to call the theme homosexuality or bisexuality, because what is presented—and what comes across—is not a variety of sexuality but a sensation of the ambiguous. Like alienation or violence, that is what is sold. That people are buying it must mean something about the needs and fears of the new audiences.

Sexual repression being what it is (and repression is what makes ambiguity sensational and saleable), male rock musicians who play around with gay mannerisms or themes feel constrained to assert their *machismo* at opportune moments. Just at the point that Mick Jagger seems to be gayer than ever (*Sticky Fingers*) he gets married. J. Geils's sly puns (*The Morning After* album shows all the band members in bed, looking altogether *louche*) are belly-to-belly with such macho masterpieces as "First I Look at the Purse." Elton John's most sexually ambiguous lyrics are in "Rocket Man":

> *And I think it's gonna be a long, long time*
> *Till touch down brings me round again to find*
> *I'm not the man they think I am at home*
> *Oh, no, no, no . . .**

They are preceded by the line: "I miss the earth so much, I miss my wife."

Whatever the "sexual orientation" (as they say in the psycho-liberal world) of these musicians may be, the issue they raise is the effect of their sexual games. If sexuality is just a gimmick and ambiguity is promoted for its own sake, nothing much will change, and the culture will become that much more corrupted. Alice Cooper's constant conjunction of violence with sex (it's a one-word concept now, sexnviolence) is so corrupt that he/she seems to come out the other end into innocence—but not quite. The others are less pathological, perhaps.

It is possible, however, that the ambiguity trend is extremely short-lived, and that it points the way to a substantial shift beneath the gimmicks. At present, that next step seems to exist uniquely in David Bowie, *a k a* Ziggy Stardust, the first, and as far as I know, only rock-and-roll star to come out.

Well, almost. Some of Bowie's press releases claim that he is the first "bisexual" rock star, which appears factitious on many levels. All outward

*Dick James Music Inc. BMI. 1972

indications are that he has jumped out of the ambiguity cult and is about to try to become an authentic gay superstar, authentically a superstar and authentically gay at the same time—for the first time in our culture since Oscar Wilde.

Bowie's live show, which was in Boston last week, was about as gay a performance as I've seen topside of the caverns of the sexual netherworld. (Except that as a sop to traditionalists, the impresarios put on Bowie's bill an excruciatingly heavy cock-rock group.) Many of Bowie's songs are about gay love and its special pain. His costumes are at least semi-draggy. His movements on stage seem to be choreographed with a gay lyricism that makes the usual posturing of male musicians ludicrous by comparison. He and his lead guitarist, Mick Ronson, exchange erotic glances, gestures and dance steps that would have heretofore been acceptable only between a man and a woman in a band.

Bowie/Ziggy is an event in rock music, but he's also an event in changing sexual culture, and I wouldn't be surprised if it's that latter event that will prove the more significant in the long run.

A great deal has been written about "cock-rock" since the term was invented by the women's movement some years ago, and it should be self-evident by now that rock music is a pretty heavy male trip. In recent months, some of the heaviness has gone out of fashion, perhaps under explicit or implicit pressures from anti-sexist sources. Already there's a critical backlash to that development: male rock critics in New York, for instance, have been calling the Carole King–Elton John–Cat Stevens–James Taylor trend the "limp dick" axis. All that phallic imagery speaks for itself.

The mellow trend in music (I'll call it that and hope for the best) is easy to take, but it is not necessarily antithetical to male rock. There are a few expressions of feminist culture creeping into the rock scene, but most of the money, most of the audience, most of the industry, is at best wary of up-front feminism, and at worst hostile. Still, women can occasionally find female groups or, more likely, a female lead singer with whom to identify.

But until David Bowie, there has been no forthright gay rock that can be generally heard and seen. Gay men have had to choose between watching a closet tease (Jagger) and a sadistic straight queen (Alice Cooper) as they try in vain to identify with the culture that rock music expresses. (There's nothing new in that, of course: gay forms rarely find their way into straight art except in the most "devious" terms—which are then denigrated for the very deviousness forced upon them.) Before he was Ziggy, Bowie was writing songs about coming out—that is, about the process of getting to gay experience. For example, "Changes" (on the album *Hunky Dory*):

> *I still don't know what I was waiting for*
> *And my time was running wild*
> *A million dead-end streets . . .*

> *So I turned myself to face me*
> *But I've never caught a glimpse*
> *Of how the others must see the faker . . .*
> *Ch-ch-ch-Changes*
> *Don't want to be a better man. . .*
> *Ch-ch-ch-Changes*
> *Don't tell them to grow up and out of it . . .*

He was fascinated with "space" in a Kubrickian way, in the same way that he seems now to be taken with Kubrick's most recent *Clockwork* fantasies. (His current show, "The Rise and Fall of Ziggy Stardust and the Spiders from Mars," begins and ends with Walter Carlos's rendition of the *Clockwork* version of Ludwig Van's Ninth Symphony, and words like "droogie" crop up in Bowie's songs.) I'm not sure what the space motif means to Bowie, but it seems to me to be a way of making ambiguous, and thereby escaping to a degree, the anguish of coming out: and at the same time looking to a future of transcendent sexuality. "Is there life on Mars?" Bowie asks bitterly and hopefully at the end of one of his songs about the horrors of life on earth. And in "Oh! You Pretty Things" he exclaims:

> *Oh! You Pretty Things*
> *Don't you know you're driving your*
> *Mamas and Papas insane . . .*
> *Let me make it plain*
> *You gotta make way for the Homo Superior . . .*
> *Look out at your children*
> *See their faces in golden rays*
> *Don't kid yourself they belong to you*
> *They're the start of a coming race*
> *The earth is a bitch*
> *We've finished our news*
> *Homo Sapiens have outgrown their use . . .**

In the new Ziggy album, Bowie's even deeper into space, but he's also writing songs explicitly about love and pain, and not just about the anxieties of sexuality.

A one-line gag was going around the promotion party for Ziggy and the Spiders after their concert here: "This is the group that asks the question, 'Are two sexes enough?'" I suppose it was a comforting joke to some, with its implication that the confining norms of sexuality can be transcended—perhaps without passing through any unpleasant intermediary stages—to Ziggy Stardust and Beyond. But it doesn't seem to me that such transcendence is in the cards, or the stars. The ch-ch-ch-changes being rung now are likely to be accompanied more by cries of pain and exorcism than by angelic hums.

*Tantric Music Corp. 1971

David Bowie is still a freak: a permissible freak, but less than threatening because of his uniqueness. If he seriously promised to breach the walls of rock culture, real battles would be fought. But perhaps he is only a herald, and the battles are shaping up somewhere else. It's still terribly ambiguous. As Mick Jagger sings: "Well, it just goes to show: Things are not what they seem . . ."

October 10, 1972, THE BOSTON PHOENIX

✦

Us and Them: A Death March for the Sixties

Washington

There is a fearful symmetry between the death of Lyndon Johnson and the inauguration of Richard Nixon, a sinister *denouement* of a classical play: the funeral of Caligula balanced by the inauguration of his horse. The events of the long Inaugural weekend seem too perfectly plotted: the great war is ending; the new king is anointed; the people rise up in anger; the old king dies. A Mass in Wartime is offered (Bernstein's concert); an overture commemorating the Victory of Czar over Emperor is played (Nixon's choice of Inaugural music).

The scenes in Washington were all too familiar. For the umpteenth time, "the people" assembled at the Lincoln Memorial for a protest march down Constitution Avenue to the Washington Monument. In front of the Capitol, another President raised his right hand and opened his mouth for a string of generalities, ending with a cue for the parade down Pennsylvania Avenue to the White House.

Johnson's death on Monday (leaving, it was said, no living President) provided a vantage point from which to perceive the swelling scene, if only in retrospect. From there, it appears that the strange career of the Liberal Sixties has ended and its consequences are all but resolved: the American ground war in Vietnam, Great Society welfarism, racial integration, a New Left. In the four years since Lyndon Johnson sent himself down from power, the remnants of his programs and policies—and of John Kennedy's before him—have been discredited by their own contradictions, have collapsed from their own weakness or have been dismantled by Nixon. The movements and the politics that developed in the wake of Johnson, or in opposition to him, have been liquidated or transformed.

The war in Vietnam will always be Johnson's war to me. Of course, Kennedy started it and Nixon couldn't let it go. But Johnson, the sentimental old imperialist and tragicomic war criminal, was the star of that show. Vietnam had all the qualities of a pure Johnsonian fiasco: the madness and vain delusion of a monstrous masterpiece, against which Kennedy's cold caution and Nixon's ragged rhetoric are puny minor works.

Vietnam—America's Vietnam—had grown out of Kennedy's plan to save capitalism (this time) by expansion into the Third World, the other two worlds being oversold already. Kennedy fought the 1960 election on the issue of American corporate expansion. Having won, he proceeded to make good on his promises with an orchestrated strategy of imperial probes, domestic expenditures and economic regulations. In the imperial sector, Kennedy put together a package of Green Berets, the Peace Corps, the Alliance for Progress, AID, the CIA, the World Bank, tactical nukes and mobile military strike forces. The object was to produce and protect liberal, mildly democratic, pro-American regimes all over the "underdeveloped" world so that US business could develop it and US military interests would be secure. Counter-insurgency was a crucial tactic, and its first test was Vietnam. Kennedy had the good sense to achieve sainthood before the strategy collapsed, and Johnson was left to preside over the debacle.

LBJ's intervention in the Dominican Republic in 1965 was a shorter, sweeter disaster. Kennedy had ordered Dictator Trujillo bumped off in 1961 and had the CIA install the liberal Juan Bosch, who was expected to complete the *embourgeoisement* of the island for the good of his people's welfare and American industry. Bosch couldn't put together what history, class and economics had torn asunder, and a right-wing coup deposed him. When authentic reformers and rebels tried to return to power outside the American umbrella, Johnson sent in the marines—"to prevent another Cuba"—and ultimately assured an authoritarian regime perpetual control. In the process, however, the plan for the quick development of a native middle class ready and eager for the effluent of American industry had to be shelved. Variants of that scenario occurred all over Asia, Africa and South America as the sixties raced to conclusion and the Third World strategy for US corporate expansion was abandoned. In its place, Nixon has embarked upon a program of probes into the Second World (Russia and China), which has stepped up the terms of America's economic war with Japan and Western Europe. Vietnam is practically irrelevant to the Nixon plan.

The domestic sector of Kennedy's expansion strategy was the Great Society scheme—a way out of the debilitating cycles of recession and boomlet that characterized the postwar economy before the sixties. The idea was to promote relationships between industry and government in the domestic sector that would parallel the chummy relationships between the two in the military sector. In other words, what government could do for aircraft companies it could do for teaching-systems companies. The proliferating programs of the Johnson era would tie industry in with long-term contracts as well as supply industry with a new crop of satisfied customers—blacks, the poor, various disadvantaged minorities.

As it turned out, the Great Society was slow, naive and so off-the-wall that even if it had not been shot through with theoretical contradictions it would never have worked. Inflation, politics and greed obviated any hope of establishing stable relationships between government and domestic producers; and the same factors prevented a significant redistribution of wealth that might have developed a viable new internal market.

Nixon has abandoned "program-throwing" because it can't do what Johnson said it would. Nixon may or may not believe the work-ethic drive he emits, but it doesn't matter—any more than it mattered whether he believed his anti-communist cant. When he needed money, markets and political support from Brezhnev and Chou, he dragged himself above the principles he had always espoused. He's turned off welfarism because it just isn't good business. Unlike Johnson, Nixon is rarely trapped by his rhetoric.

Most of the minor memoirs I've read about Johnson in the days since his death skip the politics and concentrate on his enormous quirks—his compulsiveness, his irascibility, his "bigness." I can't imagine why people from so many political positions now find Johnson's craziness, his crassness, his malevolent *machismo* so charming. I'll always remember LBJ as a demented half-drunk mockery of manliness, a dirty young, middle-aged and old man who called in secretaries to give him head and generals to give him body counts with equal relish, while mind-bent America lied to itself about him.

For me, the single most grotesque moment of the sixties came in 1965 when Lyndon Johnson pulled himself up before a joint session of Congress and mooed, "We shall overcome." I was sitting in the House of Representatives Press Gallery that night, having just come North from Selma, where the marches—and the police attacks—were in progress. When Johnson spoke, I grew suddenly dizzy in the head and queasy in the stomach and nearly pitched over the railing.

Johnson's nasty little flirtation with "civil rights" had nothing to do with confronting racism, but was rather a stratagem for supporting his "consensus" majority of city-dwellers, minorities, labor and Texas millionaires. Johnson's economic and bureaucratic policies stabilized racism; indeed, he had built a career and a politics on white power. But when the "civil rights" movement failed to dent institutional racism, all the programs and policies founded on the liberal integrationist theory failed, too. Nixon, of course, was able to discard "civil rights" and keep the Texas millionaires, a nicer trick than Johnson could have pulled off in his years.

The movements of the sixties—the New Left—seem now to be phenomena of the Age of Johnson. The left flourished as a radical reformist force because there appeared to be space for some success. The organizers and the managers of the Great Society were hardly about to turn America upside down, but they let issues be debated, and the debates needed a left. But as managerial liberalism creaked to its paralytic conclusion, radical reformism abandoned all hope of victories in its present condition. What had been a confusion of possibilities became a strictness of sides: Us and Them.

Washington during this latest Inauguration was more divided between Us and Them than I had ever seen it. The parallel parades were not only out of communication with each other; they were out of touch. Few demonstrators even wanted to *trash* the official march, so great was the repulsive force. Recognition of the existence of one march by the other was almost out of the question. Down Pennsylvania Avenue, the floats and the marching bands came drifting by eerily as the President stood behind bullet-proof shields in his white sculptured reviewing stand, like the embalmed manager of a new Exxon station under the pump canopy. Down Constitution Avenue, the spirits were high enough, even though the politics seemed a bit obscure: a demand to end a war that appeared to be ending already, a protest against the times rather than one or another policy. These days national demonstrations have come to serve as camp reunions or lodge conventions for the movements: Pentagon in '66? May Day? Chicago?

They called this one a March Against Death, and it was true that some kind of obsequies seemed to be in progress. But for whom it was difficult to tell. As much as anything, perhaps, it was a funeral march for the sixties, for Lyndon Johnson's world.

January 30, 1973, THE BOSTON PHOENIX

✦

How the War Won Me

"The War" had always meant the Second World War to me: images of German bombers sweeping in over Long Island Sound, my father's draft card in the living room desk drawer, rationing cards and gasoline stamps, an air-raid fire extinguisher made from a garden pesticide sprayer, Glenn Miller's Air Corps Band parading on the town Green, the photograph of a distant cousin killed when his plane was shot down over—I can't remember. That war was not only a historical event; it was a complete environment, like a siege or a plague or a long hurricane, dangerous and exhilarating, shattering. The struggle was immediate, and at stake was survival.

To feel the intensity of this war "in Vietnam" requires, for most Americans, an intellectual leap across a wide gap of experience. I'm different: I was in Saigon ten years ago, in Hanoi five years ago; I've met "the Vietnamese" there and in Paris, London, Canada and Czechoslovakia. But most Americans know this war second-hand. Except for those who have suffered wounds or the loss of a man of the family, this war is an abstraction of politics, a figment of morality, a construct of reason.

The burden is all on the Indochinese people, so far from us. The ways we experience the war seem petty: prices are higher, but that's nothing new; welfare priorities are askew, as always; political morality is debased, no change. We encounter Vietnam as we do the events of a novel or a movie or—more to the point—a television play. It is reality mediated by conscience or conviction, scenes of horror viewed in the middle-distance. Now I know people who have been shaken to the center of their souls by this war, and I have felt those shocks, too. There's no denying the power of the events of Vietnam—however they may arrive—to affect our lives. But unlike World War II, the war in Vietnam must in some measure be understood intellectually rather than perceived empirically (by Americans, of course), and it is not at all strange that this war has most strongly influenced those who can readily experience life through the mind.

As America's war in Indochina seems to be approaching a watershed, and although it is still unclear (as I write this) how the waters will part, I detect a need, widely felt, to "make sense" of the war and its effects. No doubt historians and the pseudo-scientists of politics will soon begin the job of classifying and cataloguing the data of diplomacy and strategy in the long conflict. My own interests tend to be more *ad hominem*. For whatever else the war in Vietnam has done, it has deflected a generation of Americans from its predictable course—and me with them—and thus into a new history. It remains to be seen who (if anybody) has won the war. It is already certain that the war has won us.

Unlike most of the "radical" generation of the sixties, I was not propelled into politics by Vietnam. Although I had been pushed by a Red rabbi, a difficult childhood and a mildly socialist education, it was not until I came into contact with the civil rights movement in the South and its analogues in Northern ghettoes that I saw "politics" as something other than Democrats-and-Republicans. I never cried, never shouted with joy, never loved comrades in "politics" until I was moved by those struggles. They created a purpose for work and action that obliterated the emptiness of the life I had grown up with in the fifties. Perhaps it was only sentiment; I'm not sure I knew in the days of the early sixties how the black movement was a part of *my* life; and I guess it was Vietnam that explained it.

Vietnam taught me about two things: privilege and liberation. It taught me by the example, not by the design, of the Vietnamese. My strongest image of the last ten years is the fantastic mind-picture of an angry and strong Vietnamese shooting down—me; capturing—me; driving out—me. And yet it is not me, because I am by the Vietnamese soldier's side.

It had been easy for us all to adopt a politics based on sympathy—for that poor Negro, this disadvantaged child, another starving Indian. Liberalism, almost by definition, needs victims to feel sorry for. When I marched for "freedom and justice" in Alabama, or sat-in at the mayor's office in Newark, I had only the slightest inkling that those actions had to do with white "us" as well as black "them." I knew I could hardly talk with black people or, for that matter, working-class white people in a way that made me feel good, whole or real. I knew that although I demanded equality for everyone under the law, I didn't feel that equality in my bones. I think I half assumed that at the end of the civil rights movement or when "poverty" was eradicated those distances across race and class would be narrowed: not by my changing, of course, but by the others moving towards me.

My meetings with the Vietnamese radically changed that perception. They did not want my sympathy (although they did not refuse it); they wanted my support in what they insisted, calmly, was a common struggle. In time I learned to love the Vietnamese people—not in a saccharine way as martyrs or victims, but as gunners by my side.

I had been to Saigon just before the coup against Ngo Dinh Diem, when the city had been de-Vietnamized if not yet completely Americanized. I was in a ghastly position as a fill-in *Time* reporter on a three-week stint. I thought the war was a stupid blunder and I hated having to be associated with *Time,* which then jingoistically supported the American intervention. But as long as I stayed with *Time,* I had to rationalize war politics in some way or lose my sanity from the crashing dissonances of personal belief and work obligations. Like most journalists of that era, I did it with cynicism and "objectivity": America was failing in Vietnam, but the war—"the quagmire"—had nothing to do with me, or my job, or my career, or my life.

By the summer of 1967, I was far away from *Time* and objectivity, though not yet free of cynicism. I was on the roster of Movement trippers in that period, and I hopped a jet to Czechoslovakia to join a group of thirty Americans meeting for a week with twenty representatives of the North (DRV) and South (NLF) of Vietnam. Madame Binh led the Southern delegation; Mr. Vy led the Northern one. I was never clear about my mission in Bratislava; I had a long private talk with Madame Binh one afternoon during which I think I proclaimed fealty to the revolution, but I'm not sure. The only moment of clarity came at the end of the week, when the Americans (a motley assortment of Movement freaks and soldiers) caucussed to decide on the content of a "communiqué." Several in the group wanted to express nothing more than the fact that we had all met and that it was very interesting. I was furious when another Movement journalist spoke in favor of the absolute minimum statement so as to preserve our "objectivity." I wanted to say we were on the side of the NLF, that we would fight for them in whatever way we could, that our Movement was in comradely support of theirs.

The next year I went to North Vietnam, on one of "those trips" that was presumably informational ("inform the American people, tell the world, show others what you have seen . . .") but was totally inspirational. I could never communicate the things I felt about the Vietnamese resistance. The information had little to do with it; what was overwhelming was the quality of human and social experience, interaction, purpose that I perceived—gathered—as I moved about Hanoi and the countryside. I knew I'd have few chances in my lifetime to walk in the midst of revolution, and that the exhilaration I felt might never be replicated.

We were in Hanoi, as we had gone to Bratislava, because the Vietnamese were concerned with the course and development of a broad movement in

America that would oppose "Johnson's war" and perhaps pressure the Administration to withdraw American troops. But it was also true that the most active and leading people in that anti-war movement had to see themselves as comrades of the Vietnamese in common combat.

After that, the American liberal line that spoke only of the cost of the war to Americans, the loss of American lives, the perverted priorities ("we could spend the money we're wasting on Vietnam at home"), the memorials to fallen American soldiers—all that seemed one-dimensional, as a line always is. The signals from North Vietnamese and NLF comrades were mixed. No one was ever told what to do—just to do something.

In Hanoi in 1968 I talked at some length with Premier Pham Van Dong. The primaries for the upcoming presidential election were in swing in America; we talked about McCarthy, Bobby Kennedy, Humphrey, the Movement (which at that time eschewed all contact with Democratic politics). It was my impression that Pham Van Dong told me to go back and work for Bobby Kennedy, but nothing in my notes of that conversation confirm anything close to that. What he really meant was: do it. Because of their tactical needs and their strategic histories, the North Vietnamese and the NLF I've met often mute their revolutionary demands (unlike the Chinese, who, I hear from recent visitors to China, are Marxist-Leninists on all levels and that's that). But the lesson of the Vietnamese struggle—the ethic of liberation and resistance—was unmistakable.

The lessons of liberation certainly came the long way around; they could have been found much closer to home if I had been prepared to look. But I wasn't quite prepared. With the example of Vietnam slowly sinking in, I could experience the black movement, class struggle—even what is sometimes called "existential" or personal liberation—in a different way. Vietnam is often credited with "turning on" people to a wide variety of issues. But what that means, I think, is that the radical implications of the Vietnamese resistance gave people a consciousness that made sense of all those other issues. In particular, the war and the resistance have helped me to make sense of privilege and power: what it means to be white, American, bourgeois, a man, technologically competent; how the power that flows from those privileges is used to oppress others; and what it feels like to be on the short end of the stick, as well as the long one. The quantity of oppression (if measures can be made) differs hugely from case to case. But there is a common quality of anger, fear, intimidation, threat, selflessness that a Vietnamese in American-occupied territory shares with a black person in an urban ghetto, a woman typist in a male-dominated office, a Native American in this Europeanized land . . . the list is long, but true for its length.

Vietnam has not let me come to terms with the privilege of being an American. But it has helped to show me how destructive—and self-oppressing—privilege is. The attempts that so many people have made to "de-role" themselves in the past half-decade have not simply arrived out of thin air. Those who have tried to shed privilege—by "dropping out" of middle-class styles, or professional jobs, or nuclear families, or whatever—have done so because they couldn't bear to live with the self-alienation that the privilege entails—after such knowledge of Vietnam, black America, whatever.

Of course there will be backing and filling, two steps back for every two forward, at least for a while. A lot of Americans have made a lot of money off this war—from Lockheed Aircraft to David Halberstam (who just got a reported $750,000 for the paperback rights to his book on the personalities that got America into Vietnam). I was lucky, too: I learned enough to make myself permanently and constitutionally unable to accept America and its external and internal empires.

Most Americans, of course, haven't been so lucky. The war in Vietnam was never much closer than the other end of the TV camera, in hot-dot land. The young, educated, acculturated middle-class could *feel* about Vietnam because they knew how to make real the moral and political notions that they conceive. Others don't usually have the leisure or the inclination to do that. That's why the anti-war movement was so impermanent, so easily diverted by a simple trick of Kennedy, Johnson or Nixon, so quickly factionalized by the ego-interests of its own "leaders." I suppose the Vietnamese always knew that the consciousness of a politically powerful mass of middle-Americans could not be raised high enough "in time" to stop the war, this war, before Vietnam would be totally destroyed. So they concentrated on their own resistance and encouraged Americans to do what they could with the political resources available. No Vietnamese ever called us "revolutionaries."

January 23, 1973, THE BOSTON PHOENIX

✦

Only in America

Nashville is an event in film criticism as well as an event in films. In both ways it is phenomenal. Not since the post–World War II epic *The Best Years of Our Lives* has a movie been taken to express the spirit of a generation, the character of America in a particular time and place. Director Robert Altman has called his film *War and Peace* with country music. Accordingly, *Nashville* has inspired political columnists to flights of analysis and sociologists to lyrics of descriptive prose at the same time it moves professional cinéastes to rhapsodies of praise. It is the Big Thing, the movie—as Pauline Kael said—against which all movies will be judged for the next decade.

Kael actually threw out the first pitch in this critical rollerball game with a preview of *Nashville* several months ago in *The New Yorker*. The picture did not even have a distribution date then, and Kael saw an uncut version of the still-long final print. Her excitement was unalloyed. She chided United Artists for withdrawing support from the project and predicted that UA would rue the day it turned *Nashville* loose. Kael's piece generated enough excitement to convince Paramount to distribute the movie, and to prepare the critical community for what was to come. (It also allowed Kael to predict, create and review the movie-of-the-decade all at the same time; if she had waited for its release date, she would be on her annual six-month sabbatical as *New Yorker* film critic, and her rival Penelope Gilliatt would have had first crack at it.)

What all the fuss is about is a long, confusing, imaginative, amazing and profoundly disturbing movie about two dozen people in Nashville, Tennessee, for the better part of a week. There is something operatic about *Nashville,* and it is not particularly the use of music that produces that effect. The characters seem to be milling behind the screen, continuing the action (or the inaction) we see only occasionally before the footlights. Lily Tomlin as a receptacle for the milk of human kindness sign-talks with her deaf children and sings as the only white in an all-black choir, while she also fiddles around with her sexual fantasies; she speaks a few "arias," has one major "duet" and produces a few "recitativos." And yet she is always *in* the movie. Barbara Harris has two or three scenes, but she does not have to be seen to be believed. She's in Nashville—and *Nashville.*

Almost all of the characters improvised their own lines in rehearsals and repeated them for the final take. Script writer Joan Tewkesbury created what she calls "constructs"—scenes and situations leading from point A to B to C, and so on. Within those constructs, the actors spoke as they understood the characters to feel. Some of the material was taken from external sources (Tewkesbury had a friend who mothered two deaf children), other material was the stuff of the actors' own lives. The whole crew lived together in a motel in Nashville during the entire shooting of the film. They helped and criticized one another in what Keith Carradine (who plays a country-rock stud with hyperactive guitar and phallus) calls "a running encounter group." The singers wrote their own songs, and in a rare way almost *became* their songs. Altman directed the scene with masterful aplomb: again, like a maestro for *Don Giovanni* in Salzburg rather than a director of a movie in Hollywood. All the difficult, disparate elements of *Nashville* ran through his creative intellect, were ordered there and came out orchestrated with his remarkable taste.

As well as his lapses of taste. The biggest character problem is Geraldine Chaplin's absurd parody of a BBC reporter on the prowl for sex, stars and stories in Nashville. It's too bad Altman does not have the feel for British manners that he has for American ones, but it is not crucial either.

What *is* crucial is the sense of *Nashville* as Altman's (and the critics') metaphor for America. It is not surprising that middle and upper-middle brow reviewers and audiences will find it staggering. It projects a desperate conception of America, dancing a do-se-do on the edge of the volcano, empty and hypocritical, valuing only glitter and fame, degrading sex and sensitivity, pretending to be humane when it is merely maudlin, passing off patriotism as politics, despising the will to be free.

"You may say that I ain't free, but it don't worry me," Barbara Harris sings at the end, pounding home one more time Altman's vision of deadly emptiness. Throughout, there has been a sense of impending disaster that is only metaphorically the specific act Altman springs at the last minute. No fiery skyscraper, no Richter-8 tremor, no crippled 747, no giant shark. We are the disaster. The perfect Bicentennial antidote! "We must be doing something right to last 200 years," Henry Gibson (a Nashville version of Buck Owens) chants. The opposite, of course, is true.

Nashville is the final bourgeois vision of America, hopeless and—in a sense—celebratory of the end. These characters, after all, are not bad; they just have nothing important to live for, nothing worthwhile to do. They are not provided with even the faintest outline of a path down from the volcano's rim. Other movies that have the same fashionable view of the degradation of American society—*Alice Doesn't Live Here Anymore* and *A Woman Under the Influence*, for instance—offer some small sense that things could be different if people were free to create new relationships, new institutions, new ways to work, to love and support one another. No such luck in *Nashville*.

Altman does not mock his characters (at least not most of them), nor does he treat them with contempt. Indeed, he seems moderately fond of them. But he has absolutely no faith in their ability to act with any more integrity than they do in his 159 minutes. Every second is dripping with bad faith. Every character is selfish, competitive, tight-assed beyond redemption. Lily Tomlin is not really a humane and caring mother and gospeleer; she's on a death trip like everyone else. Karen Black and Ronee Blakley (the two top female country singers) are locked in deadly competition for the dubious distinction of Opryland's leading lady. Gwen Welles and Shelley Duvall are so starstruck they will never regain normal vision. Barbara Baxley (as a country music club owner) will never recover from her mawkish attachment to the dead Brothers Kennedy. Geraldine Chaplin and Keith Carradine are too disgusting to sympathize with on any level except the biologic.

The critics call this the archetypal post-Watergate movie, and so it is: *Nashville* is as American as—American pie. The fact that it is so unreservedly embraced says more about the consciousness of film critics than it does about Altman's filmic genius. It is, after all, an entirely brilliant movie, and quite as fascinating to me as it was to Kael. But it ends where it should begin. It inspires the last worst disgust rather than the best hope. It reeks with the politics of decadence rather than the politics of progress. There must be another alternative—different from Nashville and *Nashville*. If Altman is right, and there is not, it's bye, bye, American pie, and no kidding.

July 2, 1975, THE REAL PAPER

Chapter VIII

✦

ADAMANT MEMORIES

Lowndes County, Alabama:
The Great Fear Is Gone

Once upon a time in a country called America, in a county called
Lowndes, lived a man named Mr. Blackman. One day while walk-
ing by the courthouse, Mr. Blackman thought, "Us colored people
been using our mouths to do two things—eating and saying yes suh.
It's time we said NO. Yes, it's time we get in this mess.
                    —From a comic book, "A Vote for the Lowndes County
                        Freedom Organization Is a Vote for Us," 1966

The mess in Lowndes is not yet cleaned. The central Alabama county, where "black power" politics began almost a decade ago, is dirt-poor as it always was. Its population of black farmers and their families who live on the margins of the cotton fields and grazing pastures is still economically subservient to the small white minority in the sprawling farmhouses and the columned stately homes of Lowndesboro. The whites who still control the board of education and the county commissioners give blacks few benefits and little recognition, and that grudgingly. The schools are still segregated. But the more Lowndes stays the same, the more it changes. For although the sleepy villages and rolling farms may appear untouched by the movements that swirled through them in the sixties, the atmosphere is profoundly new. The great fear is gone in Lowndes.

To outside agitators and observers who used to treat Lowndes as a living specimen of the problems and promises of Southern civil rights organizing, the use of atmospherics as a measure of progress may seem naive or cynical. We projected "power" in more tangible terms in those days. But the march to the commanding heights does not always proceed through plotted points; in Lowndes, a sense of freedom from fear is the base that supports both blacks and whites as they enter a long transition from the unreconstructed old order to a social design that is at best still sketchy.

The landmark event of this early period was the election in 1970—after several years of trying—of a black sheriff and two other black county officials: coroner and circuit court clerk. Of course, some folks in this slow and somnolent land will never see their elected officers from one term to the next, never feel the direct effects of government. But the very fact of the election of black people in what was the center of Southern white supremacy shattered the stability of the old system.

"It has made all the difference in the world," William Bradley, the black director of the local Head Start program, told me. Bradley, who is in his early 50s, grew up in Lowndes. "Do you know what it was like here before? It isn't anything like it was before John Hulett was elected sheriff. Blacks and whites agree on that."

Harassment, and worse, had been the way of life for blacks in Lowndes since anyone can remember and before. The county is tucked in the middle of what was once the cotton kingdom of Alabama, the buckle on the fertile Black Belt. Lowndes had more than its share of slaves to work those rich fields, and even after the Civil War they were kept in a state of *de facto* peonage from which they did not begin to emerge until the 1940s. John Cashin, a leader of the National Democratic Party of Alabama, the predominantly black alternative to the state's regular Democrats, told me that when the Selective Service agents went into the Black Belt counties just before World War II they found "black people who didn't know they were free. There were 2,000 blacks in Gee's Bend who had no last names, no marriages, no family structures except what existed in slavery."

The bus boycott, led by the young Martin Luther King in 1956, stirred Montgomery but hardly touched Lowndes, although the county borders the western limits of the capital city. Lowndes seemed to be embedded in the past, while the rest of the Deep South began to move and march.

Precisely because Lowndes was the heart of darkness—and because it had a clear black majority—young activists of the Student Nonviolent Coordinating Committee chose it as the focus of a unique and daring political experiment. Lowndes was to bring forth the first all-black political party in the country, to "take the courthouse" and the county offices and give blacks control of their land and their lives. Thus was born, in the summer of 1966, the Lowndes County Freedom Organization.

The SNCC leaders came to their notions of black power after a series of bitter and frustrating experiences with local, state and federal power structures. They also had appropriated bits and pieces of strategy and ideology from different Northern and foreign sources: the urban ghettoes, the universities, Africa, the anti-imperialist Third World. The Freedom Organization took as its emblem the crouching black panther, and immediately became known as the Black Panther party. Stokely Carmichael brought the symbol and the strategy of black party politics to Oakland later that year, when urban blacks met to form a national political organization with the same name. It was the year of "black power," and it was only logical that it was born in Lowndes, the blackest and most powerless place in America.

The slate of Black Panther candidates for county office lost in the Lowndes election of November 1966. Another slate, under the same emblem, lost two years later.

"We had a majority going into those elections, but the people just weren't ready to make the break—not yet," one of the older party members told me. Part of the problem was the panther symbol itself—more fearsome to supporters and opponents alike than the regular Democrats' rooster. The panther had already become a national radical design, and the blacks of Lowndes were uneasy about their new identification with urban militants and insurgents. Even those who knew nothing of Northern politics felt there was something wrong with voting for a party that didn't bear the name "Democratic" in Alabama.

Those difficulties were repaired, to a degree, when the LCFO abandoned the black panther and folded itself into the National Democratic Party of Alabama (NDPA) in 1970. In some sense, it was not a drastic change. The Freedom Organization had been a forerunner of the NDPA, an earlier version of a black alternative to the regular Democrats that sought to win national support against segregationist control of the regular Alabama party. The NDPA had ties with Northern blacks and white liberals dating from its struggles against the Wallace organization at the 1968 Democratic National Convention. Those ties made it suspect to the radical SNCC organizers in Lowndes, but more attractive to the local leaders after the isolation of two lost elections. SNCC was long gone, in any event, by the time of the 1970 campaign, and fears of a loss of ideological purity were overcome by the real possibility of victory under the NDPA eagle. The LCFO abandoned the panther (as did the organizations in the few other Black Belt counties that were using the same symbol), joined the NDPA and won its first offices in Lowndes County.

John Hulett, the first president of the LCFO, was elected sheriff and two other blacks won minor offices, but the county did not come under black control in the way the organizers had once hoped. Whites in Lowndes had begun to accommodate themselves to the new reality of black voting power before the 1970 vote: they appointed a few black deputy sheriffs and generally started "talking" to black leaders across the distance of lifelong apartheid. Even after Hulett was elected, however, the whites maintained their position in critical areas.

"The sheriff is an important figurehead, but whites found out that it doesn't matter much to them that a black man has the job," a white Alabama journalist said recently. "The whites say, 'It's a nigger's job, let him do it.' They know that the state legislature and the governor will protect them if it comes down to a question of property." Even hardened segregationists support some black candidates these days in the Black Belt, and blacks support whites as political strategy dictates. It all seems like "politics as usual"—with the startling addition of black faces. For example, the Lowndes black leadership backed a segregationist white probate judge because he was becoming more accommodating to blacks, because blacks were not yet ready to run for the office or vote for a black judge, and because, as the NDPA's John Cashin said, "Leaving a *white* figurehead in office is a good cover for what we want to do. It works both ways."

The Lowndes blacks also have supported a white woman for the board of education (she happens to be the probate judge's wife)—not primarily because she seems genuinely more "moderate" than other whites but because she maintains an alliance with the blacks against another white political faction. Hulett admits it is a matter of supporting Tweedledum against Tweedledee. But blacks can now exploit the ancient enmities of Democratic intraparty factions, for leverage if not for control.

There are factions, too, in the black community, and the whites have become more adept at working within them to keep an upper hand in key sectors of county politics. For instance, the corps of black teachers constitutes a cautious and conservative class that has traditionally acted as power brokers between the whites and the poor black farmers. It was this black "elite" that continued to support white candidates in the two elections in the sixties, and that still votes for whites for school superintendent, board of education and county commissioners. The white board of education picked a black "friend" from the thin anti-movement elite for its one appointed member.

"He's what we called a white-black," Head Start director Bradley said of the black appointee, in the sad and angry way militant blacks always speak of "Uncle Toms."

"He got up once at a school assembly and told the kids, 'You be submissive and obedient to the white folks and you'll get along.' You see, the board of education is still the largest single employer in the county, and it's being used effectively to sway or control people. There's a lot of uncertainty in the black community as to employment. Even black teachers don't know whether they're going to be employed until the day before school opens. Most teachers in Lowndes live outside the county, in Montgomery or Selma. They have no concern about what goes on here, except to keep their jobs. And it's hard to dismiss them because of the teacher tenure law. They're a very strong force, and they have an influence on our children that lasts for a long time.

"If we can get control of the board of education, we can speed up the process here and make some real progress, but not until then."

The "process" has been tedious. The tempo of the sixties has slowed, the sense of movement has waned. Then there were marches and mass meetings every week; demonstrations, confrontations and projects everywhere. The Christian Movement and the Freedom Organization were actively organizing the mass of black people for political power and, in a series of co-op projects, for economic self-sufficiency. The black organizations purchased 200 acres of land, with help from former residents who had moved to Northern cities: a Detroit-Lowndes axis for money and support was established to help the projects. The land was to be used for farming and for pulpwood sales. Later, the American Friends Service Committee invested enough money to start a small sawmill business for the black community. The LCFO started a credit union and set up a grocery store in a neighborhood called Moss's Community.

But movement economic growth has been slow in a county that has practically no large industry or business to speak of. The one big plant in Lowndes—a Dan River Mills textile factory—hires few local residents for its automated operations, and in any case is just outside of Selma (in neighboring Dallas County). It also has a relocation-inducement tax break from Lowndes, which makes it practically worthless as an income source at this time. Sheriff John Hulett said of the attempts at building an economic base: "It's our biggest problem. We have a long way to go."

Part of the problem is the control that the county board of commissioners and the board of education still maintain. One black man was elected in 1972 to the five-member board of commissioners, and although he is not known as a movement firebrand, his presence there has made a difference to the black community in some cases. The most important instance concerns the Community Health Center, a former Office of Economic Opportunity operation that was a point of local pride as well as a shining example of federal service to the poor before it was shut down in 1973.

The center—the only building in the county with an elevator—went up next to the jail in Hayneville in 1969, at a cost in excess of a million dollars. Another million went into equipment and appurtenances—including fourteen vehicles for getting around the thirty-square-mile county, and getting residents into Hayneville. The Lowndes "board of health," which consisted of extant doctors—all white—was the grantee. A community advisory board, including many poor blacks, tried to assert its authority, and in time moved to replace the doctors as grantee. But the resulting controversy embittered the OEO in Washington, which ceased to fund the whole project out of a mixture of confusion and spite.

The one practicing physician, Dr. Henry H. Meadows, set up an office a few yards away on the Hayneville square. He never had much faith in the local blacks, anyhow; he once told the Alabama Medicaid director that emigration of "the most ambitious and intelligent Negroes" from Lowndes had "left behind the indolent and perhaps mentally defective, and they began to inbreed." He later modified his genetic theory to take into account the effects of malnutrition on IQ and general competence. He would tell people that obesity was the major health problem in Lowndes; the result of federal food giveaways and a tradition, as in certain exotic Asian countries, that women are purposely fattened as a symbol of wealth and status.

The OEO building lay dormant for a year, while the old community advisory board changed itself into the Lowndes County Health Association and tried to get funds for a clinic. The need was demonstrable: in its four years of operation, the old center, with a staff of 108, had delivered free comprehensive health care to more than 10,000 people, a great many of whom had never been to see a doctor in their lives. But the blacks in the new association could not get their hands on the facilities. The county commissioners succeeded in transferring title to the building from OEO to themselves, and set about removing every stick of equipment and all the vehicles, and shipping them to the Lister Hill Health Center in Montgomery. The blacks looked on in dismay as their facilities drained away.

"See the holes on the walls," Steve Wilson, the acting administrator of the Health Association, pointed out as we sat in a bare office in the center. "They snatched every damn thing they could disassemble—bookcases, everything."

After a year, however, the commissioners—prodded by their one new black member—made the skeletal building available to the Health Association for $1 a year—plus the maintenance costs, which amount to about $1,000 a month. In March 1974, the Health Association opened its clinic on the thinnest of shoestrings, and with no encouragement from the local white doctors.

"The whites on the square write off the Health Association," Steve Wilson said. "They pretend it doesn't exist." But business is booming. Since it opened, some 6,800 people come through for treatment each month. There are two young white doctors on the staff; their salaries are partially subsidized by the Public Health Service. (The other two white doctors in the county—the third recently died—will not let the HA's doctors into the County Medical Association or the "health board.") The clinic gets no outside funding, except for third-party reimbursements from Medicare, Medicaid and an Agriculture Department program for mothers of infant children.

"There's no funding for people not on these programs, but of course we help them anyway," Wilson said. "We're a service program, but that's not all. The delivery of health services in Lowndes is essentially a political act—when the people have a hand in it," he added. The board that runs the clinic is now all black, as are most of the patients (though some white mothers come in under the Agriculture Department program). The board's chairman is William Bradley, also the director of Head Start. "We don't have 'leaders' here who tell people what to do," Wilson concluded. "We try to make decisions all together."

Wilson is one of only a few young blacks in Lowndes who have the style—and the background—of the civil rights workers of the sixties. He was raised in Philadelphia, worked in movement projects in Mississippi and now is "on loan" to Lowndes from a community organizing job in Tuskegee. He sees the clinic as a real victory for the movement in Lowndes, and a measure of the success of black organization. It also seems to be a metaphor for the difficulties that remain: the physical incompleteness, the uncertainty of support, the cold indifference of the powerful whites. Lowndes now is on its own; it is not likely that marches will pass through again.

The future of the movement in Lowndes is not entirely dependent on the energies, or even the success, of the black leadership that formed the Freedom Organization. The election of more black officials, especially to the school board, the commissioners and the school superintendency, would certainly give more impetus to social and economic progress. But changes in Alabama politics, in the patterns of regional emigration and immigration, and larger national trends far removed from Hayneville are as important as local developments.

First, the Alabama Democratic Party—the regulars—is more open to black support than anyone in 1966 would have thought possible. Several black county officials—including John Hulett—have declared sentiments of support ranging from outright approval to mild acceptance. Hulett remains on the most suspicious edge of the blacks-for-Wallace wave, but he now figures he can get more for Lowndes by acceptance rather than antagonism. In fact, he said he could vote for Wallace a few days after the governor helped the black Health Association get control of the medical center building from the Lowndes County commissioners.

The openings to the blacks made by the regular party have eroded the position of the alternative National Democratic Party. In 1974, for instance, Lowndes blacks chose to run in the regular Democratic Party primary rather than stay in the NDPA. They defeated the white Democrats and in some measure "took over" the old party, although the county committee still has a white majority. To an extent, the new formation in Lowndes signals the end of separate—and separatist—black politics in the South, although that process may not be completed for many elections to come. In Lowndes, at least, there was no longer any reason for the black majority to have its separate organization.

Second, the Black Belt is becoming less black. About 2,000 blacks have left Lowndes, reducing the black population by about a sixth since the movement began ten years ago. Some blacks may move in (or move back from the North), but the whites are immigrating at a much faster rate. Part of Lowndes is just beyond the current limits of Montgomery's suburbia, and it won't be long before the capital area stretches well into the county. The change in Lowndes land usage from cotton to beef production has meant less work for black farmers. The younger men and women are still leaving for Northern industrial centers. Blacks make up 90 percent of the under-5 population but only 77 percent of the total for the county. The voting-age population of blacks is getting closer to minority status.

Only ten of Alabama's sixty-seven counties have black majorities, and of those, only seven have majorities over 65 percent—generally considered the margin needed for the election of blacks to a controlling position in county offices. The total black population dropped to 26 percent in the state in 1970, from 30 percent ten years earlier. Faced with a declining percentage of voters in the state (birth rates by race are also evening out), black politicians are less interested in all-black parties and more concerned with forming the kind of coalitions that can produce tangible political gains—for themselves no less than for their constituencies.

Finally, the deceleration, if not the demise, of the national civil rights movement—and the loss of many anti-poverty programs at the federal level—has forced local blacks to concentrate on county and state resources, for both economic aid and employment. The heady dreams of economic cooperatives and socialism-in-one-county ended long ago. The few remaining projects—the sawmill and the grocery store—are beneficial but hardly the foundation of a new economic and social order.

Because the revolution that SNCC predicted (or projected) did not occur according to its 1966 timetable, some Northern—and Southern—radicals have tended to overlook the slow and painful progress that Lowndes blacks have made. None of the people I spoke with in Lowndes offered any neat prescription for sweeping change, as they had in earlier days. Incremental improvements based on interim tactics of accommodation and challenge to powerful white institutions seem to form the dominant black strategy.

Stokely Carmichael, who left Lowndes long ago for national and international activism, returned to the Black Belt last summer to see what had changed in the landscapes of his youth. A black television reporter interviewed him, in a yellow dashiki, on the steps of the state house—the first capitol of the Confederacy—in Montgomery.

"If I came through here today and said 'Burn, baby, burn'—it wouldn't happen," Carmichael said. "The objective conditions just aren't there. Six years ago the oppression was too blatant. Now the contradictions are blurred. The white power structure has some black people on television and some black elected officials. Undeniably, black people have made some progress. Your being on television is because black people spilled blood on these streets. And George Wallace," he said, looking back at the state house, "has had to come and *beg* black people to vote for him."

The reporter, rather ingenuously, asked him what black power was all about.

"Black power," Carmichael answered, "is black people coming together and making a power base to do what they have to do to assure their liberation, to be in control of their lives."

"By any means necessary?" the reporter asked.

"By any means necessary," Carmichael answered with a small smile.

April 1975, RAMPARTS

✦

The Boys in the Barracks

Love and death are both military moods. The armed force that creates a culture of killing also produces passions more profound than inhabit any civilian community. Romance in the trenches, brotherhood in the barracks and intimacy in the cockpits of combat are as much a part of military life as the lessons of war. But the affections that might seem the most natural—of soldier for soldier—are also the most unacceptable; and until now, the American armed forces have reacted to homosexuality with fear and loathing that is excessive even by the puritan standards off base. Long after there were publicly gay priests and politicians, there are no openly gay PFCs—at least none who is not under some kind of prosecution.

Suddenly, but not so surprisingly, an army of gay lovers is gearing up for battle with the army of straight soldiers. Or perhaps the formation is on the order of a platoon against a division. It's not always easy to see the lines, or the action, but it is clear that a decade's liberation movements, counter-cultural styles and political activism have penetrated deep into the reaches of the most regimented and restrictive establishment in America. Soldiers, seamen, airmen; women and men; officers, enlistees and reservists, are challenging the military's strictures against homosexuality—where even an unexpressed "tendency," according to the rules, is enough to warrant a dishonorable discharge, or worse.

The opening gun, or at least the biggest blast in that fight so far, was fired by Tech. Sgt. Leonard Matlovich, who decided last March that twelve years in the air force closet was too long, and in the style of thousands of homosexuals in the past few years, "came out" to his employer, co-workers, parents and friends. Unlike those other hundreds of servicemen and women who are mustered out of their units and less-than-honorably discharged each year for loving against Government Issue, Matlovich was not under suspicion, investigation or prosecution. He was not caught *in flagrante delicto,* but trapped in the schizoid world of hidden homosexuals.

"I was tired of hiding from myself and everyone else," Matlovich said recently as we talked above the air-conditioner hum in his bungalow in Hampton, Virginia, near his post at Langley Air Force Base. He was going about his business in the steamy summer weeks before the authorities responded to his simple disclosure. Not much had changed on the surface of his life. He dressed in air force blue each morning, travelled the few miles to his office on post, did his paperwork, chatted amiably with the others in his office. Throughout the day he would meet other gay NCOs in the cafeteria, the parking lot or by the water cooler down the hall from his desk. They talked furtively, quickly, about developments in Matlovich's "case," or about news of the local community of homosexuals. Then they parted without even much of a goodbye.

No one else among the hundreds—perhaps thousands—of homosexuals at Langley and the surrounding military posts has joined Matlovich in coming out, unasked. But although it was his own solitary choice to reveal his sexual orientation to his superiors—and thereby provoke discharge proceedings against him—Matlovich was in some sense not alone. He stands at a peculiar juncture of cultural history, between conflicting systems of values about sexuality, masculinity, privacy and self-identity. The military system has the force of tradition behind it, but it has lost its forward drive. Younger homosexual servicepeople never forget the regulations, but cannot resist expressing those aspects of gay culture that are tolerated—even chic—in civilian life. They live as lovers, travel to gay resorts, dance at the bars and socialize within the gay sets on every military post. They tell their straight friends about their lives and loves—and hope they won't be reported. They rarely are. Change is evident everywhere at the lowest echelons of the military order, but it has not yet gained the top. Matlovich is a victim as well as an agent of change, and it is his dangerous mission to draw fire to the system, as a point man on patrol presents himself as a target.

By coincidence—but not without some historical logic—a band of other servicepeople have joined Matlovich this summer at that cultural crossroads. Two WAC lesbians—PFC Barbara Randolph and Pvt. Debbie Watson—are contesting their less-than-honorable discharges from the service; they had gone to the authorities at Fort Devens, Massachusetts, for help in sorting out their difficulties as army lovers, and the army responded by giving them the boot. At Dover Air Force Base, in Delaware, Sgt. Skip Keith declared his homosexuality to a roomful of fellow students in his "race relations" class; he thought his double oppression as a black homosexual might be relevant to the class's discussion of discrimination. He is now awaiting formal discharge hearings. Navy nurses and army reservists are at various stages of appeals from administrative discharge boards.

None of them knew—or knew much—of the other challenges, but they all express an idea of resistance whose time has come. The pace is sometimes slow, but private and public institutions—from AT&T to the US Civil Service Commission—have relaxed or abandoned their restrictions against homosexual employees. Twelve states have stricken their sodomy laws, and twenty-two cities have enacted various sexual freedom and anti-discrimination laws. At last, as the movement for sexual civil rights reaches the most inflexible, intolerant institution of all, the military is closing ranks against the acceptance of homosexuality. Lest current trends of sexual tolerance cause reluctance at the local level to search out and destroy illicit love, the Secretary of Defense issued orders in June for the "prompt separation" of homosexuals and the preclusion of their service in the armed forces "in any capacity."

"Sooner or later, one of these cases will produce a court decision declaring discrimination against homosexuals unconstitutional," said ACLU lawyer Jerry Cohen, the man who defended the two Fort Devens women. "It's likely to happen in the armed services because their intolerance is so blatant, and it has the force of law. The military is the key institution. Just as the racial integration of the military in the late forties set the stage for a national social policy of integration, the critical sexual battles are going to be fought here."

It is not as if the handful of homosexuals now putting up a fight, or even those others cashiered every year in semisecret shame, constitute the entire gay population in the services. Careful research is hard to come by, and the Pentagon's figures are skewed, but two Kinsey Institute scholars estimated in 1971 that the percentage of homosexuals in the military hardly differs from the number in civilian society. The various defense lawyers and experts in the current cases use a standard estimate of "10 percent gay," in and out of uniform, although Alfred Kinsey believed that "the active incidence of the homosexual in the . . . U.S. population among men of Army and Navy age is nearly 30 percent." One gay sergeant I met thought even that larger figure was low: "If all the gay people in the military were laid end to end . . ." he began, and laughed instead of ending the gag.

The evidence of one's eyes and ears is more telling than the statistics. In the days I spent around Langley Air Force Base, I travelled easily in the gay subculture, and watched as it collided with and accommodated the dominant military culture. Gay people know each other—or know about each other—in every office and barracks. Everyone knows stories about homosexual generals and colonels. A former commanding general of the air force in Europe is widely reported to have been gay. One young airman told of his relationship with an air force general in the Far East that included weekend "R&R" holidays to romantic places aboard military planes. I mentioned to one sergeant at Langley that I had just talked with the (straight) wing information officer, and that he seemed uptight about the gay issue. "Well, you should have seen the guy who had his job a while back—he was a real queen!" the sergeant reported with a mocking flip of the wrist—a ghetto joke that he would not have made among straights.

Homosexuals have a hundred ways of "signalling" their identity to one another. Rarely do those mannerisms conform to the broad stereotypes of gay behavior—male and female—that fill ghetto humor as well as straight cruel comedy. They are simply subtle and sometimes subliminal expressions of a different culture. That "difference" is crucial. Gay people learn to act out the apartness they feel either in broad parody or careful imitation of straight styles. Non-gays invariably seize on the parodies. Hollywood's version of a homosexual soldier is either a mincing transvestite or a suicidal "butch" psychotic like Rod Steiger's caricature in *The Sergeant*. The gay men I met at Langley had nothing to do with either image. They could spot one another, perhaps, but they were necessarily invisible to the rest of the military world.

Beyond the signals, gays meet in one another's off-base apartments, or at beaches, or in the "cruising" areas that serve as pick-up points for the kind of encounters that straight people find it possible to achieve in better-lighted environments. Not the least irony of the military's confrontation with homo-sexual life is the gays' use of the Iwo Jima Memorial atop a hill in Arlington, Virginia, as a nighttime cruising ground. Lovers can meet, or make out, with a breathtaking view of the Pentagon, the Capitol and the Washington Monument, for whatever symbolic value any of those edifices may carry.

Gay bars are still the favorite meeting place, and there is probably one or more within shooting distance of every major military post in the country. The custom spreads rapidly, as well, to the outposts of empire. Skip Keith recalled that there were at least two exclusively gay bars on Tu Do Street in old Saigon, and the USO "service clubs" at the big air force bases—Cam Ranh Bay, Bien Hoa and Danang—were "very cruisy."

"The best place to cruise was the military swimming pool just by Tan Son Nhut Airport," Keith said. "It was subtle, of course, but people cruised there left and right."

In Norfolk the place to go these days is the Cue Club, a large warehouse of a building on a back street of town. What makes it popular is that it stands virtually in the center of the largest concentration of military manpower in the country.

At midnight on a weekday night the bar was crowded. The disco-soul music was loud, the dance floor was active with male and female couples bumping and jerking just as they do in New York and San Francisco. A sailor from the aircraft carrier *Nimitz* walked in, and Matlovich gave him a big hug and kiss. "We once had a brief 'thing,'" an air force major standing next to me said as the sailor walked away, "but I got sent to Indochina, and when I got back he'd found somebody else." The major chuckled and shrugged his shoulders.

Other servicemen in civvies came over to greet Matlovich, who is already something of a gay hero in Virginia Tidewater military lore. There were sea-men from their ships, soldiers from Fort Eustis and Fort Monroe, air force officers from TAC headquarters at Langley, marines, medical corpsmen, WAFs, WACs and WAVEs—and civilian gays who work on all the bases. Almost everyone I spoke with was in the service, and Matlovich estimated that the crowd is 75 to 80 percent military on an average night. No one seems to worry about raids. "Once in a while there's an intelligence agent in here, but he's usually working on a specific case," Matlovich said. "The mili-tary could bust 10 percent of its personnel in this area just by rounding up the people who come here, but it's the last thing they want to do."

The coexistence of gay and military communities presents scores of such paradoxes, and none of them is easy to explain. The harsh regulations against the admission or retention of gays in the service are enforced only selectively—but then with accompanying flights of rhetorical contempt. At the "hearing" for Barbara Randolph at Fort Devens—it was more like a trial or, at times, a medieval inquisition—the prosecuting (male) army captain railed against "this insidious, sinister thing," whispered "psychosis" and warned, "Don't let this spread." And yet more and more accused homosexuals are retained in the service each year, or given honorable or general discharges, instead of dishonorable ones, as was once the case. And the gay communities around the bases continue to grow.

"Everywhere I've been in eight years in the services I've found a gay social life," Steve Lockhart, an air force captain, said. He and his lover—a civilian hairdresser—sat around the living room in the house of a gay retired air force major and talked with a half-dozen other gay servicemen about the homosexual military subculture. ("Lockhart," like others in this account who have not made their homosexuality public, are referred to by pseudonyms. Perhaps it may not be necessary much longer to be so guarded in such reports.)

"I joined the air force hoping it would make me straight," Lockhart said. "That's how much I knew. I was stationed at Nellis Air Force Base [in Nevada] and everyone would come into the gay bar in Las Vegas, and pretty soon I was in the gay community. As long as I'm careful I don't think I'll have any trouble. At this point, I hope to stay in for twenty years."

Gary Jones and Tim Vasquez are both sergeants. They've just become lovers and are sharing their first apartment.

"I enlisted to *forget* I was gay," Jones said. "I guess for some people it's like joining a monastery or a nunnery. It's another way you can find security and a kind of family, without being married and living in the suburbs with the wife and kids."

"Gay people are never satisfied," Lockhart joked. "They either want to get in or they want to get out. A lot of people enlisted as medics or some special service to get out of the draft. Then they said they were gay and wanted a discharge."

"The thing is, they don't know what it's going to be like," Jones added, and everyone agreed.

"I tried it for years," another sergeant said finally, "but the military is no place for gays."

Not everyone agrees with that. Skip Keith likes the air force so much—at least he likes maintaining C-5 transports—that he re-upped after briefly trying out civilian life between periods of service. Barbara Randolph and Debbie Watson fought hard to stay in the army. They were enthusiastic about their schoolwork at the Army Security Agency at Fort Devens. They were eager to do whatever electronic surveillance analysis they were supposed to be trained for, and they were proud not to be able to tell me about it. They valued their top-secret clearance.

But the army's way is to take away what its members prize, and give them exactly what they do not want. Randolph and Watson were relieved of their school assignment and their clearance. Worse, they were drummed out of the honor drill team, where they had spent some of their happiest hours marching together. Still, they maintain an almost inexhaustible affection for the army. "It's not the military or the people," Watson said, "it's the regulations."

Many gays I met—Matlovich and Randolph, for two—were "air force brats"; that is, their fathers had been career airmen. In some ways, the military became a surrogate for their fathers in later life. But for some, "coming out" has been accompanied by a rejection of military regimentation and the authoritarian values they once found attractive. Matlovich, for instance, is hardly the "flag-waving, right-wing racist," he says, with horror, he once was. The very process of self-disclosure and the inevitable conflict it produces can easily bring gay servicepeople to make important political connections; to feel an affinity, if not an identity, with blacks, the poor, women and (in the case of Vietnam) the "enemy." Liberation is hard to contain in only one area of consciousness.

Civilian political activists find it contradictory to support gay enlisted men and women who want to stay in the service, and they often seem impatient about the process of consciousness-raising. At an anti-militarism demonstration at Fort Devens that was supposed to—but did not—include support for the lesbians' rights, I encountered almost as much hostility to the women's pro-army position as to the army's homophobia. "We can't get excited about their fight to stay in the army and do all that surveillance stuff," one demonstrator said huffily.

But oppression is where you find it, and for gays in the military it is never farther away than the anxious heterosexual in the next office—or the next bunk. Paranoia runs deep, and fears of discovery—and self-discovery—keep many homosexual servicepeople locked tightly in their closets, entirely coloring the lives of those who have to any degree "come out." To military authorities, self-disclosure is a confession of crime.

Regulations define gays as mentally unstable and a threat to good order. Straight or presumably straight servicemen are reinforced in their fears and prejudices against homosexuality. A system of anxiety and hostility is developed in which good order *is* undone and mental stability *is* often impaired. The military's prophecies are thus fulfilled, and the gays are discharged.

At Barbara Randolph's hearing, expert witness Frank Kameny, a Washington gay activist, tried to explain that triple bind to the panel of colonels and captains with an analogy to the military's experience with racial integration: "When you had problems with racism, you didn't throw out the blacks," Kameny argued. "You threw out the recalcitrant racists."

Randolph had been the "soldier of the month" in March, as a shakedown of sexual habits in the WAC barracks began. But prosecution witnesses said that her lesbianism had made her a "bad soldier" (in the same way, Matlovich's overall efficiency rating was automatically dropped from a nine—the highest—to a zero when he came out to his superiors). "It affects the girls," Randolph's WAC company executive officer said on the stand.

Could it be that the bigotry of straight women and the army's enforced intolerance created the tensions in the barracks? the defense asked. No, the captain said primly, "that's an individual matter. The army is not responsible for bigotry." In other words, sexuality is private when it suits the military's terms, but political when it does not.

The politics of sexuality in the armed services are not qualitatively different for heteros or homos, but the effects are widely disparate. Straights get lessons in avoiding heterosexual VD. They are encouraged by the macho military culture to "sow their wild oats," have pin-ups of big-breasted women, pick up dates at singles bars, frequent brothels in places where they exist. There is a voluminous literature of wife-swapping among the officer class, and many military posts have "key clubs" where group sex is not only tolerated but institutionalized. Straight men have the regulation version of the fantasies of fighting in the day and fucking at night, and straight women in the service have the correct-gender expectations of finding true love in olive drab.

But gay fantasies are said to impair morale and order. It's hardly surprising that gay servicepeople half believe that their expectations of love—and the infrequent expressions of it that they are allowed—are somehow perverse, if not exactly pathological. With friends, they are eager to tell their stories, as if they were tales of combat and danger.

"I was once in love with my co-pilot," an air force navigator with fourteen years of service began. "He was straight, and when he figured out what was happening, he wouldn't talk to me for two weeks. Finally, we discussed it in the Officers Club one night, and everything was okay after that.

"But I would get very depressed, and I couldn't tell anyone what was bothering me. About ten years ago I was going through a very bad time and my roommate, my closest friend, tried to get me to say what it was, but I was afraid to let it out. One night in Tokyo we had a few drinks and he looked at me and said, 'What you need is to go to bed with a man.' Well, we started a relationship, and it would have gone on but he was killed a little later in Vietnam. Also, he was married and he had two kids."

Most gay men in the service have stories like that. Fred Seligman, a medical corpsman in Vietnam, was deeply attracted to his marine sergeant:

"I guess I was in love with him. He was a kind of substitute father for me, the top man in the platoon, a real tough guy who knew his shit. One day we were out on patrol near An Wa. We were walking along a river when I heard an explosion and everyone started screaming. I ran back and looked down. His body was by the side of a crater. I tripped over his foot, which was strewn further on down the path. His guts were over everything. I took my poncho out and put him in it and went back and put his foot in the poncho, too. His bones were poking through the plastic. I carried him half a mile back to camp. It's taken me six years to be able to cry about it."

Seligman (who is now a civilian physician in the South) thinks of his love for the sergeant as "ethereal, pure—and unconsummated." Death was part of it, too: the military drenches everything with death and danger, and then uses the banal bureaucracy to keep the hearts and minds of its subjects off the subject. Repression merely feeds the fantasies.

"This may be a kind of sado-masochistic trip, you know," Will Gerzon, an air force buck sergeant, said mischievously as we talked near the jukebox at the Cue Club in Norfolk. "Everything in the military is 'yes, sir'—with boots on!" Uniforms as drag, weapons as gear, military manners as bondage and discipline: life in the army, for straights no less than gays, is porn by other means. "It's like being a diabetic in a candy shop," Seligman joked. "You can look, but you can't touch."

Matlovich hears it all the time. His house is filled with boxes of letters from gay servicepeople around the country who believe that at last they have found someone who understands.

"I left a small town to join the service," an air force staff sergeant in the upper Midwest wrote Matlovich. "I knew what I was when I enlisted. I did it to be around guys, even if I couldn't touch. At least I could look and wonder what it would be like. I've met guys in the air force who make it quite obvious what they are after, but I never mess with anybody. I couldn't afford it. Like so many other gay military men and women, I walk on eggshells, but for now I've learned to live my life of loneliness and pain behind a mask of smiles."

It was that loneliness, in fact, that led Matlovich to his own startling act of defiance: "I just adored the military. I joined the air force when were were stationed in England. I wanted to go to Vietnam to 'kill a commie for mommy,' the whole patriotic thing. I rang doorbells for Goldwater in California until they told me it was against air force regulations and threatened to court-martial me. I was continuously volunteering for Vietnam. I guess I wanted to prove myself as a man. Being gay, you hear all the stereotypes and you want to prove them wrong."

Matlovich did three tours in Vietnam. On his second, he nearly blew himself to bits on a land mine—an American-made anti-personnel cluster grenade that had not detonated when it was dropped in a bomb. Vietnamese guerrillas replanted it as a booby trap, and Matlovich touched it off digging with his shovel. He got the Purple Heart, then tried to go back to Vietnam. "Maybe it was a death wish. I don't know," he says now.

But whatever else it was, combat in Indochina was a way for him to avoid the reality of his emotional life. For almost ten years he was on the run, alighting for only a few months at bases at home or abroad. Then, two summers ago, he settled in at Eglin Air Force Base in Florida. His job was instructing airmen in race relations. Something had turned him from the "right-wing racist" to a civil rights advocate. Maybe the same thing—a psychological awakening at a critical historical moment—was propelling him into the struggle for his own sexual liberation. In that certain summer he met other gay people for the first time.

"I never found any other homosexuals in the air force," Matlovich continued. "I thought the whole gay world was dirty bookstores and fuck books. I'd never heard of gay liberation; I didn't know there were gay bars. One day I went to a dirty bookstore in Pensacola, hoping to meet someone—anyone—

and I saw five airmen from my base. I overheard their conversation and I could tell they were gay. Later I saw one of them on base and I got my nerve up and walked up to him and said, 'Listen, can you help me?' He said he'd introduce me to a civilian friend of his who worked at the base. The two of us went to the friend's house; I looked around and it dawned on me that there were three gay people in the room! I wasn't the only faggot in the world!"

With additional increments of nerve, Matlovich made it to the gay bar in Pensacola, where he saw hundreds of military homosexuals—men and women—dancing, touching, feeling fine together. "I was 30 and I not only was still a virgin, I had never held another person in my arms, never kissed another person since I was a child."

Matlovich sensed but did not articulate that he was moving with the gay liberation campaign. Like so many others, he was already on board that train and there was no getting off. Magazine articles appeared with stories about "coming out"; he somehow had missed them before. A special issue of *Family*, a weekly magazine published by *Army/Navy/Air Force Times*, was devoted to "Homosexuals in Uniform," and while an introductory editorial included an obligatory judgement that homosexuals should be kept out of the service, the article itself was sensitive and positive about gay experiences in the military. It all had its effect on Matlovich.

Soon he was flying to Washington to talk with gay activist Kameny and a civil liberties lawyer, David Addlestone. The two of them were looking for the "perfect case" to test the constitutionality of the military's regulations against gays. Matlovich, obviously, was it.

It took him nine months to summon up the guts to do what he knew on that first night in Pensacola he had to do. He composed, revised and rewrote his coming out letter. On stationary from Addlestone's Lawyers Military Defense Committee he informed his commanding officers: "After some years of uncertainty, I have arrived at the conclusion that my sexual preferences are homosexual. . . . I have also concluded that my sexual preferences will in no way interfere with my Air Force duties. . . ."

He held the letter for two weeks more, then one day in March stopped his boss, a black captain who runs Matlovich's section of the race relations instruction office.

"I have something to give you, but you'd better sit down," Matlovich told the captain. The officer remained standing. Behind him, over his desk, was a poster declaring: "I Don't Discriminate—I Hate Everybody."

"I mean it. You'd better sit down." The captain did not oblige. Matlovich handed him the letter.

"What is this?" the captain asked incredulously, after a quick read. He read it once again.

"What the hell does this mean?"

"It means," Matlovich said, staring straight ahead, *"Brown v. Board of Education."* The captain sat down.

Matlovich v. Schlesinger (if it ever comes to that) may or may not be a landmark case in civil rights law. It is barely possible that Matlovich will be reinstated in the air force before his case makes it to the end of the judicial line. Even if he isn't, lawyer Addlestone is far from convinced that the Supreme Court could ever find a majority to vote against the Defense Department, should the case go before the justices. As likely as not, the job of forbidding discrimination against sexual minorities may have to be left to Congress—or to a military command that finally catches up with the newer values it now despises.

But at bottom, the contest between gay soldiers and the military is not simply a civil rights issue. If being gay were merely a matter of sexual preference, then it would be easy enough to establish a principle of official tolerance and be done with it. Mere sexual orientation is the way the cases must be framed, but both the military and gay people know that the "problem" of homosexuals in the service is not primarily a question of sex. Being a homosexual means being part of a special culture, with its specific manners, perspectives and values. That culture and all its attributes didn't "just grow" out of the blue, but has been formed from the special experiences of gay people. It is defensive, ghettoized and xenophobic. It has its own language and mores, as do the subcultures of all minorities forced by law or circumstance out of the mainstreams of life.

In that, the gay subculture is remarkably analogous to the black community or the new "counterculture" as they both exist within the military environment. The services have had an enormously difficult time adjusting to those alien units in the regular armies. Black consciousness was a real and present danger to the morale and good order of the military's mission in Indochina; in fact, the appearance of a black "movement" in the services that related to the politics of American black and Third World liberation in the 1960s was a factor in the defeat of that imperial mission.

The armed forces have in some ways accommodated the disruptive presence of blacks and countercultural "freaks" who would not adjust to the white, straight (in the older sense) military command. From the late forties on, the services have committed themselves to a policy of racial desegregation that is still incomplete but has gone farther than any other major public or private institution in the country to equalize the participation of blacks and whites within the ranks. Lately, policies to make service life more comfortable for the turned-on generations of the sixties and seventies and make the male-dominant military more accepting of women, have changed the character of the forces—and the minds of the troops.

The Defense Department's rules against homosexuals grow out of its unwillingness to accommodate another conflicting community, and its real fear of change. Whether from basic instinct or the insights gained in coming out, gay servicepeople are more inclined than straights to question the necessity of the most authoritarian aspects of the military. Homosexuals can of course be just as hell-for-leather as any straight macho marine, but many gays find that coming out dulls the hard edge of the killer instinct.

That is not to say that homosexuals have not, or cannot, make successful careers in armed service. Ancient military history is practically a gay chronicle. "The reason why, before the battle of Thebes, the Spartans offered sacrifice to Eros," the historian Athenaeus wrote, "was that they were convinced that in the comradeship of a pair of friends, fighting side by side, lay safety and victory." Eros was the god of sexual love; "friends" in that context were anything but platonic. More romantic gay military lore can be found in the novels of Mary Renault, who has built an impressive library of books (*The Persian Boy*, *The Charioteer*, etc.) about homosexual affections in archaic armies and imperial courts. No one in the Macedonian military seemed particularly scandalized by the Great Alexander's love affairs.

The Greek ideal seems to have been abandoned over the centuries, but the practice certainly continued. There's a famous story in gay academic circles about the regiment of homosexuals the Germans formed in World War I. The soldiers had taken the option of hazardous duty rather than be discharged for their sexual preferences. The German High Command put them in the front line in the battle of the Marne, and they very nearly whipped the Allies, while the straight German divisions fell back in disarray.

What would it have been like if they did not have to *prove* that they were good soldiers? In the documentary film *The Sorrow and the Pity*, a British officer who completed all sorts of daring exploits behind enemy lines during World War II tells the interviewer that he did his derring-do because he was a ho-mo-sex-u-al (he enunciates the syllables carefully) and thought to be less than "a man." Perhaps such feelings motivate many gay men and women to join the armed forces. But the army is not yet ready to let them prove their worth, nor will it encourage the idea that may not have to prove themselves according to the old strict standards of "manliness."

Under order from Congress or the courts, or under pressure from gays within its ranks and activists outside, the military will sooner or later decide that it must deviate from its policy of exclusion of homosexuals, and that it can no longer ignore the large gay population in its barracks. The size and importance of the military as an institution make that a crucial event in social history. And the special role of the services as a repository for values that are antithetical to sexual liberation means that the conflict will be sharp and the eventual changes far-reaching. The army that emerges from that battle will not be an army of lovers, but it will not despise love in the way it does today.

August 8, 1975, New Times

Afternote: Following years of legal wrangling, Leonard Matlovich was reinstated by the air force in 1980. He died of AIDS on June 22, 1988.

America's Ultimate Strategic Hamlet

Fort Chaffee, Arkansas

On Arkansas's green and pleasant land, Americans have at last created the ultimate strategic hamlet, a secure and sanitary city of 25,000 Vietnamese, completely controlled by military authority and anti-communist to the core. According to the tragic logic of the long war, Fort Chaffee—and its counterparts in Florida and California—is America's victory, the fulfillment of the mission to win the people's hearts and minds by any means necessary. The refugees bestow on their keepers the desperate loyalty of the displaced. They left their country and their culture behind in the panic of flight, and they must adopt their master's ways or perish.

Now the refugees wander aimlessly along the paths and roads of this vast army camp, shivering in the temperate spring weather, queuing up for meals, clothing and processing. Some hold parasols against the mild sun, more out of habit than heat. They might as well be in Irkutsk or Uruguay as Arkansas; most were sped out of their Asian homes, plunked for a few hours on a Pacific islet and carried in enormous jet transports on a long night's journey to an unknown destination.

"I like to swim," one man told me as I stood near the rude barracks that is now his home. "If I go outside the gate, will I find the sea?" Fort Chaffee—on Arkansas's western border with Oklahoma—is 600 miles from the Gulf of Mexico, but there are no maps, no one to teach US geography and no way through the gates. They are "in quarantine," as a State Department agent delicately put it, until they are matched with American "sponsors," who will vouch for their physical and moral well-being for at least two years. Until they find sponsors, or sponsors find them, they are stuck in this anomalous Vietland, like characters in a Disney political theme park, or extras waiting for their big scene in *The War in Vietnam.*

While they walk and wait, the "processing" grinds exceeding slow. A Health, Education and Welfare Department office occupies the top floor of a barracks building, and the few refugees who make it to the anteroom sit patiently until they can get to a desk to sign up for their Social Security card. Steve Roper, an HEW clerk from Dallas assigned to process the refugees, explained that "*everyone* has to have a Social Security card; they're *all* eligible to work once they get security clearance." Work will make them free, and they know it. A middle-aged Vietnamese man approached me on the street in front of the PX and waved a wrinkled, tattered letter in my face; it was written on United States Navy stationery, and it was addressed "To Whom It May Concern." The letter attested to the construction work the man had done for the navy in Vietnam. "You know a contractor to sponsor me?" he asked in fairly fluent English with a heavy French accent. "I come with my family, my wife and one daughter; I would like to know some US contractor to cooperate with me. Please," he smiled, "do you know?"

Perhaps he will find work to fit his profession or his skills. At least he is well educated and proficient in building. Others are clearly not so privileged. The refugees who came to Fort Chaffee in the first few days are supposed to be the "elite" of the population that fled, but that is a relative description, and even in the time I spent at the camp, I could tell that thousands were simply low-level civil servants in Vietnamese or American offices, or ordinary military personnel caught up in the traps and confusion of war and defeat.

"I am commissary officer in the Vietnam marine corps in Vung Tau," one man told me, using the present tense incorrectly out of ignorance or wishful recollection. His family included seven people: his wife and his child and his sister and three children. He was evacuated from Vung Tau on April 27. "We have good luck, you know. We stay in airport. And we saw one aircraft landing and American just call, yes, 'hey, c'mon, let's take off.' So we put our family in a seat and they take off, five minutes after they land."

Why did the commissary officer leave his country? "I have been in the United States for two times; I study US commissary management and audit," he explained. With that history, he was afraid of what "the communists" might think of him. He has no friends or relatives in America, no sponsors. Now his family has to wait for one of the religious agencies to find sponsors for him. The Baptists seem interested in his soul.

Fifteen hundred refugees had "departed government control" during the first week and a half Fort Chaffee was operating. They must have been a real elite. Of the seven "high-ranking" Vietnamese officials reported to be here, five had already left by May 14. Four of these five went to Washington. Who are they, and who are their sponsors? The army and the State Department were not saying.

Perhaps they did not constitute a "security problem," but in any case the clearance process suddenly tightened after the first thousand or so Vietnamese had been sponsored out of Arkansas. "We were playing fast and loose with the Immigration and Naturalization Service's thirty-one excludable categories," John King, the State Department deputy at Chaffee told me. "There was a feeling in Washington that we got the politically malodorous types—the crooks and pimps and prostitutes. The House judiciary committee and a lot of people on the Hill said, 'wait a minute,' and INS put a choke on out-processing."

"But what are we supposed to do? This is a Catch-22 situation," King said, shaking his head. He has the air of a seersuckered minor diplomat in a Graham Greene version of an American imperial outpost: smart, cynical, Roman Catholic, rutted in the reaches of an intractable government bureaucracy run by unseen authorities thousands of miles away. He went on to explain his problem: "Prostitution and felonious record hang-ups were nonissues. The embassy in Saigon didn't keep records; they called the Saigon police when they had a question. But there's no Saigon police to call any-more." At least, there's no Saigon police for the US embassy to call.

"Technically," King continued patiently, "these people are not in the United States. They are seeking parole. If they are excludable, we don't know what we'd do. We're not going to send them back to Vietnam. We're just sitting and waiting. Many who made it out were US government employees, and there's a verification process for them in government agencies. I don't know what we'll do about the others."

Not even the army commander and the State Department officials know who is in their charge. The Vietnamese pour out of the jumbo jets at an airport in the nearby town of Fort Smith, or in Little Rock, and are quickly bussed to Chaffee. Near the gates to the post, they see a billboard in English and Vietnamese: "Welcome to America." No census is made, not even an accounting by age and sex. King and his military counterpart, an army colonel, were so ignorant about the composition of the refugee community that they decided to watch a load of refugees from Guam deplane at the Fort Smith airport.

"Of the 256 people on board, fifty-six were men over the age of about 16 or 17," King reported. The rest were women and children. Officials now estimate that less than a third of the total of 130,000-odd refugees who fled Indochina in the last weeks of the war may be male heads of households: that is, those best able to find jobs in the crunched American employment market.

Some may go back to Vietnam, despite their fears of dire peril at the hands of "the VC," who have been made into monsters by the decades-long flood of French, American and Vietnamese colonial propaganda.

"I'd like to return to my country," a young Vietnamese man told me, "but I have a sister married with an American, my father is a big, how you say, 'farmer,' and my brother is a former minister under Vice President Ky. It is impossible for me to try to stay in my country, but in the near future I return." He was walking with his wife, a Swiss woman he had met when both were students in Paris: he at the prestigious Institut des Etudes Politiques and she "studying little things." The young man escorted his wife to the Swiss embassy in Saigon during Evacuation Week, and she managed to get aboard an American ship out of Vung Tau, bound for Subic Bay. He flew out to Guam; they both were on that crowded island at the same time, but failed to meet. They caught up with each other walking the paths of Fort Chaffee.

The science-pol student, the striking blonde Swiss woman, the US navy "contractor," the commissary manager—they all talked freely and almost eagerly. So did a man in a long tan raincoat, almost down to his ankles, who stopped me to ask where he could find a telephone. I pointed to a nearby row of booths. He didn't seem to see them, and we walked closer. Still he asked where the phones were, and I realized he did not recognize the familiar Bell System booths as places where telephones were likely to be found. In any case, it was unlikely that he could complete his call by himself. There was no distance-dialing equipment on the post, and he had a complicated task—to call his son in Baton Rouge, Louisiana, in a department of LSU, with an extension number off the main switchboard. Someone had written the instructions for the call on a piece of paper but had put the area code after the main number. He spoke a little English, but not enough to deal with two or three Arkansas and Louisiana operators. I offered to help. We stood in line for the phones, but all three of them proved to be out of order, so we went to another building where even longer lines had formed. In the meantime, I asked him what his life had been like in Vietnam.

"I was airman," he said. What exactly did he do? He smiled: "I was major general. My name is Nguyen Van Chuan. I commanded the I-Corps in Danang. I organized three divisions. I retired in 1966, and a few years after, I became senator."

What party? I asked, somewhat startled.

"Anti-communist party," he said, his smile broadening to an engaging giggle. Quickly he added that he was in "opposite bloc" to President Thieu. I thought of all the Germans I had seen in Germany in the 1950s who assured me right off the bat that they had fought on "the Eastern Front." I never understood how the Russians beat them back, with all of the German military facing East. It may soon be impossible to meet a Vietnamese refugee who wasn't against Thieu.

"But I am, too, anti-communist," he insisted, just to get that straight. "But I disagree with Thieu, with his policy, *en general.* I don't believe we can destroy all communists in the world. Thieu failed because he did not have the people. In the last election he was alone."

Could the senator have stayed in Vietnam after the government's surrender?

"Oh no," he replied, his giggle now expanding to a full-throated laugh. "Surely it is impossible. In 1945 the communists put me in jail already." I could imagine the content of his long career.

The waiting queue for the telephone was interminable, and he wandered off to find some new office for processing. Across the path from the telephones, a group of sullen Vietnamese rangers, in commando drag but unarmed, hunkered beneath a tree. My military escort, a warmly jive second lieutenant who was working off his ROTC commitment from Southern University, said that the rangers at Chaffee were the ones who had beaten their way aboard the boats at Danang, murdering and looting as they went. The civilians feared and resented them. "They're isolated here," John King said later. "We're worried they're going to start trying to screw the [Vietnamese] people here, like they screwed them in Vietnam."

Down the road was the PX devoted to "Outdoor Living," with a complement of patio furniture and barbecues for graceful Arkansan recreation. Inside, two young blonde girls dressed in paper Uncle Sam hats and red-white-and-blue miniskirts were passing out free cake and coffee to celebrate the eightieth birthday of the PX system. A few Vietnamese wandered through the store. One woman all dolled up as if she were stepping out for cocktails on Tu Do Street emerged with a large paper bag. All I could see in it was a box of Converse sneakers at the top. I asked her what she had bought.

"I buy food, candy, something for the baby, some things for my face," she said, making a motion as if to powder her nose. I asked her whether those without money could find a way to buy things—by borrowing, bartering, working. "I'm sorry I don't know about it," she said, and hurried away.

A high school teacher named Hung had attached himself to me and was acting as interpreter and guide through these bizarre scenes. I asked him whether any crude economy had yet formed in the camp.

"There is no way to get money," Hung said. "A little number of people have dollars. We have a few thousand piasters but no dollars, and they will not let us change them."

Later, I visited the hastily established Fort Chaffee branch of a Fort Smith bank: a trailer parked away from the main barracks area and guarded inside and out by burly MPs. The trailer was fitted with wall-to-wall carpeting and finished in wood paneling. At one end was a door leading to a back room: the gold assaying office. The assayer agreed to let me see his set-up, but would tell me nothing: not how much gold he had assayed, what the largest amount anyone had was, how many people he had seen. He spoke with a middle-European accent: a gnome imported from Zurich for the occasion, perhaps? No comment.

The State Department man, John King, told me later that some refugees had come out with gold wafers stashed in fancy belts, and others had dollar travellers checks or greenbacks. He had seen a woman at the central travel ticket office buying $3,500 worth of airline tickets with her Diner's Club card; the ticket seller had checked the purchase with the Diner's Club authorization office and had been told to give the lady anything she wanted.

"But most of these people are flat-ass busted," King said. "Especially the ones who worked for the US in Saigon. Those who had bank accounts couldn't convert them to dollars at the last minute. The piaster declined 1,000 percent a day. The Saigon society went apart at the seams, too fast for anyone to save anything but their ass. The smart crooks took their money out of Vietnam long ago, and it's true, some of the first refugees had their belts lined with gold. But the great majority have nothing. In the cargo hatch of the plane I saw unload the other day there wasn't 800 pounds' worth of luggage for 250 people."

The Vietnamese are not given to blatant expressions of emotion before strangers, and I could not get a strong sense of their collective reaction to the traumas of the last two or three weeks. Everyone I spoke with had been evacuated on April 27 or 28. None had been prepared. Hung had just moved into a new house built a month before his family fled. His father, an army lieutenant colonel, was still in Vietnam: "Where he is I do not know," he said sadly. Hung came with his mother and seven other family members. He showed me his living quarters: a billet for eight people in a barracks building that contains fourteen billets. His building had elected a "leader," who was also an army colonel. Hung was anxious that I meet him; I sensed that he identified the "leader" with his father, but the man never appeared.

The refugees eat in any one of twenty-three mess halls. They stand in endless lines. I was in one mess hall for lunch; the menu was a cup of rice, a half of a banana, a scoopful of reconstituted powdered milk. There was a rumor that flakes of fish had been mixed with the rice, but if so, it was impossible to detect with the naked tongue. A few diners had bottles of red-hot sauce or Kikkoman soy, which they were substituting for the beloved Vietnam condiment *nuoc mam*, a surprisingly mild and salty liquid made of fermented fish. Although you can buy similar fish sauces in Oriental groceries in the biggest American cities, the local Fort Smith supermarket is unlikely to carry them—even if anyone at the camp could get out to the supermarket. One man, however, had a plastic package of Oscar Mayer bologna, which he was eating with his fingers. Babies were drinking from individualized plastic formula containers.

"The food is not very good here," a man named Trong, who identified himself as a Saigon stringer for Reuters, told me outside the mess hall. "But we have no complaint. They have to feed 25,000 people in such a short time. You have done your best to help us."

The gratitude began to be suffocating. Far from the hostility that officials feared the refugees would find from surrounding locals, expressions of cloying charity clogged the camp. When an American general, a veteran of the war, sponsored two young refugee girls back to his home in Oklahoma City, the publicity was so compelling that caravans of cars and campers formed and descended on Fort Chaffee.

"The emotional outburst was so strong," John King said with distaste, "that they started pouring in for 'shopping' expeditions: they'd shop around for the refugees of their choice, to sponsor." King wasn't sure what the potential sponsors wanted of the Vietnamese—just grateful wards, or perhaps domestic servants. But in any case he put an end to the shopping caravans.

"There's still a big, favorable reaction here for the 'victims of communism,'" King reported. Americans love victims—more, even, than fighters, except when fighters lose. There's nothing that quickens the liberal spirit like the sight of a miserable wretch in an inescapable plight: a sharecropper in Mississippi, a child in a rat-infested ghetto attic, a naked Vietnamese orphan aflame with napalm. Should the victims take up arms against their victimizers, however, all sympathy is lost. It makes no difference how the victimization took place. Those who supported America's war in Vietnam are the most charitable to the refugees they, in effect, helped create. But they see no connection between their own politics and its consequences. Sidney Schanberg, the grotesquely overpraised *New York Times* reporter in Cambodia, once epitomized the blindness of the American eye on the world: "The only enemy here [in Cambodia]," he wrote, "is war."

Drenched in such mawkish self-righteousness, the townspeople surrounding Fort Chaffee are getting their kicks on the biggest thing to hit these parts since the interment of Judge Roy Bean in Fort Smith. The town, by the way, was the last outpost of the United States for many decades; just across the Arkansas River was Indian territory. Crimes committed in that savage land were punishable in Fort Smith; suspects were trundled into town for daily hangings. Nowadays, Fort Smithers are slightly more sophisticated, but not much. The local reporters and television anchorpeople who gather at "1100 hours" for the daily military and civil briefing at the Fort Chaffee information office are most concerned about such dangers as the possibility of epidemics of exotic Oriental diseases.

"Is there leprosy in Vietnam?" one of the local press crew asked Col. Joe Rogers, the army information chief. Affirmative, he answered, fearing the next question. "How many cases of leprosy are in the camp?" the newswoman wanted to know. "None, as far as I know," Rogers answered sincerely. The woman went on to other diseases.

"I hear there are tropical diseases which *they* can't get, but we are susceptible to," she pressed. Colonel Rogers said that might be true, but he had checked with the hospital and there were no cases of such complaints. "They affect the skin," the woman continued, not hearing Rogers's denial.

Another reporter had heard rumors that there was a huge VD epidemic raging through the post. John King said he hadn't heard of that, but it wouldn't surprise him if the American GIs were infesting the local populace. "Naturally, the off-duty GIs are 'interested' in the refugee population," he said delicately. "Fraternization is a problem. But the Vietnamese are healthier than the GIs. The low VD rate in Vietnam would put to shame some of our major cities in this country." Someone from Arkansas in the briefing room volunteered the information that one of the nearby counties is said to have the highest VD rate in the country. King said he wouldn't be surprised about that, either. "You said it, I didn't," he grinned.

In one way or another, the whole ghastly panorama of the American "presence" in Vietnam has been reproduced in Arkansas: the VD rate, the daily PsyOps propaganda newspaper in Vietnamese, the 1100 hours briefing, the PX mentality, the processing and the packaging. The only entertainment the refugees get are cowboy and Frankenstein films, without subtitles. Hung, the high school student, was not pleased with the selection. "I don't like to see cowboy movies," he said angrily. "They show only guns that kill. I don't want any blood scenery."

But the Vietnamese are on their way to becoming Middle Americans, whether they want to or not. The officials must believe that the Americanization of the war's consequences, like the Vietnamization of the war itself, constitutes a kind of justice. Americans despise the culture the refugees left behind, so there is nothing to regret. Who in the world wouldn't welcome a free hop on a C-123 to the USA? The Vietnamese are considered luckier than the billions of other potential immigrants who cannot get in. America is suspending the immigration rules now; no gratitude could be excessive.

How it will end for these refugees is impossible to predict. After a long visit with them, I had only the smallest comprehension of their expectations, a slight glimmer of their fears. Only a few could have been guilty of war crimes so heinous as to deserve the fate of exile, and yet they seemed thankful for their new condition. But the sense of relief and escape may not last.

"As far as they're concerned, their old life is through," King said. "They're going to have a whole new life, and their kids are going to grow up and be Americans and have cars."

"But what are they going to do," he asked at the end, "when they find out that it's not one big PX out there?"

May 28, 1975, THE REAL PAPER

✦

The Adamant Memory of Vietnam

Most Americans know Vietnam as pictures on television, headlines in the papers, propaganda from politicians. What was real were the young soldiers dying in vain, the veterans, the deserters, the POWs, the mass demonstrations every spring and fall. The film *Hearts and Minds* uses those images and accepts that reality. The war is what it was and not another thing. Here are the mind-searing pictures: the Saigon police chief blowing the brains out of a young rebel suspect; the NLF cadre occupying the American embassy during the Tet offensive; naked children fleeing the bombs on a battlefront road. And the politicians and warriors: the coldly cruel and professorial Walt Whitman Rostow; the aristocratic and repentant Clark Clifford; the ambiguously apologetic Robert Kennedy; Gen. William ("life is cheap in the Orient") Westmoreland; Gen. George ("I've got a bloody good bunch of killers") Patton III. The soldiers and veterans and deserters and POWs: Randy Floyd, who sees his life as a soldier of empire as a tragic mistake; and Lieut. George Coker, who will never cease to be proud of his mission representing America in Vietnam, which, if it were not for the Vietnamese, would be a "very pretty country."

Running like insistent snatches of songs through *Hearts and Minds* are the fragments of conversations director Peter Davis and photographer Richard Pearce had with the veterans, POWs and a deserter. What they think about their war, their country and their lives becomes a central theme of the Vietnam-era consciousness that the film must explore. A haunting hollowness rings from them all.

WILLIAM MARSHALL: You know, you let us all go off to war and said, "Yea team," you know. "Fight in Vietnam," and all this kind of shit. Now 1968 comes along and "Boo team, come on home," and all this shit. "And don't say nothin' about it 'cause we don't want to hear about it 'cause it's upsetting around dinner time," you know. Well, goddamn, it upset me for a whole goddamn year. It upset a lot of people to the point where they're fuckin' dead, you know, and all this shit. Now, you don't want to hear about it. I'll tell you about it every day and make you sit and puke on your dinner, you dig, because you got me over there and now you done brought me back. And you want to forget it so somebody else can go do it somewhere else. Hell no. And you going to hear it all every day, as long as you live, because, hey, it's going to be with me as long as *I* live. When I get up in the morning, when John gets up in the morning, a lot of dudes that sit around here get up, man, their gut hurts because they got shot there. I got to put on an arm and a leg 'cause they ain't there no more, you dig. Now you do something about that. Make that all disappear, you dig. You know, make it all go away with the 6 o'clock news, turn it off or switch it to another channel and all that shit. The hell with that, you dig. It's here and it's for real, and it's going to happen again unless these folks get up off their ass and realize it has happened, you know.

ROBERT MULLER: And I got a colonel that's flying upstairs and he's getting down on me and he's saying, "Take the hill, take the hill." So I popped up behind the lead tank and started to go up the hill and everything was cool until we started taking fire, and that's when I got it. I said, "Oh my God, I'm hit." I couldn't believe it, you know. I can't believe it, I am really hit, and my first, first thought was Kay, my girl, you know. It's gonna sound stupid, but my thought was, "She'll kill me." But then I realized that I didn't have to worry because I was dying. It's all over and for what? My last conscious thought was, "I can't believe it. I'm dying. On this shitty piece of ground I'm dying. And I can't fucking believe it."

What hurts the most—and this is a purely personal thing; right, wrong or indifferent, that's how I feel—when I was in the marine corps I remember I was down in Washington, and they had the marine corps drill team there, and I was standing at attention, in my uniform, and they were playing the "Marine Corps Hymn" and then they played "The Star Spangled Banner" and I actually started to cry. I cried because I was so proud to be an American, you know. And I was so proud to be a marine, and in uniform standing there at attention. That . . . that represented so much to me in the way of life and . . . that's gone, you know, and that hurts, that hurts.

RANDY FLOYD: It can be described much like a singer doing an aria, you know, he's totally into what he's doing, you know, totally feeling it. He knows the aria, and he's experiencing the aria, and he knows his limits, and he knows what he's doing, and whether he's doing it well. Flying an aircraft can be a great deal like that.

I can tell when the aircraft feels just right. I can tell when it's about to stall. I can tell when I can't pull another fraction of a pound. I could pull the "commit" switch on my stick and the computer took over. A computer figured out the ballistic, the air speed, the slant range, and dropped the bombs. So it was very much of a . . . a technical expertise thing. I was a good pilot, you know. I had a lot of pride in my ability to fly. And the excitement, the sense of excitement, especially if you're getting shot at, is just incredible.

During the missions, after the missions, the result of what I was doing, the result of this, this game, this exercise of technical expertise, never really dawned on me. That reality of the screams, or the people being blown away, or their homeland being destroyed just was not a part of what I thought about. . . . We as Americans have never experienced that. We've never experienced any kind of devastation. . . . When I was there I never saw a child that got burnt by napalm. I didn't drop napalm, but I dropped other things just as bad. But I look at my children now and . . . I don't know what would happen if . . . what I would think about, if someone napalmed them.

April 1975, RAMPARTS

✦

Boston's Bitter Bicentennial

In Boston, where they say it all began, it all ended with cannons booming and bells pealing. No embattled farmers popped musket balls to the tune of "Yankee Doodle"; the apocalypse now featured Arthur Fiedler conducting massed orchestras, an arsenal of howitzers and the complete urban campanile in *The 1812 Overture*. The choice of music honoring Czarist Russia's triumph over imperial France was left unexplained: Boston always mixes its metaphors. And in this case, pomp rather than patriotism was the order of Independence Day.

With the Bicentennial orgies come to climax at last, Boston has struck its historical set. The media networks are losing interest in the re-enactment of dubious battles 200 years old to the day, and the swarms of tourists—having successfully dodged the rash of terrorist bombings—will float away in due course. But the metaphors march along, and the mixture is turning to the sour side.

More than the tourist posters proclaim, Boston *is* America—only worse. New York may be more desolate, Los Angeles more anomic, Houston hotter and Seattle rainier. But Boston is the most infuriating place of all, because it is the most deceptive. Beneath the Victorian charm and the Brahmin culture is a society strangling on its old pride, struggling against the civilization it invented and fighting the freedoms it won. What began here so grandly seems to be ending vaingloriously all too soon.

A metaphor far more menacing than the Boston Pops' Fourth of July birthday concert could be found not very far from the Charles River epicenter of the celebration. In a room at City Hospital, one victim of Boston history lies in a chronic vegetative state, plugged into the machines that are our best approximation so far of the bionic experience. Robert Poleet, a 34-year-old auto mechanic, was brutally beaten April 20 in what the newspapers called an "incident with racial overtones"—a bit like saying the Tea Party was an incident with revolutionary overtones, or the Crucifixion an incident with religious overtones. Poleet happened to be a white attacked by blacks, in the wake of another incident (same overtones) in which black lawyer Ted Landsmark was attacked in City Hall Plaza at high noon by a gang of young white toughs. There are certainly political differences in the two assaults: the dominant pattern of violence is by whites against blacks. But they appear side by side as positive and negative prints in the same grim exhibition—a show at least as characteristic of Bicentennial Boston as the fancy dress charades.

Landsmark, who heads an affirmative action committee seeking contracts for minority firms, was on his way to a meeting with Mayor Kevin White when he ran into a splinter group from an anti-integration demonstration. The mayor watched the scene below from his office window. Landsmark was bloodied but not critically hurt. Poleet's appointment with Boston's rich ethnic heritage came in the dark of night in a slum section of town. He was torn from his car by a couple of kids, less determinedly political than the marching whites but more lethal. Half of his brain was destroyed; the other half is now barely functioning, and degenerating. "He can't sustain spontaneous respiration," an attending nurse told me in polite hospitalese. "Once he was off the respirator for four hours, but he's on all the time now. We do hourly monitoring of his vital signs, his urine output, all his body functions. We have to suction his lungs, and he almost died of massive infections." An experimental antibiotic, the product of Boston's pre-eminent medical establishment, cured the bacteriosis and restored his vegetative state to stable.

Poleet's wife and a former wife have asked that he be allowed to "die with dignity," but while the remaining bits of his brain show some blips on the EEG, doctors refuse to pull the plug. The right to a life of suffering, after all, is an honored principle at Boston City Hospital. It was there that Dr. Kenneth Edelin, a black obstetrician, was arrested for the "homicide" of a fetus in a perfectly legal abortion operation. Edelin was targeted as the subject of an elaborate political *auto-da-fé* by a group of anti-abortion crusaders and an inquisitive DA up for re-election. A jury not exactly of the black physician's peers agreed that it was a crime as well as a sin to abort a "viable" embryo and found him guilty.

Poleet, Landsmark and Edelin are tied in many ways by the same threads of race hatred, religious fervor, political cowardice and moral blindness that make Boston today a unique and poignant emblem of the American malaise. Some people in Massachusetts still boast of local liberalism and recall the one-and-only McGovern victory here in 1972. But Boston's political complexion is far less genteel today. The city swung decisively to George Wallace in this year's Democratic primary; there are no black elected city officials and no identified liberals on the at-large school committee or city council; and Louise Day Hicks, avenging angel of the segregationist white lower classes, is city council president and practically a moderate compared with the comrades on her side.

The symbolic issue in all of this is "bussing," but it is hardly as simple as that sounds. There is a complex of crises that makes victims of all Bostonians, whether they participate in the bussing fight or not. Like many cities, Boston is dying without much dignity. It is the heart of an economic region on the economic skids, without much hope of another boom. The city is losing population, and costs are soaring. The US Labor Department figures it takes $18,090 for a family of four to enjoy an "intermediate" standard of living here—the highest figure in the continental US. The weekly "market basket" price—$72 for a family of four—is also the highest in America, including sales taxes. The median income of $9,133 is among the lowest for big cities. Centuries of nepotism and favoritism have bloated the public employee rolls and produced endemic corruption. The physical "plant" is old and crumbling: the subway is the second-oldest in the country, the ancient lead-pipe water mains are poisoning parts of the city, and the schools have a Dickensian character that is quaint for the tourists but not terribly conducive to good education.

In the face of such conditions, and many more, the bussing controversy (another neutral nonsense word, like "incident") seems to have a life of its own. More than a decade ago, a committee of liberal educators responded to the black civil rights movement and discovered segregation right here in the birthplace of free public education. The state legislature promptly passed a Racial Imbalance Act to right these wrongs, and it became a model for progressive integration laws elsewhere in America. And like many progressive models, it was never really copied and never obeyed in Massachusetts.

Nine years later, federal district Judge W. Arthur Garrity found that a directed policy of segregation had created a dual system for blacks and whites, as distinct as any in the Old South. Garrity initiated a series of integration programs—Boston is up to Phase 2-B at this moment—that involved bussing about a third of the school population. No one really wanted bussing for itself, but blacks recognized that it was an unavoidable mechanism if the ghetto school system was to be broken. When the school committee continued to evade the intent of Garrity's plans, the judge seized one of the schools—South Boston High—and placed it in a federal receivership, as if it were a bankrupt business. Liberal politicians, such as Mayor White and Governor Dukakis, have caved in to various degrees on the controversy. White, who made a national reputation battling the venomous Mrs. Hicks, filed a federal suit on the side of the Hicks forces to overturn Garrity's bussing order. Last month the US Supreme Court turned down all the Boston challenges to Garrity, so the legal aspect of bussing seems to be closed for now.

The political aspect may be just beginning. Mrs. Hicks and those more militant even than she—in the anti-bussing organization ROAR ("Restore Our Alienated Rights")—vow a fight to the death, and invoke the spirits of the dead revolutionaries to bolster their claims to divine right. South Boston—a grime-poor Irish-American neighborhood that is still the center of the fight against black rights and black political power in the city—is a sea in which violent fish can safely swim. James Kelly, the leading spokesman in that neighborhood, rushed in after Ted Landsmark's beating and vowed "legal and moral support" for his white attackers. When Mayor White, Governor Dukakis and the center political establishment called a "march against violence" after the Poleet incident and a courthouse bombing raid, Mrs. Hicks refused to participate, saying "the only march that will mean anything will be on Judge Garrity's courtroom." Last week, Mayor White gave a chatty little television speech in which he called for more jobs, more federal funds and the removal of Garrity's control over South Boston High School.

In no way is Boston more emblematic of America than in its inability to confront racism. It's been said that racism is one "problem" that America cannot outgrow, and hence cannot solve. It certainly appears to be intractable here. It is built right into the institutions of Boston's mythic liberal tradition as well as in those of its reactionary heritage. The liberal suburbs wash their hands of the issue, preferring to curtail voluntary integration plans, and of the city. A recent report of yet another "violence committee," set up by Mayor White after the events of "hot April," recommended the usual complement of economic half-measures and goodwill. No one mentioned that the institutions represented on the committee use their mighty economic power to solidify the system of segregation, to keep control in the hands of the elite "Vault" (a committee of self-appointed notables) and to track the populace into economic patterns that meet corporate needs rather than advance the dynamic of change.

So Boston's dilemma is America's, and while it is obviously exaggerated here, it is not our exclusive privilege. President Ford, Candidate Carter and politicians of the center stripe have generally endorsed the intent, if not the slogans, of South Boston's campaign for ethnic purity. To do otherwise would mean wholesale shifts in the nexus of political and economic decision-making, and no public figure bent on election or eager for support can advocate that.

"Please come to Boston in the springtime," the folkies crooned, and in fact the country did send its visitors to wander along the Freedom Trail. They stopped at Paul Revere's house (undamaged by a bomb, probably planted by anti-black terrorists, that exploded in a shop nearby), the Old North Church, the patriots' graves. Fortunately, they managed to avoid the dozen bombs exploded in Boston and environs in the last several weeks, perhaps the work of ex-con radicals as well as the anti-bussing extremists. But they must have missed South Boston High, the Roxbury ghetto, Robert Poleet's hospital room. A pity: for those present addresses have more meaning for Bicentennial America than most of the monuments to the ghosts of the past.

July 23, 1976, NEW TIMES

Chapter IX

✦

CULTURE CLASH

Kitsch for the Rich

The Quincy Market was born again last summer in one great epiphany of urban renewal. The accompanying chorus of hallelujahs praised the downtown Boston project in all its facets: architectural gem, historical treasure, planning perfection, business boon. Critics as well as customers were ecstatic: "I walk these [waterfront] streets now with particular pleasure," wrote *The New York Times*'s Ada Louise Huxtable, whose seal of approval redevelopers covet above all others; "there is no impossible dream."

Six months later, the renaissance is still in full flower down by the waterfront, but its character appears more commercial than cosmic. The Quincy Market restoration is a success by many measures, but its deeper function in the life of the city is still in doubt. Its designer (Ben Thompson), developer (the Rouse Company), producer (the Boston Redevelopment Authority, or BRA) and promoter (Mayor Kevin White) maintain that it is the key to the revitalization of Boston. Seen another way, it is also the key to the appropriation of a sizable chunk of urban territory by one class of people out of the hands of another.

The Quincy Market does not stand alone. The stately 150-year-old Greek Revival arcade is, first of all, the centerpiece of the three-building Faneuil Hall Marketplace, which will be completed in uniform style by the end of the decade. It lies next to the larger Waterfront Urban Renewal District and, beyond, the near-North End, which is now undergoing extensive rehabilitation. It continues to coexist uneasily with the scruffy old Haymarket produce stalls, and it peers over the elevated lanes of the Central Artery, hoping (if markets could hope) for a government decision to sink that roadway into the sand.

All told, the Quincy Market is crucial to a development process that creates no "new town" of mixed uses and dynamic neighborhoods but a new ghetto. It will remake an area of warehouses, wharves, working-class markets and ethnic enclaves into a high-life playground, a theme park of nostalgia and a theater of consumption. Unless glaciation, revolt or economic collapse aborts that process soon, the entire district from Government Center to Copp's Hill will be one vast stack of exposed brick, a forest of butcher block, a jungle of asparagus ferns.

It is a bitter battle for territorial rights, and victories for the defenders are few. The warehousemen have gone to Chelsea, the wharf rats are fleeing inland, Haymarket has to compete with Malben's-in-the-Market, and the old North Enders are being pushed to the fringes of their quarter as the new gentry moves in. The only barrier to a complete push to the sea is the Central Artery, and some politicians and social planners are trying to eliminate that obstacle as well. "The Expressway is the only thing protecting the North End," Cambridge planning consultant Justin Gray said recently. "It's a moat around the neighborhood. When that sinks, the whole package is complete, and you can wrap it up for the chic and the middle class."

Quincy Market's piece in that action looms large not only because of its history and its hype but also for its real success in its class. On the drawing board as well as in its drawing power it is the best of a breed of urban restoration projects now found in almost every American city. San Francisco has its Ghirardelli Square and The Cannery, Seattle has its Pioneer Center, Denver its Larrimer Center; there is Underground Atlanta, Gas Light Square St. Louis, Old Town Chicago, Newmarket Philadelphia, The Garage in Cambridge. In a relentless search for roots or relief from boredom, suburbanites, tourists and high-rise dwellers swarm into decrepit car barns, old pasta factories, abandoned firehouses and gutted tenements—all from a past the newcomers never knew or only dimly understand.

Almost everywhere, the new uses of the old slums entail no organic relationship to that past. The Ghirardelli candy factory is now a shopping center, the Old Spaghetti Factory is a nightspot, the Firehouse is a gay club, the Garage is a Harvard Square shopping center. But Quincy Market was always a market, and still is—more or less. Designed by Alexander Parris, it was built by the city of Boston under Mayor Josiah Quincy in 1826 to replace derelict buildings in a blighted area around the old City Dock: America's first urban renewal project.

The elegant domed Doric agora was Boston's central market for more than a century, but its two flanking buildings (North and South Markets) were redecorated with Victorian facades and broken down into warehouses so thoroughly that their granitic skeletons were undetectable. At length, even the Quincy Market seemed to have outlived its usefulness, and an impatient BRA contemplated its demolition to make way for more architectural modernisms of the New Boston. But the tide of taste was turning. Preservationists protested that the market complex was one of the most precious heirlooms in the city's cellar. Architect Ben Thompson, whose own focus had moved from Marimekko fabrics (he founded Design Research and designed the building that houses it) to the preservation of colonial Harvard, drew up a restoration plan for the markets and presented it to the city.

Thompson's proposal and pressure from a prestigeful lobby of local antiquarians succeeded in reversing the BRA blitz, but not only because roots suddenly came into fashion. The economics of redevelopment was changing. New construction had become prohibitively expensive, while restoration was affordable by middle-income buyers. Moreover, the politics of "community action" in the late 1960s contained troublesome barriers to the destroy-and-rebuild strategy of redevelopment. Neighborhood activists organized enough power to stop or delay new building so that developers were wary of taking on projects and architects found their best opportunities in restoration.

"Preservation" became the favorite rationale for the middle-class takeover of urban territory—in Boston's South End, Washington's Capitol Hill, Manhattan's Soho, San Francisco's Mission. Such projects could be economically feasible, however, only when the poorer residents and marginal businesses of the area were removed and wealthier residents installed. Only then could developers profit from their projects, and cities "increase the tax base" by inflating the value of the territory.

"You could call the process 'reverse blight,'" MIT urbanologist Lisa Peattie said, only half jokingly. British planners call it "gentrification"—the imposition of a higher-class population in a lower-class area. With the new population, of course, come its paraphernalia of play and business: boutiques and crêperies, clean well-lighted places to shop and schmooze, pubs and parking garages. It is all expensive and chic, excluding those who have neither the necessary money nor the appropriate tastes.

Quincy Market didn't just *happen* the way it did: the textures, the costs, the culture and the quality were determined by the vectors of "gentrification." When all is done, the 6.5-acre Faneuil Hall Marketplace project will have cost public agencies and private companies upwards of $40 million. To cover a nut of that size, the markets have to be organized to encourage heavy consumption by a mass of customers.

In Boston, that means "tourists"—not necessarily from Sweden or Iowa or Springfield, but from the suburbs. Visitors from Roslindale or Brockton come to the Quincy Market as tourists, eat their popovers, buy their piece of pottery, quaff their ale and clear on out. Downtown office workers check out the market during the day and head home at dark to the safer outlying towns. It is not much of a neighborhood market—not even as much as a suburban mall is for its surrounding communities. The market is in its own world, different from that of the tourists it traps and different from that which surrounds it. And even when the North End is gentrified, only a small proportion of the customers for the business at the markets will be indigenous to the area.

The reliance of Boston's urban "revitalization" on a tourist economy represents a major conceptual flaw in the project. Tourist dollars are notoriously weak building blocks for economic development. Tourism waxes and wanes

296 ✦ THE THIRTY YEARS' WARS

in unpredictable rhythms: today's fashionable hang-out is tomorrow's last resort. Tourist services provide low-paying jobs to "marginal" workers. Too many of the 400 jobs at Quincy Market already are $2-an-hour, dead-end positions for a transient work force of young single men and women.

Low-paying employment is only one of many economic drawbacks. Although sales in the Quincy Market have been brisk, much of the money may not be "new"—in other words, these are dollars that would have been spent elsewhere in the city. Nor do the profits all enrich Boston. Although there were supposed to be no national chain department stores there, some of the most successful operations in Quincy Market are in fact "hidden" chain outlets, such as the Magic Pan and Proud Popover restaurants, which are owned by Quaker Oats and return their profits to (and buy much of their materials from) Milwaukee. All in all, not many of the dollars spent at the Market trickle down deeply into the parched Boston economy.

Nineteen seventy-five came and went, and the Bicentennial Year itself was almost over when the Quincy Market opened last August—150 years to the day after Josiah Quincy dedicated the original building. A hundred thousand visitors jammed the site, swamping the frozen yogurt and souvlaki stands, mauling the craftsmen's pushcarts, pushing and shoving among the mimes and the mayor, the balloon sellers and the businessmen.

Thompson's design was clearly a triumph. The shop signs were similarly styled but not standardized, the traffic patterns were fluid but not strict, the scale was personal as well as monumental. Even the glass garage doors that serve as "canopies" over aisles of pushcarts sandwiching the main colonnade were pronounced acceptable. (Rouse wanted those additional selling areas in order to double the rentable space; Thompson rationalized them as evocations of the tin sheds that once protected carriages and animals alongside the markets.) The designers and developers had paid meticulous attention to detail. The trash barrels were old hogsheads with the inscription "Please Use Me" stenciled on top. The janitors wore uniforms emblazoned with a print of Faneuil Hall's weathervane grasshopper. And over it all hung Alexander Parris's marvelous copper dome.

But on closer and longer inspection, not only the brick seemed to be exposed. Doubts began to show up too, and they concerned two related issues: social culture and social use.

"Ben Thompson is superb in his idiom," Justin Gray remarked not long ago, "but maybe that idiom isn't the only thing that ought to be down there." In fact, the preservation idiom is already a cliché as empty of imagination as skyscraper curtain-wall was in the sixties. "Ye olde" design is the new kitsch of advanced capitalism, self-conscious for all its charm and boring for all its originality. Even the best use of the cliché cannot give it the life that mass culture has already drained from it.

Something happened to the rootedness of the old buildings when they were scrubbed and arranged and organized. Thompson did not purify them in the Williamsburg style, but he changed their relationship to the world around them, related them instead to a timeless, airless, placeless standard that exists outside any specific context. Blindfold a tourist and drop him in Canal Square in Washington or Ghirardelli Square in San Francisco or Quincy Market in Boston, and it would be impossible to say whose history he is re-enacting or remembering. Like airports, television series, suburban malls, garden apartments, cinema complexes and Hilton hotels, restoration redevelopments are interchangeable in design as well as content—and for similar reasons. Common denominators must be found, cues must be provided, signs must be posted to tease out expenditure. The tourist areas take on a Disney quality that even good architecture cannot reclaim for reality. And Disney begets Disneys: it is altogether logical that the Proud Popover and the Magic Pan locate in the market, spreading ersatz haute cuisine on portion-controlled platters from the same kitchen.

Intentionally or not, the BenThompsonization of Boston provides the cultural artillery to establish and protect a class beachhead on the Waterfront. In the territorial wars now raging, there can be no lasting truces between the hostile parties. A French political scientist, François D'Arcy, said at a recent international symposium on urban conservation that "the economic rules of the occupation of space no longer allow the coexistence of different income groups on the same space." Those who have to make a profit from the use of land cannot do so unless there is a linked housing and shopping economy that automatically excludes the poor or the rich.

Design marches in the service of one or another of the warring parties— either the conscious use of design symbols or the avoidance of them. The surest way to take over a neighborhood bar for the silk-shirted singles set is to clear out the bubbling beer displays and expose the brick. At the Quincy Market, the genius of Cambridge's most notable architect was to remember a distant past and enact a familiar present—the superimposition of the safe suburbs on the risky city. The result is the creation of an environment that automatically produces a class clientele.

It *could* have been different—but only if the community around such a development project were different. "There could have been a 'new town' in the existing city center," urban economist Jerome Rothenberg says. With financial subsidies and a will to redistribute power and privilege from well-off to hard-put parts of the population, a mixed mini-society with housing, jobs, educational and cultural facilities, and shopping services could have been built. It did not turn out that way, Rothenberg says, because there is "enough political muscle and money only for the benefit of the middle and upper class." This is no time to think of the others. "I should not like to fault an imaginative program like this just because it does not help the poor."

In fact, there are no scale models for new mixed communities in city "cores" in America. Only in countries or regions where integrated economic and social planning is possible can the iron logic of profit be contradicted in the construction of communities. In Bologna, Italy, for example, the communist government is rehabilitating the ancient buildings of the central city according to their historic use. Research into the social history of the neighborhoods is as extensive as study of the original architectural designs. Workers' quarters will stay in the hands of their comrades; subsidies are given to families so that they may remain in their houses after rehabilitation. By contrast, the Rome municipal government, until very recently, had no interest in social planning. The "market" was allowed to determine the character of the neighborhoods, and in quarter after quarter, poorer residents have been forced out as their space is "rehabilitated" into fashionable antique shops and expensive apartments. Back in Bologna, craftspeople may still live upstairs from their modest ateliers. The result is a kind of "revitalization" that has nothing to do with the cosmetic affectations of the Faneuil Hall Marketplace and the Waterfront.

Some commentators argue that whatever its shortcomings, the Quincy Market and its surrounding projects at least occupy an "underutilized" and undertaxed area of the city at relatively small cost to the public treasuries. But a city of classy playgrounds and retail amusement parks, of tourist-shoppers and rootless workers, eventually will decay of its own irrelevance, despite the early economic benefits. The long-term failure of Quincy Market will result from trying to substitute superficial vitality for real social dynamism. By destroying true life, Quincy Market will likely contribute to the demise of Boston, rather than to its resurrection.

February 19, 1977, THE REAL PAPER

✦

Culture Clash: America's New Right

The talk of Bensenville, Illinois, is all about women's liberation, homosexual rights and abortion. Like thousands of communities around the country, this placid, featureless town in the far western reaches of suburban Chicago has suddenly been ignited by the burning social issues of the decade. The *Bensenville Chronicle* is heavy with hortatory letters and earnest editorials. The auditorium at Blackhawk Junior High School rings with righteous rhetoric. Groups of militant women have left their noodle rings and needlepoint and meet into the night to draft pamphlets, plan demonstrations and raise their consciousness. As this short summer wanes, the grass-roots movements in Bensenville show all the familiar road signs of popular political struggle that Americans have been reading about since the sixties: that is, every sign but one. In Bensenville, the arrows all point right.

Dorothy Waldvogel, a 46-year-old mother, Mormon and militant in the Bensenville backlash, sells sweet corn by the streetside on the outskirts of town. In the lush, late harvest season, her farm wagon is laden with the ripe vegetables she and her husband grow on fifty-three acres of leased land. Behind the stand, her 1968 Buick LeSabre is filled with propaganda produce no less ripe than the corn: copies of "The Phyllis Schlafly Report" ("International Women's Year: A Front for Radicals and Lesbians"), a wallet-size comic book denouncing the Equal Rights Amendment ("Do you want the SEXES fully integrated like the RACES?") and Xeroxes of a letter of commendation from North Carolina's Senator Jesse Helms, a Washington anchor for the anti-ERA, anti-homosexual and anti-abortion axis.

"You sort of hear things that you don't really feel good about," Waldvogel said, recalling the first phases of her radicalization in right-wing politics last winter. "There was abortion, and then the homosexual movement was getting *so big*. And then Illinois was the key state for the ERA. You know something is wrong, but you need someone to tell you how to get involved.

"So some of the girls down at the church made up a list of state legislators—I don't know how they got the names, but they did. I sat down and wrote sixty-five letters, all about the importance of the family and how male and female are different. I mean, how can a law make males and females the same? To me, the ERA is an attack on our system of life—call it tradition—the way that God intended it to be."

Waldvogel's convenient theology may be widely disputed; the unisex hell prophesied by ERA opponents could exist nowhere on this earth. But she can find convincing confirmation of her belief system in the mundane success of her comrades' campaigns to make God's Word into common law. Beyond Bensenville blow winds of change that have dramatically shifted direction since the late storms of liberal and left protest subsided.

The ERA was defeated in Illinois and every other state (save Indiana) where it's been at issue in the past two years; chances for its ratification by at least four more states in time for the 1979 deadline now seem bleak. Ordinances guaranteeing homosexuals protection against discrimination lost decisively in the South Florida referendum as well as in city councils and state capitals across the nation; previously progressive Austin, Texas, for example, voted down a gay rights bill that the local Civil Liberties Union director said "would have passed with all flags flying" two years ago. Congress, the Supreme Court and several state legislatures have grievously wounded the new body of laws giving women the right to choose abortion, and the Catholic hierarchy is steamrolling the drive for an anti-abortion amendment to the US Constitution.

Behind the New Right vanguard on the "pro-family," anti-liberation front are troops fighting scores of battles that may seem separate but appeal to the same backlash sensibilities. Sooner or later, pro-family activists find themselves *pro*: death penalty, Laetrile, nuclear power, local police, Panama Canal, saccharin, FBI, CIA, defense budget, public prayer and real estate growth. More likely than not, they are *anti*: bussing, welfare, public employee unions, affirmative action, amnesty, marijuana, communes, gun control, pornography, the 55 mph speed limit, day-care centers, religious ecumenism, sex education, car pools and the Environmental Protection Agency. Of course there are exceptions everywhere; Boston's leading conservative theorist, David Brudnoy, is as passionately for gay rights as he is against abortion rights. Former John Birch Society director John Rousselot, now a California congressman, says privately that he is for freedom of choice with marijuana as well as Laetrile. But the overwhelming political significance lies in the new conjunction of all those issues, not in the exceptions.

Liberals, radicals, reformists and progressives who have done battle these many years on the opposite side of those questions would like to believe that the ideology and the logistics of the new right-wing movements are devised and controlled by a few conspirators at the top: Phyllis Schlafly, Jesse Helms, a Catholic cardinal here or a John Birch birdwatcher there—a handful of Reaganites, racists and young Republicans. But the left's devil theory is no more plausible than the right's. There is a great social upheaval at the heart of America that now finds expression in the new constellation of traditionalist, individualist and fundamentalist movements. It feeds the established politicians and practitioners of the right, and it is well fed by them. But to disregard its authentic roots in home-town America is to misread the new national mood, and to become its more vulnerable victim.

Nobody's perfect, but Dorothy Waldvogel is as nearly perfect a product of the new social backlash as may be found in its Midwest heartland. "I'd rather be home cooking and caring for my family, doing embroidery, than what I'm doing," she told me earnestly. "But a force greater than myself is magnetically drawing me to pursue it. I guess I feel a responsibility to inform other women what's going on. We've just got to protect the family."

"The family!" she repeated excitedly. "Where else can you go at Christmas but back to your family?"

If a lonely holiday Whopper in a deserted Burger King is the pervasive fear-fantasy of the American seventies, turkey and the trimmings en famille is surely an alternative of choice. There may be other credible options, but none is immediately apparent in Bensenville. For Dorothy Waldvogel, as for many other women of her social location, "the family" is the best available rock in a storm-tossed sea of contradictions.

Out there on Thorndale Road where she sells her produce and peddles her pamphlets, the contradictions tumble down at every turn. The pastoral peace is shattered by the artillery thunder of jets streaking across the cornfields from O'Hare Airport, just a few miles to the east. Suburbia is approaching almost as fast: a "Locate Your Business Here" sign has gone up a few hundred yards from the Waldvogel farm stand, and a fast-food franchise occupies a nearby intersection. Soon enough, there will be no land left for planting.

Bensenville's biggest billboard advertises the Unisex Hair Styling shop, and despite Waldvogel's nostalgia for strict sex roles, she shows up each morning at the old stand in men's shoes, white socks, blue jeans, a plain shirt—and hair as long and loose as Peter Frampton's. Only a thin veneer of pale lipstick prevents her full participation in the integrated sex model.

"I understand what women go through," Waldvogel confided. "I've been divorced. I know about unequal credit laws. I couldn't get the water company to put the bill in my name. I needed that law against sex discrimination. But I don't know what these women libbers are trying to do with this country except get us stirred up. I think to myself, What are they doing to me out there? *What are they doing?*" Her voice rose in passion and evident fear, just as a customer pulled up to the stand for two dozen ears.

Married and a mother before she was 17, Waldvogel held her first family nucleus together for a quarter of a century. She and her husband built a successful janitorial service in an Indiana town, then sold it to a partner whose business behavior was a bit too sharp for their liking. They had moved to Arizona and begun a similar business when she decided her husband was no better than their previous partner. "We just didn't hold to the same values," she said flatly.

One day during the worst years of her domestic turmoil, Mormon missionaries came to the door on a proselytizing tour, and in a flash Dorothy Waldvogel saw the light. "I had been hooked on cigarettes and I hated myself for it, but when I started going to church I was able to stop smoking," she confessed. "That's what churches are supposed to do—to teach us to understand ourselves and to do what's good for us."

What was good for her was to leave her husband, pack up the kids and return to her roots in the Midwest—where she promptly met a Mormon widower; she was remarried in a year. Life was complete with the new family, the farm stand, embroidery and church socials—until the ERA vote came up in Illinois. In the supporting warmth of Mormon conservatism, Waldvogel began her activist career by lobbying legislators against ratification. Then she "and a bunch of the girls" made a bigger plunge into politics. One night last June they piled into a car and headed for their state's preparatory meeting for the International Women's Year National Conference, scheduled for November in Houston.

The fifty-state IWY meetings have provided the battlegrounds this year in the eruptive war of women against women. The purpose is to set agendas and choose delegates for Houston, but the real prize of battle is the definition of feminism: whether Americans will accept the new terms of liberation, or restore an earlier concept of womanhood based on separation and inequality. Sizable stores of political power reside in each camp. Despite furious fights, feminists of the left—led by the National Organization for Women in a coalition of liberationist groups—have been able to withstand the fire from anti-ERA, anti-lesbian, anti-abortion forces of the right. There have been some disasters for the NOW side: Mormons in Utah, fundamentalists in Mississippi and Catholics in several Midwestern states have routed the left with religious fervor. But at the June meeting in Normal, Illinois, 500 women bearing backlash banners were beaten by the NOW liberationists after bitter political confrontations.

Whatever else that event was, it became a major milestone in the political odyssey of Dorothy Waldvogel.

"I have never been the same since," she said with a shake of her long hair. She and "the girls" walked out in protest against the left's "manipulation" of the meeting and caucussed later with the assistance of organizers from Phyllis Schlafly's ferocious Eagle Forum, the nationwide anti-ERA commissariat, based in a suburb of St. Louis. What they all decided was to make a permanent counterrevolution against women's liberation in Illinois.

Waldvogel hurried back to Bensenville and began writing letters and pamphleteering. She broke into print on the opinion page of the *Bensenville Chronicle*, decrying the resolutions of the Normal IWY meeting, which advocated "rights for homosexuals, gays and lesbians to marry and adopt children," and arguing: "We need to unite if we are to stop the destruction of our families and the decline of moral values being thrust upon us."

So enthusiastic was the response to that letter that Waldvogel was propelled to the leadership of the backlash movement in Bensenville. She easily got the use of a hall at Blackhawk Junior High for a rally of her partisans. By the merest coincidence, Phyllis Schlafly was passing through Bensenville that night on her way to the airport (by a circuitous but opportune route) and agreed to address the throng. Almost 300 people packed the room, donated $105 in small change (reimbursing Waldvogel for the cost of printing flyers) and convinced Waldvogel that her immediate future, at least, lay in political organizing.

"I've gone all around town," she reported proudly. "I went over to the Catholic church and talked to the priest. I told him that we as Christians have to unite against the evil that's taking over this country. It's evil to allow murder of little babies under our Constitution. It's evil to allow homosexuals to marry and be adoptive parents. It's evil to have federally funded day-care centers, although it's not evil to have babysitters of your own—as long as you don't encourage it in the whole country. It's evil to bus your children across the city when you live across the street from a perfectly good school."

She gave me a perfectly good ripe red tomato and a tiny cardboard amulet of Morton's salt. It was perfectly delicious. I jumped down from my perch on her wagon and prepared to leave Bensenville when she indicated she had one last thought to convey.

"You see," she said, "there are evil things and there are good things and we are put on this earth to choose. That's our whole purpose. My own belief is that Lucifer is trying to make it hard for people to have children, to have families. So I *have* to get involved. I can't just stay home and do nothing. After what I've learned, I can't think of anything anymore. I put down an afghan I was making for my daughter's graduation that day I went to the meeting at Normal, and I can't even finish it."

Far from Thorndale Road, the "magnetic force" compelling Dorothy Wald-vogel to action may be less mysterious than she imagines. The contradictions of her life and hard times and her own social predicament seem genuinely perplexing; but its political display in particular issues is arranged by cynical and often sinister figures in the institutions and offices of the organized right. For although Lucifer and the Lord may be contending for Waldvogel's soul, it is more immediately Phyllis Schlafly, Jesse Helms and other earthlings who are fighting for her body—for the phalanxes of their movements, their organizations and their election campaigns. The New Right of small-town women, urban Catholics and working-class whites starts only with unformed fears and perplexities. Someone else, with different interests, other agendas and wider connections, will translate them into a coherent political force.

"The New Right is led by the old fascists," argues NOW president Ellie Smeal. "It's the same old people who have been around since Joe McCarthy's time and the beginning of the John Birch Society. But now they're wrapping themselves in the cloth of 'the family,' instead of racism and super-patriotism. The old right of the fifties never died; it's just been reborn."

What is *new* about the New Right is its generation in the "pro-family" issues and its creation of a logical place for women leaders in those concerns. The "traditional" family is indeed being transformed; no right-wing fanatic has to convince Americans that the old styles of long, stable marriages, lots of loving children, extended family structures and firm sex-role stereotypes are out of fashion—if not yet out of existence.

But while the hidden economic and political pressures that distort the old forms are extremely complicated, symbolic enemies are easier to conjure out front. Dorothy Waldvogel in Bensenville and her New Left counterparts in Berkeley or the Bronx may have similar problems with their marriages, their work and their utility companies. They may feel attracted and repelled by strict sex roles, consumerist capitalism and government interventions in their everyday affairs. They may both yearn for a peaceable kingdom, a happy home and a turkey dinner. But one chooses the women's movement and the other the backlash.

The bussing battles in Boston, Louisville and Los Angeles have all been led by newly politicized women. Women were in the vanguard of the furious campaign in Wheeling, West Virginia, to rid school libraries of "progressive" and "permissive" textbooks. Women helped organize the successful recall election this summer in LaCrosse, Wisconsin, which removed five members of the local school district who had voted to fire a brutally authoritarian school principal (the principal is now back on the job). Ellen McCormack made startlingly strong showings in many states last year with her anti-abortion presidential candidacy. Governor Ella Grasso of Connecticut, elected as a conventional liberal, has made most of her political hay on backlash issues, such as her opposition to gay rights, marijuana-law liberalization and abortions for the poor. Anita Bryant and Phyllis Schlafly are perhaps the two most powerful "populist" political figures of the year: they have slowed, though not stopped, the forward march of the two great movements for human liberation of the seventies.

What is *old* about the New Right is its manipulation by the old men in the old institutions. Politicians such as Georgia Representative Larry McDonald, Illinois Representative Henry Hyde, Utah Senator Orrin Hatch and North Carolina Senator Jesse Helms have seized upon "pro-family" sentiment in the way they and their fellows once used "pro-American" patriotism to rally reaction and build a right-wing movement in America.

Suddenly this summer it is growling again. Informal meetings of right-wing organizers have begun in Washington to swap strategies and make plans for the coming campaigns. "The first meeting consisted of about a dozen people from conservative organizations who committed themselves to the opposition on a number of specific issues, like the Panama Canal treaties," a veteran Washington lobbyist reported. One key strategist was Paul Russo, once a Reagan campaign field worker, who now works as a liaison between the Republican National Committee and the far-right movements.

Russo represents his boss, Charles Black, campaign director of the GOP committee, who until recently headed up a militant new-right outfit called the National Conservative Political Action Committee (NCPAC). NCPAC's fundraiser is Richard Viguerie, the mercurial reader and adviser for extremist campaigns and causes—from George Wallace ($6 million) to Senator Strom Thurmond to former California education superintendent Max Rafferty, and indirectly to Anita Bryant and Phyllis Schlafly. Viguerie is also among the key strategists in the Washington area meetings.

Viguerie's publication, *Conservative Digest*, lays out the lines of the new political strategy in an interview with Mike Thompson, the publicist for Bryant's successful campaign to defeat the gay anti-discrimination ordinance in Dade County, Florida.

"We will bring together people who have never been politically involved before," Thompson enthused, "or people who have been involved but not on the same side. We will probably be a catalyst, and these people will go on to work together for other issues and candidates."

Thompson is a PR man and perennial rightist candidate (he has run for Congress and state offices) who struck gold—or at least orange—with the Bryant crusade. Now he has left the OJ Queen and is striking out on his own: on the trail of what he sees as the "new majority" of Democrats, blue-collar workers and Jewish voters who are liberal on other issues but conservative on "the family." Thompson chairs the Florida Conservative Union— the local arm of the American Conservative Union—and is preparing the advertising blitz to defeat the Panama accords.

The relationship between the militant mass movements and the manipulative elite organizations is extremely complex. Beside NCPAC and the Republican campaign committee, some of the groups and personalities involved are:

§ The American Legislative Exchange Council, a new network of conservative state legislators and national congressmen, which is drafting backlash bills for introduction at all levels of government.

§ The Heritage Foundation, a tax-exempt, right-wing think tank, funded last year by Joseph Coors of Colorado beer fame, which gives "intellectual content" to right-wing projects. One early idea was Coors's plan to create a "Fourth Network" for conservative television programming and production.

§ The Committee for the Survival of a Free Congress, headed by Paul Weyrich, formerly of the Heritage Foundation. Weyrich says, "My bag is organizing"—specifically, the defeat of liberal congressmen and their replacement by reactionaries. Viguerie has raised substantial funds for the committee in direct-mail campaigns.

§ The Conservative Caucus, thought to be the "key connection" of New Right grass-roots organizing efforts for candidates and causes. TCC is run by Howard Phillips, a former Young American for Freedom, who was Nixon's last director of the Office of Economic Opportunity. Phillips's job at OEO was to scuttle the anti-poverty program—as scuttle he did. His dream for the Caucus is to place hundreds—thousands, even—of activists in every congressional district in the country; something like a network of Committees for the Defense of the Counterrevolution.

§ Citizens for the Republic, the personal political vehicle for the future travels of Ronald Reagan, wherever they may lead. Reagan's recent presidential aspirations have been heavily subsidized by Coors.

Beneath the bland names of those general groupings, the issues of the New Right connect in byzantine ways. The campaign to legalize Laetrile, for example, is organized by an ad hoc Committee for Freedom of Choice in Cancer Therapy, Inc., a virtual subsidiary of the John Birch Society. The "legislative representative" of the group is Larry McDonald of Georgia, author of the anti-gay legislation. Similar overlaps can be found across the range of conservative issues and ideologues.

And like anti-war and civil rights workers of yore, the New Right takes its campaigns from the streets into the election booths, concentrating huge amounts of energy and time in targeted districts.

"There's no question that the right is getting increasingly successful on Capitol Hill," Vicki Otten of the Americans for Democratic Action said nervously. "The *anti* people are winning bigger and bigger majorities. In 1976 a partial anti-abortion bill was defeated two-to-one; this year the House accepted a *total* prohibition by almost the same margin the other way. In the Senate, it's been the Democratic liberals who have gone over to the right on this issue—Ted Kennedy, Humphrey, Leahy—all of a sudden they're scared.

In the House, the new freshmen of '76 were supposed to make up the most liberal Congress in history. But they've made it one of the most conservative. Their mail is running ten-to-one, a hundred-to-one against bussing, abortion, gay rights. It's phenomenal! They believe that 'lifestyle' issues will re-elect them or defeat them, and so they're voting with the *antis*."

The growing strength of the New Right showed itself in Congressman Larry McDonald's success in passing an amendment to a legal services bill that forbids government-funded legal aid in cases of discrimination against homosexuals. McDonald was practically laughed off the floor of Congress when he first proposed his amendment. Then he called for a vote on the record, and the frightened representatives passed it 230 to 133.

It is already a cliché of columnar journalism in Washington that the political vectors of the country all run right. But in their divinations of a "national mood" the columnists ignore the essential importance of right-wing organization and its purposes. Real power and commanding interests rest on the nexus of "moral" and "emotional" issues. Dorothy Waldvogel and the girls in Bensenville may not realize it, but their outrage in Illinois can be redeemed for cash benefits and political privileges in Washington. In the not-so-old days, politicians on the left understood that functional importance of grass-roots activism and used it for their own schemes, wise or foolish. White civil rights sympathies and middle-class anti-war sentiments were converted into progressive policies that began to redistribute power and wealth somewhat: from the well-off to the poor, from whites to blacks, from the countryside to the cities, from South to North, from old to young. Suburban liberals who joined one candlelight vigil were enrolled as troops in the war on poverty, as supporters of Chicano unions, as voters for liberal candidates, as participants in a "culture of the left." In time, everyone of that tendency felt part of a movement, many movements, or "the Movement."

Suburban conservatives and small-town moralists are now drafted as soldiers for the armies of the right and consumers of its culture. "The Movement" now is located 180 degrees from the 1967 position. What counts now, as then, are the deeper connections of power and politics beneath the pious rhetoric, the strong currents beneath the surface froth.

The reborn right began organizing at the bottom of the political pyramid, much as the New Left did in the sixties. In fact, the parallels between the two native movements, one progressive and one reactionary, are striking.

"We learned a lot from the left organizations," Bircher Representative John Rousselot told me one afternoon as we chatted over bean soup in the House dining room. "Sometimes it's been conscious, sometimes not. But a lot of conservatives have learned from groups like Common Cause, the unions and the ACLU."

"One thing we learned," he continued, pounding the table with his finger, "is that organizations like Right to Life have paid off in votes right here."

Rousselot knows how the grass-roots right has turned Congress around, how it has profoundly shaped the Carter Administration, and how it is succeeding in every state legislature in the country. The governors who still have the temerity to veto anti-abortion and pro-death penalty laws are often overridden. Gay rights hasn't a chance now in any major constituency in the country (with the possible exception of San Francisco's gay ghetto).

Former liberals are hiding their progressive pasts in the nearest available closets. For example, the latest anti-homosexual crusader is Adam Walinsky, a campaign adviser to New York mayoral candidate Mario Cuomo and a former legislative assistant and speechwriter for Bobby Kennedy. I can remember the day in early 1968—in my Washington apartment—when Walinsky made plans to leave congressional politics and join Tom Hayden's movement in the streets to end the war and bring socialism to America. At the last minute, Kennedy's decision to run for president kept Walinsky out of the Chicago "conspiracy." Now, not even ten years after, he has joined the anti-liberation lobby.

There is no single simple way to explain the success of the New Right, much less to predict its future trajectory. The victories of the right this year have been permitted, to some extent, by the failure of a liberal opposition— the consequence of the left's own cynicism, disillusionment and isolation.

The New Left and its descendants have been notoriously maladroit in reaching people whose background and behavior diverge from its young, white, cool, cosmopolitan styles and middle-class status. Serious and progressive urban feminist organizers are impatient with Middle American housewives who are not quickly captivated by the blinding truths of women's liberation. A depressing case in point concerned a clutch of pro-feminist Catholic women from a working-class district in Chicago who attended the Illinois International Women's Year planning session as partisans of the NOW liberationists. They were soon dismayed at the way their own "leaders" demanded strict adherence to the ideologically pure position on abortion. The Catholic women personally favored the right of women to choose abortion, but they knew they could not go back to their neighborhoods and organize other women on the basis of the purist platform that the middle-class, largely Protestant and Jewish feminists pushed through in Normal.

Nothing is gained by the left in dismissing their antagonists as "right-wing nuts," as one bitter Chicago feminist called them. There is too much nuttiness around these days and a fair portion of it can be found in the precincts of the New Right. It's hard to discern much logic in any of the stated arguments that Larry McDonald or Phyllis Schlafly make against the ERA. But the women who oppose the amendment are as diverse a lot as those in favor. There are the jeans-clad young mothers of the suburban New Right and the blue-haired Republican ladies of the old; there are those who believe every far-fetched fantasy of the Schlaflyites—that the ERA will foist coed toilets, battlefield breastfeeding and compulsory female ditch-digging on helpless American womanhood—and there are others who treat the anti-ERA campaign as a symbolic confrontation with modernist doctrine.

"I feel sorry for people who are trying to hold on to yesterday," NOW's Ellie Smeal said sorrowfully; but she has no good way to help them loose the grip. No one has yet devised a believable alternative to the old family forms and social values, the decay of which has thrown so many Americans into a reactionary snit. The left experiments with communes, collectives, open marriages, living together, same-sex couples and the like. The right clings to the old formulas for marriage, religion and sex roles—long after their content has been compromised and only the skeletal structures remain. Accidents of class, ethnicity and geographic context—as well as quirks of character—can determine which side a person will choose.

For, in the end, we are all squeezed in the same inexorable vise. Dorothy Waldvogel and her unknown feminist counterparts are natural allies, not enemies. As Congressman Rousselot told me, the pro-pot and pro-Laetrile issues are virtually identical—except that one has been captured by the left, the other by the right.

What is breaking up the family are the demands of the system—call it what you will—for women workers at low pay, for routinized work schedules, for education tracked to job slots, for high rates of consumption, for waste and for profit. Scraps of the proceeds of that system have for years been thrown to the most underprivileged members of society in hopes that they will not upset the social apple cart; the rest stays in the board rooms at the top. Inevitably, the Waldvogels of this world get the short change, and it is they who are crying in pain. It is a pity that they yet mistake their fellow sufferers for their true tormentors.

September 30, 1977, NEW TIMES

✦

The Dialectic of Disco

The moral is, take care of the sense, and the sounds will take care of themselves.

—the Duchess, to Alice

Disco is the word. It is more than music, beyond a beat, deeper than the dancers and their dance. Disco names the sensibility of a generation, as jazz and rock—and silence—announced the sum of styles, attitudes and intent of other ages. The mindless material of the new disco culture—its songs, steps, ballrooms, movies, drugs and drag—are denounced and adored with equal exaggeration. But the consciousness that lies beneath the trendy tastes is a serious subject and can hardly be ignored, for it points precisely where popular culture is headed at the end of the American seventies.

Disco is *phenomenal*—unpredicted and unpredictable, contradictory and controversial. It has spawned a new $4 billion music industry, new genres in film and theater, new radio stations, a new elite of promoters and producers, and a new attitude about the possibilities of party-going. It has also sparked major conflicts: "Death to Disco" is written on Soho walls, and "Disco Sucks!" rises from the throats of beleaguered partisans of rock, punk or jazz who find their cultural identity threatened by disco's enormous power.

Scenes from disco wars erupt across the landscape. Gangs of rockers and hustlers (the dancing kind) fight furiously in the streets outside disco clubs in provincial cities. When Mick Jagger or Rod Stewart "goes disco" (with "Miss You" and "Do You Think I'm Sexy?" respectively), their cultural conversion is debated in hip salons as well as in *The New York Times*. The rock critical establishment still treats disco music as an adolescent aberration at best; many cultural commentators look on the whole sensibility as a metaphor for the end of humanism and the decline of the West.

Not many months ago, during a frenzied dance party on a summer lawn in Vermont, I found myself struggling with an old friend in a tug of war over what record we would play next. I wanted to hear Linda Clifford's popular title cut "If My Friends Could See Me Now." The good-natured contest suddenly developed an edge of bitterness that I had never recognized before. The lawnful of post-sixties migrants to that idyllic rural setting seemed divided along lines of sight, taste and feeling. And across the lines, despite the deep communality of that group, there was obvious hostility.

Since it was my yard and my stereo, I won the night with Linda Clifford. It was several days later, when passions had cooled, that my friend put the silly struggle into a serious context. "I can see what you're doing," he said. "You're trying to drag us holdover hippies kicking and screaming into the seventies." I protested, of course; but he was dead right in seeing our argument over such a banal issue as a severe clash of sensibilities.

The sense of the sixties provided coherence and validity to rock when the critics of an earlier era proclaimed such sounds to be junk. Rock was "our music": only "we"—whoever *we* were—knew that it was good and what parts of it were best. The music was riding a historical tide; it was the sound of the politics, the expectations, the explorations and the institutions of an era. It was the background music as well as the marching melody for civil disobedience, sexual liberation, crunchy granola and LSD. The Buffalo Springfield's "For What It's Worth" was perfect music-to-avoid-the-FBI-by. "Street-Fighting Man" was made for trashing draft boards. "Mr. Tambourine Man" was for smoking dope. "Up the Country" was for dropping out of the city. "Let It Be" was for letting it be.

The music conveyed no special meanings to those who did not share the sensibility. The songs may have been pretty and popular, but Mantovani's version of "Piece of My Heart" has no historical validity, while Joplin's original surged with an emotional power born of place and time. Bitter battles raged across the famous gap of generations, but the gulf was not a creation of chronological age; rather, it expressed different sets of values. Teenage straights used to beat up on 30-year-old hippies as often as Mom and Dad fretted about their kids. The film *Easy Rider* was the most direct statement of the sixties sensibility as well as the hostility it generated, and the two sides of America it showed were not so disparate in their generations as in their attitudes. As much as the action, the music of that movie epitomized what the difference was.

History hardly stops. Disco in the seventies is in revolt against rock in the sixties. It is the antithesis of the "natural" look, the real feelings, the seriousness, the confessions, the struggles, the sincerity, pretensions and pain of the last generation. Disco is "unreal," artificial and exaggerated. It affirms the fantasies, fashions, gossip, frivolity and fun of an evasive era. The sixties were braless, lumpy, heavy, rough and romantic; disco is stylish, sleek, smooth, contrived and controlled. Disco places surface over substance, mood over meaning, action over thought. The sixties were a mind trip (marijuana, acid); disco is a body trip (Quaaludes, cocaine). The sixties were cheap; disco is expensive. In a sixties trip, you saw God in a grain of sand; on a disco trip, you see Jackie O at Studio 54.

In describing "camp" in her influential essay fifteen years ago, Susan Sontag remarked that "a sensibility (as distinct from an idea) is one of the hardest things to talk about." It is "not only the most decisive, but also [the age's] most perishable aspect. To name a sensibility, to draw its contours and to recount its history, requires a deep sympathy modified by revulsion."

Not only the camp and disco aesthetics—which resemble each other in their characteristics as well as their relationship to historical periods—create such conflicts in the minds of their beholders. Vanguard sensibilities in any age must contain all the awful contradictions of set and setting, the negative and positive parts of the whole; the good, bad and ugly in the rush of creativity. Certainly the spirit of rock and radicalism a decade ago was not composed of unalloyed virtue; nor was the Silent Generation wholly banal, the War Effort of the forties completely uplifting, the Jazz Age entirely liberating, or Victorianism uncompromisingly repressive. We remember what we choose to celebrate.

I knew that night in Vermont that I am drawn to disco's dazzling physicality, its style, it controlled energy; and I am revolted by its empty excesses, it superficiality, its desperate trendiness. Nor can I dismiss the aesthetic originality under the tawdry facades as an irrelevant fad. It must be clear by now to everyone with an ear or an eye that this era—of whatever duration—is already the Disco Years, whether it will be called by that name or not.

The performance and production of disco music creates a technical and economic foundation on which the intangible aspects of culture and sensibility develop. Disco is not a natural phenomenon in any sense. It is part of a sophisticated, commercial, manipulated culture that is rooted exclusively in an urban environment. Disco music is produced in big cities and its fashions are formed in big cities, at considerable expense, by high-priced professionals. Almost as an afterthought the product is then disseminated to the provinces. All the sparkle, speed, cynicism and jaded irony associated with metropolitan life is attached to disco. It is far from wholesome. Provincials may either envy or abhor it, but it belongs to the city.

"Disco is a New York thing. It happened here," says Kenn Friedman, the 26-year-old promotion wizard of Casablanca Records. "And it still happens here." On a weekend evening in the city, Friedman may commandeer the label's limo or slip out on his own and make the rounds of the hottest New York clubs: Infinity, Flamingo, Les Mouches, Studio 54, 12 West. He holes up with the disc jockeys in their sound booths, then quickly moves out onto the dance floors, soaking up the spirit of the music and catching the response of the crowds. He and his crew at Casablanca are eminently successful because he can feel the hits.

"I *know* what will be number one, what the hottest record is going to be on the street this weekend," Friedman told me matter-of-factly. At the time we spoke he predicted it would be James Wells's "My Claim to Fame"; and sure enough, when I went round to the clubs the next Saturday, it was the song that provoked the peak excitement of the night. "I can't tell you exactly how I know, but it's because I'm part of the culture, I love to dance, I love the music."

Dancing is what does it. Last week at the "Casbah"—Casablanca's New York digs in an arabesque town house on 55th Street—I found the company's top disco director, Mark Simon, boogying excitedly in Friedman's cramped office. Just back from the world record industry's annual congress in Cannes, Simon was effusive about the "completely new sound" his label will introduce as its 1979 line later this month. The first group making this as-yet-unknown music is called Nightlife, and Simon says he's banking his business ($100 million last year) on his intuitions.

"I heard a different producer's sound every fifteen minutes, five hours a day, all the time I was in Cannes," Simon says coolly, "and I picked the ones I felt were going to be the dance hits."

While the sounds of disco are highly synthesized, the hits cannot be completely determined. Nobody dreamed up the whole disco promotion campaign in the first place. "In the beginning we used to dance to the best rhythms from Motown and other rhythm-and-blues records," Simon recalled. "There was nothing called disco back in the sixties—just Diana Ross, Freda Payne, the Temptations." Then the producers in Philadelphia—Gamble and Huff—started making a specific disco sound, with the familiar heavy beat and the modified samba rhythm.

By reckonings, the first big disco hit—*as disco*—was Gloria Gaynor's 1974 top-of-the-charts "Never Can Say Good-bye." Others pick "Love's Theme," by Love Unlimited Orchestra. But the record companies seemed bewildered by what they had, and promo people continued their quirky disregard for the disco category in their portfolios. Instead, they inflated passing fancies into seismic cultural events: Peter Frampton, reggae and punk, for example. Not that some of the sounds or stars lacked merit; certainly Springsteen, Bob Marley and the best of the New Wave deserve seats high in rock-and-roll heaven. But disco would soon swamp them all, and nobody was watching.

Disco has authentic roots in America that punk and other more fashionable genres never found. John Rockwell was still writing Hegelian analyses of the Sex Pistols in the Sunday *Times* when two-thirds of the city was listening to Donna Summer and couldn't tell Mr. Rotten from Mr. Respighi.

The big hits of disco music still seem to happen in spite of the hype. Polydor guessed that "Substitute" might be the next Gloria Gaynor success late last year, and the company pushed that unknown tune over the "B" side of the single, "I Will Survive." "Survive" became the runaway best-seller.

The fact is that while disco is racing to new levels of sophistication and elaboration at high speed, there is yet no reliable test for a hit. The reason is that the disco phenomenon has turned the pop industry upside-down, as no development has since the advent of sixties rock.

The disco wave crashed on unseen shores, catching producers and musicians without adequate cultural or commercial bearings. There were few critics to say what was good or bad—that is, what their readers or listeners should buy. There were no researchers to test the market; no one knew what questions to ask. The one or two music writers who dove into disco often felt overwhelmed by the legitimacy and power wielded by the rock establishment, and they hid their opinions under barrels or in closets.

The low regard in which the titans of rock hold the upstarts of disco has created a new, self-conscious elite of performers, producers and promoters. "Before disco there was one pie; Warners, Columbia and RCA had it, and no other record company could get a piece of it," says John Brody, Casablanca's promotion man in New England. "So along came Neil Bogart from Buddha Records—the bubblegum king of the sixties—and he said, 'Let's make another pie.' That's how he started Casablanca."

Today, the disco record industry is a mammoth enterprise—bigger than television, movies or professional sports in America. "Disco accounts for about 40 percent of all the chart activity," Friedman estimated. By the end of the decade, half the top 100 songs on *Billboard*'s lists will be disco numbers. Disco radio stations are sweeping the country. New York's WKTU is a story in itself: in nine months of disco programming (it used to send out "mellow rock") it has gone from the dregs of stations too low to rate to the number one broadcaster in the country, either AM or FM—beating out the gargantuan WABC. Boston's WBOS was minuscule before it went all-disco; it now tops the biggest FM rock stations in America's hottest "youth market." And there are 200,000 disco clubs, earning $6 billion annually.

What all this means is that a sizable chunk of capital in the entertainment industry is now in the hands of the disco elite—a mixed breed of newcomers, switchovers and fast dancers who had the sense to accommodate themselves to the sensibility of the seventies. The new disco elite has its own vocabulary and values, and these are quite different from those of the rock entrepreneur. For one thing, the disco people have to feel like dancing—not autistic, explosive fits of movement but the more controlled, stylized dancing of the clubs. And for another, they have to be able to mingle and mix in gay settings as well as straight ones, for the locus of the emerging disco culture is pointedly in urban male homosexual society.

"There is a big cultural difference between rock and disco," Kenn Friedman said firmly, "and it's gayness. Some people don't like to talk about it, but it's true. Disco began in gay clubs. At first, it was just a case of speeding up the gap between records on the jukebox. But that's how the concept of continuous music began. The disco club was the first entertainment institution of gay life, and it started in New York, as you would expect."

Disco promoter John Luongo agrees. "In the beginning, there was the gay audience for disco. The 'primo' disc jockeys were gay. Gays couldn't find any rock bands to play in their clubs, so they had to make records their own form of entertainment."

Not long ago, Friedman took John Brody around to several clubs on his Saturday night rounds, and Brody gave me this report:

"The intensity was different at Infinity, which is predominantly straight, and at 12 West, which is mostly gay. At Infinity the energy was lower, there was less emphasis on dancing. At 12 West everybody was dancing, and it was a kind of sexual thing. It was very powerful. There was a strong smell of poppers—amyl nitrate—in the air, and I guess a lot of people were high on whatever. That must be part of the mood. But the gays seemed a lot less hung up in their environment than the heterosexuals seemed in theirs. At 12 West, I looked at these people dancing at 4 in the morning; it looked like the last night of their lives."

Even so, Friedman did not take Brody to Flamingo, the most intense gay disco in New York. "I didn't think he could handle it," Friedman joked. What Brody would have seen was this:

Flamingo is an enormous loft on the edge of Soho, undistinguished by signs or lights. Members (who pay $75 a year plus a substantial fee for each visit) start wandering in well after midnight on Saturday nights, the only day of the week the club is regularly open. By 3 AM, several thousand people, almost entirely men, mostly shirtless and universally stoned, are dancing feverishly to the most imaginatively mixed, most persistently powerful music ever assembled in one continuous set. One wall of the dance room is panelled with colored lights which flicker and race at appropriate intervals in harmonious correlation to the music. Along another wall, a dozen or so men dance by themselves on a raised banquette, acting as erotic cheerleaders to the swirling crowd. The fume of poppers is overpowering.

Many Saturday night dances at Flamingo have a theme, like a senior prom. Late last month there was a "Western/Tattoo" night, which featured a raised platform in the lobby where party-goers could be tattooed in their moments of relaxation from dancing. Another annual feature is the "Black Party"—named not for the race of the customers but for the suggested color of attire, the decorations and the mood of the evening. Last spring's Black Party was one of the final Saturdays of the season—before Flamingo closes for the summer while its thousands of members repair to Fire Island for whatever adventures await them in the dunes. Now, this was some senior prom. In the entrance hall there were cages, platforms and theatrical sets where various happenings were in progress, all in accordance with a vaguely s&m, "black" leather-gear theme. Some of the goings-on were semi-mentionable: people (actors?) were in chairs, under the whip, grovelling and groping, dishevelled. Other attractions were unmentionable, and getting more so as the evening wore on. There were more people in the loft at 6 AM than there were at 1. When *do* these people sleep?

A strange fascination kept me at Flamingo past my bedtime, and I have returned many times in the months since. Most often, the mood is lighter than on that black night (the "White Party" is coming up later this month), but the extravagant sense of theatricality is maintained. The throbbing lights, the engulfing sound, the heightened energy and hyperbolic heat of Flamingo gives me the sense that the world is enclosed in this hall, that there is only *now*, in this place and this time. It can be extraordinarily assaultive; I have felt trapped in a theater of sound, of flesh, like a character in Buñuel's *The Exterminating Angel*, unable to leave a party even after its positive appeal has fled. But what is worse is the prospect of a chill gray Manhattan dawn outside. Leaving is more depressing than staying: the disco beat is like a life rhythm, and to stop would be to create a killing thrombosis.

Danae—it's his *nom de disco*—is a well-known disc jockey on the New England and New York circuit. I asked him what he does to make the special blend of music that distinguishes the disco club sound from just "playing records."

"The mix starts at a certain place, builds, teases, builds again and then picks up on the other side," he explained. "The break is the high point. It's like asking a question, repeating and repeating it, waiting for an answer— and then giving the answer. That is the great, satisfying moment."

In practice, a "hot" disco mix in a dance club is a sexual metaphor; the deejay plays with the audience's emotions, pleasing and teasing in a crescendo of feeling. The break is the climax.

"That's the rush," Danae said. "The dancers cheer, they pump the air with their fists, they wave and shout. It's very exciting. I played at 12 West last Christmas, and its was one of the best nights I've ever had. After a while, someone came up to me, all excited, and said, 'You were fucking me with your music!' I took it as a great compliment."

"There's gay disco and straight disco, although there's overlap between the two," Danae continued. "Straight disco is heavy-duty funk, the driving sound, that has all the power without much of the emotion. Gays like to hear black women singers; they identify with the pain, the irony, the self-consciousness. We pick up on the emotional content, not just the physical power. The MFSB sound was gay, Barry White was a gay sound, so is Donna Summer, Gloria Gaynor. We knew 'Disco Inferno' was a great song years before it got into the *Saturday Night Fever* soundtrack. To me, the epitome of gay disco this year is Candi Staton. She's all emotion; you can feel it when she says, 'I'm a victim of the very song I sing.'"

There are contradictions within contradictions in the sexual implications of disco. Consider The Village People, the singing group that claims to hail from Greenwich Village and parodies the macho styles of its homosexual culture. One of the members is dressed as a leather biker, another as a construction worker, a third as an Indian, a fourth as a cowboy and so on. They perform songs that extend the parody—notably "Macho Man" and "YMCA." For gays, the line "I want to be a macho man" from the mouths of these butch-impersonators is a bit like "I want to be white" if it were sung by Stevie Wonder for a black audience.

Gays are amused by The Village People, but the group is finding its biggest fans among straights. "YMCA" is never heard at Flamingo. Kenn Friedman, whose Casablanca label produces the group (one of the most profitable in his stable) agrees: "'Macho Man' did not happen in gay clubs but in straight ones. The Village People is the first gay-to-straight 'crossover' group. The funny thing is that straights don't really believe the group is gay. They love 'em in Vegas and in tacky suburban dinner theaters in Midwestern shopping centers. Did straights ever catch on with Paul Lynde? With Liberace? People will protect their identity at all costs, they'll pretend to the last possible minute that it's all an act."

Gay activists have protested that Casablanca is deliberately closeting The Village People to make the act "safe" for straights. A Casablanca PR functionary says that producer Jacques Morali (who reportedly picked all the members, except possibly the accomplished lead singer, because of their tough good looks rather than their musical talent) became visibly upset when a *Newsweek* interviewer began probing into the gay issue. But the group is coming out, as it were, with ever more outrageous lyrics and postures. Their biggest hit to date is "YMCA," which concerns a young boy who comes into the big city, looks around for a place to hang out and lands in a hostelry that is legendary in the gay community as a cruising spot. What did Middle America think it all meant when The Village People sang that number, with all the appropriate gestures, at the height of the Macy's Thanksgiving Day parade on national television?

There are two levels on which The Village People's campiness works: the first is with the "knowing" gay audience, the listeners who are in on the joke, the images, the allusions (Fire Island, the bushes, Castro Street, Key West, the Y). The other is with the "naive" straight audience, the listeners who either don't know (or mind) what's going on in the lyrics, or think it's all theatrical drag. In much the same way, disco music as a whole appeals to a knowing audience that sees what Friedman calls the "cultural gayness" in it, and a naive audience that simply likes the fashion and the beat.

"The straights don't see the gay culture; they've only seen what they've made—the styles," Friedman says. Just before Casablanca's disco movie, *Thank God It's Friday,* opened across the country last year, Friedman took a short segment of it to several cities and showed it to selected audiences. Casablanca boss Bogart was worried that straight Americans would be offended if they detected the goings-on in the background of one sequence: two men dancing together and sniffing amyl nitrate.

"I interviewed hundreds of people, showed it to thousands, and as far as I know not one straight person ever saw the men dancing, even after I showed the segment to them two or three times," Friedman reported. "And yet the gay viewers saw it immediately."

One more example: Paul Jabara's song "Disco Queen," on the *TGIF* soundtrack, concerns a "queen" who is "known from LA to San Francisco to the Fire Island shore." She "even sleeps with her tambourine." She flirts with a handsome young marine. The chorus asks: "Where does she get her energy? Where does she get her energy?" *Really.* The images in the song are all attached to male homosexual styles. This queen is certainly a queen. But I'll bet heterosexuals never even consider the possibility that the disco queen is not a woman. To them, it's just another nice dance tune—which it is.

Disco became the theme music of gay culture in the seventies (not only in America but in Europe and Latin America as well). Of course, the straight audience now far outnumbers the gay one, but the music still has a special meaning for gays: if sixties freaks could say that rock was "our music," gays now say the same for disco. It is the background music for the activities and institutions of the burgeoning urban gay culture—for the shops, the bars, the restaurants and the offices where gays go about their business. It is music for sex, for dancing and for watching the straight world go by. It is reassuring and supportive; in an important way, it is the sensational glue that unites a community.

But disco has deep roots and strong attachments in other cultural groups as well. Disco is, after all, a mixture of certain black rhythm-and-blues sounds, Latin forms and an African beat. New York's first major disco station was WBLS, a black radio outlet. Many of the best disco performers are black—while rock is bleached and white. For years disco suffered severe disadvantages to total acceptance: major disco artists were black or Latin, many were women, the principal white audience was gay, and the non-gay white audience was located in the urban ethnic working class—all reasons for cultural disability.

Saturday Night Fever illustrated the class aspect of disco for urban whites. While rock was infused with middle-class attitudes (although often downwardly mobile in its aspirations), disco was originally proletarian. One clue: the "weekend" theme reappears in disco lyrics, as in "Thank God It's Friday," "I Just Can't Wait for Saturday," "Funky Weekend" and, of course, in the film title *Saturday Night Fever* itself. Working-class kids toil all week and wait for their one big shot at fun, escape and dreams on the weekend; they dress up, get drunk and play out sexual fantasies in a community context. Quite the other way with the rock culture: hippies hang out all week and can't tell Saturday night from Tuesday afternoon. They don't do much dancing, and when they do, they do not care much for dressing up, spending money, having dates and controlling their movements on the dance floor.

There are certain immutable characteristics of rock culture: it is white, straight, male, young and middle-class. The exceptions to those rules prove them. Female stars and their songs must conform to male sexual fantasies—Linda Ronstadt, Christine McVie. Black musicians and their music must be chlorinated to make it up the rock charts—Jimi Hendrix, Stevie Wonder, Chubby Checker. What may appear to be lower-class images in rock usually turn out to be middle-class myths and fantasies: punk violence, "Working Class Hero" radicalism, drop-out dreams. And performers who tinker with sexual stereotypes must remain determinedly "ambiguous" or turn up alongside partners of the opposite sex from time to time, to beard their offensive nakedness. Jagger may French kiss Ron Wood on *Saturday Night Live*, but it's fortunate that he can lose a paternity suit with, figuratively, the same breath. Sexual deviation (like gender, class and race aberrations from the norms) must be playful and let's pretend: it cannot seriously threaten straight identity.

For a time, it appeared that disco culture might change those rules to a degree, particularly in the case of sexual identity. It now looks as if the dominant demands of American society will prevail, to no one's great surprise. The past year has seen several disco stars achieve the "crossover" effect, bringing the music out of the subcultural ghettoes into mainstream life. The Bee Gees were crucial to that passage: they made disco safe for white, straight, male middle-class America. What Elvis Presley did for black rhythm and blues, and Diana Ross did for soul, and Elvis Costello did for punk, the Brothers Gibb have done for disco. Now all of Nassau County is lining up for disco lessons. Sixties survivors who steadfastly resisted disco because it was apolitical, or dehumanized, or feminine, or homosexual, or too Bay Ridge, are suddenly skipping to the beat. They have found what Gladys Knight calls out, in one of the best songs of the season: "It's a *better* than good time."

The rise of disco music occurred alongside the decline of rock, but whether there is a connection between these two aesthetic events is not at all clear.

"Rock-and-roll is at an all-time low in creativity," promoter John Luongo fretted. "It's all rehashed material, there's no freshness. I love rock; it's where I started. But the music has let people down. There was a big hole, and disco filled it. There's no other form of music that offers the power, the excitement, the party atmosphere of disco."

A few months ago I discovered that my friend Janet, who had been thoroughly indoctrinated in rock culture in Radcliffe in the sixties, had suddenly discovered disco. I asked her what it was that got her out on the dance floor after all these years of mooning about her living room listening to Dylan and his progeny.

"There did get to be a point of no return," she allowed. "The sixties was so solitary, so solipsistic, so narcissistic: look at the way people dance! Disco is just as exhibitionist, but you create it with someone else, with another person on the dance floor. It's a retreat from that scary chaos into patterns. You get high with someone else. Back in '64 we started dancing to the Beatles in a way that was a rebellion against dancing-class dancing. The chaos began there; it was energy for its own sake. Now we've returned to a more formal routine, to stylization. That's not necessarily reactionary. It's infusing form with the energy of the sixties. And it's beautiful to watch. Maybe it's pretentious to say, but this seems to be the end of a process—of rebellion, excess and transformation. In our end is our beginning."

"Anyhow," she concluded, "you can't listen to that music and not want to dance. I really don't believe there is life after disco; it's what people will always want to dance to."

Disco is the word, as grease was the word. It is a handle for the seventies, as the other was a metaphor for the fifties, for in the extraordinary cultural and commercial success of disco several of the new elements of this generation can be identified. Disco has many functions, but one of the most essential may be as a drug: it feeds artificial energy, communal good feelings and high times into an era of competition, isolation and alienation. As drugs go, it is not egregiously harmful, but it is easily abused, quickly tolerated and naggingly addictive.

Sensibility is dialectical—which is to say that it grows from the material of history and the experience of society. It does not descend from the heavens of invention or corporealize out of thin air. The seventies sensibility emerged from the achievements and excesses, the defeats and triumphs of the years before. Our end is *always* in our beginning, and we are, as Candi Staton croons, the victims of the very songs we sing.

February 12, 1979, THE VILLAGE VOICE

✦

The Rise and Decline of Cocaine Culture

Between the blizzards of 1977, a man I'll call Wally flew to Bogota and back to his suburban neighborhood of nondescript ranch houses on the perimeter of a large mid-Atlantic city. In Colombia he had made a deal for $50,000 worth of cocaine, as pure as it can be in these days when the pressures of world demand and the restrictions of Colombian suppression force honest traffickers into minor frauds. After three years of price stability—at $18,000 a kilo—the cost of 2.2 pounds of export-grade cocaine has been inflated to $22,000 in the past three months. Wally never carried the coke; he ordered it shipped to a third country, where it was brought into America by confederates who would never arouse the suspicions of customs inspectors. "If I ever get busted," Wally says, "it'll be because of a tip-off in South America, not an inspection at an airport."

Wally got five pounds of coke to his house, where he stashed it in 8" x 11" Ziploc plastic bags. Opinions differed as to its purity at the point of export: Wally maintained it was "90 percent uncut." But no one suspected that it had yet been "stepped on" in the United States for the domestic market. As such, it was the purest, most potent cocaine that anyone but the top dealers in the country will ever see or snort.

Word went out quickly that a high-quality shipment was in the States. Second-level dealers began flying into Wally's tract community from distant centers of the drug culture: Slim from Atlanta, Robert from Seattle. They pulled into the driveway in modest rent-a-cars, made themselves at home in the ranch-style comfort of Wally's living room, and waited for the big man to do his deals.

Wally was in wretched shape. Once slender, strong and vibrant, he had recently put on forty pounds around his middle in several abortive attempts to give up personal use of the drug. Now he was fat and wired like an electrical generator. The subdealers stood by in helpless anticipation as Wally flew from room to room, brandishing a hypodermic needle, which he was using every forty minutes or less to shoot himself up with liquefied cocaine. A few drops of blood dripped from the point and they spattered against the white walls of the rooms as he gesticulated. One minute he was sprawled on a couch, another he was prostrate on the floor, then he went careening from wall to wall, babbling almost incoherently and calming momentarily after each "firing" of coke into his veins.

Various friends and hangers-on watched the grim scene with compassion and horror. Wally had been up for four days and nights, dealing and firing and descending into a cocaine psychosis. He had just recovered from an attack of hepatitis; his eyes—like many of his friends' eyes—were still deep yellow. His face was pitted with bloody wounds where he had gouged small blemishes in the belief that they were "bugs"—impurities that had to be torn from his flesh. The subdealers were not optimistic about future dealings with Wally, but his coke was always reputable, and he promised to "stay off" use for himself after the huge stash was sold.

Slim left in his snappy rented Camaro Z-28; Robert remained. "We have only five minutes more work to do," he said optimistically. In the dealing room, a half-pound of delicate crystalline cocaine was dumped casually on a marble-top table. Puffs of it blew around the floor. There was as much wasted dust from the mound as many people would snort in a year. The extravagance was mind numbing.

"You know as well as I do," Wally said, taking me into his confidence, "that there's no way to control yourself. Whatever's on the mirror, you're going to consume it before the night's over. You can't do it in moderation forever, not if it's available like this"—he wiped a huge fingerful of the stash onto his nose—an amateur would smear it on his gums. "But if it's not around, I'll be okay. Come back after all this is gone, and I'll be in great shape. You'll see. I promise you." Then he sent me out and asked Robert to come back to finish the deal. By the end of the day, he had made a quarter of a million dollars.

Dick Cavett calls cocaine "the drug of the 1970s." *Newsweek* publishes a five-page puff piece on "The Cocaine Scene," and confirms that its "popularity has spread so vastly within the last few years that it has become the recreational drug of choice for countless Americans." Dr. Peter Bourne, the former Carter aide and White House pill prescriber, reports that some eight million Americans have "tried" cocaine and perhaps two million use it on a regular basis—a fivefold increase in the last few years—with remarkably "few problems." Sal, a well-known South End dealer, says there's been "a Hiroshima" explosion of cocaine sales in Boston in the last six months.

Unlike almost any other potent drug, licit or illicit, cocaine conjures a positive image nowadays to users and non-users alike, a connotation of the euphoria and innocent exhilaration that correspond to the drug's physical effects. Even cocaine's slang names suggest the drug's breezy delights: toot, blow, snow. If it were legal, or necessary, to advertise the product, the appropriate spread would show a Salem cigarette couple leaping through a leafy glade, the wind rippling through their hair, an autumn snow flurry frosting their pink noses.

The myths about cocaine are mostly reassuring, and they are built into the structure of the cocaine culture, so much so that Americans have become snow-blinded to the deeper hazards. To most occasional coke users, and to the millions more who read about it in *People* and wish they could take a whiff, the picture of a nation of *coqueros* is pretty in all respects. But there is trouble lurking in this paradise. All of a sudden, and just as it is established as the best drug of all, coke is found (by many long-time users) to be too good to be true. Cocaine has a time-bomb effect or, as one confirmed coke-head told me recently, a "theory of revenge" whose infernal machinery may take many years to work.

The seeds of cocaine's destructiveness can be seen in its popularity. Above all else, coke is a drug of paradoxes. Its very mildness, its lack of physiological addictiveness, its euphoric effects and its subtle support of a user's ego are the elements that contribute to its long-term danger.

"It's the devil," one friend said painfully. His identity, like that of all those interviewed, has been disguised. "It took me six years to find that out when I was snorting. Now it's taken me two months to find it out because I'm shooting. It's the apple in the hands of Eve. You can't resist. It's out of control," he groaned, and then repeated his complaint in a roar: "OUT OF CONTROL!"

Personal accounts of addiction to any substance from opium to Chinese food convey similar sounds and familiar fears. But there are significant differences between dependence on cocaine and addiction to other drugs, and they result not only from the chemistry of the product but the social context in which cocaine flourishes.

First of all, coke has *class*. Its exorbitant price ($80 to $130 a gram, depending on purity and quality, in Boston this month) makes it a plaything of the upper brackets, but there is more to that status that the simple determinism of economics. Something about cocaine's effects, its ability to make the drab dazzling, the vulnerable self-confident, the boring brilliant, has secured its role in high society.

Cocaine was Freud's favorite drug (although he smoked tobacco longer and eventually died of mouth cancer, which smoking probably induced). It was Sherlock Holmes's legendary weakness. It was the drug of decadence and Art Deco: Bertolucci used cocaine in his film *1900* to symbolize the doomed self-indulgence of the European upper classes between the world wars. In Hollywood of the Babylonian era, cocaine was used by the racier stars: Errol Flynn daubed it on his penis to prevent premature ejaculation. Other members of his set may have been less clinical in their application of the drug, but it remained a staple of the entertainment industry.

Then in the 1970s, cocaine use rocketed up from that plateau of popularity into general acceptance among the stars. "It's very hard to go to a party in [Hollywood]," Cavett says, "where at one point it doesn't divide into the cocaine users, or maybe doesn't even divide." Naturally, fans everywhere seek to imitate the habits of their idols. As quickly as it took *Annie Hall* fashions to infiltrate Filene's, cocaine found its mass market.

The class-to-mass progress of cocaine sets it apart from other recreational drugs. "When I lived in Berkeley, we used to use a rolled-up hundred dollar bill for a 'straw,'" reported Eric, an old coker. "It was crisp, and therefore better for inhaling than a rumpled one-dollar bill. But it was more than that—it was the style of it—the look of a rolled hundred left casually on a mirror in a room with a lot of people."

"Cocaine is where marijuana was five years ago," a psychiatrist commented recently. In the past year or so coke has trickled down from the Hollywood Hills and the East Side of Manhattan to high-school parties and college dorms in lower-middle-class America. Last summer a friend who works at a country inn in New England told me that the young dishwasher at his hostelry went in with a chum from the village every week on a gram or a half-gram of coke, whatever their meager paychecks allowed. What startled my friend most was not the extravagance of the purchase but the ease with which the teenagers could find dealers in the backwoods.

Second, cocaine is *seductive*. First-time snorters typically cannot identify the "high" because it does not resemble, in intensity of feeling or alteration of reality, the intoxication of other drugs. It is no doubt true, as the medical experts claim, that cocaine does not produce physical addiction, which is to say its withdrawal after significant use does not produce a package of painful symptoms, such as heroin entails.

"The big problem is that very few people know they're addicted," says Harold, a middle-level dealer in an East Coast town. "There are no detox centers for coke, as there are for other drug addicts or alcoholics. The only thing that contains the problem at all is the accessibility and the economics. If I were the head of the KGB, I'd tell all the generals in the Kremlin to dismantle their missiles and make toot available to everyone in America."

I was amazed at Harold's vehemence. It is not easy to set up an interview with a dealer, especially one in a distant city who is not a close friend. But Harold's first words were, "I hope you do a negative piece."

"Coke can remove you from acting in the rest of society," he explained. "It doesn't do the obvious things other drugs do. Marijuana hits you like a club. Coke takes time to get you. I worry about my customers, and I worry about myself. I've never known anyone with access to more than three grams at a time, three grams a week, who is in control of it.

"When you're a dealer, or a heavy user, you become part of an in-group, people who take care of one another. It's part of the dramatic intimacy that's the bottom line of coke, the impetus to share everything because of the legal problems, the effects of the drug itself, the social dynamics. A little while ago, my in-group here said they didn't think I was in control. They asked to make tests, and after the tests they decided to limit my usage. I have a very strict 'bookkeeping' system now. I have to account for every toot I take."

"Coke is a wonderful thing," Harold said as we parted from a meeting in a roadside diner. "I expect to be involved with it to the day I die. It's very positive in its way. But make it legal? It would be disastrous! Now *that* would frighten the hell out of me."

Third, coke is historically *relevant*: its popularity is peculiarly attuned to this generation at this point in history. Cocaine gets you up for dancing, for work, for sex. It creates a sputtering sparkle and ephemeral warmth that seems to suggest that the world is all right. I'm okay, you're okay, coke's okay. It is the pre-eminent antidote to alienation, a release from the rigors of competition, a methodology for confronting cutthroat individualism. The awful end, of course, is that you have to come down. And soon.

Other drugs deaden the senses or bend the mind, and, of course, deactivate the user in the process; the depressant effect of various dopes were much discussed in political days gone by. But coke activates and euphorizes at the same time: an appropriate response to the accelerating pursuit of happiness, with no concern for expense and little care for the consequences.

The ultimate paradox of cocaine is that it gives the user the illusion of control and at the same time erodes the reality of control, too slowly to catch the degeneration in time, but surely enough to destroy it in the end. In the end, the loss of control invades every area of cocaine culture. Bob, a friend of mine from Berkeley, left the Bay Area for a year and then returned for a short visit. He called his old dealer, who announced that he had given up tooting and dealing. Through another old coke buddy, he was put on to a new dealer; they made a connection, and then another. After the third deal, the new source let him in on the secret: the old dealership had been "franchised" out to the new man because the old one was "hot," visible to potential police agents. Bob and a list of other customers were transferred to the cooler new dealer, along with $15,000 worth of high-quality cocaine, and an unwritten promise of a percentage share of the proceeds. The old dealer laid low and became a "bathroom tooter": to his circle of friends he had given up the drug, but he still snorted his lines in private. Bob had been sold and bought, like an indentured servant.

Like so many other highs in this age of summit experiences, cocaine creates a perplexing puzzle of choices: how much is enough, who makes the decisions, and what is the place of authority in the control mechanism that at some point must keep it in check?

"When you come down against coke, as I think you should, you're on the side of the narcs and the puritans and the assholes who want to regulate our lives," said a friend who admitted that not long ago his only ambition in life was to have a shoeboxful of coke. "The experts and *Newsweek* and Cavett are right when they attack the drug puritans, but they don't know the scene, they do it from the wrong side. We have to do it from the inside, from having been down and come up again."

"The problem is minute compared with other drugs, if you look at the figures on some computer print-out," he continued. "A lot more people get in trouble from downs, from speed, from cigarettes, from booze. Coke problems affect only the filthy rich and the dealers, and their friends. But we're like those monkeys in the test: they gave them their choice of food, water, sex and cocaine. They all went to the cocaine until they died."

December 2, 1978, THE REAL PAPER

✦

Gay Life: Present at the Creation

The lives of great cities are ordinarily organized by the imperatives of class, race, religion and authority. The temper of Boston is Brahmin and Celtic; the tone of Dallas is Baptist and *nouveau riche*; the mood of Chicago is bourgeois and bossy. The texture of New York is woven of all cults, castes and nationalities, but now there is another, wholly new strand in the social fabric: affection. For the first time in history an affectional community—comprising a million or more homosexuals—occupies a territorial base, and it has begun to promote its power and assert its attitudes in ways that are rarely recognized and little understood.

New York has become a gay place. The material of the new homosexual culture pervades its life, from lowbrow to highbrow, on the streets and in the shops, the theater, the cafes and the apartments of at least a dozen neighborhoods. What is startling about this cultural explosion (the city has seen many others) is that it flows from a source of sexual identity, just as the stuff of ethnic and religious communities grew from their more familiar roots. We know about Polish peasants, African slaves, Prussian burghers, Cantonese coolies, Latins, Litvaks and Levantines. We can trace their influence in our politics, our literature, music, business, language, dress, cuisine, morality and everyday attitudes. We speak of the Jewish novel, black jazz, Calvinist work ethic, Latin rhythm, Oriental patience, Irish politics, Italian filmmaking. We may relish, detest or simply describe the regional flavors that blend in the melting pot, but their origins are hardly mysterious anymore.

But there are no evident precedents (in this civilization, at least) for the development of an "ethnic" culture based on sexuality and centered in a single geographical district. Scholars may fetch far for parallels in the myths of Amazon woman-nations or the tales of Greek homoerotic cultures; but there are no ready records of self-conscious communities formed around a shared, exclusive sexual trait—masculinity, femininity, homosexuality, transvestism or whatever—to compare with the extensive gay society that has developed in the American metropolis in the few short years since its birth in 1969 in Sheridan Square, in the battle of the Stonewall bar. It is no exaggeration to say that we are present at the creation of a stage of society and a style of life that is unique in the world we inhabit.

Two important distinctions should be set down. First, the new gay city includes both men and women, of course, but for many reasons (not least of which is plain sexism) the gay male elements are more noticeable than the lesbian ones; and many of the descriptions used to characterize the common culture come out of the male experience. Patterns of lesbian culture are often included in the larger category of feminism—for which there is no gay male analogue. Second, the development of a visible gay community in New

York—in Manhattan, most of all—is replicated in other cities around the country. The birth of the various gay communities is really a vast "invasion," a migration that is both external (from the hinterlands to regional centers and then to the largest cities) and internal (from the closets into the sunlight and moonglow). Gay life elsewhere may be more intense or perfected, but nowhere is it as much of a model, on a scale so mass, as in Manhattan.

The elements of gay style are both banal and extraordinary, as unimportant as the short cut of men's hair and as weighty as the invention of Pop Art, as trendy as the redevelopment of Columbus Avenue and as serious as the emergence of gay psychiatic and medical services. Gay sensibility can be sordid (the dives along the Hudson River way after midnight), or elegant (the ballet, the musical theater, the opera), or glitzy (Studio 54, Saturday afternoon "tea" in the Pines on Fire Island, a roomful of Art Deco *tchotchkes*), or angry (a march through the Village after a homophobic incident, or a flood of letters to the *Post* after a know-nothing column by Harriet Van Horne).

All told, there are as many separate—and often contradictory—styles as there are homosexuals, and the assertion of any one of them, or of any set or system, may provoke vehement attacks and vigorous exceptions from those who do not feel themselves included. No heterosexual is as bothered by the bars and baths as are gays who do not frequent them; no Brooks Brothered straight man will rail against the leather look as furiously as a preppy partisan of Shetland sweaters and penny-loafers in an East Side gay garden; no one hates gay disco more than a gay punk.

For like the evolving, expanding ethnic sectors in New York—black and Latin, for instance—the gay community is fragmented, disparate and heterogeneous while it is profoundly self-conscious. Differences in class, gender, age, race, ideology and psychology give the culture its many-sided surface: it can be as radical, reactionary, racist, tolerant, snobbish or democratic as any other social grouping in these times. But what unites homosexuals on a deeper level are the common condition of oppression, the shared history of liberation and the sense of permanent separation from the prevailing social definition of normality. We may be teased, tolerated or loved; we must always be different. From such difference comes a unity in spite of ourselves, a sense of pride as well as fear, struggle as well as acceptance, superiority as well as vulnerability.

Straight society sees homosexuals (the flamboyant few), but it does not readily recognize the presence of a gay culture. Last winter, *The New York Times Magazine* published a cover story on the city's "renaissance," replete with color photographs of all the fashionable features of born-again Gotham: discos, musical comedies, Bloomingdale's, rehabbed brownstones, warehouse neighborhoods, Deco restaurants, designer boutiques, gourmet kitchens. There was hardly an item on the list that was not tinged with gay sensibility—or created by it. And yet the influence of the new sexual community on the revitalized city was never once mentioned—not even in the coy euphemisms ("neighborhoods of single adults") that the genteel press prefers. Gays who read the *Times* were astounded by the omission. It was as if a newspaper had described the New South without mentioning the blacks of Atlanta or Birmingham, or had recalled pre-war Vienna without admitting the existence of its Jews. The oppression of gays takes many forms—from brutal discrimination in employment to psychological submission in the family—but the most devastating of all is the cloak of invisibility imposed by the straight powers that be.

It is hardly surprising that gays themselves often participate in the unorganized conspiracy of silence about the very existence of gay culture. Gays are all still in the closet to some degree, the militant no less than the mouse. Invisibility may be frustrating and stifling, but it is also protective. Homosexuals who are entirely comfortable in an all-gay environment often find it difficult or disturbing to communicate the quality of that experience to their straight friends, no matter how approving the straights may be: "they don't understand"; "they have no idea what goes on in our lives"; "they don't think like us." Every gay person knows that the mood of a roomful of homosexuals is abruptly and irreversibly changed when straights enter.

The straight world is what it *is*; to be gay is to be aware of a special reality. Depending on how a particular homosexual may feel about himself or herself at a given moment, that reality may be glorious or ghastly, enlivening or deadening. But gay reality stands out against ordinary life in sharp relief. There are neighborhoods and gay neighborhoods, newspapers and gay newspapers, resorts and gay resorts, bars and gay bars, doctors and gay doctors, dinner parties and gay dinner parties (compare: judges and lady judges, or theater and black theater). The very awareness of a distinction constitutes the primary closet, whether gays are conversationally open about their sexuality or not. For liberation, after all, is both a personal and a social process. Heterosexual consciousness imposed closets on gays in the first instance, through religion, the ideology of family life, *machismo,* puritanism and gentility. Gays cannot fully escape without changing the greater world as well as their own smaller selves.

From the moment gays begin to test their identities against straight "norms," they learn to pretend: to hide behind straight masks, to perform straight parts in straight plays, to divide gay selves from straight roles. Only the eyes betray the truth: gay men check out everyone within eyeshot for the sly glance, the subtle mannerism, the hidden smile, the measured gait, the clothes, the posture—all to find fellow members of the tribe and announce their own "ethnicity," in ways so covert that outsiders (those whom other tribes may call strangers, barbarians, *ofays* or *goyim*) seldom catch the exchanges. It happens all the time: on the subway, in an office, on a movie line, in all-night banking centers, airport lounges. The universal gay checkout glance may be a kind of "cruising," but its basis is survival and support more often than sex. Until recently, a gay man grew up believing he was the only queer in the world; the search for others is essentially a means of re-assuring himself that he will never again be alone.

There were millions of homosexuals before Stonewall, of course, but there was no coherent, self-aware gay community. There were bohemian elites and quiet cliques of closeted homosexuals, but no gay culture, no visible gay presence on the street except for the odd "queen." For the most part, homosexuals were allowed to express their identity in purely sexual terms (hence the clinical, Latinate name *homosexual*), and only after dark, in bars and in bed. Homosexuals had straight jobs, socialized with straight friends within a strictly heterosexual culture, participated in straight politics, talked straight talk. Homosexuals bought records of straight popular music, whose lyrics told of guys and their dolls. The straight theater consisted of plays based on the formula: boy meets girl, etc.

Only after the straights dropped of fatigue or boredom could homosexuals "go out"—that is, present themselves in a gay setting. But the night trips of that era were always furtive, dangerous and often humiliating. What gay culture existed before 1970 was pre-eminently a culture of oppression, in which homosexuals conformed to the perverse and prejudiced definitions of sexual "deviation" dreamed in the worst heterosexual nightmares. Gays were sissies, tramps, sadists, drunks, neurotics, hysterics. All expectations were confirmed, all prophecies fulfilled.

The few homosexuals honored in the heterosexual world were forgiven their bad habits if they did not flaunt them, or if they made a valuable contribution to straight culture. Tennessee Williams was lionized as long as he kept the sexuality of his dramatic characters properly ambiguous and his own predilections nicely sublimated. What Benjamin Britten and Peter Pears did after the opera was their own business. Similar rules held in other oppressed cultures: Ralph Bunche did not flaunt his blackness, and Margaret Chase Smith did not trumpet feminism; the occasional homosexual celebrity was expected to keep his or her own quirk hidden as well.

Looking back, the world seemed positively medieval; in these post-liberation years, gays have been able to integrate their lives with the facts of their sexual identity to a degree considered impossible a short time ago. In New York now, gays may live in supporting surroundings, in heavily gay districts, within a social and economic infrastructure shot through with aspects of gay culture. Gays may work in gay-run businesses catering to a gay clientele, or they can get jobs through the gay network in larger establishments, such as department stores, where gays occupy top managerial positions. They eat in gay restaurants, shop on gay avenues in gay boutiques, listen to gay-oriented music, share gay living quarters, dance in gay discos, vacation in gay garden spots, worship in gay churches, read gay magazines and gay novels, snack on gay pizza and gay burgers, see movies by gay directors featuring gay actors and actresses, play softball in gay leagues and hope for victory in the Gay World Series, sail on gay cruises, get high on gay drugs pushed by gay dealers, and spend all their social hours with gay friends.

Both straights and gays debate the value of gay exclusivity, but the trend appears to be firmly established. The need for it is evident beyond argument: gay culture strengthens the fragile self-image of homosexuals, and the more complete the community, the stronger the image. The development of a more or less total gay culture is analogous to the experience of other ethnic minorities at similar moments in the history of their liberation movements: read Miami Beach for Fire Island or 125th Street for Christopher Street, and gay exclusivity does not seem so strange. Many homosexuals will continue to spend their hours in heterosexual culture, too, but the developing gay community in New York will certainly set the terms for the next phases in all of gay life. There is power, energy and innovation in the creation of a separate gay society, and it has already had an enormous impact on the lives of all New Yorkers.

What makes a hamburger gay? Certainly it is not a genital attribute. What counts is the context: like the space "around the fish" in Klee's famous painting, the surroundings of the ordinary burger on the bun give it a cultural meaning. Walk into Pershing's on Columbus Avenue or Clyde's on Bleecker Street: the sound is disco, the texture is grainy, the pitch is high. A youngish man with a dark mustache, short dark hair, and a tight T-shirt and jeans approaches with a certain smile. He nods in a familiar manner and recites the list of burger possibilities (cheddar, "blue cheese," bacon) in a litany laced with a little lilt. Almost everyone in the room seems to be a male homosexual. Even the plants are well hung; and so a neuter burger becomes recognizably gay.

Sometimes the defining characteristic of the new gay institution is the specific make-up of its clientele: the sheer size and aggressive good taste of Bloomingdale's gay trade makes the store a center of the New York gay marketplace. Often, gayness is a matter of attitude—the way a certain veneer of camp irony may characterize a gay neighborhood. Columbus Avenue—the main street of the "Swish Alps"—is lined by shops with such names as The Sensuous Bean (coffee), Kiss and Make Up (cosmetics), Le Yogurt (yogurt), The Cultured Seed (flowers). Decoration, of course, is also telling: the To Boot cowboy boot store on West 72nd Street—"Queens Boulevard"—features "situation windows" that suggest the presence of odd couples rather than the conventional kind. In one display, two pairs of empty boots appear in a room set with an elaborate Sunday brunch which the occupants have hastily abandoned. One can only imagine what is happening "offstage."

Bars are still at the core of gay social life (there are more than seventy in Manhattan), and the baths, backrooms and warehouse barracks where sex is easily and anonymously available remain popular from that earlier era when they were, in a sense, pressed on the gay population by the straight definition of homosexual encounters as strictly zip-fuck meetings. While many gays deplore the exploitation of affection that bar life entails, the priapal palaces still serve a social and emotional purpose that will last until the next level of ascent to a more sincere and non-sexist society is reached. But while gays attack "cock culture" from the inside, there is something disingenuous about straight criticism of gay social institutions from the outside—as if masters condemned servants for participating in the culture of servitude.

The specific vision, manners, protocols and imagination of gay culture were first forged in response to the prevailing definitions of homosexuals as "different" in their sexual affections from ordinary people. Those who are called different and treated as such will naturally develop different ways of life. At bottom, it matters little what the original difference was thought to be: Jewish culture began many millennia ago as a function of the oppression of Jews for their monotheism or their curious tribal rituals; but theology is not primarily what concerns that culture today. Blacks were oppressed because of the amount of melanin in their skin and because of their African habits of life; but black culture in America is more than a color code or a continental curiosity.

And yet many heterosexuals still admit the existence of only sexual differences between themselves and homosexuals. Jeff Greenfield, for instance, wrote in this paper last year that "gay rights are different from all other rights" because they merely concern sexual practices, which are private, not community demands or cultural needs; thus they are unworthy of liberal support or legal protection. He went on to lecture his readers that "the cultural majority always sets the rules, and minorities have the choice of conforming, defying those rules or finding a community where they are the cultural majority." In other words, act straight and you'll have no problem.

For such heterosexual critics (and there are homosexuals still stuck in their closets who want desperately to agree) there is no gay culture, no gay lifestyle, no gay consciousness—just isolated units of homosexuals doing their thing in the sack.

Such denials of a gay sensibility lead to bizarre lapses of comprehension. For example, *Time* and *Newsweek* have both published long cover articles on the masters of Pop Art, which detail every conceivable influence brought to bear on the works of these artists—except the overwhelming fact of the homosexual culture to which they belong. The Pop artists and their followers attacked the analytic traditions of modernism that held sway for fifty years, and promoted instead a romantic "camp" attitude that profoundly changed American tastes in art, performance and design. It is impossible to understand these breaks in cultural continuity without accepting the reality of a gay aesthestic—and yet it seldom appears in straight art criticism. Only when artists paint homosexual pornography, or when writers describe sexual acts, is their own sexual "preference" considered relevant.

The struggle for visibility—for social acceptance of a gay identity beyond mere sexual practice—is long and tedious, with lags and leaps at unexpected times and in improbable places. Failures in the political forum—such as the repeated refusal by the city council to pass an anti-discrimination ordinance—may turn out to be less significant than success in community development. For the most important changes in the lives of gay people since Stonewall have come from the creation of a new ecology of gay institutions—commercial, cultural, political and intellectual—which provide the material basis to protect and extend the community.

The gay "movement" after Stonewall was largely radical in its analysis of sexist society and militant in its practice of confrontation with the straight male "ruling class." It had personal and ideological ties to the equally radical and militant anti-war, civil rights and socialist movements of the era. There was a moderate wing as well, but it too was part of a movement of structured organizations—even if the total effort often seemed disorganized and the relationships were usually strained. Only in the loosest sense does a definable gay political movement still exist in New York; rather, there is a social earthquake, without significant organization or clear direction. If there is a discernible theme to this enormous event it is, simply, change: very little that can be seen in metropolitan gay culture today will last the year, perhaps not even the week.

For example, the macho styles of dress and attitude so much in vogue in Village gay life in recent times seem to have lost their power and punch. While the "look" is still prevalent, it is no longer on the front edge of historical necessity. Gay macho (which was never really macho at all, if the truth is told; under those leather jackets lurked a lot of pussycats) expressed and exaggerated the suppressed masculinity of gay men, now made legitimate by the ideology of liberation. In the old days, homosexuals were "nellies" and "femmes." Suddenly, it was possible for homosexual men to be *men,* and they clutched at society's symbols to validate that difficult definition. Some gays with a well-developed radical approach were able to avoid the butch look and the violent symbols. But macho had to work itself out. As macho naturally followed sissy, its own negation will arrive when the time is ripe—probably soon, from the looks of things.

One clue to the new shape of things could be found at the annual Black Party held last month at the Flamingo disco, attended by several thousand of the most self-conscious gay circuit-riders in the city. This year, costumes were fanciful and ethereal rather than heavy metal—headdresses of silver-tipped black feathers replaced executioners' hoods of leather. Moreover, the mood of the party shifted from sinister to rollicking, from heavy duty to good fun.

If one factor in the change of attitude is the passage of time, another is the arrival of the second post-liberation generation to positions of status in the gay community. Homosexuals who came out when they were already adults will never lose their closet consciousness as thoroughly as young gays who come out now, in a vastly changed social universe, during adolescence or before. The latecomers see the issues in their own way, conditioned by the pain and confusion of years of real repression. The task of self-definition as gays was arduous and confused; the ways were uncharted.

Younger gays are relieved of some (although not all) of the problems that plagued the first generation. While there is more open "fag-baiting" and less genteel obliviousness found in many areas of the city, the psychological security of a vast, visible gay world is drawing out people who would have been intractably closeted in the sixties. At least there are available models now by which young gays can begin to define themselves. And those who will come out in future years into a much more supportive and well-posted gay community will have a still clearer sense of who they are. How that will affect their behavior in the full society is impossible to predict with any certainty. But it is clear that homosexual life ten years from now will present scenes as different from those visible today as our own pictures are rearranged from the pre-Stonewall era.

Take one example: there is a group of men in New York these days that one writer I know describes as the "killer fruits." They are rich, powerful and manipulative businessmen, lawyers and designers who hold court in East Side duplexes, chic discos and the Hamptons with a retinue of young "twinkies"—attractive boys who are kept amused, kept busy and simply kept by their older protectors. Competition among the "killers" is fierce, pressures are intense and humane values are held in abeyance as the men jockey for position, status and the favors of their followers. The "killers" are only partly out of their closets; they gain power by keeping their sexual identity ambiguous to the straight world in which they operate. But they are of a certain age and history that suggest they will soon vanish as a breed. The closet that produces them will cease to be so attractive as the gay community widens and its opportunities for a fulfilling life improve. Closets are places of personal as well as social oppression; they torment their inhabitants and diminish their functional capabilities. The end of the closet—as a concept of mind—is the essential goal of gay liberation.

Because there is no politburo, legislature or gay town meeting to establish priorities and set goals for the gay community, the scene in New York is every-homosexual-for-himself. Contradictions tumble over one another: for instance, every phase of liberation becomes a base for commercialization— which in a certain sense replaces one form of oppression with another. The demands of vanguard capitalism on the consciousness of the gay community are in some ways as strong as the strictures of puritanical heterosexuality. Gays have more disposable income these days than their straight counterparts in class and age: there are few, if any, children to educate, families to support, heirs to provide for. Gays may be easily led into traps of conspicuous consumption.

There is a final contradiction in the construction of a complete gay society, which may prove to be the most difficult to resolve: the backlash of heterosexuals against the accumulation of power, privilege and status by gays. The difficulties here will arise not primarily from the Anita Bryant end of the right wing, nor from the traditional homophobic centers in orthodox religion. The more serious problem will come from the majority of straight men who find their own emotional mobility and social comfort circumscribed by the growing influence of gays—in business, entertainment and everyday life. Heterosexual men used to take their privileged positions for granted, but all at once it seems they are threatened by the success of gay liberation and feminism. It is not impossible to conceive a scenario for severe backlash. In a time of economic hardship, straight men may come to believe that gays have the good jobs, the most spending money, the least responsibility—and the most fun. Gays could be seen not only as "different" but also as threatening. At that point, the gay "ethnic" community could be a target as easily as other groups served as scapegoats for mass social failure in the past.

Gays will be vulnerable for years to come—as far into the future as we can see. But gay liberation and feminism are allied in function as well as form, and together they infiltrate so much of the majority society that it would be hard to re-isolate and destroy them. The gay ghetto is primarily a function of consciousness, not class or race. Gays are, literally, everywhere—in every family, in every business. The backlash seeks to re-closet gays, but before it can succeed, it must erase the liberating experiences of millions of men and women. It would be a cruel endeavor indeed, and also self-defeating. Gays have valuable lessons to teach the world—about freedom from roles, the importance of emotion, the varieties of sexuality—and if given the chance, people will learn what is best for them.

June 25, 1979, THE VILLAGE VOICE

Chapter X

✦

COLD WAR II

Cold War II

Washington in the week before Labor Day looked like a city that had just suffered a neutron bomb attack. The solid stone buildings stood unmarked under a heavy haze, yet not a soul moved in the streets. Jimmy Carter and his crew were rafting in Idaho. Congress was junketing around the world, bureaucrats were at the beach and tourists were back home in the hinterland preparing for school or work. In the Everett McKinley Dirksen Senate Office Building, a few hold-outs huddled in air-conditioned isolation, like survivors awaiting doom in a disaster movie. One of them, a determinedly anonymous foreign affairs adviser to a Midwestern senator, welcomed me into his chambers with cold coffee and whispered words.

"Don't be deceived by the peace and quiet around here," he warned, clanking his cup on its saucer. "The war has started."

The war on his mind—and the one that worries much of official Washington—is not the shooting kind. No one scans the skies for missiles from the east. Rather, there is a growing fear that America is now entering another cold war, a replay of that epochal conflict that gripped the globe for two dangerous decades between the end of the world war alliance and the beginning of détente—between the Truman freeze and the Nixon thaw.

Cold war fever already had infected the capital before the late summer evacuation and the brief spell of Camp David, and it seems sure to recur in the weeks ahead. "It's been like an epidemic," the senator's aide continued. "It spreads from office to office. The senator and I were away for ten days in July, during the trials of the dissidents in Russia. When we got back, there were stacks of letters waiting from other senators: 'Dear Colleague: Join with me in denouncing this, deploring that, condemning, criticizing, viewing with alarm; boycott the ballet, cancel the Olympics, cut off the computers, build the B-1 bomber.' And these were not from the hawks, as you'd expect, but from the sweetest liberal doves that ever flew into this room."

The Cold War, Part II, has not yet erupted in full fury, but these initial skirmishes are startling enough after several years of steadily improving relations between the superpowers. Most of the action is still far removed from everyday American life. Fear of foreign invasion or internal subversion does not grip neighborhoods, campuses and countryside as it did during the fifties. The scenes of battle then were congressional investigations, demagogic demonstrations, spy trials and lurid confrontations across the iron curtain. There was a culture of the cold war, implicating everything from hula hoops to Elvis Presley to Francis Gary Powers. Now the war games are played to a more selective audience in the upper reaches of government, in think tanks and publishing companies. Whether the ideology will ultimately take root deep in the popular imagination—whether that is even possible now, or necessary—it is too early to say.

Although the cold war may not finally subvert the structure of détente, neither will it soon abate. There are deep divisions among the brokers of power in America—the result of a disastrous war, an unstable economy and a fractious society. The threat of Soviet domination is being used as a weapon in their power struggle, and it is a weapon that already is making its mark:

§ The new Strategic Arms Limitation Treaty with Russia (SALT II), which President Carter a year ago said was ready for the final dotting of i's and crossing of t's, is still shuttling from continent to continent in a diplomatic limbo, and Senate leaders have told Carter to hold it back from consideration until after the November elections. Even then, the treaty may fail to win ratification.

§ Under pressure from foreign policy adviser Zbigniew Brzezinski, Energy Secretary James Schlesinger, Pentagon chief Harold Brown and key Brzezinski aide Samuel Huntington, Carter took personal charge this summer of all sales of high technology equipment to Russia. First off, he blocked the sale of a computer to Tass, intended to facilitate compilation of statistics for the 1980 Olympics. Next, he held up the sale of oil-drilling machinery for arctic exploration. Later, he approved the deal, only to reconsider it when the security crew raised a fuss. Meanwhile, the Russians are easily procuring similar equipment from other Western countries.

§ No one talks much anymore of "reordering priorities" from guns to butter. During his presidential campaign, Carter repeatedly promised Pentagon reductions of $7–$8 billion; since he took office, he has projected increases of $9–$10 billion every year.

§ In early August, 148 members of Congress announced formation of the Coalition for Peace Through Strength. Its goal: military superiority over the Soviet Union (a condition considered eminently secure already by everyone from Gerald Ford to the liberal Center for Defense Information). The organizer of this bipartisan group—which includes a number of admirals, generals, former presidential advisers and chairmen of the Joint Chiefs of Staff—is John M. Fisher, president of the American Security Council, one of several private research institutions and think tanks that form the Washington base of the New Right.

§ In eleven months, US policy turned from recognition that the USSR would have a role in any Middle East settlement, to a plan—the Camp David accord—that specifically isolates Russia and its allies in the region. At least one skeptical congressman believes that Camp David will be a "nail in the coffin of détente" and make Russian-American cooperation in other regional conflicts "difficult if not impossible" for the foreseeable future.

"I have trouble with the proposition that the cold war ever stopped," says Harvard Sovietologist Richard Pipes. Pipes is the academic cold warrior par excellence, a thoroughgoing opponent of détente who sees Russia "continuing its subversion in Western Europe and its support for wars of national liberation in Africa and elsewhere."

"It's true that Nixon and Kissinger declared the cold war over," Pipes says. "Then they borrowed the word 'détente' from de Gaulle and used it for domestic political purposes, for a PR campaign. But this 'détente'"—the word rushes out with startling intensity—"lasted only two years or so. We're heading now for very difficult times, I think."

If the declaration of détente (in Pipes's perspective) was a high-powered hype perpetrated in the aeries of Washington, the resumption of the cold war seems at least as much a gambit of media politics.

"At the top, there aren't more than ten men running this cold war issue," a California congressman guesses. He ticks them off: Brzezinski, Senators Daniel Patrick Moynihan and Henry Jackson, former presidential aide Paul Nitze, former Johnson Administration undersecretary of state Eugene Rostow, Pipes, conservative Democratic strategist Ben Wattenberg, columnist George Will, Jackson assistant Richard Perle and Sam Huntington (who, this summer, left the National Security Council and returned to his Harvard teaching post). He may have missed one or two, such as Energy Secretary Schlesinger, *Commentary* magazine editor Norman Podhoretz, Georgia Senator Sam Nunn or former Treasury Secretary John Connally. But it is true that these few politicians, writers, professors and freelance diplomats have been able to engineer a major reversal of American foreign policy with uncommon swiftness.

In the summer of 1974, Democratic politicians who had supported the war in Vietnam to its bitter end issued an anti-détente manifesto. It warned of the "Soviet threat" and argued for a continuation of the American global role that had been so thoroughly discredited in Vietnam. The broadside was written by a foreign policy task force under the direction of Rostow, one of the Vietnam era's superhawks. Rostow's task force was formed under the auspices of the Coalition for a Democratic Majority, a collection of Johnson-Humphrey Democrats who had been beaten by the McGovernites for party power in 1972.

Three days after Jimmy Carter's election in 1976, the Coalition for a

Democratic Majority reanointed itself as the Committee on the Present Danger; in its opening ideological barrage, the committee called for an aggressive policy to counter the "Soviet drive for dominance based upon an unparalleled military build-up." Rostow was on the board of the new committee, along with other leading members of former Republican and Democratic administrations: Kennedy's Secretary of State, Dean Rusk; Nixon's undersecretary of defense, David Packard; and former political switch hitters Connally and Nitze, who served both parties.

In the perspective of the members of the committee, the "present danger" was characterized by the "Soviet build-up" in ground troops, missiles and naval power. It included Russian "adventurism" in Angola and Ethiopia, and aid to black independence groups in Rhodesia, South Africa and Namibia. The committee's moral justification for saber-rattling was the treatment of Jews and dissidents inside Russia (which, predictably, has grown worse ever since the new cold war winds began blowing).

Throughout the first year of his Administration, Carter maintained the momentum of détente, with only an occasional glance over his shoulder at the angry gestures emanating from Present Danger adherents, who had tried but failed to get cold war hard-liners appointed to important foreign–policy making positions. The President left African policy to UN ambassador Andrew Young, who believes that America stands to gain more by supporting black militant movements than by opposing Russian or Cuban influence on that continent. Carter encouraged SALT negotiator Paul Warnke to come up with a new treaty. And a year ago this month, Carter and Brezhnev issued a joint statement on the Middle East, which tied peace in the region to a general East-West accord.

But early this year, cold war fever struck again, this time in a more virulent strain. The problem now was the Horn of Africa, a dry and primitive peninsula comprising Ethiopia, Somalia and Eritrea, where Soviet influence has been strong but inconsistent. The Russians, after all, were summarily kicked out of Somalia (losing their vaunted naval base astride the route of oil tankers from Arabia), and the Cubans have been reluctant to help Ethiopia take control of its rebel province of Eritrea.

For years, Ethiopia had been an American client state. There were secret US intelligence bases there even after the feudal empire of Haile Selassie was overthrown in 1974 by a Marxist military junta. The idea that the Russians would pick up a rebellious American client when the going got rough—as they did—wounded the pride and patriotism of the cold-war-mongers, and soon high-pitched warnings of a Soviet thrust in Africa were being issued by the Present Danger people. Carter's Secretary of State Cyrus Vance tried to cool the issue, but the image of a Russian takeover of a continent had begun to take hold.

The continuing Cuban presence in Angola added to this new sense of peril. Andy Young's observation that the Cubans "stabilized" the political situation in that country—still reeling from a civil war in which South African whites intervened and the CIA meddled—was roundly denounced.

Then, late last May, rebels from the province of Katanga in Zaire reinvaded their homeland. The invaders were part of a contingent of Africans trained in military maneuvers by Cubans in Angola. The cold war lobby promptly tried to sell the invasion as a major setback in East-West relations. While European countries flew in troops to safeguard their extensive mining interests and maintain their economic control, Zbigniew Brzezinski accused the Russians of masterminding an African takeover with Cuban surrogates. (Cuba denied it had any direct involvement in the Katanga invasion, and the CIA now agrees.)

President Carter's popularity was beginning its long spring and summer slump, and his aides decided the image of presidential "softness" was largely responsible. As the rag-tag Katanga invasion ended with the dispatch of French and Belgian paratroops, Carter opened a NATO meeting in Washington with a call for $60 billion in new military expenditures and a warning that "the Soviet Union and other Warsaw Pact countries pose a military threat to our alliance which far exceeds their legitimate security needs." Carter had bought the Present Dangeroid line, at least for a season. In a Naval Academy speech delivered the week after, Carter rattled his MIRVs and told the Soviet Union to choose "confrontation or cooperation." In the ensuing days, he ordered the National Security Council to review all trade deals with Russia to see that American industry was not "transferring technology" to the Soviets.

The cold war scare intensified during the July trials of Jewish dissidents Anatoly Shcharansky and Alexander Ginzburg. When Shcharansky and Ginzburg were found guilty and sentenced to long prison and exile terms, Moynihan called on Carter to cancel Vance's summer trip to the SALT conference in Geneva. "To send Vance to Geneva is to participate in the butchery now going on in the Soviet Union," Moynihan fumed. Carter let Vance go anyway, but he cancelled lower-level contacts. At the same time, Brzezinski went off to Peking; he scrambled up the Great Wall and met with Chinese leaders for eleven hours of talks. "Zbig" called the Russians "international marauders" and joked about whether the US or China should be the first to go into Ethiopia to oppose them.

Meanwhile, former Vietnam doves like Representative Robert Drinan of Massachusetts suggested a US boycott of the Moscow Olympics. Senator Gary Hart of Colorado, who had been George McGovern's campaign manager in 1972, now frequently finds himself in accord with hawkish Senator Nunn in calling for a stronger NATO build-up to meet the Soviet "threat." McGovern himself declared Cambodia an outlaw state and suggested that the US invade the country with other members of the United Nations.

As for the President, he instructed Attorney General Griffin Bell to arrest two suspected Russian spies and put them on trial—a violation of the tacit agreement long honored by the superpowers to repatriate agents rather than subject them to public prosecution. In retaliation, the Russians published the story of an American CIA agent named Martha Peterson, whom they expelled (under the old agreement) last year. Then they arrested an International Harvester tractor sales agent, and accused him of buying rubles on the black market. Charges of slander were lodged against the correspondents of *The New York Times* and *The Baltimore Sun*.

In the space of half a year, the promise of "Nixon's spring" was gone, the hopes of Carter's platform of peace seemed to be buried. If America and Russia were not back at square one, relations had sunk to the lowest point in sixteen years, since John Kennedy faced off with Khrushchev over Berlin and Cuba.

Carl Marcy was staff director of the Senate foreign relations committee during the reign of former Senator J. William Fullbright; now retired from the corridors of power, he continues to watch East-West accords and discords from a perch in a research institute housed in a refurbished slum on Capitol Hill. White haired and soft spoken, Marcy has seen wars hot and cold come and go, and he knows the difference between transient contests and long-term trends. "Relations with the Soviet Union are much, much worse than they've been for many years," Marcy says sadly. "They've seriously deteriorated since Carter took office. I don't know whose fault it is, but I doubt if there will be any improvement at all during the rest of Carter's term."

October 30, 1978, NEW TIMES

✦

Jamaica: Trouble in Paradise

Kingston

The news in Jamaica is all bad. The treasury is bare, the classes are warring, scandal is rife, violence is flaring, and last summer brought floods. But the bigger news this year is a story about the news itself: the wide and wounding war between the island's major newspaper and the government now in power.

It is no small story. *The Daily Gleaner*—Jamaica's dominant daily—has stood as an immovable object in the island's social landscape for 145 years. It now confronts the government of Prime Minister Michael Manley and his Peoples National Party (PNP), which has swept along as an irresistible force in Jamaican politics for the better part of a decade. The result, so far, is a stand-off: neither side will yield, but neither can yet triumph.

The clash between the island's leading newspaper and the Manley government is part of a drama being played out, often with violent results, throughout the Third World. In the Caribbean, the governments of Haiti and

Grenada have clamped down on hostile journalists, and in Guyana, Prime Minister Forbes Burnham recently cut off newsprint supplies to the opposition paper, *The Mirror*. Elsewhere, newspapers have already helped topple regimes: Chile's *El Mercurio* is credited with subverting Allende's Marxist republic; Nicaragua's *La Prensa* led the fight against Somoza.

The issues involved in all of these conflicts—the role of powerful newspapers in climactic social crises, the use of news as a weapon of political warfare, the mobilization of support around the issue of press freedom—stand out in sharp relief against the tense Jamaican background, and the stakes become uncomfortably clear.

The positions of the two sides are easy enough to describe: the *Gleaner* stands for capitalist enterprise, alliance with the West and a conservative sensibility. Manley's government is moving towards socialist development, Third World alignment and an insurgent spirit. But that is just the snapshot view. The daily course of battle reveals the complexities of the conflict, as the *Gleaner* reports and editorializes on what it considers the incompetence, corruption and totalitarianism of the administration and the ruling party. Many of the paper's journalistic themes coincide with those voiced by the opposition Jamaica Labour Party (JLP) and its leader, Edward Seaga. SEAGA: KINGSTON BECOMING THE SUBVERSION CAPITAL OF CARIB., announced the *Gleaner*'s front-page banner one day last October. Other headlines read: JLP DEMANDS PROBE OF POLICE 'RAMPAGE'; PUBLIC SECTOR LABOUR UNREST CONTINUES; SOMEBODY HAS TO STAND UP FOR JAMAICA—SEAGA. Day after day, the headlines hammer away not only at the government's policies but at its very legitimacy.

Inside, a combat brigade of columnists has been sniping at the *Gleaner*'s enemies in the PNP. "These men are irresponsible political juveniles," wrote Wilmot Perkins. "It is now almost impossible to argue in public; one can only abuse," wrote David D'Costa. "If Michael Manley stays in power much longer there is not only increased misery but murder at the end of the road," concluded John Hearne.

But the *Gleaner* is no mere mouthpiece for Seaga and his JLP. It also formulates strategies and orchestrates their execution—as in the pivotal campaign it waged last summer against Cuba's ambassador to Jamaica, whom the paper used to symbolize the evils attributed to Manley's government: seduction by Castroism, affinity for Latin and African radicalism, repression of the press. In many ways, in fact, the *Gleaner* carries more clout than the politicians whose views it favors. "When you come down to it," says Kingston lawyer and journalist Ronald Thwaites, "the *Gleaner is* the opposition."

Across the battle lines, Manley's PNP government charges the *Gleaner* with mendacity, lack of patriotism and subversion. "It's one of the most corrupt journals publishing in the English language," Manley told a private gathering of friends and journalists in his suite at the Plaza Hotel in New York during a visit last fall. He blames the paper for creating a climate of social tension and political violence, which it then presents as news to its local readers and journalistic contacts abroad. The result, Manley says, is civil instability and foreign suspicion, which together could make the country increasingly difficult to govern. Manley supporters tell me that he is convinced that the *Gleaner*'s goal is not merely to topple his administration but to return to power the landed and monied interests that have suffered from recent socialist policies and austerity measures. This "plantocracy" fears continued government attempts to parcel out agricultural lands to peasants, expand state enterprise and control investments and imports.

Gleaner chairman and managing director Oliver Clarke acknowledges a certain class basis to the conflict. "The business community here feels it is under siege from the government," Clarke tells me, "and it looks to the *Gleaner* to be its advocate for free enterprise and a Western style of life."

The *Gleaner*'s advocacy finds resonance in major newspapers and magazines in North America and Britain: *The New York Times*, *The Washington Post*, *The Miami Herald*, *Newsweek* and the London *Daily Telegraph*, among others, seem to accept and repeat the *Gleaner*'s perspectives on Jamaica at face value. The *Gleaner* frequently reprints reports of local events from the foreign press and often amplifies the stories in its news columns. A FREE PRESS AT STAKE IN JAMAICA, read the head over one such reprint of a James Nelson Goodsell article in *The Christian Science Monitor*. "One of the Caribbean's oldest and most courageous newspapers is fighting for its life," read the text.

But nothing promoted the newspaper's international prestige last year as much as the special citation of merit it received from the Maria Moors Cabot Prizes, awarded by Columbia University's Graduate School of Journalism. The citation honored the *Gleaner* for earning "the wholehearted esteem of all who value freedom through its unbiased, fearless and comprehensive reporting and its high standards of journalism."

The Manley government has its overseas friends, too, but they are increasingly detached from Western centers of power. Although he has tried to maintain Jamaica's traditional ties to the United States and to the West—which still provide the bulk of the country's aid and business—Manley has recently emerged as a leader of the Non-Aligned Movement. For him politics has become an intricate, even death-defying, rope dance.

In the final analysis, of course, the contest between the government and the *Gleaner* is about power: each party believes, or at least claims to believe, that its survival is at stake. Tolerances are fine and balances delicate in the social machinery of this small, poor, newly independent island nation of two million people. The opposition of a single paper could not only bring down a government but wreck its entire program of social reform. By the same token, one act of government, such as the restriction of newsprint imports, could silence the only powerful voice of the opposition. Almost everyone here would agree with the conclusion of writer and radio commentator John

Maxwell, a persistent *Gleaner* foe: "It is *journalism* that today is the major political issue in Jamaica, and it is right that it should be."

Both protagonists in the conflict occupy central roles in the life and imagination of the island. To friend and foe alike, Manley is a charismatic personality of heroic stature; the *Gleaner* is, equally unarguably, the island's leading cultural institution. Moreover, their struggle takes on almost mythic proportions by being rooted so deeply in Jamaican history—centuries of slavery; a long struggle against British dominion; the trials of independence within a tightly defined economic framework; and the search for a national cultural identity that every Jamaican can share.

To an American visitor, the *Gleaner* may seem a bit amateurish to have assumed such a pivotal role. Slightly wider and longer than *The New York Times*, it typically prints about 50,000 copies of a daily edition containing twenty to thirty pages and circulates 82,000 copies on Sunday; its afternoon sibling, a racy tabloid called *The Star*, has a circulation of about 45,000. (The government-owned *Jamaica Daily News*, by contrast, has a daily circulation of only about 10,000.) The *Gleaner*'s circulation seems small until one considers that a third of the population is illiterate and that the paper's cost (2.55 Jamaican dollars for seven issues) represents a sizable part of the average weekly income of 50 Jamaican dollars (US $28). Almost everyone who can afford the *Gleaner*, and who lives where newspapers are available, reads it.

Like many less controversial newspapers, the *Gleaner* is more often dull than dashing. The instances of editorial savagery are few—if increasingly frequent—and therefore memorable. But the persistence of the paper's campaign against Manley, its very banality, infiltrates readers' consciousness more effectively, perhaps, than would an uninterrupted stream of horror-tale headlines. Of late the friction between the newspaper and the government has ignited into a wildfire of bitterness, with tensions high and politics polarized as never before.

Months of conflict came to a head last September 24, when, exasperated by coverage in the previous day's edition, Manley angrily adjourned a cabinet meeting and marched most of his ministers to a protest demonstration before the *Gleaner*'s gate. There he joined leaders of the Marxist-oriented Workers Party for a rally that featured expressions of Cuban-Jamaican solidarity, along with denunciations of the *Gleaner*.

The escalation had begun early in the summer, with the *Gleaner*'s campaign against Cuba's new ambassador, Ulises Estrada. In a major story published in late June, before Estrada arrived in Kingston, the paper reported that members of the opposition JLP suspected Estrada of being a Cuban intelligence officer with links to African and Palestinian revolutionary movements. Should these suspicions be confirmed, the newspaper declared, the JLP would "launch demonstrations and pursue him to every corner until he departs." Subsequent editions of the *Gleaner* elaborated on the threat by playing up JLP leader Seaga's charges that "over 5,000 Cubans" were already in the country and that Manley was planning to close the *Gleaner* and to establish a "Cuban-style apparatus" in Jamaica.

In July, Estrada flew into Kingston. Asked at a press conference to comment on the *Gleaner*'s allegations, Estrada called them "lies," and added: "We have means to answer all over the world and to begin to say our truths. . . . If war is declared by anyone, the Cuban revolution has always been characterized by accepting the challenge, and as Comrade Fidel has said, 'When the Cubans say we fight, we fight seriously.'"

Manley interpreted Estrada's retorts as metaphor; the *Gleaner* took them literally, as threats of violent reprisals. In Kingston the street demonstrations which the *Gleaner* had predicted in June began, as the JLP called out protesters to demand the ambassador's expulsion.

The *Gleaner* provided the daily call to battle. In edition after edition, the "Estrada affair" filled news and comment pages alike. Manley and his ministers denied the *Gleaner*'s charges (never documented) that Estrada was a master spy and terrorist *kapo*, and they called the *Gleaner*'s characterization of Estrada's statements "malicious lies." But, urged on by the *Gleaner*, the street marches escalated during the summer and early fall.

The polemical peak was reached on September 23, the day before Manley led his demonstration, when the paper bannered MOUNTING TOURIST CANCELLATIONS across three columns on the front page. The story reported that hotels in the North Shore resorts were swamped with cancellations from American tourists "following [Manley's] anti-American speech at the Non-Aligned Summit in Havana." It added that his statements "could seriously affect the predicted bumper 1979-1980 winter tourist season." Few news stories could have shocked Jamaicans more; tourism is the country's second-largest industry, a major source of foreign exchange, an essential means of financial survival.

But that wasn't all. Next to the "tourist cancellations" story was a large chart reporting a *Gleaner* poll that showed the PNP trailing the JLP in popular support and losing ground to the Workers Party on the left. And, in the ultimate addition of personal insult to political injury, the paper carried a full-page "poster" advertisement calling Manley a JUDAS (in giant letters) who had "sold out Jamaica to the Cubans for less than 30 pieces of silver!" The ad was signed by a spurious "League for Social and Economic Reform" which was assumed by Jamaicans in both parties to be a creature of the JLP. (Hector Wynter, the *Gleaner*'s editor and a former JLP chairman, just shrugs and smiles when asked whether the committee actually existed.)

Both the substance and the style of the paper were startling even for *Gleaner* readers. Manley was humiliated, his finance minister devastated. And so, with that edition, the government itself went into the streets. Arriving at the *Gleaner* building on North Street, Manley climbed into the back of a truck, which served as the speakers' platform, and waited for silence. "I have no speech to make," he told the crowd. "You have made the speech for me and you have made the speech for the progressive forces. . . . But next time . . . next time . . ." Not only the crowd in North Street but also the *Gleaner*'s editors and managers behind the windows overlooking the scene were left to wonder what strictures the Prime Minister might have in mind.

Part of the answer became clear in mid-October, when, further angered by *Gleaner* coverage, a PNP delegation—including five cabinet ministers and the party's general secretary—stalked into the *Gleaner*'s offices to answer the paper's accusations and to present a dossier of countercharges. The group reviled the managers and editors for "publishing articles which are calculated to undermine the confidence of the Jamaican people in public institutions" and "breach the normal standards of decency." The delegates claimed the *Gleaner* was "inciting the people to overthrow the duly constituted government of the country." This went beyond mere political opposition, remarked one of the PNP officials in attendance, who also conceded the right of the *Gleaner* "to give support to the free enterprise system" and "to be pro-imperialist." Said the speaker: "What we charge the *Gleaner* with is that it has breached that basic responsibility" to be "objective and to be fair."

Other PNP officials at the meeting presented the government's responses to the sensational stories run by the *Gleaner*. But the real drama of the event was produced more by what was *not* said—by the history that divided the participants, by class conflict, racial tension, political polarization and the cultural ambivalence that assails the country's elite. Both sides are reported to have been shaken: the PNP because it took on the surviving symbols of colonial power in person; the *Gleaner* because it felt the rage of its enemies face to face. The two sides use the event now for their own purposes. The government claims it has taken the offensive to prove its case against the paper. The *Gleaner* says the delegates' visit was an example of intimidation and an implicit threat to press freedom.

Months later, however, talking to an outsider, some *Gleaner* writers are willing to abandon the official *Gleaner* position—that the paper is doing nothing more than reporting the news. "This has been a ferocious campaign," columnist Hearne tells me. "It would be idle to pretend that there has not been a systematic attack on the government by the *Gleaner*. For myself, my one intention is to get this man Manley out of office, by any fair means at hand."

Despite the rhetoric of the September 24 demonstration before the *Gleaner*'s gates, the Manley government has so far limited itself to replying to the paper with libel suits, verbal attacks in interviews and press conferences, and the ministerial meeting. "The *Gleaner* has been extremely dangerous— ruthless—because they know we're committed to press freedom," Manley said bitterly in New York. "We've been meticulous about setting down our respect for freedom of the press."

While Manley's ideological commitment to democratic freedoms may be one restraining factor, so too is his political sense. He is well aware that the *Gleaner* has the ear of foreign journalists and politicians who together can make or break an economy still heavily dependent on Western business, tourism, aid and credits. A final solution of the *Gleaner* problem would—as a Jamaican teacher put it delicately—place Manley "on the other side of President Carter's human rights issue."

But there is something else about the *Gleaner* that may explain Manley's commitment to its survival: its importance as a cultural institution, one whose very name is invoked by Jamaicans as a synonym for "newspaper" when they ask for "a gleaner" in New York or London. As Jamaicans struggle to achieve an authentic national identity in the wake of centuries of colonialism, the *Gleaner* has something to offer them—whether they like it or not—and that is *legitimacy*. For whatever the political consequences of independence, the cultural links between modern Jamaica and its colonial past remain powerful, particularly for the middle class.

The *Gleaner,* in fact, is the most important institution to survive the colonial period. Founded in the nineteenth century by the deCordovas, a family of Portuguese Jews, the paper developed into the voice of the ruling white plantocracy and of the small, predominantly white commercial elite. Independence, won in 1962, did not alter the paper's colonial-era outlook. The Ashenheims, who married into the deCordova family and now control the largest block of the paper's stock, are interlocked into most major enterprises in Jamaica. Oliver Clarke, the *Gleaner*'s present chairman, is the scion of the family that owns one of Jamaica's biggest plantations, "Paradise," on the island's southwestern tip. Clarke is white; Jamaica is 95 percent nonwhite. He is irretrievably a member of the plantocracy, which is now trying to protect its status, despite pressure from the "brown" middle class and the black peasantry and urban masses.

Much of the *Gleaner*'s potency derives from its plantocratic traditions, its orientation towards the best of Britain and the wealth of America. But the *Gleaner* is no longer a purely "white" institution; the complex political sociology of the island does not break down into discrete racial categories. Nor are the paper's class allies confined to the old colonial elite. In fact, the complexities of race and class on the island give the conflict between Manley and the *Gleaner* its special texture. Manley himself, for example, is a leading member of a new Jamaican elite—the light-skinned, British-educated native bourgeoisie which organized a "brown revolution" against the colonial plantocracy in the 1930s and which came to power at independence.

Until the mid-seventies, there was a tacit agreement between the leading political forces—confirmed in an important measure by the *Gleaner*—to maintain the structure of institutional relationships that existed in 1962. The JLP—supported by the *Gleaner* as the party of the white colonial remnants, the plantation peasantry, and unionized labor dependent on industry and tourism—emphasized foreign investment, maintenance of the plantation economy and a free hand for the foreign bauxite extractors. The more nationalistic PNP—comprising a coalition of newly urbanized black poor and the brown middle class which wanted a share of the wealth and status still in the hands of overseas whites—emphasized expansion of local business, a greater Jamaican share in the profits from bauxite and the development of national cultural institutions. But these were differences in emphasis within a general consensus that assumed Jamaica would primarily follow a Western and capitalist road with only brief excursions into nationalistic welfarist byways. The system seemed to be working well; the sixties brought a strong bauxite market and a tourism boom. A social contract seemed possible.

The JLP was in power from independence through the prosperous years until 1972, and the *Gleaner* generally supported its administration. Towards the end of its run, however, the paper began to pick at the ruling party for the failures of management and innovation common to entrenched administrations. *The Gleaner*'s unhappiness with the JLP helped Manley and the PNP win the elections of 1972. But since the PNP's platform staked out positions well within the post-independence consensus, the *Gleaner* could fairly expect business-as-usual from the Manley administrations. Manley had defined his party's ideology as "democratic socialism," but he had always left the term conveniently vague so that policies of opportunity could be pursued without risking ideological integrity. Grateful for the paper's support, Manley had seized the occasion of the opening of the *Gleaner*'s new offices on North Street in 1970 to praise it. "This is a truly great newspaper," he gushed. "It is sometimes difficult to tell whether your paper is an extension of Jamaica's collective personality or whether that personality is an extension of your paper."

Less than a decade later, Manley's praise had turned to scorn. In that short span of years, Jamaican life had broken sharply along several faults. The consensus that had held together the Jamaican system—a basic agreement on political forms, economic direction and social relations—had ruptured.

By the time Manley came up for re-election in 1976, Jamaica's economic position had deteriorated. The demand for bauxite—Jamaica's leading mineral resource—had fallen off; the market for sugar—the island's primary agricultural export—had sagged; meanwhile, the price of oil was soaring. As inflation and stagnation weakened Western economies, foreign investment dried up, bringing the country to the brink of bankruptcy.

The myriad—and interconnected—economic hardships of the seventies produced a climate of rancor between the government and the *Gleaner*, even as they also began to polarize politics and society. Manley's strategy for survival had domestic and international components: extensive socialist development for a more self-sufficient economy at home—including land reform, diversification of agriculture, expansion of state-run enterprises—and new alliances with non-capitalist countries abroad to help finance the domestic programs. Preparing for the 1976 elections, PNP secretary D.K. Duncan systematically mobilized the most beleaguered part of the population—the unemployed poor of the West Kingston ghettoes—into an unbeatable electoral organization. To the PNP, "DK" was a political marvel; to the *Gleaner*, he was a dangerous radical.

As the PNP developed its new platform for the 1976 elections, the *Gleaner* began warning its readers that Manley's program entailed revolutionary change in Jamaica's political economy, that private investment would fall off and that tourists would be frightened away. The newspaper's fears reflected those of the JLP, which, under Seaga, recently elected as its leader, was moving towards the right.

Political differences turned into social crisis in the summer of 1976, a few months before the elections, when Manley's government declared a state of emergency after claiming to have discovered a plot among opposition militants. The government charged that they planned to launch a campaign of civil disorder that would wound the economy, discredit the administration and so destabilize the society that its democratic foundations might crumble. With the example of Allende's Chile—destabilized only three years earlier—foremost in party leaders' minds, the PNP accused the United States of supporting the campaign.

The JLP charged the emergency was merely an invention to subvert the democratic process during the election. The *Gleaner* kept up a barrage of warnings about a communist threat to Jamaica, and its reports were soon reflected in American newspapers and magazines: *The New York Times*, *Newsweek* and *Business Week* carried scare stories, and a great fear swept through the Jamaican and foreign business communities like a hurricane. The aluminum companies reduced their production by 30 percent. American aid was cut. Jamaica was unable to find a single American bank to give the government a loan, while wealthy Jamaicans and foreigners spirited $300 million out of the country. Private investment dried up. Tourism revenues fell by half.

If, as PNP supporters claimed, the *Gleaner*'s stories were part of a campaign to discredit the Manley administration just before the election, the tactic did not work: the PNP went on to win a smashing victory. But almost from the moment of triumph, Manley was obliged to discard much of his electoral program and, faced with an acute fiscal crisis, to turn for help to the International Monetary Fund.

Primarily a creature of American foreign economic policy, the IMF required that Jamaica comply with rules designed to keep its programs consistent with American models for economic development. The fund demanded a drastic devaluation of the local currency, liberal allowances for the export of capital and profits by foreign investors, controls on wages and the removal of controls on prices. As a result, the cost of living skyrocketed—and in 1978 alone the standard of living for most Jamaicans dropped 35 percent.

Manley paid dearly. The left wing of his party, led by Duncan, walked out *en bloc* when Manley agreed to the IMF demands, and the communist Workers Party suddenly seemed able to command 5 to 10 percent of the national vote, according to various polls. The Prime Minister found himself isolated in a shrinking middle ground—unable, on the one hand, to rouse his popular base with promises of radical change and incapable, on the other, of convincing the business community that he could manage the country along traditional lines.

Discerning Manley's vulnerability, his enemies attacked. Once again siding with the JLP, the *Gleaner* struck repeatedly at the government's economic failures, and, as last summer's heat set in, the paper promoted the opposition's campaign to topple the government with street demonstrations, the agitation against Cuban ambassador Estrada and the consolidation of foreign support around the issue of press freedom.

Manley was faced with the choice of placating his foes in the JLP by adopting programs that would win favor among Western governments and investors, or moving decisively to the left. Finally, believing that the IMF and other Western development strategists were placing unacceptable strains on Jamaican society and, moreover, that Western economies were no longer able to provide sufficient development assistance, Manley chose to go left. The most dramatic evidence of his decision was D.K. Duncan's return to the PNP as party secretary last summer, when he began organizing in the ghettoes and outlying cities as he had successfully done for the 1976 election.

The *Gleaner* and its friends now fear that if Manley does manage to stay in power (he must call elections before March 1982), Jamaica will forsake the "Westminster model" of parliamentary democracy in favor of authoritarian rule. In that process, they believe, the *Gleaner* will be taken out of the hands of its present owners and managers. Such fears have been fed by statements such as one made at an Inter-American Press Association dinner by Arnold Bertram, the minister of information and culture. The *Gleaner*'s "negativism," he told the journalists, is "not freedom of the press; this is freedom of property. They simply own the press and from this position dictate what is to be put in it." Those more favorably disposed towards the Manley government saw nothing more in Bertram's distinction than a Caribbean echo of A.J. Liebling's famous dictum that "freedom of press is guaranteed only to those who own one." Its enemies thought otherwise.

Trouble in paradise always takes time to detect: the tropics splash a lush and lazy humor across the surface of the most desperate scenes. Not that Kingston is an obvious Eden; the capital contains more than a third of the island's population, crowded into shantytowns whose wretchedness is unrelieved by the vista of high-rise hotels and, beyond, the Blue Mountain foothills, among which lie the shady suburbs, perched out of harm's way.

The tension runs high in Kingston, and the social polarization is so extreme that everyone is drawn into the drama—even a visitor who comes down for a few days—and every incident is charged with significance. To talk to Jamaicans is to learn that few common assumptions survive or agreements exist. There is really no longer a social contract here, and the question of how Jamaican society is to be ordered remains to be answered. Differences over rights and privileges within the social order now resolve themselves into one primary question: Who shall rule?

It's easy for Americans to resort to First Amendment principles and the certitudes of a consensual society. But in Jamaica such concepts as freedom of the press or loyal opposition no longer have an absolute definition. "We all believe in freedom," a teacher friend said one afternoon as we strolled across the campus of the University of the West Indies on the outskirts of Kingston. "But we do not agree on what it means. Does it mean the freedom to destroy freedom? The freedom of the powerful to deny the freedom of the weak? Or will it be the freedom of the many poor to gain power over the few rich?"

"It is getting to that point down here," he continued. "This is no abstract argument about freedom of the press. This is a bloody class struggle, man, and you're in the middle of it. You'll be lucky to get out of here alive."

March/April 1980, COLUMBIA JOURNALISM REVIEW

Afternote: For the remainder of 1980, Jamaica was awash with violence; 500–600 died, many in the month preceding the October elections, which Manley lost to Seaga. Manley had finally broken with the IMF's "stabilization" programs, and relief from the US, in the form of aid or debt relief, was not forthcoming. ("It's . . . the Castro thing," one New York banker explained.) After the election Congress hurried $40 million to Jamaica, which the *Congressional Quarterly* described as a reward for the country's voting in Seaga.

✦

One-and-a-Half (Strangled) Cheers for the USSR

"If pigs had wings," Nikita Khrushchev liked to say, "they could fly." If global politics were described in pleasant patterns, if might and money were apportioned in even measure, if the manners of great nations were ruled by sturdy morals—then the new Carter Doctrine might be graven on tablets, set on high (perhaps at the Khyber Pass) and honored as revealed truth. But pigs still wallow in the slime, and this unpleasant, unequal and unstable world is not a single battleground where one superpower of darkness wages a bitter struggle against the other of light. Carter's creed is a contrivance of error and slander, designed to defend imperial greed and to assault historical fact. "It is wrong," as the Caterpillar says to Alice, "from beginning to end."

The real world (as it has evolved since World War II) is convulsed in a crisis of revolution and reaction, imperialism and liberation, insurgency and repression. For reasons neither pure nor simple, the Soviet Union has almost invariably sided with the revolutionaries, the liberationists, the insurgents. The United States, with equal consistency, has supported the enemies of rebellion. There is nothing tidy, honorable or even predictable in this reality; alliances shift, support is ephemeral, intentions are suspect and even definitions are arguable. But the balance at the bottom is clear enough: without the power of the USSR present as a global threat, hardly a single war of colonial liberation or social revolution would have succeeded in these three decades.

Looking from present to past, Russian power is in some large degree responsible for:

§ the success of the Patriotic Front in Zimbabwe;

§ the abdication of the Shah of Iran;

§ the victory of the revolution in Mozambique;

§ the success of the MPLA in Angola;

§ the victory of the PAIGC revolution in Guinea-Bissau;

§ the defeat of the American invasions of Vietnam, Laos and Cambodia;

§ the revolution in Ethiopia;

§ the revolution in South Yemen;

§ the revolution in Somalia;

§ the attempted revolt of the Dhofaris against the feudal lords of Oman;

§ Northern Yemeni independence from Saudi Arabian rule;

§ mobilization of international support for Allende's government in Chile;

§ consolidation, defense and upkeep of the Cuban revolution;

§ the revolution in Afghanistan;

§ Sukarno's successful independence struggle against the Dutch in Indonesia;

§ Ben Bella's fight against the French in Algeria;

§ Nasser's overthrow of British colonialism and American neocolonialism in Egypt;

§ success of nationalist movements in Ghana and Mali;

§ survival of North Korea when the American troops pushed north of the 17th parallel to the Yalu River;

§ survival of the Western European left during the cold war;

§ survival and growth of the Chinese People's Republic in the dicey days when many Americans urged Eisenhower to "unleash Chiang" against the mainland;

§ maintenance of the independence of India;

§ and, perhaps most important of all, creation of political space for the development of a bloc of nonaligned states which can maneuver, bargain and maintain independence from both great imperial powers. From

Jawaharlal Nehru to Joshua Nkomo, leaders of national independence and revolutionary socialist movements owe at least some of their success to the *presence*—if not the material aid—of the one superpower willing and able to provide a counterbalance to Western expansionism.

All of this, however, took place in the real world, with its dreadful complications and depressing contradictions. In another kind of Wonderland, all the rebellions and revolutions would have progressed in orderly fashion, the masses would share in the decisions that affect their lives, and the power that aided their struggle would retire once the battle was won. As it is, one Washington researcher who helped me compile this list found little to cheer.

"In some cases," he said, "one imperial tyranny was exchanged for another; in many cases, independent local regimes are as repressive as the colonial ones, or worse; in a lot of cases, the Russians didn't come through with any economic aid or military support at a crucial point and the revolutions failed; in some of the most important cases, the Russians got booted out, and became enemies of the people they helped put in power. What I would like to see is a situation in which these movements didn't have to go to Russia for help."

Unfortunately, there seem to be no other alternatives. The Vietnamese revolutionaries, for all their legendary courage, fortitude and ingenuity, could not have lasted long with only General Giap's guerrilla handbook; they needed SAMs, AK-47s, food, trucks and technical help. The MPLA would have been demolished by the other two Angolan nationalist groups and incorporated into the US–South African system if they had not let tens of thousands of Russian-backed Cuban troops into their homelands. And despite the imagination and momentum of the Cuban revolution itself, Castro could not have withstood alone the multiple pressures from America ninety miles away.

They all paid a heavy price for that help. But anyone whose sympathies lie with the enemies of American intervention in Vietnam, Portuguese and South African exploitation of Angola, the Batista/Mafia tyranny in Cuba and even the feudal tradition in China must acknowledge the USSR's historic help. Those on the other side know the score very well.

In many instances, the mere fact of Russia's power is enough to help rebellions, even if no tangible aid is forthcoming. With its nuclear arsenal and military might, Russia provides a permanent check on extravagant adventures of the West. Moreover, Russia's ability to align itself with revolutionary movements in the most oppressed places often forces the United States to enact "moderate" reforms when its allies prove intractably cruel. To diminish the likelihood of Soviet inroads in strategic countries, the CIA carried out the assassination of Trujillo in the Dominican Republic; Kennedy agreed to the overthrow of Diem in South Vietnam; and Carter convinced Somoza to leave Managua and the Shah to flee Tehran—all to insure that the left parties in those countries would not grow strong enough to control the government.

All too often, at that point, the USSR abandons those who profited from the global stand-off. Russia hardly raised an eyebrow when the Ayatollah Khomeini cracked down on the Iranian left. In Chile, despite expressions of support, Russia let President Allende twist slowly in the wind, refusing even to "signal" retaliation against the Nixon Administration's successful destabilization program.

In Afghanistan and Ethiopia, where the USSR supplied massive material aid, the revolutions paid a different price—pervasive control by Moscow and the imposition of Russian institutional models drawn from the sterile, rigid forms created by the Soviet bureaucracy.

Now it seems that the United States is making another in a long series of attempts to diminish both the Soviets' latent power of tremendous amounts of retaliation and its access to various revolutionary movements, by provoking and capitalizing on its intervention in Afghanistan. Afghanistan is clearly a pretext for the current crisis. As early as last summer, the promotion of a phony confrontation over the Soviet "combat force" in Cuba—which had been there for years and posed no threat at all—signalled a new strategy in Washington. The mood was intensified by Brzezinski's insistence on linkage of Soviet good behavior to ratification of SALT II. Yet when the Russians removed tanks and troops from East Germany to prove their good faith, Carter denounced the move, decided to go ahead with the MX missile, ordered a 5 percent raise of the Pentagon's budget and okayed new long-range missiles for Europe (that is, for Germany—Russia's historic enemy). SALT was dead.

That strategy has become the Carter Doctrine. It purports to set down principles for confronting Soviet power, but on closer analysis it reveals more about American preoccupation with Third World revolution and American imperial shrinkage than with the "Russian threat."

Even at its superpowerful best, the Soviet Union is as far from "burying" Western capitalism today as when Khrushchev prophesied the event back in 1961. By the accounting of several Washington defense analysts and tank thinkers, the Western bloc (with its new ally, China) commands about 70 percent of the world's military and economic power; the Soviet bloc controls about 20 percent; and the remaining 10 percent is genuinely uncommitted to either side.

On a good day, Russia can demand the allegiance of nineteen countries (out of the 152 in the UN), and the good days are getting fewer and far between. Many of that small coterie defected recently on the vote against Russian troops in Afghanistan. Russia has "lost" more important allies in recent years than it has gained: Egypt, India, Iraq, Indonesia and Somalia are now either distant or hostile to the USSR. Russia's historic fear of "encirclement" by hostile forces can hardly be diagnosed as political paranoia, what with US Defense Secretary Harold Brown negotiating military deals with China and the US Navy cramming ships in the Indian Ocean like rubber ducks in Carter's bathtub.

Outside the Western Hemisphere, the United States has about 200 military bases and a force of some 450,000 military personnel—in countries like Saudi Arabia, Japan, South Korea and West Germany. Outside of its bordering satellites in Eastern Europe, the Soviet Union has about 10,000 military personnel stationed in its friendly states of Cuba and Ethiopia—as well as its invasion force of 100,000 soldiers (according to Pentagon figures) in Afghanistan. America's borders are so secure that it needs no similar military defenses of the homeland: the US military force in Canada numbers 600. But when a Western Hemispheric state is threatened by leftist insurgency, America can move its troops quickly: Lyndon Johnson sent 40,000 marines into the Dominican Republic in 1964 at the merest hint of a pro-Cuban revolt. The Dominican Republic is about 7 percent the size of Afghanistan, with a quarter of the population.

According to foreign policy analyst Richard Barnet, the United States intervened militarily in foreign countries on the average of once every eighteen months between 1947 and 1965. The USSR has intervened militarily on three occasions between 1947 and 1980: in Hungary, Czechoslovakia and Afghanistan. Barnet's figures do not count "surrogate" interventions, such as the United States' war against Patrice Lumumba's revolutionary government in the Congo in the early sixties, or the Soviets' support for Cuba's role in Angola. A Brookings Institution study showed that there were 215 American "shows of force" between 1947 and 1975.

It may be true—as many sincere leftists in the US and Europe argue—that the USSR has been the worst possible champion of revolutions all over the world. The fact remains, however, that it is the only possible source of support in the world of real possibilities. The only other candidate for that role was China, but despite its size and zeal, its military and industrial power is limited. More than that, China has rarely been in the position or the mood to give more than rhetorical support to other revolutions. After its foray into neighboring North Korea (an act of self-defense against a real and present danger of US invasion) it withdrew to contemplate and construct its own society. Its aid to Vietnam during the French and American wars was problematic. I was in North Vietnam in early 1968, and one day, on a trip through the mountains to the northwest of Hanoi, I asked my government guide how much help the Chinese were giving. Usually guarded in his comments about Vietnam's socialist comrades, he suddenly showed emotion: "They're crazy," he said forcefully. "They've stopped the trains and they're holding political meetings instead of sending supplies. They're completely hopeless." Even the promises of aid stopped after the war ended, and in 1978 China invaded its comrade neighbor.

Soon the Chinese were backing every reactionary butcher they could find:

Pinochet in Chile, Zia in Pakistan, the Shah in Iran, Mobutu in Zaire (with a military mission and economic aid), Pol Pot in Cambodia. Their favorite European political leaders are Conservative Prime Minister Thatcher in England and the ultra-right Franz-Josef Strauss in Germany, both of whom have been enthusiastically received in Beijing. And, of course, Nixon . . .

Khrushchev—alone among recent Soviet leaders—used to spout off about the revolutionary morality of Russian support for wars of liberation, but such morality is of course entirely conditioned on self-interest. The global game is played by a set of rules established years ago: the US gets the dictators and the ruling classes, and the Soviet Union gets the masses and the revolutionary movements. Occasionally the rules are suspended: the USSR supports the right-wing junta in Argentina against its guerrilla rebellion, and for that charity the generals will supply the Soviets with wheat (enough to make up for the current US embargo). Russia also has withheld support from the worthy Polisario movement fighting the US-backed Kingdom of Morocco.

For its part, the United States occasionally inherits anti-colonialist governments when the Russians really muck up: Egypt, Somalia and Iraq are recent examples. In most instances, the US soon attempts to turn its new wards into imperial outposts: the Pentagon is preparing to build its Indian Ocean base in Somalia this very month, and Sadat's Egypt has become a complete client of the US.

But outside the Wonderland where the Carter Doctrine is recited, self-interest rules, and those who make the most of it win the day. If the Soviet Union did not exist, revolutionaries would have to invent a substitute. Perhaps it would be better engineered, without the deformities, malfunctions and ubiquitous bugs. But for now we have to live with the state-of-the-art model, even if we condemn its grotesque design and dangerous demands. After all, as E.H. Carr—the great chronicler of the Russian Revolution—wrote, "an historian can praise the achievements of the reign of Henry VIII without being supposed to condone the beheading of wives."

I came face to face with Carr's unresolvable contradiction one drizzly August morning in Prague a dozen years ago. While most Americans were watching the radical anti-war movement and the youth culture suffer its finest hour in Chicago at the Democratic convention, I rode into the Czech capital on an unscheduled train called the Mozart Express, which somehow managed to run the Russian blockade of the Austrian border after Moscow's invasion of the newly "liberal" Czechoslovakia. I was one of two passengers to alight at the Prague station; there were no taxis, porters, trams or buses, and I lugged my suitcase and a portable typewriter through deserted streets to the great central Wenceslaus Square. It was filled with Russian tanks and Russian soldiers, and small bands of Czechs stood around each man and machine, arguing and shouting in a language I could not fathom.

The walls were covered with slogans: "Vietnam=Czechoslovakia" seemed to be the favorite. There was no shooting, but no work or business either, and it was easy to meet people—especially students—who spoke English. That first night I joined a group of them as they roamed the city spray-painting anti-Soviet graffiti and throwing paving stones and beer bottles at the tanks. My sympathies were with their cause from the start, and we spoke about the similarities of Lyndon Johnson's invasion of the Dominican Republic—a client moving out of America's grasp—to Russia's invasion of its satellite. Here was a clear case of the "beheading of wives" no humane observer could condone. Soviet imperial control of its satellites, I always believed, has a drastically different meaning than its imperial support for Third World independence movements; there could be no revolutionary apology for the Eastern European policy, only a military rationalization.

The next noon I visited the mission of the National Liberation Front of South Vietnam, whose struggle I found equally worthy in that year of Tet. To my dismay, an NLF representative told me how much he welcomed the Soviet invasion. One of the features of liberal Premier Dubcek's "Czech Spring" was the total withdrawal of all aid to Vietnam. As I remember it, the Czechs suddenly stopped work on a telecommunications system they were building in North Vietnam and brought their men and money home. They pursued a similar withdrawal from Cuba. With their savings, they would concentrate on developing the kind of consumer society many Czechs envied in the West. So much for liberation in the Third World.

I know I gave no intelligent response to the NLF man's argument. I detested the Russian intervention, but I also understood the Vietnamese support. They had no other option in the real world. In a different history, both Czech independence and the Vietnamese revolution might have been mutually compatible. And I remembered another Russian proverb: "If grandma had a beard, grandma would be grandpa."

April 11, 1980, THE VILLAGE VOICE

✦

Lennon Without Tears

John Lennon's global send-off Sunday was more a coronation than a funeral, an act of elevation rather than a last goodbye. In a way that was unpredicted and unpredictable, "our Beatle" is now our king, the immortal incarnation of the spirit of the sixties, the defining figurehead of a formless generation. In the parks and public squares from Liverpool to LA the multitudes mourned, but that show of grief was also an act of homage—to the single songsmith, saint and symbol who now sums up everything we are.

Mere mortal monarchs express the essence of their bounded realms. In their years on the throne (or, in the case of democratic royalty, in their terms in office) they serve to unify their subjects by the ritual affirmation of the national character—that special Englishness, Dutchness, Frenchness. But death can confer a curious immortality and an unbounded domain on heroes. "Lennon Lives"—a conspicuous slogan scrawled on signboards in Central Park—rings true: the posthumous president (he might prefer the democratic form) of Woodstock Nation will permanently define the specialness of a generation that transcends frontiers, class and ideology. Young insurgent workers in Gdansk, lawyers in Atlanta, nurses in New York, supermarket stockmen, computer programmers, wheeler-dealers, stars and layabouts who came of age in the Beatle years have finally found a focus in John Lennon.

The appointment of a spiritual leader presents a crisis in personal identity as well as social history, and Sunday's ceremony contained both of those elements. The cab driver who drove us home from the park had been listening to a live broadcast of the event on the radio, but he was curious about the "feeling" in the park. "Will you remember it for the rest of your life?" he asked.

I was momentarily startled by the gravity of his question, but I hardly hesitated to answer yes. It had the "feeling" of Woodstock, of the 1969 antiwar mobilization in Washington: those massive gatherings that served as identity checks as well as historical blips. People in the park last Sunday stared intensely at one another, as they might study themselves in a mirror. What they saw, at the very least, was the persistence of their past.

There have been crowded concerts and sectarian rallies in the past decade, but none of them have had the inclusive, definitive character of the great gatherings of the sixties—until the Lennon memorial. Once more, ten years after, we recognized the specialness of our "nationhood," appraised—and maybe mourned—our history. Everything was the same—and different.

My friend Roger, a lawyer in his early 30s, told me that he wandered through the throng alone, trying to detect the collective sensibility he knew "in the old days." But although the people *looked* right, they emanated isolation instead of community. "There was nothing to connect us," he said sadly, "except the memory of how we once were connected."

Lennon knew all about isolation; he wrote a song about it nine years ago. Indeed, his creative genius and his historical importance consist in large measure in an unerring sense of prophecy and timing. Fans be damned, he broke up the Beatles at the moment he saw that the group had lost its dynamic of artistic development. His politics were sincere but safe: give peace a chance rather than struggle and trash. "The war is over," he exclaimed, but the wish did not make the fact. "All you need is love" was comforting but inadequate. Soon he recoiled at the increasingly revolutionary adventures of the militants and proclaimed that he didn't want a revolution at all; in fact, he counselled his fans simply to "let it be."

As the counterculture drifted into drugs, mysticism and exotic psychotherapies, Lennon led the parade, acid-tripping, Maharishi-grouping and primal-screaming. Long before Tom Wolfe, Lennon announced the advent of the Me Generation, declaring his disbelief in every cause, cult hero and movement—the Kennedys, Gita, Zimmerman, the Beatles: "I just believe in me; Yoko and me."

Once a working-class hero, he now was a captain of the *haute bourgeoisie,* multiplying his fortune by dealing in ranching, real estate and other diversified enterprises. Like the rest of the Beatles generation, his work and his life were becoming private rather than communal. Even his good deeds were personal: for charity, he gave turkeys and woolen scarves to the needy in his West Side neighborhood. At last, he idealized the nuclear family ideal with a pluperfect marriage, a quiet life in the Dakota and a new record of unrelenting sentimentality. He could be inducted into the Moral Majority. No wonder he succeeded; more than any other performer of his era, he was a "crossover" phenomenon, adulated by the mass media and the alternative culture. He no longer posed a threat to the arbiters of good manners and the protectors of public order. Quite the other way: here was a living lesson of how an unruly, undisciplined youth of the lower class could acquire good manners and morals, not to mention an estate of $235 million.

Lennon's life is replete with contradictions—as are the lives of those for whom he is now a spiritual avatar. The generational character he defines is informed by the same dreams and delusions, the confrontations and evasions that Lennon experienced. There is no way, of course, to avoid the contradictions—to defeat isolation, pretend that money is unimportant, forget charity, deprive oneself of loving intimacy. They are facts of a larger social reality that rock musicians can never revise. The best anyone can do in the face of history is to act with as much inner honesty and authenticity as possible— and that, above all, is how Lennon achieved his heroic stature.

A week ago no one would have imagined the immense impact of John Lennon's death. If a list had been drawn up of potential cult heroes of the 1960s, his name might well have been included, but in fact he had slipped out of the limelight for so long that his social significance was drastically diminished. Only in death did his real role become clear. Who else is there? No political activist, no movie star, no other performer comes close: Dylan is too bitter and guilt-ridden, Jagger suffers from retarded adolescence, the other Beatles are ordinary people, Tom Hayden is abrasive, Abbie Hoffman is a goof, Jane Fonda is shallow.

Lennon had honesty, authenticity, courage, depth, warmth and vision— the best qualities of the sixties generation. He projected a dream of utopia where peace, love and community reigned unchallenged by meanies. Cynics may scorn, but that utopian vision is what gave the people of the sixties a measure of meaning to their lives that they remember well but may never see again.

Even the remembrance of utopia gives that generation a unique coherence as it travels through the decades—the rat moving through the body of a python, intact and isolated from everything before and behind it, still self-conscious and undigested. Imagination of perfection does not create utopia, but it offers hope that can make action and living worthwhile. Its opposite— despair—is all too prevalent in this day and age, and it leads nowhere. John Lennon never was a nowhere man.

December 17, 1980, THE SOHO NEWS

✦

Slow Bay of Pigs

A merica's secret war in Nicaragua is not so secret anymore. The remnants of former dictator Somoza's brutal National Guard—trained, equipped and directed by US military and intelligence agencies—are moving out of their camps on the Honduran border in increasing numbers, penetrating deeper into Nicaraguan territory and striking at economic and political targets. The Somocista platoons terrorize villages, disrupt commerce, sabotage transportation and communications. Their ultimate objective is the overthrow of the Sandinista revolution in Managua. But they have a long way to go.

The cover on the covert action was blown last winter by *Newsweek* and other publications, which ran astonishingly detailed reports on the US-run training camps, the shipments of military equipment and the general plans for the Somocista invasion. The Reagan Administration never contradicted the reports or denied the details, but neither did it confirm the American involvement. Since then, the war has escalated in the field and in the headlines, but Washington remains silent on its role and steadfast in its fantastic assertion that the conflict is an "internal" affair of the Nicaraguans. No one except America's Honduran and Salvadoran proxies believes the official version; Jeane Kirkpatrick is utterly isolated when the issue is raised in the United Nations Security Council. But in Congress, opposition to Reagan's war has been slow to build, and the press seems to have upped its evidentiary demands from smoking guns to full confessions.

What is actually going on is an invasion by degrees, a slow Bay of Pigs, a stop-go counterrevolution waged without apology or explanation. Presidents have become more sophisticated in their foreign adventures since 1961, when John Kennedy sent a go-for-broke battalion to Cuba. But after Vietnam, the United States became more circumspect about precipitous intervention in Third World affairs. The plan now is for cautiously increasing pressure to destabilize the Sandinistas, to destroy Nicaragua's developing social order and cripple its vulnerable economy, to make life miserable for the people and to make government impossible for the revolutionary leadership.

The lesson of Cuba is still clear. Despite Kirkpatrick's claims, there is no internal military resistance to the Sandinistas in Nicaragua, and the idea that an outside invasion force will be joined by a spontaneous uprising of the populace is as absurd as it was in Cuba two decades ago. But the success of the new fallback strategy of invasion-by-attrition is not so assured as the Administration believes. It may require the use of Honduran troops along-side the Somocistas, with full US support in the air and great infusions of money and equipment. The Pentagon has already built a huge air traffic control facility in Honduras, and its purpose can hardly be to facilitate tourist flights to Tegucigalpa.

When the Administration came into office, it put out the word that it wanted to "take one of *their* pieces off the board"; that "somebody armed by *us* must beat somebody armed by *them*." It tried Libya; that didn't come off. It worked on Poland; no-go there, either. Now the target is Nicaragua, and time is running out. It is a moment of enormous danger, not only for the Nicaraguans but for the region—and the hemisphere—as well.

April 9, 1983, THE NATION

✦

The Return of Cold War Liberalism

"**L**iberalism is out of fashion," Arthur Schlesinger Jr. wrote from the lower depths of the 1950s, "and liberals are out of office." The cold war of that decade did more than freeze East-West relations. It produced a profound chilling effect on the exercise of progressive politics on the home front. Excluded from power and denied prestige, the liberal brokers of the New Deal generation had to scramble merely to stay alive. And out of their isolation and insecurity—and their struggle for survival—came a new category of political behavior: cold war liberalism. It was both a sensibility and a strategy, a defensive posture towards the warriors of the right and an aggressive attack on the rebels of the left. Looking right, the cold war liberals affirmed the end of ideology, the vitality of the center, the failure of the socialist god. Looking left, they baited the hell out of Reds, fellow travellers and "progressives" in general.

Now a new chill is in the air. The powerful producers of the plays of history have opened a sequel to their old cold war hit, and many of the cultural props that supported the first run are coming back into style. There's a retro look to the political landscape, the feel of the Dulles days. Rebellion, utopias and tender-mindedness are out; conformity, realism and hard-heartedness are in. Liberals—who always managed to mediate the terms of discourse—are out of high office and high fashion, and once more many of them have enlisted in a cold war, with their familiar postures and attacks.

The liberal media are in the forefront. CBS's *60 Minutes*, that exemplar of electronic liberalism, hounds the National and World Council of Churches for allegedly supporting Marxism, revolution and lesser heresies, with a ferocity its correspondents usually reserve for corrupt politicians and quacks. *The New York Times* baits the old left, the New Left and lefts yet unborn for a variety of political sins and ideological errors.

The Washington Post's editorial page is suddenly strident in its attacks on certain leftist organizations within the nuclear freeze and disarmament movement. *The New Republic* lets hardly a week go by without detecting the rebirth (or the persistence) of Stalinism in all the old familiar places on the left. Similar seizures occur with increasing frequency in the editorial chambers of *Harper's, Newsweek,* even *The New York Review of Books*, and at the major television networks.

There are more examples every day, but the new cold war liberalism goes far beyond a simple series of journalistic attacks on leftist positions in a few *causes célèbres.* It is a wide, deep and diffuse campaign against the left itself, a contest to define history, to capture political icons, terms and totems. It is a battle for legitimacy, waged by leading lights of liberalism against those on their political and cultural left flank. It is the first wave of an advancing cold war culture, propelled by the neoconservative and New Right tides of the recent past, which will touch all that we think and do in the period ahead.

It is Susan Sontag in a speech at a Solidarity rally at Town Hall in New York City in February 1982, accusing many of her former comrades of countenancing communist authoritarianism and aggression. It is Irving Howe, in his recently published book, *A Margin of Hope: An Intellectual Autobiography*, berating the New Left of the 1960s for its immature tolerance of Stalinism. It is David Horowitz and Peter Collier, in *Rolling Stone*, trashing the SDS and the Weather Underground as orgies of sex and violence, without regard or sympathy for the radical movement's historical context or political analysis. It is Timothy Garton Ash, in *Harper's*, comparing the antinuclear Green Party to the Nazis because of its idealism. It is the *CBS Evening News* insinuating that President Mitterrand's compact with the Communist Party has brought a wave of terrorism to France. It is the uncritical broadcasting of rumors about KGB plots, Libyan hit squads, Bulgarian conspiracies. It comes from Flora Lewis, Ronald Radosh, David Denby, the brothers Kalb, Morley Safer: liberals all, to some degree, writing and speaking in ideological phrases and accusatory tones not heard in this country since the end of the 1950s.

Anyone with an eye and an ear for the nuances of a new sensibility should be able to detect the telltale signs of the new cold war culture. Political discourse has shifted rightward; whole topics are excluded; fundamental arguments—about revolution, for example—have been dropped from conversation. There is an inordinate amount of talk these days about national security, military strategy, subversion and terrorism. The Soviet Union is again a pariah state. Throughout, discussions of public issues have an ideological spin, and criticisms are hurled with a prosecutorial power that is strongly suggestive of the fifties. Politics *feels* different.

The new cold war liberals are not to be confused with the New Right or the neoconservatives, who are illiberal across the board—on social welfare, civil liberties, racial and sexual equality, the environment and cultural styles. The cold war liberals are still left of center on most of those issues most of the time. CBS is committed to "soup-line journalism," exploring the downside of Reaganomics. *The New Republic* is staunchly civil libertarian. *The New York Times* is for clean air and pure water, even at corporate expense. *The Washington Post* speaks out strongly for civil rights.

What unites these still-liberal voices is a concern with loyalty, subversion and national security reminiscent of that displayed by the old cold war liberals. The issues are defined with more sophistication than they were three decades ago, but the objectives are basically the same.

Take the matter of loyalty. In the 1950s, the working definition was simple: allegiance to the United States and not to the Soviet Union. CP membership was considered *prima facie* proof of disloyalty, and non-card-carrying fellow travellers had only to be shown to be adherents of the "party line" to be outlawed as well. In the 1980s the loyalty issue is more ambiguous because the limits of the left are not coterminous with the membership of the Communist Party (or *any* radical party), or even with an identifiable conspiracy of communists-cum-fellow travellers who slavishly follow Moscow's orders. The new loyalty battle is being fought largely in a single arena—the nuclear freeze and disarmament movement. Some of its liberal sympathizers call for the expulsion of communists, as well as their "stooges" and "dupes," from the movement.

Some of the critics (who often have personal histories of radical activism in the 1960s) claim that the communists, by dint of their single-minded dedication and demonic energy, will "take over" peace coalitions and "subvert" them to their own ends, thus weakening the potential for mass mobilization. For example, Ronald Radosh reported in *The New Republic* that a communist member of the executive board of the June 12 Rally Committee wanted last year's giant pro-freeze demonstration in New York City to endorse "such demands as a call for an end to U.S. intervention in Central America." That and similar appeals to "mushy logic," he warned, would drive out clear-thinking types who might otherwise demonstrate against nuclear war.

Here is a classic case of the "mush shift," a deft maneuver practiced by the old cold war liberals. The purpose, then and now, is to deflect right-wing accusations of being muddle-headed and tender-minded onto the far left. It was practiced in antiquity by Arthur Schlesinger, who drew the line between the tender and the tough in his 1949 book, *The Vital Center*, the bible of cold war liberal thought. The maneuver was part of the larger process of blame-shifting that became the liberals' standard technique of cold war survival. Of course, they insisted that their motives were moral rather than self-interested, patriotic rather than protective. They saw the evil of communism and the perfidy of communists, they said, and it was their duty to condemn wrong thinking and wrong doing. But while their intentions may indeed have been high-minded, their actions subverted their motives. What they did was destroy the left while hardly denting international communism (that fight was carried on by the generals of capitalism, not their liberal lieutenants). Cold war liberalism's pre-eminent preoccupation—and its primary target—was the American left, and it succeeded mightily in its destructive work.

Why has that preoccupation returned, like a long-buried fear-fantasy in the still of the night? Why are the new cold war liberals so concerned with loyalty, legitimacy and limpness of mind? It cannot be that a handful of American communists pose a clear and present danger to Reagan's republic by their putative disloyalty, even if all the dupes, stooges and fellow travellers are lumped with them. Nor does their presence in the peace movement seem to be having any deleterious effect on its organizing efforts, or on its success in recruiting Middle Americans. In fact, the cold war liberals are more worried about pressure from the right than any danger to the disarmament movement from the left. The calumny originates with President Reagan: the peace movement is "inspired by not the sincere, honest people who want peace, but by some who want the weakening of America and so are manipulating honest people and sincere people." With Senator Jeremiah Denton: four groups advising Peace Links, the women's organization sponsoring National Peace Day, "are either Soviet controlled or openly sympathetic with, and advocates for, communist foreign policy objectives." With *Reader's Digest*: the "patriotic, sensible people who make up the peace movement have been penetrated, manipulated and distorted to an amazing degree by people who have but one aim—to promote Communist tyranny by weakening the United States."

And how do the new cold war liberals respond? Just as in the old days, by calling the dogs off themselves and sicking them on the left. The objective effect of such attacks, whatever the claimed motive, is to destroy both radical consciousness and radical activity as legitimate parts of political life.

Loyalty as an issue is now complex. The left of the 1930s, which became the "generation on trial" of the 1950s, had an alien cast—in origin or allegiance—whereas the contemporary left has an all-American look. It was spawned on native soil, derived largely from the New Left, nurtured in the civil rights and anti-war campaigns, and multiplied by the myriad movements of the succeeding years. It is hardly alien, and attempts to brand it disloyal require more elegant arguments than those used before.

Irving Howe, perhaps the greatest living arbiter of acceptable and unacceptable styles of leftism, unveiled some of the arguments against the New Left in a landmark article, "The Decade That Failed," which was published in *The New York Times Magazine* last September. In this excerpt from *A Margin of Hope*, he looked back in sorrow for the movement and in anger at those who did the damage: the "self-styled revolutionists," the "rigid" author-

itarians, the white Marxist-Leninists, the black "Mau Maus," the naive
utopians, the student Stalinists—all the familiar terms in the arsenal of
charges that liberals now use against the New Left.

Describing a decade as "failed," as Howe does the 1960s, is rather like calling a generation "lost." It is an expression of one's own disappointment and
despair rather than a description of historical reality. Certainly there are
arguments enough for those who would maintain that the social and political
upheavals of the sixties had enormously positive as well as negative consequences, even measured against the rigorous standards of a social democrat
like Howe. But the inquests on the sixties performed by Howe and others
who have taken to baiting the New Left radicals are not primarily efforts to
understand history; they are attempts to write it in their own terms, for
their own ends.

The decade of the 1960s is a cultural artifact up for grabs—just as other
decades were on the block when the earlier cold war liberals began grading
their own loyalty tests. The far right of the McCarthy period thought the
1930s a season of treason perpetrated by communists and New Dealers.
The old cold war liberals then made their favorite distinction: the decade
had failed because of the Reds, and the loyal New Dealers were not to
blame. The new cold war liberals make an analogous distinction: the 1960s
failed because of the aforementioned intellectual crimes and political trea-
sons of the radicals, but the true "democrats" should be spared in the general disgrace.

The battle to define the history of the 1960s is nowhere more noisy than
in the contest for the hearts and minds of scholars and students of the
Vietnam War. A fight has been brewing for some time, but it burst into public debate and into print just this year, at the Vietnam Reconsidered conference at the University of Southern California and in an exhaustive cover
article in *The New York Times Magazine*, "The New Vietnam Scholarship,"
by that paper's former Saigon correspondent Fox Butterfield. The
antecedent of the contest was the right wing's indiscriminate assault on the
whole anti-war movement, from the quagmire theorists who believed that
the war was simply not winnable to the anti-imperialists who hoped the
Vietcong revolutionaries would, in the words of one Vietnam veteran who
spoke at the USC conference, "kick the US in the ass." In response to the
right, the liberal "revisionists" have declared the anti-war movement another failure of the left because it enabled communists to win in Indochina
(with the usual blood baths and re-education camps) and because it weakened the power of the United States to work its good will elsewhere in the
world. To give native color to the argument, *The New York Review of Books*
published a rather bizarre complaint from the first major defector from the
revolutionary National Liberation Front of South Vietnam. Truong Nhu
Tang said that the NLF had all along wanted the United States to leave
behind a neutralist, liberal Vietnam, but that the Tet offensive and the

American anti-war movement had delivered his country over to the communists. Tang now lives in Paris.

Naturally, the liberals absolved themselves from blame for events after the war in Vietnam; it was the fault of the other guys—the radicals who tripped to Hanoi, who waved NLF banners, who expressed solidarity with the "enemy." That is, the ones who were disloyal to flag and country.

What's wrong with the liberal blame-shifting in this case is that it revises history in such a way as to make it fantastic. The anti-war movement had only one objective: the disengagement of the United States from Indochina. There was no disagreement between liberals and radicals (or anyone else in the movement) on *that* score. It was a movement in America, not in Vietnam; its targets were the policy makers in Washington, not in Hanoi. It did not demand that the United States disengage itself from the war only if social democracy were installed in Saigon; it was for the reign of peace, not for the establishment of a parliament in Vietnam or the victory of the Communist Party. The sympathies, the rhetoric and even the behavior of many radicals may have been tasteless or provocative, but that was irrelevant to the shape of the peace. Nor could the radicals conceivably have damaged the anti-war movement; the radicals *made* the movement. Insofar as American policy was shaped by domestic pressures (rather than by the situation in Vietnam), the disruption of the social fabric on the home front was certainly critical to stopping the war.

Subversion as an issue in the culture of the new cold war liberalism has surfaced in somewhat the same way as loyalty: in response to repeated rumblings on the right. And like the loyalty issue, subversion has an antiquated as well as a contemporary aspect.

The subversion problem in the 1950s was stated thus: spies for the Russians were stealing secrets (the Rosenbergs), manipulating policy (Alger Hiss in the State Department) and brainwashing the masses (the Hollywood Ten). Subversion was the objective act; it was produced by disloyalty, the subjective state. The great subversion trials of the cold war era were meant to provide proof that disloyalty had a perilous predicate. When cold war liberals bore witness against leftists before congressional committees, or when they enforced blacklists, or when they voted to outlaw communism, they tacitly (or loudly) accepted the theory, enshrined in the Smith Act of 1940, that American communists posed a danger to America.

In time, and with the cold war thaw, the operative sections of the Smith Act were declared unconstitutional, after which espionage was treated as a criminal act, not an ideological statement. Now, as the new cold war settles in, there is a revival of interest in the old spy stories. Two books about the Rosenbergs are due this year (the thirtieth anniversary of their execution), Alger Hiss's case is flaring up again in the courts, and the British cold war spies are forever popping up in one connection or another. Michael Straight comes out in his book, *After Long Silence*. Donald McLean and Anthony

Blunt die, and the obituary writers celebrate their contributions to Soviet espionage. It all serves to create a credible context for cold warriors: what happened once could happen again.

But subversion has a different face in the 1980s. Just as the right is more worried about the disloyalty of native New Leftists, so it is fearful of a new kind of home-grown subversion: the name is terrorism. The right is apt to lump everyone it doesn't like into one terrorist group, so it has fallen to the cold war liberals, again, to take cover and direct the fire to their left. The far right, for instance, figures that mainline Protestant churches in the United States and abroad are fomenting revolution on every continent. *60 Minutes*, however, does a two-part special on the peculiar perfidy of the leadership of the National and World Council of Churches (as opposed to the lcyal, conservative membership) and their grants to such groups as the North American Committee on Latin America and the Committee in Solidarity with the People of El Salvador. Various shots of "leftist" church people are intercut with shots of Fidel Castro, unidentified marching Asians and unnamed black Africans carrying (according to correspondent Morley Safer) revolutionary rifles.

It is not a very great leap from there to the conclusion that those who support revolution in the Third World are soft on terrorism, or worse. Since we know, or have been told by Alexander Haig, Jeane Kirkpatrick and President Reagan, that terrorism is international, that the Palestinians who kill innocent people in Jerusalem are allied with the Black Liberation Army and old Weatherpeople who kill bank guards in Nyack, New York, it must follow that anyone who holds to the politics of insurrection is a potential terrorist.

There is a perdurable debate within the left, and between liberals and leftists, over both the morality and the efficacy of non-violence, revolution, guerrilla warfare and even standard-brand terrorism. The debate has cropped up in the course of hundreds of political upheavals, from the French Resistance and the Warsaw uprising in World War II, through the anti-colonial wars in Asia and Africa, to Cuba and Nicaragua, and to the black liberation movement in the US. But the kind of treatment *60 Minutes* gave to the subject was quite different from the old debate: it was a prosecutorial campaign. "Terrorism" as a term thus becomes an ideological weapon, like "Marxism" (which Safer also hurled at the church leaders) or "Stalinism." The words are not meant to have descriptive value, only firepower.

Like loyalty and subversion, national security has also made an unexpected comeback on the list of liberal concerns. After the fearful fifties, it seemed that the question of American military security was settled; its last gasp came during the Kennedy Administration, with its apocalyptic vision of a missile gap, the Cuban missile scare and the Berlin crisis. JFK's *"Ich bin ein Berliner"* were famous last words of the old cold war. After that came a period of concentration on internal problems (poverty, racism), the war in Vietnam, détente and Watergate. But *voilà!* The missiles are bristling once again, the bomb looms large and militarism is in command.

After the setback in Vietnam, the New Right and the neoconservatives set out to kill détente and restore American military supremacy. Their method was to raise the specter of the "Soviet threat," that is, the Red menace in Russian uniform. But their strategy could never have succeeded without the participation of liberals in a revived cold war discourse.

The liberal reaction to pressure from the right worked on two levels. The ideological groundwork was laid by placing communism—as an ideology— outside lawful limits of thought. "Communism *is* fascism," Sontag said at Town Hall. If that is true, then communism in any national accent— Russian, Cuban, Ethiopian, Nicaraguan—is dangerous and must be destroyed before it destroys us. (Communism in countries that happen to be soft on America can be redefined as something else, such as Yugoslav "Titoism" or Chinese "revisionism," and need only be patronized, rather than liquidated.) Marxism—when it wears a guerrilla uniform or a kaffiyeh—is simply communism waiting to shoot its way into government. The cold war liberals can thus condemn Salvadoran rebels and Palestinian fighters with the same fervor they display towards Soviet soldiers.

On the second level, the new cold war liberals offered a political platter of fine distinctions and sophistries about the arms race and the nuclear freeze and disarmament movements. These were definitively stated by Leon Wieseltier in his exhaustive rumination in the January 10/17, 1983, issue of *The New Republic*, titled "Nuclear War, Nuclear Peace." Wieseltier's very comprehensiveness defeats analysis, let alone characterization; but it is fair to say that after demonstrating that both the "hawks" and the "doves" are neither all wrong nor all right, he concludes that there is indeed a Soviet military threat and that nuclear deterrence is the only possible political and moral method for meeting it.

This is an important conclusion for cold war liberals, similar in significance to the decision of their predecessors to stand behind, or under, Dullesian "massive retaliation," and to sanction containment, brinkmanship and the various permutations of confrontational policy. And while Wieseltier and like-minded theorists begin by responding to the fears of the right about Russian domination, they end up by attacking the left—the freeze movement, the disarmament prophets (Jonathan Schell and E.P. Thompson) and the naive, sentimental, tender-minded troops in the ranks.

Culture, like history, is dialectical; it develops in response to the interplay of political and intellectual forces on a scale of time in the real world. Cultural developments do not appear out of nowhere, or float free of the basic relationships of power that they reflect. The culture of the new cold war has a history and a reason that are related to its times. And it has a future that can be presumed, though not precisely predicted.

In its current phase, the cold war resumed at the moment détente was declared—whichever date one may care to name: when Nixon announced his mission to Moscow in 1971, when he signed the SALT I arms treaty in May 1972, when Congress authorized its approval in September. In any case, six months later, the Coalition for a Democratic Majority—soon to be renamed the Committee on the Present Danger—was in business, plotting a campaign to restore the *status quo ante* détente.

In the mid-1970s, the coalition, and the infant cold war campaign in general, was run for the most part by neoconservatives; it flourished in the world of the formerly liberal. There were historical reasons for that, particularly the long memories from the 1950s. But there were practical reasons as well. The neoconservatives were closest to power, and they used the cold war threat as a means to consolidate their position. It had, after all, worked before.

There was another source of heat on the issue of communism and national defense. The old right had been utterly out of power, office and fashion since the McCarthy days. In the post-Vietnam political trough the New Right— McCarthyism rehabilitated—was making its bid. Eventually, these far rightists would merge into the Reagan campaign (and Administration). In the late 1970s, they were still outside the political mainstream, firing away at the liberals and the left with indiscriminate enthusiasm, while the neoconservatives—a more tasteful, pin-striped bunch—were more precise in their aim. *Their* target was the tender-minded liberalism of the Vietnam period, now embodied in the McGovern wing of the Democratic Party and in what journalists called the "left" of the Carter Administration. The jousting between these two forces that had gone on between 1974 and 1978 was a preliminary to the main event: Carter's capitulation to the new cold warriors halfway through his term and the eventual flight of the Administration's McGovernite wing into the descending night. It was at that point that cold war liberalism was born, a brand-new political baby, the product of—but distinct from—a set of neoconservative and right-wing forebears.

As much as anything, Carter's surrender to the New Right and the neoconservatives on defense and national security issues deprived his Administration of an independent foreign policy. It may well have led to his defeat in 1980, for the liberal members of the Vietnam generation, whom Carter had courted and who had helped provide his small margin of victory four years earlier, were demoralized and disillusioned—and bored, to boot. Carter had given the left a declaration of amnesty for Vietnam-era draft resisters and deserters. He had tried to curb the most rapacious imperial instincts of US policy in Africa and Latin America. He had gone all gooey for human rights. But then he changed tack, even reinstituting draft registration, and his Administration offered the left only an echo of a right-wing foreign policy, not a meaningful choice.

This dynamic of pressure from both neoconservatives and the New Right is very much like the one that produced the cold war liberalism of the 1950s, which was a response to the Republican far right and the new conservatives who became ensconced in the last year of the Roosevelt regime. They had engineered the dumping of Henry Wallace in 1944, and had advised Truman to assume his cold war positions in the early postwar period. But there is another dynamic at work in the return of cold war liberalism, which has its origins in the personal history of a generation, the evolution of its ideas and the development of its consciousness.

History, Hegel said, is the problem of consciousness. The generation of the 1960s cut its consciousness on a liberationist, activist, sometimes utopian view of the world. Only a few members of the sixties cohort actually acted out the vision in a purposeful, dedicated way. The great majority watched, sympathized or dabbled with the passing radical causes and countercultural styles: civil rights, anti-war protest, Third World revolution, sexual liberation, communalism, high times, working-class militancy.

Their sympathies were based, for the most part, on sentiment rather than ideology. They felt a shiver of excitement when civil rights organizers raised their fists for "black power," even though the slogan—and the politics behind it—contradicted the idea of integration that they affirmed when challenged. Many secretly approved of the most violent expressions of social protest and personal rage, even if they stated their opposition to violence as a matter of policy. I remember lunching in Washington with a leading black official in the Johnson Administration during the bloody Detroit riots in 1967. His job was to keep the lid on racial conflict, to defuse tensions and maintain social peace. But he told me that he and his wife watched the news every night and cheered, "Burn, baby, burn!" as Detroit went up in flames. There were other cheers for the Vietnamese communists' victory of Tet, for various Weather Underground exploits, for blows against the American empire struck throughout the world.

Many of the cheering liberals on the broad fringes of the radical issues never stopped to think that what was happening in the movement and in the streets would be inimical to their own class and career interests. They revelled in the sit-ins and the freedom marches, the campus strikes and the smoke-ins, the cane-cutting expeditions to Cuba and the encounters with the Vietcong in Canada and Czechoslovakia. Now, however, they feel guilty about—or have been made to take the blame for—a rigid communist regime in Vietnam, murderous black cults like the Symbionese Liberation Army, the desperate junkie society that replaced the pot-and-flowers communes. When the right wing—both the neoconservatives and the New Right—began its attack on the politics and lifestyles of the 1960s, many members of the vast liberal fringe, now grown up and settling into conventional jobs and marriages, realized they had to fight for their own legitimacy. Their loyalty, broadly defined, was questioned in the context of a new cold war that was revived for that very purpose—to delegitimize the radical consciousness of a generation. Without many second thoughts, the liberal fringe turned right—and pointed left, with accusing fingers and hostile words.

The new cold war liberals were prepared to disown their history for both a personal and a practical reason. Many members of that generation found themselves facing choices in their own lives that required them to deny or redefine their earlier experiences. Whatever else the sixties did, the decade seemed to promise its children an honest, humane, useful and communitarian life. Those promises were always exaggerated, and when they could not be fulfilled, the ageing children labelled them "lies," and the whole decade a "failure." It was tempting for them to condemn the expectations when confronted by their own accommodations to a competitive, individualistic, illiberal and often inhumane world. And those who feared they had "sold out" resented those whose continued activity according to the old patterns of thought presented a constant reproach.

The practical reason for the turnaround was simple: the sixties no longer sells. Liberal in government, the media and academia are the ideological entrepreneurs of the American system. Their power is that of the broker. In the last two decades they brokered peace in Vietnam and social tranquillity, racial harmony and economic opportunity at home. It worked this way: liberals delivered the support, the votes and the good behavior of their constituents "at the base" to the political and corporate governors "at the top." The pay-off, which the liberals negotiated, was civil rights legislation, a Vietnamese settlement, anti-poverty transfer payments to the underclass, and relaxation of social and sexual norms.

Today the currency of pay-offs is in short supply—or no supply at all. What the people at the top have to offer is national security, patriotism and good feelings about America: cold war values. And liberals must adapt to this new marketplace. The hysterical popular response to the Iranian hostage affair and the reception accorded the returning hostages, the celebration of the US hockey team's Olympic victory over the Russians in 1980 and the great fear of Soviet military "superiority" all helped create an aggregate demand that the cold war liberals' entrepreneurial skills are now devoted to meeting.

The personal and practical dynamic in the rise of the new cold war liberalism is also identifiable in the old version. The left of the 1930s also had a broad liberal fringe, which sympathized with the radical causes of the era in a vague, sentimental, non-ideological way. Liberals then were generally approving of militant labor fights, the Spanish Civil War, resistance to fascism and the activities of the artistic avant-garde. After World War II, the liberals, now grown up and settled in, pulled back, first into a self-absorbed apathy and privatism which anticipated the "personal liberation" and "human potential" movements of the 1970s, then into downright hostility to their past sympathies and to those who still maintained the old ideals. The liberals' transformation was accompanied by name-calling ("Stalinist") and name-naming ("fellow traveller"); they beat a retreat from the concerns of the radical decades to the safety of the cold war issues.

As the cold war culture spread across the land, the liberals began address-ing new questions, or redefining old ones. They fought for the ownership of icons and issues. They began a debate over Freud: is psychoanalysis a panacea for the individual or a means to social change? Over Marx: dead determinist or live methodologist? Over sociology: prescriptive or descrip-tive? Over philosophy: concerned with words or things?

The liberals sought to depoliticize all aspects of culture, to emphasize tech-nique over ideology, the instrument over the idea. Daniel Bell's book *The End of Ideology* decreed the cessation of class struggle in America. The sur-viving form of liberalism was "managerial" rather than ideological; it offered a method for adjusting social imbalances rather than a blueprint for reform-ing society. The technical approach became the Democratic Party's "pro-gram" in the 1950s. Liberalism is, of course, non-revolutionary by definition, and even in the headiest days of the New Deal, liberals opposed the transfor-mation of the capitalist system. But with the death, or dormancy, of the radi-cal left in the fifties, liberalism lost even its reformist character, and it too became depoliticized.

Militarism, individualism and consumerism invaded the cultural life of the fifties. The emblematic cold war television program was *Victory at Sea*, a Churchillian celebration of World War II, minus the politics. The represen-tative novelists were J.D. Salinger, James Gould Cozzens and Ayn Rand. Social criticism was aimed at the tasteless or debilitating effects of the politi-cal and economic system, not the system itself: Vance Packard on advertis-ing (*The Hidden Persuaders*), David Riesman on alienation (*The Lonely Crowd*), William White on suburban conformity (*The Organization Man*).

The new cold war of the 1980s has already had similar success in refram-ing cultural discourse. A rapid and radical depoliticization has seized the country; it is obvious in the media, in the universities, in literature, in social criticism. There is even a depoliticization of politics itself. Public issues are not discussed in terms of power, justice, idealism and morality, as they were in the 1960s, but as a kind of theater, or a category of aesthetics. Compare, for example, Joan Didion's *Salvador*, published this year, with the "literary" reportage of the Vietnam era: Susan Sontag's *Trip to Hanoi*, Mary Mc-Carthy's *Vietnam*, Norman Mailer's *Armies of the Night*. Less high-flying reports are similarly depoliticized, and they evince a "pendulum" theory of history: things are one way, then the other, but nothing really changes. In the more starkly politicized journalism of the sixties there was a sense of movement rather than stasis, of evolution (or revolution) rather than termi-nation, of optimism rather than cynicism.

There are clashes over the issues and icons of the 1980s corresponding to the cultural battles of the 1950s. Now there is a fight for Foucault and semi-otics: tool for change or for analysis? For the Holocaust: failure of the human spirit or tragedy of the war against fascism? For Poland: working-class struggle or anti-communist revolt? Even for peace: disarmament or deterrence? And for the history of decades and wars gone by: the thirties, World War II, Vietnam, the McCarthy era, the sixties.

Ever ready to grasp new issues and broker them to their customers, the liberal media have picked up on the new cold war culture and are selling it by the pound. Overall, there is a new "spin" to the discussion of public policy and social issues. Militarism, individualism and consumerism are back in fashion. The first great TV show of the emerging culture was *The Winds of War*, a (long) brief for the cold war liberals in the contest for intellectual property rights to World War II, the Holocaust and attendant events. The debate over the role of the left in the McCarthy era has flared anew with the publication of William L. O'Neill's *A Better World*, which is subtitled *The Great Schism: Stalinism and the American Intellectuals*. O'Neill (and his sympathetic reviewers in *The New Republic* and the daily *New York Times*) argues once again that CP members and leftist intellectuals who refused to denounce American communism were doing Stalin's work under the cloak of constitutional liberties. No historical debate can ever be finally settled, especially one in which the historical participants are still alive. But the O'Neill book arrives as an offensive weapon in a political fight: to discredit the left, to link what leftists thought with what Stalin did, to prove past guilt by association.

The world-shaking movements connecting personal and political change— feminism and gay liberation—have also been transformed into little more than support systems for getting ahead and having it all. Betty Friedan, who inspired the first wave of militant feminism twenty years ago, now, in *The Second Stage*, argues for the traditional values of family life in a home full of upscale appointments. The impetus towards retrenchment in liberation ideology is rationalized in the name of realism or pragmatism—those reborn cold war virtues from the earlier age. Contempt for idealism and blindness to the visions of utopia are hallmarks of the emerging culture, for both idealism and utopianism are necessary for radical change.

Analogies are logically imperfect. When historical events happen for the second time, as Marx remarked, they are likely to make farcical what was initially tragic. The first cold war culture not only imposed a stultifying, conformist creed on creative work and thought; people really suffered. There were purges of leftists from unions, political parties, public organizations, the news media, academia, show business, publishing, government. The woods are full of "McCarthy victims" who survived. But a lot of them did not survive. They were all victims of the cold war liberals as well as of the McCarthyites. The liberals were well placed to do the dirty work, for they were in charge of the great institutions sheltering the left.

Can it happen here, and now? In a very small sense, it may be happening already. Journalists who consider themselves (or are considered) leftists say that many publications that once welcomed their work have shut tight in recent months. The big publishers, often subsidiaries of vast conglomerates, are showing less interest in issues as leftists frame them. Hollywood, which has not been markedly political since the 1940s, is extremely sensitive to the current ideological crosscurrents. One film released this year, *The Lords of Discipline*, which takes place in a Southern military academy, was set in 1964 (pre–Gulf of Tonkin) rather than in 1966, when the novel on which it was based was set. The change was made to avoid any mention of the war in Vietnam, though that was crucial to the author's theme. It's a wonder *Reds* wasn't set in 1904. The unexpected success of the Academy Award–winning *Gandhi* seems like another symptom of cold war fever. The Mahatma, after all, was the favorite foreign rebel of Americans after World War II, the liberal alternative to Mao.

Outside of the peace movement, where, as mentioned, the fiercest fighting is centered, the left today is dispersed, fragmented and isolated. It is even difficult to speak of "a left," a unitary, self-conscious political cohort such as existed before the old cold war. Thus, the destructive tactics traditional to cold warriors—both the right-wing and liberal varieties—are inappropriate in the current situation.

But if there is not a left, there are leftists—that is, there are countless heirs to the political and countercultural traditions of the 1960s, as well as older radicals and newly organized sympathizers—who occupy positions (generally in the lower ranks) in the established liberal institutions: unions, schools and colleges, social welfare agencies, service organizations, the media and even government. They also can be found in thousands of activist organizations—tenant unions, environmental lobbies, labor insurgencies, legal aid offices, health groups, women's and homosexuals' support groups, foreign policy study and action projects. These, and many more, represent a largely innovative development in American institutional life. Their members are not always aware that they are playing a wider political role—that they constitute an ad hoc left or radical presence. At least, they do not function that way. But the presence is there, it is important, and it is felt. In a sense, the emergence of the new cold war is logically connected to the development of a new class of post-sixties activists. It is this new political class, however incoherently its politics and its class demands are expressed, that the cold war liberals are engaging.

How successful the liberals will be in determining the course of the conflict is impossible to gauge. Cold war liberalism, in its new form, is a phenomenon whose meaning has only begun to "mean itself"; events that have yet to happen, developments that have yet to develop and consequences that have yet to occur will make the determination.

But at the core of the process is war—the militarization of American society, the obsession with national security, the preoccupation with loyalty, patriotism and power. War, Orwell said, is the engine that drives society. It is certainly the motivation for neoconservatism, the New Right and, now, cold war liberalism. The issue of war and peace has shaped every aspect of American policy in this century, from highway construction to education to economic strategies to the preservation of civil liberties. If the country moves towards war, the pressure will increase on all the forces in the land that seek to open institutions to popular participation, change and equality. If we move towards peace, the space for freedom will begin to expand again.

April 23, 1983, THE NATION

PART THREE

Chapter XI

✦

NEGLECT OF THE LEFT

Neglect of the Left: Allard Lowenstein

There is a rare and curious condition sometimes observed in victims of stroke in which the patient loses all sense and perception of one half of himself, of his surroundings and indeed of his universe. The lost side is typically the left. Neurologists call the condition "neglect," perhaps because it suggests a certain moral deficit as well as a perceptual one, as if the patient, through no fault of his own, becomes constitutionally unable to appreciate dialectical reality. To see only one half of the world is to miss the meaning contained in its relation to the other. To apprehend only good and not evil, beauty and not ugliness, truth and not falsehood—or the other way around—is to lose the integrity of opposites and the possibility of choice. Sufferers from neurological neglect of the left often are aware that they have misplaced their faculty for intuiting relationships and, as best they can, try to find it in the reaches of the right. Doctors on hospital rounds tell of watching patients inching towards the right side of their beds until they are up against the railing, in an attempt to create a left side within right reality, and thus establish a center for themselves, a vantage place, a point of view. The search, of course, is by definition futile. Metaphysically, they are on the wrong side of the bed.

As striking as that image appears as a medical symptom, it is positively breathtaking as a metaphor for a certain political sensibility, a turn of mind and a mode of behavior that marks a good part of liberal society in America in the last four decades. To get down to cases—and now the doctor's terminology elides with the reporter's—it is eerily apt in describing the phenomenal figure of Allard Lowenstein, plotting his peculiar progress from teenage activist to martyred hero, and explaining the bitter controversy that still attends his name.

Few personalities of contemporary American political culture so young, so marginal to power and so removed from great institutions have been more exhaustively examined, diagnosed, treated, mistreated and re-treated, buried and exhumed. A popular subject for journalism, gossip and heated conversation during the 1960s and '70s, the two decades of his most newsworthy achievements, Lowenstein has not ceased to inspire discussion in several genres even after his murder, by a psychopath who was once his friend and protégé, in 1980. Here a biography, there a memoir, now a play, somewhere a film, a *Festscrift*, a Pulitzer Prize-winning article, a treatise of sexual analysis, a major critical essay, a packet of affidavits, a lawyers' brief: the continuing multimediation of Al Lowenstein is a cultural phenomenon in itself. Friends gather regularly in Georgetown drawing rooms and Manhattan apartments to honor his memory, which has been institutionalized, so far, in a charitable foundation, a congressional symposium and a prize for public service. There is an Allard K. Lowenstein Library on Long Island, and an Allard K. Lowenstein Square near the United Nations in New York. In all of that, the Lowenstein iconography is hardly crisp and clear; critics and canonizers have darkened the shadows or applied the gilt according to their own beliefs. But throughout the stories, the dramas, the yellowing clips and even the affidavits, that image of Al keeps recurring: a young man searching for his center, trying to create reality, inching towards the side of the bed.

The contest to capture Lowenstein's past is part of the wider struggle to write the history of liberalism in the time before the first cold war and its recent resumption, which amounts to a version of the history of America in that same era. It is no idle pastime. The power to write history is, in effect, the power to use it, to keep it, to make the most of it. The issues that have been isolated in the often tendentious debates about Lowenstein's life are emblematic of the great topics of the period: radicalism and anti-communism, the end of ideology and the practice of politics, American imperialism and the war in Vietnam, complicity with authority and the oppositional stance, racism and the limits of revolution, sexuality and the social role of personal liberation.

Lowenstein's nose for a *Zeitgeist* was like a pig's for a truffle, rich and ripe below the unsuggestive surface. As a student at the University of North Carolina just after the Second World War, he fought the anti-Semitic fraternity system, combining two worthy and popular causes in one effort. He worked for Hubert Humphrey just as liberalism was re-emerging from the long night of reaction. He travelled to Africa when the world's eye shifted there from Central Europe and the Far East. He dabbled in anti-fascist agitation as the democratic opposition developed in Spain. He dove into student politics in its prime, the civil rights movement as it gained steam, the antiwar campaign when that caught on, the insurgency against Lyndon Johnson at an opportune moment, congressional elections when that was the thing to do and, ever so tentatively, gay liberation when that was becoming legitimate. Like a smart missile he homed in on hot targets: Martin Luther King, the Kennedys, Eugene McCarthy, Andrew Young, George McGovern. John Kenneth Galbraith, who, like Lowenstein, was once chairman of the Americans for Democratic Action, said his own political strategy consisted of figuring out when a parade was about to come around the corner, waiting for it to turn, and then jumping in front to lead. Lowenstein had the same idea.

Lowenstein did so much, knew so many important people, filled so many spaces in his truncated career that it is hard to fix on any one activity as supremely representative of his life's work and thought. He seemed always to be on the move, as if something were pushing him, or somebody pursuing. But three major issues—more accurately, three existential areas—remain unresolved, and they retain the power to set his foes to fuming and his friends rushing to the defense. The first is the question of his association, if any, with the Central Intelligence Agency or other covert-action agencies of government or private enterprise. The second is his responsibility, at any level, for the failure of the black delegation from Mississippi to unseat and replace the white delegation at the 1964 Democratic National Convention in Atlantic City—and, by extension, for the failure of the civil rights movement to establish a radical position apart from the liberal Democratic Party. And the third is the nature of his sexual identity, which calls into the question the relation of Lowenstein's personal and political agendas.

I first encountered Al at Stanford in the early 1960s, when he was a teacher, a dean and an immediate inspiration to a generation of students, almost exclusively male. His self-presentation was fashioned as a kind of caricature, the messiness of dress and appearance, the habitual tardiness, the neglect of daily routine, the explosive delivery of movement and speech, the intensity and, always, the secrecy. In an article in *The New York Review of Books*, Hendrik Hertzberg remembers Lowenstein with his "thick weight-lifter's neck and torso which made his head seem a little too small for his body, and he had thinning hair, Coke-bottle glasses, a big nose, and a delicate mouth." "Yet he had presence," Hertzberg wrote, "from his limitless self-confidence and from the infectious urgency of his mind and voice."

Yet? Lowenstein's cartoon physicality—part Batman, part Robin—was hardly beside the point, but at the very heart of his commanding personality. His famous wrestling bouts with friends and comrades contained clearly choreographed subtexts as dominance dances and sexual play. In the play *Dennis*, James Ryan made the opening scene a wrestling match between Lowenstein and Dennis Sweeney, the boy who much later would be his assassin. As a dramatic device it was too obvious and easy, but as an existential exclamation point it was just right.

One virtue of Richard Cummings's new, contentious biography, *The Pied Piper*, is that it recalls much of Lowenstein's early career that is largely glossed over in the admiring memoirs. It's not that anything horrible happened then; Lowenstein seemed always to do what was right, according to his lights, for the time he was in. But many of his early activities prefigure the later ones, or at least illuminate them. At Chapel Hill, for example, Lowenstein quickly fixed on the legendary Carolina liberal Frank Graham, who was the university president. When Graham left home to accept an interim appointment as a US senator, Lowenstein attended him as a staff member. He agonized when Graham waffled on a crucial anti-filibuster vote—the most important moment in his brief senatorial term, since the choice would mark him as a true son of the South or a Negro sympathizer— but the young staffer ultimately decided that the maintenance of political office took precedence over the maintenance of pure principle. Graham later lost his seat in spite of (or because of) the waffle, and Lowenstein moved on.

Lowenstein became president of the National Student Association in the summer of 1950 after delivering an enthusiastic speech to the NSA convention supporting American intervention in the Korean War. He returned to North Carolina and student politics for a spell, and in 1958, with two young Princeton students, he visited South Africa. Out of that trip came Lowenstein's first book, *Brutal Mandate*, a solid study and passionate brief against Pretoria's colonial oppression of South West Africa, now Namibia. The book may fairly be considered a cornerstone in the development of the American movement against the policies of the white South African government. Like many others, perhaps, I first heard of Lowenstein when a friend showed me an advance copy of the book, at a small party of mostly Peace Corps office aides in Washington. But my friend was not much interested in the contents. She opened to the acknowledgements and began reading aloud a list of names that seemed to contain every single member of the liberal establishment of the day, beginning with Eleanor Roosevelt (who wrote the foreword) and Hubert Humphrey, and running over hundreds of entries and nine densely printed pages. I still can hear the raucous laughter as she droned on with the list, and I see now that this was the beginning and end of Lowenstein's world, his wish list and his pantheon. It describes, without annotation, who he thought he was and who he wanted to be.

Lowenstein went to work for Hubert Humphrey. He spoke out against the House Un-American Activities Committee, that great liberal cause of the hour. He sought out Walter Reuther, president of the United Auto Workers, and formed an association with the mainstream labor leadership that would last over many years and countless issues, from union organizing in Spain to black participation in the Democratic Party. He went to Stanford and travelled in Europe with one of his students, a man who—like Sweeney—soon was to side with the radical New Left against Lowenstein's liberalism. When they were in Spain, that student told me many years ago, he and Lowenstein motored from city to city, meeting with members of the anti-Franco opposition, talking to strangers and occasionally dropping in on American consuls. Lowenstein would disappear for hours on end, leaving his companion to sit in the car or wait at a cafe. Where was Al? The student, like many of Lowenstein's travelling companions on several continents, over many decades, in a variety of social contexts, could only guess. The student from Stanford thought Lowenstein was engaged in intelligence work. But later, when such things were thinkable, his fellow-travellers guessed that Al was out cruising for sexual contacts. Maybe he just wanted to be alone. Maybe his huggy-bed sessions with his friends, as described by various biographers, were unfulfilling. No one would ever know.

Richard Cummings constructs an elaborate case for the theory that Lowenstein did CIA work throughout his career, from Africa and Spain to Mississippi and wherever liberal Democratic politics took him. It is a theory constructed of old stories, plausible guesswork, unsupported rumors, ambiguous memoranda, suggestive recollections, an understanding of how officialdom operates and a willingness to believe the worst. It uses fragments of classified documents with important words deleted and a good deal of filling in of blanks with arbitrary inferences. For example, Cummings acknowledges that the CIA's well-reported collaboration with certain officers of the National Student Association began in the year after Lowenstein's tenure as president, but he suspects that a still-unreleased index of agency operations would show that an informal arrangement between the spies and the students existed some years earlier, which would thus implicate Lowenstein by association. Moreover, Cummings quotes colleagues and observers from Lowenstein's years in student politics to the effect that "Al must have known" about the CIA connection.

That sounds right. There is a pattern of coincidence so wide in scope and so long in time that it is not credible for anyone to hold that Lowenstein was oblivious to the activities, the interests and the expectations of not only the CIA but the larger intelligence community, the Foreign Service and private political forces working in the same fields as he was. Everyone else supposed that anti-communist student congresses, labor organizations and foreign political oppositions to leftist (or ultra-rightist) governments were on the CIA dole; why would Lowenstein think differently? Surely he "must have known" that one desk in the crazy-quilt intelligence services supported the Pan-Africanist Congress against the African National Congress, as he did; that some sector of the State Department wanted to get rid of Franco, as he did; that certain people in the Johnson Administration and the FBI hoped to keep the black and white movements of the 1960s out of radical hands, as he did; that the liberal foreign policy establishment was always looking for a "third force" to mediate revolutions from Vietnam to the Dominican Republic, as he was; that the CIA worked for its ends through student organizations, foreign and domestic labor unions, political parties and cultural institutions, as he did.

But where's the point? Hard evidence of Lowenstein's specific collaboration with the CIA is still lacking after Cummings's broad pattern is drawn.

Hertzberg convincingly countered a few of Cummings's accusations, and many others were attacked by Gary Bellow, Jeffrey Robbins and Ronald Tabak in their "privately circulated" tome, *Documentation Concerning Serious Factual Errors in Forthcoming Book by Richard Cummings Purportedly about Allard K. Lowenstein.* But nothing is finally proven, nothing is demolished beyond the shadow of a doubt, nothing is revealed. In fact, the pattern that Cummings produced is actually confirmed by his critics when they try to explain all the coincidences.

What remains in contention is the meaning of the pattern. Lowenstein's obvious complicity with governmental authority for years on many levels could fill a volume, but it makes an ambiguous book whose text is impossible to deconstruct with certainty. One can be a salaried agent, a freelance informer, a volunteer, a friend or even a part-time opponent of the CIA and still do its work, be complaisant, at least, with its affairs. It is not widely remembered now, but Frantz Fanon, the great Martiniquan writer and psychiatrist who wove the ideas and practice of the Algerian revolution into a classic work of liberation literature, *The Wretched of the Earth*, was in cahoots with the CIA at the end of his life. He actually died in the care, if not in the arms, of a CIA agent in the Dupont Circle Hotel in Washington, where he had been brought by the agency for medical treatment. Certainly that collaboration invalidated neither Fanon as a political actor, his work nor the revolutions he supported. The CIA—or that part of it that Harris Wofford, a Kennedy Administration official, calls "the good wing"—wanted a foothold in post-revolutionary Algeria. It thought it could co-opt amenable parties. Fanon, who was dying of leukemia, wanted help for himself and for his movement. He got both, in the short run.

In the long run, the CIA must be destructive, for it demands that one thing of its clients and assets that is death to surrender: independence of mind and action. Some collaborators realize the danger, some in time and some too late to terminate. For others it is hardly an issue, because they do not conceive of themselves in an independent opposition apart from the overriding purpose of the authority they serve. Whatever Lowenstein's association with government may have been, it was his membership in the community of liberal political managers—that list he acknowledged in *Brutal Mandate*—that is very much the point that Cummings misses and Hertzberg et al. ignore. Lowenstein was part of a cultural and ideological nexus that sanctioned covert operations and mounted public movements against radicalism at home and abroad. While maintaining a rhetorical respect for civil liberties, the liberals drove the left out of the labor movement, out of the Democratic Party, out of academia, government, communications, and out of the civil liberties field itself. In the age of McCarthyism it was the rabble-rousers who created the climate for those expulsions, but it was the liberals who did the expelling. Hubert Humphrey, not Joe McCarthy, wrote the bill to outlaw the Communist Party. The American Civil Liberties Union, not the reactionary right, kicked Elizabeth Gurley Flynn off its board. By neglecting the left, in a manner of speaking, they sought a new legitimacy within the right, a vital center, a new political reality.

Lowenstein pursued that elusive reality throughout his career. No sooner was the Mississippi Summer underway, in 1964, than he drew the line for acceptable participation. The leftish National Lawyers Guild was pariah, the radical Student Nonviolent Coordinating Committee was suspect, and even the Mississippi Freedom Democratic Party, which he helped invent, would have to surrender its independence to the demands of the liberal national Democrats, as formulated by Johnson, Humphrey and Reuther, and conveyed by Lowenstein.

The split between Lowenstein and the left that week in Atlantic City was one of those nodal points in politics that defines an era. To this day no one who took part in the fight to seat the black Freedom Democrats can forget the lines that were drawn, the curses that were cast. Perceptions formed then are unchanged twenty years later. Hertzberg and other friendly memoirists neglect the left side of the crucial debate on the compromise and hold simply that the Freedom Vote and the formation of the Freedom Democratic Party "led to . . . the destruction of Jim Crow in the national party."

But wasn't it quite the other way? The line begun with the white liberals' refusal to accept the equality of black activists led to the maintenance of white power with only token black representation in the party. It led to the formation of black-power groups in reaction to exclusionary policies. It led to the fragmentation of the multiracial civil rights movement and its eventual dissolution. In a sense, it led to the Jesse Jackson campaign and perhaps the rise of Louis Farrakhan. It led to the neglect of the entire left side of the broad and popular movement for racial equality and created a new reality for racial assimilation in the right.

I last saw Lowenstein in the mid-1970s, on a warm June day in Washington Square Park, at a rally that was held to commemorate the anniversary of the riots outside the Stonewall Bar in Greenwich Village in 1969, generally held to herald the birth of the modern gay liberation movement. I was surprised and pleased to see him, and I noticed that he seemed less driven, less distracted and more comfortable in conversation than ever before. He actually listened to what others around him were saying, without seeming to attend only to those items on an agenda in his own head. He stood by the speakers' platform—a familiar position—with his wife, Jenny, and their children; it must have been a year or two before his divorce. We didn't talk much about politics of any kind. I asked him what he was doing at the rally and he told me he thought that the gay movement was "terribly important." I remarked later that his earnestness seemed sincere but naive. It was a bit late in the day.

I sensed the power of Lowenstein's homoerotic libido the first time I met him with his student charges in Stanford so many years before. Who could miss it? I also heard rumors of homosexual affairs he was supposed to have had over the years, especially during the civil rights and anti-war campaigns, but you heard that about a lot of powerful men with adoring disciples. Hertzberg, who apparently felt Lowenstein's libidinous energy too, thought it helped him "turn his appeals to reason and idealism into powerful bonds between himself and thousands of young followers."

Lowenstein never "came out" as a homosexual, at least not in public, but he began meeting with leaders of the gay movement and acted as a kind of emissary/organizer to the gay community in Florida during Edward Kennedy's presidential primary campaign there in early 1980. Larry Bush, who wrote the only extensive article about Lowenstein's sexuality (it was refused by the *Soho News*, which had commissioned it, and later published in the gay biweekly, the *New York Native*), told me recently that he spoke to so many primary sources who described homoerotic contacts with Lowenstein that he had no doubt "Al was struggling to understand his sexual identity in the months before he died."

"Rather than sweep such questions aside," Bush wrote, "we would be better served by thoughtful consideration of what these issues mean as public figures reclaim their private lives." The trouble is that we do not have a readily available vocabulary for such consideration. Surely Lowenstein's sexuality was central to his life and to his work, and not in the ordinary way that that observation is often made. Intimations of sexual outlawry place those who have them in a social and cultural opposition. Escape is impossible. Only by acting to change the external environment can the outlaws gain confidence, feel legitimate, indeed establish their identity and reclaim their lives. Lowenstein, like so many others similarly situated, neglected his outlaw side for most of his years. He reached into his respectable half—marriage, career, traditional politics—for the legitimacy he must have missed. It could not have been there. Bush, Hertzberg and Cummings, who disagree on many things about Lowenstein, all suspect that he was poised for change at the age of 51. He never got the chance.

Spring 1986, GRAND STREET

✦

Movin' On Up

A veritable Niagara of ironies drenches the selection of the first black Miss America, New York's Vanessa Williams. First of all is the Faustian victory of sexism over racism. The venerable Atlantic City beauty pageant—which excluded black beauties for the first thirty of its sixty-two years—still stands as a bastion of every mystique that feminists have attacked. Williams told an interviewer after her coronation that she did not want to be seen as a black heroine; apparently she has no qualms about a career as a sex object.

Then there is the way the beauty packagers, image enhancers, judges and contestants conspired to project a winning "look" that is deracinated, depersonalized and devoid of ethnic energy or charm. It was almost impossible to pick out Williams from the collection of Linda Evans look-alikes and shampoo salesladies that paraded down the runway. If this was a triumph of "pluralism," as some have said, it had an oddly homogenized cast. A long-ago line of the humorist Harry Golden, on the occasion of Barry Goldwater's presidential nomination, seemed more apropos. "I always thought," Golden said, "that America's first Jewish President would turn out to be an Episcopalian."

The final irony is that a society that is still profoundly racist along its entire institutional base can thrill to the symbolic success of an individual from an excluded minority. Last week it was Vanessa Williams; the week before, black astronaut Guion Bluford Jr.; before that, a sports star or TV comedian or fast food tot. The key, of course, is individual symbolism rather than collective power. Minority heroes tend to lose their appeal when they travel in large groups.

And yet—Vanessa Williams's story has a particular political resonance this year, and it would be wrong to discount it for the obvious problems and contradictions it presents. The past year has seen a startling surge—or resurgence—of black demands for power and privilege, after a decade of battered quiescence. "Our time has come," Chicago Mayor Harold Washington proclaimed in his campaign. "We want our share," Jesse Jackson insists. White America is not ready, by a long shot, to meet those implicit demands. What it can do, at least, is come up with singular success stories, new symbols of liberal good intentions. If that's what Miss America is, more power to her. But more *power*. After all, as they sing every week on *The Jeffersons*, "It took a whole lot o' tryin' . . . but we finally got a piece o' the pie."

October 1, 1983, THE NATION

Afternote: Williams's tough luck was to be locked in a series of double binds more secure than most jails, and part-way through her "reign" she was forced to cede her crown for having once been a pornographer's model. The whole point of beauty pageants is that the fox on the runway must never be caught—or caught in the act, least of all with another woman!

Prayer Power

More things are wrought by prayer than this world dreams of, and although Tennyson had his own poetic take on that issue, President Reagan understands better than anyone what politics may be made with folded hands, murmuring lips and lowered lids. His appeal for prayer in the schools is, so far, the centerpiece of his re-election strategy. It galvanizes his conservative constituency, intimidates his liberal opponents and deflects such unpromising issues as unemployment and nuclear war from intruding on the electoral debate.

Reagan is helped immeasurably by the confusion of his critics, who take the prayer campaign solely as an attempt to deregulate the separation of church and state and to establish an official religion. The arguments they derive from such a vision, however worthy, are couched in constitutional terms and appeal to the Jeffersonian conscience that liberals hope is lurking in the mind of the modern majority. Senator Lowell Weicker, the Connecticut Republican who is leading the fight against the Administration's amendment, bases his case on the theory that the imposition of any moment of meditation in a public school is a denial of freedom of speech and religion. It is a theory that might win in the Supreme Court (the *old* Supreme Court), but it misses the political point of the current confrontation.

This is not, after all, merely a replay of constitutional conversations that took place in Philadelphia 200 years ago. The prayer proposal is a leading part of a wider campaign to subvert the humanistic culture that characterizes America in the twentieth century much more than it did in the eighteenth. It is this year's symbol of the New Right's attack on modernism, secular democracy, egalitarianism and personal liberation. It is profoundly reactionary in its assault on history, and it is perfectly political in its organization of power against an appeal to reason.

Prayer is hardly horrible. Nor does a bit of mumbo-jumbo in the morning lead a nation into blind obedience to hooded priests and an unseen God. Britain, which has suffered its own state religion and compulsory school prayer since Tudor times, is the most atheistic nation in the world. Italy, with the Pope and his retinue in its midst, produced the West's biggest Marxist party. Obviously the opiate has lost its punch.

No one, not even Jesse Helms, believes that prayer in public schools will make much of a difference by itself. Most kids will hardly notice the minute of silence squeezed in between the last toke in the schoolyard and the food fight in the cafeteria. Those in the better public institutions who may take prayer seriously will soon have to translate the King James words into BASIC or FORTRAN in order to glean their meaning; and all for nought, because the Deity is notoriously unresponsive to bits and bytes. Many more will be permanently alienated from religion when they discover that, as

Sister Mary Ignatius tells her students in Christopher Durang's delightful play, "God always answers prayers, but sometimes the answer is no."

God, in one form or another, is easily exploited as the answer to the problems of modern life. "A whole lot more of Jesus and a lot less rock-and-roll" was the country music prescription a few years back. What's most disturbing about the current campaign, however, is that it is embodied in a powerful movement to impose intellectual and cultural hegemony on the whole society. The New Right agenda not only includes compulsory prayer; it demands compulsory militarism, compulsory surveillance, compulsory pregnancy-to-term, compulsory heterosexuality, compulsory sobriety, compulsory racism, sexism and imperialism. The campaign against that movement must be waged in terms appropriate to its political message, for the target is the right and its power, its politicians and its patrons. There's a cultural war on, and it will not be won by lawyers and logic alone.

March 17, 1984, THE NATION

✦

The Left, the Democrats and the Future

With hardly a backward—or forward—look, the bulk of the surviving American left has blithely joined the Democratic Party center, without the will to inflect debate, the influence to inform policy or the leverage to share power. The capitulation of the left—a necessarily catch-all word, here covering the spectrum of progressive politics from old socialism to recent radical activism—is almost without precedent. This time out there is no McCarthy of 1968, no McGovern of 1972, no Kennedy of 1980; not even a John Anderson or a Barry Commoner to raise a standard of dissent or develop an alternative vision against a Democratic Party whose project is overwhelmingly conservative in attitude and action. The excuse for submission is easy to discern: Anybody But Reagan. But the consequences are likely to be dire, and they are already taking shape. By accepting the premises and practices of party unity, the left has negated the reasons for its own existence.

In the beginning, of course, there was a certain Somebody within the Democratic fold who was a candidate not only of principle but of opportunity for the left. Jesse Jackson and the Rainbow Coalition he proposed represented the historical base, the organized movement and the radical program for which the left has been hunting the last thirty-five years. But . . . no. Jackson is usually taunted for failing to broaden his coalition, but when he made personal pitches to each likely constituency, the invitees almost invariably declined. Jackson gave an impassioned call for the solidarity of racial and sexual movements last October in the keynote speech at the gay Human Rights Campaign Fund banquet at the Waldorf-Astoria; by March, gays were openly supporting Gary Hart in the New York primary and Walter

Mondale in other states. Jackson talked to unionists and women, and last November 12 he addressed marchers who had come to Washington to demonstrate against US intervention in Central America. Among the major candidates, it was left to him to stake out opposition ground on America's intervention in Lebanon, its invasion of Grenada and its proxy wars in Central America; on the nuclear arms race and corporate accountability and racial equity.* It would hardly have been an election campaign without him. But sympathy to his overtures rarely led to organized support. Barry Commoner urged the Citizens Party to endorse Jackson—if there was ever a natural white base for Jackson, it was there—but the party is putting up its own candidate.

Long before Louis Farrakhan slouched into the headlines, white leftists had run through every excuse to withhold support from the black candidate. First there was the argument that only a respectable black with a significant white following should be allowed to swim in the Democratic mainstream. Then there was the notion that any black candidacy would provoke a backlash from white voters. Next came charges that Jackson was, in turn, a charlatan, a crook, an anti-Semite, a capitalist roader, a poor administrator, a divisive force. Quickly the dark motif of Campaign '84 changed from Anybody But Reagan to Anybody But Jackson. Once again, racism destroyed the promise of a populist, progressive, internationalist coalition within the Democratic Party.

As had to happen, Anybody became Walter Mondale, and he arrived promoting a platform as immoderate and regressive as any to be found in the Democratic Party archives since John W. Davis's unremembered candidacy of 1924. With substantive objections only from Jackson's underrepresented contingent, the party's pre-convention committees adopted policies and accepted planks that contained the essential elements of Reaganism: continued military expansion; support for Reagan's allies in Central America, the Caribbean and the Middle East; further degradation of the welfare system; denial of black demands for equity; and unqualified submission to the imperatives of the corporate system.

Complicit in the first formal expression of Mondaleism are those who early and often endorsed Mondale without reservation: leaders of the National Organization for Women, organized teachers, democratic socialists, black officeholders, labor hierarchs, Hispanic leaders. They must now be foot soldiers in a campaign whose captains are implacably antagonistic to the prin-

---

*The political demands of the Rainbow Coalition, implicit in its construction and explicit in Jackson's speeches, are extraordinary. They are racial, sexual, economic and ideological. "All of us feel deprived in twentieth-century America," he told the audience at the Waldorf, "and America is still organized by cash—the cash system that is still dominated by white males." What other major-party candidate in this century has talked about deprivation in a "cash system dominated by white males"? No wonder Jackson scares conventional politicians half to death.

ciples and concerns of their constituencies. What can Mondale's tame left flank do, for instance, to rescue poor women, blacks, service workers and the young from the ranks of the growing underclass impoverished by economic policies and structures Mondale endorses? How can socialist leaders save socialist politics from the isolation, irrelevance and ultimate extinction ordained by complaisant submission to Democratic Party practices? How can union chieftains get more power for union members when the point of Mondaleism is the expansion of management control? How can black politicians win from Mondale what they have been denied by the party machinery for years on end?

Where does the left—the white left, that is, which refuses to concede Jackson's validity and hardly acknowledges his existence—stand now? It has given up on class struggle, black liberation, the Third World, even détente. It can hardly remember the nuclear freeze. Its only live demand, settled last week, was the promotion of a woman as the Democratic vice-presidential nominee: the transubstantiation of politics into symbolism. If she does anything, Geraldine Ferraro will activate the party ticket, but she is poorly placed and notoriously disinclined to shift its gravity from dead center. After all, she chaired the platform committee that codified the party's conservative cast. Those who rejoice at her appointment should remember as well the politics it is being used to ratify. To what degree, therefore, will symbolism become sedative?

Is this bleak prospectus the inevitable consequence of what Michael Harrington recently extolled as the necessary strategy for any left in America today: that "the Democratic Party, with all its flaws, must be our main political arena"? Harrington, co-chairman of the Democratic Socialists of America, and Irving Howe, editor of *Dissent* and avatar of democraticsocialism as an unhyphenated ideology, chatted at great length recently in *The New York Times Magazine*, which touted them as "Voices From the Left." The import of their conversation, which ran 8,000 words without one mention of the difficult name Jackson, was the denial of any vital role for the left in current politics.

They are wrong. There is a way to salvage something of the left's presence even this late in the year, to broaden its constituency and sphere of action, to begin building a role for the next decade—and still engage the realities of the two-party system. But the left must first accept the invitation of history.

Heedless of the seismic convulsions in the American economic and social landscape during the last two decades, the left continues to read old history: the chronicles of the New Deal and its successor deals in the postwar boom. In that long-ago time, the Democratic coalition offered industrial workers, the new urban and suburban middle class and white ethnic minorities (overlapping categories, to be sure) a certain measure of economic security, social mobility and political influence in return for their cooperation in the governing strategies of state and business in the American Century.

The bargain began to unravel in the early 1960s, when the underclass mutinied. The Democratic response was the War on Poverty, a kind of federal trust fund for the civil rights revolution. But the war was lost. A few statistics illustrate the size of the rout. In 1965, the poorest 40 percent of the population earned 11 percent of the total US market income; nearly a decade and a half later, that same group's share had shrunk to 8.5 percent. From 1945 to 1983, black male participation in the labor force fell from 80 percent to 60 percent. The poor got poorer and the blacks got unemployed. In his trenchant résumé of postwar American history, Mike Davis, writing in the January/February 1984 *New Left Review*, stresses that the civil rights revolution "fundamentally failed in its ultimate goals of achieving the mass incorporation of black labor into the high-wage economy, or of surmounting the barriers of *de facto* segregation in Northern schools and suburbs. A generation after the first March on Washington for Jobs and Freedom, black unemployment remains double that of whites, while black poverty is three times more common. Sixty percent of employed black males (and 50 percent of Hispanics) are concentrated in the spectrum of the lowest paid jobs."

The number of working women doubled between the Eisenhower and Reagan eras, but in the same period their earnings declined to 59 percent of the average wage for men. In 1980, one-third of full-time women workers earned less than $7,000 a year, as against a white male median of $17,000.

A populist, progressive Democratic Party could have entered the 1970s with a renegotiated social compact, an expanded coalition and a renewed vision. It could have proposed to bring women and blacks into better-paying jobs; to reform tax and spending policies to expand public services and collective consumption; to apply Keynesian theories to a peace-building rather than a war-making economy; to answer increasing demands for better health care, education, recreation and a clean environment. And, indeed, there was a ready-made activist base and an eager constituency for change in the civil rights, black liberation, women's and peace movements of that period.

It was the road not taken. The Democratic Party leaders and their allies—Hubert Humphrey, Henry Jackson, George Meany—were unprepared to accept the necessary conditions for a directional shift. They could not imagine converting to a peace economy when the war economy (and the ideology that rationalized its expansion) had been the foundation of Democratic fortunes since 1939. Labor leaders could not countenance the threat to their power implicit in the demands a militant and unified work force would make for integration, participation in management decisions and conversion. And, finally, the party bosses would not allow disenfranchised blacks, poor people, women and low-wage workers to challenge their hold on the party and its agenda.

Instead, the party traditionalists counterattacked. Labor leaders forced blacks out of training programs, bucked affirmative action and literally assaulted those who protested the war system. In 1972, Democratic hierarchs and their labor lieutenants decided to defect from the campaign of their party's candidate—standard-bearer of the popular alliance at its strongest hour—rather than permit a new politics to develop. On that scorched earth was built the fractured architecture of the next period.

With its crumbling coalition and its old commanders, the Democratic Party now faces an entirely changed landscape. The road the country did take as the postwar boom ended led to the famous split-level economy, with its vast low-wage ghetto (containing a third of the labor force, mostly in the expanding service sector), its newly employed and scandalously underpaid female component and its powerful echelons of the new rich.

To sustain and expand their privilege, the new rich have mounted one of the most successful campaigns in American political and economic history. From the tax revolts of California to the tax programs of the Republican Administration and the Democratic ways and means committee, the large upper class has devised schemes to make a better living for itself at the expense of the even larger underclass. Despite spasms of opposition, the Democrats are incapable of challenging the basic corporate campaign. They cannot meet the enemy; they are it.

The Democratic weakness is much more structural than spiritual, though the party's profound lack of imagination cannot be overstated. For instance, the present phase of military expansion, projected from 1977 to (at least) 1986, is the longest in US history. Amid long-term stagnation, it is the engine of what vigor remains in the economy. To cut back on such spending in any substantial way without innovative, indeed radical, alternatives would be to assail steel, machine tools, aerospace, shipbuilding—all of which are, in labor terms alone, core parts of the Mondale coalition. Mondale could no more allow anti-militarist sentiment to threaten the war industry than he could let insurgency threaten Third World regimes in hock to the American banking system.

Mondale pretends to include members of the newly expanded underclass in his old coalition, but the programs he espouses leave no place for them except as voters on election day. Gary Hart could have undercut Mondale by embracing the popular alliance that the old Democrats ignored. Instead, he chose to clothe his neoliberalism—the politics of lowered expectations—in bogus generational rhetoric. In the end, his only issue was the difference between Mondale's birthdate and his own, whatever that might be.

So, in control are the Democratic "pragmatists," as the pollsters and pundits call them: the ones who argue for party unity at the expense of movement and who propose that the way to beat Reaganism is to denounce its excesses while accepting its premises. The pathos of their opportunism lies in its short-sightedness. As every tactician attests, the key to defeating Reagan is turnout. But turnout has political content and context. People will not simply vote for Anybody But Reagan; they want somebody who speaks to their interests, who promises them more than they've got and who offers them hope. The enormous non-voting constituency of today is located in the lower precincts of the split-level economy. Its participation in the election is by no means assured. But it is there that the left must look for its opportunities and discharge its responsibilities in the next period.

The only way the left can work within the Democratic Party is to act without it. That is, the future of the party will be determined by the development of forces operating on its margins or beyond its boundaries (just as the developing American political economy—late capitalism—faces its most serious challenge at the hands of the Third World, both within and outside the national frontier). The constituency that formed in response to Jackson's campaign is a prime example. Its votes are absolutely necessary to defeat Reagan, but its priorities set it directly against the power and position of the Democratic mainstream. The pragmatists who want the votes will soon see that those votes don't come free and that without a significant reordering of the Democratic agenda, the new voters will not stream to the polls.

Ironically, the blacks of the Jackson campaign may have learned a lesson from the strategy Jewish leaders have employed since 1968: that it is at least as important to assert power in a coalition as to submerge it, and to withhold support from a candidate as to endorse him. Good alliances imply clear threats. Mayor Richard Hatcher of Gary, Indiana, chairman of the Jackson campaign, was recently quoted as saying, "Better four more years of Reagan than four more years of disrespect from the Democratic leadership."

The left has a history of attachment to a political logic that admits two equally unacceptable alternatives: isolation in purist parties (activists and intellectuals doomed to life on the margins of social practice), or total immersion in the belly of the Democratic beast. Once the left sees that party as the only possible vehicle, it is trapped in the lesser-of-two-evils paradox and ends up as a cheering section for the most reactionary elements in it. To see a way around the paradox, and escape the logic, the left need look no further than the Jackson campaign's project to form a popular coalition of people who need change most and can be counted on to fight for it hardest. Rainbowism is certainly the most interesting news in this political season, and potentially the most wrenching historical development since the labor struggles of the 1930s. It offers an example of how an alliance of the disenfranchised can approach the Democratic Party, use it when necessary and work at some remove when that seems propitious.

An election campaign, it should be stressed, is only one avenue of action in the process of building power. The methods developed by Ralph Nader, which organize coalitions of consumers at the point of consumption, aggrieved citizens at the point of their grievance and workers in the context of their workplace, make enormous sense for left activism. Parties are important but they are not all-important. The Democratic Party is a vehicle, not the only vehicle.

As the fall campaign begins, the left should remember that there's more to politics than is suggested by that self-deprecating formulation of *Realpolitik*: hold one's nose and vote for Mondale. Barbarism with a human face may be preferable to barbarism with a barbaric one, but there are hundreds of other campaigns, scores of local coalitions in formation and numerous activist projects that carry greater weight in an electoral year. The Democratic call for unity is a guilt trip when party whips—the ones in the press as well as in power—use it to extinguish all signs of life on the left side of the universe. It is not the left's business to shore up the party and cheer on its candidate every four years. There is a bigger job to do in creating radical alternatives to dead-center politics—and that means regarding the Democratic Party without sentiment or illusion.

July 21, 1984, with Alexander Cockburn, THE NATION

✦

'Our Parents Are a Little Weird'

The last time I saw Maris, she was sitting on a large stone that served as the front step of a commune house in Putney, Vermont, watching the war come home around her. A pickupful of local punks had roared up the road the night before, shouting oaths at the long-haired hippies who lived inside and tossing the odd Bud can onto the communal property. It seems like the slightest provocation today, but in the summer of 1972 there was a madman in the White House, an Underground in the hills, a holocaust in Indochina and a world in generational turmoil. To the Putney settlers, those punks came clothed as the President's men, Hoover's agents, Westmoreland's army.

The communards swung into action. The boys—few of them were yet 30—wheeled an old, dead Land Rover across the driveway, assembled a pile of sticks and stones, and shouldered pieces of gear that might well have been real weapons in the hands of real guerrillas. The girls—they had not yet been certified as women—hung back, worried and confused. Maris looked as though she had been crying.

There was no engagement of the enemy that warm day in the gentle hills of the Connecticut River Valley. Perhaps the punks never knew they had been counterattacked. The repression of the radical generation, of which the Putney communards had been active members, was softer and subtler than the fantasy of armed assaults they enacted. The revolution in Vermont just ran out of steam, and the rural radicals were soon ready to split. In two weeks, Maris was in Miami. Within a few months, the men—game time over—had left for other lives in other places. Many of the women—they had put down more roots, taken up local responsibilities and in some cases borne children—stayed to make new homes in New England.

It is not true that there are no second acts in the lives of Americans; there are reunions. Twelve summers after the brief battle of the Putney commune, some 300 communards and other survivors of Vermont collective living at the turn of the last decade gathered at the YWCA's Camp Hochelaga on Grand Isle in Lake Champlain to reprise some of their old lines, untie some of the stubborn knots and see how the years had weathered the cast.

They called the event the Free Vermont Recollective, and what it brought back were the denizens of a score of communes and collectives that once dotted the countryside: in Glover in the Northeast Kingdom, in Guilford on the Massachusetts border, Franklin on the Canadian frontier, Mount Philo, Plainfield, Richmond, Burlington, Putney. Free Vermont was a concept that never quite made the leap into an organization. Under its banner (the old pre-federal Vermont flag, with the imperishable warning "Don't Tread on Me"), young urban radicals spread out to pursue their politics *al fresco*. At length, the communes withered away, but many Free Vermonters kept in touch, and last winter some of them—mostly the women—began planning a summer reunion. But there were unexpected snags. Life in the commune had been resolutely vague; no membership lists, no job descriptions, hardly any last names. The Recollective organizers sent out calls seeking the whereabouts of "Sharon from Glover" and "Strawberry (runaway) from Brattleboro."

Strawberry is still missing. But Maris came up from Miami, and Robert flew in from Paris. Most people still hadn't acquired last names; others had gone through several. And it still didn't matter. As John said, "We lived with people for three years and never knew who they were."

People brought snapshots and buttons with forgotten slogans, and someone displayed a diary she kept in the days when so much was happening and short-term memory was at a premium. Its pages were filled with particolored, rock-resounding visions of the brave old world: swimming at the quarry, long collective encounter sessions, the first time someone said "Sisterhood is powerful." The past is media, too; nostalgia carries messages from one country to another.

There was volleyball and boating and, on Saturday afternoon, movies about the wars in Central America. Like the old days, the weekend was a fluid but not always plausible mixture of politics and hanging out. The social arrangements had a familiar sixties slant. The women did all the organizing and the men walked around, slightly bemused, wondering about their appropriate parts. The kids enjoyed a remarkable measure of command. They greeted the reunionites, explained camp layout and scheduling, and ticked off pertinent details on computer sheets.

The children of this generation are now racing through adolescence, and they carry their ironies with aplomb. They have names like no others: Dylan, Rain, Leaf, Amerin, Zephyr, Eurydice. I didn't hear of anyone who changed to Mark or Melissa. "We think our parents are a little weird," one of them told Paul, a former Free Vermonter who now works for National Public Radio. The judgement was lighthearted, Paul reported to a group sitting on the grass. His analysis (these people are nothing if not persistent analysts) was that the kids have a collective memory of an anarchic time when there were no rules or prohibitions. It was wonderful but unreal. Since then they've watched, with approval and some sympathy, their parents grow up.

Everyone looked great. Not as terrific as Tom Berenger or Glenn Close in *The Big Chill*, but healthy and whole at 40 or more. Hardly anyone has a good steady job on the inside track of business or the professions. Robert makes movies in France. Jane works in an LA bookstore with a Buddhist name. Bobby is a gumshoe for the NAACP in Oakland, investigating cases of police brutality all over Northern California. This first multimedia generation is hip deep in publishing, broadcasting and filmmaking, but in most cases with that fringe sensibility that defines the age.

Many of the women from the old Vermont communes settled around Burlington. Without much strategic planning, they have built an impressive network of social services and political institutions: day-care centers, women's crisis facilities, legal aid offices, health-care clinics, cultural programs, solidarity committees. Some of them came in on the ground floor of Socialist Mayor Bernie Sanders's successful campaign. All of them see a connection, however indirect, between the ideas they explored in Free Vermont and the development of a remarkable modern culture in a state that caters to the New Age and the older ones with a high degree of tolerance and support. It wasn't always clear how, but they can see now that in 1972 the punks lost and the Free Vermonters won, in ways they never imagined.

October 1984, NEW ENGLAND MONTHLY

✦

The Changelings

The convert plays a favored part in social history and ideological drama. Armed with the certainty of revelation, the authority of confession and the conviction of sin, the convert leaps ahead of those poor souls who have had the misfortune, or bad sense, to keep a foolish consistency. From all accounts, St. Augustine was a pretty fair pagan—coveting this and that, and generally indulging his paganistic vices with relish and determination. But he really came into his own after the prayers of his mother, Monica, converted him to Catholicism (for her efforts she was sainted as well; the benefits of conversion are not strained). Thousands of patient monks and anxious abbots who had hoped to place in the heavenly sweepstakes were left in the dust by the born-again Bishop of Hippo.

David Horowitz and Peter Collier, former editors of *Ramparts* and more recently authors of best-selling books on the Rockefellers and the Kennedys, may have less world-historical impact than the Catholic converts of antiquity, but their embrace of Reaganism has given them enormous cachet in this intellectually chaotic season. They have been in the process of spiritual transformation for some time. Their well-researched biographies of America's dynastic families are stuffed with scandal, high on inside dope and devoid of serious analysis, from any perspective, of the kind Horowitz, at least, constructed so eloquently in the 1960s. (His *Empire and Revolution* and *The Free World Colossus*, which documented the disastrous dynamic of American imperialism, were pioneering revisionist works.) Of late, the two have turned up in mass-circulation magazines with rambling, vicious ad hominem attacks on former comrades, allies and friends from the anti-war and black power movements. One article defined the difficult association of white and black radicals as a problem of interracial lust and class guilt, with names named for easy identification. Another rewrote the history of the final years of SDS as an orgy of drugs and pansexuality, complete with an illustration of Bernardine Dohrn's bare breasts.

The message of the books and the articles, beyond simple sensationalism, is that society is irrelevant, that historical forces are inoperative and that only ego, id and libido—especially libido—are useful categories to describe and understand "an imperfect world." The rich man's quest for power, the adolescent's lust for pleasure, the white woman's guilt about her skin color, the black man's rage to dominate: such is the stuff of history, so why grapple with difficult abstractions like class, race, revolution, empire and ideology, which cannot be illustrated with anatomical detail?

Horowitz and Collier's latest broadside is an article published last month in *The Washington Post Magazine*. It's called "Lefties for Reagan," and it takes the cake. "Casting our ballots for Ronald Reagan," they write, "was indeed a way of finally saying goodbye to all that—to the self-aggrandizing romance with corrupt Third Worldism; to the casual indulgence of Soviet totalitarianism; to the hypocritical and self-dramatizing anti-Americanism which is the New Left's bequest to mainstream politics."

Why a vote for Reagan was specifically an antidote to these psychological and existential horrors ("self" is the authors' favorite prefix) is never made clear. They admit, in a parenthetical phrase in the penultimate paragraph of the seven-page article, that they are less than enthusiastic about the President's "domestic policy," but there's no time for that now. They are very upset about Soviet policy in Afghanistan, about the brutality of certain Third World governments (only a few leftish ones are mentioned—nothing about Chile, South Korea, the Philippines, El Salvador, Guatemala, the Sudan, South Africa, etc., etc.), about Abbie Hoffman, Tom Hayden (in his old days), Fidel Castro, "the Beverly Hills cocktail circuit," Noam Chomsky, the Khmer Rouge, *The Nation* and me.

This magazine comes under attack for an editorial that argued that the United States bears some responsibility for events in Cambodia and could contribute to a solution to the troubles there. I am criticized for a column I wrote for *The Village Voice* in 1980 which credited the Soviet Union with supporting (albeit inadequately) popular insurgencies and revolutions in dozens of places around the world where the United States supported (much more generously) the ruling dictatorships, juntas, oligarchies and tyrants.

Nevertheless, one would think that a vote for Mondale would have been just as legitimate an affirmation of the electoral process, a protest against selfism in all its ghastly forms, an expression of anti-communism and pro-Americanism, and a symbolic whack at Abbie, Noam and me. But only a Reagan vote is a ticket to heaven, a true confession of error and a credential for a place at the head of the line. Converts to Reaganism must be more radical in their convictions than ordinary adherents of the ideology; the born-again are less mannered in their behavior than are those to the manner born. Conversion hysteria, after all, is not a character disorder, like "self-hatred," "self-aggrandizing romance," "casual indulgence" and the other psychological and sexual aberrations Horowitz and Collier diagnose in the American left. It has specific social and historical functions, and it is a way for a political culture to create ideological momentum and legitimacy.

Horowitz and Collier rationalize their transit from Red to dead as an aspect of maturity: "Anyone under 40 who isn't a socialist has no heart; anyone over 40 who is a socialist has no brain." I don't suppose they're thinking of Mussolini or Chiang Kai-shek; perhaps Susan Sontag and Arturo Cruz, both of whom are mentioned favorably, are more palatable models. The left has had its share of changelings, and it is certainly every polemicist's prerogative to go back on his or her word. But we should understand that reality does not change with each passing birthday, and that confessions made under the duress of history can easily fail the test of time.

April 6, 1985, THE NATION

✦

Handwriting on the Wall

In the Fourteenth Street subway station at Sixth Avenue in Manhattan—Bernhard Goetz's home stop—a new piece of graffiti adorns the grimy tiles: "GOETZ RULES NIGGERS." There's nothing special in the sight of filth and bile scrawled on the city's walls, but that terse emblem may be unique: of the millions of words written and broadcast about the "Death Wish" Vigilante since his attack on four black youths in the subway last December, those three most frankly and directly state the racist sentiments that infuse the case.

Racism is hardly a secret, and the significance of a white man emptying his revolver into the bodies of four blacks is lost on no one. It is what everyone talks about in their homes, at work, on the street. Race is the referent when people recount tales of their own muggings or of assaults on friends and neighbors. But now the media display an unaccustomed tact. Last week, *The New York Times* published almost a full page of research on Goetz in which the word "black" appeared only once, in a quote from Goetz's description of a 1981 mugging; the racial aspect of the recent shooting was never mentioned. Goetz's campaign against neighborhood crime was detailed, tenants in his apartment house were interviewed, and his life and career were chronicled. The reporter, Robert McFadden, apparently thought it was relevant to relay the story that Goetz's father was indicted for molesting two teenage boys in 1960, but he omitted one highly charged item that was published in another paper just after Goetz's surrender: some neighbors who attended a tenants' meeting Goetz once organized were appalled at his "bigotry."

Even the tabloids, for whom no sensation is too lurid, present the racism only by inference: pictures of the assailant and his victims, the coy use of journalistic code words and the repetition of telltale descriptions ("the blond, well-dressed engineer"). Public officials, including Mayor Ed Koch and Police Commissioner Benjamin Ward (the first black man to hold that position), were quick to condemn the shootings, but they seemed more concerned about the challenge it posed to the city's monopoly on police power, the affront to the city administration's competence and the effect on November's local elections than about the racial crisis that it expressed.

Apparently, the media and the officials believe that if race is not mentioned, it need not be confronted and might somehow disappear as an issue. Other justifications, some of them valid in part, are applied to fit the crime and the public reaction. Self-defense is a natural right; the public is sick of crime, mistrustful of the police and despairing of justice from the courts; people need to take revenge, personally or vicariously, for all the unpunished "little murders" of urban life; the social contract ran out in the 1960s and has not been renewed. Local television news shows bolster arguments for those theories with sidewalk interviews that confirm the racial component by seeming to deny it: a black woman supports Goetz; the mother of one of the shooting victims says her son deserved it; a "civil rights lawyer" and a CORE leader express approval for the vigilante's attack. If race were not at the heart of the matter, such pointed responses, marshalled to influence public opinion, would not be necessary.

Avoiding public discussion of the issue that is on everyone's mind does not dampen hatred but gives it a measure of legitimacy. The subway shooting has loosed a lot of ugly thoughts and unworthy opinions not only in New York City, where it is hard to view one's fellows of all varieties without fear and hostility, but in peaceable corners of the country, where street crime is rare and social relations are generally cordial. Storekeepers in New Hampshire, farmers in Iowa, suburbanites in Georgia, reveal to reporters and talk-show hosts an anger that hardly comes from personal experience. Rather, it is a metaphorical rage, the function of a pervasive sense of powerlessness that fixes primarily—though not exclusively—on race as a cause and revenge as a cure.

In fact, the subway shooting has become a mythic expression of the illness of American society. It is a drama strong enough to arouse a country inured to ordinary acts of violence, able "to hit a raw nerve" as people are saying, to subvert the facts of the case to the construction of an instant social myth. Goetz himself is called an unlikely hero, but he seems perfect for his part in this modern morality play: the story of a lonely yuppie terminator, neurotic, freelance and divorced in the anomic city; but blond, brave and Germanic in battle against the invading dark barbarians. It doesn't matter in the myth, as opposed to the event, whether he was hassled or attacked, whether he saw the youths' screwdrivers or not, whether he meant to kill or defend. In the play, the blasts from his silver gun arouse a powerless people, and the wounds of his victims redeem a fallen land.

The myth as well as the reality evoke frightening historical analogies. Our nightmares are filled with images of tribal violence rationalized as political necessity. We know what results when racial tension is exploited to empower a populace whose pride and patriotism have been offended. Nothing good comes from acts of social vengeance. The subways and streets of New York are no safer now, the courts are still clogged, the police are no more efficient, punks are not cowed and ordinary citizens are not confident. To change the conditions that gave rise to the myth, the myth must first be destroyed. Fear, hatred and hostility are private emotions, but they are also public issues. And they are written on the subway walls.

January 19, 1985, THE NATION

Chapter XII

✦

A SEASON FOR REPENTANCE

War and Memory

If the lesson of the fortieth anniversary of the end of the war in Europe is "Never Again," the message in many of the celebrations marking the tenth anniversary of America's withdrawal from Vietnam seems to be "Wait Till Next Time." The parades and the fireworks, the voluminous media retrospectives and the fulsome political rhetoric seek to mobilize sympathy for Vietnam vets. But behind the patriotic fuss is a desperate desire to ennoble the American war, to cancel the country's shame and to prepare for the next defense of imperial power.

Although America lost in Indochina, no de-Vietnamization campaign was created to cleanse the culture of the ideology that sanctioned the war and of the personalities who waged it. After a brief period of unpopularity produced by military defeat—not moral compunction—the generals, the diplomats and the intellectual apologists of the Vietnam intervention are back in favor and in power. In California, the state assembly recently passed a resolution calling America's war "a noble and honorable defense of liberty," and the bill's sponsor attacked Assemblyman Tom Hayden, who spoke against it, as a "traitor." It passed 52 to 0, with twenty-seven abstentions. The men who ran the assassination programs in Vietnam, who called in the strikes that incinerated and defoliated the peninsula, who deceived and manipulated the American people, are now in positions to try their hand at targets much closer to home, for another defense of freedom against the Nicaraguans.

In Germany, the allied de-Nazification effort at least established the moral culpability of those who made the apocalypse then. The millions who followed Hitler, or simply remained silent, and the soldiers who did their duty were victims of a kind, but they were also executioners. President Reagan and Chancellor Kohl may claim that the Nazi army was made up of 15-year-olds snatched from school, and we should feel sorry that they were used by criminal men for evil ends. But the forces of the Reich cannot escape historical or moral condemnation. The soldiers may not have welcomed their assignment, but they carried it out.

The American invasion and occupation of Vietnam was of a different order from the Nazi campaign in Europe, but murder is murder is murder (as Margaret Thatcher so nicely phrased it); torture is torture; racism is racism, whether aimed at Jews and gypsies or the Vietnamese. The veterans of that war repose in quiet graves or survive in troubled times, and they deserve our pity but not our praise. Their presence is our Bitburg, and they should rest in peace, not rise in revenge.

May 18, 1985, THE NATION

✦

Rambo: Metamachismo Carries the Day

Vietnam has suffered invasions, interventions and expeditions by every great power in this century; it has endured the visits of foe and friend, from Robert McNamara to Jane Fonda; it has survived almost half a century of bombing, mining, corruption, incineration and defoliation. All that, and now this: along comes Rambo, the ultimate weapon in humanoid form, winning with biceps and pecs the war that the mightiest nation in history lost with mere B-52s and Agent Orange. At last, William Westmoreland's dishonorable defeat has been avenged by Sly Stallone.

Rambo: First Blood Part II is at once hilarious and disgusting. It's hard not to howl at Stallone's apish ambition, the blind egomania of a lowland gorilla who looks at his reflection in a jungle pool and sees a limpid Narcissus. It is to laugh when Stallone slaughters whole battalions of Vietnamese and Soviet soldiers ("damn Russian bastards!") with crossbow, bazooka and bare hands; steals a helicopter and destroys native villages (the ones the US army missed); rescues American POWs from the Vietcong tiger cages where they have been languishing since *The Deer Hunter*. It is even worth a chuckle when Stallone finally manages to grunt out a complete prepositional clause ("for our country to love us as much as we love it") in the closing thirty seconds, even though we may have to wait for Part III for a whole sentence, with subject and predicate like they have in those European films. When Brando mumbled through *Julius Caesar*, it was tolerated as sheer Method madness; with Stallone, mumbles are the very best he can do.

But even Stallone's camp followers will have a hard time swallowing the twisted history, the racist images and the political line of Rocky's latest horror show. Its premise is that certain villains—bureaucrats, politicians, CIA operatives—sold America down the river in Vietnam and afterwards, thus losing the war and preventing the return of uncounted MIAs. The lowly grunts would have won if left to their own devices, and when they were sent home the society that surrendered despised them precisely because their presence was a constant reproach. *First Blood*, which introduced Rambo, glorified the bitter and violent veteran in his struggle against cowardly authority and a complacent citizenry. In that effort, Rambo turned his wrath against small-town rednecks in the Pacific Northwest and against wave after wave of the national guard. For the damage done, he was sentenced to a season on the prison rock pile.

Post-imperial frustration is a familiar theme in twentieth-century history: cf., Hitler after Versailles, the Tory right after Suez, the China Lobby after Mao's march. The syndrome has several phases. First blood is always drawn internally, from those at home held responsible for the unaccountable defeat. Then come the overseas revenge fantasies, sometimes enacted in terrifying reality. No doubt there are worse scenarios in store for America than the one Stallone and James (*The Terminator*) Cameron created for Rambo, but until the real thing comes along, we are asked to sublimate our death wishes in the Hollywood version.

Rambo is sprung by his old special forces colonel (Richard Crenna) and sent back to Nam. "Do we get to win this time?" he asks in a moment of foreshadowing which epitomizes the subtlety of the plot to follow. The Green Beret replies that it's all up to Rambo, but in fact the same wimps and sell-outs in Congress and the CIA who collapsed after Tet are setting Rambo up for failure. They want him to find no live Americans in-country so that they can continue their dirty diplomatic games of appeasement and accommodation.

Aided only by Co, the Vietnamese girl *contra* (apparently no authentic ethnic actress has succeeded France Nguyen as the all-purpose Pan-Asian heroine, so the part is played by the round-eyed Julia Nickson), Rambo has to do battle with Charlie, Ivan, a band of river pirates, assorted leeches and snakes, the CIA mission commander, the legacy of Henry Kissinger and the ghost of the anti-war movement. It's no contest. Metamachismo carries the day. Rambo sheds only a tear when Co takes an Aka burst in the back (those damn Russian bastards always shoot you as you're running). When, dying, she implores, "Don't forget me," he merely grunts, "Uh-uh." War love is never having to say anything, and these big guys really love making war. Stallone is a Bill Broyles with muscles, but his passion for carnage is no big secret. "You're of Indian-German descent," the CIA man notes approvingly as he reads Rambo's dossier. "It's a hell of a combination." I'll say!

June 22, 1985, THE NATION

✦

Are You Game?

I do not come from a household of hunter-gatherers. In the postwar suburban world where I learned about the provenance, preparation and consumption of food, meat trotted through the kitchen door once a week in the arms of Albert the Butcher. Wild berries were thought to be toxic until proven edible by a foolhardy friend, and root vegetables were considered unclean unless julienned or minced by Birds Eye. Aside from the gray squirrels who romped under the adolescent oak on my father's manicured lawn, the only wild game I ever saw was the odd dead deer strapped across the bumper of a car racing along the Merritt Parkway on a Sunday evening in the fall.

Now I can't say much about the evolution of gathering as a social phenomenon since then; the movement sparked by Euell Gibbons in the late sixties never became more than a pleasant pastime for those with the leisure to stalk the roadside berm, and a taste for parboiled milkweed. But it seems clear that hunting, or at least the fruit of hunting's labor, is making a major comeback.

A sizable bookshelf of new frontier culinary texts is growing, with such landmark volumes as *The L.L. Bean Game & Fish Cookbook*, in which Angus Cameron and Judith Jones offer recipes for "crumbled and fried beaver tail" and "baked young woodchuck in sour cream and mustard." At Christmas time the great urban gourmet boutiques are decked out like natural history museums, with stuffed swans suspended from the ceiling, enormous salmons snarled in *aioli* nets, and menacing boars poised against the patrons on the countertop. Smaller shops along gentry row in several cities are stocking quail and venison where just recently they were content to carry franchised patés and frozen quiches, limp relics of an earlier trend now fading.

The transit from mousse to moose is marked by the emergence of the hunter as a defining figure of American life. The solitary figure of the frontiersman, clad in the skins of dead animals and armed to the teeth, has come to signify the new American cuisine, which is to effete old-world cookery as the ringtail coonskin cap is to the starched white tocque. It certainly must be a powerful myth if it can get city people to eat baked woodchuck, of any age.

Far from the swinging swans of Soho and long before Cameron and Jones created "ground billy [goat] with peppers, zucchini and eggplant Parmigiana," folks began trooping to Bradford, Vermont, for an extraordinary supper of wild game laid on each year at the end of hunting season in November by the gentlemen and ladies of the United Church of Christ. The frontier never quite died in the Vermont historical identity; it merely hibernated during the middle decades of this century while local inhabitants made a kind of peace with the stockyard system and the supermarket culture. But in villages like

Bradford, where 1,200 souls huddle between the Green Mountains foothills and the upper Connecticut River, the men still hunted and trapped, and sometimes they would get together for a feast of their prey.

"The men really liked beaver the best," Eris Eastman, a townswoman who has helped run the game supper for almost twenty years, told me not long ago. There was beaver on the menu that night in 1957 when the men decided to convert their occasional meals together into a benefit supper for the fund to build a cement sidewalk from the street out front to the vestry-room door. A hundred people paid $1.25 each—75 cents for children—to eat venison, roast raccoon, 'coon and rabbit pies and, of course, roast beaver. The church made $83.15, as the story goes, so the sidewalk was built and a ritual pageant of the hunt was born that persists to this day.

For ten years the local exemplars of frontiersmanship ran the show as a male preserve, Eris Eastman recalled with a slightly rueful smile. The men brought in the game, cooked it to their taste, organized the whole affair and served the guests, whose number steadily increased as the years went by. Women were allowed to make the gingerbread for dessert, in their own kitchens, and they were invited to dinner, but the pageant maintained a strictly masculine cast. By 1966, some 300 game-hungry diners would arrive at the church, and the contradictions of the tumultuous times as well as the limitations of the modest facilities began to impinge on the peace of the pageant.

"It was a cold, cold night that year," Eastman recounted, dropping her voice and drawing closer as we chatted across the table in her kitchen, not far from the church in Bradford. "Hunters came in from the field, maybe they had had a few beers, and things got a bit rowdy in the vestry. The men thought they had to wait too long for their food. If it hadn't been a church, there would have been a fight, I think," she continued, "but when things calmed down, the men decided they'd better let women run things from now on."

Eastman took over as co-chairwoman in 1967, and there has been no trouble at all since then. These years, upwards of a thousand people are served in shifts running from 2:30 in the afternoon to 8:30 at night, the tariff is $15 for adults and $7 for children, and the menu has expanded to included, at various times, wild boar, moose steaks, buffalo, Catalina goat, mouflon ram, Dall's sheep, caribou, elk, pheasant with rice, bear sausage, mixed-game sausage, venison in three or four different styles, and the old stand-bys of raccoon, rabbit pie and beaver.

There have been fewer gastronomic disasters than one might have expected. "The time we had woodchuck, everyone said it tasted just like chicken," Eastman said, "but for some reason it was not popular. We never had it again. Then there was the year we served pigeon pie. One pie went the whole meal, and there was some left over. We never had that again, either."

"The worst was when we lost our beaver," she continued with a faint shudder. There was big trouble in Bradford that year. "Some people come just for the beaver, although a lot think it's too gamy. Well, the beaver is shot early in the year, in January and February, and one of the ladies put ten beavers in her freezer and went away to Florida. Her husband had just passed away and she didn't come back by the time we started to prepare the meats. We *do* keep track of where our food is stored, we have a system," Eastman insisted, "but that year, for some reason, no one could remember who had the beaver. We looked *everywhere*. Finally, we had to go without it, and a lot of people were *very* disappointed."

It would be exciting to think that every species that hits the table roams the wilderness on the edge of town, but in fact few of the target animals are brought down by local townsfolk *in situ* with their .22s. "We don't go out and kill anything specifically for the supper," Eastman emphasized. But bear, beaver and raccoon are indeed trapped in the area, their pelts taken for sale and their meat donated for dinner. Buffalo comes from a rancher in South Dakota, and the exotic viands, such as Catalina goat and mouflon ram, are culled from the stock of Web Keefe's private game preserve in neighboring Ely, Vermont. Pheasant and rabbit are provided by commercial suppliers (wild hare cannot be legally sold in the state), and the occasional moose, elk or caribou turns up when a friend or parishioner happens to shoot such a beast in the distant wilds.

Venison has a more problematic provenance. Thousands of bucks (and in some years, does) are bagged in Vermont's sixteen-day big-game annual shooting spree, but hunters cannot easily sell their prizes, and the church cannot rely on the generosity of parishioners who might have an extra haunch to donate. So, much of the deer meat is collected, hit or miss, throughout the year. The hitting is, unfortunately, often done by cars, and game wardens around the state are alerted to scoop up road kills and turn over illegally shot animals to the supper's organizers, who place dressed meat in villagers' freezers for eventual preparation.

The men still do the grilling and roasting, a gender-identified ritual in hunter mythology that contemporary sexual politics has not yet altered. The women whip up the fancier concoctions—the loaves, stews and game pies— as well as the vegetables and dessert. A hundred or more townspeople are engaged in supper activities; they store the meat, cook at home or at the regional high school's institutional kitchen, tidy up the church and serve the food. Minister John Knight has a crucial responsibility; he is in charge of dyeing 15,000 toothpicks in rainbow hues to color-code the meats. Guests are handed a small mimeographed card with the key for each year's menu: aqua for boar, for instance, yellow for mouflon ram. Nowadays, the supper makes a heady profit: a good $10,000 is cleared with a capacity crowd, and that goes for church repair and redecoration and a scholarship fund to send local youngsters to the Green Mountains Conservation Camps in the summer.

I first heard about the Bradford supper in the early seventies, when it was already well-established but not yet part of the gentrified trend of frontier cuisine. With a rather jolly group of friends from Boston, I drove up Interstate 91 on another cold, cold afternoon in the late New England fall. There was ice on all the ponds and a thin crust of snow over the brown meadows, and by the time we got to Bradford, the main street was full of cars with out-of-state license plates disgorging people dressed in heavy winter gear. No wonder L.L. Bean is pushing game recipes this year; they might have outfitted the entire guest list that night.

We had sent in for our reservations a month earlier. Each year a date is set for applications—usually in mid-October—and would-be diners are accepted according to the postmark on their letters. The event is generally sold out after one or two days' mail. We had been assigned to a 6 o'clock seating (you can list three choices), but like eager beavers we arrived at the lodge before nightfall. A state policeman directed us up the steep front steps of the white wooden church to the main sanctuary, where we would await our call to supper in the vestry below.

Katrina Munn, the church organist, was seated at her instrument behind the pulpit, facing the pipes at the rear but watching the crowd in a mirror. "O God, Our Help in Ages Past" was the Sunday service hymn but Saturday supper was show-tune time, and "I'm Gonna Wash That Man Right Outta My Hair" set the expectant diners to humming and toe-tapping. Retired folks from Rhode Island like to sing the old songs, but hunters can be boisterous as well. One night one of them let out a moose call that was heard halfway to Fairlee, they say.

The wait in the sanctuary allows visitors to fraternize, and also to pick up copies of the church cookbook, subtitled *From Beaver to Buffalo*. I took a menu for the night's meal from a stack on the hymnal table and saw that mouflon ram loaf was the special feature of the supper that year. I couldn't imagine what that animal was—I had not yet learned much about game beyond gray squirrels and dead deer—but none of the women selling cookbooks or keeping the reservations clipboard could help me. I was, at last, directed outside behind the church, where the premier venison chef was grilling cutlets on a barbecue. "Mouflon ram?" he repeated. "I guess it's one of these," whereby he dropped his long-handled fork and made swirling, counterclockwise motions with his fingers around his ears. He then let out a short, deliberate bleat. I got the picture.

Only a few minutes behind schedule, we were sent downstairs into the food line. Politely but firmly, the servers hurried us along. "We serve three people per minute, 180 per hour," Eastman noted with Taylorist efficiency. Once, she clocked her own movements as chief hostess and figured she travelled seven and three-quarters miles during the day of the supper.

Bits of this and smidgens of that were plopped on our plates. The pheasant with rice was easily identifiable by the rice, and rabbit pie by its crust; the bear sausage looked like a tiny hamburger patty. But everything else needed the Reverend Knight's colored toothpicks. In three minutes we were through, just as the efficiency expert claimed, and seated at a refectory table loaded with baskets of bread and bowls of vegetables. An apple-cheeked cider girl came around to fill our cups, and before the gingerbread lady arrived with dessert we were back in line for seconds of the best dishes, which were the bear and the venison.

The cuisine, to be honest, is not the greatest attraction of the day. Eight or ten different meats cooked in fifteen or twenty different ways tend to blend into an indistinguishable common denominator of cooked animal protein, and only the gamiest items retain any memorable character of their own. Perhaps the new American cuisinards have the right idea; a dollop of dilled sour cream and mustard sauce, or a ragout of provençal vegetables atop the bobcat, or whatever that was, might have made a delectable difference.

Still, the food is part of a scene in the church that is incomparable for its pageantry, something between a Texas chili contest and the Oberammergau passion play, with sounds of Rodgers and Hammerstein, textures of flannel and flavors of deep woods and upland meadows. And on the best nights, a bellowing moose call. My friend Charles, who is on the radio in Boston, had driven four hours for the food and the scene, and as he contemplated the long return trip home he wondered whether it was worth all the trouble.

"It's a long way to go for beaver," he chuckled. But two years later he came back for more, and I think he's now a regular.

February 1985, HOUSE & GARDEN

✦

Heroes Are Made . . .

When Italian partisans entered the Tuscan town of San Gimignano behind the fleeing Fascists, they toppled the statue of Mussolini that had adorned the central piazza and inscribed a motto on its base: "Blessed is the people that has no need of heroes." Peoples in the throes of liberation like to smash their icons, disavow their myths and begin to create new ideals and models. Societies bound to repressive authority, on the other hand, build ever bigger statues and adhere to stricter cults.

It's not hard to see which way the wind is blowing nowadays. The elevation of heroes is a full-time occupation for the media, and politicians regularly appeal for obedience to orthodox morality as if it were synonymous with citizenship. Celebrities are expected to fuel the bandwagon. Susan Akin, the new Miss America from Mississippi, pleased the arbiters of patriotic behavior by denouncing rock-and-roll in one of the first dicta of her "reign." Hardly a week goes by without one or another star performer denouncing the evils of drink and drugs, or promoting the virtues of hometown and the Statue of Liberty. If, as Andy Warhol said, everyone in the 1960s was entitled to fifteen minutes of fame, everyone today is eligible for a brief fling with hero-ism: the astronaut-of-the-month, the latest artificial-heart recipient, the freed hostage, the megabucks lottery winner, the record-breaking baseball player or the latest sports champion. Win a basketball game and get a locker room call from Ronald Reagan and a Rose Garden reception the next day.

Sports celebrities are favored candidates for heroism because they best meet the complex demands and fill the unique requirements for veneration in Reagan's America. They get prime-time media exposure, make millions of dollars and exhibit manly virtues, even when they are women; they are com-pulsively physical, habitually apolitical and usually God-fearing. What is equally important is that they are vulnerable to temptation and acquainted with sin. For heroism is always measured against failure, as winning must be validated by losing.

The baseball-and-drugs "scandal" is the cautionary tale in the heroic saga of the sport. Pete Rose (this month) expressed the positive lesson, but it was incomplete without its negative counterpart, the fallen idol. After all, the Book of Genesis would never have sold without the part about the Expulsion. Myths of every kind are composed of contradictory forces, the hero and the goat: Christ and Judas, George Washington and Benedict Arnold, Paradise and Inferno.

It's all too bad for the ballplayers who used cocaine and amphetamines; apparently the ratio of them to the "clean" players is about the same as would be found in the general population, adjusting for their higher salaries. After oil, illegal drugs make up the biggest industry in the country. The banking system in many states would be shattered if drug money sud-denly stopped flowing, and some rural economies would collapse if the mari-juana crop failed. Any investigation of truck drivers, stock traders, students and who knows what other group would surely turn up enough speed-ballers, pot smokers and coke snorters to swamp the judicial system. But the baseball players now in court and on the nightly news should know that they were set up by the system, in the same way as they are fashioned into heroes, for symbolic value. That system needs bums (also informers) along with champions, and it's anybody's guess who will be chosen for one role and not the other. In this atmosphere of social repression, traitors to the American way of life will be hauled up for judgement—not as they were in the 1950s, when political suspects were rounded up by congressional com-mittees. This time, the dupes are dopers, the radicals are rockers and the sub-versives pose nude for *Penthouse* rather than give secrets to the Russians. And they will pay for their sins not primarily with jail terms or political exile but with cancelled contracts for commercial endorsements and a bum rap on *Entertainment Tonight*.

September 28, 1985, THE NATION

✦

The Revenge of Ahab

What did the killer say as he pumped four .22 caliber bullets into the body of a young female Beluga whale cavorting in New Haven Harbor? "You've had it, pal"? "Go ahead, make my day"? What insult was avenged, what crime punished, what principle upheld?

B.W., the ten-foot, 950-pound cetacean, dropped out of her school a year ago and took up residence along the Connecticut coast, amusing herself and delighting the nearby humans in playful encounters. She nuzzled small boats, tickled swimmers and performed such self-taught tricks that many terrestrial mammals came to believe their marine relative possessed an intelligence comparable to their own. B.W. was not, scientifically speaking, a great whale, but she was a very good one, a veritable Girl Scout. She was trustworthy, loyal, friendly, brave and perhaps even reverent. She was certainly harmless. She cruised the waters unarmed, she never demanded spare change, she did not sponsor terrorism or export revolution, she did not come ashore to take someone's job or go on welfare.

Whoever killed B.W. one fine day in May must have seen her as a symbol suitable for slaughter. Whales have been problematic partners of men at least since Jonah, and long after Moby Dick. Whale catching was the economic foundation for the flowering of New England, and although whale watching is now a peaceful pastime, it may be simply a sporting sublimation rather than a moral equivalent of the cruel hunt.

As a beast, B.W. was perhaps too good, too intelligent and too trusting to survive in man's jungle. The will to kill has never been stronger, and a complete catalogue of means and motives are retailed in the media, in the proud boasts of politicians, in the triumphant toasts of national heroes. The trick is to keep from becoming a target, which is the one B.W. did not learn.

May 31, 1986, THE NATION

✦

Chickens Come Home to Roost

It is not enough that President Reagan slough or shuffle his National Security Council staff. It is not enough that an independent counsel pursue evidence of criminal activity. It is not enough that congressional committees probe the proliferating reports, rumors, connections and discrepancies that constitute the Iran/*contra* arms sale scandal. For at its core the crisis that has already diverted and may permanently derail the Reagan Administration concerns the conduct of foreign policy and the democratic legitimacy of presidential authority; and until those issues are met, the crisis cannot be resolved honestly.

In less than six years the Reagan Administration developed its system of covert operations, extended its string of secret wars and refined its schedule of shady deals to a level of sophistication and a point of pre-eminence unknown in the history of US foreign relations. Apologists for Reagan will surely claim—as William Safire did so doggedly for Nixon—that the pattern of secrecy and manipulation had been firmly established by presidents long gone. And so it had. But until now no president has so vastly replaced open policies with covert ones, has so cynically removed the major issues of his Administration from the possibility of public debate, has so brazenly and hypocritically done one thing with a closed hand and the exact opposite with the other. The arms deal—variously called Iranagua, Gippergate and, by Reagan, "our Iran policy"—did not take place on the margins of policy but at its very heart. The ghoulish alliance of reactionary, repressive and aggressive governments that the White House forged to turn its tricks was the centerpiece of its strategy in the Third World, the most active and volatile arena of global politics for the past quarter-century. The same complex of deals that gave money to the *contras* at a time when Congress expressly forbade such aid was also supporting the whole wretched network of terrorists, mercenaries, rebels and death squads from Angola to Guatemala.

Reagan ordered the covert war against Nicaragua in the first weeks of his Administration, and it has naturally received the most publicity. It has never been debated straightforwardly because the Administration still does not call it by its rightful name but insists on the fiction that a genuine rebellion seeking to gain leverage for "negotiations" with the Nicaraguan government is in progress in the remote regions of Central America. For some reason most politicians and the major media have not conceded that the war to overthrow the Sandinistas is headquartered in the White House.

America's war against Angola, fought in conjunction with the white minority regime in South Africa, gets only a footnote in current conversations. The US effort in Afghanistan, which is presented to Americans as a selfless defense of democratic struggle in the face of Soviet aggression, is in reality a self-serving intervention that sponsors covertly the same kind of terror, torture and subversion that the Russians are practicing overtly. It now turns out that profits from the Iranian arms deal also went to Unita in Angola and the mujahedeen in Afghanistan, and perhaps freed up some funds so that South Africa could pour more into the Renamo guerrilla operation which is bleeding Mozambique.

CIA-watchers estimate that there are at least fifty live covert-ops around the world, from Algeria to Zambia. Many of those involve terrorism on a scale so grand that they make the odd Arab hijacking or kidnapping look like a quiet day in Miami. The Administration managed the election of Duarte in El Salvador and then conceived of the tactic of terror-bombing civilian villages in the Salvadoran countryside, supplying the training, the technology and the money to do it. Reagan has approved money and arms for his chosen guerrillas in Chad and in Cambodia. He has sanctioned training of troops in Guatemala, and he has made Honduras into a permanent US staging base, on the order of Camranh Bay, in South Vietnam.

With the willing participation of the government in Tel Aviv, the White House strategists have hastened the process by which Israel is becoming a mercenary state bound to serve America's interests and support America's interventions anywhere in the world. Just as Israel arranged the Iranian deal and may have facilitated the financial transfers to the *contra* war (Israel and US officials are blaming each other), it has done dirty work in South Africa, in Guatemala and in El Salvador when for various reasons the US government would rather keep its white gloves on. Israel said last month that it has no particular interests in Central America, but it has supplied right-wing forces in that region for years, and even now Israelis are training Nicaraguan *contras* based in Honduras. Israel promoted and continues to feed the anti-terrorism campaign that has defined Reagan's foreign policy in the public sector. There is evidence that Mossad, the Israeli secret service, obliges the common effort by contriving acts of Arab terrorism when there is not enough news to print.

Israel and Saudi Arabia do share a similar interest in destroying Arab radicalism—by bombs if necessary, by more subtle means if possible. The United States throws billions into that effort as well. The Saudis get AWACs (arranged by Lieut. Col. Oliver North and Maj. Gen. Richard Secord, among others) and finance the Afghani mujahedeen. The United States also rewards its various friends and allies with intelligence software as well as military hardware. Lost among the sub-scandals of the past month was the poignant item that in 1983 the CIA fingered some 200 Iranian leftists to the government in Tehran, which promptly executed them. Reagan's gift of 200 lives was apparently part of the same deal meant to woo "moderates" in Iran and free hostages in Lebanon.

The Saudi-Israeli-Iranian triad fits nicely into the world anti-communist front that was set up by right-wing fanatics, but it is an important element in the geopolitical project of mainstream US policy makers as well. Nazi collaborators whom the CIA saved from prosecution after World War II are put together with fugitive assassins from the Somoza regime in Nicaragua and black Africans acting on behalf of South Africa in an International of the Right pledged to do battle against popular revolutions and socialist struggles wherever they occur. At the same time, Washington has helped secure a permanent funding network of foreign governments, political parties and private institutions to support global counterrevolution without being subject to the vagaries of local elections, changes of officials or the whims of public opinion in any one country. The West German government was recently reported to have administered a fund for anti-left politics around the world. Among its recipients are El Salvador's Duarte and South Africa's Buthelezi, who visited President Reagan on November 25. The Bavarian arm of West Germany's ruling Christian Democratic Party participates in the same effort. From the United States, several outfits tied to private foundations and organized labor have traditionally done CIA jobs in Europe and the Third World, and during the Reagan Administration they have been especially active in Africa and Latin America.

The "low-intensity conflict" in which the Administration is engaged is directed not only against nationalist and leftist forces abroad but against the progressive opposition in this country. From the very beginning the strategy was assumed to be antithetical to democratic debate. An army study that lays out the doctrine of low-intensity conflict declares:

> As Americans, we consider democracy to be the best form of government, but it is not always the most efficient. The cumbersome decision-making and consensus-building process inherent in a democracy can be too slow to respond to dangers before they become critical.

The "enemy within" is clearly targeted: a consensus on Third World wars has not existed since the Vietnam era, and no one in Washington overlooks the role that liberal and radical anti-war and solidarity movements have played in blocking or at least moderating the government's interventionist impulses since that time. Reagan was forced into the covert mode of foreign policy by the legacy of Vietnam and the history of democratic opposition to imperial adventure. Nixon came a cropper of the peace movement of the 1960s; it is wonderfully ironic that, after all this time, Reagan has fallen victim to the same syndrome he has so often pronounced cured.

December 2, 1986, THE NATION

✦

Suffering Succotash

Christmas will come late this year—if it comes at all—for the family of James Wentzel in Annandale, Virginia. Reviled and pursued like Jean Valjean for the petty theft of food to feed his family, fired like Bob Cratchit from his job almost on Christmas Eve, the wretched Wentzel will find a lump of coal in his stocking when more fortunate fellows get their glittering prizes. Who will tell the Wentzels in their impoverished state, "No, Virginia, there is no Santa Claus"?

This Christmas dirge, however, is not completely without redeeming moral consequence. Wentzel was the president of the Legal Services Corporation, a government agency once charged with defending the rights of poor people but lately restricted in scope and purpose by an Administration steadfastly opposed to its very existence. Appointed to the position a year and a half ago, Wentzel was widely assumed to be supervising the slow extinction of his agency, by hook or by crook.

Now his work on behalf of the government of the greedy against the interests of the needy has been cut short. A security guard at a Magruder's super-market identified Wentzel as the man he caught in the store's parking lot concealing a fifteen-ounce can of succotash in his back pocket, several slices of ham in his suit jacket, and two packages of chocolate snack cakes, each in a different pocket of his overcoat. The guard reported that Wentzel pleaded for mercy on the ground that he was president of the LSC, saying an arrest "will ruin me."

The items on this little shopping list were priced at $5.66. Wentzel, who was earning $68,700 a year in his government job, resigned "in the face of overwhelming information," a legal aid lobbyist said—which only proves that the Christmas spirit works in mysterious ways, by hook or by crook.

December 16, 1986, THE NATION

✦

Cold War Camp:
Amerika—It Can't Happen Here

Somewhere in the murky midlands of *Amerika*, ABC's fourteen-and-a-half-hour miniseries on the extension of Soviet hegemonism to the Western Hemisphere, a native-born American wonders how his country ever fell under the jackboot of communism, and without a fight. It seems that somehow a morally soft and politically weak-willed democracy bought a totalitarian line, and before long they were wearing babushkas in Iowa and teaching kids in school that "Marx is the father of our country."

"They promised us peace and harmony," his friend says, by way of expla-nation. "Yes," the unhappy man replies, "we know a lot more about disinfor-mation campaigns now than we did then."

At the ABC screening last December, when I saw a ninety-minute mon-tage of the miniseries, the audience howled at that anachronistic zinger, and I won't be surprised if they excise it from the broadcast version. But it will not be easy to keep the rest of the material on the intended target. The scan-dals of the summer and fall have undercut the premises and reversed the referents of Donald Wyre's leaden script. When characters talk of political infiltration, subversive operations and covert wars, they may be thinking of the Kremlin, but they will be heard referring to the National Security Council. The KGB agent assigned to engineer the devolution of the United States into bioregions and encourage the ascendancy of a collaborationist governor in the five-state Midwest seems a lot like Ollie North with his quest for "moderates" in the Mideast. Indeed, the Soviet clique of colonels, spies and terror-specialists who run the Amerikan operation are dead ringers for the junta that, at least until a few weeks ago, held paramount power in Washington.

The origins of *Amerika* go back to the 1983 doomsday document *The Day*

After, ABC's last look at nuclear holocaust. Ben Stein, who wrote speeches for both Richard Nixon and Gerald Ford, suggested in a newspaper column that the network give equal time to the better-dead-than-Red crowd by showing in fictional form that Soviet communism is much worse than incineration or radiation sickness. Right-wing lobbies like Accuracy in Media were also exercised by the pacifist message of *TDA* and agitated for a tele-militarist answer. ABC heeded their calls. After all, Reaganism was rampant, the nuclear freeze was rapidly fading and bear-baiting was all the rage, not only in Washington but throughout the neoconservative West. The network set its corrective project in motion.

But now, on the eve of correction, all the lines are garbled. A lot has happened since launch. Who could have known that the dreary Soviet interregnum of Andropov-Chernenko would be replaced by the sparkle of Mikhail Gorbachev's *glanost*, that the *gulag* would lose its potency as a symbol of evil empire, that the Russians would occupy the high ground in the arms control and nuclear deployment debate, that the Nicaraguan *contras* would never transcend their image as mercenaries and drug-runners, that American family farms would die by deliberate government inaction before they could ever be converted to collectives by Soviet central planners. And so on. Like so many Hollywood efforts, *Amerika* became an anachronism before it ever saw the light of day.

As far as I could tell from the conflated segment I saw and from the synopses ABC has dribbled out to the press for the past several months, *Amerika* posits a day ten years from now when the Russians, in the guise of a United Nations peacekeeping army, have taken control of the United States without a thermonuclear exchange—at least without one big enough to write home about. (Frequent criticism from early screenings that the takeover was ludicrously easy has apparently resulted in the addition of material explaining that an electromagnetic pulse—the exceedingly trendy EMP—was used to accomplish the conquest.) Life is hard in the Soviet States of America. There are no fresh tomatoes in the shops, political slogans have replaced commercial advertisements on billboards, and many people sound like the late Andy Kaufman doing Latka on *Taxi*. For some reason a lot of homeless people have been taken off the streets of cities and placed in refugee camps with poor sanitation facilities. Tecumseh, Nebraska, where some of the series was shot, is made to look like the heart of the Uzbek SSR, with women walking around wrapped in blankets and sporting the ubiquitous babushka (*vinter vear?*). Queues, the constant companions of communism, are mandatory for all activities. Where once Nebraskan housewives sailed through supermarket check-outs laden with Lean Cuisine, they now have to line up for soyburgers.

Back to this bleak scene, his boyhood home, comes Devin Milford (Kris Kristofferson), a Kennedyesque figure who was the last *bona fide* candidate for president of the United States before *they* came. The Russkies have released Milford from detention to further their devolution scheme, but he will have none of it. Instead, he starts to form the Resistance, a sort of armed civil liberties movement reminiscent of the African National Congress or the Palestine Liberation Organization. (As a matter of fact, many of the meanest policies of the conquerors, such as banning the patriotic flag and outlawing resistance organizations, refer directly to Israel and South Africa, rather than to the Soviet Union.) Violence escalates. The Russians swoop over and bomb a refugee camp, rather like an attack on a peasant village in El Salvador. There's something about a helicopter raid that will always remind American television audiences of a search-and-destroy mission.

Like a prime-time soap opera, *Amerika* cuts all over the lot. But even the ninety-minute version was loaded with class, sexual, racial and political signifiers. The sinister people greet one another with kisses on both cheeks. The decadent collaborators drink champagne from tall, narrow glasses. The Russians have put a woman, Milford's ex-wife, in charge of one of the bioregions; she is to be the nominal lieutenant governor but hold the real power. Naturally, she is keeping Milford from seeing their two sons, but he gets a couple of construction workers to arrange a meeting in the little boys' room of the school where they are boarded. There are crusty farmers, drunken women, ambivalent blacks (make that black), cheeky waitresses, punks with mohawks and young lovers. The "UN" soldiers are made to be generic, their faces covered with Darth Vader masks. They do, however, understand Spanish. When a Soviet general orders his men to burn down the Milford house, he obligingly translates the command for them. Now we know where bilingual education will lead us.

For a while, the bits have a certain allure, like the scenes in *Star Trek IV*, *Back to the Future* and similar movies in which time frames are skewed and we see familiar relationships or activities with an unusual consciousness. Here we are supposed to see the ordinary material of American lives from the extraordinary point of view of an oppressed population. That's not a bad idea. But the vision is refracted by ideology and the images are unreal.

Amerika seems to have been concocted by the idiot ideologues who made John Birch Society home movies in the late fifties. There is no wit or sophistication to its anti-Sovietism, no hint of a human face behind the Stalinist mask, no plug for social democracy as a hedge against Marxism. This is not a movie made by Ben Stein, who is actually quite amusing, or even by Pat Buchanan, who is a masterful performer of reactionary camp. As a political tract and a week's entertainment it is the kind of stuff storefront ministers in Los Angeles suburbs used to make for Tupperware parties, at the level Cardinal Mindszenty would have enjoyed in his quarters in the US embassy in Budapest, sitting around having a few beers with the marine guards while the cold war raged outside.

They can't be serious. The fury now being directed at ABC by liberal academics, UN bureaucrats and responsible political personalities (the list grows daily) for putting such a program on the air may not be unprovoked, but it is surely inappropriate to the gravity of the project. If the network's secret team had come up with a plausible scenario for socialism in America, or had made an honest attempt (even an incorrect one) to play out a logical confrontation between the superpowers, or had found a way to exhibit the real failures and weaknesses of liberalism, they might have had cause for worry. But *dreck* is *dreck* is *dreck*. At worst it will fill the niche in American consciousness where *Hollywood Wives* and *Princess Daisy* and most miniseries reside. At best it will lay bare the intellectual and dramatic poverty of the lunatic right, and inform millions of conversations for weeks to come. Don't mourn for *Amerika;* watch it and laugh.

February 14, 1987, THE NATION

✦

Subways Are for Shooting

What victory did the Bernhard Goetz trial jurors celebrate when they raised the "V" sign as they left the New York City courtroom? Who are the good guys who triumphed? What system worked? How has justice been served and society defended? Every question that was raised following this sad and sordid event two and a half years ago remains unanswered today, just as the meaning of Goetz's mad act of social revenge is unresolved.

Only one thing is clear, and that is the polarization of caste and class that has attended the case from the start. The legal arguments about self-defense, the pragmatic concerns about copycat attacks, even the philosophical debates about violence in the modern age, are overwhelmed by the stark realities of white fear and black anger, of privilege and alienation, of power and powerlessness.

The defense contended that we all live in an urban jungle, where only the law of lions and wolves applies. It is an attractive but incomplete metaphor. Some beasts are more equal than others in this part of the forest, and the most successful predators don't always have the sharpest teeth. Or the sharpest screwdrivers.

People here prey with land and laws, with college degrees and stock exchange seats. They kill with redlining and maim with snobbery. They mark their territory with sweetheart deals, political patronage and special favors. They use wealth as a weapon, race as a prison, status as a stick.

Those who created that kind of jungle cannot now in good faith blame the ones least fit to survive for their pathetic strategies and bad manners. There was a bitter bumper sticker popular years ago, when Native American rights were in the news: "Custer Died For Our Sins." This time Goetz was tried for our sins—and found innocent. It must not have been a fair trial.

June 27, 1987, THE NATION

A Season for Repentance

A ll summer long, Jim Bakker sat on a mountain looking over Gatlinburg, Tennessee, imprisoned by the celebrity he craved, isolated from the community he created, denied the salvation he sought. It was a comfortable confinement in a pretty penitentiary, a sprawling, solitary retreat hidden in hickory woods off a winding road that begins at the back of the Howard Johnson's parking lot and climbs past resort condos and the fancier estates of Gatlinburg's rich and famous. But the picture was not perfect. The garish strip-scarred town beneath is a hideous jumble of discount outlets and T-shirt stands, storefront creep shows and mallettes that mix redneck nick-nacks with Christian curios. On weekend nights the horny *Hee-Haw* culture bubbles over, and beery kids chase one another through the bars and cruise the back streets. If Pastor Jim still thinks in biblical paradigms, he must have noticed the blasphemous clash of commerce and nature, the discrepancies of flesh and spirit, man's desecration of God's gorgeous Great Smokies that rise and stretch beyond his window. For once again, and perhaps not for the last time in his life, he has found himself afoul in a temple of the Lord.

Early in the season, Jim's older brother Norman came to town to oversee construction of thick stone walls, spiked iron fences and armored steel gates around the property. Video cameras and microphones were activated for early warning of intrusion, and unsubtle signs were posted to fend off visitors, but the elaborate fortifications seem designed as much to keep Bakker in as to keep intruders out. After the several sexual and financial scandals broke over his head, Bakker began serving an indeterminate term of house arrest. His few contacts with outsiders were disastrous; in July he stormed out of a meeting with a *Time* reporter when the interviewer indelicately questioned Bakker's heterosexuality. The media had fashioned his fame, they had broadcast his name, and they had brought him down, exposed his avarice, defined and magnified his guilt. There were no more interviews.

Tammy Faye was freer to go abroad; shame, after all, is far less personally repressive than guilt (unless you're a samurai), and God knows she could well afford to lose a little face. When the forlorn couple got evicted from church-owned homes in Palm Springs, California, and Tega Cay, South Carolina, and fled to Gatlinburg, she sniffled to the network cameras that she was, after all the bright lights and big cities, "just a small-town girl at heart" whose purest joy was shopping on Main Street. But what could she buy? Perhaps a few black-and-red splattered I BUMPED INTO TAMMY FAYE AT THE GATLINBURG MALL sweatshirts, the hottest item in the shops last summer.

They say that the past is another country, and that people are different there, but Jim and Tammy Faye were small-town kids all along. They still are small. It's only the towns that have got bigger. Jim was born in Muskegon, Michigan, in 1940, on the very cusp of the Depression and World War II generations, and he lived through good times, perhaps the last period of unbridled prosperity the place will know in the lifetime of anyone now resident there. When Jim left Muskegon in 1959, it still had the purpose and coherence of postwar American life. The foundries and auto-parts factories were humming, social and racial relations were stable, conservative conventions of behavior were in full force, the future was blindingly bright.

The Bakkers on his father's side, and the Irwins on his mother's, had such wide roots in such constricted ground that by the time Jim came along, the family seemed socially pot-bound. There's a Bakker Road out by the new airport and an Irwin Street near the church of Jim's youth. Grandpa Irwin, a livestock dealer, was a wily businessman, Jim once wrote. Grandma Irwin was doting and consoling and nurturing to his dreams. Jim later dedicated a TV production studio in her name in Charlotte, North Carolina, before the whole operation moved to Heritage USA, his lavish inspirational theme park in South Carolina.

Grandpa Joe Bakker was a truck farmer, a descendant of Dutch Calvinist immigrants who settled the eastern shore of Lake Michigan in the nineteenth century. Muskegon lumber had rebuilt Chicago after the Great Fire. Then the sawdust from the mills that had made that miracle went ablaze and the center of town was burned to the ground. Dust to ashes, in a manner of speaking, and then Muskegon rose again to become a manufacturing feeder for Detroit's insatiable industrial appetite.

Social evolution is never as orderly and effortless as it seems in historical outline, and the pathways of change are littered with those who cannot or will not keep pace. In the case of Joe Bakker, the streets of Muskegon were also littered with pamphlets he'd throw at passers-by as he pressed them to give up the licentious ways of the new industrial society, return to the fundamental Christian values of the old land-based order and be reborn. Jim called his grandfather a "fanatic," perhaps not as affectionately as he'd like it to sound today. Jim's Uncle Charles ("Lonnie") Irwin allows how "Joe was a great radical fellow. Before he had a church to go to he just walked around handing out hundreds of tracts. He worked among black people, too." After several years of curbside ministering, Joe got a permanent church together in the mid-1920s. Among the charter members of the Central Assembly of God were his son—Jim's father—Raleigh, and Raleigh's brother-in-law, Lonnie Irwin.

Like millions of Americans similarly situated between farm and factory in those days, Joe Bakker embraced the new fundamentalist "revival" that seemed to provide a haven from the chaos of a rapidly urbanizing, industrializing, modernizing America. The genus of fundamentalism had numerous species, and it is still spinning off sorts and varieties. Aimee Semple MacPherson's International Church of the Foursquare Gospel was one variant. Southern Baptists mutated into subsects with widely differing affects: Billy Sunday, Billy Graham, Jerry Falwell and Pat Robertson are all of the ilk. Joe's was the town's first church of the new Pentecostal order, founded only a decade earlier, in 1914. Pentecostalism took its cues from the New Testament account of Jesus' return to the world fifty days (Greek *pentecost*) after he was resurrected. So ecstatic were his disciples to get a visit from the Other Side that they began babbling in "tongues of fire," apparently gibberish which, though ordinarily incomprehensible, was now understood by all who listened. Most Christians read the applicable biblical text (Acts 2) to mean that the gift of tongues was temporary. Pentecostals hold that God was no Indian giver, and that the ecstatic experience is available for all until Judgement Day, at which time there will be no need for any of it.

For many small-town families in the Midwest and poor whites and blacks in the South, the verities of biblical literalism and the ecstasies of Pentecostal ritual were effective bulwarks against the demons of relativism and rationalism loose in the land. Moreover, the church offered a caring, including community—an assembly of the godly—arranged against the worldly powers that were isolating and excluding Americans. Not quite as demanding as political fascism, religious fundamentalism nevertheless represented a similar reaction to radical transformation in a society ill equipped for change.

In return for spiritual services rendered, the Pentecostal church demanded strict adherence to a code of conduct of Pentateuchal severity. Amusements that might distract a follower from obedient attention to God were strictly forbidden. Sexual and marital practices that contradicted the patriarchs' commandments of wifely submission, gender specificity and conjugal inseparability were expressly outlawed. Dancing was out, drinking was prohibited, the movies were off limits, divorce was a disgrace, and non-missionary, non-heterosexual intercourse was an abomination in life as it was in Scripture.

In the Bakkers' Muskegon, church was an organizing center of everyday life. "Most kids spent more time in church than in their homes," Richard Rolfe, Jim's high school classmate, reflected. "Depending on your denomination, there were prayer meetings every Wednesday, junior choir, Sunday school, camp meetings, catechism—something to take up your time every day of the week."

The Central Assembly was also a center of support for Muskegonites who were ignored or condescended to by the professional and manufacturing elites. "It was not with great pride that you told someone where you went to church if you were a Pentecostal in the Assembly of God," Jim's Bible-college roomate, Pastor Robert Cilke, explained. "If you were in one of the traditional denominations you were accepted. We were not accepted. Then, we were from the wrong side of the tracks."

The Bakker family—father Raleigh, mother Furnia, brothers Bob and

Norman and Jim, sister Donna—inched their way up through the forties and fifties from working-class modesty to middle-class ambition. When Jim came along, the last of the line, the Bakkers lived in a tiny bungalow that stands today with a new coat of pumpkin paint. About 1946, feeling cramped, the Bakkers moved to a more substantial three-story house in Muskegon Heights, less than a mile beyond the Sealed Power piston-ring plant, where Raleigh worked as a machinist. Pumpkin must be a favorite hue in Muskegon; that house was also painted an organic orange when the Bakkers lived there, but it so offended young Jim that he asked friends to drop him off several blocks away so that they would not see his secret shame.

"It's really strange," his uncle Lonnie Irwin said, sitting on a divan on the porch of his own house, next door to the original pumpkin bungalow. "Raleigh wasn't poor, their house wasn't bad, they got a Cadillac through the—what do you call it?—credit union, and I can't understand why Jim thinks that way." But Bakker is retrospectively obsessed with the poverty of his youth and his ramshackle surroundings. The fantasy of a restricted youth must validate his expansive expectations. His oddly revealing but often obtuse autobiography, *Move That Mountain!*, written "with Robert Paul Lamb," is full of self-pitying descriptions of a deprived childhood—uninteresting presents at Christmas and tattered hand-me-down clothes, the traditional Cratchit-family syndrome.

In fact, the family was steadily moving on up in the postwar industrial society, and by the time Jim was 14 it was established in an elegant Victorian mansion on Webster Avenue, once the toniest street in town and still a prestige address in the mid-fifties. Jim was in his glory in their new digs. He threw fabulous parties in the rambling wooden house; they're still talking in Muskegon about the one with the reigning Miss Michigan in attendance as his personal guest. "I was in the limelight—the center of attention," Jim glowed. He always loved celebrity, however primitive.

"Jim was a typical fifties kid," Richard Rolfe recalls. "He was *Ordinary People*. If you watched *Peggy Sue Got Married*, you'd know what it was like back then." Rolfe recently returned to Muskegon as general manager of the local UHF "inspirational" TV station. He seems to have a cinematic imagination. "When I saw *Back to the Future*, it was as if my own life and high school were on the screen. The worst thing we ever did was try to talk someone over 21 into buying us a six-pack of beer. We were like the guys in *Diner*, which was our year, too." On summer nights Jim would play out his Elvis dreams. He'd plaster back his black hair, jump into the family's two-tone blue '52 Cadillac, and cruise up and down another main street in that other land, bopping to "La Bamba." Then he'd head down to the town beach on Lake Michigan and watch the girls go by. Or whatever.

"Jim wore red crewneck sweaters and khaki slacks and penny loafers, and you could lube your car with his hair," Rolfe continued. He had his dates, including a "cute blonde named Sandy." At church camp in the summer he was celebrated as quite the skirt-chaser. "Jim was well liked," says Rolfe. "He mixed well, like me, but . . . he was distant; he wasn't committed to anyone or any group; his one interest was photography."

Jim liked to watch—watch and direct and spin his dreams. He edited the *Campus Keyhole* and staged a fundraiser for the paper; he directed variety shows; he presided over the Camera Club. He deejayed records over the school intercom, and after hours, at neighborhood hops. A dreamy landscape of innocent amusements and wholesome pleasures drifts up from the pages of *Said and Done*, the Muskegon High yearbook, retrieved from the basement of the Hackley Library, a stone-solid American Romanesque building. On a sultry morning in August 1987, I sat looking at life in 1959. The kids were all white, the girls had Gidget smiles, the boys looked like retro Ollie Norths. The senior play was *Tattletale*; the class motto was "The wheel of time rolls downward through various changes."

Outside of Muskegon, the wheel was already rolling. Jim's last year there was a watershed year for America. The auto-industrial age was declining and with its Muskegon's fortunes. Some factories folded; others fled to the Sun Belt, taking workers with them.

During the forties, recruiters for the auto-parts plants and machine factories had toured the South, mustering workers for the war effort. "There's still a lot of the Old South in Muskegon," Clayton Hardiman, a black reporter on *The Muskegon Chronicle*, observed. "There's a great deal of racism." Chestnut Street, where Jim first lived in the pumpkin bungalow, is "90 percent black," according to Uncle Lonnie, who is a retired Lutheran minister, having jumped denominations when he was courting his wife, and "The Heights," where Jim moved at the age of 6, is predominantly black. Muskegon High School, which more than any other institution seemed to express local identity, is no more the Wonder Bread soul of the town. Jim's old Central Assembly used to be tastefully integrated. But on a Sunday morning last summer, in the church's new digs out by the K Mart shopping center, the congregation was 100 percent white.

Desperate for new development in the late fifties, officials ordered Webster Avenue widened into a one-way, four-lane expressway. Some houses in the district "became rooming houses for little gray men on Social Security who drank a lot," a neighbor said. A local adman bought the Bakkers' house and remodelled it into a version of San Francisco Victorian camp, complete with a tiny Italianate garden and bubbling fountain in the back. That particular irony, however, is lost on the locals, who have little taste for postmodern conceits. Successive attempts to transform Muskegon into a yuppie service center have been unsuccessful. "Internally, we suffer from an inferiority complex," the adman told me. "Externally, it's just an ugly, dirty factory town." Last summer, *Money* magazine voted it America's second-worst city to live in, out of 300 rated.

"There was an innocence then," William Harrison, Jim's Muskegon High teacher and mentor, remembers. "People thought the most evil in the world was Elvis Presley. In the summer Jim would go to church camps and dream of what he'd like to do. He had big plans. He told me he wanted to go off to the South American jungle to change the world. But it seemed he wanted to create that safe and secure world that was in his dreams."

Innocence is a charm, and also a trap. Jim was the " baby" of the family, a prisoner of his own immaturity. He felt safe when his sister Donna "mothered" him, and he resented the emotionally severe Bakker family: "I knew they loved me but they just weren't vocal about it." What love they gave was conditional upon Jim's religious obedience and his school performance, neither of which earned him high marks. Brother Bob, the firstborn, had escaped the church, the family and Muskegon, but baby Jim was enthralled and chastised by all of them.

"Fear had constantly pervaded my life," Bakker confessed in his autobiography, "from the first time I saw the big 'eye' in church. It was a black-and-white picture of a human eye standing about three feet high on the wall of our Sunday school classroom and, to me, that eye was God Himself. And he was looking directly at me. . . . Almost as a precaution, I'd read one verse each night from the New Testament. It was like a ritual I felt I had to do. One night, as I sat on the edge of the bed, I opened the New Testament to read my nightly verse. My eyes fastened strangely on Romans 6:23 and seven words came right off the page at me, 'For the wages of sin is death. '. . . Death!'"

What immortal hand or eye had framed his fearfulness, and why? Maybe he had lust in his heart for Sandy and the girls, or yearnings of the kind that Jerry Falwell would condemn in him years later. Maybe both. For whatever reason, guilt was a constant, looming presence in his life. One night while he was deejaying a sock hop he heard a voice challenging him from way beyond the loudspeakers: "Jim, what are you doing here?" Another time when he was spinning the platters in the gym he looked up to see his father standing silent in the doorway, like Leopold Mozart or the commendatore come hot from hell through the trapdoor to warn the unwary sinner.

But the most traumatic sign was sent one terrible Sunday night in the winter of '58, when Jim and Sandy sneaked out of the church before the service was over, in that part of the fundamentalist ritual when the faithful are called to the altar to let the spirit enter their souls and opt for Christ. "I simply couldn't sit through an altar call," Bakker wrote. "There was something about it that bore heavy on me."

Jim and Sandy went cruising through town in the blue Caddy. Fats Domino was singing "Blueberry Hill" on the radio. Life was a dream. Then Jim noticed the lateness of the hour, and he hurried to get back before church let out. The snow was high on the curbs as he tore into the parking lot, and ran over 3-year-old Jimmy Summerfield.

The child survived but Jim's sock-hopping, car-bopping, church-skipping days did not. He diagnoses his own religious rebirth from that event, and no doubt the accident added to his burden of guilt; but the load was already large. The great fear and the watchful eye predated the brush with tragedy, the harmless amusements, the misspent evenings. It haunted him and it closed him.

"There was an area of Jim's mind that you were never privileged to know," Bob Cilke told me. "There's a mysterious point at which he stopped confiding. We lived together but I never felt I was dealing with the real Jim. He confided to me about dating and so forth, but there was that part of him that was removed, a hidden place. You always felt you weren't hearing the whole story. It wasn't lying; it's just that there was something that was not accessible. Maybe because of the secretiveness, he uses friends up quickly."

More than many do-it-yourself denominations, Pentecostalism guarantees God's forgiveness for sinners as soon as they "come down" to the altar and get reborn. In black gospel song, the forum for redemption is a court of law, where "Jesus drops the charges" if sinners pray for his mercy. In white liturgy, it is often a kind of game show, a redemptive *The Price Is Right* that only the initiated are entitled to play. The trouble is that the guarantee is not always honored by the Maker.

"Guilt is part of the theology Jim grew up with," a longtime associate who left Bakker's organization to work for another televangelist explained. "With Catholics, the guilt is left there in the confessional; that is, the act of confession is a sacrament that confers absolution, no questions asked. With fundamentalists, you have to believe you left it there. You walk out in such an emotional state that you're bound to screw up before the weekend."

Jim Bakker walked out of Muskegon in 1959, and except for family visits and a sentimental sermon at the Central Assembly of God, he never came back.

Dave Kolb, the editorial writer for *The Muskegon Chronicle*, is one of many in town who believe the "Jim Bakker story" really begins after he left home. He took with him not only the accumulated guilt of his fundamentalist past but memories of mid-century America that would seem more idyllic as that old wheel of time rolled downward. Everything he built, every fantasy he spun, every dream he realized in the next quarter-century, can be seen as part of a strategy to get back to that Edenic time and to ensure his salvation.

In the fall of 1959, Jim enrolled at North Central Bible College in Minneapolis, a small, strict Assembly of God training school for preachers, missionaries and attendant church personnel. He had heard the call to the ministry—or, more accurately, he had read it—shortly after a visit to little Jimmy Summerfield's hospital bed. Jim went back to his own room, opened his Bible and out leaped the words, "And He commanded us to preach." *Stichomancy*, the venerable practice of reading random text as prophecy, has many followers among fundamentalists. Jim was pleased to try it, as well as other Delphian aids to decision making, at important junctures in his career. NCBC seemed a logical next leg on his journey out of Muskegon. Housed in a gloomy former Methodist hospital near the center of Minneapolis, it was not then an accredited college, despite the name. "Basically, they just taught guys how to put together a sermon," a friend of Bakker's explained. Women were admitted as students, and a few were ordained as ministers (many more make it today), but relations between the sexes were strictly controlled.

The Reverend John Phillipps, a retired Assembly of God pastor, was on the faculty at NCBC in 1960. "That old building was a coed dorm, with the boys on top and the girls on the lower floor—and never the twain shall meet!" he said. "We had hall monitors who walked the floors. We discouraged PDA, that is, the Public Display of Affection. We didn't want them to be holding hands and kissing around the campus, but where we didn't see them they could do anything they wanted; it wasn't a penal colony." It was Church Lady country.

"Students were under surveillance, but the way they got around it was to join a ministry team," Phillipps continued. "They went out to rundown neighborhoods or small towns far away. The boys preached and the girls played the piano; it didn't count as a date. Jim got involved in 'practical work' at rescue missions and storefronts in the slums. He'd feed derelicts soup and sandwiches, but after the sermon, as a come-on. When I asked him what he wanted to do in life, he said, 'I want to win the world for Jesus'—he joked about it later."

Jim had been conveniently reborn just before classes began, a kind of spiritual freshman orientation accomplished during an altar call at a downtown church known as the Minneapolis Evangelistic Auditorium. Freshened for spiritual exploration, he soon fell in with, or hung around, a group of the most ritualistically adventurous students at school. These were the notorious "Holy Joes," who would rather pray than study. "They were eccentric to the point of being unbalanced," Phillipps said. Jim wrote that he was known as a Joe, that he "turned [his] back on the world completely," that he didn't date at all, that his "life just didn't have time for girls." Apparently sex and Joedom did not go together.

"There was singing, speaking in tongues, praying out loud," Phillipps recalled, "but although Jim has said he was a Holy Joe, he really wasn't. He gave you the idea that he had a special mission. There was always a reserve; he held back. I don't think anyone ever penetrated that reserve, not even Tammy, until his moral collapse over the [Jessica] Hahn girl."

Bible school had its share of scandals. One of the worst infractions occurred just before Jim entered, and it must have been an ominous lesson for all newcomers in the late fifties. It seems that a male student complained that his male preaching partner on a ministry tour to a small town in western Minnesota had made a sexual approach in the bed they shared. "The two students came in, and the homosexual made no objection to the charge," Pastor Phillipps said. "He acknowledged his guilt and he said he was the aggressor. He was expelled. The other fellow turned out okay. He's even had a couple of kids of his at the college."

Jim met Tamara Faye LaValley, a girl from a broken home in International Falls, Minnesota, during his second and her first year at North Central. She had come to the school as the girlfriend of a minister's son from back home, but the romance wilted and Tammy was available. Jim described their historic first encounter, in a hallway at NCBC, rather like Dante's first sight of Beatrice. "Even without makeup, she was a little doll," Jim says of his "little holiness girl." In fact they were both little dolls, Pentecostal Ken and Barbie.

"I was absolutely, totally infatuated with this effervescent eighty-three-pound blonde. She didn't wear a touch of makeup," Jim wrote; he does have a way with the devastating compliment. Bob Cilke filled in the scant details of their whirlwind courtship. "They met one week, he proposed the next month, and in another month or two they were married." The ceremony was at the Minneapolis Evangelistic Auditorium, where Jim had been reborn and had spoken in tongues. Cilke was best man. It was April 1, 1961, and they had broken another rule of the school, that students were not allowed to marry during term time. Both were expelled.

"They couldn't wait to get married," a former executive at PTL, the Bakker televangelist operation, told me. "They couldn't wait to have sex. Jim looked at himself as being a very sexual kind of person. They were always talking about their sexual life and their fantasies—where they made love the night before, how it was. They liked doing it in public places, just on the edge of being found out." Reporters in Charlotte, North Carolina, near Heritage USA, say they heard Bakker bragging that he and Tammy had sex on a swing in a park, but they had managed it in such a way that the frolicking families nearby hadn't even noticed.

Expulsion was not such a big deal. No college degree—not even a Bible-college certificate—was necessary for ordination in the Assembly of God. Out of school with nothing to do, Jim and Tammy cast around for a world-saving mission. Jim met up with an evangelist from Burlington, North Carolina, named Aubrey Sarah, who invited the young couple to make a revival tour of the South. They set off at once, travelling through mill towns in the Carolinas and TVA country, preaching salvation (Jim) and playing the piano and accordion (Tammy) in the heart of the Bible Belt. The factories of the North had moved to the Carolinas, and in a sense it was appropriate that the preachers should follow them. The Rust Belt was religious, but the South was historically hot.

As itinerant evangelists, Jim and Tammy toured around in a 1959 Cadillac, stayed mostly with parishioners and preachers, and for long stretches of time had no fixed address. But Someone was always looking out for the prayerful couple. Jim would have but to mention their need and they would receive a hot meal, black-diamond rings, a new shawl, a travel trailer. You name it, they got it. After a shaky start, Jim got a lot of converts for Christ (that is, conversion from "unborn" to reborn status) and a reputation for fluent sermonizing and successful fundraising.

The textile culture of the Carolinas was beginning a wrenching change just as the old auto-industrial culture of the North was being transformed. The wheel of time had rolled below the Mason-Dixon Line. Another social metamorphosis, another opportunity for authoritarian, salvationary religion. Desegregation was coming to the largely white work force in the mills, as it was to the schools, and the Klan was newly noisy in the red-dirt hills and scrub fields of the Piedmont. Unions were stirring, too, in the mills, and there were early hints of factory flight and Third World competition that would ravage the textile economy. And it was, after all, the sixties, with the war and the kids, the marches and the sit-ins, and the radical recodification of moral values. In the great Pentecostal tradition, Jim Bakker preached salvation not only from personal sin but from the objective sin of the material world.

The problem was that somewhere along the line the material world began to look more useful than sinful. Jim had preached poverty and had lived the simple life, but in the go-go sixties he heard America singing. Back in Muskegon the Central Assembly of God had moved next to a shopping center. In Minneapolis, the NCBC had embarked on an expansion program that would add more buildings to the campus, gain the school collegiate accreditation and send preachers out to rich suburban ministries. And all over, poor fundamentalists were getting on the satanic TV and becoming celebrities. As below, so above. Don Hardister, the Bakkers' personal bodyguard, advance man and PTL executive for many years until his break after the scandals last year, noted how Bakker began to practice "blab it and grab it," the ministry of prosperity.

"He had a thing about being poor and his deprived childhood," Hardister told me late in August in his office in the Heritage Grand Hotel, the Ritz of the Christian vacation world. "He had a thing about coats in particular. He bought every kind of coat that you could imagine 'cause he didn't have any when he was young. He said he was getting part of his heaven right here on earth."

The break between preaching and praying and getting and spending may be dated from the day Tammy got the idea for a puppet act to add to their gospel show. Call it retail *stichomancy*, but all she did was look up on the shelf in a grocery store and there she saw the future, and it would work. Cartons of bubble bath were topped with plastic animal heads that, she believed, could be molded into puppet characters. Soon the previously childless couple was travelling with Susie Moppet and Billy, Johnny, Dad, Grandpa, Grandma and Mom. Sometimes Tammy would enter as the character of Susie Moppet and express her emotions through the doll. The Bakkers' appeal has always been to the infantilistic sensibility of American life. Jim's an effective preacher, but not a great spellbinder. He was best as the Disney version of himself, just as his PTL network is a Disney Channel of the spirit, and his theme park is a Christian universe parallel to Disney's. Tammy's only shtick is the presentation of herself as a cartoon character. Fortunately for them, the pool of believers out in TV fundamentalist land is large enough to accommodate widely disparate appeals. Jimmy Swaggart goes for the spiritual jugular, Falwell likes to preach national security policy, and Oral Roberts deals largely in hocus-pocus. The Bakkers made revival hour into a Punch and Judy show, and it was a hit.

Pat Robertson, the begetter of televangelism, was also a perceptive impresario, and he reckoned that the Bakkers' puppets would be an ideal treat for a fundamentalist kiddie show. Letters were exchanged and in 1965 the couple, plus Susie Moppet et al., left the mill towns for the airwaves out of Portsmouth, Virginia. Things started happening for them. They ran an innovative fundraising telethon to save the young network from ruin. They moved from puppetry to talk-and-variety, and soon they were the stars of Robertson's *700 Club*. Then another bad bolt came from on high.

One night in the spring of 1969 Jim fell ill with bizarre and unusual symptoms: nausea, vertigo, hypersensitive skin, bone-deep exhaustion. Worst of all, he felt he "was losing all the restraints that held [his] life together." Prayer was not immediately effective. A physician was consulted who diagnosed his illness as a case of "nerves" and prescribed a cream-and-milk diet. Later, Tammy's doctor suggested that she become pregnant for Jim's sake. God also told Jim he should "go fishing," and a combination of all therapies indeed pulled him through. But what of the restraints? Once loosened, the bonds of repression never again seem to hold the inner demons as securely as when they first were tightened. Jim had to work harder to maintain his balance. He lost himself in the ever-widening gyre of dream and ambition. He and Tammy travelled around staging telethons for local inspirational TV outlets. His celebrity grew, and he seemed to be having more and more direct conversations with God. Once God told Jim to disregard the denominations that divided Christians and maintain a kind of fundamentalist ecumenism, which as luck would have it dovetailed nicely with his national televangelist strategy.

At last God decided it was time for Jim to leave Pat Robertson and strike out for himself. Jim heeded the Word; after all, it had come just at the moment that Jim and Pat were beginning to claw each other to bits in competition for the limelight. After some to-ing and fro-ing, divine direction headed Jim and Tammy back to North Carolina. This time, however, they eschewed the mill-town scene for the promotional possibilities in Charlotte, the regional metropolis. Charlotte is, among other things, the hometown of Billy Graham, who really is a local hero, with a parkway named after him and other tokens of civic esteem in evident abundance. The Carolinas have always been fertile fundamentalist ground, and the Bakkers decided to set up a TV network of their own. It was tough going. Jim nearly failed in his first attempt, and he narrowly escaped a brush with bankruptcy. But he got his books in order . . . and the rest is historiography. PTL (variously Praise the Lord, People That Care and Pass the Loot) became a staple of daily televangelist fare, Bakker raised hundreds of millions of dollars, and the whole operation moved to nearby Fort Mill, South Carolina, where Heritage USA was built.

What people see in Heritage USA is a perfect recreation of a safe and wholesome life. "He created a world of 1950s innocence," said Bakker's former teacher Bill Harrison after visiting Heritage last year with his wife, Marge. "It was cheerful and friendly, no one ever grabbed a kid, nobody hit anybody. People helped homeless men and unwed mothers and handicapped children, and respected their elders. Jim still called us 'Mr. and Mrs. Harrison.' I wouldn't want to live there—the wine list was awfully short," Marge Harrison said mischievously. "It was too bland. But it was an alternate world, a parallel universe."

True, but what the eye divines is a worldly effluent of Jim Bakker's soul, a monument to his subconscious, a slow emergence of the repressed. There are two important strains in American Protestantism, and Heritage combines them in color, paint and plastic. One hard-nosed tradition holds that salvation is predestined—you're either saved or you're not—and nothing a man does on earth can redistribute the allotment of grace. Another holds that grace is a state whose blessings may be seen in symbols of earthly success. It is understood that the rise of capitalism in Europe owes much to the latter belief. A rich man may have as much trouble getting to heaven as a camel passing through a needle's eye, but on the other hand his wealth could prove that he's already made the passage.

With its thrusting hotel tower, its lavish shops, its water sports making a bigger splash than any baptism, its passion plays and healing services and entertainment for the whole family twenty-four hours a day, Heritage is more than just a Bible Belt version of a Borscht Belt resort. It is Jim Bakker's investment in salvation, a vehicle for his ride to heaven. Unfortunately, he may not complete the trip. Like those Sunday rebirths in Muskegon, this *auto-da-fé* is not foolproof. Good works may signify a soul redeemed, but salvation does not come automatically; it still requires unswerving faith in the power of prayer and the efficacy of great monuments to remove one's worldly sins. Bakker's doubt had always overcome his faith, and his preoccupations with cash and flesh could not cancel his fears.

As Bakker became more obsessed with his monuments he also seemed to delve deeper into sin. No doubt the two obsessions made a single syndrome. In a perverse way, the reality of sin legitimizes salvation; at least it identifies the mysterious, inaccessible guilt that only the eye can see. Jim grew jealous and petty about real or imagined affronts, both personal and commercial. He competed with rival televangelists the way Rather battles Brokaw. When Tammy had her breasts enlarged (she let close friends feel their new fullness after surgery), Jim had his face lifted. He began laying in cases of Asti Spumante, and an ex-bodyguard, Michael Richardson, has written that he began taking nips of vodka.

He worried about his manliness, Don Hardister recalls. "He was very concerned with his sexuality. He always said to me that supercreative types were sexual people. I guess at first I took it to mean that he had a healthy sexual life at home." Another associate remembers Jim as "exhibitionist and narcissistic. He was fixated on himself but he didn't really believe in himself."

In December of 1980, Tammy Faye fled to California. She had been telling her girlfriends that Bakker was neglecting her and had become a "workaholic." At the same time she was said to be having what the guys at PTL call "a flirtation" with a burly, bearded, born-again gospel singer named Gary Paxton, who appeared regularly on the *Jim and Tammy Show*. Tammy denies it. Divorce was still "a no-no" in the AG church, so the Bakkers tried to act as if nothing were amiss. In the thick of their separation they flew to Hawaii to conduct a marriage seminar. There, Jim melted down Tammy's wedding ring and re-presented it to her remolded into a "twenty years' service pin." Tough love. Then Jim dashed back to Clearwater, Florida, for his legendary ten minutes with Jessica Hahn. Bakker told her his sex life with Tammy was no good because she was "very big" and he couldn't be satisfied by her (but was the glass half full or half empty?). Hahn has told interviewers Jim was an "animal" in the throes of their copulation.

It looks as if Bakker was also dabbling, at least, with the ultimate prohibition of fundamentalism, the no-no that dares not even whisper its name. There were stories all around Charlotte that Jim was into guys. "I had worked for PTL for a long time and nothing ever happened that way," a former confidant of the Bakkers began (the man is still in the evangelism industry and he requested that his name not be used). "And then several years after I had left I was in Charlotte and I got a call from him to go to his house in Tega Cay, on Lake Wylie, near Heritage. Some people called it 'Tacky Key,' but it was quite a place. I found Jim lying in bed. He wanted to discuss hotel construction at Heritage—whether to put phones in the bathrooms, whether to have in-room air conditioning, computer jacks, remote-control TV service, that sort of thing. He was going non-stop at ninety miles an hour. Then in the middle he stopped and asked for a back rub. I had seen this happen before, but I had never given him one. I started in, and then he said, 'Do my leg," and 'Do my knee.' All of a sudden he grabbed my hand and placed it on a part of his body it shouldn't be on. Then he reached for my zipper. He asked me to close the curtains. I broke out in a cold sweat and got out as fast as I could."

There are other stories that detail more serious affairs, and Jerry Falwell has said (on *Nightline*, among other forums) that he's heard that Bakker has been gay since 1956 in Muskegon. So what? "There is strong connection between evangelism and sexual conflict," Jim's high school teacher Bill Harrison remarked. One of the features of fundamentalist revivals is the explosive discharge of emotion through ritual, after years of repression. Sex of whatever kind, power in whatever form, money in whatever denomination, and religion on any pulpit make up a continuum of expression and action that will out, no matter how determinedly it is controlled.

Dreams mediate conflict, and fantasy defuses emotion. Americans have mastered the art of avoiding the intractable struggles of life with infantile illusions. Jim Bakker prospered in an auto-reflective culture of video images, mascara and make-up, puppets and theme parks. It is a universe without death, without sin, without decay or incompetence.

Not the first of the media-hot performers to retreat into his own performance, Bakker was never sure of his own value away from his medium. "Jim had very low self-esteem," his old aide and companion Don Hardister thinks. In the fall he was making plans to come down from the mountain and go on the road again with Tammy Faye, in a new revival-cum-variety show, as if he had no identity without an audience. "He didn't think he was successful. He'd ask me, 'What is it that makes people come here [to Heritage USA]? What is it that draws people to me?' I saw him wrasslin' to grasp his identity like a brass ring on a merry-go-round. He never felt legitimate. Jim was not in touch with himself. Everything he did he did to gain approval. He was proud of what he accomplished, but it wasn't pride that drove him, it was approval."

He was, at the end, a captive of his own childish, narcissistic dreams. Along his route to Heritage USA he had made little memorials and commemorations to those who had believed in the dreams, and in him: Grandma Irwin, Bill Harrison, Aubrey Sarah, assorted relatives and hangers-on. But finally the charm wore off. "Jim dealt in a fantasy land," an old friend told me at the end of a long conversation. "He built one, he lived in one. The fantasy worked for a long time. And then it failed. These dreams can't go on forever."

December 1987, ESQUIRE

Chapter XIII

✦

LIGHT AND SHADOW

A Populist Message Hits Home

Des Moines

It is impossible to get the full flavor of a presidential caucus campaign in Iowa without attending a kick-off celebration in the Grand Ballroom of the Hotel Savery, a hot and airless space in which you will see every resident or transient politician, lobbyist, journalist, contributor and promoter in the capital, not one of whom should you trust with your wristwatch. It was to such a gathering that Democratic Senator Joseph Biden of Delaware came one night early last month, on the last leg of a movable announcement festival that began when he officially declared his candidacy in a train station in Wilmington, Delaware; continued in the rotunda of the Russell Senate Office Building in Washington; and ended up in the boondocks, where America's heart belongs.

Iowa's party caucuses next February 8 will provide the first test of popularity for the countless candidates (there seem to be at least sixteen real or prospective entrants so far), and the long and expensive campaigns for a few votes constitute a major economic boost and cultural fillip for a state otherwise in desperate decline. It behooves candidates not only to woo voters by taking tough stands and making bold promises but also, by their presence, to provide moral support for the heartland that many Iowans feel the rest of America has forgot.

The Biden strategy was ballyhoo. Hours before the candidates winged in from Washington, a convoy of chartered buses from the Iowan outback pulled up to the Savery and disgorged their loads of wide-eyed passengers wearing Biden buttons, carrying Biden banners and humming Biden tunes. "We sang all the way from Council Bluffs," one elderly woman said, and another woman handed me the official Biden song sheet. I scanned "Ev'ry Thing's Coming Up Biden" and "Biden This Time" but saw that the hit of the sheet would surely be "Io-wa, Io-wa," sung to the tune of "New York, New York," a combination sales pitch and anthem to state pride.

Start spread-in the news,
Joe's announcing today.
We're gonna be a part of it,
Io-wa, Io-wa.

His leadership style
And warm winning smile
Will step right to the front of it,
Io-wa, Io-wa.

He's gonna wake up in the state
That doesn't sleep,
To find he's king of the hill, top of the heap.

Our little towns here
Are for you today.
They're gonna be a part of it,
In ol' Io-wa.

If he can make it here,
He'll make it anywhere,
It's up to us
Io-wa, Io-wa!

The crowd lined up for registration and drink tickets and jammed into the narrow ballroom, which seemed too constricted for any dance more expansive than a fox trot, even when empty. A local comedian took the stage and delivered topical one-liners, performed magic tricks and made birdcalls. A Dixieland band played "Happy Days Are Here Again" and an array of dignitaries was introduced, including a delegation of US congressmen flown in for the occasion. The last warm-up act was the candidate's sister and campaign chairwoman. She seemed about to explode with excitement when Himself arrived, that warm winning smile framed around a truly estimable set of choppers. Like top models, the most successful politicians usually have the best teeth. But the imagery was not perfect. Hot lights set up earlier by the television crews brought out beads of sweat on Biden's brow, and the brightness glinted off his transplanted hair plugs.

Biden introduced his wife, Jill, and his children, all of whom carry prime-time soap opera names: Ashley, Hunter, Bo. I can imagine what they call their dog. He launched into his speech, full of the Kennedyesque cadences, Sorensenian formulations and Schlesingerundives that are supposed to make audiences think of the New Frontier (the good parts). "I don't want America to compete," he said, "I want America to *win*." He spoke of a "new generation" poised on the lip of power, but from the look of the room it was not evident that this particular generation has the historical self-consciousness or the outsider identity of the post-Eisenhower cohort to which Biden alluded. There were a lot of fresh-faced white kids with no sign of alienation from the good life the Reagan years have provided them. Nevertheless, Biden, who is 44 years old, believes he can corner the youth market—if he can create one.

Jesse Jackson, a year older than Biden, had come to the same hotel ballroom four days earlier, but the scene couldn't have been more different. Jackson spoke to a local convention of the American Federation of State, County and Municipal Employees and gave a detailed populist sermon meant to rouse a coalition of "the displaced and the dispossessed" that has no other obvious haven in the party. Biden had talked about "excellence" and warned that "foreign workers are better educated and work harder" than Americans. Jackson said, "Foreign workers are not better than American workers; they are cheaper workers."

Jackson's was not a speech about the new social compact between business and labor that other Democratic candidates are proposing; it was a demand for "economic justice." US corporations, he said, are fleeing these shores and setting up "slave labor" shops in the Third World, from which they export cheap goods back to America in a flood that destroys jobs, lives, communities. As he does in nearly every talk, Jackson exhorted the unionists to make "common ground" with others similarly situated; to forget racial divisions; to accept women, minorities, immigrants and the unemployed as comrades in arms; and to change the distribution of power to their own advantage. "The fight is not at a pizza parlor in New York, not on a lonely road in Georgia," he said in one of several preliminary crescendos before the final, familiar rhetorical arpeggio that has become the hallmark of his style. "The fight is at the shipyard, where they bring in goods made by slave labor. We should turn to each other, not on each other."

Since he came to Iowa on Super Bowl Sunday, six months ago, Jackson has been so warmly received that even his most ardent supporters have trouble believing or understanding the phenomenon. Dixon Terry, a 38-year-old dairy farmer and political organizer, was instrumental in getting Jackson to his own Adair County on that cold January day, and he even supplied the cow Jackson stood beside when the campaign's most memorable news photo was snapped.

"We brought Jackson to Adair to get him interested in family-farm legislation," Terry told me, "but we had no idea he would catch on this way. Eight hundred people on Super Bowl Sunday left their TVs on and came to see him, 300 stayed for the potluck, and Jackson launched a rural strategy after that day. Average folks turned out by the hundreds. Old folks were coming out to see the preacher preach, some were crying; he really touched a nerve."

Terry and I sat in the back room of the Iowa Farm Unity Coalition office on the town square in Greenfield, the Adair County seat, where Jackson has set up his statewide headquarters. It is a modern populist's dream setting. The beautiful old courthouse dominates a perfectly symmetrical arrangement of wooden buildings, cut by roads at the corners and compass points like the plan for a Renaissance chapel. Mornings, farmers drive their pickups into town for one thing or another, and at noon people gather at Toad's Place for lunch. The Jackson office is just off the square, and the young woman who runs it is just getting used to the influx of strangers from parts of the country she has seen only in the movies.

"America must be changing," Terry said, looking out the back window on the drizzly day. "Jackson came here and met Jay Howe, a local lawyer whose father was a banker and whose grandfather owned the newspaper. Now Jay is Jesse's state co-chairman. Jackson's been good for the whole progressive agenda, for the farm fight, for peace groups and Central America issues. He's moved the whole debate here to the left. I don't really know how it happened."

Everywhere he goes Jackson gets the crowds and the response, with a speech or merely an appearance, that most candidates will spend millions, perhaps, to buy with television ads and professional staffs. Jackson is currently running second to Representative Richard Gephardt, of neighboring Missouri, in the *Des Moines Register* poll of Democratic voters. It can't be blacks—Jackson's principal constituency in 1984—giving him that standing, since they make up only 1.4 percent of the state's population, and the farm communities where Jackson is doing so well are immutably monochromatic.

What no one knows for sure is whether Jackson's media celebrity accounts for his political popularity. Among Democrats his is the only familiar name and face now that Gary Hart has retired from the race. Most people think that Paul Simon is the fellow who used to sing with Art Garfunkel, that Babbitt is a book or a town in Minnesota and that Dukakis is where you go next January to register your presidential preference, as in "I'm going down to do caucus."

Actually, Dukakis is worse than unknown in the farm areas. On his first trip here in the spring, he recommended that the feed-corn and bean growers, virtually the entire agricultural sector, start raising Belgian endive and blueberries, like the trendy truck farmers beyond the Boston suburbs. The idea didn't go over in a big way.

Jackson has different ideas about Iowa farming. The threatened demise of the family farm system cannot be averted by managerial maneuvers or market gimmicks. What is required is a wholesale assault on the political economy of American agriculture. The Reagan Administration has accelerated a process that began decades ago, in which the family farm is being replaced by "megafarms" increasingly owned by absentee management firms and agribusiness corporations. Some companies are building vertical monopolies in the industry, with land as the bottom layer of a structure that will include feed-lots for cattle, meatpacking houses, machinery manufacturing plants, grain exporting companies, supermarkets and shopping malls—all in a transnational system.

Like Stalinism in the Soviet Union in the 1930s, Reaganism in America in the 1980s seeks to rationalize agriculture to make it responsive to centralized planning and presumed economies of scale. Here the centralization is corporate rather than collective, but many of the methods of forced removal of farmers and the consequences to traditional communities are remarkably similar to those used in the Soviet Union. No kulaks have been shot in Iowa, but tens of thousands of families have been driven from their homes, many after three, four or five generations on the land, and sent to distant towns where they shovel chicken manure in poultry "factories" or fast food in roadside stands. They migrate to the losing end of the agricultural chain they once helped forge. Unless radical reforms are instituted—a most unlikely prospect, to be sure—half the farms in Iowa will go under in the next ten years.

Seventy miles north of Adair County, in the little town of Churdan, the remaining farm families are watching their community dissolve and their lives change for the worse with no recourse to the established political means of reform. Johnny Maguire (he'd rather I didn't use his real name) took over the family farm when his father retired, and he works several more rented pieces of land for a total of some 1,200 acres—a large spread by local standards, but he sees himself as one of a dying breed.

"I'll be 29 in September," he said, "but there's probably not more than a dozen that's younger than me in the whole area." A quiet, rather reserved man, he swung his arm to indicate the extended region to which he referred. "A lot of the farmers, they're 45 years old and up, so they'll be retired in fifteen, twenty years, and that'll be the end of it. Most of my friends in my class at Iowa State went into jobs where they got $20,000 or more to start, and they didn't want to come back to the land. Oh, this ground will always be farmed, one way or the other, but not by the people who live here. As for me, I'm going to stay a farmer for the rest of my life."

What Jackson calls a "new feudalism" is settling over the rural heartland. Farmers default on their loans; banks and insurance companies (and sometimes government agencies) foreclose; sometimes they burn and bulldoze the lovely old white farmhouses, the barns, the silos and the stands of trees that protected the homeland from the prairie winds. Scorching the earth lowes the property taxes. Families who simply cannot tear themselves from their birthplaces are sometimes allowed to stay on the land by the new management companies or megafarmers, in return for work done. Those new tenants represent the saddest sector of a shift in productive relations that will amount to billions or perhaps trillions of dollars by the end of the century.

Another Churdan farmer, whom I'll call Don Davis, saw his brother-in-law go under last year, and just the other day read in the paper that his best friend from high school had been foreclosed on. "The community is dwindling," he told me one hot evening in his kitchen. He and his father farm a large tract planted in corn and soybeans, the usual mix here, and his house sits in the middle of lovely land, green as far as the eye can see and dotted here and there with old white buildings. Away on the horizon, in a shimmering mirage, a complex of grain elevators stands between the earth and the sky, like a great ship at the end of the ocean.

"There are twenty-five or thirty empty houses in this town, and you can't sell them," Davis was saying. One friend would let her big home go for $13,000, but she can't find a buyer. The local high school football team won the state championship two years in a row in its class but next year it won't have enough students to field a team; there's talk of going in with a school far away just to get a squad together. "Half the houses you see out there," Davis pointed through the window, "will never be lived in again." "I'll tell you," he added softly, "I don't go down to the coffee shop anymore. It's all gloom and doom in there."

On the trail in Iowa, Jackson excites voters more by promising them participation in the power structure—the organizing principle of the old civil rights movement—than by offering them specific programs and policies to cure their complaints. Unlike most other Democrats campaigning in the state, he does not hurl a string of neoliberal proposals from the hustings. His delivery is at once personal and political rather than procedural and managerial. At a district Democratic picnic in a scenic park in Decorah, on bluffs overlooking the Upper Iowa River, Jackson moved the audience with a promise to "go to Central America" and end the war there, as Eisenhower did in Korea. Later that day in a hot town square in Iowa Falls a crowd of recently laid-off workers cheered when he said, "We must change the equation. There's no sense of corporate justice, of fairness. We'd better wake up and fight" to stop the "merger maniacs." The town was reeling from the decision of Farmland Foods to close its pork packing plant and idle one-quarter of the local industrial work force. Efforts by the mayor and a committee of employers to sweeten the economic terms for the Kansas City–based firm had been unavailing. Fred Gandy—the local congressman who previously won celebrity in the role of Gopher on *Love Boat*—was promoting his efforts to get a small retraining grant for the displaced workers, but surely was not concerned about "corporate justice." Jackson was there to say that only a radical political realignment could achieve some semblance of equity in the economic equation. "We have the money to bail out the American farmer," he said, "but we don't have the priority to do it."

It's not hard to see how Jesse Jackson can make populist politics in a place like this, and the strategy seems to be working, at least in this early stage of the campaign. Farmers who have never seen a black person in their town, let alone in their kitchen, told me they'd vote for Jackson because, as one of them put it, "he's meeting the issues." Dick Butler, a farmer who moonlights as a coach at the school in Churdan, said he wouldn't vote for a Catholic— "the Vatican's got too much power as it is"—and he wouldn't vote for Pat Robertson "if my life depended on it," but he thinks that Jackson "understands the farmer, the blue-collar man, the working man."

"I don't think the fact that he's black will hurt him here," Butler's wife, Rona, added. "The presidency is so far away. Now, if he was going to marry my daughter, that might be a different story."

July 18, 1987, THE NATION

◆

Flo Don't Know

Detroit

In 1950, when she was 19, Bertha Gillespie left the hot, rich farmland of Columbus, Mississippi, and rode the train a thousand miles north to Detroit to find good work and raise her family. She had high hopes. Right away she got a job as a housekeeper in the new Howard Johnson's motel, the perfect orange-and-aqua symbol for the triumph of the auto-industrial age and the mass car culture it spawned. She already had two children, and they moved into the sprawling Brewster housing project. Her new neighbors were black migrants from all over the rural South who had come to work in the factories—and make the beds—of the corporate families that had fashioned Detroit into a great war machine and the foundation of the consumer civilization.

"Oh, things were nice then," Bertha Gillespie told me as we walked around Brewster-Douglas, as the project is now known, just behind Jesse Jackson and a platoon of Secret Service men on the afternoon of the Michigan Democratic caucuses. Gillespie, her daughter and several friends had joined hundreds of residents in an impromptu march to get out the vote and drum up enthusiasm for a campaign that was already at fever pitch in the projects.

"It was a real nice place to live in, most times," Gillespie recalled. "The buildings were so new, they wouldn't let us barbecue outside, 'cause they said we'd smoke up the bricks." The place was full of possibilities. Joe Louis, the Brown Bomber of Detroit, was a Brewster boy. "See over there, that's where Diana Ross grew up. I used to see her all the time," Gillespie said proudly. "And on the second floor of that high-rise there, that's where Mary Wilson lived. And behind, the other Supreme, the one who died, she lived there." They don't remember Flo so well.

"Things started to go down after that," Gillespie recounted. "We lacked police protection. There was a lot of drugs and guns, and the police would come and circle the block, they'd pull over somebody and take their money and drugs and keep on going. They still do it, but they don't come around that much anymore."

Detroit went up in flames in the riots of 1967, and there are still broad fields of dirt and rubble where nothing has been rebuilt. The bricks of Brewster grew grimy and the paint peeled, but it wasn't from the smoke of barbecues. The entry to Diana Ross's apartment and hundreds of others are boarded up with plywood; the windows in Mary Wilson's high-rise are broken and the stairwells are littered and foul. They closed Bertha Gillespie's apartment block and moved her out of the project, but she still works as a housekeeper in one of the buildings, where old people live. Her seven kids are grown; the "baby," she says, is coming out of school this year. She's thinking of going back to Mississippi. "Things down there ain't so bad anymore," she thought. In Detroit, hopes are no longer high.

It is impossible to understand Jesse Jackson's extraordinary political achievement in Michigan without some sense of the social transformations that have produced the conditions his campaign addresses. When Jackson talks about the "dispossessed and the disenfranchised," he does not refer only to the poor or the voteless but to people who are radically removed from the nourishing institutions and the enlivening spirit of American society. In Michigan, especially, that includes whites as well as blacks, and people who are just getting by in the economy as well as those who are suffering on welfare. Hundreds of thousands of white workers have lost their jobs, and the ones who are still working live with a permanent sense of insecurity. A pall of pessimism has settled over the scene.

"We work every day," Jackson reminds crowds of the underemployed, who invariably respond with knowing assents. "And we are still poor. We pick up your garbage; we work every day. We drive your cars, we take care of your children, we empty your bed pans, we sweep your apartments; we work every day. We cook your food, and we don't have time to cook our own. We change your hospital beds and wipe your fevered brow, and we can't afford to lie in that bed when we get sick. We work every day." By the end of the speech the nods of approval are mixed with tears.

The precipitous decline of "the industry" has ravaged souls as well as cities. It has exacerbated racial and class differences and has called into question all the old strategies for economic development and social improvement. Detroit Mayor Coleman Young, a hero of black political power in the early 1970s, has failed utterly to redistribute resources from the declining corporate coffers in the suburban ring to his miserable base in the core. His *de facto* endorsement of Michael Dukakis, who represents the old politics, was a last act of loyalty that was rejected by both the base and the ring.

Jim Settles, an official of UAW Local 600 in Dearborn, explained that Jackson's "message" was getting through to workers of all stripes in his union, but it was not merely the promise of paychecks or food stamps. "Jackson does something no one else has done," Settles said. "He gives people hope." Richard Gephardt, who was favored for a time by the union's top brass, scored some emotional points with his Hyundai-bashing, but Jackson won by locating villainy in the system rather than in Asia. Dukakis halfheartedly appealed to white workers on the basis of their ethnicity and certain cultural icons. He endlessly repeated sentimental stories of his parents' arrival at Ellis Island, and in the Polish enclave of Hamtramck he told a small and dispirited audience that his wife, Kitty, "the love of my life," is supposed to "look just like Jackie Kennedy." At which point his sponsors presented him with a signboard with his name spelled out in kielbasa. Not too many of those folks came out to vote for him the next day.

Jackson has known all along that a populist campaign runs on hope and the prospect of power. His jingly chant, "I am somebody" (heard more frequently four years ago than today), turns out to be the essential statement of the populist ideology. He is more sophisticated now, but no less consistent.

In Michigan he could be recognized as a great communicator of hope to the victims of transformations that he himself has lived through and triumphed over. The Brewster kids have a new model for success. What Flo don't know (in the Supremes' phrase) is that a new level of political possibility has come out of the projects, out of the shuttered factories along the Rouge, out of the dead city and the besieged suburbs. It's a powerful tide that Jackson is riding now, and it energizes constituencies in ever-widening rings.

Although anything *could* happen in this highly volatile primary season, not everything *will*. Jackson's appeal is still limited—as evidenced by his second-place showing in the Connecticut primary last week—by the class character of his campaign, his race base and the historical conditions he engages. Michigan displays virtually every difficulty of postindustrial America. Connecticut is about as good as the new entrepreneurial service society can get. If Jackson can get from the one to the other, he will make his own history.

April 9, 1988, THE NATION

✦

Light and Shadow: Where Do Jesse's People Go?

They used to say in the civil rights movement of the 1960s that "the people need victories" to keep going in what is always a bitter and frustrating endeavor. Jesse Jackson says over and over that the people need hope, which is also a kind of victory. Jackson won 6.7 million votes in the primary round, against Dukakis's 9.7 million, although the delegate line-up does not reflect that remarkable success. He won in many of the major cities of America (including New York, Chicago, Philadelphia, San Francisco, Houston), much of the Deep South and many important "demographics," including a majority of all voters between the ages of 18 and 29. Again, he raised the level of political excitement and brought thousands of politically inactive people into the political process. But if the campaign to win power in the nation's political institutions—what his candidacy represented—is to continue and grow, those who join must have the reasonable expectation of some pay-off for their efforts. If they can't get a big piece of the pie Dukakis controls this year, they will have to win some of those battles in the Farm Belt, the big cities, the states, the unions, the schools and workplaces, the points of production and consumption. A complete movement creates useful activities and a political culture that will carry its members through the long years on the margins of power.

Perhaps there were a few moments—between the Michigan caucuses and the Wisconsin primary—when Jackson and his supporters indulged their fondest fantasy of winning the nomination, but they always knew that the dream was impossible. At best, the campaign could organize a force mighty enough to demand a share of power in the general election campaign, in the Democratic Party and in a Democratic Administration. And that best would be very good indeed.

But no matter how successful Jackson is in getting a share of power for himself or his campaign this year, he has demonstrated that an expanded electorate and a coalition of the disempowered is the only likely route for progressive politics in the foreseeable future. Democrats who will not or cannot expand the party to include that half of the population that does not now participate (and that would in great measure support progressive programs), and candidates who offer no plan for the reorganization of power at the base, will be stuck in the center and dependent on the interests of the corporate class that dominates politics. They are obliged to cater to the most regressive "swing" constituencies in the electorate, as Dukakis has been told he must. They make unseemly compromises with racism (however humane their rhetoric) in order to placate the swing voters, who—surprise!—turn out to be white and conservative. Such candidates may win, but they cannot make change. In boom times and in periods of low-intensity social conflict (e.g., in Massachusetts in the mid-1980s) they may deliver modest benefits to the needy and civilized management for the middle class. But they cannot, and will not, attempt the kind of *perestroika* that progressives glimpsed this year for the first time in almost a half-century of trial and failure.

The search for "new ideas" that occupied Democrats during the 1984 primary season turned up nothing but recycled or repackaged old ideas. This year there are enough new ideas around to choke a horse. There is the idea of conversion from a military to a civilian economy, of realigning US foreign policy with the forces of independence in the Third World, of public control of corporate behavior in the social sphere, of universal health care, of redistribution of wealth and power, of democratizing the processes of politics, of empowering the powerless. Unfortunately, those are not the kinds of ideas that the people who finance and direct the established Democratic Party believe should be tried or even mentioned in genteel company. You will not find them written in the party's platform or contained in such legislation as a putative Democratic president may offer in the next four years.

The Jackson campaign has produced important proposals for change, but more than that it has been a prelude to a possible movement. Now the choice to wither away or fight for the future must be made in the next few weeks. To be credible after Atlanta, the Jackson faction must fight for power at the convention even if it must lose the big battles to the party establishment, which has superior numbers there. Fighting is itself a way of gathering strength, as the civil rights movement also showed. If the Jackson campaign allows itself to be folded into the Democratic Party like egg whites into a soufflé, it will have betrayed all those who put their faith in and pinned their hopes on empowerment.

July 16, 1988, THE NATION

The Old Gringos

For a dead duck, the cold war still has a lively kick and a lot of squawk. However much superpower tensions have been relieved in Europe and the peril of nuclear exchange reduced, the century-old campaign waged by American political leaders and cultural arbiters against "the left," as they define it, remains in full force. It can be seen every day in various forms: in bipartisan support for the ultraright Cristiani regime in El Salvador, in the Administration's reluctance to underwrite real working-class democracy in Poland, in Jonas Savimbi's reception in Washington, in the refusal of the nation's economic strategists to consider redistributive policies or new social investments.

The extreme reaction in Washington and in the national media to Nicaraguan President Daniel Ortega's announcement of the resumption of military operations against *contras* inside his country is explicable only in a cold war, counterrevolutionary context. Of course, Nicaragua never posed any clear or present danger to US domination of Central America. But while the Soviet threat was still a viable myth, security fanatics and neoconservative propagandists could claim that with the Sandinistas in power in Managua, Russian tanks were only a stone's throw away from Harlingen, Texas. Now with Moscow's radical retrenchment away from Third World struggles, its admission of error in Afghanistan and Gorbachev's irreversible policy of diverting military expenditures to the civilian sector, not even the wildest fantasies of Soviet expansionism are credible.

But the ideological campaign against Nicaragua continues unabated. For it is the example of independence and the potential for contagion from that dread disorder (however small, alas) that sets Washington's wings to flapping. The day after Ortega's slightly gauche declaration in Costa Rica, the capital was seized by the war spirit. Bush made snobbish and snide comments about Ortega's size, his uniform and his behavior—the sort of thing British blimps used to say about uppity colonials. Reporters tried to drum up interest in the resumption of "lethal" aid (as if " humanitarian" aid hadn't killed hundreds of Nicaraguans just since the cease-fire), and Ortega was denounced by Democratic liberals and Republican reactionaries alike in a sense-of-Congress resolution that passed by a whopping 379 to 29 in the House and 95 to 0 in the Senate.

After a few days, the mood began to mellow. It dawned on a few sane commentators that the Nicaraguans had a point or two in their favor. After all, the United States has been waging one of the most deadly wars in the history of the hemisphere against one of the poorest countries in the world. Nicaragua has suffered more than 57,000 casualties, with almost 30,000 killed (*contras* included) and economic damages estimated at over $12 billion. The US-imposed trade embargo and the US veto of international aid to Nicaragua amounts to another $700 million lost. For more than a year and a half, the Nicaraguan government has observed its own unilateral cease-fire, which the *contras* have refused to join. And the United States has refused to heed the most important planks of the Central American peace plan (which Bush castigated Ortega for disobeying), which calls for demobilization of the *contras* and their bases in Honduras by early December. Finally, *contra* attacks have been escalating in the last months, as thousands of the armed rebels roam the Nicaraguan countryside on a rampage in a last-ditch terror campaign before the scheduled national election.

Although any awful thing is possible in the bootless Administration and craven Congress now ensconced in Washington, it looks as though Ortega—and Nicaragua—will survive one more time. For despite all the screaming for blood, no one in power really wants to put the war in Central America back on the national political agenda. There's no percentage in it for Bush, even though he must constantly play to the hard-right crowd that got him where he is. The Democrats hate having to prove their military *machismo* every time a crisis occurs, and they would rather get back to endorsing fat checks from corporate PACs, which seems to be the party's sole activity and *raison d'être* these days.

And yet the counterrevolution continues. It is clear that the "lessons of Nicaragua" will make no more of an impression on America's political and intellectual rulers than did the lessons of Vietnam. Unlike that other superpower, which has taken the unimaginable step of encouraging grass-roots revolts, movements of independence and self-determination for people long in its orbit, the United States maintains an imperial mentality with all the mean-spirited consequences for the wretched of that part of the earth under American control. Which is what the cold war has always been about.

November 27, 1989, THE NATION

✦

Race, Class and Murder in Boston

Murder is war on a very small scale, and like great battles, a single slaying can define and focus the history of its time. What has become known as the Stuart murder case (a headline that hardly begins to describe its layers of meaning) is a paradigm of late-century American popular pathology, a pre-eminent social parable that links rampant racism, pervasive sexism, media sensationalism, class competition, political opportunism, corrupt justice, repression, tribalism, narcissism, greed—and much, much more. Not really an American tragedy (there are no flawed heroes or fallen ideals), the Stuart saga is essentially a case of bad attitudes and morbid symptoms in a society turned too tabloid to be tragic.

The murder of Carol Stuart—initially blamed on a black robber and now attributed to her husband, Charles, perhaps with the help of accessories or conspirators still to be named—fits as many categories of plot as there are critics and commentators. Connie Chung, on her low-rated Saturday night television "magazine," presented it as a "hoax" in a package with the story of a woman who, as a prank, told reporters she had won the New York lottery. That made as much sense as linking the deaths of John Kennedy and Billy Martin as traffic accidents.

The New York Times, as well as several Boston columnists, bracketed the Stuart murder with the Tawana Brawley case, narrowing the hoax to a racial accusation. But that ignored the vast power differential between the two incidents. When Chuck Stuart described a black man as the murderer of his pregnant wife, the white authorities in Boston sent a small army of occupation into the black neighborhoods. Police invaded the housing projects of Mission Hill, knocking down doors, bursting into apartments, slamming and insulting residents. White cops taunted the terrified people: "Where's the nigger with the trigger?" Young black men were stopped, searched and detrousered on the street for no cause more reasonable than their skin color. The cops called the blacks "pussy" and "faggot," and sexual humiliation— white male power against black male impotence—became another tactic of the occupation. In short order, a likely suspect by the name of Willie Bennett (cf. Willie Horton) was located and evidence produced to get him into a line-up, where Stuart identified him as his assailant. No comparable assault on the white community in New York State followed Brawley's charge that white cops had brutalized her.

In Boston, the media went certifiably berserk. There was nothing else in the papers for weeks. Television provided live coverage of Carol Stuart's funeral, with the ultraconservative Bernard Cardinal Law officiating, lame duck Governor Michael Dukakis and Mayor Raymond Flynn, a gubernatorial hopeful, leading the official mourning, and the entire roster of local political leaders in attendance. Once in the ground, Carol was almost completely forgotten. Even after Chuck became a "suspect" in her killing, the category of violence against women was not prominently applied, except by the daily papers' three female columnists. It's far more likely that the murderer of a woman in Massachusetts will be her husband or boyfriend than a robber who enters her car—or her house. But somehow interspousal murder is less gripping to media managers than is interracial, interclass homicide.

Anyone with a pen or a PC (which in literate Massachusetts is almost everyone) mongered an opinion. Liberals diagnosed the social malaise of the ghetto (cf. the pathology of the black family) as the root cause of the murder, and prescribed increased funding for programs to combat poverty, drugs and crime. Conservatives suggested that a permanent, intractable criminal underclass infests minority neighborhoods, and they demanded more jail cells and police protection and reinstatement of the death penalty.

Some whites argued that the search-and-destroy tactics of the police were "strong medicine" for the blacks' own good. "It may be true that this crime focussed our attention because this time it was one of us bleeding in the street," a woman from a suburb south of the city wrote in *The Boston Globe*. "The massive police response no doubt came from the outrage of a public broader than a single city neighborhood. . . . Roxbury [synecdoche for "black people"] will still benefit from the police sweep."

Some black leaders were offended by Mayor Flynn's "aggressive" police penetration of their community, while others (including a number on the Flynn payroll) internalized white fear and loathing and agreed it was for their own good, much as certain leaders of a poor and despised country welcome imperial invaders. But the mood in the projects was sullen and resentful. "It's always us black people who suffer, no matter what," one woman said. There was clearly no agreement on who "us" were in Boston.

Despite the liberal cast that Boston assumes, the place is a racial nightmare. White ethnics fought school integration so viciously that a federal court took over the system for years. Ray Flynn was a segregationist *kapo* in Southie in those days. Michael Dukakis, in his first term as governor, cravenly ducked the issue. Segregation in public housing is worse than in the schools, occasioning more federal judicial intervention, and although Flynn turned around on public integration issues as his political ambitions rose, he still refuses to let blacks, Latinos or Asians (who together form 45 percent of the population) make decisions in his administration. The mayor's inner circle is all white and all male, and tribalism keeps an iron grip on power.

Flynn, who says he'll decide for sure in a month or so whether to run for governor, has refused to apologize to the Mission Hill neighborhood (the epicenter of the police invasion) and the black community in general for the calumnies and cruelties. "We're all guilty," he says. (What is Mission Hill guilty of, other than the crime of "I-wouldn't-put-it-past-them"?) He wants to be a "healer" and hopes that he can funnel some funds into Mission Hill to combat crime, drugs, poverty and the general low life that white Bostonians still believe, somehow, killed Carol Stuart.

Chuck Stuart sought to rise to Back Bay gentility (he was a $100,000-a-year manager of a fur boutique on the best shopping street in town) from the bars and backyard basketball courts of Revere, an all-white, working-class suburb where Irish, Jewish and Italian immigrants landed a century ago. He lied about his life (he never went to Brown, as he claimed) and about his love for Carol DiMaiti. A bright, well-educated tax lawyer with considerable earning power, she was useful to him for a while. But she got pregnant and that seemed to threaten his plans for advancement into restaurant ownership, a Revere boy's dream. It was the same season—probably the same week—that Sam was trying to buy Cheers, on Channel 4. So why not "do" Carol (in the native lingo) and blame it on the blacks? It's a local tradition.

February 5, 1990, THE NATION

Afternote: For Boston in 1990, now read Union, South Carolina, in 1994. For Chuck and Carol Stuart, read Susan Smith and her drowned little boys. Once again, an easy racism first figered an entirely fictional black man.

Cycle of Madness

Madness has its uses, both for the lunatics and for the society that produces them. The Nazi leaders may have been certifiably insane, but Nazism had a diabolical internal logic; in its own terms, it worked. Psychokillers who shoot up schoolyards and shopping malls in America hear their own private voices, but louder still is the message of anomie, isolation and alienation broadcast by a consumption-driven society. In short, derangement has social resonance. Nowhere is there "the lone gunman." The title of a French film about capital punishment some years back had it just right: *Nous sommes tous des assassins.*

Israeli government officials predictably attempted to normalize the massacre of seven Arab day laborers at Rishon le Zion by comparing the "isolated incident" to other acts of wanton violence in the United States or Canada. But the murder of Arabs by a recently discharged Israeli soldier is too horribly logical to rationalize by saying that "everybody does it." Others may attempt murder to impress Jodie Foster, redress a labor grievance or take vengeance on generic Asians for humiliation in Indochina. The Israeli assassin took his aim in the context of a Jewish political culture that despises Arabs, wishes them dead or deported and cheers their brutalization. And when his bullets were spent, the supposedly sane and calculating forces of the state continued the carnage by killing and wounding hundreds more in the name of public order.

According to the Hebrew-language daily press, the "lone gunman's" victims lay unattended for the better part of an hour by the side of a major highway near the "slave market" where they had gathered to seek work. Before any ambulance arrived, no Israeli stopped to offer help. Many drivers passing by raised their fingers in the "V" sign. One newspaper reported an Israeli motorist getting out of his car and dancing among the bodies, shouting, "What, only seven killed?"

It was not until the Shamir government realized that it had a major escalation of protest on its hands that officials began to offer apologies and express regret—more or less in the tone of voice US officials used when navy gunners on the *Vincennes* blasted an Iranian airbus with 290 civilians on board into the Persian Gulf. That was an "unavoidable accident." The plane was in the wrong place (a "war zone") at the wrong time (when the US navy was shooting at every blip on the screen). This was an act of derangement, the unfortunate and utterly inexplicable act of a madman.

In fact it was a set-up, an "irrational" piece of a very rational pattern of murderous repression, dehumanization and racism developed and endorsed by a large number of Jewish citizens for many years. At once Shamir and his crowd turned on their victims, blaming Palestinians for responding with rage. Amazingly, President Bush had the courage to take a stand, however mild, with the Palestinians. He sent his condolences to the families of the slain workers and criticized the Israelis for their "lack of restraint" in handling the protests in the streets. The United States can do a lot more: just stop the money that finances the occupation and immiseration of the Palestinians. Congress has cut off aid and imposed sanctions on terrorist organizations and outlaw states before, from Guatemala to South Africa. It is no longer politically unthinkable to pressure Israel in the same way. Indeed, it is madness to continue as if nothing had happened in Rishon le Zion.

June 11, 1990, THE NATION

✦

Blood, Oil and Politics

Why does it sound so familiar? The undisputed bully of the region, seeking to protect and extend his hegemony, launches a midnight attack on a small but strategically located country to his south—in his "backyard." Deep in debt from past failed military adventures and extravagant arms build-ups, the bully is worried that the principal resource of the targeted country is out of his control, and might actually be used to his detriment. Crucial shipping lanes are at stake. The small country is a major financial center. Previous attempts to subvert, realign or otherwise squeeze the offending country have been ineffective. But the regime of the small country is no great shakes either. It was created and delineated as a fiction of a nation by an imperial superpower only at the beginning of this century, and it has existed by and large for the superpower's benefit.

When the bully strikes with his gleaming weaponry and well-trained troops, it falls within hours and its undemocratic, authoritarian leader is sent into exile. Stirring sentiments are presented as a rationale for the invasion, which has killed at least several hundred civilians and introduced an army of occupation into the no-longer-independent country. But the pretense hardly hides the naked power play. Out of the blue, a jury-rigged government of the bully's choosing is installed in the middle of the night, a new army and police corps are created to enforce the new order, and the bully announces he is "withdrawing" as soon as peace is restored.

The international organization responsible for the region votes overwhelmingly to condemn the invasion, but that hardly deters the bully, whose hegemonic appetite is insatiable and whose "national interest" provides the moral justification for every violent act. Not entirely accidentally, the invasion is wildly popular at home—the people are mad for victory after a succession of dismal defeats—and the bully's ratings rise to historic heights, at a time when intractable domestic problems are mounting.

The bully of the week is, of course, Saddam Hussein, conqueror of Kuwait, but the idea that, with a few allowances for difference in scale, the paradigm fits George Bush, scourge of Panama, should give the pious politicians and smug policy rats in Washington some pause. It wasn't too long ago that they were cheering the destruction and occupation of America's own bad neighbor to the south, which had become uppity and unreliable. Kuwait was breaking the OPEC rules and overproducing oil. That was deeply damaging to Iraq's economy, which needed high oil prices to make up the deficit incurred in its war with Iran. Panama was refusing to go along with US Central America policy, Noriega seemed to be getting chummy with Washington's enemies and the country's great resource—the canal—could conceivably have slipped from US control.

The comparison in no way excuses the activities of Saddam Hussein, who by all accounts is a real rotter. But it wasn't so long ago that the Reagan Administration was tilting mightily to Saddam, and Bush was opposing congressional cut-offs of loans to Iraq. No one complained much when he invaded Iran—and later bombed an American warship, killing thirty-seven sailors—or even when he used poison gas. Saddam's elevation from greedy adventurer to world-historical monster (the *New York Times* columnists liken him to Hitler, while *Time* prefers Nebuchadnezzer) suggests that something else is going on, a dynamic different from the simple one of law and outlaw promoted most of all by the United States. No ordinary despot could produce the war fever that has taken over the country and allowed Bush to begin the biggest military mobilization since the end of the war in Vietnam.

At bottom, the larger war of which the current conflict is a part has been going on for years, in episodes of heat and cold. It's the new war of resources that replaced the old superpower cold war as the pre-eminent international conflict long before the Berlin wall came down. The industrialized "West" has long relied on the extraction of cheap resources from the rest of the world for its increasingly lavish lives. To keep prices low, political control was necessary, and when direct imperialism was no longer a viable option, suitable methods of indirect domination were applied.

What President Bush meant when he called the establishment of an Iraqi client government in Kuwait "unacceptable" (as a replacement for the Western client emir) was that Iraqi power over the price of oil is unacceptable. The problem is not that Saddam is a madman (which has become the cliché description of all our darker-skinned enemies—and if you're looking for real horror shows, the Saudis, after all, cut off heads and hands and run a barely postfeudal society of unspeakable repression) but that he is no longer *our* madman. Like Noriega, he struck out on his own.

The United States, which is leading—indeed, compelling—the international attack on Saddam Hussein, has been itching for a war against the Muslims at least since Iran took its hostages. First there was Carter's Desert 1 fiasco, then the bombing and forced retreat of the marines from Beirut, the Palestinian *intifada*, the acts of terrorism, the hostages in Lebanon, Abu this and Abu that. Nothing seemed to work. Even the bombing of Tripoli was a bit of a dud. The top guns in their billion-dollar bombers missed Qaddafi, and things are about the way they were before. Now the Christians are ready once again to have at the Saracens.

War sounds good to Bush now for many reasons, domestic and diplomatic. With the economy teetering and about to go over the edge because of the "oil shock," there will be cries for action and Bush can be ahead of the pack by sending in the troops. The specter of Jimmy Carter must be looming large in the night corridors of the White House. Nor is it difficult to detect a fine Israeli hand in the preparations for war. The elimination of Saddam Hussein and Iraq's military potential has long been a priority for Israel. And demonizing the Butcher of Baghdad diverts attention from Israel's own occupied territories. Above all, Bush—who goes way back in the oil business—wants to control that commodity in its most abundant reserves. The risk that he may be starting a version of Vietnam in the Middle East will be taken so that the United States can maintain dominance. Resource wars, like the other kinds, are hell.

August 9, 1990, THE NATION

✦

The Dish on Nancy

Gossip serves as justice in a corrupt world. In a more perfect place, Nancy Reagan would have been brought to trial for crimes against sincerity, candor and taste, and surely judgement would have been terrible and swift. The United States penal code, however, omits such offenses, so there's only Kitty Kelley to even the scales. We can all sleep more easily now that gross hypocrisy has been exposed and moralism revealed as turpitude.

In a real sense, the Reagans are getting the comeuppance they deserve. They created a myth about themselves and their "values" that had a specific purpose of social manipulation and control. Reaganite preachments about drugs, fidelity, volunteerism, charity, common sense and old-fashioned morality were not just broadcast but targeted to a generation, a cultural sensibility and a political class that had very different ideas about how to behave in this day and age. Institutions—schools, foundations, corporations—responded to the Reaganite canon, which is what truly has been politically correct in America since the couple came to power.

Now the myth has been punctured, perhaps for good. Many of the revelations in Kelley's book have been known, or at least suspected, for years, but Americans and their media minders have until now not seen fit to believe them. Exposés have their historic moments, which are impossible to predict. Washington's political set knew all about John Kennedy's wicked ways (they called him "Mattress Jack") from the start, and reporters and rival candidates on the 1988 campaign trail bandied about stories of George Bush's extramarital affair(s), which Kelley also retails. But neither of those rumors made a scandal or destroyed the myth. Obviously, the time for Reagan-bashing is now ripe.

Is it just coincidence that not one but two tabloid-quality sensations are now in banner headlines? The media seemed to be suffering from postbellum depression since the Gulf War, and in the unseasonably hot doldrums of April (at least in the Northeast, where the news is made) the doings at the Kennedy compound in Palm Beach and the disclosures about the Reagan White House had a tonic effect.

The Kennedys have hardly been immune from gossip, as the Reagans have, but the current crop of the clan seems to have got what's coming to it. There's a lot of hypocrisy to answer for in the myth of Camelot. It's unclear what happened after Willie Smith's skinny-dip in the wine-dark Atlantic, and someone in the party that night may have to pay with real time. But tabloid gossip will be the only retribution for the crimes against myth, modesty and *mesure* that by any measure have been proved without trial.

It goes without saying that malicious gossip—the kind that Nancy Reagan allegedly spread about many of her closest friends—is hurtful and unjust. But turnabout against hypocrites is always fair play, whatever their politics, and no system yet has devised a more exquisite form of punishment than the unauthorized biography.

April 29, 1991, THE NATION

✦

Pee-Wee's Bad Trip

As TV's first postmodern kiddie icon, Pee-Wee Herman carried a lot of cultural luggage. His Saturday morning hit show was a campy commentary on gender, authority and the television industry itself. Full of sexual innuendo, double-entendre and auto-referential visual puns (Pee-Wee once "went camping" on the set, complete with flaming campfire), *Pee-Wee's Playhouse* played house in the wreckage of American innocence.

Now Pee-Wee's human animator, Paul Reubens, has been permanently deconstructed by the very forces he targeted. The industry that makes big bucks exposing sexual fantasies to millions and selling mutilation toys to tots has declared Pee-Wee a non-person for getting caught in a position of self-abuse inside a darkened "adult" movie theater.

CBS pulled *Pee-Wee's Playhouse* reruns off the air, toy stores pulled Pee-Wee items off the shelf, iconographers pulled Pee-Wee's hand prints and his gold star from the sidewalk on Hollywood Boulevard and parents are said to be "counselling" their children to withstand the revelation that their idol has feet, or whatever, of clay. It brings to mind the moralistic eruption that ended the career of Fatty Arbuckle (so named in an earlier, unenlightened day; now he'd be Weight-Challenged Arbuckle), though the silent-screen comedian was found innocent of the death of a starlet at an orgy. The moral? Orgies can go awry, and don't go camping in the wrong playhouse. And don't think you can survive as a rebel, however hilarious, in TV's well-fortified cultural garrison.

August 26, 1991, THE NATION

Chapter XIV

✦

GRINCH CAPITALISM

Clinton Already?:
The Manufactured Candidate

Manchester, New Hampshire

It was said of Belgrade after World War II that there was nothing in the shops except dead flies and pictures of Tito. So it is this winter in Manchester, minus the pictures. There are enough empty storefronts on Elm Street to serve as headquarters for a hundred candidates in the February 18 presidential primary. Once home to the biggest textile mill complex in the world, Manchester seems to have no future save as a theme park about the devolution of America. In this Decline World, factories have flown, malls are empty, condos are bankrupt, banks are failing, the service-sector boom of the Reagan 1980s has gone bust, unemployment has almost tripled since the 1988 primary. And the elms are all dead.

On a damp Sunday morning in January, traffic lights on Elm Street blink on and off gratuitously to lanes devoid of cars. Torn sheets of green plastic flap idly around an abandoned construction site. Except for a posse of transient advance men, handlers and media persons gathered to start the day campaigning with Bill Clinton, only one local citizen is visible, a tall, dishevelled youngish man with a graying beard, camouflage cap, tattered parka and dark aviator glasses. His hands are plunged in his pockets and his shoulders seem permanently hunched against the cold.

"Going down, isn't it?" he says suddenly as we pass, in front of a shuttered porn mart the Clinton people call "the adult book store."

"It looks that way," I agree tentatively.

"Going down," he repeats, and walks away without turning.

In many ways, Bill Clinton is the prophetic candidate of decline. The young and personable Arkansas governor begins his basic rap—at house parties, club meetings, nursing homes and wherever else a crowd is collected—with a litany of economic deterioration. "We [candidates always assume the identity of the places they seek to represent] used to be the world's banker, now we're the world's biggest debtor," he says. "American workers used to be the best paid, now we're tenth. We used to be eighth in income equality, now we're dead last. The Fortune 500 have announced 300,000 lay-offs in the last thirty days." Infrastructure is crumbling, education doesn't work, pollution is pandemic, there's no health system to speak of, manufacturing is disappearing: Clinton counts the woes. Clinton is arguably the most articulate and certainly the best informed of the candidates chronicling decline in this recession season. It is not unreasonable, however, to ask, "Compared to what?" Jerry Brown has a strong but one-note message about a single "incumbent party" and the "corruption" of the political system, Paul Tsongas is passionless and unpresidential, Tom Harkin is bombastic and unattached to any populist movement he pretends to lead, and Bob Kerrey is fixated on his own war record and sinking fast.

That leaves Clinton in front of the pack and perhaps unstoppable except by an obstacle of his own erection. The experience of 1988 suggests that Democrats are eminently capable of destroying their own campaigns, both by suicidal behavior (Gary Hart's philandering, Joe Biden's plagiarism) and by sudden blackouts of imagination (Dukakis's collapse after the party's national convention). The primary season has just begun, and a slip of the tongue or a fall on a banana peel could derail any one of these characters.

Barring such disasters, Clinton has a clear shot at the nomination. He is now winning the all-important "first primary"—fundraising—and already media heads are swooning in his wake: Joe Klein of *New York* and Michael Kramer of *Time* act as if they're part of the campaign (Klein actually "spins" for Clinton and explains his policies to reporters on the trail; he maintains for all to hear that Clinton is "the smartest politician I've ever met"). Economics columnist Bob Kuttner of *The Boston Globe* detects "a genuine bandwagon" for Clinton, "a Democrat . . . who is not only adroit as a candidate but who also might govern competently." He neglects to say he helped assemble said wagon. Even *New York Times* columnist William Safire, an anti-Bush Reaganite, is boosting Clinton, for his uncompromising defense of Israeli demands on the US Treasury.

The favor of the intellectuals has been the key to Clinton's success so far. While Harkin has some Big Labor, Tsongas some high-tech business and Brown some self-identified progressives, Clinton has organized the opinion-leaders and gatekeepers in the cool center of the political establishment. It didn't happen by accident. A founder (and recent chairman) of the Democratic Leadership Council, he directed the development of an ideology to support his campaign. As Clinton and friends begat the DLC, so the DLC begat the PPI, the Progressive Policy Institute, a Washington think tank that fires off neoliberal proposals like a Salad Shooter spews lettuce shreds.

Not only that, but PPI heavies and adherents have converged on Op-Ed pages all over the United States in a deliberate drive to legitimize Clinton and the ideology of Clintonism that the institute has created. For example, Elaine Ciulla Kamarck, a PPI senior fellow and Clinton groupie, is now a regular contributor to both the *Los Angeles Times* and *Newsday*. Her first effort posed six "killer questions" for the candidates, all of which only Clinton would answer to her liking; the second was an out-and-out endorsement of Clinton's "centrist ways" as the best antidote to Bush. In a similar conceit, the op-edible Abe Rosenthal of *The New York Times* listed ten "errors" he said Bush made in foreign policy, virtually all of them on the "left" side of the issues (failure to devastate Iraq fully and murder Saddam, skepticism on Israel). Clinton alone among the Democrats is on the Rosenthal side.

As for the voters, the more America declines, the better will Clinton's chances be to become president. If the recession is as deep and intractable as now seems the case, the candidate who can give voice to suffering citizens and provide clear plans for action at least stands a chance against the expected Bush blitzkrieg.

The only problem for Clinton at this point is Clinton himself. His policy papers have great preambles and solid introductions, but then they go blank. If there are no second acts in Americans' lives, there are no second pages in Clinton's proposals. On economic strategy, for instance, the devastating statistics of decline he cites do not lead to ideas of equal weight. He does give New Hampshire audiences a taste of his short-term plans for the economy: speed up work under the new transportation bill, help small businesses with capital gains and investment tax breaks, beef up federal housing loans and, tastiest of all, cut "middle class" taxes by 10 percent, giving the average family about $400 to spend "paying off credit card loans" and, perhaps, sending the kids to Yale or buying a new Buick.

The United States is the only major country in the world without an economic strategy, Clinton points out, and that's why manufacturing is dwindling, the Japanese are winning and wages are dropping. His solution is to "deliver quality, affordable health care," encourage manufacturing, reduce interest on the national debt and train young people for skilled work. Is it my imagination or is the dog chasing its own tail? Everything is dependent on a contingency. American cars, he says, have more than $700 in health insurance costs "built into them," while Japanese cars roll off the line with only 200 health care dollars in each chassis. Provide cheaper health care and Detroit will boom and spark a significant reindustrialization of America, Q.E.D. Tax revenues will rise and the debt will decrease. There will be skilled jobs at high wages for young people who go through Clinton's apprenticeship program. Cut military spending and use the "peace dividend" for social improvements. But wait. Re-examine the premise, and the logical train is derailed before it leaves the station.

Like Michael Dukakis in 1988, Clinton refers to the marvels of his home state as models for national action. Dukakis's promise of "good jobs at good wages" had as its basis the high-tech, service-rich "Massachusetts miracle," fueled by the Carter-Reagan military expenditure extravaganza and by the explosion of consumption in the 1980s. Elect Dukakis, we were told, and the whole country will experience Massachusetts' *Wirtschaftswunder*. Unfortunately for the Duke, the Iowa caucuses had not yet been held when the *Wunder* started to go under. A year later, when Dukakis assured his voters he would not stand again for governor of the state he helped run into the ground, Massachusetts was the basket case of the country, and it soon brought the rest of New England under with it.

Clinton also promises a "high-wage, high-growth, high-opportunity society," and he refers to many programs in Arkansas as models for his national plan. But even a cursory look at his state shows that his investment strategy over eleven years as governor there has been the opposite of what he claims. Arkansas is essentially an anti-union state with a "right to work" law that depresses wages and benefits for workers and inhibits the expansion of a skilled labor force. The vaunted Arkansas Industrial Development Commission, the incarnation of Clinton's investment strategy, paves the way for low-wage industrial growth by keeping the state union-free. Clinton has never sought to change the anti-union climate. Nor has he even gone the short distance towards curbing factory flight that Dukakis travelled in enacting a law mandating that workers be notified if their companies shut down. Quite the opposite: Clinton joined anti-union forces in endorsing President Bush's "fast track" negotiations with Mexico for a free trade treaty that would undoubtedly accelerate flight and further dampen wages.

In fact, Arkansas is closer to Mexico than anyone care to admit. It's tax structure gives enormous breaks to both new and established businesses, while maintaining a regressive and anti-worker sales tax on groceries and non-prescription drugs. Clinton has said he's against that tax, but he opposed its repeal by voter initiative and by legislative action. And his bid to be the "environmental candidate" rings hollow when seen against his state's dismal record. The current "Green Index" lists Arkansas forty-eighth among the states in overall environmental health. Businesses looking to relocate in Arkansas are pleased to find such an unregulated atmosphere.

Like Dukakis, again, Clinton offers no evidence that he can reverse the decline of politics in America that seems to have accompanied the decline of economics. Reports from his pollsters and focus group leaders recommend that he never speak of the poor, of blacks or Latinos, of labor unions, of cities, of the working class, of power. He is permitted to mention the unemployed only if it is clear that he is speaking of the temporarily unfortunate. Welfare is considered a problem, like AIDS for Bush, to be solved by changing the behavior of the afflicted. Clinton projects a spurious idea of "unity," "personal responsibility" and "citizenship" that codifies middle-class manners and interests.

For two decades, Democrats have debated electoral strategies. Some have suggested that only a campaign that brings non-voters—the young, the poor, minorities and the uneducated—into the polls can create a new majority to overcome the white middle-class suburban vote for Republicans in national elections. Others, like Dukakis (until ten days before the 1988 election) and now Clinton, seem to have given up on democracy for the many and concentrate on appealing to the relative few who do vote. At this writing, there can be no proof that either strategy will be successful. Expansion has never really been tried, and no Democrat has managed to trash blacks, the poor and the peace people enough to please a sufficient number of swing voters. It remains for Clinton to try again.

Barring an accident (and as William Burroughs said, there are no accidents), Clinton's campaign will demand the attention and energy of everyone within the Democratic Party's ambit for the next nine months. For progressives and the left, it will not be an easy gestation period. Although Clinton does have a valid claim to a personal history in progressive politics, he has abandoned all but a few of its traces in the discourse he now employs. His trajectory is a lot like Gary Hart's. Both moved from the McGovern campaign of 1972 into a fuzzy neoliberal project that spoke of "new ideas" but decried "special interests"—that is, the insurgent constituencies that gave both of them their start.

It is virtually impossible for the remaining progressives within the Democratic Party to have much influence on Clinton's political direction. In terms of making any meaningful change in the way America works—from the delivery of health care to the redistribution of power—Clinton offers nothing of interest. The transformative moment that seemed at hand four years ago has passed. This is a status quo election. America is still a one-party state.

Clinton's success must be counted in the devalued currency of American politics. His is a masterpiece of manufacturing, a triumph of positioning rather than positions, an encyclopedia of first pages and a political dictionary of few words. "It's prime meat," a veteran liberal activist said of Clinton's campaign in New Hampshire. "The voters will be drawn to it like dogs to sirloin steak. But it may be *too* good, too perfect. Then they'll sniff for a long time, and walk away."

February 3, 1992, THE NATION

✦

Grinch Capitalism: No Miracle in Lowell

Lowell, Massachusetts

The big deal in Lowell this winter was an all-day "motivational program" given by a TV self-esteem pitchman named Tony Robbins to a crowd of some 2,700 people, each of whom had paid $179 to scavenge vicariously in what Robbins calls "a warehouse full of cutting-edge technology . . . to create success." Early on the appointed morning in February, a parade of smartly dressed men and women, briefcases in hand, headed for Lowell Memorial Auditorium, a handsome neoclassical building rising above one of the ancient canals that powered the many textile mills here 150 years ago and gave the city the noble sobriquet "Venice of America." These were the canals that a young city councilor named Paul Tsongas once proposed be paved over to facilitate vehicular traffic.

The youthful managers and eager professionals in Robbins's audience need all the technology he can deliver. The growth, prosperity and success promised them just a few years ago, by Paul Tsongas in particular, are in short supply. His ballyhooed experiment in urban revitalization for Lowell has not only run out of steam, it seems now to be running in reverse. Lowell's troubles, while in some cases less acute than those of its sibling Merrimack Valley communities not blessed with pork-barrel funds, are nonetheless grave. Jordan Marsh, the only big department store in town, is closed for good. The Hilton hotel that Tsongas coaxed into town (with a federal grant) as a development anchor has become a Sheraton and may well be a Motel 6 by the time the tourists return this summer. Wang Laboratories (another federal beneficiary), headquartered here, has taken a serious bath, and its red-brick high-rise training center is now a community college library. An immigrant influx of some 25,000 Cambodians and other Asians has produced soaring unemployment and predictable symptoms of urban decay. It had somehow slipped Tsongas's mind to include the poor, the working class, the unemployed, the unions or the discount shoppers in his experiment, and now in the general slump they are paying doubly for their exclusion. No wonder that Tony Robbins, not Paul Tsongas, is the major motivational source in the city today.

Before he came down with cancer in 1983, Tsongas was planning to run for president on his record in Lowell, the success story par excellence of urban renaissance in America, at least for a few years in the 1980s. It seems crazy now, but his economic philosophy was informed by the optimism of expansion, not the gloom of decline. He had every reason to take credit for the city's flashy prosperity, its national reputation, its creative attractions. By acclamation he was acknowledged the patron of the city; "Saint Paul" was born again on the way to Lowell. Pre-eminently, if not quite single-handedly, Tsongas put together the pieces of the new Lowell and in many cases micromanaged the result. With characteristic (and slightly suspect) modesty, Tsongas did not take all the credit he deserved; he told Harvard urban development researchers, "Eliminate a dozen people and none of it would have happened." But the researchers knew better; they wrote later in their case study that "Tsongas is too modest. . . . Eliminate one individual, Tsongas, and Lowell's revitalization would not have been nearly as dramatic."

The plan (that word is central to this story) Tsongas imagined and to a large extent executed does not make sense without an understanding of Lowell's place in American history. In the second quarter of the nineteenth century it became, quite simply, the most concentrated industrial center in the nation, the showplace of the Industrial Revolution and the birthplace of industrial capitalism in the New World. In 1810 a Boston Brahmin named Francis Cabot Lowell travelled to England and saw for the first time the incredible benefits of water-powered looms to elevate the profit positions of textile-mill owners in the Midlands. In a feat of legendary industrial espionage and unauthorized technology transfer, Lowell memorized the mechanics of the operations and sailed home with the blueprints in his head.

Back in Boston, he put the workings down on paper, organized a posse of friendly entrepreneurs and scouted locations for mills on the Midlands model. Ur-Lowell was a place called Chelmsford Neck, at a bend in the Merrimack River about thirty miles north of Boston. The Pennacook Indians, who had once been given deed to the area, were on the losing side in King Philip's war and were forced out by the European settlers. The Neck had the right specifications: a perfect drop in the river (to turn the machines), abundant cheap labor (teenage daughters of hard-pressed farmers) and proximity to good ports and stores of raw materials (slave-picked cotton came into nearby Massachusetts Bay landings). In other words, fair nature, hard times and inhuman exploitation all conspired to turn Lowell into a gold mine for the infant capitalists. (Readers will be spared further commentary on the ironies of that dialectic for our candidate's time.)

In any case, before long those pesky contradictions that bedevil smooth-running economic operations, like hidden viruses in computers, sent the whole system crashing. The farmers' daughters were unhappy with their long hours, unhealthy work environment and brutal living conditions, and went on strike for a better lot. Most quit anyway after a few years at the loom. Their places were taken by a succession of European ethnic immigrants—Irish, French Canadian, Italian, German, Greek—who overwhelmed the Yankees and transformed the culture and politics of the city. The new technology of the 1820s became obsolete by the 1860s, and newer mills on other rivers, or powered by steam, took the competitive edge.

The immigrant workers, inspired by European socialism and American labor activism, organized themselves against the mill owners and struck, as the Yankee mill girls had done. What with the terrible depressions that hit in the 1890s and again in the early 1900s, Lowell's competitive edge dulled to disappearance. In the years just after World War I the factories began fleeing south in the vanguard of what would become the wholesale evacuation of manufacturing from Massachusetts, which continues to this day despite the state's brief economic "miracle" of recent memory. (Or was it a dream?)

World War II brought a bloom to Lowell's sallow cheeks, but it turned out to be no more than the evanescent blush of a dying consumptive, and the city coughed its last when the war factories were demobed. Or so it seemed. The economic decline drove thousands to booming regions, and those who remained wallowed in self-disregard. Tsongas told the Harvard researchers, "It was difficult to be proud of your hometown if you came from Lowell."

Tsongas grew up in Lowell at its nadir in the 1950s and early 1960s, mired in the swamp of deindustrialization and depression. He worked in his father's dry-cleaning business (he suspects that fumes from the chemicals may have caused his lymphoma) and, like most ambitious young men of his generation, got out of town as soon as possible: Dartmouth for college, Yale for law school, Ethiopia in the Peace Corps. But like his rival Bill Clinton, he went home again to fashion a political career from the building blocks of his heritage.

It took some time for the light bulb to go on. His idea of 1972 to pave over the wonderful canals, built primarily by Irish contract labor, was unheeded. Well, here's Plan B: a privately organized development project primed with a huge flow of public money directed to transform the working-class and welfare-dependent city into a middle-class tourist attraction, an upscale shopping zone and a high-tech haven. Bingo.

The cornerstone of the edifice was not industrial development but historic preservation. Tsongas—by the late 1970s a member of Congress—got on the appropriate subcommittee, wrote the pertinent legislation and shepherded a bill through to passage that established the country's first urban national park in his old hometown. Not just a national *monument* like the Indian mounds in Iowa, or a historic *site* like the Herbert Hoover birthplace: Lowell now has a proper park, with Smokey the Bear rangers, a museum, canal walks, mill tours, a display devoted to local antihero Jack Kerouac, ethnic fast food, fake trolley cars, *real* trolley cars—the genuine article, like Yellowstone or Yosemite. Without the bears.

At the same time, a web of interlocking agencies was spun to supervise economic development. As a US senator, Tsongas produced the Lowell Plan, a dreamy 1979 scenario for community renewal based on improbable cooperation between all sectors of society. In the local legend, the muse of development came to Tsongas in a Greek restaurant and caused him to draw up the Plan on a paper placemat. (That would put it in a category with supply-side economics, first published by Arthur Laffer on a cocktail napkin over lunch.) Parts of the city not quite up to national-park importance were set aside as a heritage state park and other lesser categories. Tsongas also set up the

Lowell Development and Financial Corporation as a non-profit to funnel private and public funds in the form of low-interest loans to businesses and developers in the city.

Lowell itself became a kind of economic theme park, parallel to the national historical one. Money was cadged from Washington to restore the drab old buildings, repoint the crumbling brick and install ersatz gaslights along the narrow streets. A great swath of territory was cleared for the federally aided hotel, né Hilton. Shops that sold staple goods at a discount to the poor, the elderly and the unsophisticated were rudely forced out of business to make way for boutiques. There's a folk music festival in the summer. In all, a deliberate attempt was made to turn plain old Lowell into one of those new yuppie quarters that draw shoppers and immigrants to Boston, Minneapolis, Seattle and places in between.

Tsongas's role in all of this was almost Medicean: a humane philosopher/aristocrat creating, managing and protecting a flourishing city-state by the force of his own vision and the political tools at his command. Cosimo the Competent, Lorenzo the Managerial. His loyal princelings ran the various agencies, held office as city manager and sat on the city council and the school board. There was occasional friction and Tsongas didn't get his way every time. For instance, he fought with a school superintendent over a piece of prime property. The superintendent wanted it for a "magnet" high school; Tsongas, who makes a big deal out of his promotion of education, wanted it for upper-middle-class private development. Tsongas lost.

But he had many more wins than losses. He convinced An Wang to locate the world headquarters of his computer company in a new industrial park in Lowell. Wang already had a facility on the outskirts of town, so it wasn't that much of a stretch. But Tsongas used both his economic leverage with the development agencies and his princely powers of persuasion to draw Wang into the Plan. In fact, he got the government to give $5 million to the development corporation, which in turn lent it to Wang. The tycoon built a training center and other handsome structures, and Lowell was suddenly a major pushpin on the high-tech map of America.

Tsongas utilized the development corporation as the vehicle for pressuring local banks to contribute one-twentieth of 1 percent of their deposits to a loan pool for redevelopment. Some bankers figured there would never be any more development, so why protest? New England's most prominent rent-a-quote economist, the Bank of Boston's James Howell, gave the verdict on Lowell in 1975: "[It] has no future . . . no economic hope." But when other bankers balked, Tsongas ratcheted up the campaign, reminding them that he sat on the House banking committee and they had best do his bidding. He had been extremely helpful to the industry by leading the fight to deregulate savings and loan associations in the early 1980s, a legislative triumph he curiously omits from his speeches now.

A city-state also needs a city university, and Tsongas helped convert two

minor-league colleges—Lowell State and Lowell Tech (the latter a relic from
the textile industry days)—into Lowell University, a part of the University of
Massachusetts system; last year it was further upgraded into UMass-Lowell.
Its mission is frankly to aid the development of the region, and its engineer-
ing and management schools are closely allied with high-tech businesses in
Lowell itself and in the vast techno-zone around Route 128, the East Coast's
Silicon Valley, not very far to the south.

Naturally, Tsongas was given a seat on the board of trustees of Lowell U,
and later he headed the regents for the whole UMass system. His reign
there, as it was in the cultural affairs of the city, was largely benevolent. As
one academic put it, "He allowed good things to happen." For instance, he
did not object when the university's president set up a work environment
department in the engineering school and staffed it with some of the most
progressive—and renowned—occupational health and safety professionals in
the country, who could be considered hostile to some of Tsongas's corporate
allies. Years ago, when socialist Michael Harrington came to speak at Lowell
University, Tsongas approved because, as he said at the time, "these guys
keep us honest." Nor has he questioned the national park's stunning presentation of the class struggle in Lowell. A slide show run every half-hour (there
were 800,000 visitors last year) describes the old Lowell as "a city based on
the exploitation of a permanent working class," a line that is seen nowhere
in the Plan.

But Tsongas still keeps his hand in the minutiae of academic and cultural
life. He strewed art in public places (none of it up to Florentine *quattrocento*
standards), and in the middle of his campaign for the presidency he is trying
to get the university to move its bookstore into downtown Lowell, which now
has none. Tsongas was reportedly dismayed to see that Nashua, another old
mill town and a rival to Lowell just across the New Hampshire border, has
a Barnes & Noble right on its Main Street. The students strongly object.
Tsongas, however, would override their demands for his dreams.

If Lowell's success in the 1980s was a model for America, its sudden failure must have heavy resonance for the country as well. It's why you don't
hear much about Lowell from Tsongas in his current campaign, and why
the great experiment in urban revitalization is not touted as his plan for the
country. But to a large degree what happened to Lowell *is* what happened to
America, and Tsongas's own failures in that regard should be instructive as
he tries to sell himself as an economic savior. All the points mushed up in his
famous booklet, *A Call to Economic Arms*, are illustrated in the living city.

To begin with, the Lowell Plan and its various projects completely ignored the working-class neighborhoods, the poor, the immigrants and the
aging ethnic populations that make up the bulk of the city—just as Tsongas
never mentions those sectors in his economic manifesto. The implicit idea is
that prosperity trickles down from upper-class development into the worlds
of the deprived.

It simply didn't happen. Worse than that, Tsongas's henchpeople in city government tried to bulldoze—literally—the lower orders out of the picture. City manager Joe Tully, for years Tsongas's key man on the ground, planned in 1982 to raze a large part of an old working-class district called The Acre, which lies on the edge of the national park and the boutique belt. Many of the 15,000 inhabitants were Latinos of various national provenances. The Lowell *Sun*, not always a Tsongas fan but a Lowell Plan booster of unbounded proportions, ran vicious editorials against the inhabitants; one editorial cartoon depicted them as hideous rats jumping the good ship Acre: "LET THE CRIMINALS LEAVE . . . and we'll have a better ship." Only the successful struggle of a local grass-roots organization, Coalition for a Better Acre, saved the area. And as for Tully—he was on the grift and went to jail, though Paul Tsongas came to his trial as a character witness.

The business and political elites Tsongas commanded were in effect an army in a war for territory—some of it geographical, some cultural, some ideological—with other classes, races and interests. The same fight has been waged in most major cities, most fiercely when urban land is contested by redevelopers on the one hand and poor residents on the other. In Lowell, however, it was total war, for the contested territory included the whole city and its society.

In a sense, the battles began 300 years ago when the British replaced the Pennacook Indians. More recently, middle-class, "Americans" in advanced assimilation have taken territory from poorer ethnics. "Little Canada," where the mill-working Québécois had lived, was largely flattened and the cultural community devastated. The Acre survived because the Coalition was able to outsmart the central planners, but the life of the neighborhood has been severely circumscribed by the elimination of cheap stores, restaurants, services and attractions. Its citizens, as well as Latinos and Asians in other quarters, lost ground in schooling, social mobility and political influence.

In a revealing passage in his memoir of cancer and its aftermath, *Heading Home*, Tsongas recounts how he broke the news to his twin sister, Thaleia, that there is no Santa Claus. He has been telling the country the same thing this year on the campaign trail. But it was in Lowell that he acted out the "truth" that he insists we learn: that government is best which aids the upper middle class and lets the poor fend for themselves.

Grinch capitalism has its own contradictions, however, and they became as apparent in Lowell as the contradictions of early industrialism did a century ago. Without a steady dose of public tax money (for parks, for housing and urban development, for welfare) the private sector can't cope. At the same time, an industrial policy can't be sustained in one city without regard to regional and national conditions. Even in the good times, most Lowell residents riding the boom worked outside the city in the defense-based and electronics companies along Route 128. Many professionals "blow in" daily from their homes in the more desirable suburbs closer to Boston. Those at the bottom of the scale took the leavings. The Cambodians, for instance, were low-tech workers in high-tech industries: many of them assembled circuit boards in electronic sweatshops under contract to Wang, Raytheon, AT&T and other big-name companies. The Cambodians were non-unionized, poorly paid, denied benefits, kept in poor conditions—and laid off when the companies began downsizing. Now there are no jobs for them, nor will there be in the future unless there's another military build-up or the companies successfully convert to civilian production at the same level and in the same location they were when their decline began. That would probably require public investment in corporate equity, an idea utterly anathema to Tsonganomics. After all, there are industrial policies and there are industrial policies. Meanwhile, the plight of the displaced workers—an enormous chunk of the local population—replicates that of the Yankee mill girls and their immigrant successors.

When the regional industries declined, the city's economy suffered more severely than it might have if a better class mix had been maintained. The boutiques that had been brought in to replace the discount stores went under, and the center-city streets are now lined with shuttered shops. The infrastructure built to support upscale Lowell is falling apart, and it is doubtful the downscale tourists who visit the national park in summer will shore it up again. For some reason, the planners were too short-sighted to see what would happen when the economic and demographic conditions of the early 1980s changed.

Tsongas goes around the country promising high-wage jobs in new manufacturing industries by means of a program of public aid to business for research and development, tax cuts for capital gains and investments, job-training programs and educational reforms, an aggressive policy of opening foreign markets and an easing of anti-trust laws. Many of those ideas have been tried in the laboratory of Lowell. The university, publicly funded, contributes a kind of R&D to industries, and other schools and colleges train and track workers into local businesses. The city has given out tax breaks until it's blue in the face. Boosters have touted Lowell's wares beyond the Merrimack, and have especially hard-sold its attractions to tourists, a lucrative kind of "foreign trade."

What's wrong with Lowell is what's wrong with Tsongas's industrial policy: it won't work unless everyone affected by it participates in making the decisions, setting the agenda and allocating the resources. Who decides? is at least as important a question as Who benefits? Certainly the consequences of "planning," in the Tsongoid sense, differ widely as to how those questions are answered. The Harvard researchers who studied Lowell in the mid-1980s saw even then the flaws in the picture: "The revitalization story of Lowell illustrates that the trickle-down aspects of development cannot be assumed; it often requires an engaged citizenry to ensure that the benefits from development are more evenly distributed." In other words, the time when "aggressively pro-business" policies were successful has long passed, and Paul Tsongas might think again about paving over the canals.

March 30, 1992, THE NATION

✦

Necromania

Eastertime is as good a season as any for a ritual public execution. The fact that a presidential campaign is also in progress makes it doubly appropriate. More than an administration of justice, the gassing of Robert Harris in California seemed designed as a national catharsis and a display of power. Nobody mentions deterrence anymore; the death penalty is about social control of a far more pervasive kind. It is a reaffirmation of the state's franchise on terror, its totalitarian dominance and its license to treat the lives of humans in the way that vengeful deities trifled with their subjects. After such a spasm of official bloodletting, people are impressed with their own powerlessness: "As flies to wanton boys are we to the gods; they kill us for their sport."

As Americans feel their sense of control slipping away, their cries for more state murders grow louder. It makes perfect sense that the movement of consciousness against the death penalty slowed and stopped in the middle of the 1960s and has been racing in reverse ever since. Insurgencies, ethnic and sexual struggles, imperial defeat and the extraordinary persistence of violence in everyday life have created a post-civilized society in which quite cultivated people are given to the most barbaric sentiments. A nation that can rejoice over the slaughter of tens of thousands of Iraqis on the highway out of Kuwait City last year is hardly going to be upset about snuffing one—or 300—inmates on California's death row.

There is a connection between the form of state terror called war and that which is known as the death penalty. Both are antithetical to democracy, for they deny the essential autonomy of the individual and deliver total power to the executioner, whether it's a faceless hangman or Governor Pete Wilson, a bearish general or President Bush. Politicians and military men love death (unless they're moral radicals, like Mario Cuomo or Jerry Brown) because they can use it to exercise authority without regard to democratic scruples. Bill Clinton flew home to Arkansas on the eve of the New Hampshire primary to oversee the now-famous execution, by lethal injection, of a brain-damaged black convict. It gave him the opportunity to exploit that knot of hatred and anger in the American soul, the one that makes approval ratings rise ten or twenty points in the polls. The model, of course, was Bush's somewhat grander invasions of Panama and Iraq, which gave the voters more deaths than they knew they wanted, with commensurate ratings hikes.

Those who oppose the death penalty in America must realize that it will be in use for the foreseeable future, and increasingly employed by liberal and conservative politicians alike for their own ends. The Supreme Court is hopeless on the subject well into the next century. The eleventh-hour dissents of Justices Harry Blackmun and John Paul Stevens in the Harris case were passionate and compelling, but two out of nine is not a promising division of the court. And those particular two are old and ailing.

It is grotesque that the self-described "world's leading democracy" is also the world's leading imprisoner of its people and the world's leading executioner of its wrongdoers. Although the political institutions are solid (rigid, some would say), civic society is so weak that it relies on a vast system of punishment and cruelty to keep the peace. The death of Robert Harris, while perhaps a small event in the sweep of horrors seen in recent history, is nonetheless a token of America's failure to produce a good society, much less a great one.

April 23, 1992, THE NATION

✦

LA Lawless

"**L**A is America—only worse," Paul Jacobs said a generation ago, and neither place has improved much since. The latest events in LA prove Jacobs's point. The several disasters of postmodern America converge in the sprawling desert basin. Now they have produced an explosive reaction, some combination of race riot, shopping spree and rebellion, and in the pictures of violence erupting at the corner of Florence and Normandy and beyond, the whole world could for a moment glimpse the core of pain and the persistence of rage in the lives of black people in America.

LA is one of the most segregated cities this side of Johannesburg, which it resembles in frightening ways. The decline and flight of industries that summoned and employed many blacks during and after World War II has left a large population confined in forgotten townships, or perhaps internal refugee camps. Education is so inferior, prospects are so dim, the contempt of the white community is so strong and the culture of the black community is so estranged that "gangster" warfare seems positively progressive, or at least inevitable.

The Rodney King riot, as it is being called, is horribly perfect in its expression of the destructive elements of African-American experience: the stereotyping of an entire people, the powerlessness of even physically strong men, the prison culture of the ghetto, the cruelty of the law, the despair, discrimination and injustice. Once again shut out of the system, people in their fury took their grievances to the streets, the only place in this country where African-Americans have ever found redress, or the beginning of it.

In retrospect, no one should have been surprised that the jury let off the police who beat King last year with a savagery that, preserved on video, has now entered the iconography of the culture. From the testimony of the first of the twelve to speak up after the verdict, the panel was predisposed to believe the "thin blue line" theory put forth by the defense: the police are all that protects law-abiding citizens from the predations of a criminal class. Race never entered the jury's mind, the juror said, but then it didn't have to.

The whole setting of the trial encouraged a prejudiced verdict. The venue was moved from multicultural Los Angeles to the suburban Simi Valley in the far reaches of Ventura County, conveniently close to the Ronald Reagan Library in case anyone wanted to dash over during a break to see how racism was instituted in America on a truly grand scale. Nor was the figure of "Willie" Horton, perhaps the most potent racist metaphor in recent political history, entirely absent from the courtroom. In addition, the prosecutor, an African-American named Terry White, presented a good excuse for acquittal for jurors who believe somewhere in their souls that black men cannot be believed, especially when they are on the side of their brothers. And the silent specter of Rodney King himself, frightening to the jurors by his presence but invisible to them in his humanity, persuaded his peers in the box to believe the ideological arguments and video technicalities of the defense rather than the evidence of their own eyes. It was King, one more victim turned perpetrator, who was on trial, and he lost his case.

If he had won—that is, if the policemen had been found guilty—the masters of law and directors of government would have quickly patted each other on the back and declared that once again "the system worked." But of course the system does not work, despite the occasional conviction of those who abuse authority, kick people when they're down and malign races they consider inferior. It malfunctions precisely in the way the King episode illustrates: there is a double standard of justice that extends from the lowest traffic court right up to the Supreme Court, from the police car on the prowl or the cop on the beat up to death row. Indeed, the system is getting more spiteful rather than more tolerant.

Five years ago, LA Police Chief Daryl Gates launched the first assault wave in a program he called Operation HAMMER, which amounted to a military campaign against the ghettoes of South Central LA. The helicopters that are now a constant feature of the city's skyscape were called in for surveillance, intimidation and ground attack support. Commando SWAT teams arrested thousands of black boys and men. Mike Davis chronicled one raid in his superb book on LA, *City of Quartz*:

> Like a Vietnam-era search-and-destroy mission—and many senior
> police are proud Vietnam veterans—Chief Gates saturates the
> street with his "Blue Machine," jacking up thousands of local
> teenagers at random like so many surprised peasants. Kids are
> humiliatingly forced to "kiss the sidewalk" or spreadeagle against

police cruisers while officers check their names against computerized files of gang members. There are 1,453 arrests; the kids are processed in mobile booking centers, mostly for trivial offenses like delinquent parking tickets or curfew violations. Hundreds more, uncharged, have their names and addresses entered into the electronic gang roster for future surveillance.

That short passage illustrates only a few of the many ways Los Angeles has provided a model for systemized social control that other cities are sure to copy as the need to suppress unrest grows. The military tactics recall the recent triumphs of Bushismo in Panama and the Gulf. Deconstruct LA and you find allusions to South Africa, Israel in the Occupied Territories, science-fiction dystopias such as *Blade Runner*, European colonial wars and tribal anarchy. Indeed, some of the young blacks interviewed during the riots referred to the cops as "the police gang"—heavily armed, well-organized but with no more authority than the Crips or the Bloods.

The riots were horrifying to many Americans who watched the live coverage on CNN. This time—contrary to the old verse—the revolution *was* televised. The nation's leaders piously claim that the violence was "counterproductive," but in fact it put the issues of race and poverty on the political agenda for the first time in many years. Clinton as well as Bush has studiously avoided even mentioning blacks or poor people this year. As LA burned it was clear that neither one has a clue what to do beyond immediate measures of crowd control, short-term damage control (retrials for the cops) and long-term studies of the "root causes," which you can bet will have nothing to do with the effects as seen on the streets of LA. The crisis of leadership is seen everywhere. The black mayor of LA and the traditional "leaders" of the black community seem as out of touch with the residents as the white politicians downtown and in the statehouse.

It's not polite to say so, but with their matchbooks and their expropriated VCRs, the blacks of Los Angeles and the Latinos who joined them have reordered the political priorities of the nation, if only for a short while. Without further organization, without the politicization of the rebellious outburst, without a strategy for action and a vision of the future, that order will revert to the same deadlock that has deadened progressive development since the mid-sixties. Twenty-seven years ago Watts burned. Now the rest of the LA ghetto and large tracts outside went up in flames. More than fifty people were killed in what is now officially known as the worst instance of social unrest since the Irish riots in New York City 130 years ago.

There was no central organization to the action, and hence no strategy. There was, however, a high degree of tactical sophistication. Groups made much more headway into the bunkered white enclaves of downtown than is generally understood, and similar forays into white neighborhoods such as Hollywood were well planned. It was no accident that Koreatown sustained the most damage. As infuriating to blacks as the "not guilty" verdict in the Rodney King case was the absurdly light sentence (probation, with no jail) recently imposed on a Korean grocer who killed a black girl, Latasha Harlans, in a dispute about payment for a $1 carton of orange juice.

Who the "organizers" of the riots were remains a mystery. Perhaps some of them are among the 9,000 people arrested, but it is doubtful that anyone will ever know. Most of those detained were "looters," and most of them (overwhelmingly Latino) were taking food and baby supplies, such as Pampers and purées. Although the media showed the happy looters carting away expensive electronic equipment (one group pried loose an entire cash machine from the wall of a bank building), many just loaded up on staples. In any case, a society that imposes consumption-fetishism on its citizens can hardly complain when desire explodes out of the unconscious with furious force.

Now that it's all over, the incident that provided the first spark is no longer quite the issue. The Los Angeles District Attorney made plans to retry one of the officers who beat Rodney King, but even if the new trial is held and the cop is convicted, it will convince no one that there is "equal justice under the law." Not only do blacks suffer brutality and disrespect at the hands of police all over America but studies show they have little access to qualified legal assistance, they are not favored in plea bargaining between prosecutors and defense lawyers (which constitutes the bulk of judicial procedures), they are stigmatized by their records as miscreants, and they come to hate the courts and prisons as the fixed representations of the authority that is repressing them. Furthermore, a recent survey in Washington revealed the staggering fact that nearly three-quarters of all black men between 18 and 35 are in jail, awaiting trial or on parole. A few dollars— even a few hundred million dollars—can do nothing to resocialize an entire population that can be extrapolated from those numbers.

Slavery and cheap immigrant labor built America in the beginning. Not only blacks in the feudal South but Irish, Italians and Greeks in industrial New England, Chinese along the railroad lines of California and the river levees in Mississippi, and Mexicans in the great farmlands of the Southwest. Some of those groups have been accepted or assimilated; others will be tolerated. But the descendants of African slaves may never be truly free or legitimate in the land that they have worked for 400 years. But still they persist, and neither will they disappear. And the irony is, their anger and agony will afflict the land for as long as they must suffer.

April 30–May 13, 1992, THE NATION and IL MANIFESTO

✦

Anybody But . . . Who?

The electoral system in America is now being convulsed by the broadest, fiercest voter insurgency in perhaps 140 years, and the left is watching from the sidelines. The two formerly major parties are a shambles, institutions of government and the press despised, political authority disdained, and every measure of popular anger overflowing. And yet those who have long expected this transformative moment to come are—if they are realistic—confronted primarily by their own irrelevance to this historic hour.

Worst of all, the receptacle of these volatile political humors is one man, Ross Perot. No significant institutions are forming, no vital new party is poised to challenge, no coherent movement of revolt is discernible save the closely held campaign of the picayune populist billionaire. As genteel suburbanites network for Perot and speak of revolution, great slabs of the left can find no better correlative for their political desires than exhumation of JFK as the dead king whose murder must be requited before America can be made whole again. But the specter arising from Dallas this time is Perot.

Despite the mayhem he can inflict on an unresponsive system, Perot is a catastrophe for the progressive/activist spectrum. Insurgent labor, minorities, feminists, lesbians and gays, environmentalists, community organizers, peace internationalists—the coalition that once made up the Rainbow—are in varying degrees offended by Perot's campaign but, more important, excluded from it on any terms but his.

In that great Might-Have-Been, there was the possibility that the Rainbow Coalition and Jesse Jackson's two presidential campaigns in the 1980s could have engendered a permanent political force capable of bargaining for power, promoting a progressive agenda, forging new institutions. Constituencies already mobilized by the Reagan counterrevolution, by deindustrialization and the reorganization of work, by the wars in Central America, were ripe for larger coalitions. But the hour came and went. That failure was ordained by Jackson's insistence that he remain securely within the Democratic Party and that the Rainbow refrain from any initiative other than what the Reverend commanded. He fulfilled his own satiric characterization of the role he imagined the party's helmsfolk expected him to play in 1988: "that I will go out in the field and be the champion vote picker and bale them up and bring them back to the big house."

Along with his undoubted strengths and skills, Jackson displayed many shortcomings of political imagination, chief among them his inability to see that without a permanent grass-roots presence, the organizational Rainbow would be as evanescent as its name implies. His relentless deference to centrist Democrats made impossible any role for the Rainbow other than as vehicle for his own political ambitions. The coalition's source of power would have been its independence, its ability to withhold as well as confer support, to produce alternatives that threatened the party's elite. Above all, it could have decisively turned the flank of those Democratic liberals whose destiny has always been to sell out progressive principle for the dream of a piece of the action. Jackson denied his coalition that independent existence, and in the process betrayed his own base, the African-Americans whom he had urged to "keep hope alive." Those hopes were unrealized, and the consequences of his failure were to haunt the left, fragmented and atomized as it now is.

But Jackson's folly is almost secondary to the prolonged campaign of that motley crew of Democratic liberals who for twenty years have fought determinedly—and successfully—to keep the party anchored in the bipartisan consensus. In the wake of George McGovern's defeat in 1972, the liberals— young Bill Clinton among them—learned the wrong lesson. Liberals misread Jimmy Carter's victory in 1976. It seemed he won because, as a white Georgian, he made inroads in the Republican South. But the deeper reason was that with the aid of black leaders, including Jackson, Carter was able to win newly mobilized black voters, who came into the electorate in huge numbers for the first time since the civil rights legislation of the previous decade. That, coupled with a weak semi-incumbent President Ford and a Republican Party reeling from Watergate, produced what now can be seen as a Democratic blip eccentric to the trendline.

By the late 1970s, Carter and his Administration were echoing the ascendant ideology of Ronald Reagan, and while some liberals dallied with Ted Kennedy in his 1980 challenge, most fell head first into the second Carter-Mondale campaign. In 1984 Gary Hart's premature yuppie campaign—the spiritual antecedent of Bill Clinton's candidacy this year—moved the party even further in the wrong direction. White liberals attacked Jackson that year for every conceivable reason, not least their desire to woo the racist "Reagan Democrats." But of course what happened was that they lost the bigger boost the mobilization of his base would have provided. The great irony is that in the 1986 midterm elections Jackson's registration drive netted upwards of 2 million new Democratic votes, a prime reason the party regained control of the Senate and defeated the nomination of Robert Bork for the Supreme Court. Nonetheless, in the 1988 presidential race, when Jackson again sought support, not one white personage in the party, even down to the third and fourth rank, came forward. There was a show of unity on nomination night at the convention in Atlanta, but two weeks later Dukakis was in Neshoba County, Mississippi—where Ronald Reagan had launched his re-election bid in 1984—and his appeal to white voters took the form of a conspicuous refusal even to mention the three civil rights workers who had given their lives in the cause of racial justice in that very place two decades earlier. It was as though he had gone to Memphis and disdained any reference to Martin Luther King.

Bill Clinton's carefully planned slap at Sister Souljah, the black rap singer who had dissed whites to a *Washington Post* reporter in the heated aftermath of the Los Angeles riots, was this candidate's version of Dukakis's Neshoba speech, and for the same effect: to dissociate his campaign from everything Jackson symbolizes to white voters. It was of a piece with an earlier action by Clinton's campaign chairman Mickey Kantor, who seized upon Jerry Brown's embrace of Jackson to drive Jews into Clinton's column. If racism is not in Clinton's heart, as he blandly insists, it is evident in his behavior, which is after all what counts.

The Sister Souljah affair, while small in itself, was nonetheless a watershed in the ideological contest within the Democratic Party. The Democratic Leadership Council, which Clinton helped found seven years ago as a white Southern (and later neoliberal Northern) institutional antagonist to blacks and New Deal constituencies, has been advising its candidates to identify their campaigns with military and police power and against the aspirations of blacks, women, union members and other "special interests." The council and its political expression, Clinton, have faced but two serious threats. First there was the insurgency of Jerry Brown, who made the intellectual case against neoliberalism and who anticipated Perot in sensing the rot of the party structure. The assault on Brown in the crucial New York primary was merciless. He faced squadrons of inflamed columnists, from A.M. Rosenthal through Anthony Lewis and Pete Hamill. In the wake of Brown's suggestion that TV licenses might run for limited periods, ABC News staged the Tsongas "comeback," which took thousands of votes from Brown, and, as the *coup de grâce*, prominently retailed the wild, anonymous allegations of drug use at Brown's Los Angeles house when he was governor.

Much of the contest this year within the Democratic Party has been to establish a tone—a set of cultural references showing dominance and direction. The lines clarified after the Rainbow Coalition convention in June. *The Washington Post* and its columnist Richard Cohen, *The New Republic* and its Clintonette Sidney Blumenthal, *The New York Times* and a troupe of congressional Democrats, black and white, came down for Clinton as a man not afraid to shoulder the white man's burden when the time was right.

The social culture that has congealed around Clinton—the first such afflux to a Democratic presidential candidate in three decades—excludes the diversity that an expanded Democratic electorate would present. The contours of the Clinton culture are generational and ideological, and its purposes are both the advancement of careers and the confirmation of identities. In the think tanks, research institutions, non-profit foundations, campus towers and editorial offices that house the neoliberal cavalry of the Democratic Party there are people at the apex of their careers who have been waiting twelve years for access to executive power. The thrust of the Clinton culture was perfectly expressed by one of Clinton's Washington acolytes: "It's *our* turn."

Not everyone who works for Clinton, not even in his inner circle, partakes of the culture, but there is a set of sensibilities, a familiar history, that gives the crowd definition. In the beginning, the tone was set by columnists like Blumenthal, who wrote that the Clinton project had been formulated over a somewhat indefinite period by what Blumenthal was pleased to term "The Conversation," an ephemeral, unrecorded dialogue among like-minded tank thinkers, ex–Rhodes scholars, neoliberal politicians and grown-up student protesters from the late 1960s and early 1970s. Joe Klein, now at *Newsweek*, who like Blumenthal worked on "alternative" weekly papers in the Boston area twenty years ago, rapturously broadcast Clinton's brilliance to a mass audience in the early months of the campaign.

An unusual number of people around Clinton, almost all of them white and male, began their political trajectories in the McGovern campaign or similar post-radical efforts of the same period. Harold Ickes, son of FDR's Interior Secretary, got to know Clinton via McGovern. David Wilhelm, Clinton's campaign manager, began with former Oklahoma Senator Fred Harris, the last white populist of the left, who directed his 1976 presidential campaign at "the little people" but dropped out after losing badly in New Hampshire, conceding that maybe the little people couldn't reach the voting levers. The rest of the Clinton advisory circle is composed of Rhodes scholars, such as economic strategist Robert Reich, competitiveness consultant Ira Magaziner and deputy campaign manager George Stephanopou-los. Or relatives of Rhodes scholars, like Derek Shearer, whose brother-in-law, Strobe Talbott, was Clinton's roommate at Oxford and whose brother Cody, a journalist, was particularly assiduous in circulating the Brown drug story at the finale of the New York primary. Or honorary Rhodesies, like Michael Mandelbaum, who was at Cambridge during Clinton's stay at Oxford. Or odd left-academics *manqués*, like Stan Greenberg, a Marxist teacher at Yale who didn't get tenure and turned to "public opinion research." Greenberg's big contribution to the Clinton campaign was to discover that white working-class ethnics in Michigan refer to themselves as "middle class" and don't like black people. Out of that came Clinton's rhetoric and, apparently, his principles.

It's difficult to convey the *feel* of the Clinton culture. Like the Kennedy culture thirty years ago, it is a stir-fry of blatant self-promotion, unexamined idealism, cynical sophistication, suspect intellectual certainty and an arrogant race and class snobbery that can be oppressive to those without the necessary credentials. It comes on as hip and liberal, but it panders to the right (Clinton's embrace of the death penalty) and abhors any person or movement to its left. It is suffused with a gestural sentimentality about racial harmony, but its commitment is to white power and privilege. Its adherents protested the Vietnam War, if they were old enough, but they hold no internationalist values and, as Clinton now famously explained to an Arkansas ROTC director, are ever-willing to sacrifice principle to "political viability within the system." In another age, cultural Clintonism would have been called cold war liberalism or vital centrism. One would think such a set had been marginalized in American life. After all, *thirtysomething* was cancelled due to low ratings. But since many of its traits are shared by journalists recently arrived into visible roles in strategic publications, politicians on the make and an arrant cadre of entrepreneurs, entertainers and culture-vultures, the Clinton gestalt has achieved a certain presence in the national consciousness.

There is, of course, another vital quadrant of Clinton's circle, and here we find the unsentimental reality of the Arkansas financiers, chief among them the Stephens family, which introduced BCCI to America and to whom Clinton—his campaign all but broke—now owes millions of dollars and political IOUs the length of the US Treasury building.

Of a piece with the culture of Clinton is the candidate's economic plan, launched in late June. Dutifully garnished with slogans about "empowerment" and about education as the solvent for a better America, the plan offers scant purchase upon America's predicament. As with his initial campaign manifesto, Clinton reserves his fieriest passion for vocational training, even pledging a 1.5 percent levy on corporate payrolls to help finance such training. And as with his initial manifesto, the obvious question is never answered: training for what? Behind the ringing phrases about a better-educated America and a new civilian research agency, a computer network linking home, library, workplace (also perhaps the field offices of his proposed 100,000-strong National Police Corps?), lurks the budgetary vision of a small-town chamber of commerce. For investment in transportation, the information network, vague ideas about the environment and conversion, the new police force, community financing (including block development grants), Clinton allocates just $20 billion. By contrast, sixty heavyweight economists recently advocated an investment of $50 billion just to get the economy moving.

Behind uplifting wordplay lies the bleak reality. Clinton has no specific allocation for primary education. His welfare proposals are similarly hollow: "We will scrap the current welfare system and make welfare a second chance, not a way of life. We will empower people on welfare with the education, training and child care they need for up to two years, so they can break the cycle of dependency. After that, those who can work will have to go to work, either by taking a job in the private sector or through community service." Read literally, "community service" might suggest a pledge to full employment and a guaranteed job. But Clinton is pledging nothing of the sort, so the entire passage is merely opportunistic, obscuring the reality of desperate mothers forced into low-wage jobs while leaving their children in day care and simultaneously having to endure Clinton's sermons about stronger families and enhanced parental responsibility.

When the bulk of Clintonomics was incorporated into the proposed Democratic platform, the longtime Jackson adviser Robert Borosage hastened to call it "the most progressive platform, with the most redistribution in it, since 1972," ignoring its lack of strategic direction and its abandonment of basic principles of economic justice. That Jackson himself could have welcomed Clinton's plan is yet more evidence of the Reverend's willingness to swallow any offal so long as he can attend the banquet.

The salient feature of the political year so far is the spectacular deconstruction of the two parties. The coalition of white ethnics, middle and high suburbanites, God-fearing reborns, neoconservative intellectuals and stalwart country-club Republicans that Reagan led into the White House has come unstuck in the late years of Bush. David Duke and Pat Buchanan dislodged part of the package, and various Democrats were able to co-opt elements during the primaries. The result is that Bush has an unsure base—hence, Dan Quayle's attempts to regroup the reborns by attacking *Murphy Brown* as the cause behind the LA riots. Risible though such efforts may seem, they represent smarter thinking than anything evinced by Clinton and his strategists. Bush and Quayle understand that in a three-way race, you concentrate on your core support. It should be stressed, however, that the Republican Party is still an immensely powerful institution, part of the glue holding together most of the significant sections (Western chapter) of the world's ruling class. The Democratic Party, whatever its fortunes this year, is in a far more advanced stage of decay.

The Perot phenomenon has been the logical consequence of the vacuum created by the decomposition of the two-party system, in which the only "political" idiom available to a distraught citizenry is self-consciously antipolitical: against corruption, against Washington, against vested power. The fundamental psychology derives from the inexorable realities of American decline, parsed first in the disruptive challenges of the insurgent sixties, then in the slow slide downhill from economic security. First comes fear, then depression, then anger and finally, if the traditional political safety valves fail, outright rebellion.

Back in the mid-1970s, intellectuals who had flocked to Carter's Washington formulated the "crisis of democracy"—said crisis being heightened citizen confidence in democratic activism in the wake of the Watergate scandals, in which corporate America reached its nadir in popular esteem. Sam (Mad Dog) Huntington and similar savants brooded about the dangers of this popular distemper. A decade and a half later, with democratic institutions and safeguards relentlessly abraded, veterans of the Huntington school (whose true trustee was Nelson Rockefeller) can gaze with complacency upon the political landscape. The people now trust in nothing. Fifteen years of corporate chicanery are forgotten amid the bogus check-kiting storm. Legislators flee the light like hunted things, despised and, where possible, limited to brief terms under the watchful suzerainty of the business lobby.

The hero of the hour is a billionaire entrepreneur, with all the disadvantages of Richard Nixon—paranoia, vindictiveness, intolerance, opportunism—and none of his cynically brilliant political vision. To the degree that political intention has been coaxed from the sphinxlike Perot, his economic vision is as stunted as Clinton's, with rhetoric about "the mess in Washington" commingled with crass ravings about a war on the deficit. His politico-economic stance is instantly recognizable to anyone who interviewed high-tech entrepreneurs in the boom years. Fatted on government contracts, they combined vivid anti-regulatory, anti-Washington passion with commensurate zeal for protectionism, the whole hypocritical stew larded with thunderings against the idleness of the Fortune 500.

Perot's strength derives not from the marginalized redneck cadres of a George Wallace or a David Duke but from the core suburban "middle class." The origin of his support is in the "radicalization of the moderates," as political theorist Theodore Lowi puts it, which began its current phase in the post-Watergate era, at the same time that the Clinton cadres were forming. The voters' revolt had its first expression in the anti-tax campaign in California, which then-Governor Brown belatedly joined. In fact, the history of neoliberalism is intricately tied to the moderates' revolt, as ambitious progressives and leftists sniffed the *Zeitgeist* and headed where they thought the votes were.

Last month Lowi and a pollster, Gordon Black, published an opinion survey that provides the first categorical assay of voter discontent. The survey shows that the revolt has moved beyond specific issues, such as taxes, the congressional pay raise, the deficit and talk-radio favorites like the 55 mph speed limit, mandatory seat belts and the spotted owl, to serious electoral reform.

"The most moderate, middle of the road voters are the voters most in favor of fundamental reform in the American political system," Lowi wrote in his introduction to the survey. Those identifying themselves as conservatives were next, and liberals were far and away the least amenable to radical change. In other words, liberals have become the most conservative element in American politics today where systemic change is involved.

"There is a dirty little secret that sophisticates have been hiding from the masses for three or four decades," Lowi continued. "The secret is that the two-party system is dying. The two-party system is a 19th century, largely Anglo-American phenomenon that has failed to make the adjustment to the requirements of modern, 20th century democratic government. The two-party system has been kept alive with artificial respiration through state laws biased against third parties and through artificial insemination by federal subsidies and other protections sold to the public as 'campaign reform.' The two-party system would collapse in a moment if all the tubes were pulled and the IVs were cut."

Now hands are extending towards those tubes, and knives brandished against the IVs. It would be premature to write off at least one of the major parties, just as it would be foolish to underestimate the capacity of George Bush to rally the legions of Republican loyalists against the would-be Bonaparte from Texarkana. But as we observed at the start, it is not premature to emphasize the utter marginalization of the left in the political narrative now unfolding. Is there a chapter in this narrative yet to be written that sets the left nearer the center of the drama?

July 20, 1992, with Alexander Cockburn, THE NATION

✦

Back Off, Jack

There's an election in America; run for the bomb shelters! No one in the world is safe when the presidency is at stake. George Bush's threats to pulverize Saddam Hussein and surrounding populations over the "stand-off" at the Iraqi Agriculture Ministry were obviously occasioned by the imperatives of the campaign rather than any menace to the new world order. The response from opposition Democrats, particularly the chicken-hawkish Al Gore, had a similar origin.

Clinton—the "good cop" of his team—emphasizes the importance of including the United Nations in moves against Iraq, but his is a spurious internationalism. Ever since Harry Truman used the UN to cover America's entrance into the Korean War, presidents have tried to put a multilateral face on self-interested military adventures. When world organizations have pushed policies that contradict Washington's wishes, for example on Israel or Nicaragua, the Americans go it alone. Of late the UN has been unusually successful in arranging settlements in trouble spots from Namibia to Phnom Penh. But the impetus for those efforts came from a genuine consensus of UN members, not a bought and bribed coalition imposed by Bush and his Secretary of State.

When Saddam—or was it Bush?—"backed down" over inspection of the building in Baghdad, the danger of a presidential sneak attack diminished but did not disappear. Bush is doing so poorly in the polls that one can imagine the assassination of Saddam, or perhaps capture à la Noriega, as the only move that might win him the election. A life for the presidency—isn't that a trade-off with just cause?

Bush has nothing else to show for his presidency (or his vice-presidency, for that matter) except bully-boy raids on weaker countries, covert deals with tyrants and support for counterrevolutionary clients. It's true that his ratings rise with each foray, but his popularity does not have what Hollywood calls legs, and it belly-flops as soon as the ink is dry on each executive order. He has done nothing to organize his own base around its real interests, which always come down to prosperity and peace.

The Gulf War lobby in Congress and in the press tempts Bush and Clinton with promises of invaluable support if either candidate commits himself to "finishing the job" against Iraq, with or without the United Nations. They all insist, however, that it is not enough to remove Saddam; as Gore would have it, he must be replaced "not with his killer cronies but a decent government of the opposition." No doubt such an outcome would get wide applause.

For the past forty-five years, though, the world has suffered more from American intervention than from the lack of it, and if the quotient of liberty is to increase, the United States must learn to back off. Most times it is better to let people fight their own battles, bloody though they will be, than to choose sides and intervene. For the choice will always be based on this country's interests, and the targets of intervention will become clients or enemies. In the end, neither will be independent.

August 17, 1992, THE NATION

Chapter XV

◆

STARTING OVER

From Russia With Love and Squalor

In the summer of 1991, when a diehard, generally drunken crew of plotters tried to overthrow the government of Mikhail Gorbachev, anxious Soviet citizens crowded around television sets to watch the dramatic play of events. The year since then has been one of enormous upheaval, much misery and fear for the future, and now the citizens of the former Soviet Union—the FSU in current lingo—are back in front of the TV. Last summer the program that got the ratings—an inconceivable 70 percent of the population, or 200 million daily viewers, making it the most popular series in world history—was a fourteen-year-old, 249-part Mexican soap opera called *The Rich Also Cry*. When the first episode of the day came on at 9:15 in the morning, all work, such as it is, seemed to stop. Men and women stared into communal screens in hotel lobbies, public buildings and factory canteens. Mothers at home in the highrise suburban ghettoes of modern Moscow parked their babies and escaped into the high-class barrios of Mexico City in the 1970s. After the death of utopia on earth, TV is the new workers' paradise of the mind.

At a late dinner I attended in September in an apartment on the outskirts of St. Petersburg, eating and toasting ceased while the entire extended family gathered to watch the midnight showing of the soap opera on a huge set adjoining the dining-room table. But what really caught everyone's eye were the glamorous commercials for American products like Head & Shoulders shampoo, one dose of which would cost the family a day's income in rubles. In Volgograd (once Stalingrad) a well-connected woman of recently reduced means, the mother of an émigré friend of mine, watches the same installment three times—in the morning, at night and the rerun the next day—because, her son Alexander* reported, "It's about good and evil, very stark, like good guys and bad guys in the 1950s in America."

_____

* Some names have been changed or shortened at the request of the subject.

The soap's characters have become superstars. Years ago, in a more instrumental age, Soviet babies were given names like Elektrifikatskiya and Oktyabr; this year the names in the nurseries are romantic: Mariana, Marisabel, Luis-Alberto and Jaime. Veronica Castro, the Mexican leading lady who plays the noble but needful Mariana, made her first triumphal trip to Moscow at the beginning of September, just as the first anniversary celebrations of Russian Federation President Boris Yeltsin's own triumph against the coup plotters were ending. Yeltsin personally welcomed *la* Castro at the Kremlin and swept her away in his black Mercedes to lunch with parliamentary leaders, and to *Swan Lake* at the Bolshoi, where she was seated in the imperial box and mobbed by frenzied fans. They did not notice, or perhaps were too loyal to remark, that the actress had weathered considerably in the decade and a half since the series was made, and that the luscious Mariana was somewhat more . . . grandmotherly than she appeared on TV.

1.

The stupefying ironies of everyday life in the FSU are not lost on its people, who sometimes seem as if they are trapped in their own endless soap opera, another world-historical production where the banal and the cosmic clash, dead villains are reanimated, wicked twins appear out of nowhere, families fall apart, joy dissolves into despair, and evil always trumps good. Very stark. The break-up of the Soviet Union has accelerated the fall into an abyss of hyperinflation, shortages, unemployment and economic shrinkage. Rumors of coups, communal conflicts and civil war fill common conversation and the press. A very few have very quickly become very rich and are pleased to find an array of available consumables, from Cadillacs to Chanel, while many more have been plunged into poverty and can only window-shop for the new imports. The loss of communist control has created a kind of Hobbesian battleground where the worst instincts of ethnic hatred, cutthroat competition, corrupt enterprise and personal violence can flourish without hindrance or restraint. Privatization has so far meant little for economic relations (96 percent of the economy is still state-owned), but the public-service sector has deteriorated and millions have been cast adrift without recourse or redress. In September, TV talk-show host Vladimir Pozner assembled a group of teenagers from around the FSU to hear their thoughts about the events of the past year. Some non-Russians from the sovereign republics said they were proud of their newly won independence, but at the same time even they deeply regretted the end of the Union. None of them had much hope for their own future.

The distance between Mariana and Moscow, between soap opera and reality, between late-capitalist mythology and post-communist fact, is no longer than the flight of stairs that thousands of Muscovites descend after watching the rich cry in the morning. Out on the street they take up positions shoulder to shoulder in long silent lines—not to buy sausages, as Western TV always shows them doing—but to sell their household possessions: a lamp, a picture frame, a lace antimacassar, a pair of shoes, a leather pocketbook or a suit jacket without the pants. Some women buy a bottle of milk in a store and sell it for a few rubles' "profit," while their children stand equally silent by their side. Many spend the whole day in lines, stretched single-file along Tverskaya (formerly Gorky) Street from the Pizza Hut almost to the Kremlin, on the sloping sidewalk down from the old KGB headquarters on ex-Dzerzhinsky Square or around Metro stations quite far from the center. The lines continue into the night, but after dark the inventory tends to change from milk and shoes to Marlboros and sweet Soviet champagne; a pack and a bottle cost about the same—a third of the price of a flask of Head & Shoulders.

The lines I saw were composed largely of middle-aged, "middle class" (if that term has meaning here) women and some older men; not hard-core street dwellers, gypsy beggars or punky youths (although there are plenty of all of those) but people who are spiralling downward in the dawn of the free market. They are the pensioners who are helpless against hyperinflation (perhaps as high as 2,000 percent this year in Russia, worse in Ukraine), widows or single women who are unemployable in an imploding economy (1992 production will be down 20 or 30 percent, in the fifth year of "negative growth") and people without access to the world of Westerners and their hard currency. When the long lines began to be seen earlier in the year, the press was full of irate denunciations; the practice was condemned as humiliating to a once-prosperous and proud citizenry. Some people called on the authorities to clear the vendors off the street, as Americans have wanted the police to sweep the homeless from Lafayette Square in Washington, or the beggars from Grand Central Station in New York. "For you they're images," Sergei Kozlov, a Kazakh journalist, said when he detected a bit of bleeding heart in my description of the lines. "For us it's real life."

Just a jump up from the single-item sidewalk vendors on the capitalist ladder are the kiosks, which sprouted with the sycamore leaves last spring and are now the dominant feature of the Moscow commercial landscape. Some kiosks are proper wooden stalls set up at the edge of squares, surrounding Metro stations and along wide sidewalks; they sell a variety of goods, from vodka *ordinaire* to gilded Orthodox icons of dubious provenance, cold doughy *kolbasa* to Mars bars and M&Ms. Billboards, in English, entice candy cravers to "make a mess in your mouth." One-stop shopping at a kiosk can often provide the four basic food groups of Russian nutrition: lard, refined sugar, booze and tobacco, with an icon as spiritual supplement.

Other kiosks are nothing more than folding tables or upended wooden boxes, on which a few wares are displayed: soap, carbonated drinks, audio-cassette tapes. Along the highways leading to the countryside around the capital, *babushkas* sit on folding chairs hawking apples and cut flowers to weekenders heading to their *dachas*. Across from McDonald's in Pushkin

Square, young men in the traditional graduate-student gear of bulky sweaters and wire-rimmed glasses sell Havana cigars at a dollar apiece; they complement the standard meal of *Beeg Mak gamburger*, large *kartofel fri* and a thick milk *koktel* (cost: 300 rubles, also a dollar, at the going exchange rate in early autumn). Many of the vendors will flash a card with the symbols $-DM-£, indicating their willingness to exchange currency on the spot. And almost anywhere you can buy sets of *matryoshka* dolls in ascending size, painted to represent Russian czars, commissars and presidents, from a tiny Peter the Great to a jumbo Yeltsin.

American economists and business journalists aswarm in Moscow survey this scene and with wide grins announce the birth of a vibrant free market. But neither kiosk capitalism nor card-table arbitrage seems remotely like the familiar Western versions of corporate enterprise and finance, featuring Wal-Mart and Citicorp, not to mention nameless Zurich gnomes, transnational agribusiness and conglomerates after the manner of Engulf & Devour. For one thing, the primitive Russian market is overtly and entirely corrupt, while the Western corporate system has managed over the centuries to write its own rules, regularizing what was once out of bounds and legalizing its corruptions. For another, the FSU economy is expanding primarily in one sector—trading—while all else shrinks and capital flees to safer havens. And finally, while the late-industrial West has a way (if there's the will) to provide social and physical supports that serve the system and modulate its ravages, the ex-Soviet infrastructure is rickety or ruined and the safety net is ragged.

"Mafia" is the ubiquitous descriptor for every small trader, petty hood, prominent politician and enterprise manager in the FSU. The trouble is that the term is so inclusive as to be of dubious value. The ersatz taxi drivers who cruise the avenues of Moscow looking for fares, whom they kidnap, rob and often brutalize, are mafia. So are the train robbers who roam the corridors of the midnight express to St. Petersburg, occasionally lobbing tear-gas canisters through the air vents of locked compartments, so that passengers have to open their doors and let the robbers in. Mini-mafias own "chains" of kiosks, and mafias composed of members of the many ethnic groups in and around Russia demand protection money from everyone who sells anything on the street. The two semi-underground, permanently floating gay discos that appear in various Moscow locations on weekends must pay 25 percent of the door each night to a *gay* mafia. In St. Petersburg, the nightly rumbles, rub-outs and drive-by shootings among mafia groups have earned the city the nickname "Chicago on the Neva." Elsewhere, the hard-core criminal violence is not nearly as prevalent as in any large American city, but its novelty in ex-Soviet sociology exaggerates people's sense of danger. What most do not yet understand is that it could get a thousand times worse in a very short period of time.

"Mafia" is also widely used to describe almost every political leader from

Yeltsin on down, including the acting mayor of Moscow, Y.M. Luzhkov, who has been charged in the press with profiteering from privatization—a pandemic symptom in the chill changeover to capitalism. According to Denis Molchanov, a hotshot young investigative reporter for *Komsomolskaya Pravda*, Luzhkov was in league with Gavril Popov, the previous mayor and one of America's favorite new Russian "democrats." Luzhkov later succeeded Popov, and has been delaying the municipal elections demanded by the more popular-based Moscow City Council—still known by the old name of Mossoviet. Despite the accusations, which are widely believed, no one in the network is in serious trouble with the law.

At the apex of all the petty crimes, sleazy deals and grand scams there is rumored to be a high command of corruption, a "Black Empire" that ties the directorate of the old Soviet *nomenklatura* to military chiefs, the KGB, the Italian Cosa Nostra, and both illegal and legal Western banking, finance and political cabals, from BCCI to P-2. This ultimate conspiracy is of course unproved, and in a sense unprovable, because it concerns not only abnormal figures against a normal ground but criminal figures against a criminal ground. If absolutely everything is corrupt, corruption has no meaning.

At times, "mafia" is a term of respect, or at least grudging admiration. Mischa, a young taxi driver in St. Petersburg, told me that he and a few of his old army buddies who also were "chauffeurs" put together a mafia and commandeered a choice spot at the city's airport. "It's hard to make ends meet in the taxi business these days," Mischa complained. A burly amateur boxer who grew up in frigid Arkhangelsk on the White Sea, he moved to "Peter" after army service, rented a beat-up old yellow Lada and started hustling fares. Along the way he got married, had a little girl and set up with his wife, her parents and an unrelated boarder in a cramped apartment near the airport. In Soviet terms he would be downwardly mobile. His parents were professionals—father a neurosurgeon with international connections, mother a professor of education—but he never went to college and preferred hunting wild dogs in the frozen forests to a life in the professions. The stick shift of his car is covered in dog fur, suggesting the tail of a Siberian husky asleep at his foot. But in post-Soviet society chauffeuring is one of the few trades that provide ready access to the beloved *valyuta*—hard currency—without which ends can never be met.

Even so, he reckoned, "I need to make 1,500 rubles a day to pay the rent on the car, and if I charge passengers what I need they'd pass out on the ground." But no sooner had his "mafia" taken over its turf at the airport than the real racketeers moved in—Mischa calls them "the Chechens," members of a legendarily fierce ethnic group from the Caucasus bidding for independence and now widely perceived by Russians to be gangsters—and demanded protection payments of 3,000 rubles a month. "It's a lot of money, but we have to pay or we can't do business."

Mischa's mafia is the kind of network of friends, relatives and co-workers that many Soviets developed simply to survive in a system where institutional life was monopolized by the party/state. The personal networks are the basis of new private economic activity and also of non-governmental public organizations—what would be called non-profits, charities and activist groups in the West. There are networks of the right and the left, and ones that have no obvious ideological spin. Even the most vicious businessmen have their networks, and there are new networks dealing with gay rights, feminist issues and the Russian version of New Age concerns—with everything the government has ignored, suppressed or tried to make dependent on state power.

Although Mischa is surviving on the fringes of the hard-currency economy, his network is not making him rich, and he is pessimistic about the future. When he is asked The Question that every former Soviet hears from a foreigner—"Is life better now than before *perestroika*?"—he answers quickly, "Of course not." Some of his close friends have immigrated to America—one is a taxi driver in New York—but Mischa hasn't the means to take his young family abroad. Democracy isn't working, he insists. "Democracy here just means letting a lot of people yell and scream." In the United States, there's "real democracy. People can vote for whom they want. Things won't get better here until the bunch of guys running things is thrown out." And how will that happen? "Ordinary people can't do much," Mischa said, and then added, brightening, "except maybe line them up against a wall and shoot them."

2.

The tremendous changes of the past year have not seriously affected the power of the old communist *nomenklatura,* members of which remain in public office, in managerial control and in the top echelons of the military. Nameplates, job descriptions, salaries and perks are the same as they always were; only party affiliations or ideological identities have been altered to protect the accused, or the vulnerable. The vaunted anti-communist revolution was more like a switcheroo, no groundswell of insurrection but a shell game at the top of the system in which programs and politics acquired new names while the personnel stayed the same, give or take a few forced retirements, traded offices and new portfolios. Ideology, after all, was of minor importance compared with power.

Privatization of large enterprises, where it has occurred, mostly puts commissars in CEO suits. "*Nomenklatura* privatization" has spawned whole strings, if not galaxies, of new stars, men such as Vadim Polovnikov from Rostov-on-Don, a fiftysomething engineer from a *nomenklatura* family who sits on top of one of the biggest chemical companies in the FSU. His trajectory to the new ruling class is instructive. After graduating from Odessa Polytechnic College in 1964, he worked his way up in the state chemical industry and became, in the middle of *perestroika,* director general of the October Revolution Amalgamated Chemical Works of Rostov.

Then the big switcheroo: Polovnikov privatized his company, first turning it into a "collective" and selling shares to the workers, then securing total control for himself.

Alexei Pankin, himself the son of a top reform communist who was foreign minister for a few days under Gorbachev, finds Polovnikov the very model of the new Russian tycoon. He marvels at how Polovnikov converted the October Revolution works into the Empils Stock Company, a diversified enterprise (chemicals, paints, electrical products, consumer goods) that does business with 400 other FSU companies, earns hundreds of millions of dollars in hard currency with American and Western European trading partners, and is developing joint ventures with US corporations.

"These guys know how to survive," Pankin said in that easy American idiom that Russians of his class and background often employ. "They've had lots of experience. Speaking of Polovnikov, Rostov is where the Cossacks come from; the entrepreneurial spirit never died there, it just went into criminal activity, so they're better prepared for entrepreneurship. They're releasing people from the jails for activity previously condemned as criminal, which is now normal economic activity. In the Soviet Union the laws were so absurd that there was no way *not* to violate them. Now, there's a situation of total chaos and you have to violate laws to get something done. . . . Even the so-called democrats are being sucked into the system very quickly."

Like many youngish Russian intellectuals, Pankin is fascinated by the new entrepreneurial class—so much so, in fact, that he is thinking of leaving his job as deputy editor of the staid bilingual journal *International Affairs* and starting an institute to study the new *biznesmany* (another fractured English word in the protocapitalist Russian vocabulary). Funding, he thinks, will come from the objects of examination.

"These people are the new masters," Pankin continued. Behind him in his editor's office, an open window gave out on a leafy lane where chauffeurs chatted beside their cars, waiting for the diplomats, academicians and journalists who worked or were visiting in the stately pre-revolution mansions of the quarter. "The new masters have no ethics; everything is permissible. These are the initial stages of capitalism, and a man is guided only by his own motives. There has to be room to limit them, to be independent from them. But this is inevitable, like the United States after the Civil War. We'll pass through it in less than the several decades it took the United States. The later you start on the capitalist road, the quicker it takes to get there."

These days, the road is bumper-to-bumper with self-starting traders. Anyone with the slightest inclination and the smallest means to trade goods for hard currency will forsake education, talent and even high status for a crack at the dollar market. A journalist told me about a friend of his named Max, a former diplomat in the Soviet foreign ministry who left the government and, using his old contacts, has virtually cornered the market on viper venom, a valuable pharmaceutical raw material that is collected in Turkmenistan and sold at $10,000 an ounce to Western drug companies. The Russian companies that used to process the venom can pay for it only in worthless rubles, and thus are practically out of business. Many hundreds of Russians are out of work, and aggregate output has been pushed down a notch. On the other hand, the diplomat makes a thousand times more selling snake oil than he ever did in the Soviet civil service.

Then there's Yuri, a prominent physicist who holds three important patents, who has gone into the cigarette business. He travels to Germany and buys large quantities of Marlboros for 54 cents a pack, smuggles them into Russia and sells them for $1.50 or $2, depending on the demand. He does not bank the hard currency in Russia—no one does, especially since Yeltsin taxes bank accounts at the rate of 40 percent, and banks pay tiny interest—but smuggles it back to the West, often through Hungary, the easiest route now.

And Irina, a keen sociologist expert in Western European studies, who started a second, lucrative career facilitating adoptions of non-Russian babies in Russian orphanages by American parents. Russian law currently forbids the adoption of healthy, ethnically "pure" Russian children under the age of 4. But exceptions are made for children with illnesses or birth defects, as well as for children of Asian or other non-Russian parentage. Racism in Russia is pervasive, but it is strangely qualified. Tens of millions of Russians are intermarried with non-Russians, and often with non-Slavs such as Georgians, Armenians, Jews, Kazakhs, Tatars and various Turkic or Mongol peoples. Nor are the children of such multiethnic unions oppressed or ashamed of their heritage, as are, for example, the Amerasians and Afro-Amerasians of Vietnam. I don't know whether Russians and other ex-Soviets share my perception that grace and beauty seem to increase in proportion to the number of ethnic traces in an individual, but I can report that I saw ordinary people walking down the streets of Kiev, Tashkent and St. Petersburg with natural cheekbones that film stars in Beverly Hills would pay untold thousands to acquire from plastic surgeons. It doesn't make sense for orphanages and government agencies to sanction a kind of ethnic cleansing adoption policy when the country seems so casually mixed and coolly multicultural. Yet old hatreds die hard, and ethnically speaking, there's a lethal disjuncture between the personal and the political.

By coincidence, I met in Moscow an old and dear friend from the Boston area. He and his wife were maneuvering the bureaucratic and commercial minefields of the adoption process. Irina had found them a baby of mixed Central Asian blood, had fixed them up with a host family where they could stay for the two to four weeks the process might take and had provided a car and guide to expedite their visit. The package cost my friends $10,000, which went to unnamed officials at the orphanage and in government offices, to the stateside organizers, as well as to the host, the driver, the interpreter and, of course, Irina. Not a ruble went to the baby's mother, who is not supposed to know her child has been adopted by foreigners. The new parents adore their baby and admire the organization, which indeed is saving many babies from a childhood in horrendous conditions. Last summer Irina was riding around Moscow in a Mercedes with a cellular phone. Late word has it that she was fired by the American organizers for skimming funds off their adoption fees.

"This is a brothel society," an Italian editor said contemptuously when we were trading tales of the new open market. The defense ministry is selling missiles, nuclear warheads and the best scientific minds of the generation to the Pentagon and NASA. Kazakhstan is bargaining away its trove of mineral resources and bidding to *accept* nuclear waste. Local game wardens are turning a profit by opening protected reserves to big-game hunters (and big spenders) from the West. And all over the FSU, families are stripping their homes and looting their legacies of art, icons, furniture and *objets* for sale to antique shops and salons in the West. What capitalism has meant so far is not the democratization of prosperity but the commodification of practically everything.

"Socialist man never existed; capitalist man does not yet exist," Andrei, a newly rich, 29-year-old entrepreneur said while sipping white Georgian wine in his communal flat near the Nevsky Prospekt in St. Petersburg. The room was a hilarious jumble of books and papers, junked household appliances, computer paraphernalia, rock-and-roll memorabilia and Hare Krishna posters. Andrei is an interstitial figure, caught in the moment between a system that was secure but, he insisted, offered him no possibility of expression, and a system that promises no security but endless possibilities. Lean, angular and articulated like a tailor's dummy in blue jeans, he ranged around the cluttered room with barely restrained ferocity as he talked about life on the edge of capitalism.

"What you may say is that I'm an entrepreneur," Andrei began. "I'm not a *biznesman*. I work for a small venture, I do everything, sell everything, trade everything. I work in an office, on the street, in a car. For example, we own some oil wells and we have connections with other owners of oil wells who do not belong to our company. Connections are important. There is a pool of people, networks, people who find things to buy, whether it's china or coffee or wine or precious metals. We trade all the time. Now I can sit in the car and make deals."

Andrei was the son of a man whose job description in America might be national forest ranger in a remote conservation area. Andrei would accompany his father as he guided Soviet bureaucrats from Moscow on hunting parties through the dense, cold pine and birch forests. At 14 he left the countryside and moved to St. Petersburg, where he lived by himself, took care of his own needs and fell under the protection of the manager of the local Intourist office ("a drunkard," Andrei's girlfriend interjected), who lived in an adjoining flat. The tourist chief, Andrei said, taught him many things, among them the craft of buying goods cheap from Intourist and selling them dear to foreigners.

Olga, an astute, ex-hippie feminist intellectual of 38 with whom Andrei has been living for the past year, said that "his heart is still in the forest" but that he is caught up in the fiercely competitive, corrupt and often violent culture of the new entrepreneurs. "It's a world of young males, almost exclusively; there are some women's businesses, but they're small and scarce, and the women are less successful because they're more law-abiding. Most of the young males are illiterate; that is, they *can* read, but they *don't* read. They don't even speak correct Russian. There's quite a low level of education and socially, education has lost its prestige; it's meaningless. The most popular academic institutes today are involved not with literature or even pure sciences but with business."

Olga believes that the entrepreneurial culture is profoundly affecting male/female roles and relationships. "Andrei's attitude towards me changed tremendously when he started making a lot of money," she said as he paced around the room, his internal spring almost visibly tightening. "A man we know who has become an entrepreneur now says he hates his wife because she's 'stupid' and 'dull.' He's looking for a replacement."

"Before," Olga continued, dropping the unnecessary object of the preposition, "in a proletarian family, a wife would take all the money coming in every month, because otherwise the husband would drink it. She'd give him a ruble a day to take to work. That was the reality. Now, men find that something is missing in their lives. They want to spend their money on flats and foreign cars, on nightclubs, on travel, on expensive clothes. And they want their wives to stay home and take care of the kids."

Olga told me of a recent poll that showed that women are lowering not only their expectations but their desire for financial independence and career advancement. In 1988, 20 percent of the women polled said they would stay home and not work if their husbands made enough money for the family. This year that figure is 30 percent, and it's rising. Increasingly, women no longer say they want to be engineers or doctors or managers, regardless of their previous education, but think "secretary to a *biznesman* who earns hard currency" is the top job.

Almost none of the money the young entrepreneurs are making leaves the trading sector. "They put no money into productive investment," Andrei said. "It's so easy to make money. I go to Germany, buy a big consignment of cigarettes, come back and sell them, and ship the money out to a bank in England. At this level of inflation, I need huge amounts of money to live. I can't afford to invest. I'd risk bankruptcy if I invested. Also, the tax laws and investment laws change overnight. No one's interested in production."

What Andrei *is* interested in is joining the ranks of what Alexei Pankin calls "the new masters," the embryonic bourgeoisie. Andrei as Julien Sorel: "I'm a simple village boy but I have become rich," he said proudly. "I will be a member of the aristocracy"—his word for the economic ruling class. "I have a big bank account in London. I own a film studio in Odessa. I've made $30,000 this year, which can buy what a million dollars buys in the States. In this economy, cash is the only secure commodity, not real estate, not factories. So I buy things for myself, things I can carry or drive or throw away: clothes, a laundry machine, silk sheets and silk suits, a cordless phone. I've bought a car—a Zhiguli, not an expensive one," he added modestly, "and I invest in art, made by a friend who's an artist."

At the mention of art, Andrei suddenly softened his affect. He seemed to be in a trading mode. "What do you think this is worth?" he asked me, pulling a cloth-covered object from behind an empty carton. Underneath was a small jeweled cross with a tiny luminous painting in the center. I hadn't a clue, and insisted I was not in the market for an icon. "Just tell me how much this would fetch in the States," he pleaded. I figured the sales pitch signalled the end of the conversation and made for the door. He followed me down the dark stairs, past a rusted, wrecked motorcycle on the first landing, into the past-midnight St. Petersburg gloom. "Well," he said as we waited for a taxi, "There's an oil well for sale. What about it?"

3.

"It's easier to change a name than to create a bourgeoisie," the political journalist and historian Daniel Singer remarked as we stood near the old Gosplan building—the center of the Soviet command economy—in downtown Moscow. The switch from Leningrad to St. Petersburg took the Lensoviet (now, City Council) a few minutes of discussion and a vote. Actually existing capitalism, with a developed bourgeoisie and a surrounding bourgeois culture, is still light-years away.

A first—perhaps false—glimmering of it, however, may be seen in an apartment just off one of the wonderful wide canals that are the main feature of St. Petersburg, and the only part that is not in a state of decay and decrepitude. Nevsky Prospekt, the Hermitage Museum and the rows of eighteenth-century buildings along the canals are in sorry shape, and the crowds thronging the avenues look shabbier and more forlorn than pedestrians in Moscow, Kiev or even in central Asian capitals like Tashkent and Alma-Ata. But the apartment I visited was brazenly bright in bourgeois Russian colors, all red brocade and gold silks, with expensive, campy light fixtures that revolved and twirled to hidden hums.

Volodya (he was adamant that his real full name not be known) was born thirty-seven years ago on a train hurtling between Odessa and Leningrad. His family had been evacuated to Uzbekistan during World War II and later moved west to the Black Sea port, but towards the end of her pregnancy Volodya's mother split and had *almost* reached her Baltic home when she gave birth. The family's route around the vast Soviet Union was not unusual in those days for Jews, who were relocated not only for their own safety from

German troops but to break up a potentially independent and therefore troublesome "nationality" in the Stalinist order.

"My family suffered a great deal under Stalin," Volodya began, puffing on
a Marlboro and twisting a tiny glass of cognac in the fingers of one hand.
"My mother's father was shot by the KGB," he said without much emotion.
"I'm Jewish but I never practiced religion. My wife is not Jewish and I didn't
have many Jewish friends, and those I had all immigrated to Israel, and so
did my parents and my brother.

"When I was in the army a drunken officer berated some Lithuanians for
being hypocrites because they killed Jews during the war and now they were
'Jew-lovers.' I went on a hunger strike then, and another time because of
anti-Semitism. I encounter anti-Semitism all the time, in every sense of the
word. Today I was out walking my dog, who has a long nose, you see," he
chuckled. "There were some people walking by, just there, downstairs from
my apartment, and they called out, 'Hey, the dog's a Jew just like you.' They
were not being friendly. You see, I'm identifiable to Russians as a Jew. It's
very frightening; it always has been and it always will be. Today at my business I got a phone call from a man who said, 'Even though you're a Jew, you're
a great guy.' Was that a compliment or an insult? Even though my dog has a
long nose, is she a great dog?

"Things are different now than they were ten or twenty years ago. It was
more frightening back then. This is how I was kicked out of the university: it
was 1977 and I was 22; the dean called me in and said, 'You're a Jew, you're
already in your fifth year [of law school], you're a good student, but the KGB
is always asking about you. You don't have *good* relatives. You cannot as a
Jew work in government legal service, so it's better for you to leave, do something else.'"

Like many Jews of the FSU, Volodya's experiences with anti-Semitism
never brought him deeper into his religion. I asked him if he had had a
bar mitzvah. "What's that?" he wanted to know. The translator (Volodya
could understand some English but could not speak it well) went on about
the coming-of-age ritual performed by Jewish men at the age of 13, and it
seemed to ring a bell. "Oh, yes, I know what you mean, but I didn't do that."
He knows only a few words of Yiddish—like *meshugeneh* and *putz*—and he
has never set foot inside a synagogue. But last year he sent his non-Jewish
wife and their two children to Israel to live with the rest of his family. Why
hadn't he joined them? "I wouldn't fit in," he replied, somewhat cryptically.
"I sent my kids because here they are considered ugly, because they are recognized as Jews. Here, the rich kids are beaten up by poor kids. There's an
attitude against people who rise up from the crowd." The reasoning was
unconvincing, but Volodya changed the subject to business, which he loved
and which had made him the father of rich kids and a budding bourgeois in
St. Petersburg.

"Today I sold two tons of nickel, and in two hours I made 3.6 million rubles," Volodya said, cheering considerably after the unpleasant stories about his family. "Sometimes I sell cognac, furs, coats. But we don't buy the nickel for money. We exchange 400 bottles of 'royal spirit' [grain alcohol, which is cut into four bottles of vodka or nondescript rotgut] for one ton of nickel. The royal spirit costs us 450 rubles per bottle, or a total of 180,000 rubles for the lot. We then can sell the nickel for 2 million rubles a ton, for a profit of 1.8 million rubles. We sold two tons today and that's how we made so much money!"

"There's no 'normal' law on land or property," Volodya continued. "I'll be able to invent it. We can figure out where the reforms are going, what the government is thinking, and then we do our business on what we learn. Frankly, I think the government will change. [Former Acting Prime Minister Yegor] Gaidar is not in favor of low-interest loans to industries, but the new head of the Central Bank, Viktor Geraschenko, wants the loans. Well, he doesn't care. He just wants to ride around in a Mercedes."

Volodya himself rides around in a thirty-two-year-old Volga—"from before Gagarin flew into space"—because a newer car would attract too much attention. A few years ago he bought a new Volvo and went out to a restaurant for dinner. As he was parking, two "hoodlums" approached and demanded 10,000 rubles *not* to break the windows. He paid. In the next two days he was stopped by the "militia" three times and had to pay 6,000 rubles in bribes to continue on his way.

"They stop you for any reason, to check your documents, to check for weapons, or if the guy is bored or needs rubles right then. If there were a real reason for stopping you and he gave you a fine, it would be okay. But he wants to feed his family. You see, we do not have a normal bourgeois democratic system. They haven't even started yet, and if they started tomorrow it would take fifteen years to have a 'normal' system, to get new people in power who know how to be civilized. The kids now in school—in the *best* scenario, they'll become criminals. Then future criminals will take power. It's very frightening."

With his new apartment (which cost a million rubles "officially" and 3 million more in unofficial pay-offs), his vintage car, his wide-ranging business interests and his civilized values, Volodya would seem ready to run with the new St. Petersburg elite, even with the suspect nationality written in his passport. But there is one horrible contradiction to his success, a secret that both explains the peculiarities of his life and obliterates his future. Volodya has AIDS.

"I had the flu last January. I didn't get better and I developed pneumonia, so I went to the hospital. They tested me and I was positive. I almost jumped out of the hospital; they had to hold me from the window. The health authorities threatened to call my business, to call my wife unless I gave them the names of all my sexual contacts. I gave them the names of all the women and the men I had slept with. One man came in and tested negative, but he began to blackmail me. I paid him a lot of money. I changed my address five times; I still try to avoid having my last name mentioned in my business affairs. When I delayed paying him, he hired thugs to beat me up. I lost my front teeth—look—and when I called the militia about it they threatened *me* rather than investigate the beating. They threatened me with Law 121, which makes homosexuality a crime, and with Law 115, which allows the militia to keep lists of gays. Then the blackmailer started threatening my children and my wife, and that's when they went to Israel."

We had moved from his brocade and silk apartment (the decor suddenly seemed to make more sense) to one of St. Petersburg's most interesting restaurants, built in the wall of the fortress of Peter and Paul, the low, looming citadel and prison on the Neva where Lenin's brother was held and executed by Czar Alexander III. A party of twenty *biznesmany* and their wives sat behind us, gulping large glasses of vodka with each toast. "In an hour they'll take out their own bottles, to save money," Volodya sneered. His jaunty, proud facade of the afternoon had disappeared as he told me of his loneliness and dread, his love for his family and, just recently, for a man who could never become his lover. Business had become an escape from the reality of his illness and his isolation. "Here I'm making all this money," he said, "and I have nothing to do with it. I'll make sure my wife and my children are comfortable and then I'll give the rest of it away to help AIDS patients. It's better to give money away than to give it to the government," he smiled slightly. "Anyway, I don't give a shit."

AIDS—called SPID—is not high on the public's list of worries. Nor do Western analysts or journalists ever examine the social context of the disease, which is full of meaning for the transformation of Soviet life. Sexual mores, family values, gender roles, social service structures and the organization of civil institutions are all implicated in the epidemic and the response to it. The Russian government says that fewer than a hundred people have died so far and under a thousand have been infected with HIV, but the World Health Organization estimates that there are a hundred or more unreported infections for every known HIV-positive individual, which would mean more than 100,000 may actually have the virus in Russia alone. The government still tries to deny the extent of the looming epidemic. Yuri Kobishcha, a gentle, saintly doctor who runs an AIDS outreach program in Kiev, thinks that by the end of the decade there will be at least 10,000 people with HIV in Ukraine, "but there are no reliable methods of verifying this." There is very little AIDS education, condoms are in short supply and those available are dangerously unreliable. And there are unique patterns of socio-sexual behavior, involving a kind of institutionalized bisexuality, that create new categories of risks.

What the epidemic has done in startling degree is to bring Russian gay people hesitantly but irreversibly out of a closet so deep and dark that Western homosexuals would hardly recognize it. AIDS has stigmatized gays to some extent, for here, as in the West, it is known as a "gay disease"—although the Russian model is in some ways closer to the African or Southeast Asian paradigms of primarily heterosexual as well as homosexual transmission. But under the prodding of a few gay American "expats" residing in the country, including my interpreter, Kevin Gardner, an indigenous gay community is forming, with AIDS activism as an organizing principle.

A half-dozen men in their late teens or early 20s gathered one night to talk about AIDS in a small two-room apartment in a bleak Khrushchev-era housing project far from the center of Moscow. To get there, we drove forever in a dark drizzle, long past the point that the asphalt ended and the road degenerated into mud and ruts. It was not easy to find the right entry among hundreds of indistinguishable doorways. At length, we asked some kids who were playing with a soccer ball in the fading gloom and mounted a rickety staircase in a pitch-black hallway. At the top we were met by a slight, blond teenager with a peach-fuzz beard. "My name is Viktor. This is my wife," he said, nodding to a heavily made-up woman in jeans and high heels, with a great deal of hair. "And this," Viktor added, "is my husband." A man in his mid-20s, with a dark stubble of whiskers stepped forward.

The *ménage à trois* of young gays and straights is not unusual in Russian cities because it satisfies critical economic and social needs, if not psychosexual ones. Young singles can't find apartments for themselves, and the kind of group housing common in the United States since the 1960s has not been introduced. It is extremely difficult for gays to meet one another. There are no gay bars or cafes; Russia does not now have a developed stationary bar or cafe scene of any kind. But even if there were opportunities for forming alternative families, Russian parents insist that their children follow the old family values by marrying, setting up a household and bearing children, as soon as possible.

The meeting was chaired by another young man, named Kolya, who was trying to start a Moscow spin-off of the Names Project, the San Francisco–based organization that put together and sent on tour the huge quilt with its hand-sewn patches memorializing lovers, relatives and friends who had died of AIDS. The problem the gay men (there were no lesbians) had to solve was how to register their group with the Moscow authorities—a necessary step if they were to open a bank account, receive contributions and spend money. Non-registered groups cannot easily do any of that, but Law 121 made registration difficult. The men smoked Marlboros furiously and drank tea from delicate china cups; the two wives present went off to the other room and talked. An American filmmaker preparing a documentary on AIDS in Russia wandered in and shot some footage. A British journalist came by and offered a substantial contribution to the organization. The Russian men came up with no good answer to their dilemma, but a few months later I heard that Yeltsin had announced he would ask parliament to repeal the discriminatory law.

Many hundreds of gay men and a smaller contingent of lesbians were out in great force one weekend at the Rainbow Disco, a dance that moves from place to place each week to avoid trouble with gay-bashers, as well as to keep the authorities off-guard. So loose is the construction of law and morality now that no one knows whether the gatherings are completely legal or not. The organizers sometimes hire city militia for security, but there's always the fear that the hall could be raided.

The dance that Saturday night was held in the *dom kultury*—literally, "culture house," but in effect a kind of recreation hall—in the basement of one unit of a midscale housing project just outside the inner ring girdling Moscow's center. The decor and lighting were sparse and primitive, but the sound system was impressive and enhanced by a man doing what looked like *karaoke* to hip-hop and acid house music of current vintage. Two bars served warm champagne, vodka and surprisingly appetizing cold food plates. Every so often a few people would leave to walk around the block and share a joint of marijuana, but that seemed to constitute the drug scene. There was hardly a dancer in the room older than 30, but very late, or rather early in the morning, mixed couples of Westerners began arriving. The word around town was that it beat the glitzy hooker clubs as the hot place to be.

"Six months ago these dances were taking place with about thirty people in someone's flat," the principal organizer told me. But the end of Soviet rule has brought increased sexual permissiveness, not only for gays and lesbians but for everyone, to buy, sell, make, do and simply *see* sexual things, from prostitution to erotic art. Some of it is over the top. At the Red Zone, where the new high-rollers and mafia *biznesmany* meet Western businessmen, naked women dance in cages that descend from the ceiling, there's a VIP room with a special strip show (the chorines take off Cossack costumes out of the 1940s Ice Capades) and the only hard thing a man has to have to get a bar girl is his currency. A Ukrainian who speaks Russian fluently but with an accent boasted that he routinely gets a date by claiming he's an American from New York.

The commercial, competitive, often hostile and even violent ambience of the big chic clubs contrasted sharply with the communal feeling at the Rainbow Disco. Except for small personal networks of friends and business partners there are few new active "communities" in the Western sense, large groups of people who not only share a social identity but in some ways act out that identity together in a visible way. There have always been homosexuals in Russia, of course; I remember a friend returning to America from a visit to Leningrad in the mid-1950s with reports of a small clique of artists among whom were several gay ballet dancers, including a young local star named Nureyev, thought by the rest to be the one destined for greatness. But until this year it has not been possible to speak of a gay community, or even a gay identity.

It is even more difficult to talk about a feminist community, let alone a women's movement in the terms most Americans now know it. The beginnings of a movement might be located, however, on the twelfth floor of a high-rise Academy of Sciences building, again quite far from Moscow's center, where Anastasia Posadskaya runs the Gender Studies Center, the only really advanced women's studies institute in the entire region.

"Two years ago, the *word* 'gender' didn't even exist," Posadskaya said as she began to explain the difficulties of feminism in Russia. "We took the word from English, as so many have been adopted wholesale. In Russian, we say 'socially determined sexual role,' or 'social sex,' which sounds erotic, or perhaps like sex under the Bolsheviks."

Posadskaya was raised by women (her mother and grandmother), taught political economy at the University of Moscow, got married, had a child and got divorced. "I took academics seriously," she continued. "I wanted to be a mathematician, then a philosopher, but my professor said, 'I never heard such a silly thing. You should be a teacher, something compatible with having a family.' Many economists recommended that women be removed from the labor force to make the economy more efficient.

"I was in the Lenin Library researching my thesis on women's employment in the USA when I came across a picture album of women workers in America. There was a picture of a woman coal miner, with the caption, 'American women win the right to work underground.' I wondered, why do they *want* the right? I started to think how women want to be protected. It made me feel constrained, rather than secure."

Somewhere in the Soviet communist culture, however, were the seeds of feminism. "Socialism brought an agenda for women's liberation," Posadskaya said. "But that was the idea of socialism. Socialism as a system was terrible. For me it was a reality, it meant millions of people killed. It took my family, my life. When we met Western feminists we were struck by their social frame. They were Marxists. We argued with them so much I even cried. How could I say that the system that did all this to me was good? No one wants to hear about solidarity in this country anymore, because for years it was imposed: solidarity with South Africa, solidarity with Cuba. For Western women socialism was a question of values. They said, 'At least the communists had liberation down on paper.'"

Many of the budding Russian feminists (and there aren't many) continue to look with suspicion on certain of their Western counterparts, not primarily because of their socialist values but because of their focus on what Americans used to call "the politics of personal identity" rather than on the economic and social status of women. There's no question that women in Russia and the other republics are suffering far more than men in the deepening morass.

"The Soviet pattern was that a woman first got an education, then a lifelong job and finally a pension," Posadskaya said without noticeable nostalgia. "It was very stable and secure. Now all this pattern is smashed. Women make up 70 percent of the unemployed. And of these unemployed women, 85 percent have higher or specialized educations. At the same time, education is being privatized, there are more places for pay, so competition for the few free places is more intense and women are losing out. In the government's plan, health, preschool, education, child care, and some pensions and social security should be increasingly privatized. And it's all the fault of a woman—Margaret Thatcher!"

"*Before*," there was a quota that reserved one-third of all the seats in the soviets (parliaments) for women. "Democracy" has removed the quota, and women's participation is down to 5 percent. When I asked various politicians if there were any women in positions of power now, they repeated rumors that such-and-such wife of a leading figure was "the power behind the throne."

In the space of a few months, Russians have adopted some of the West's most reactionary gender roles and sexual stereotypes. "There are help-wanted ads in the newspapers," Posadskaya concluded, "'We need beautiful girls without complexes for rich gentlemen,' and 'We need secretaries—our uniform is miniskirts.' And there's no reaction to this! To say that anything is 'Western' is a form of legitimation. I interviewed a girl who was a participant in a beauty contest. She had the idea, told to her by the men who ran the contest, that the contest was an art form, when it was just a striptease, it was semipornographic. She got no money for it and she was told, 'Art is its own reward.' When I questioned her about it, she said that this was 'normal,' that it was 'civilized,' that it was true and right because it was 'just like in the West.'"

4.

Moscow in the Soviet era—"the seventy years" in the stock phrase—was "drab, drab, drab" to Western eyes, primarily because of the absence of neon signs and the omnipresence of military colors on soldiers, trucks and buildings. There's nothing like a lit-up Fuji Film sign, a fire-engine-red Bronco or a pomo-pink office block to brighten up a cityscape. There's still little color or neon, but it's clear after only a few hours in Moscow that this is a great world-city, brimming with mysteries and the unexpected, alive but unwell and definitely down in the dumps.

What is missing now, however, is the revolutionary excitement of early *perestroika*, when there were informal debates in every setting, daring new films opening weekly, experiments in the arts, literature, journalism and social organization going on at every level. There's almost nothing left of that brilliant moment. It's difficult even to find a Russian-made movie playing in the capital. Most of the films are third- and fourth-rate American rejects, with a couple of hits—*Pretty Woman*, anything with Arnold Schwarzenegger—to add a touch of class. The reason for the sudden death of the local film movement is said to be the commercial machinations of a certain Uzbek entrepreneur who monopolized the import market and won't let Russian product into the theaters. The same Z-movies are on television, occasionally with synchronized dubbing, but more often annoyingly narrated by a single voice over low-volume English dialogue in the background. In culture as in commerce, cheap is cheap.

Tens of thousands of the most innovative and imaginative Russian (and other ex-Soviet) intellectuals are immigrating, primarily to the United States and Israel, but also to Western Europe, South Africa and Australia. What used to be called "defection" is now the less politically charged "brain drain." It is hard to find anyone anywhere in the FSU who has a mind or a skill marketable for hard currency who is not considering a move. Batir, a rising foreign service officer in the government of Uzbekistan, said on an afternoon's walk through Tashkent that although he was proud of his newly independent country, he was applying for a scholarship to do graduate work in Pennsylvania, where he hoped to find an American wife and settle down. "Americans have everything," Batir said enviously. "Buick cars and Kim Basinger."

People are mad for American culture and its artifacts. Not only in western Russia but also in the farther reaches of the late empire, the highest style and the most sought-after goods are American. Schoolkids in Tashkent have the look down perfectly, which this year is straight out of GAP ads. In Manezh Square beyond the Kremlin, young guys with roller blades race around passing out fliers for the twenty-four-hour casino in the Intourist Hotel and bumping into pretty girls' behinds. On Prospekt Marx, two young skateboard rats practice flips on the low platform supporting the monumental bust of Karl Marx, under which are written the immortal words, "Proletarians of all lands unite!" Late at night, knots of young Russians, dressed in a version of Soho chic, wander Gorky Street bumming cigarettes and looking for something to do.

MTV clones blanket the land, and kids are as *au courant* about Nirvana, the Red Hot Chili Peppers and grunge as an older generation of Russians might have been about Louis Armstrong and jazz. Across a street behind the KGB headquarters in ex-Dzerzhinsky Square, where once banners exhorted workers to meet production quotas or comrades to express solidarity with Cuba, a streamer now advertises, in English: ROCK 'N' ROLL TV. There are at least four all-music stations in Moscow with American formats (golden oldies, hard and soft rock, heavy metal, current pop—but little rap or r&b and no country). Turner Broadcasting has a management crew in Moscow negotiating with "a bunch of Russians" to start a private, independent news-and-movies television outlet early this year. A CNN type told me proudly that advertising will be "integrated with programming" on the US model. Culture wars are also imported; one of the most ferocious arguments I had in a month was with a Russian Kazakh who insisted that McCartney was the greatest Beatle, while I, of course, held out for Lennon. He got the pun, too.

The American expeditionary force has established beachheads in almost every category of life and work. American (and, to a lesser extent, British) lawyers have built a business not only as clients' representatives but as advisers to the authorities creating the new laws. The American firm of Baker & McKenzie, known as the world's biggest, has offices in both Moscow and St. Petersburg, as well as in Kiev. The Ukrainian operation was begun by two Ukrainian-Americans, who first got a foothold in-country by staffing the International Advisory Council, a board of notables set up at the time of independence to deliver acceptable and appropriate positions on economic and political issues to the Ukrainian Parliament and to President Leonid Kravchuk, who, as a former communist, suffers from a certain credibility deficit in Western (and domestic) circles.

The council included several British and American moderate-to-conservative economists and politicians, such as Roy Romanow, premier of Saskatchewan; Shirley Williams, a founder of the British Social Democratic Party and now a leading neoliberal theorist at Harvard's Kennedy School; and MIT economist Lester Thurow. The council was privately funded by the Hungarian-American financier George Soros, whose footprints can be seen all over the developing institutions of post-communist Europe. Ivan (formerly, John) Hewko and Borys (formerly, Boris) Dackiw, the two Ukrainian-American lawyers who staffed the council, are among the thousands of members of the Ukrainian diaspora who have visited—or immigrated to—their ancient homeland since independence.

So flimsy is the institutional infrastructure of even big countries like Ukraine (the largest nation wholly in Europe) and Russia (still the largest nation in the world), and so few are the precedents of actually existing capitalism, that "foreign" bodies like the International Advisory Council, foreign advisers like the ubiquitous Jeffrey Sachs of Harvard, and foreign philanthropists can have considerable influence over so-called democratic development.

A British journalist who regularly covers economic news in the FSU pointed out that Sachs, for just one example, has "dozens of 'Sachsettes' in government ministries—24-year-old students from Harvard, many without graduate degrees, yet they are drafting Russian commercial law." No one is especially worried that Sachs himself will derive great financial benefit from his academic/political activities (although there's nothing stopping him or any of the members of Team Sachs from cashing in on their contacts and making efficient use of the laws they are writing). But elsewhere, lawyers and advisers are networking like crazy, and clearly making deals with *nomenklatura* capitalists they only recently advised in government offices.

Borys Dackiw said he foresaw many troubling ethical problems when he set out for Kiev last summer to help launch the Baker & McKenzie office. For guidance, or perhaps moral support, he brought with him a complete set of the Bar Association's ethical guidelines. What happens, for instance, when (not if) a foreign client asks for advice on whether to pay a bribe, by whatever name, to a local official or manager so that a deal can be struck? Dackiw said the easy answer is that a lawyer must say he is not allowed to give advice on such matters. But in the post-Soviet system things are never that easy. The foreign company seeking the deal does not usually offer or pay the bribe, but gets a local front to take care of the sleazy business, giving the upright Westerners "deniability." There's very little commercial law, and no applicable conspiracy law, so the foreigners are home free. Dackiw said that not long ago a German tycoon completed an especially lucrative deal with a state enterprise in Ukraine (where virtually nothing of consequence is privatized yet), and at the signing ceremony presented the Ukrainian manager with a bundle of marks worth about $100,000. "These are for the children of Chernobyl," the German said unctuously. The manager put the bundle in his briefcase.

5.

The lobby of the Hotel Uzbekistan in Tashkent is one of those intergalactic way-stations where you can see the strangest people in the universe all in one place. On one warm Sunday evening in September there were robed and hooded Arab men, women in black chadors, fat German businessmen and their thin wives, Sikhs in turbans, a delegation of Bahai followers from LA, wide-eyed and seersuckered American Peace Corps workers, a representative of the British Mint in Savile Row regalia, Uzbek (recently Soviet Red) Army officers in full metal jackets, and a wide assortment of Mongols, Turks, Pakistanis, Koreans, hustlers, hookers, moneychangers, interpreters and tourists. Long after dark a bedraggled complement of Americans from the National Democratic Institute for International Affairs in Washington arrived with overstuffed suitcases, backpacks and a rather prominent guitar. The group had spent the day in the boonies, spreading the democratic word, outreaching like crazy and, presumably, selling neoliberalism to the natives. Yurt to yurt.

Tashkent is a peculiar but agreeable city, with a large Western quarter mostly rebuilt in Early Brezhnev style after the devastating earthquake of 1966, and a sprawling (but not "teeming," as in Calcutta) "native" area of narrow streets and low houses behind high mud walls. Inevitably, creeping Westernization is gobbling up the traditional neighborhoods, and Uzbeks are moving into the high-rises that are standard in cities of the FSU from Lvov to Vladivostok. This is no backwater. Tashkent is the fourth-biggest city in the former Union, and it has all the amenities the central government was pleased to provide: a Metro, an enormous permanent circus and wide plazas where hundreds of thousands could assemble to cheer the commissar *du jour*.

The multitudes who massed in Independence Square (changed from Lenin Square) for the declaration of Uzbekistan's removal from the Soviet Union in the summer of 1991 were no doubt optimistic about the promise of sovereignty, but as elsewhere, the reality has been bitter and the future holds many threats. Chief among them is the growing conflict between Islamic nationalism and authoritarian secularism, with almost no prospects for liberal democracy. The barely restrained civil war in neighboring Tajikistan could spill over into Uzbekistan at any time; there are many who say that it already has, along with the Tajik-speaking refugees who have moved across the tortuous border to live among their ethnic siblings in the region of Samarkand, Uzbekistan's second city and the still-glorious capital of the ancient Silk Road between China and the Mediterranean.

Partly because of the ethnic tension, Uzbekistan's president, Islam Karimov, another Soviet-era hack who changed the name of his party but not much else when independence came, has tightened his rule. The opposition—both fundamentalist and secular—is harassed and repressed, and prominent opponents are cruelly assaulted. One Saturday morning I had an appointment with Shukhrat Izmetullaev, the acting head of Birlik, the main opposition movement (it is not allowed to call itself a party). The meeting was slightly surreptitious, by his request. We were to meet in someone else's office in a building near the Hotel Uzbekistan, but the details were vague and he did not offer—as everyone else did in Central Asia—to pick me up, guide me and generally make all the arrangements. Moreover, he was an hour late, which was unusual, and when he finally arrived, in a run, he apologized mightily. It was not until the interview was finished and he was walking me home that he told me the reason: that very morning he had been fired from his job teaching mathematics at the university merely for being a visible member of the political opposition; another colleague got the same notice. Furthermore, Karimov ordered that anyone active in opposition organizations be fired from *any* job controlled by the government, which includes state-run industries, schools and universities as well as official agencies.

"Uzbekistan is like the old days," Izmetullaev said, sighing. "If you want to know what things were like in the Soviet republics, you have come to the right place. We are not allowed to hold meetings in the open. Birlik cannot be a normal party. Two of our leaders were beaten by Karimov's men and must be in exile in Moscow. Several others are political prisoners." Perhaps the most humiliating betrayal has been the recent rehabilitation of a hated tyrant of the late communist era, Sharaf Rashidov, who, among many more heinous acts, was linked to a corrupt deal with Chevron Oil. Rashidov had once been buried in an elaborate tomb in central Tashkent. His body was removed at the time of independence, but on the first anniversary of the new republic in August, his coffin was trotted out again and reburied with great ceremony, and his memory and good works were celebrated. It was not taken as a good sign for the future.

The small Russian minority in Uzbekistan—about a million souls in a country of twenty-one million (and roughly the area of California)—feels increasingly unwanted as Islamic nationalism intrudes from the south.

Uzbekistan borders Afghanistan, which is now recognized as the arms bazaar of the world. "There's no frontier to speak of," a Western diplomat in Tashkent shrugged. "Whole convoys of arms move out of Afghanistan every day. You can't even call it smuggling; it's basically a highly developed export system." Russian and Uzbek troops from the barely breathing Commonwealth of Independent States—Yeltsin's jury-rigged spin-off of the Soviet Union—have been sent to the Afghan border in increasing numbers, but they have failed to stanch the flow of weapons.

Many ethnic Russians have left Uzbekistan for Russia, and almost all of the country's Jewish population is on the way out, either to Israel or points west. Originally many Jews came to Uzbekistan from the western Soviet Union, ahead of the advancing German invaders in World War II, but there is also a sizable community of Farsi-speaking Sephardim, called "Bukhara Jews," who have been in the area for centuries and are the most fearful of creeping Islamization.

Bukhara, the spiritual and geographical center of the Sephardic population, is an oasis city between the Red and Black deserts in central Uzbekistan. It's known as the place where the famous rugs come from, except that they don't: Bukhara was the entrepôt where "Oriental" carpets from all over Central Asia were brought for sale, but none were ever made in the city itself. The old part of town lies astride the historic trans-Asian trade route and is still a wonder of domed markets, blue-tiled mosques and plazas and pools lined with ancient mulberry trees. Men with black and white embroidered Turkish skullcaps sit on raised platforms in the open streets and play chess and dominoes, sip tea from glasses and while away the idle hours.

Just off the central square with its wide pool and shaded mosques is the Jewish quarter, which looks very much like the rest of old Bukhara, except that over a door in a mud wall there's a sign in Russian and Hebrew letters identifying the entrance to the synagogue and proclaiming "SHALOM. MIR." Inside, an old *shamus* showed me and two other American visitors the array of Torahs, the central lecterns and the modest decorative elements. Water for tea was boiling on a kerosene stove, and after a while another man arrived, washed his hands and then shook his elbow with the *shamus* so as not to soil himself again. Otherwise there was no visible activity.

Outside, a young girl of 10 or 11 ran up to us and began a spirited monologue in surprisingly good English. "I am going to Queens in New York in three months," she said excitedly. Her younger brother, Igor, joined her. She had relatives in America, and from the way she spoke of her trip it was clear that hers was not the only family emigrating. In the soft afternoon she was saying goodbye to Bukhara.

I left Uzbekistan a few days later, but not without a parting shot from the *ancien régime*. The visa requirements of the republics of the former Union change daily, are often hopelessly contradictory and generally involve bribery. I had already bought my way into the country with a $20 pay-off to a mid-level foreign ministry bureaucrat, who handed me my entry visa and pocketed the note. On the way out, I was stopped at the airport gate and escorted to a small room marked "Security Control," in English. A smiling, neatly dressed young man took my passport and asked, in the only English he knew, for "exit visa." I tried to make him understand that my entry visa was sufficient, but he was adamant, and finally made clear that I would not be allowed to leave the country. It was hot, I was frustrated, there were people waiting for me in Kazakhstan and shouting didn't seem to help. Finally a Finn I had chatted with told me to take the man out of the room where no one would see us and "make it worth his while." I started the bidding at $10. The security controller laughed and drew his hand around his neck to symbolize a hangman's noose. I decided to raise the offer in increments of $5. Again, the hand across the neck. I handed him a ten and two fives. He smiled again. "Okay," he laughed. "Exit visa okay."

6.

The trouble in Kazakhstan is that there are *too many* Russians. Not counting people of inextricably "mixed blood," of which there are many, Russians make up about 40 percent of the population—a figure roughly equal to that for ethnic Kazakhs. The largest of the five former Central Asian SSRs, Kazakhstan is almost twice the size of Alaska. Alma-Ata, the extravagantly green and easygoing capital, sits at the end of a dusty desert plain in the foothills of the Tian Shan range, all snowy with glaciers dropping from jagged granite peaks. Luda, a translator who works for a local joint venture, says that Americans tell her Alma-Ata "looks like Salt Lake City." Maybe, but not much. The climate and the view may be Mormon, but the ambience is of a French or Belgian colonial outpost in Indochina or Africa, though with more amenities and a thoroughgoing cultural integration.

But with independence in 1991 the long-suppressed stirrings of nationalism surfaced. As elsewhere in Central Asia, many ethnic Russians perceived the handwriting on the wall and left for a country they never knew, and in which they have not felt terribly welcome. Jews left for Israel. The ethnic Germans, some 800,000 in all, are leaving in droves, although Germany is in no mood to accept them these days. Many have had to settle for new homes in underdeveloped areas of Ukraine, where they are welcomed as "hard workers—unlike the lazy Ukrainians," a teacher told me in Kiev.

Perhaps because of the ethnic stand-off, Kazakhstan is the least tense of the republics and the most stable. President Nursultan Nazarbayev, who rules like a semi-benevolent monarch, has great press in the West, primarily because he controls one of the largest nuclear arsenals in the world. In the divorce settlement of the Soviet Union, Nazarbayev got the 8,000-plus warheads in his territory, and although he has made all kinds of pledges to act responsibly and even to become nuclear-free, he still has a nuclear button and must be stroked. To bring in hard currency, Nazarbayev has offered to sell uranium, both from ore mined in Kazakhstan and from recycled warheads, to the United States, but perhaps to jack up the demand and hence the price, he has also let stories leak that he is willing to sell to anyone else willing to pay dollars, including Iran and China.

Kazakhstan has been in the nuclear business for a long time and has suffered greatly from both the literal and figurative fall-out. The immense Soviet testing site at Semipalatinsk, about 500 miles northeast of Alma-Ata, has left a legacy of death and doom for thousands of miles around. American and Kazakh anti-nuclear activists formed a Nevada-Semipalatinsk protest organization and succeeded in stopping testing at the site, but the legacy of four decades of explosions will last an eternity. An American embassy worker told me (and the head of the Alma-Ata environmental agency, under prodding, confirmed) that super-fine low-level radioactive dust from the test site not only blankets the capital but has been detected in the glaciers atop the Tian Shan peaks, which are higher than the Alps or the Rockies. Every morning when the old men and women sweep the streets with their long brooms of wooden branches, they swirl another cloud of radioactive particles into the air.

Nikolai Dudkin, the editor in chief of the weekly environmental newspaper in Alma-Ata, *Eko-Kurier*, looked glum under a huge painting of Lenin in the national environmental agency where we talked. "Seventy percent of Kazakhstan is an ecological disaster zone," he began. "Parliament made it official this year. Semipalatinsk will be deadly for millions of years. There are chemical weapons test sites still in use in what's left of the Aral Sea, one of the largest inland seas in the world. It has lost half its water to irrigation projects, mostly for the cotton fields of Uzbekistan. There are large boats stranded on dry land where there used to be water. Now the Uzbeks are selling their cotton to foreigners for hard currency and the textile industry in the rest of the former Soviet Union has collapsed, so the ecological disaster is contributing to an economic disaster, and probably a political disaster as well."

Kazakhstan's principal exports are extracted from the land—oil, lead, copper and other minerals—and there are environmental difficulties, if not disasters, associated with every sizable mining process. The economic problems loom even larger, however. Although Nazarbayev insists his country does not want to copy the "Saudi model" of development-through-extraction, it seems to have little choice. There is no money readily available in Western countries for the kind of investments in industry and infrastructure that would enable Kazakhstan to take his preferred road to "Singapore": development via Japanese and American investment in export-driven businesses, kept competitive by a state-enforced low-wage structure and government unionbusting (some cynics have recently begun calling this the "Arkansas model").

The dilemma of development is hardly unique to Kazakhstan. It applies to almost all the fifteen republics of the old Union, and not one of them is very far on the road to renewal. Russia is in dire need of capital at a time when there is no ready source of assistance in the West. Germany's financial attention will be taken up for the foreseeable future by the overwhelming problem of integrating the Ossis with the Wessis. Japan is in a recession and, in any case, has all it can handle underwriting the much more readily developable coastal lands of the western Pacific Rim. The rest of Western Europe is stumbling along at a reduced level of growth, and the United States has neither the interest nor the capital to transform the economies of Eurasia when it cannot even repair its own.

Russia's reforms, as undertaken in the brief tenure of Yegor Gaidar, were predicated on a monumental, historic Western investment—not aid—project, which never arrived. The laughable voucher program, which is supposed to make 152 million Russians "instant capitalists," couldn't possibly work unless there were well-run, sufficiently capitalized companies that would be worthwhile to own. But there are few, if any, substantial industries in Russia that can make it alone, that are not already in *de facto* bankruptcy and kept alive only by government "credits," which are simply operating subsidies. Russia has no real money to give such credits, so Yeltsin is printing money as fast as his presses will run, and the Devil take the hindmost. Western neo-this and neo-that economists told Gaidar to cut the credits, let the workers go (and starve, if they must), shutter 30 or 60 or 90 percent of the factories if that's what it will take, and don't worry about the politics. Inevitably, Gaidar had to go instead. Even Yeltsin, contemplating political suicide, could not discount the people.

"They have ruined everything," Veniyamin said, shaking his head. He and Lida, his wife, had invited me to spend a Sunday afternoon in their *dacha* above Alma-Ata, where the apple trees thrive on the cool breezes and glacial waters (unfortunately radioactive) from the front range of the Tian Shan Mountains. Lida was preparing dinner with a friend, the Uzbek wife of a Kazakh journalist who passes for an ethnic Russian but was born a Jew named Schlomo. "It was better before Yeltsin, before Gorbachev, before *perestroika*."

That is not an opinion a Westerner hears often in the FSU, and it is certainly not a majority view, but for anyone who had achieved a fair amount of comfort, if not prosperity in the Western sense, it is understandable. Veniyamin bought his *dacha* a dozen years ago, when it cost 5,000 rubles, or about ten months' pay. A car cost about the same amount. "Everybody bought a *dacha* in those days," Lida added. Now, a *dacha* or a car costs about one million rubles, which is about seventeen *years'* salary. Plus, gas is unaffordable, food is expensive, education and social welfare are being cut back on the American model and the threat of civil war, or at least ethnic conflict, looms in the distance.

"And you wonder why we love America," Sergei, who had come to the pic-

nic table in the *dacha*'s garden, said to their American guest. I had compli-
mented Lida on her fruit preserves and mentioned that I sometimes put up
jams and froze vegetables myself in Vermont. Everyone looked astonished,
and a bit resentful. "But you can get everything in the supermarkets, all
year long," Lida said. I felt like Marie Antoinette glimpsed by the peasants
in La Ferme, her play-farm at Versailles. "It tastes better when you do it
yourself," I said lamely.

It is no good telling Russians or their ethnic neighbors about the recession, about mortgages, about brutal competition, blind ambition, social insecurity and all the many deformities of capitalism—even the moderated
form as now practiced in the liberal West. The Russians don't believe you,
and even if they do, they want a chance to experience it all, the goods and
disservices, for themselves. Until, or unless, that happens, there will not be
much of a movement to jump beyond the primitive, imitative stage of banal
capitalism into a future where a uniquely Russian system can combine the
best of many worlds.

"Look at this country," Lida said. *"Shto dyelat?"* What can you do? Or, in
another translation, What is to be done?

January 18, 1993, THE NATION

✦

Whited Out

Chris Hani's assassination, apparently at the hands of a white Polish
immigrant who belonged to a quasi-Nazi Afrikaner organization, is
more than another South African personal tragedy. It has decapitated the
minority movement within the African National Congress that remains dedicated to non-racial, egalitarian democracy, and suddenly makes the path to
a continuation of white power considerably clearer.

Hani never had the press that Nelson Mandela and the ANC's moderates
enjoyed. For long years he commanded Umkhonto we Sizwe, the hit-or-miss
guerrilla wing of the Congress, which had more success inspiring the
unarmed black masses than defeating a Boer government armed to the
teeth. When the ANC returned from exile, Hani chose not to bid for its leadership but instead took over as head of the Communist Party a career choice
unlikely to inspire cheering headlines.

But in recent months Hani had been getting an ominous sort of attention.
His split with his CP predecessor, Joe Slovo, over the direction of negotiations for a post-apartheid government centered on whites' demands for
"power sharing," which Hani considered shorthand for "power keeping." It
has been clear to many in the ANC that the Afrikaners would copy the
model of Zimbabwe, where for many years whites were given a dispropor-
tionate voice in the nominally democratic government, and where today you

find black faces in administrative offices and white ones in the board rooms.

In its Freedom Charter, promulgated forty years ago and rededicated throughout the anti-apartheid struggle, the ANC promised socialist democracy, in which the enormous riches and resources of South Africa could be enjoyed by those who had been denied them for so long. But prosperity-sharing went by the board when the Congress was confronted with the full extent of white might. After all the guerrilla raids, the township rebellions, the international sanctions and the worldwide campaign to free Mandela, the white minority never was defeated, never surrendered. With the departure from the world stage of the Soviet Union, its chief sponsor, the ANC itself was forced to surrender the principles of democratic socialism and "one man, one vote."

Hani, Pallo Jordan (the ANC's information director) and a small group of radicals had been holding out for more power and less sharing. Because of his immense popularity, Hani was in a position to bargain. The ANC leadership hoped he would bring millions of blacks to support a negotiated settlement, but it also worried that the government would abhor any settlement he approved.

A few days before he died, Hani was shown in America on PBS's *Frontline*, shouting "We hate apartheid. We hate capitalism." He meant it, too. Such men are dangerous.

May 3, 1993, THE NATION

✦

The Gay Moment

The gay moment is unavoidable. It fills the media, charges politics, saturates popular and elite culture. It is the stuff of everyday conversation and public discourse. Not for thirty years has a class of Americans endured the peculiar pain and exhilaration of having their civil rights and moral worth—their very humanness—debated at every level of public life. Lesbians and gay men today wake up to headlines alternately disputing their claim to equality under the law, supporting their right to family status, denying their desire, affirming their social identity. They fall asleep to TV talk shows where generals call them perverts, liberals plead for tolerance and politicians weigh their votes. "Gay invisibility," the social enforcement of the sexual closet, is hardly the problem anymore. Overexposure is becoming hazardous.

While gays organize what may be the biggest march on Washington ever, set for April 25, Congress ponders the pros and cons of granting gays first-class citizenship, in the civilian order as well as the military. Courts consider the legality of discrimination against the last community in the country officially excluded from constitutional protection. Senator Edward Kennedy and

Representative Henry Waxman hope to introduce a new national lesbian and gay civil rights bill soon. But until that passes—certainly not for many years—the ruling federal precedent is the notorious decision by retiring Supreme Court Justice Byron White in the 1986 *Bowers v. Hardwick* case, in which he invoked the entire Judeo-Christian tradition of patriarchy and homophobia to deny gay people the rights all other Americans enjoy. Newspapers censor pro-gay comic strips, television stations ban gay programs, schools proscribe gay-positive materials, church hierarchs forbid gay people from preaching (and parading), state electorates revoke existing anti-discrimination laws and outlaw passage of new ones, and bullies on streets of every city beat and bash gays and lesbians with escalating hatred. Some 1,900 incidents of anti-gay violence were reported in 1992. Except for a small number of enlightened workplaces in college towns and the big cities of both coasts, American institutions make it dangerous or impossible for millions of gays to leave their closets and lead integrated, fulfilling lives. In schools everywhere young gay pupils are routinely taunted and worse, and a third of all youthful suicides are gay-related (according to a government report never disseminated by the Bush Administration). Across the country, gay cavaliers must prepare to joust with Christian roundheads for the right to protect their young sisters and brothers.

But it is the contradictions rather than the cruelties of sexual struggle that define the moment. Despite the difficulties, most gays would agree that life as a homosexual is better now than ever before in American history. The Reverend Al Carmines's hopeful but unconvincing post-Stonewall song, "I'm Gay and I'm Proud" now reflects a widespread reality. Responding to the rigidity of the old order, younger gay men and "baby dykes" have created a queer culture that is rapidly reconfiguring American values, redesigning sensibilities and remodelling politics. The gay movement, broadly construed, is *the* movement of the moment. Devastated by a plague that threatens the very existence of their community, gay men have converted horror and grief into creative energy and purpose. AIDS has given a new sense of solidarity to lesbians and gay men who for years have often pursued separate agendas.

Suddenly, "out" gays inhabit high and mid-level positions in journalism and publishing, law, academia, medicine and psychiatry, the arts and creative professions. They have made it not only possible but comfortable and natural for younger lesbians and gay men to come out at the entry level. More out gays are in public office throughout the land, at least up to the sub-Cabinet level of the federal government. A quarter of a century of gay and lesbian political action has produced, *inter alia*, the first pro-gay White House—despite distressing backsliding. Gay couples are winning recognition as legal families by some city governments and a few corporations (*The Nation* is one), although valuable benefits have been extended to only a small number of registrants. And a complex infrastructure of activist, educational and professional organizations give gay life a formidable institutional base and contribute to the general appreciation of "gay power." Morley Safer was not way over the top when he suggested to his *60 Minutes* audience recently that it "face up to the gay nineties."

Suddenly, it seems, gay faces adorn the covers of major magazines; Broadway is bursting with gay plays; big book awards go to gay authors; even Hollywood is developing movies with gay themes; and gay people of every age and social stratum are shattering their closets with explosive force. "Queer theory"—also known as lesbian and gay studies—is explored by scholars and students at hundreds of colleges.

In the realm of pop music alone, stars such as k.d. lang and Elton John have come out; the late Freddie Mercury (of Queen) was outed after he died of AIDS, while others, such as Pete Townshend (of The Who) and Kurt Cobain (of Nirvana), have more or less matter-of-factly talked about bisexual times of their lives. Madonna, the premier sex symbol of the decade, is graphic about her own Sapphic activities. More important, her videos have shown same-sex couples in intimate poses—a crucially legitimizing image for the MTV generation. Prince exudes androgyny, and what more can be said about Michael Jackson in that department? Only Brooke Shields knows for sure. Perhaps the most consequential gay moment in music was a single line in the new Garth Brooks country hit "We Shall Be Free," which instructs the Nashville nation to be accepting of same-sex love. Brooks, who outsells everyone else in music these days, told Barbara Walters that he wrote it in support of his lesbian sister. *Newsweek* devoted an entire page to the song and the "turmoil" it has engendered among the hee-haw set.

Nor is a *tour d'horizon* of the gay moment complete without a mention of *The Crying Game*, the most successful mainstream movie to deal frankly with a straight/gay relationship—with full frontal nudity. Never in the history of film has a single penis shot grossed so much: $54 million at this writing.

While the arrival of the gay moment is unmistakable, its provenance and history are ambiguous and debatable. There is a feeling prevalent in the lesbian and gay community that Bill Clinton's groundbreaking pro-gay campaign and election made all the difference in the world. Jeffrey Schmalz began an important state-of-the-gays article in *The New York Times Magazine* last fall with an account of Clinton's long friendship with David Mixner, an influential, openly gay consultant and fundraiser, and how that relationship led to Clinton's stand.

The two first met, Mixner says, at a 1969 reunion for people who had worked on Eugene McCarthy's presidential campaign the year before. Mixner was still in the closet; Clinton was heading to Oxford. In time, Clinton returned to Arkansas and became a politician; Mixner went to California and became a political consultant. He came out—to the world and to his old friend Bill—in the mid-1970s, and immersed himself in gay politics. In 1978 he ran the successful campaign to defeat the Briggs

Initiative, which would have effectively barred gays from teaching in the state's public schools. (His most important ally in that struggle was, of all people, Ronald Reagan, who had recently retired as governor to run, again, for the presidency. Mixner got one of Reagan's top gubernatorial aides, a gay man who had become a department store executive, to sensitize his former boss to the issue.)

Mixner kept in contact with Bill and Hillary and, by his account, instructed the couple in the elements of gay oppression and liberation. Mixner was on the Clinton presidential bus from day one, served as the campaign's co-chair in California and as a senior adviser to the candidate nationally. He also helped bring huge pots of gay money to the campaign and to position Clinton to win in excess of 75 percent of the gay vote, a crucial component of the Democratic totals in big cities where gays are concentrated. The Human Rights Campaign Fund and the Victory Fund, the two leading gay money-raising groups in Washington, estimate that $3.5 million was contributed to Clinton; perhaps three to four times that was given to all political campaigns.

But it was the crisis engendered by the military's anti-gay policies and the many challenges by lesbians and gays in the service that set the stage for Clinton's stance on homosexuals' rights. And it was Paul Tsongas who, in a manner of speaking, brought Clinton out on the issue. Campaigning in frigid Iowa before the caucuses there, Tsongas was asked by a reporter at an airport stop whether the candidate favored letting gays into the military. "Everybody's in, nobody's out," Tsongas replied, in a phrase he would often use. Soon, all the other Democratic candidates would second Tsongas's motion. Clinton, who was plummeting in New Hampshire after the Gennifer Flowers story broke, could not afford to give Tsongas an advantage with the liberal Democrats who work hard and vote often in the early primaries, and he added his support for lifting the ban.

Clinton's national strategy, however, had targeted the "Reagan Democrats," those middle- and lower-middle-class white suburbanites, including many Catholics and churchgoing Protestants, who would respond to progressive class issues (such as tax "fairness") but not liberal social issues (such as affirmative action for minorities and civil rights for gays). Accordingly, Clinton remained mute on the military ban and other gay issues (except AIDS, which has its built-in escape clause) until the end of May, just before the California primary, when he gave an extraordinary speech to an absolutely delirious gay audience at the Palace Theater in Los Angeles.

Flanked by Mixner and an array of gay notables, Clinton reiterated his promise to reverse the military's ban, and in the course of citing a Defense Department study that supported such a move, all but outed the high-profile Pentagon "spokesperson who himself was said to be gay" who released it to the press. He promised to put gays in government jobs, to start a "Manhattan Project" crash program to combat AIDS, to appoint an AIDS czar, and to "make a major speech on AIDS to a non-traditional group of Americans," presumably gays, who had never been so addressed by Reagan or Bush. Clinton choked with emotion as he praised the gay and lesbian community for its courageous and committed work against AIDS.

A videotape was shot, of course, and it quickly made the rounds of gay activists as well as Republican "opposition researchers," who never quite got up the gumption to use it against Clinton in the campaign. Clinton asked Bob Hattoy, another gay friend and early campaign adviser, who has AIDS, to speak at the Democratic National Convention—but about AIDS, not gay rights. Clinton argued with Hattoy, Mixner and other gays on his staff up until the last minute before his acceptance speech about whether to include *the word* "gay" in his text. Reports filtered onto the convention floor: it's in, it's out, it's back in. At length, Clinton used the g-word, in the predictable litany of diverse groups he would include in his Administration. But that was practically the last time he initiated a discussion of gay issues in his campaign. In fact, when he spoke in Oregon in October he pointedly failed even to mention the battle then in progress around a virulently anti-gay ballot referendum.

As the political campaign progressed, it dawned on many gay and lesbian activists that from now on every Democratic candidate for President would be pro-gay. The reason that Mike Dukakis was so bad on gay issues in 1988 and Bill Clinton was good enough in 1992 had less to do with their characters or their ideologies than with their personal histories. For Dukakis, as for most straights and gays of the 1950s generation, the sexual closet was a reassuring structure of social architecture. He had close gay associates— indeed, one of the top men in his 1988 campaign was out in certain corners of the gay community—but none of them were open about their identity.

Openness has enormous power in the politics of personal relationships. Straight friends and relatives of gays have to confront truths about themselves and their social environment that they have long denied. Clinton, boomer child of the sixties, when Stonewall broke open the closet, had mixed easily with gays for years. More than that, he must deal all the time with openly gay journalists, politicians, lobbyists and advisers. For the better part of a year Clinton travelled day and night with *Newsweek* reporter Mark Miller, who was preparing the Clinton story for the magazine's special issue that would detail "how the candidate won." Miller, who is gay, did not hide his interest in gay issues, and Clinton apparently responded earnestly.

It was Miller who also pressed Clinton, at his first televised press conference in March, to admit that he would consider segregation of gays in the military. Miller seemed to be barely restraining his anger at Clinton's apparent betrayal of his own promise to end discrimination in the service, and it could be that if Miller had not been there the issue would have been blurred or buried. Even the presence of gay people in an office, a classroom, a legislative hall or a city room changes the political dynamics. Within hours after the press conference, Mixner and Hattoy were denouncing their friend the President with exceptional vehemence. Meetings were hastily called at the White House and in New York, where millionaire contributors explicitly threatened Democratic National Chairman David Wilhelm with a financial boycott of the party if Clinton didn't recant on segregation.

It is doubtful that Clinton knew from the start how immensely complex lifting the ban would become. But he should have. He reiterated his campaign pledge on the morning after his election, in response to a reporter's question. A brief but intense firestorm followed, and then seemed to subside. But according to a White House source, machinations continued below sea level. The Joint Chiefs and top Pentagon brass were unhappy at the prospect of admitting homosexuals into the service, but they were equally concerned about losing power in what they feared would be an instinctively anti-military Administration. They worried about budget cuts, cancellation of weapons systems and the organization of congressional forces hostile to the Pentagon.

The generals had apparently tried to stop Clinton before the election by pitching the gays in the military issue to Bush, but for some reason—perhaps because of the backlash to the gay-bashing that went on at the GOP convention in August—the Bushies passed. But soon after Les Aspin was chosen as Secretary of Defense, the brass began working with him to undermine the expected executive order on gays, and in the process stake out a perimeter around their own turf.

Clinton did not "stack" the ban-lifting order with those on the abortion counselling "gag rule," on fetal-tissue research and on experimentation with the abortifacient RU-486, all of which he issued two days after taking the oath of office. If he had, he might have outflanked the opposition—a tactic endorsed by some gay activists, *The New York Times* and others who wanted to see the ban lifted. Instead, he did the worst thing, which was to talk about lifting the ban, but not do it.

Over the weekend after the inauguration, a kind of quiet military coup was leveraged, with the gay ban as the lever. Morton Halperin, then an adviser to Aspin (he has since been nominated assistant secretary of defense for democracy and human rights), prepared a memo, which he also leaked to the press, predicting dire consequences in Congress if the ban was lifted. He recommended postponing the order until summer. The week's delay also allowed the Christian right around the country to mount an impressive anti-gay letter-writing campaign to representatives in Washington. Right-wing talk-show jocks were out in force on the issue. But the consequences were in a sense predetermined by the Pentagon, which, with Aspin's compliance, had been lobbying key legislators to form the pro-military bloc the Joint Chiefs wanted. Halperin had served on Richard Nixon's National Security Council and had suddenly turned civil libertarian after he found out Henry Kissinger tapped his telephone. In recent years he headed the Washington office of the

ACLU, where he worked on cases of gay people harassed and cashiered by the military. He was close to and completely trusted by lesbian and gay activists. During "the week" when the expected executive order seemed to slip away, Halperin's role was crucial, but estimations of his effect on events differ according to one's sense of political possibility. A gay lawyer who is still fighting to lift the ban is convinced of Halperin's loyalty to the cause, and believes he had to orchestrate a delay to have a chance of winning the issue. But there is the smell of sell-out in the air. A gay Democratic source says, ruefully, "Mort's no friend of ours." By doing the bidding of the Joint Chiefs and congressional conservatives, Halperin undercut the potential strength of a Clinton *coup de foudre*, and made it all the more likely the hearings and negotiations would produce a defeat for gay rights in the guise of a "compromise" that would reinforce the military closet and keep things pretty much as they were. (Halperin declined to talk about the issue.)

For most gay people, the military ban was not the issue of choice. As one former "gayocrat" who left gay politics in Washington rather than devote all his time to fighting the ban said, "Why should I spend my life getting queers the right to kill or be killed? The best thing about being gay was that you *didn't* have to go in the army."

But it was the issue of opportunity. For as far as gays have come, they cannot yet completely determine the order of their own social agenda. There is also a serious disjunction between the gayocracy and the millions of lesbians and gays around the country who have quite different needs and demands from the fundraisers and check-writers who are the active participants in gay politics. There is no real nationwide gay organization of activists similar to the great movements for civil rights, women's liberation and radical social change that blossomed in the 1960s and soon after. The National Gay and Lesbian Task Force claims a membership of 26,000, and it performs many useful services, such as its national campaign to counter the homophobic right and to win validation for lesbian and gay families. But for the most part membership means annual giving. ACT UP around the country has been able to muster several thousand shock troops for demonstrations and civil disobedience, but there is no national coordination and, besides, it is not specifically a gay organization. Queer Nation, which was formed on the ACT UP model to deal militantly with gay issues, is small and decentralized, and riven with dissension where it still exists. There are hundreds of new organizations formed by gays in professions, and lesbian and gay groups now thrive on many college campuses. All of them contribute to the moment, but not one has assumed a leading role.

AIDS has had a painfully paradoxical effect on the movement. At the same time that it ravaged the gay male community in institutional as well as personal terms, it has unquestionably contributed to the visibility of gay people against the social background. AIDS contains many tragedies, but first and still foremost it is a catastrophe for gay men in America. What is happening is the destruction of an affectional community very much like an ethnic or national community. Half the gay men in San Francisco are said to be infected with HIV, and the numbers in New York and other big cities are staggering; there is nothing yet to keep most of them from dying. Clinton has dithered in launching his "Manhattan Project" for AIDS. Ever fearful of the right, he refused to reverse the Reagan/Bush order excluding people with HIV from immigrating. As of mid-April he had still not appointed an AIDS czar, even though he had indicated it would be a first order of business. He has included full funding for the Ryan White Act programs to help care for people with AIDS and for education to prevent its spread, but the sum of appropriations for that and AIDS research is nowhere near what the crisis demands.

But again the contradictions intrude. Clinton is failing to live up to his promises, but at least he talked about the issues. Now homosexuality is—by presidential directive—a positive qualification for an Administration job. Gays in Washington are finding Administration jobs for themselves and other gays, but they are also trying to convince closeted gays (in the super-closeted capital) that coming out would help, not hurt, the chances of getting hired.

Donna Shalala, Secretary of Health and Human Services, had been "outed," without supporting evidence, by students at the University of Wisconsin, where she was chancellor. According to an Administration official, she was asked many times during the transition, by co-chair Warren Christopher and others, whether the rumors were true. Moreover, the Clintonites repeatedly tried to assure her that it was okay to be gay, and they would support her coming out. "It began to sound like a *Seinfeld* shtick," one Washington insider told me. When the press repeated the rumor, Shalala made a statement: "Have I lived an alternative lifestyle? The answer is no." That ended it for the White House, but lesbians and gays were upset. "Lifestyle" is *their* word, not ours. Homosexuality is an orientation or an identity, never a lifestyle.

What has changed the climate in America is the long experience of gay struggle, the necessary means having been, first, coming out, and second, making a scene. Sometimes it is personal witness, other times political action, and overall it is the creation of a cultural community based on sexual identity. The ascension of gay people to positions of authority in key sectors of society has made a huge difference in the weather. The prerequisite for their influence is being out—which is why the destruction of the closet is the most vital issue of gay life, beyond any act of censorship or exclusion. It is also the reason that "outing" has become such a charged political question.

Every opinion survey shows that people who say they have a gay friend or family member are twice or three times as likely to support gay rights than are those who say they know no gay people. What the surveys don't report is the opinion of people who know out gays. None of the political victories, the cultural successes achieved by gays in the past short period of time, would have been possible if closets were shut.

The military establishment, schools, churches all understand the importance of the closet in maintaining institutional order. That is why the services never cared a damn about gays who did not proclaim their identity, by word or deed. It is why school superintendents have lived for centuries with lesbian and gay teachers, but panic when anyone comes out. It is why churches countenance lesbian nuns and gay priests and ministers as long as they lie about themselves.

Andrew Sullivan, the gay neoconservative editor of *The New Republic*, wrote recently in *The New York Times* that dropping the military ban on gays would be a deeply conservative act, in that gays who join up would be, by definition, patriotic and traditionalist. That may be true in the particular, but in general and historical terms, nothing could be more radical than upsetting the sexual apple cart. As Randy Shilts asserts in his study of gays in the service, *Conduct Unbecoming*, "The presence of gay men [in the military] . . . calls into question everything that manhood is supposed to mean." And homophobia—like its blood relations, racism, misogyny and anti-Semitism—is an ideology that rationalizes the oppressive uses of male power. When cruel and self-hating homophobes such as J. Edgar Hoover and Roy Cohn are outed, even posthumously, the power system is shaken.

The counterpower of coming out has given the gay movement primacy this year in the unfinished civil rights revolution. It's more than appropriate that the NAACP has decided to participate in the April 25 march on Washington, along with every major civil liberties and civil rights organization in the country. Labor unions, which have not been particularly supportive of the gay movement, are also sending busloads of marchers. Modern American feminism has a natural affinity with gay liberation: the latter was, in a sense, born of the former. The two have not always been on the best of terms, but increasingly, adherents of both movements understand how closely allied are their ideologies, how similar their enemies and how important their coalition. The kind of broad "rainbow" coalition now developing was unthinkable only a few years ago.

But the gay nineties is not only about civil rights, tolerance and legitimacy. What started tumbling out of the closets at the time of Stonewall is profoundly altering the way we all live, form families, think about and act towards one another, manage our health and well-being and understand the very meaning of identity. All the cross-currents of present-day liberation struggles are subsumed in the gay struggle. The gay moment is in some ways similar to the moment that other communities have experienced in the nation's past, but it is also something more, because sexual identity is in crisis throughout the population, and gay people—at once the most conspicuous subjects and objects of the crisis—have been forced to invent a complete cosmology to grasp it. No one says the changes will come easily. But it's just possible that a small and despised sexual minority will change America forever.

April 15, 1993, THE NATION

✦

Opening Shots

The armed insurgency against the Mexican government that began New Year's Day in the remote state of Chiapas draws heavily on symbols and styles of the past. The rebels call themselves Zapatistas, after the great Mexican revolutionary Emiliano Zapata, who led a peasant uprising eighty years ago; comparisons to the followers of Augusto Sandino and Farabundo Martí, in nearby Central American nations, inevitably leap to mind. Some of the guerrillas who have been interviewed speak admiringly of the Cuban revolution and say that communism is the one correct solution. The authorities respond with their own clichéd charges of international conspiracies and outside agitation. Worse, they bomb civilians, clear villages and execute peasants death-squad style—tactics learned in dirty wars from Guatemala to Argentina, Angola to Vietnam.

And yet the revolt of the Chiapanecos is something stunningly new, the first shots of a rebellion consciously aimed at the new world order, the dire consequences of a history that did not die as predicted but intrudes in the most pernicious manner on the way of life of people always overlooked. It is a war against the globalization of the market, against the destruction of nature and the confiscation of resources, against the termination of indigenous peoples and their lands, against the growing maldistribution of wealth and the consequent decline in standards of living for all but the rich. It might be that the battle in Chiapas will end with the predictable bangs and whimpers heard whenever outnumbered, outgunned peasants without powerful international support are picked off and packed away. But the shots fired in Mexico in the first week of the new year have been heard around the world, and their echoes will not soon stop.

The Mayan tribes that inhabit the forests and secluded valleys of Chiapas have suffered without much relief since the Spanish Conquest 500 years ago; only the specifics of their misery have changed with the layers of history. Despite the rhetoric of the 1910 Mexican revolution, the Indians were excluded from its benefits, however meager and stunted. For the most part they could not own land even when land reform laws were passed. They survived by subsistence farming, supplemented with a bit of cash from coffee, corn and other agricultural commodities. And all the while they were brutally repressed by the "European" police, landlords, ranchers and politicians of the dynastic PRI—the party that is revolutionary in name only.

Things started going from bad to very bad for the peasants in the late 1980s when coffee prices slumped—not by an act of God or chance, but because President Bush orchestrated an end to the stable commodity markets to enforce his free-market ideology. Cappuccino drinkers in Seattle rejoiced; small coffee growers in Chiapas suffered.

About the same time, the Mexican government began speeding up its "modernization" program, which entailed across-the-board privatization of the economy and integration of the resulting structure into the US-led global system. In Chiapas, for instance, peasants could get ownership title or credit for their once-communal plots of land. Many took credit, but without a market for their surplus the land was soon foreclosed—and, with government and police help, wound up in the hands of big cattle ranchers. The Indians were pushed farther into the Chiapan rainforest, where they slashed and burned the land simply to survive for a few years—until that conveniently cleared land was grabbed by the ranchers. The Mayans inevitably have been forced to give up their life on the land (tiny Chiapas, with three million inhabitants and thousands of refugees from the long war in Guatemala, has the highest indigenous population in the country) and join the city slum-dwellers. Ultimately, the laws of population hydraulics push commensurate numbers of displaced and desperate people over the border to El Norte.

The passage of NAFTA provided the spark igniting the revolt, because its provisions so clearly imply the destruction of the Indian peasants' lives, culture and history. Corn in the Mexican south cannot compete with the high-tech productivity in Bob Dole's Kansas or Tom Harkin's Iowa (both of whom voted for the treaty). The indigenous people are unequipped and ill-placed to become workers in export-oriented factories. The social services and land reforms brightly packaged by Mexican President Salinas as the "Solidarity" plan are inadequate and do not protect the Mayans, who continue to be exploited by ranchers, oil companies, forest clearers, landlords and police. In fact, the horrendous abuses documented by human rights agencies have increased with the new economic pressures of the past several years. Local Catholic priests and bishops provide the only aid and comfort, but they are also under attack from the hierarchy.

The timing of the Zapatista invasion of several towns to coincide with NAFTA's implementation shows how well the processes of history are understood—mo' better in San Cristóbal de las Casas, it seems, than in Washington or LA. It's not that the treaty itself causes all the grievances the guerrillas list, but the ideological underpinnings and political effects of the new globalism have suddenly become real and clear. A small army of Mayans can't reverse those effects, but the battle of Chiapas allows untold millions around the world to see that it's still possible to put up a fight.

January 13, 1994, THE NATION

✦

Starting Over

A funny thing happened on the way to the end of history. Neoconservative theorists proposed in the late 1980s that the global struggle apparent for 200 years screeched to a stop with the fall of Soviet-bloc governments in Europe; henceforth, free-market capitalism would advance unhindered by revolts of the oppressed. Indeed, categories such as oppression and revolt had been obliterated. Struggle was replaced by management.

But many of the people of Eastern Europe who eagerly discarded the corrupt and ruthless trappings of actually existing communist governments did not realize that they would also lose the egalitarian values, social benefits and priceless security of the socialist ideal. Promises of cheap cars, tropical fruits and rising salaries were never fulfilled, except for the new, narrow entrepreneurial class, while the rest got unemployment, inflation, falling production and zero social services. Then history started running again.

The electoral victory of the Socialist Party in Hungary is only the latest in a series of defeats for Western-style capitalism imposed on the European East. Hungarians who gave the post-communists an absolute majority in Parliament knew what they were voting for: social values as well as consumer goods. According to the local Gallup pollster, "This is a revolt against the market economy. . . . People are voting for the Socialists because they are hoping they will go for more equality." Voters in Poland made a similar estimation and put a post-communist coalition in power last year. Lithuania has gone the same route. Ex-communists are making a comeback in Ukraine, and they never seem to have left in Slovakia, as well as in many of the breakaway Soviet republics on Russia's southern border. In Russia itself, post-, ex- and neocommunists have a good chance of expanding their parliamentary and regional bases and taking over the national government in the not-too-distant future. There are strong and troubling nationalist/populist tendencies in the new Russian parties—as in many of the socialist parties of the other countries—but the first principle and most important project of the new governments seems to be avoidance of forced obedience to the dictates of the IMF and the other masters of the market.

None of this looks like the return to Leninism so dreaded in the West. If anything, the post-communist parties in Hungary, Poland and Lithuania are versions of Eurosocialism—pluralistic, non-authoritarian, capitalist-friendly, with a healthy respect for economic equality and social planning. The weakness of the new parties may be evident in their inability to pursue self-sufficient policies and plans outside the Western market system. But they are committed to trying a new way.

Skeptics who refrained from expressing unconfined joy at the death of socialism a few years back pointed out that people will always have a need to join in collective efforts to secure a better life for the many against the greedy predations of the few. That struggle goes hand in hand with the attempt to free individuals from the tyranny of unaccountable authority. But just as the struggle had been blocked in the nominally communist countries of Eastern Europe, so is it under the reckless and unresponsive regimes that emerged from the wreckage of the old order. But there is always another chance to bring a better system to birth, which is what history means, after all.

June 20, 1994, THE NATION

✦

After Stonewall

A s revolutions go, the street fighting that took place around Sheridan Square in Greenwich Village on the night of June 27, 1969, lacked the splendor of the Bastille or the sweep of the Finland Station. State power did not crumble, great leaders did not appear, no clear objective was advanced. A bunch of drag queens and their friends pulled from the Stonewall bar in a police raid refused to go docilely into the paddy wagons and all hell broke loose along Christopher Street and in adjoining parks and alleys. Fighting between the queers and the cops resumed the next night, but that was the extent of the violence. And yet the Stonewall riot must count as a transformative moment of liberation, not only for homosexuals, who were the street fighters, but for the entire sexual culture, which broke out of confinement that night as surely as gay people emerged from the closet.

Stonewall became a metaphor for emergence, visibility and pride, and its historic power has been its affirmation of gay identity rather than its establishment of a particular homosexual agenda. Unlike the national days of other communities, countries and ethnic groups, the nationwide celebration of the anniversary of the riots memorializes an act of legitimation, not an act of parliament, a treaty or a war. Gay Pride Week, the name for the observance, could hardly be more appropriate. Although Stonewall came at the very end of a decade of convulsive change, and was profoundly informed by the struggles of black Americans, women, radical students and insurgent movements throughout the Third World, it was in many ways the purest cultural revolution of them all, and the precursor of the postmodern politics of identity that proliferated in the decades to follow. Lesbians and gays are surely today's children of Stonewall, but many more are stepchildren or close cousins. That June night a quarter of a century ago now belongs to everyone.

Lenin said somewhere that "revolutions are festivals of the oppressed," and although Stonewall wasn't remotely Leninist, it was certainly festive and it definitely was a low-down crowd that poured out of that bar. The prominence of drag queens in the vanguard of the insurgency always made theoretical sense: as one of the most marginal, disdained and isolated sectors of the homosexual world, the drags had the least to lose from acting out, or acting up—and perhaps the most to gain. But as much as "straight appearing" gay men (a description still found in the personals) kept their distance from drag queens, or treated them only as camp objects of amusement, the boys in "chinos and penny-loafers," as historian Martin Duberman calls them, could see that those qualities in the drags most despised by the straight world were present in all homosexuals in one form or another. The most unmodulated, outrageous and flamboyant behavior—and the most oppressed—was thus the most liberating expression of all. In the gay liberation movement that exploded after Stonewall, young lesbians and gay men were urged to "get into their oppression," to comb the crannies of gay consciousness and to feel solidarity with those who suffered the most.

Today's gay neocons deny the radical history of Stonewall as well as its relevance to the present. It's true that Stonewall was the beginning of something, but it was also the culmination of a long siege, during which protest had become a normal way of making politics, and all sorts and sizes of groups had bid for power. Many of the campaigns crossed communal lines, but there was a great deal of fear, a sense of threat and sometimes an ardent "nationalism" that kept the groups apart. Stonewall is often described as a narrowly constructed, exclusively gay male "happening" (in the 1960s sense), but lots of lines were crossed. The drag contingent, at least, was remarkably racially integrated. Although the bar was not known as a lesbian hang-out, lesbians were always in attendance, and one story suggests that a butch lesbian cross-dresser might have instigated the riot. Some original street fighters complained that political leftists didn't participate, that the left didn't "get it." But in less than a year gay liberation was on the agenda at every radical event, organizations took revolutionary names and styles (e.g., the Gay Liberation Front, after the Vietnamese guerrillas) and the roots of the gay movement were apparent in the uprisings of the decade.

Craig Rodwell, a witness to the war in the streets, said in an interview for the documentary *Before Stonewall* that what was most magical about the Stonewall riot was that "everything came together that night." Somewhere in the existential depths of that brawl of screaming transvestites were all the freedom rides, the anti-war marches, the sit-ins, the smoke-ins, the be-ins, the consciousness-raising, the bra-burning, the levitation of the Pentagon, the endless meetings and broken hearts. Not only that, but the years of gay men and lesbians locking themselves inside windowless, unnamed bars; writing dangerous, anonymous novels and articles; lying about their identity to their families, their bosses, the military; suffering silently when they were found out; hiding and seeking and winking at each other, or drinking and dying by themselves. And sometimes, not often, braving it out and surviving. It's absolutely astonishing to think that on one early summer's night in New York that world ended, and a new one began.

July 4, 1994, THE NATION

INDEX

Abernathy, Rev. Ralph, 4, 59, 170, 199-200
Abortion, 298-308, 506
Abram, Morris, 191n
Accuracy in Media, 412
ACLU (American Civil Liberties Union), 55-56, 79, 105, 110-111, 380-381, 507
ACU (American Conservative Union), 304
ADA (Americans for Democratic Action), 99, 305, 377
Addlestone, David, 275-276
Addonizio, Hugh J., 11, 13
Afghanistan, 349, 351, 352, 394, 408-409, 439
Africa, 66, 349, 410
African Americans
    See Black Americans
Afro-American Citizens' Council, 43
Afro-American Culture Association, 43
AFSC (American Friends Service Committee), 263
Agnew, Spiro, 170, 186, 213
Agriculture policy, 431-434
AIDS, 450, 486-488, 502-505, 507-508
AIM (American Indian Movement), 216
Albee, Edward, 47
Alexander, Clifford, 191n
Alexander, Sidney, 18
Algeria, 370
Allende, Salvador, 339, 346, 351
Alliance for Progress, 250
Altman, Robert, 256, 257-258
American Labor Party (NY), 99
American Legislative Exchange Council, 305
American Security Council, 334-335
Amerika (TV miniseries), 411-414
ANC (African National Congress), 379, 413, 500-501
Anderson, John, 385
Angola, 408
Anti-imperialism, 164-165, 183, 193
Anti-Vietnam war movement, 13, 23, 26-31, 55, 67-68, 76, 77, 106-107, 109, 111, 114, 123, 124, 152, 156, 218, 219, 238, 255, 362-363, 366, 367, 410.
See also Vietnam War
Demonstrations and Marches
April 1965 March on Washington, 13
November 1966 SANE March on Washington, 26-31
October 1967 March on the Pentagon, 106
October 1967 Stop the Draft Week, 158

August 1968 Chicago, 151-152, 154, 177, 199-200
October 1969 Weathermen in Chicago (Days of Rage), 176-181, 188
November 1969 March on Washington, 181-187, 201-202
draft resistance, 87, 118, 158, 198
GI protests, 109-110, 188-189
    See also Dr. Howard Levy
Mobilization Committee (Mobe), 181-187, 188
Moratorium, 181, 183-184, 187-188, 189, 217
National Coordinating Committee 26, 29
and sabotage, 146-148, 158, 210-214.
    See also Bombing
Appalachia, 15, 147-148
Arbuckle, Fatty, 447
Arica, 234-236, 238-239
Armstrong, Louis, 492
Armstrong, Neil, 169
Ash, Timothy Garten, 359
Aspin, Les, 506
Austen, Burt, 111
Ayres, Bill, 168

Baba, Meher, 175
Babbitt, Bruce, 432
Baez, Joan, 121, 175
Baker & McKenzie, 493
Bakker, Jim, 414-428
Bakker, Tammy Faye, 415, 422, 423-428
Balaguer, Joaquin, 38-40
Baldwin, James, 90-91
Band, The, 172
Barnet, Richard, 352
Baseball, 198, 406
Batista, Fulgencio, 229
Battle of Algiers, The (film), 243
Baxley, Barbara, 258
Bay Area, 158. *See also* Berkeley,
Bears, 84, 455
Beat generation (Beatniks), xx, 46, 172
Beatles, The, 24, 84, 154, 245, 318, 355, 356, 492
Bee Gees, 317
Beittel, A.D., 22
Bell, Daniel, 369
Bell, Griffin, 337
Bellow, Gary, 380
Beluga whales, 407
Benny, Jack, 170
Berkeley, California, 8, 46, 146-147, 158
Berlin Wall, 445